Homeland Security in the UK

This book is a detailed examination of the UK measures taken since 9/11 to enhance homeland security. The authors consider the potential value of these measures in the light of the changing terrorist threats to the UK and the existing counter-terrorism capabilities prior to 9/11. Major lessons concerning the effectiveness of different measures, their implications for human rights, and the experience of the US and our fellow EU member states are highlighted.

While improved intelligence has helped to thwart or disrupt a number of Al-Qaeda-linked conspiracies, the suicide bombings in London on 7 July 2005 are tragic evidence that we need to do much more to improve the quality of our intelligence and our capability to prevent terrorist attacks and to deal with emergency situations when prevention fails.

This book will be essential reading for all students of terrorism and counter-terrorism, security studies and politics, and will be of great interest to professional practitioners and informed general readers.

Paul Wilkinson is Professor of International Relations and Chairman of the Advisory Board of the Centre for the Study of Terrorism and Political Violence at the University of St Andrews. He has authored and edited a dozen books on aspects of terrorism and the problems of democratic response. His latest book on terrorism is *Terrorism Versus Democracy: The Liberal State Response* (2nd edn, Routledge 2006).

Cass Series: Political Violence
Series Editors: Paul Wilkinson and David Rapoport

Research on Terrorism
Trends, achievements and failures
Andrew Silke (ed.)

A War of Words
Political violence and public debate in Israel
Gerald Cromer

Root Causes of Suicide Terrorism
Globalization of martyrdom
Ami Pedahzur (ed.)

Terrorism versus Democracy
The liberal state response, 2nd edition
Paul Wilkinson

Countering Terrorism and WMD
Creating a global counter-terrorism network
Peter Katona, Michael Intriligator and John Sullivan (eds)

Mapping Terrorism Research
State of the art, gaps and future direction
Magnus Ranstorp (ed.)

The Ideological War on Terror
World-wide strategies for counter-terrorism
Anne Aldis and Graeme P. Herd (eds)

The IRA and Armed Struggle
Rogelio Alonso

Homeland Security in the UK
Future preparedness for terrorist attack since 9/11
Paul Wilkinson (ed.)

Homeland Security in the UK

Future preparedness for terrorist attack since 9/11

Edited by Paul Wilkinson

Routledge
Taylor & Francis Group

LONDON AND NEW YORK

First published 2007
by Routledge
2 Park Square, Milton Park, Abingdon, Oxon OX14 4RN

Simultaneously published in the USA and Canada
by Routledge
270 Madison Ave, New York, NY 10016

*Routledge is an imprint of the Taylor & Francis Group, an informa
business*

Typeset in Times New Roman by
HWA Text and Data Management, Tunbridge Wells
Printed and bound in Great Britain by
The Cromwell Press, Trowbridge, Wiltshire

British Library Cataloguing in Publication Data
A catalogue record for this book is available from the British Library

Library of Congress Cataloging-in-Publication Data
Homeland security in the UK : future preparedness for terrorist attack
since 9/11 / edited by Paul Wilkinson.
    p.   cm.
Includes bibliographical references and index.
  1. Civil defense–Great Britain. 2. Terrorism–Great Britain–Prevention.
  I. Wilkinson, Paul, 1937–
UA929.G7H65 2007
363.325´170941–dc22   2006102050

ISBN10: 0–415–38374–9 (hbk)
ISBN10: 0–415–38375–7 (pbk)
ISBN10: 0–203–08745–3 (ebk)

ISBN13: 978–0–415–38374–5 (hbk)
ISBN13: 978–0–415–38375–2 (pbk)
ISBN13: 978–0–203–08745–9 (ebk)

Contents

PART III
UK efforts to enhance preparedness since 9/11   **115**

Illustrations

Figure

Tables

Contributors

Frank Gregory is currently Professor of European Security, and holder of a Jean Monnet Chair in European Political Integration at the University of Southampton. He has been a specialist adviser to the House of Commons Home Affairs Select Committee, and in 2000 reviewed the UK National Organised Crime Notification Scheme for the Home Office. His special areas of research are linked to the terrorism, crime and policing aspects of the EU's 'third pillar' on Justice and Home Affairs. Frank was responsible for the Southampton University part of the St Andrews and Southampton Universities Economic and Social Research Council (ESRC) project on the UK's preparedness for future terrorist attack.

Darryl Howlett graduated from University of Southampton in 1988 with his PhD and now teaches courses on international security. Between 1987 and 1995 Darryl was the information officer for the Programme for Promoting Nuclear Non-Proliferation (PPNN). Darryl's recent publications include, 'The Emergence of Stability: Deterrence-in-Motion and Deterrence Reconstructed', in Ian R. Kenyon and John Simpson (eds) (Routledge, 2006) and *Deterrence and the Changing Security Environment* (Frank Cass). Darryl's research interests include arms control and disarmament, issues in international security, and the changing nature of terrorism.

Peter Lehr is a Senior Research Associate at the Centre for the Study of Terrorism and Political Violence (CSTPV), University of St Andrews, Scotland. Prior to his appointment at St Andrews in September 2004, he was lecturer at the Department of Political Science, South Asia Institute, University of Heidelberg, Germany, and visiting fellow at the Institute for Strategic and International Studies (ISIS), Chulalongkorn University, Bangkok, Thailand. Being a regional specialist on the Indian Ocean, he currently works on security issues such as piracy, organised crime and (maritime) terrorism with a strong focus on South and Southeast Asia. He has just published a book on *Piracy in the Age of Global Terrorism* (New York: Routledge, 2007), and is preparing a handbook on ISPS implementation which is due to be published in autumn 2007 by Taylor & Francis, New York.

Jez Littlewood was awarded his PhD (Bradford) in 2001 for work on arms control and international security. He joined the Mountbatten Centre for International Studies, University of Southampton, in January 2002 on a post-doctoral scholarship from the university. He was subsequently awarded an ESRC post-doctoral scholarship (2003) and an ESRC Science in Society award. Jez was seconded to the Foreign & Commonwealth Office, Arms Control and Disarmament Research Unit, from March 2005 to March 2007. Jez's research interests include; arms control, disarmament, proliferation, biological weapons, nuclear weapons, chemical weapons, terrorism and international security.

Tamara Makarenko was part of the ESRC-funded research team working on the Domestic Management of Terrorist Attacks project. Her project responsibilities included conducting ongoing assessments of the capabilities of international terrorist groups, assessing the vulnerability of potential terrorist targets in the UK and Western Europe, investigating the intricate ties that exist between organised criminal activity and terrorism, and assessing the effectiveness of counter-terrorist contingency plans and crisis management for the private sector. Her academic interests focus on the relationship between organised crime and terrorism, illicit group dynamics, arms and narcotics trafficking, and related political corruption.

Anthony Richards is currently involved with the teaching and administration of the Centre for the Study of Terrorism and Political Violence (CSTPV) terrorism studies distance learning project at the University of St Andrews, for which he has designed two modules. His research interests have included the Northern Ireland peace process, Northern Irish terrorism, and British counter-terrorism strategy in the face of contemporary international terrorism. He was assistant editor of the academic journal *Terrorism and Political Violence* from 2002 to 2005.

John Simpson is an expert of international standing on the evolution of the Treaty on the Non-Proliferation of Nuclear Weapons (NPT) and other international mechanisms to prevent nuclear proliferation. His work at the Mountbatten Centre also covers British nuclear history and missile non-proliferation. Professor Simpson was awarded the OBE in 1999 for services to nuclear non-proliferation.

Paul Wilkinson is Professor of International Relations and Chairman of the Advisory Board of the Centre for the Study of Terrorism and Political Violence (CSTPV) at the University of St Andrews. He was Director of the St Andrews and Southampton Universities Economic and Social Research Council project on the UK's preparedness for future terrorist attack. His publications include *Terrorism and the Liberal State* (second edition, 1986), *Terrorism Versus Democracy: The Liberal State Response* (second edition, 2006) and *Aviation Terrorism and Security* (co-edited with Brian Jenkins, 1998). He was advisor to Lord Lloyd of Berwick's Inquiry into Legislation Against Terrorism (1996) and wrote volume 2, the research report of the Inquiry.

Preface

The sub-title of this book gives the reader a more precise indication as to what the authors' specific concerns are. This study is an edited and updated report of the study funded by the Economic and Social Research Council (ESRC) on 'the preparedness of the UK for future terrorist attack' and undertaken by a combined team of academic researchers from the Centre of the Study of Terrorism and Political Violence (CSTPV) of St Andrews University, and the Mountbatten Centre for International Studies at Southampton University, and which commenced in late 2002. The Members of the Southampton group were: Professor Frank Gregory, Dr Darryl Howlett, Dr Jez Littlewood and Professor John Simpson. The St Andrews group comprised: Dr Anthony Richards, Dr Tamara Makarenko and Professor Paul Wilkinson (Project Director). Our Project Secretary was Mrs Gillian Duncan of CSTPV, St Andrews. As Director of the project I would like to thank them all for their hard work and excellent teamwork. We also wish to thank Sir David Veness, Former Assistant Commissioner (Special Operations) at New Scotland Yard for his encouragement and his advice and also to acknowledge the valuable advice of our consultants: Professor Yonah Alexander, Potomac Institute, Washington DC, Dr Tony Moore, expert in disaster management, Mr Roger Howsley of BNFL and Mr Ian Hutchison of BAA. The research team would also like to thank the officials and policy-makers who generously gave their time to participate in our workshops and seminars and to grant interviews to assist in our research. The authors of the present book are, of course, solely responsible for any errors.

I conclude by acknowledging once again our appreciation of the support given by the ESRC for our project and our superb ESRC Project Secretary, Mrs Gillian Duncan.

Paul Wilkinson
November 2006

Part I
Introduction

1   Introduction

Paul Wilkinson

What this book is about

'Homeland security' is a term which originated in the USA in the wake of the 9/11 attacks to denote the numerous policies and measures undertaken by the US government to enhance the protection of US territory against terrorist attack. The label has not so far become part of the political debate in the UK, although it has been adopted as a useful shorthand for a number of conferences and seminars for a whole variety of specialists in aspects of counter-terrorism, and the Conservative opposition appointed Patrick Mercer MP to speak on homeland security matters and is committed to the idea of creating a Minister for Homeland Security, a proposal discussed later in this book by my colleague, Professor Frank Gregory (see Chapter 6, pp. 127–32).

One obvious difficulty about using the term 'homeland security', however, is that it could plausibly cover security against a very diverse assortments of threats ranging from a chemical, biological, radiological and nuclear (CBRN) attack by a hostile state to a conventional military attack or even increasing violence by organised crime groups, foreign and domestic.

The authors wish to emphasise the independent nature of the research study on which this book is based. The Economic and Social Research Council (ESRC) is an independent funding body established to support academic research in the social sciences. The present study was not motivated by any vested or partisan interest or by any commercial consideration. We believe that the rigorously independent status of our project was a vital factor in securing the trust and cooperation of both public and private sector organisations and individual spokespersons and officials who were willing to be interviewed or to address our workshops and seminars. In our view this is a good omen for further academic research into policy-relevant areas such as terrorism and counter-terrorism which are particularly liable to be characterised by passionate, often bitter controversy.

The St Andrews/Southampton ESRC project team has not been afraid to tackle key policy issues and the complex moral dilemmas involved in formatting and implementing counter-terrorism strategy and measures. In our brief from ESRC we were asked to pay particular attention to the need to find the right balance between protections of national security and protection of civil liberties. A key part of our project entailed holding a major conference on terrorism and human rights with participants from the UK and 21 other countries. This was held in St Andrews in the summer of 2004 and the academic papers presented at this meeting were published in a special issue of the academic journal *Terrorism and Political Violence*.[1]

A constant concern in the preparation of this book has been to ensure that any material which includes sensitive information for potential use to terrorists is excluded. All members of the research team have taken great care to check their contributions, in addition to the checks by the editor, to ensure that there are no inadvertent errors of this kind.

The concept of terrorism

A great deal of unnecessary confusion has been created as a result of the mass media, politicians and others using the term terrorism as a synonym for political violence in general.[2] Others seek to ban the word terrorism on the spurious grounds that most of those who use terrorism as weapon prefer to be called 'freedom fighters', 'holy warriors' or 'revolutionaries', depending on the cause they profess to be fighting for. Some so-called 'post-modernists' reject the concept of terrorism on the grounds that it is purely 'subjective', implying that there are no independent objective verifiable criteria to enable us to distinguish terrorism from other forms of activity. The public would be justifiably puzzled if lawyers and criminologists ceased to use terms such as 'murder', 'serial murder', and 'war crime' and 'genocide' simply because those who perpetrate such crimes regard these terms as a pejorative.

As for identifying objective criteria for identifying terrorist activity, common sense indicates that the general public in most countries in the world recognise terrorism when they see campaigns of bombings, suicide bombings, shooting attacks, hostage-takings, hijackings and threats of such actions, especially when so many of these actions are deliberately aimed at civilians.

Terrorism can be conceptually and empirically distinguished from other modes of violence and conflict by the following characteristics:

- it is premeditated and designed to create a climate of extreme fear;
- it is directed at a wider target than the immediate victims;
- it inherently involves attacks on random or symbolic targets, including civilians;
- it is considered by the society in which it occurs as 'extra-normal', that is in the literal sense that it violates the norms regulating disputes, protest and dissent; and
- it is used primarily, though not exclusively, to influence the political behaviour of governments, communities or specific social groups.[3]

It is true that in the burgeoning of modern international terrorism in the late 1960s and early 1970s many efforts to obtain international agreements and conventions on the prevention and suppression of terrorist crimes were stymied by governments which, for their own political and ideological reasons, wished to block such measures by claiming that there was no internationally accepted definition of terrorism. Since then almost all the major democracies have developed national anti-terrorist legislation and many individuals have been convicted of terrorist offences. We have also seen a considerable amount of international law on terrorist offences developed before and since 9/11.[4] Moreover, in October 2004 the UN Security Council unanimously passed Resolution 1566 which defines terrorism and declares that in no circumstances can terrorist acts be condoned or excused for political or ideological reasons:

> Criminal acts, including [those] against civilians, committed with the intent to cause death or serious bodily injury, or taking of hostages, with the purpose to provoke a state of terror in the general public or in a group of persons or particular persons, intimidate a population or compel a government or an international organisation to do or to abstain from doing any act, which constitute offences within the scope of and as defined in the international conventions and protocols relating to terrorism, are under no circumstances justifiable by considerations of a political, philosophical, ideological, racial, ethnic, religious or other similar nature.

It is true that we may have to wait some time before we see a UN General Assembly definition. However, governmental and inter-governmental conferences on problems of terrorism no longer waste days in definitional issues: they have made genuine progress in improving cooperation against terrorism, and those who dismiss the national and international efforts to develop a legal regime to deal with various aspects of terrorism as nugatory are simply wrong. The legal framework to deal with terrorist crimes is far from perfect and very difficult to apply effectively because the more sophisticated and dangerous groups have become more skilled at evading detection, but despite this there have been some major successes in bringing terrorists to justice (for example, Ramzi Youssef, Shoko Asahara, Abdullah Ocalan, Abimael Guzman, Carlos the Jackal). Terrorism is not simply a label; it is a concept which has proved indispensable in legal and social science discourse to deal with a complex global phenomenon.

The key statutory definition of terrorism in the UK legislation is contained in the Terrorism Act (2000):

(1) In this Act 'terrorism' means the use or threat of action where–
  (a) the action falls within subsection (2),
  (b) the use or threat is designed to influence the government or to intimidate the public or a section of the public, and
  (c) the use or threat is made for the purpose of advancing a political, religious or ideological cause.

(2) Action falls within this subsection if it–
   (a) involves serious violence against a person,
   (b) involves serious damage to property,
   (c) endangers a person's life, other than that of the person committing the action,
   (d) creates a serious risk to the health or safety of the public or a section of the public, or
   (e) is designed seriously to interfere with or seriously to disrupt an electronic system.

(3) The use or threat of action falling within subsection (2) which involves the use of firearms or explosives is terrorism whether or not subsection (1)(b) is satisfied.

(Terrorism Act 2000, Part 1, (1)–(3))

The US government has employed the definition contained in US Code Title 22, Section 2656f (d) since 1983 as follows:

The term 'terrorism' means premeditated politically motivated violence perpetrated against non-combatant targets by sub-national groups or clandestine agents, usually intended to influence an audience.

The term 'international terrorism' means terrorism involving citizens or the territory of more than one country.

The term 'terrorist group' means any group practicing, or that has significant sub groups that practice, international terrorism.

(US Code Title 22, Section 2656f (d))

Typology, with historical and current examples

Terrorism is an activity or a 'weapon-system' as Brian Jenkins has termed it, which has been used by an enormous variety of non-state groups, regimes and governments. (Historically, the use of terror by regimes has been infinitely more lethal than that of non-state groups, because, by definition, regimes/governments are likely to have control of far greater supplies of weapons and manpower to implement their policies of terror in the course of internal repression or foreign conquest.)

However, in an operative democracy the major threat of terror is posed by non-state movements or groups seeking to destroy or undermine democratic government and to impose their own agenda by coercive intimidation.

Another basic division is between international terrorism which involved the citizens or jurisdiction of more than one country, and domestic terrorism which is confined within the borders of a single state and involves no foreign citizens or property. This distinction is useful for statistical purposes, but we should bear in mind that almost all protracted domestic terrorist campaigns targeting a specific state develop an important international dimension through their creation of an overseas support network aimed at raising finance, recruits, weapons and other resources for their colleagues leading the struggle against their chosen 'enemy', state authorities and security forces.

One useful way of categorising non-state terrorist movements or groups is by their political motivation: *Ethno nationalist* groups, for example ETA (Euskadi ta Askatasuna or Basque Homeland and Liberty), which has waged terrorism for 40 years in a struggle to establish an independent Basque state; *Ideological* groups, for example the Red Brigades, which waged a campaign against the Italian Republic in the 1970s and 1980s with the aim of creating a neo-communist state and socio-economic system; *Religio-political* groups, for example Hamas, which aims to create an Islamic Republic of Palestine and ultimately to dismantle the state of Israel; *single issue* groups, such as animal rights extremists linked to ALF (Animal Liberation Front) aim to change one aspect of government policy and social behaviour rather than to remodel the political and socio-economic order as a whole. While most members of the animal welfare movement are committed to restricting themselves to non-violent protest, the extreme militants are prepared to engage in arson and bomb attacks on the premises of commercial firms they wish to target and to engage in threats, and in some cases attacks, on people they describe as animal 'abusers'. It should be borne in mind that campaigns by animal rights extremists against specific firms and projects such as the Cambridge animal laboratory have caused industry research labs to lose millions of pounds.

The damage and disruption caused by violent single issue groups should not be underestimated, but so far, at least in the UK, they have not succeeded in killing anyone.

One distinction which is worth adding to our typology is that between potentially *corrigible* terrorism where there is a real possibility of finding a political/diplomatic pathway out of the conflict by addressing its underlying causes, thus very probably reducing if not ending the terrorist violence spawned by the conflict and *incorrigible* terrorism. In the latter case, the movement/group has such absolutist and maximalist aims and poses such a major threat to the lives and wellbeing of civilian communities that the only recourse is to use all possible measures to suppress the group before it can wreak more mayhem.

In order to begin to understand the implications of recent changes in the nature of international terrorism, it is essential to grasp the major differences between the new terrorism of the Al-Qaeda network of networks and more traditional terrorist groups such as the ETA and FARC.[5] Al-Qaeda is not simply another group like ETA but under a different label. ETA has certainly committed hundreds of brutal killings. However, unlike Al-Qaeda, ETA did not explicitly adopt a policy of mass killing as an integral part of its strategy. As Brian Jenkins so aptly observed, terrorists in the 1970s wanted 'a lot of people watching, not a lot of people dead'.[6]

By contrast Al-Qaeda's leader, Osama bin Laden, issued a 'Fatwa' on 23 February 1998 which announced the setting up of a World Islamic Front for

Jihad and declared that 'it is the duty of all Muslims to kill US citizens – civilian or military, and their allies – everywhere'.[7] The brutal language of this 'Fatwa' is one way in which the sheer ruthlessness and lethality of this movement is reflected.[8] Their track record of brutal mass-killing in New York, Washington, Kenya, Bali, Casablanca, Saudi Arabia, Iraq and many other places is proof positive of their remorseless use of mass terror.

Moreover, whereas ETA and other more traditional groups have limited their aims to bringing about radical change in one particular state or region, Al-Qaeda has an uncompromising/absolutist commitment to changing the entire international system. The Al-Qaeda movement aims to expel the USA and other 'infidels' from the Middle East and from Muslim lands generally. They also want to topple Muslim regimes/governments which they accuse of betraying the 'true Islam' and of collaboration with the US and its allies. Ultimately, their aim is to establish a pan-Islamist Caliphate uniting all Muslims.[9] These aims may appear grandiose in the extreme, but we need to bear in mind that bin Laden and his followers fanatically believe that they will prevail in their Jihad because Allah is on their side.

A major difference between the new terrorism of the Al-Qaeda network and more traditional groups is precisely its global network of networks, including affiliates, cells and support. These networks provide the movement with a presence and a capacity to act in at least 60 countries. It is the most widely dispersed non-state terrorist network ever seen and this is what gives the movement 'global reach'.[10]

'Traditional' terrorist movements generally confine themselves to mounting attacks in one country or region, though in some cases they do develop sophisticated overseas support networks to obtain finance, weapons, recruits, safe haven and the opportunity to enlist wider support for their cause.

The opening chapter of Part II of this book will assess Al-Qaeda's current strategy, modus operandi, targets and tactics and ask to what extent the War on Terrorism can be judged successful in its efforts to crush Al-Qaeda.

Theory and methodology

There is no universally accepted general social scientific theory of terrorism, or of counter-terrorism. This is not so surprising when one considers the extreme difficulty of developing and validating theories of other aspects of human society. On the other hand we do have a variety of different hypotheses, models and partial or limited theories derived from politics, strategy, history, ideology, psychology and sociology, for example, which can provide useful insights and understanding of aspects of terrorism and its associated activities.

The St Andrews/Southampton project team made a firm decision to allow members to draw on the theories, models and hypotheses which they found to be most valuable in their work on their specialist tasks. This proved to be the most practical and effective approach in our holistic research framework. UK preparedness was not something which could be adequately assessed simply by examining 'consequence management' and 'resilience', important though these aspects may be. To do our job properly we clearly needed to reassess the threat posed to the UK by the Al-Qaeda network of networks and other terrorist groups. How effective were the UK's intelligence agencies in gathering high-quality intelligence on Al-Qaeda and its affiliates? How far were the USA and other allies prepared to go in sharing intelligence on terrorism in the UK? How good was the analysis of intelligence? Did the newly established Joint Terrorism Analysis Centre make a significant improvement in threat assessment for government and the counter-terrorism agencies? What of the role of the Foreign and Commonwealth Office and the UK diplomatic efforts: to what extent do they assist British preparedness? Are the UK police forces adequately trained and resourced to undertake a major task in preventing terrorism, pursuing terrorists and how effective is cooperation between police and the Security Service (MI5), with the armed forces, and with other emergency services?

What is the appropriate role of the British Army in preventing and combating terrorism and in consequence management? How effective have they been in applying some of the key lessons learned from the Northern Ireland conflict and other terrorist campaigns around the world? Do they have enough troops and equipment of sufficient quality to undertake the mission they have been given in the so-called War on Terrorism? What is being done in order to enhance the protection of our National Critical Infrastructure against possible terrorist attack? How effective is the UK's emergency planning and training for contingencies such as terrorist attacks with weapons of mass destruction? Has the private sector significantly improved its own anti-terrorism measures since 9/11? If not, why not? And, perhaps most problematic of all, what should be done to counter the threat to the UK from home-grown Al-Qaeda linked cells of the kind that were involved in the London bombings on 7 July 2005, and the alleged Al-Qaeda-linked conspiracy to blow up airliners in mid-air en route across the Atlantic?

What more should be done to strengthen the UK's long-term preparedness and resilience against terrorism? And what should the UK do to help win the battle of ideas against Al-Qaeda's evil ideology?

These are just some of the questions explored in this book.

It is obvious that this holistic approach to our subject has necessitated the use of a variety of methodologies. The research team had access to the huge range of open source publications, including the burgeoning body of academic literature on terrorism, official reports and transcripts of trials, the print media, television and radio interviews and documentaries, the internet, one-to-one confidential interviews with policy-makers, legislators, government officials and members of all the security, criminal justice-related and military professions, and last but not least seminars and workshops comprised of academics, public and private security practitioners, lawyers and members of the armed forces, and members of the public, held under strict Chatham House rules. Although we did not have access to classified information we found a rich vein of research materials as a result of employing this eclectic methodology.

The historical context

Mainland Britain has experienced a remarkable degree of internal peace for over 250 years. The last instance of civil war in Great Britain was the 1745 Jacobite rebellion, brutally suppressed by Butcher Cumberland and his troops. The last major riot arising from religious sectarianism was the Gordon riot of June 1780 instigated by Lord George Gordon. He led a large mob to the Houses of Parliament to present a petition against the Catholic Relief Act of 1778. A riot ensued and lasted several days. It led to the loss of a large number of lives and considerable property damage.

In the nineteenth century there was considerable apprehension that industrial unrest would give rise to large scale violence. These fears proved to be unfounded. It is true that there was a brief armed rising by militant Chartists, members of a British working class movement for parliamentary reform, at Newport, following Parliament's summary rejection of their petition for reform in 1829. But this rising was swiftly suppressed. The main leaders of the rising were transported to Australia and other leading Chartists were arrested and imprisoned. Thereafter Chartist militancy declined and the leadership of the main working class movements remained largely in the hands of moderates. There was a brief alarm about possible confrontation at Tonypandy in 1910 when the then Home Secretary, Winston Churchill, employed troops to deal with what he perceived to be a real threat of industrial insurrection, but thankfully it receded.

In the inter-war period the internal threat in mainland Britain, as perceived by the authorities, was an upsurge of industrial unrest leading to an interruption of essential supplies and services. The Emergency Powers Act of the 1920s authorised the use of the military to aid the civil power in such circumstances, by helping to maintain essential supplies and services. The first major test of the new legislation came in 1926 with the General Strike. The government enlisted members of the public into the Civil Constabulary Reserve and used troops to run the government's Supply and Transport Organisation. The emergency passed off remarkably peacefully, largely due to the statesmanship and moderation of the trade union leaders and the caution of the government. Mainland Britain's long experience of internal peace is in sharp contrast to the continental European states' record of major civil conflicts during the same period. How can this be explained? In part it has much to do with Britain's strong tradition of civil policing by local forces with deep roots in their local communities and following the doctrine of minimal force in their policing of protest, unrest and public disorder. In Britain the police regard themselves as citizens in uniform, dependent for their success on the support and confidence of general public and not a paramilitary force sent in to coerce the population. It is true that the number of police trained and deployed to use firearms has vastly increased over recent years in response to the growth in the number of armed criminals. But the British police, in contrast to some police forces abroad, are not seen by the public as a hostile armed force of occupation.

Other factors that help to explain the relatively small levels of politically motivated violence on the British mainland in the nineteenth and twentieth centuries are: the absence of any experience of foreign occupation and concomitant violent resistance; the development of religious toleration, reducing and ultimately eradicating violent sectarian conflict; and the growing availability of peaceful channels for airing grievances and campaigning for demands (for example, trade unions, the universal franchise, the mass media and the development of pressure groups of all kinds).

It would be foolish to overlook the worrying recent developments that have fuelled higher levels of conventional crime, violent disorder, alienation and vandalism, particularly among youth. One factor is the continuing very high level of unemployment among young Muslims. Another is the worrying development of racial tensions in multi-ethnic communities and the rise in the number of racially motivated attacks. I shall be considering these factors in assessing the current and future threat of terrorism in Part II of this book.

A remarkable feature of the history of the British *mainland* since 1745 has been the absence of any civil war or major indigenous politically motivated violence. Yet, despite this domestic tranquillity successive British governments, the British Army and the British police and intelligence services have been compelled by circumstances to respond to a range of terrorist challenges even wider than that faced by the French, and more prolonged and lethal than the ETA terrorist campaign confronted by the Spanish authorities since the 1970s. There are three historical factors which explain this paradox: (1) the violent legacy of coercion, religious and political conflict, partition and suppressed civil war in Ireland; (2) in the early twentieth century, the British experience in confronting the use of terrorism by anti-colonial movements and the process of decolonisation from the end of the Second World War to the 1960s; and (3) terrorism emanating from the Northern Ireland conflict from the 1970s to the mid-1990s, the worst terrorism experienced in any European country in that period.

Terrorism in Northern Ireland[11]

The political culture and traditions in Northern Ireland, on both Republican and Loyalist extremes of the political spectrum, are so steeped in violence that the Province became a virtual laboratory for deploying protracted terrorism as a weapon within a liberal democratic state. By 1998 over 3,300 had died in 29 years of conflict. From the 'Peep O'Day Boys', the Ulster Volunteer Force (UVF), the Fenians and the Irish Republican Army (IRA), fresh generations of gunmen have emerged in the north and south. As Conor Cruise O'Brien has remarked:

Young people in both parts of Ireland have been brought up to think of democracy as part of everyday humdrum existence, but of recourse to violence as something existing on a superior plane, not merely glorious but even sacred. Resort to violence, that is, in conditions resembling those that spurred the Founders into action.

Insofar as IRA violence was directed against the British government since 1970 in order to force a British withdrawal from Ulster and the destruction of the Unionist regime, it must be described as a campaign against liberal democracy. But it must be admitted that, from the establishment of the Unionist regime in Stormont in 1922 to the 1980s, the northern Catholic minority suffered from political, social and economic discrimination. Moreover, the Special Powers Act introduced in Ulster in 1922 gave the government sweeping powers to suppress any unwelcome forms of political opposition. The outlawed IRA did attempt a campaign of bombings and attacks on policemen and soldiers in the north from 1956 to 1962, but it was an ignominious failure. The political initiative amongst the Catholics in the north was taken by the Civil Rights Association in the later 1960s, using non-violent demonstration, petition and political pressure. The IRA was compelled to involve itself in this political work to avoid complete isolation. Apparently blind to the real grievances of the Civil Rights movement, the hardline Unionists interpreted the movement as the front for the IRA conspiracy and revolution. Self-styled 'Loyalists' and the Royal Ulster Constabulary (RUC) over-reacted against Civil Rights marches and demonstrations, while the Revd Ian Paisley whipped up a campaign of anti-Catholic hatred comparable with that of Titus Oates. There is little room for doubt that the hardline Unionists mistook the angry rioting in Londonderry's Bogside in 1969 for a Fenian rising. And the Scarman Tribunal produced abundant evidence of the panic over-reaction by the RUC. As the civilian death toll in the street-fighting rose, the Londonderry and Belfast Catholics began to arm themselves and to look to the IRA as the only available armed Catholic defence organisation. The IRA leadership in Dublin were caught off guard by this escalation into armed conflict. They had, after all, recently swung over to a *political* strategy in the north. It was the 'Provisional' IRA which then formed and moved in rapidly in 1970 to fill this vacuum.[12] Led by hardline 'physical force' men like Sean MacStiofain, the Northern Republicans began to rally to the Provisional organisation because they were ready for military action, and the Provisionals became bitter rivals of the so-called 'Official' Marxist dominated IRA for the support of the Northern Irish Catholics.

It is worth keeping in mind that Belfast was the most ideal terrain for the urban terrorism. It is a city of over 400,000 people, most of whom lived in small homes in narrow streets. There were few natural boundaries within the city, and because of its featureless anonymity it was relatively simple for the terrorist to evade patrols and merge into its surroundings. Much of the property is Victorian or Edwardian, and yards are divided by high walls. There were ideal fields of fire in every street, and countless hiding places for sniping and ambush. Nor was there any shortage of privately held guns, many of them officially registered on the pretext of 'rifle-club' membership. Both the Provisionals and the Ulster Defence Association (UDA)[13] and the UVF[14] obtained up-to-date arms from abroad. The Provisionals benefited from considerable financial aid from Republican sympathisers in the USA, and from expropriations and 'donations' within Ulster. They were able to obtain the highly accurate gas-operated American armalite rifle, made in Japan under licence for the Japanese Self-Defence Force. But the major sources of IRA weapons, including Semtex, AK-47s, and machine guns were huge shipments of arms from Libya in the mid-1980s. Certainly the border with the Republic was in constant use by the Provisionals both as a source of arms and ammunition and as an escape route for terrorists. In sum, all these conditions were conducive to an extraordinarily protracted and bitter ethnic sectarian feud between the extreme Republicans and the extreme Loyalists and a war of attrition waged by the Provisionals with the aim of compelling the British Army to withdraw.

Ideologically, the Provisionals' campaign was callow in the extreme. It is true that they could depend on widespread sympathy among the Catholic population. The widespread Catholic hatred and resentment of the internment measure introduced by Faulkner's government in the summer of 1971 and the Bloody Sunday shootings[15] helped to fuel support for the Provisionals. By late 1972 the sympathy had been largely eroded by the revulsion against the particularly indiscriminate and bloody campaign of bombings in Belfast and Derry which hurt the innocent population (Catholic and Protestant alike), ruined livelihoods and which seemed to prove to the majority of the population the absolute necessity of a continuing British military presence. By continuing a stubborn policy of death and destruction the Provisionals forfeited all possibility of participation in, or real influence upon, the planning of a new constitutional structure for Northern Ireland to replace the now discredited Stormont system. Cathal Goulding's assessment of MacStiofain could really be applied to the Provisional movement as a whole:

> The whole thing I have against him is that he is a very narrow man, he is a man who won't accept or examine new ideas and in his rigidity he is sure that there is only one solution to this problem and that is by physical force. He has no time for politics of any kind – and a revolutionary who has no time for politics is in my mind a madman.[16]

There is no doubt that the Provisionals deployed an impressive range of terrorist techniques including car bombs, mortar attacks, assassinations, gaol-breaking, letter bombing and kidnapping. They repeatedly demonstrated capability in carrying terror bombings into London and other English cities. But terrorism can sink to the level of a corrupted and professionalised form of crime which is finally self-destroying. Nor did the Ulster Freedom Fighters (UFF) and UVF or the other Protestant extremist organisations in the Province have any better record.[17] Several recent studies have carefully documented the scale of their record of murder and destruction and show how they also actively incited violence and promoted sectarian hatred and bigotry.

The case of terrorism in Northern Ireland further supports my argument that liberal democracy is only seriously threatened by revolutionary terrorism when there is a general withdrawal of popular support from government, or when government appears entirely unable to deal with the problems that face it. This reassuring conclusion should not lead us to neglect the tragic costs of prolonged terror in a democracy: community values are destroyed; families are divided and bereaved; children are brought up in an atmosphere of suspicion and hatred and, in their teens, are socialised into terrible violence. Normal business and industry becomes impossible and new investment ceases. Whole sectors of cities are so damaged by terrorism that they take on the appearance of a land subjected to air attack. Political relations between parties and groups become poisoned, so that bargaining and compromise are instantly identified as 'betrayal'. Both extremes take on organisational forms and attitudes of paramilitary movements. It becomes increasingly difficult for the ordinary citizen to escape the terror of one or other of the armed camps. 'If you are not with us you are against us' becomes the rallying cry. Terrorism can corrupt and corrode democracy by establishing a kind of tyranny over men's souls and no democracy worth the name can afford to tolerate it.

Just as there were those in the Irish Republican movement who misread the history of Northern Ireland, and believed it was a case of British colonialism comparable to Cyprus, so there were some in the security forces who believed that they could simply apply the lessons of counter-insurgency acquired by the army in colonial situations and this would suffice to defeat the Provisional IRA. Both sides had to adapt to a much more complex reality. Eventually, the more pragmatic and politically astute political leaders in Sinn Fein/IRA had to recognise that they had to enter the political arena if they were to have any chance of securing the changes they desired. Following the 1998 Good Friday Agreement and its endorsement in the 22 May Referendum, it remained to be seen whether the hard-core Sinn Fein/IRA would be willing to give up the bomb and gun for good, although the IRA's announcement in May 2000 that it was prepared to put its weapons 'beyond use' and to allow independent observers to inspect its arms dumps was a major breakthrough. Eventually in 2005, the IRA announced the decommissioning of its weapons and only the use of peaceful means to pursue its goals. And on 26 September 2005, the head of the international decommissioning body, General de Chastelain, issued a statement confirming that the decommissioning had taken place.

Meanwhile, the security forces and successive British governments have had to learn that combating protracted terrorism in modern democratic society under the spotlight of the media and international opinion must be carried out in ways fully compatible with the maintenance of democracy, respect for human rights and the upholding of the rule of law. Even in this severe test, the criminal justice model of response and the police primacy worked best, with the Army providing invaluable support to the police.

As many commentators have pointed out, it is undoubtedly true that the British intelligence services were extremely preoccupied with Northern Ireland and the spill-over of Republican terrorism in the British mainland in the 1990s. This is understandable in view of the importance attached to keeping up the momentum of the Northern Ireland peace process, and the fact that the extremists in Continuity IRA and Real IRA, bitterly opposed to the Good Friday Agreement, were already embarking on a bombing campaign. In August 1998, Real IRA carried out the Omagh bombing in which 29 civilians were killed, the worst single atrocity in the history of 'the Troubles'. However, while counter-terrorist efforts were still heavily engaged in Northern Ireland matters, too little attention was being paid to the arrival of radical Islamists linked to terrorism, the dissemination of jihad, propaganda, and increasing support and recruitment efforts by radical Islamist groups, including Al-Qaeda.

Despite the increasing evidence of Al-Qaeda's growing transnational network and its capacity for suicide no-warning attacks aimed at mass killing, such as the deadly attacks on the US embassies in Kenya and Tanzania in August 1998, it appeared that monitoring radical Islamists in the UK was not given high priority by the intelligence services or the police. It seemed to many observers that there was a kind of unwritten understanding that if the radical imams and their followers refrained from planning or encouraging terrorist attacks within the UK, their preaching and propaganda activities would be tolerated by the authorities.

There were a variety of reasons for the neglect by the British authorities of the rise of the more dangerous international type of terrorism: an acute shortage of reliable intelligence from Afghanistan, Pakistan, Saudi Arabia and other Muslim countries where Al-Qaeda and its network had a growing presence; and a lack of appropriately trained intelligence officers to undertake the gathering of the vital HUMINT (human intelligence), essential for discovering the radical Islamist groups' intentions and plans. In the circumstances, it is hardly surprising to find that the British intelligence services were just as blind-sided regarding the growing Al-Qaeda threat as their colleagues in the USA and the intelligence services of Britain's EU allies. The shock of the 9/11 attacks showed that *all* the Western countries' intelligence agencies had a huge intelligence deficit concerning the Al-Qaeda network and its affiliates. There was a mountain to climb in the efforts to rectify this major weakness in the wake of 9/11.

The legislative context, pre-9/11

Prior to 9/11 the main legislation dealing with terrorism in the UK was designed primarily to deal with the severe problems of terrorism emanating from the Northern Ireland conflict. In 1969 it became clear to the government that the scale of the violence had become too great for the RUC to contend with. The Home Secretary of the day, James Callaghan, with the full support of Prime Minister, Harold Wilson, and the Cabinet, took the decision to deploy units of the British Army in support of the civil power. When the policing system was breaking down, the government had no other recourse if it was to prevent a slide into civil war. However, the militarisation of the conflict was not without cost.

Draconian measures such as internment without trial, events such as Bloody Sunday in 1972 when 14 unarmed civilians were killed by British troops and evidence of ill-treatment of detainees caused growing concern both in Britain and abroad. The decision to prorogue the Stormont Parliament and the establishment of Direct Rule in March 1972 transferred full responsibility for security in Northern Ireland to the British government. A Commission headed by Lord Diplock was set up to 'consider legal procedures to deal with terrorist activities in Northern Ireland'. The Diplock Report[18] provided the basis of the Northern

Ireland Emergency Provisions Act of 1973, providing special policing powers and special criminal justice procedures to deal with the terrorist emergency.

The most significant outcome of this inquiry was the establishment of the Diplock courts to try those charged with terrorism ('scheduled offences'). To counter the efforts of the terrorists to intimidate and coerce juries, witnesses, judges and lawyers, a single judge was appointed to hear the case and he was to sit without the jury. The judge has to be a regular member of the judiciary. And to help compensate for the absence of a jury the person convicted of a scheduled offence, the court has to give a judgement stating the reasons for the conviction as swiftly as possible in order to facilitate an appeal if the convicted person decides to contest the verdict. In spite of the doubts expressed about Diplock courts when they were first established, they have enabled the criminal justice system to deal with the most challenging series of terrorist cases in the legal history of the UK.

Far and away the most controversial measure adopted in an effort to deal with terrorism at the height of 'the Troubles' in Northern Ireland was internment or detention without trial. This was originally introduced in 1972 at the request of the government of Northern Ireland before Stormont was prorogued. The initial rounding up of large numbers was based on woefully inaccurate intelligence. When it became clear that many of those interned were not involved in the IRA or any other terrorist organisation, it caused a major outcry and became a propaganda weapon for the IRA both in Ireland and the USA. It also led to the development of a kind of 'Staff College' for terrorists among the internees. In other words, the introduction of internment was soon shown to be hugely counter-productive. By the end of 1975, Merlyn Rees, the Labour government's Secretary of State for Northern Ireland, had carried out his declared intention of releasing all internees. Many of them had been radicalised by their experience and became involved in the IRA activity when released.

The Prevention of Terrorism Act was not a panic measure. Its main provisions had already been prepared well before the carnage of the Birmingham pub bombing of 21 November 1974, in which 20 civilians were killed and 180 injured. And it was right and necessary that the government had such legislation ready, because the war in Ulster had already spilled over into mainland Britain over the previous 18 months. Indeed, before the Bill was introduced into Parliament nearly 700 people had been injured by IRA bombs in Britain. On a single day in March 1973, nearly 250 people had been injured and one killed in two bomb attacks at the Old Bailey and Great Scotland Yard. In 1974 there had been attacks at the National Defence College, Latimer, on a coach on the M62 in February, at the Tower of London in July, at Guilford in October and at Woolwich in November. But it was the Birmingham pub bombings that finally convinced public opinion, MPs and the government that emergency measures were necessary to try to prevent the spread of this barbarism.

The Act introduced by Roy Jenkins provided a valuable example of the kinds of special powers that can be used effectively to protect a society under severe terrorist attack without simultaneously suspending the constitution. One of its major provisions, the proscription of the IRA as a terrorist organisation, was, arguably 'more spectacular than effective'.[19] Security experts have long argued that proscription simply tends to drive the target organisation completely underground and makes the tasks of intelligence-gathering and detection more difficult for the police. Nevertheless, this move was politically well-judged, for it would have outraged public opinion if the IRA had been permitted to continue to meet, raise funds and recruit support openly in British cities. It was, after all, already a proscribed organisation in Ireland, both north and south of the border. Moreover the stiff penalties for belonging to, or professing to belong to the IRA, giving it financial or other support, or arranging or assisting in the arrangements of an IRA meeting were a useful token of the government's determination to crack down on terrorist organisations. And one positive benefit of proscription is that it deprives the terrorists of the opportunity to march, demonstrate and provoke affrays with rival groups. This helps to free the police from the dreary and time-consuming work of crowd and riot control on the streets and enables them to concentrate on protecting the general public and catching criminals.

A particularly controversial power under the Act was the power to exclude terrorists by denying them entry to Britain or by deportation. The Prevention of Terrorism Act enabled the Secretary of State to make exclusion orders to prevent acts of terrorism, whenever committed, designed to influence public opinion or government policy with respect to affairs in Northern Ireland.[20] This enabled the authorities to deny entry to (or deport) any person suspected of terrorist offences, or suspected of entering Britain for the purpose of committing terrorism. As the necessary instrument of this Act, port controls by police and immigration officials were considerably tightened. Port police had the power to stop, question and search any suspected person. These controls yielded much invaluable information to the security authorities.

Another very important power for the security forces is that of searching any person suspected of committing, preparing or instigating acts of terrorism. Apart from body searches of suspects, which may yield valuable evidence and intelligence, random searches of premises, and searches for specific equipment and materials used for terrorism, such as explosives and transmitters, can be specifically authorised under current anti-terrorism legislation.

The key police powers afforded by the Prevention of Terrorism Act, however, were those under section 7, clauses (1) and (2), dealing with arrest and detention. The police were thereby empowered to arrest without warrant a person whom they 'reasonably suspected' to be (i) a person guilty of a terrorist offence, or (ii) a person concerned in the commission, preparation or instigation of acts of terrorism, or (iii) a person subject to an exclusion order. Moreover, in particular cases the Secretary of State had the power to extend the period for which a suspect could be detained or questioned beyond the normal maximum of 48 hours. The additional period could not exceed five days, making the maximum period for which a person could be detained without being charged seven days. This power was an invaluable aid to the police, for it is interrogation that saves lives and provides the leads for catching other members of the terrorist organisation. And in the judgement of most intelligence experts 48 hours was not long enough for the process of interrogation to yield results. Seven days is generally just long enough for conventional police questioning methods to wear down the suspect's resistance. Frequently, the longer period has enabled the police to use bargaining power. Exceptionally, with the cooperation of the Director of Public Prosecutions, they could offer certain types of immunity from prosecution in return for everything a suspect knew. This method could be particularly effective in cases where suspects are likely to have become enmeshed in terrorist activities more through blackmail and intimidation than political conviction. For example, the super-grass system in Northern Ireland yielded invaluable information on terrorism for the RUC. This resulted in scores of arrests of terrorists from the IRA and the Irish National Liberation Army (INLA) and the Loyalist terrorist groups.

By the late 1990s it had become clear that the Prevention of Terrorism Act was urgently in need of replacement. It had been introduced to deal with terrorism emanating from the Northern Ireland conflict, and despite the efforts to broaden its scope to encompass international terrorist crimes in the UK in the 1984 Amendment to the Prevention of Terrorism Act, the legislation was still primarily configured to deal with the problem of IRA terrorism. Yet, by 1998, when the Good Friday Agreement confirmed major progress, it was becoming evident that *international terrorism* was to be the major future threat facing the UK and the international community. Last but not least, the Prevention of Terrorism Act's provisions were incompatible with the Human Rights Act which incorporated the European Convention on Human Rights into UK law, and with the Police and Criminal Evidence Act (PACE) which increased safeguards for suspects in the criminal justice process.

Lord Lloyd of Berwick headed an Inquiry into Legislation against Terrorism which reported in 1996 on the need for specific legislation dealing with Irish, international and domestic terrorism in the United Kingdom in the event of a lasting peace in Northern Ireland. The government drew heavily on Lord Lloyd's proposals to form the basis of Terrorism Act 2000, now serving as the framework of UK anti-terrorism legislation. The majority of those charged in the UK with terrorism offences are charged under the Terrorism Act 2000.

The new Act was very carefully scrutinised by Parliament, especially in the House of Lords, where there are a number of peers with expertise in anti-terrorism law and human rights. The Act eventually came into force on 19 February 2001.

In introducing the draft legislation, the government made clear that it agreed with Lord Lloyd's conclusion that there would be a need for permanent UK-wide legislation even when lasting peace was established in Northern Ireland. It also agreed with Lord Lloyd's conclusion that the time had come to put the necessary legislation onto a permanent footing. The government stated that it recognised the threat from international terrorist groups (and, to a lesser extent, from other groups within the UK), and that it was committed to changing the climate in which terrorists operate. The government summed up its aim as follows:

> To create legislation which is both effective and proportionate to the threat which the United Kingdom faces from all forms of terrorism, which ensures

that individual rights are protected, and which complies with the United Kingdom's international commitments.[21]

The key elements of the Terrorism Act 2000 show that the government achieved its stated legislative objectives. It provides UK-wide anti-terrorist legislation to replace the existing, separate process of temporary legislation for Northern Ireland and Great Britain. It covers international as well as internal terrorism, for example, inciting, planning and funding terrorism outside the UK. It defines terrorism more broadly than previous legislation, in an effort to cover all types. The Act gives the Secretary of State the power to proscribe a domestic or foreign organisation under Schedule 2 to the Act, but also establishes a Proscribed Organisations Appeal Commission to which an individual or an organisation affected by proscription can appeal against the decision to proscribe.

Under Part III of the Act, it is an offence for a person to assist in raising funds, to use or possess funds or other property for terrorist purposes, to help arrange or launder money for terrorist purposes, to fail to disclose information about a belief or suspicion that an offence has been committed, to receive or provide money or property if he intends that it should be used, or has reasonable cause to suspect that it will or may be used for the purposes of terrorism. The Act also provides new powers to seize suspected terrorist cash at borders. Customs and Excise is also given the power to apply to a court for an order to forfeit seized or detained cash. Under Part IV (39) it is made an offence to disclose any information which may prejudice a terrorist investigation or which will interfere with such an investigation.

The powers of arrest and stop and search of premises have been retained (with slight amendments) from the Prevention of Terrorism Act as amended.

As the public have argued that these powers are vital for protecting society against terrorism it is hardly surprising that we should find them embodied in the Terrorism Act 2000. Two of the most controversial elements of the earlier Prevention of Terrorism Act most criticised by human rights lawyers – that is, the power to place suspected terrorists in detention without trial and the power to exclude individuals from moving from one part of the UK – have been dropped from the Terrorism Act 2000 (though as we shall see in a later chapter, this power was reintroduced in the Anti-Terrorism, Crime and Security Act 2001, sometimes known as the Blunkett Act).

In brief, the UK already had in place, by the turn of the century, a comprehensive body of anti-terrorism legislation which was compatible with the Human Rights Act, and which could deal with the growing challenge of terrorism from an extreme radical Islamist network waging a global jihad.

The structure of this book

This multi-authored study deals with the complex problems of assessing the major types of terrorist threat faced by the UK. It opens with the editor's assessment of the changing threat posed to the UK by the Al-Qaeda network of networks, its cells and affiliates (Chapter 2). This is followed by Dr Tamara Makarenko's *tour d'horizon* of other foreign-based groups that have posed, or could in the future present, a terrorist threat to the UK. Dr Makarenko also highlights the activities of some of the leading propagandists for radical Islamist extremism within the UK (Chapter 3).

Professor John Simpson, one of the world's leading specialists in nuclear weapons and arms control, and his colleague Dr Jez Littlewood contribute an incisive and calm assessment of the CBRN threat (Chapter 4). It is conventional wisdom in some quarters to dismiss the chemical and radiological terrorist threats and to suggest that all our attention should now be directed at the biological terrorism threat. Yet this 'wisdom' rather conveniently overlooks the fact that the CBRN weapons of choice for terrorists so far have predominantly been chemical rather than biological. The threats section of the book concludes with an assessment of UK indigenous terrorist threats including Northern Ireland groups, links between organised crime and terrorism, and violent animal rights extremism (Chapter 5).

Part III covers a wide range of UK efforts to enhance preparedness in the light of the growing international terrorist threat since 9/11. It begins with Professor Frank Gregory's comparative analysis of national governance structures to manage the response to terrorist threats and attacks (Chapter 6). He draws some interesting conclusions about ways in which these structures could be strengthened. John Simpson and Jez Littlewood present a fascinating and original analysis of the role of counter-proliferation, arms control and disarmament as tools for reducing the CBRN threat (Chapter 7). This is followed by an analysis by John Simpson of the organisational changes UK government departments and agencies have made in response to the threat from nuclear terrorism (Chapter 8). Frank Gregory follows with an assessment of intelligence-led counter-terrorism in the UK in the same period (Chapter 9). Because of its key role the analysis of the UK police response to terrorism since 9/11 by Frank Gregory is undoubtedly one of the key elements in the overall assessment of the UK's homeland security performance. It is remarkably balanced and perceptive about the difficulties and sensitivities of the policing task.

Tamara Makarenko examines the role of agencies other than the police and the courts in law enforcement and inter-agency cooperation, and follows this with a useful guide to the relationship between immigration and asylum and security issues (Chapters 10 and 11).

There follows a case-study by the editor of the problems of enhancing the security of UK civil aviation since 9/11 (Chapter 12) and an assessment of UK maritime security improvements since 9/11 by Dr Peter Lehr (Chapter 13), thoughtful analysis of terrorism and public information by Anthony Richards (Chapter 14), efforts to enhance our cyber security by Darryl Howlett (Chapter 15), and the private sector's role in counter-terrorism by Frank Gregory (Chapter 16).

In Part IV, Frank Gregory opens with a timely examination of the UK's Civil Contingencies Act 2004 (Chapter 17). This is followed by Anthony Richards's balanced and sympathetic account of the efforts to enhance the UK's emergency response capability for dealing with terrorist attacks (Chapter 18).

The editor concludes the book in Part V by looking at the broader international and foreign and defence policy implications (Chapter 19). He then identifies what he suggests are the key components of a winning strategy to unravel the Al-Qaeda network of networks. There follows a very brief summary of the major findings of the contribution to the book (Chapter 20).

Needless to say, each team member has been free to make their own proposals and recommendations in their individual contributions to this book.

Notes

1 (2004) *Terrorism and Political Violence*, 17(1–2), Winter.
2 Schmid, A.P., Jongman, A.L. *et al.* (1988) *Political Terrorism: A New Guide to Actors, Authors, Concepts, Data Bases, Theories and Literature*, Amsterdam: North Holland Publishing.
3 Wilkinson, P. (2000) *Terrorism Versus Democracy: The Liberal State Response* (1st edn), London: Cass, pp. 12–14.
4 (1979–2005) *Terrorism: Documents of Local and International Control*, multi-volume series, Dobbs Ferry, NY: Oceana Publications.
5 Bergen, P.L. (2002) *Holy War Inc.: Inside the Secret World of Osama bin Laden*, New York, NY: Touchstone, and Gunaratna, R. (2002) *Inside Al Qaeda: Global Network of Terror*, New York, NY: Columbia University Press.
6 Jenkins, B. (1975) 'International terrorism: a balance sheet', *Survival*, 17(4), p. 158.
7 World Islamic Front (1998) 'Jihad against Jews and crusaders', available at www.fas. org/irp/world/para/docs/980223-fatwa.htm.
8 Lewis, B. (1998) 'Licence to kill: Osama bin Laden's declaration of jihad', *Foreign Affairs*, 77(6).
9 Gunaratna, R. (2002) *Inside Al Qaeda: Global Network of Terror*, New York, NY: Columbia University Press.
10 Mannes, A. (2004) *Profiles in Terror: The Guide to the Middle East Terrorist Organisations*, Lanham, MA: Rowman and Littlefield, pp. 3–112.
11 For the historical and political background to this conflict, see O'Brien, C.C. (1972) *States of Ireland*, London: Panther; Rose, R. (1971) *Governing Without Consensus*, London: Faber; Townshend, C. (1984) *Political Violence in Ireland: Government and Resistance Since 1848*, Oxford: Oxford University Press; Buckland, P. (1981) *A History of Northern Ireland*, Dublin: Gill and McMillan; and McKee, R. (1987) *Ireland: A History*, London: Weidenfeld & Nicolson.
12 On the emergence of the Provisionals, see Bishop, P. and Mallie, E. (1987) *The Provisional IRA*, London: Heinemann.
13 The best analysis of the Loyalist terror groups is Bruce, S. (1992) *The Red Hand: Protestant Paramilitaries in Northern Ireland*, Oxford: Oxford University Press.
14 Ibid.
15 For a collection of hitherto unpublished eye-witness accounts of Bloody Sunday, which threw into doubt the findings of Lord Widgery's official inquiry see Mullan, D. (ed.) (1997) *Eyewitness Bloody Sunday: The Truth*, Dublin: Wolfhound Press.
16 For accounts of the bitter disputes and tensions between Goulding and MacStiofain, see Bishop, P. and Mallie, E. (1987) *The Provisional IRA*, London: Heinemann; Maloney, E. (2002) *A Secret History of IRA*, London: Penguin Books; and English, R. (2003) *Armed Struggle: The History of the IRA*, London: Macmillan.
17 See Bruce, *The Red Hand*, op. cit., for example.

18 (1972) Report of the Commission to consider legal procedures to deal with terrorist activities in Northern Ireland, Cmnd 5185, London: HMSO.
19 (1974) *Economist*, 30 November.
20 Prevention of Terrorism (Temporary Provisions) Bill, 1974, Explanatory Memorandum.
21 (1999) *Legislation Against Terrorism: A Summary of the Government's Proposals*, Home Office, p. 2.

Part II

Threat assessment

2   The threat from the Al-Qaeda network

Paul Wilkinson

Is Al-Qaeda still an organisation?

Al-Qaeda is a transnational network of 'ism' rather than a traditional highly centralised and tightly controlled terrorist organisation. Its worldwide network of networks is bound together with a shared ideology, strategic goals, modus operandi and fanatical hatred of the USA and other Western countries, Israel, and the government of the regimes of Muslim countries which Al-Qaeda's leaders accuse of being 'apostates' on the grounds that they 'betray' the 'true Islam' as defined by bin Laden.[1]

This network of networks consisting of affiliated groups, operational cells and support networks in over 60 countries gives the Al-Qaeda movement a greater global reach than any previous international terrorist network.[2] It also provides Al-Qaeda with the flexibility and resilience to adapt and sustain its global jihad in spite of the many severe blows the movement has suffered. Al-Qaeda's core leadership, communication and training capabilities suffered major disruption and damage when the Taliban regime in Afghanistan, which had provided Al-Qaeda with safe haven, was overthrown in autumn 2001. Since 9/11, 15 leading Al-Qaeda militants have been captured or killed, and over 3,000 suspected Al-Qaeda followers have been arrested or detained. Moreover, millions of pounds of Al-Qaeda assets have been frozen in the banking system. Yet despite all these setbacks the movement has continued to recruit and raise more funds worldwide and to commit atrocities such as the bomb attacks in Madrid and London, massive suicide bombings in Iraq and the beheading of hostages.[3]

It is a dangerous illusion to assume that because Al-Qaeda's core leadership does not carry out the detailed planning, organisation and implementation of all the attacks carried out in its name the movement no longer exists or has a purely marginal role. Bin Laden and Ayman Zawahiri provide the crucial ideological leadership and strategic direction of the movement. It is they who inspire new recruits to join the global jihad and to be ready to sacrifice their lives as suicide bombers for the cause. Al-Qaeda videotapes and websites demonstrate the great importance they attach to propaganda.[4] Recently, they have expanded into broadcasting their own news programme called 'Voice of the Caliphate' which attempts to use world events to put over their movement's perverted doctrines.

Al-Qaeda's leaders are well aware that they cannot rely on the mosques as the sole channel for spreading their ideas. Clear evidence that they continue to win the hearts and minds of those who are attracted to joining Al-Qaeda affiliated cells around the world is the way the websites of these affiliated groups swiftly claim the Al-Qaeda connection in their claims of responsibility for attacks, and the way the Al-Qaeda core leadership are so quick to claim 'ownership' for successful attacks. However, there are some clear risks involved in this decentralised network of networks structure. What happens if there is a schism over strategy and tactics between leadership and one of the affiliates? And what happens if a splinter group challenges the leadership by defying its decrees?

Aims, capabilities and plans

The main aims of the Al-Qaeda movement are:

- to eject the USA and its allies from the Middle East and all Muslim lands;
- to overthrow existing Muslim governments/regimes, on the grounds that they are 'Apostate' regimes which betray the cause of the true Islam, as defined by bin Laden and Zawahiri; and
- ultimately to establish a pan-Islamist Caliphate to bring all Muslims under the rule of an Islamist super-state.

Al-Qaeda believes that the use of the weapon of mass casualty terrorism and the belief that Allah is 'on their side' will ensure that they win ultimate victory. The aim of killing as many of their 'enemy' including civilians, wherever and whenever the opportunity arises was spelt out in bin Laden's notorious Fatwa of February 1998.[5] It is Al-Qaeda's explicit commitment to mass killing, so horrifically demonstrated in its 9/11 attacks, that makes it by far the most dangerous terrorist network in the modern world.

What do we know of Al-Qaeda's capabilities? The key resource for any terrorist organisation is its membership and their level of commitment, training, expertise and experience. In attack after attack Al-Qaeda's network of networks has proved its ability to deploy large numbers of operatives and to recruit more than sufficient new members to replace those lost by capture and death in suicide bombing or in armed confrontations with security forces. We should remember that it only takes relatively small numbers to carry out attacks which can kill thousands and inflict severe economic damage and disruption. The 9/11 attacks were carried out by 19 suicide hijackers and a support network of a handful of people.[6] There is no evidence that the movement is unable to obtain the funds and explosives it needs to carry out major coordinated mass killing suicide bombing attacks. There is overwhelming evidence from a whole series of police investigations into Al-Qaeda movement activities that the local networks are not only carrying out the planning and execution of operations, they are in most cases raising the cash to fund such operations and obtaining the explosives and other materials and vehicles or other equipment through thefts, corruption and organised crime in their own areas.

However, although small-scale terrorist bombing is a very low-cost activity for the local networks, the cost of mounting a coordinated mass-casualty attack may well be beyond the resources of a local network. It has been estimated that the 9/11 attacks cost Al-Qaeda around $500,000. The freezing of Al-Qaeda assets in the banking system has not been extensive enough, however, to deprive Al-Qaeda of all its resources but it has compelled the terrorist leadership to rely more than ever on local networks for the resources to carry out local attacks.

By far the more important capability for carrying out local attacks is the availability of expertise, especially in bomb making, operational planning and tactics. The Al-Qaeda network's supply of well-trained and experienced terrorist operatives has been enormously increased as a result of the field experience provided in the Iraq conflict. Foreign terrorists who have been involved with the Al-Qaeda jihad in Mesopotamia are now able to return to their countries of origin, including the EU member states, battle hardened and with skills acquired and honed in Iraq. It is also noteworthy that in recent months we have seen tactics methods copied from the terrorist campaign in Iraq being used in Afghanistan by Taliban and Al-Qaeda-linked groups and their Afghan warlord allies to attack members of North Atlantic Treaty Organisation (NATO) forces deployed to assist President Karzai's government. For example, the terrorists have rammed vehicles carrying British personnel using vehicles packed with explosives.[7] In another close parallel with Iraq, the terrorists have also started to mount attacks on recruits to the newly established Afghan Army.

It is possible to obtain a clear idea of the Al-Qaeda leadership's long-term strategy from their writings. Zawahiri's Knights Under the Prophet's Banner, for example, stresses the importance they attach to the dual strategy of seeking to establish control over a base area within the heart of the Muslim world while at the same time carrying the struggle to the homelands of the USA and its allies.[8] The US military intercepted a letter from Zawahiri to Abu Musab al-Zarqawi, former Head of Al-Qaeda who was killed in 2006. Zawahiri is confident that Al-Qaeda will gain a victory in Iraq, and sees this as the first step, the setting up of a base area initially in Iraq, but followed by waging jihad in Syria, Lebanon, Egypt, finally leading on to the destruction of Israel. The US Department of Defense is convinced that his document is genuine, and, if so, it provides an interesting glimpse of Al-Qaeda's strategic plans. The letter also reveals evidence of divisions within the global Al-Qaeda network. Zawahiri warns that Zarqawi's particularly cruel measures such as the mass killing of Shia Muslims and the beheading of hostages may alienate public opinion in the Muslim world. If this letter is genuine, as the American government believes, it confirms that the core leadership is unable to control all activities carried out in the name of Al-Qaeda. It also confirms the point made earlier re schisms: such a major split on questions of tactics suggests the possible development of deeper and more lasting splits in the movement.

As for plans for specific operations, alas we do not have adequate human intelligence on the precise intentions of the operational planners, cell leaders and support networks. However, we can learn from the investigations carried out by police and judicial bodies into previous successful and failed attacks, in order to learn more about their modus operandi. We know enough from the case history to understand the care and sophistication Al-Qaeda network groups use to plan attacks. A vivid example was the information found on an Al-Qaeda laptop computer captured in Pakistan which showed that the operation's planners were closely examining not only the details of the security provided for key financial targets they planned to attack in the US, but also the precise structure of the buildings in order to decide on the type and strength of explosives to use. It is typical of the Al-Qaeda network to engage in detailed reconnaissance and intelligence gathering in preparation for any major operation.[9]

How the Iraq factor has been exploited by the Al-Qaeda movement

One of the most significant developments in the evolution of Al-Qaeda since 2003 has been the way the movement has exploited the allied invasion and occupation of Iraq. Whatever view one may take on the decision to invade Iraq it is simply ignoring reality to deny that the invasion and occupation have been a big boost for Al-Qaeda and a setback for the coalition against terrorism. The invasion was a propaganda gift to Al-Qaeda because it could portray it as an unprovoked imperialistic attack on a Muslim land. Al-Qaeda poses as the defender of Muslim lands and people everywhere. It used this as a recruiting sergeant and as an opportunity for fund raising for its global jihad.[10] Moreover, the conflict provided a rich concentration of US and other Western military and civilian targets in a country which the militants could enter all too easily across virtually uncontrolled borders.[11] As this fragile experiment in establishing a democratic government moved forward in Iraq, Al-Qaeda had a growing incentive to attack because the last thing it wishes to see in Iraq, or anywhere else in the Muslim world, is the successful establishment of a democratic political system. Having failed to prevent the free elections in January 2005 it is now desperate to disrupt the efforts to secure a stable democratic government for Iraq and to provoke an all out civil war between the Sunnis and the Shiite majority. This is what the brutal Al-Qaeda bomb attacks on Shiite civilians and clerics are designed to achieve. The Iraq conflict has also deflected valuable military assistance and finance away from Afghanistan at a time when the Kabul government has desperately needed help to counter the resurgence of the Taliban.[12]

It is absurd to suggest that recognising the way Al-Qaeda has exploited the war in Iraq to its own considerable advantage in some way 'excuses' Al-Qaeda's terrorism. In my view there can never be an excuse for the use of terrorism, whoever the perpetrators.[13] Terrorism involves the deliberate mass murder and injury of civilians and is a crime against international law and humanity. However, understanding more about the motivation of terrorists and how they are attracted into extremist groups and groomed to be suicide bombers is a vital subject for research. 'Know thine enemy' has always been a key maxim of successful strategists. How are we to unravel Al-Qaeda if we do not understand what makes them tick? Nor should we overlook unforeseen consequences of foreign policy decision-making, especially when the key decisions are taken by a more powerful ally which may also have failed to anticipate and plan for the implications of their policy for the struggle against international terrorism.[14]

Know thine enemy: the nature and strategic implications of the Al-Qaeda threat

The Al-Qaeda movement is the archetype of the new terrorism; and its absolutist and grandiose ideology, pledged to recasting the entire international system, and its record of mass murder of civilians, help to explain why it is now the most severe international terrorist threat ever posed to international peace and security in the entire history of non-state terrorism. One does not need access to classified intelligence sources to reach this conclusion. The evidence is all too clear from open sources available to all who profess a serious interest in the subject. What are Al-Qaeda's key characteristics?

A track record of terrorist attacks aimed at mass killing

This characteristic was apparent well before the 9/11 attacks. For example, Al-Qaeda was responsible for the August 1998 bombings of the US Embassies in Nairobi and Dar es Salaam that killed over 200 and injured over 5,000. On 11 September 2001 Al-Qaeda suicide hijackers crashed two commercial airliners into the World Trade Center towers in New York, another airliner into the Pentagon building in Washington DC and one into a field in Pennsylvania, causing the deaths of almost 3,000 people. This death toll exceeded the numbers killed in the Japanese attack on Pearl Harbor and the total number of people killed by the IRA in 25 years of terrorism in Northern Ireland.[15] Since 9/11, Al-Qaeda's network and its affiliates have killed hundreds more civilians in terrorist attacks around the world including the Bali bombing and the Madrid train bombings, each of which killed over 200 civilians.

Absolutist ideology and commitment to global terror war

Al-Qaeda has a universalistic ideology aimed not only at forcing the USA and its allies to withdraw their presence from the Middle East and all other parts of the Muslim world, but also at toppling the government of all Muslim states which it sees as betraying the 'true Islam' by collaborating with the West, and ultimately establishing a new pan-Islamic Caliphate. In February 1998 Al-Qaeda issued a declaration in the name of 'The World Islamic Front for Jihad Against the Jews and Crusaders', stating that 'it was the duty of all Muslims to kill US citizens – civilian as well as military – and their allies, everywhere'.[16] This explicit commitment to mass killing is another feature which differentiates Al-Qaeda from more traditional terrorist groups. As Brian Jenkins rightly observed, 'the terrorists of the 1970s and 90s wanted a lot of people watching, not a lot of people dead'.[17] The Al-Qaeda network wants a lot of people dead *and* a lot of people watching.

It believes that this greatly increases the efficacy of the weapon of terror, and that mass terrorisation of its enemies, including even the US superpower, will ultimately work as a means of undermining its opponents and securing the victory which it believes is ultimately inevitable because, it believes, Allah will ensure it.

High propensity for using chemical, biological, radiological and nuclear terrorist weaponry

It follows logically from Al-Qaeda's utterly ruthless commitment to mass killing of 'infidels' (non-Muslims) and 'apostates' (those Muslims who betray 'true Islam' by cooperating with the West) that it has an intense interest in acquiring and deploying unconventional weapons which would greatly increase its capacity for mass killing; for example, chemical, biological or radiological weapons. This is not just a vague speculation by the mass media or by security experts. Al-Qaeda has *already used*, or attempted to use, unconventional weapons on occasion. Mercifully, there have been cases where Al-Qaeda's efforts to employ such weapons have been thwarted by intelligence service and police action. In addition, there is ample evidence that it has been actively pursuing additional materials for CBRN weapons and the technical knowledge to weaponise these materials. For example, Al-Qaeda exploded a tanker truck containing gas to attack a Jewish synagogue in Djerba, Tunisia, in April 2002.[18] Its plan to attack the US Embassy in Rome by poisoning its water supply was fortunately thwarted by the police. The training manual used by Al-Qaeda found by the police in Manchester contains a whole section on poisons, and the *Encyclopaedia of the Jihad*, used by the organisation, includes a volume dealing specifically with CBRN weapons. Important evidence, including documents and videos of chemicals being tested on animals, was discovered by the Allies' forces in Afghanistan, in buildings which Al-Qaeda had been forced to vacate in a hurry. Whitehall sources are also reported to have been told, that in Operation Anaconda in Afghanistan, US troops found an Al-Qaeda biological weapons laboratory. Although suicide car and truck bombings and shooting attacks are likely to remain the standard tactics of Al-Qaeda it is only a matter of time before it carries out a chemical attack or possibly a 'dirty bomb' combining radioactive isotopes with high explosives.

The inherent advantages of Al-Qaeda's structure as a 'network of networks'

By using a global network of operational cells, preparative cells, support cells and affiliated groups such as Jemaah Islamiyya and the Salafist Group for Call and Combat, which it has penetrated and manipulated, Al-Qaeda has been able to sustain its global terror campaign on a number of fronts simultaneously.[19] It has by this means been able to adapt despite losing its state sponsor, the former Taliban regime in Afghanistan. The multinational composition of the Al-Qaeda network, its presence in over 60 countries and the inherent difficulty of identifying the links between the different components of the network, and monitoring their linkages and communications, makes Al-Qaeda far more difficult to defeat than a traditional terrorist group with a single vertical structure and a single territorial focus for its terrorist operations.

Why is the UK a top target for the Al-Qaeda network?

The reasons why the UK is a prime Al-Qaeda target may seem too glaringly obvious to rehearse. However, in case there are some who still believe that the UK is magically immune from such attacks it is worth summarising the grounds for the UK authorities' firm conviction that the UK homeland and British citizens and facilities overseas are prime Al-Qaeda targets.[20]

- Al-Qaeda has repeatedly threatened to attack Britain in messages released to the Arabic media.
- Some terrorist attacks against British targets overseas (for example, the HSBC building and British Consulate in Istanbul) leading to deaths and injuries have shown the Al-Qaeda network's continuing effort to attack UK targets.
- Some major terrorist conspiracies to mount terrorist attacks in the UK such as the alleged plot to blow up nine or 10 airliners en route from Heathrow to the USA, have been thwarted or disrupted by police action.
- The UK is the closest ally of the USA and has been a key participant in both the Afghan and Iraq conflicts.
- Britain has a sizeable Muslim minority population, small numbers of whom are known to support or sympathise with Al-Qaeda and associated groups.
- The Security Service has concluded that Al-Qaeda has regrouped and strengthened its organisation in Pakistan and that one of the reasons why the UK has become increasingly vulnerable is that Pakistan is visited by tens of thousands of people each year. Also, intelligence agencies have found it extremely difficult to penetrate the camps there.[21]
- Britain is a very open society, therefore vulnerable to terrorists seeking to hide within its heavily urbanised population.
- Al-Qaeda sees the result of the 2004 Spanish General Election[22] and the new Socialist government's decision to withdraw Spanish forces from Iraq as a major victory. There is therefore a real possibility that Al-Qaeda will use similar tactics to intimidate the UK, especially in the period leading up to the next General Election.
- In November 2006 the then Head of the UK Security Service, Dame Eliza Manningham-Buller, stated that her service was aware of over 1,600 hard-core militants in the UK capable of involvement in terrorism, and 200 groups and 20 significant terrorist conspiracies, thus underlining the threat from a rapidly growing number of 'home-grown' terrorist recruits in the UK.[23]

The 7 July 2005 suicide bombings in London which killed 52 civilians were carried out by a group of this kind, though it seems probable that it had strong links to Pakistan-based extremists. The phrase 'home-grown cells' may be slightly misleading.

Al-Qaeda targeting

One of the most frequently asked questions about Al-Qaeda is 'which potential targets are most at risk of attack?'. Sadly, there is no simple answer. The track record of Al-Qaeda and its affiliates and the information on targeting contained in its training manual show that it aims to strike at targets over a very wide range, both in geographic and functional terms. It is interested in attacking 'hardened' targets, such as political leaders and military, maritime and aviation targets. It also aims to cause maximum economic damage and destruction by attacking key economic infrastructure targets with a modicum of security protection, such as major financial institutions and energy installations. However, it has also shown a readiness to attack soft targets where it can cause large-scale loss of life with minimum problems of access, such as tourist bars, hotels, shopping areas and other places where the public gather in large numbers.[24]

It is understandable that the possibility of attacks on civilian aviation has been given such close attention: 9/11 was carried out by suicide hijackers turning airlines into weapons of mass killing, and we have abundant evidence that the Al-Qaeda network tends to return to targets and tactics which they regard as particularly successful.[25] To them, 9/11 was a great victory over their hated enemy, the USA.

In August 2006 the UK police revealed that they believed they had uncovered an Al-Qaeda-linked plot to mount suicide sabotage attacks on airliners flying from the UK on transatlantic routes. If this alleged plot involved nine or 10 airliners and aimed to blow them up over urban centres, the scale of lethality and destruction caused could have been even larger than 9/11.[26]

However, Al-Qaeda and its affiliates have also attacked a wide variety of other targets. The attack on the USS Cole and the Limburg and its plans to attack shipping in the Straits of Gibraltar show that the maritime dimension is also seen as an attractive alternative transportation target in its eyes, perhaps all the more so because shipping, ports and harbours have been very slow to take really effective security measures. Also, its attacks on underground trains in London and train bombings in Madrid on 3 November 2004 show that they have also been attracted by the opportunities of attacking rail passenger services, a particularly difficult target to protect.

Al-Qaeda and its affiliates have also attacked Christian churches, restaurants, banks, buses, consulates, residential compounds and civilians and members of the military as part of the coalition presence in Iraq and Afghanistan, and many other targets. The targeting and tactics are undoubtedly shaped by its ambitious long-term aims of undermining its perceived enemies' economic and military power and political leaderships, but it is also determined to sustain a campaign of terrorising the public in its target countries. Hence it sees bomb attacks on civilian soft targets as valuable in creating this climate of fear and undermining the will of the USA and its allies to resist its 'jihad'. For all these reasons it would be foolish and misleading to predict the 'next target' or to rule out certain targets. Maximum vigilance across the board is what is required if we are to improve the chances of picking up early warning signs of imminent attack.

Tactics

The same caution needs to be entered in regard to the Al-Qaeda network's choice of tactics. It has frequently used suicide vehicle bombings, but it has also used or planned to use shooting attacks, suicide hijacking, suicide sabotage bombing, man-portable air-defence system (MANPAD) attacks, an LPG truck, poisoning water supplies, ricin, conventional high explosive bombings, suicide maritime attacks, booby traps and many other tactics and methods. Once again, it would be dangerous and foolhardy to lay stress on one or two particular tactics. It has shown great flexibility and the ability to innovate and to plan terrorist operations with extraordinary thoroughness. To know the Al-Qaeda enemy is not to underestimate it.

In assessing possible targets and tactics, the question is often posed: 'Is deterrence still a useful objective for the anti-terrorism agencies and governments threatened with attack?'. Obviously, individual suicide terrorists, by definition, are not amenable to the logic of deterrence in regard to their own physical survival. However, this does not mean that deterrence has no validity in relation to Al-Qaeda strategy and tactics.[27] Al-Qaeda planners want their operations to *succeed*. They do not want to waste 'martyrs' in unsuccessful actions. Hence, if the targeted country can cause attacks on certain high-value targets to be potentially costly to the terrorist movement, and so unlikely to give a chance of real Al-Qaeda 'success', the logic of deterrence can still apply.

Structure of Al-Qaeda-linked groups

In the course of numerous investigations into terrorist conspiracies over the past two years the Security Service and New Scotland Yard's Anti-Terrorism Squad have discovered that Al-Qaeda-linked groups are adapting some of the features of the self-contained cells which characterised the IRA cells which operated in the UK in the 1980s and 1990s.[28]

Each group is commanded by an organiser, a planner who exercises tight control over the members of the group. There will also be the equivalent of the old IRA 'quartermaster' responsible for the group's supply of explosives and firearms. The groups are engaged both in planning and carrying out attacks, and in support work such as obtaining funds through criminal activity such as fraud and intimidation and courier activity, in addition to training new volunteers.[29]

In its investigations of terrorist conspiracies involving Al-Qaeda-linked groups in the UK the Security Service has discovered that the core leadership of the movement in Pakistan continues to delegate initiatives to different cells, but that the movement's structure is more coherent and with far more linkages between the groups and the core leadership than it had thought hitherto,[30] and far more sophisticated planning of attacks than had earlier been believed.

Recruitment and training

Considerable care is taken in targeting the right kinds of potential recruit, mainly alienated young Muslims in their late teens or early twenties. It is a mistake to think of mosques as the major places where recruiting takes place. Many of the young men attracted into the movement have had little or no contact with traditional mosques and religious leaders. If they are second or third generation Muslims who have been born and bred in the UK, many find it difficult to relate to many of the imams in the mainstream mosques: many imams do not speak English and, except in a minority of cases, they preach mainstream interpretations of the Koran and appear to have no message to appeal to angry Muslim youths. Some recruits may be converted by radical clerics operating in radical mosques. Many are recruited through contacts in a whole range of social institutions, such as university campuses,[31] gymnasiums and summer camps. Some are recruited in the prison system.[32] Many more are recruited by the internet websites of extremist groups, taped messages from Al-Qaeda's leader on TV or radio. All the evidence is that the flow of new recruits is far outstripping the capacity and resources of the Security Service to carry out surveillance of their activities.[33]

Conclusion

This chapter has argued that Al-Qaeda is the most dangerous international terrorist network in the history of modern terrorism. This is because of its commitment to mass killing and economic destruction and disruption, and because it has absolutist religio-political beliefs which make it incapable of political pragmatism and compromise.

Moreover, the Al-Qaeda network is particularly skilled at hiding among the civilian population. Three other characteristics make it particularly hard for an open democratic society to prevent its attacks:

- its attacks are generally carried out by suicide bombers or hijackers;
- it does not give warnings of its attacks, thus maximising the carnage and destruction that is likely to result; and
- on numerous occasions it has carried out coordinated attacks on several targets simultaneously, thus creating additional challenges for the counter-terrorism agencies and the emergency services' first responders.

Notes

1 For useful accounts of the origins and ideology of Al-Qaeda, see Corbin, J. (2003) *The Base: Al-Qaeda and the Changing Face of Global Terror* (revised edition), New York: Simon & Schuster, and Gunaratna, R. (2002) *Inside Al-Qaeda: Global Network of Terror*, London: Hurst & Co.

2 On the importance of networks, see Roy, O. (2004) *Globalised Islam: Deterritorialisaton and the Search of the New Ummah*, London: Hurst & Co., and Abou Zahab, M. and Roy, O. (2004) *Islamist Networks: The Afghan-Pakistan Connection*, London: Hurst & Co.

3 For an interesting attempt to explain Al-Qaeda's capacity to adapt and survive, see Gerges, F.A. (2005) *The Far Enemy: Why Jihad Went Global*, New York, NY: Cambridge University Press. For Al-Qaeda's training manual 'Guidelines for Beating and Killing Hostages', see Al-Qaeda Manual UK/BM-76 Translation, Eleventh lesson in Laqueur, W. (ed.) (2004) *Voices of Terror*, New York: Reed Press, pp. 406–7.

4 There are countless references to the Iraq conflict by propagandists supporting Al-Qaeda's terror campaign. See, for example, 'Iraq's Al-Qaeda Leader Mocks Bush and Republican Defeat While Singling Out Donald Rumsfeld', available at www.pipelinenews.org/index.cfm?page=alqaeda111106.htm; and www.memritv.org/Transcript.asp?p1=862.

5 For the text of Osama bin Laden's notorious statement 'Jihad Against Jews and Crusaders' put out in the name of the World Islamic Front, see Laqueur (ed.), op. cit., pp. 410–12.

6 For a detailed analysis of the 9/11 conspiracy and the way in which it was implemented, see (2005) Report of the National Commission on Terrorist Attacks Upon the United States, *The 9/11 Commission Report*, New York, NY: W. W. Norton & Co.

7 See Nawa, F. (2006) 'How the West Short-Changed Afghanistan', *The Sunday Times*, 29 October, pp. 48–59, and Loyd, A. and Luddin, T. (2006) 'The Face of Afghanistan five years after the fall of the Taliban Knights', *The Times*, pp. 37–8.

8 For example, Al Zawahiri, A. (2001) *Under the 'Prophet's Banner'*, London: Al-Sharq al-Awsat (in Arabic), 12 December, translation from FBIS, Document No. FBIS-NES-2001-1212.

9 See also report of the trial in London of Al-Qaeda terrorist Barot: he studied the structure of buildings he intended to target to calculate the type of bomb that would be needed to wreak maximum carnage and destruction.

10 The intelligence service in both the USA and the UK had warned their respective governments prior to an invasion of Iraq in 2003 that one of the consequences would be that the Al-Qaeda network would exploit the invasion and ensuing occupation to mount terror attacks and to boost their support. Both in the USA and the UK the intelligence services warned their governments of Al-Qaeda efforts to mount further terrorist attacks in 2006. However, the reaction of the UK government was either to deny any connection between foreign policy and vulnerability to terrorism, or to attempt to totally ignore or play down its significance.

11 One of the great strategic mistakes made in Iraq after the invasion was the failure to establish tight border controls for Iraq, thus allowing large numbers of terrorists to drift into Iraq.

12 The author warned of this danger when he gave written and oral evidence to the Parliamentary Select Committee on Foreign Affairs in 2002 and again in 2005.

13 See Wilkinson, P. (1977) *Terrorism and the Liberal State*, Basingstoke: Macmillan.

14 See Gregory, F. and Wilkinson, P. (2005) ESRC Research briefing, *The World Today*, June–July, Chapter 2, pp. 46, 47.

15 See McKitterick, D. *et al.* (1998) *Lost Lives*, Edinburgh: Mainstream – the most comprehensive and accurate record of deaths from terrorism and sectarian conflict in Northern Ireland; in the Pearl Harbor attack there were over 3,000 casualties of which just over 2,000 were fatalities.

16 See bin Laden, 'Jihad Against Jews and Crusaders', op. cit., n. 5.

17 Jenkins, B.M. (1975) *Will Terrorists go Nuclear?*, Santa Monica, CA: RAND Paper, p. 5541, P4.

18 See description of the attack in (2002) *Patterns of Global Terrorism*, Washington, DC: Department of State, country report for Tunisia.

19 This phenomenon is brilliantly analysed by Jessica Stern in (2003) 'The Protean Enemy', *Foreign Affairs*, July–August, and Rashid, A. (2002) *The Rise of the Militant Islam in Central Asia*, New Haven, CT: Yale University Press.

20 For confirmation that the UK is a prime target, see Cowan, R. and Norton-Taylor, R. (2006) 'Britain Now No. 1 al Qaida target – anti-terror chiefs', *Guardian*, 19 October, p. 1, an article based on a briefing by UK terror chiefs.

21 Ibid.; see also Abou, M. and Roy, O. (2004) *Islamist Networks: The Afghan–Pakistan Connection*, London: Hurst & Co.

22 For Al-Qaeda's claiming the credit for the outcome of the 2004 Spanish General Election, see Moghaddam, F.M. (2006) *From the Terrorists' Point of View: What They Experience and Why They Come to Destroy*, Westport, CT: Praeger Security International, p. 5.

23 Mile End lecture by Dame Eliza Manningham-Buller, 9 November 2006.

24 See Gunaratna, op. cit.

25 See (2005) *9/11 Commission Report*, Washington, DC: W. W. Norton.

26 In a press briefing at New Scotland Yard, Peter Clarke, Head of the Anti-Terrorism Branch, provided a very positive picture of the progress of this huge investigation.

27 See, Davis, P.K. and Jenkins, B.M. (2002) *Deterrence and Influence in Counterterrorism*, Santa Monica, CA: RAND.

28 See Cowan, R. and Norton, R. (2006) 'Britain Now No. 1 al-Qaida target – anti-terror chiefs', *Guardian*, 19 October, pp. 1–2.

29 Ibid.

30 Ibid.

31 See Taher, A. and Fradher, D. (2006) 'Islamists infiltrate four universities', *The Sunday Times*, 12 November, p. 4.

32 See Brady, B. (2006) 'Imams bid to convert radicals in prisons', *Scotland on Sunday*, 12 November, p. 2.

33 See, for example, (2006) *Report of the Parliamentary Intelligence and Security Committee into the 7th July bombings*, London: The Stationery Office, for evidence of the security service problem of overstretch.

3 International terrorism and the UK

Assessing the threat

Tamara Makarenko

The UK has had vast historical domestic experience with terrorism. Protracted conflict and ever-elusive peace prospects in Northern Ireland have preoccupied the attention and resources of British government and security institutions for decades. Despite the government making decisive inroads in alleviating the threat posed by domestic terrorism, its very focus on developments in Northern Ireland has deflected attention from producing complete assessments of the threat posed by foreign-based terrorist groups to the UK. Although the UK has not experienced 'spectacular' acts of terrorism perpetrated by international groups such as those that occurred in the USA on 11 September 2001,[1] it would be a gross exaggeration to suggest that international terrorism has not gained an important foothold in Britain.

Regardless of the relative absence of international terrorist acts committed on British soil, international terrorist groups have used the UK as a base from which logistical operations have been organised in support of acts of terrorism conducted in other countries. Offering an open society that respects the rule of law and prioritises the rights of individuals (at times to the detriment of the security of the state), the UK – directly and indirectly – has facilitated terrorist financing, recruitment, and political support. In many respects the UK has come to represent an important node in many international terrorist networks. For the UK, therefore, the greatest threat posed by foreign-based terrorist groups for much of the past decade has been indirect (that is, contributing to criminality and community tensions) via the support structures they have established. However, following the terrorist attacks of 11 September 2001, the British government has increasingly voiced its concerns that the UK – like America – had moved from posing an improbable target for international terrorism, to becoming a vulnerable and likely target for international terrorist groups such as Al-Qaeda.

The security of the UK, as with other liberal democratic nations, has been greatly affected by the events of 11 September – an event that exemplified the dangers expressed by terrorism analysis throughout the 1990s, expressing the dangers posed by the emerging 'new terrorism'. Characterised by terrorist groups that are inherently transnational in nature, utilise sophisticated communications and financial structures, seek mass casualties without necessarily claiming responsibility, and seriously entertain the possibilities of using CBRN weapons, the emerging terrorism necessitates a dramatic refocus of the predominant British view that it is not in the interest or remit of foreign-based groups to conduct major acts of terrorism within their borders.

Among the most pressing lessons of 11 September is that all states throughout the world have been forced not only to remain vigilant to the international terrorist threat, but also to realising the importance of proactively preparing preventive and responsive measures capable of addressing the terrorist threat as it exists at any given moment. For the UK, this specifically means that authorities must acknowledge the operational threat it now faces from foreign-based terrorist groups while seriously addressing the issue of how international terrorist support structures could be dismantled within the domestic arena in order to pre-empt (if not eliminate) any possibility that these support structures could be mobilised to act as operational units. For these reasons it is essential that the motivations, capabilities and support structures of foreign-based terrorist groups are monitored closely and continuously so that the relevant British authorities can establish and employ effective and efficient counter-terrorist measures at home and abroad.

The UK: a magnet for international terrorism?

Historical overview of international terrorism and the UK

As previously mentioned, the UK has limited experience with international acts of terrorism perpetrated on British soil. Apart for the 1988 Lockerbie bombing, the only other significant act of international terrorism in the UK that received significant domestic attention was the hijacking of an Afghan Ariana Airline aircraft in February 2000. Despite a relative lack of experience with international terrorism at home, international terrorism has affected British citizens living abroad and British tourists. Although many of these incidents are limited to kidnapping for ransom, British citizens have also been among the victims in indiscriminate terrorist attacks. Most recently, these include the US attacks of 11 September 2001 and the Bali bombings in 2002. Finally, British officials have also been directly targeted by terrorist groups abroad, as exemplified by the murder of Stephen Saunders (UK Defence Attaché, Athens) by the 17th of November Revolutionary Organisation.

Even limited experience with international terrorism has not deterred the British government from becoming party to the 12 existing United Nations conventions and protocols that seek to counter the threat posed by international terrorism, from the Tokyo Convention (1963) to the International Convention for the Suppression of the Financing of Terrorism (1999). In addition to these, the UK has also signed and ratified the 1977 European Convention on the Suppression of Terrorism, and has worked on counter-terrorism issues within the framework of the European Union (EU), G8, NATO, and the Organisation for Security and Cooperation in Europe.

International commitments, however, did not appear to have a significant practical impact on how domestic UK legislation was written in response to the pre-11 September threat posed by international terrorist groups to British territory. Primarily focused on Irish terrorism, it was not until the Terrorism Act 2000 that the UK released a list of foreign-based proscribed groups.[2] Despite identifying these groups, prior to the counter-terrorism drive initiated at the end of 2001, few official resources were directed towards controlling the extent to which international terrorist groups established a presence in Britain. Combined with the benefits of establishing a presence in the UK as discussed in detail in the next section, the reluctance to address international terrorism in the domestic context has undoubtedly further attracted foreign-based terrorist groups.

Committed to domestic, regional and international agreements designed to counter terrorism, the UK still remains largely acquiescent to foreign-based terrorist groups that have penetrated British society. As a generalisation it may be preliminarily concluded that efforts have largely failed to apply existing legislation to deter foreign-based terrorist groups from taking advantage of the liberal democratic environment offered by the UK. Thus, for example, despite the fact that inciting hatred is a crime, individuals such as Abu Hamza al-Masri and Abdullah el-Faisal (see section 'Groups of potential concern') have been allowed to freely preach radical anti-Western rhetoric in public venues. This radical rhetoric is believed to have fostered the rise of militant extremists such as Zacharias Moussaoui, Ahmed Ressam, and Richard Reid – a fear that had been noted by Muslim community leaders as early as 1999.

The benefits of operating in the UK

A liberal democracy by nature, the UK offers many benefits for British society and its citizens. In addition to providing several freedoms, such as the freedom of speech and the freedom to assemble, the country also offers a comparatively high standard of living and opportunities to attain economic stability. It is precisely these advantages inherent within British society that have attracted criminal, and subsequently terrorist, groups. Taking advantage of constitutional freedoms and rights, in addition to diaspora communities, and sophisticated communications and financial systems, the benefits of establishing a presence in the UK have thus far exceeded the risks.

Manipulating British rights and freedoms

Throughout much of the 1980s and 1990s there appeared to be a sense among terrorist groups that the liberal democratic freedoms could be taken advantage of in the UK because there was little indication or evidence that authorities enforced associated criminal laws. For example, despite it being illegal to publicly incite hatred, there have been no known cases of somebody being arrested on these grounds. In all reality, democratic governments generally appear afraid to enforce laws that deal with fundamental freedoms because of the potential community backlash that it may create. As discussed in greater detail in the section 'Groups of potential concern', this has allowed radical Islamists to freely preach their extreme views. Concerns for civil liberties thus appear to outweigh the direction given to law enforcement to conduct surveillance and investigate activities related to overstepping the boundaries of democratic freedoms.

Another important factor attracting terrorist groups to use the UK as part of their logistical base is that historically the UK has shown that it does not extradite individuals unless the requesting country is deemed 'safe'. Based on the human rights laws integrated within British legislation, extradition requests are denied if extradition may lead to death for the individual being repatriated, or if such cooperation with a requesting country is not in the political remit of the government at that time. In many cases then, even if an individual is suspected of involvement in a terrorist group, it is unlikely that they will be imprisoned in the UK or extradited to their country of origin. Furthermore, the UK has often granted 'freedom fighters', especially from the Middle East, status of asylum seekers and therefore legal sanctuary – in a sense allowing their perceptions of terrorism to be coloured by foreign policy issues. As a result, the UK has revealed a high degree of tolerance for international terrorism, allowing groups to use British territory to distribute propaganda, recruit members, raise finances, and establish a support network.

There are numerous recent cases to support this conclusion. For example, Anas al-Liby, wanted in connection for his alleged role in the 1998 US Embassy bombings in East Africa, has been refused extradition to Egypt on the grounds that the UK is unsure that the Egyptian authorities will give him a fair trial that will not lead to a death sentence, but Al-Liby was later reported to be in Afghanistan. Authorities have also refused to extradite Abu Hamza al-Masri, sentenced in Yemen for his alleged role in terrorist acts, including the killing of Western tourists in 1999 but, at time of writing, Abu Hamza was still in the UK fighting deportation to the US.[3] British authorities also initially resisted Jordan's demands for the extradition of Abu Qatada;[4] Shafiq ur Rehman was initially allowed to remain in the UK despite originally being ordered deported as a 'danger to national security',[5] but lost his case against deportation in 2001.

Diaspora communities

Related to rising immigration and asylum claims has been the growth of diaspora communities within the UK. Given the close-knit nature of diaspora communities, combined with an overbearing sense of uncertainty felt about their new home, they have served as an important logistical support base for terrorist groups. For example, community members – either through cooperation or coercion – have provided safe houses, and the community itself acts as a spiritual and communications hub. Taking the Algerian community as an example (explained in further detail in 'Algerian connection' below), evidence indicates that radical UK-based Algerians have preyed on vulnerable youths for spiritual indoctrination into radical brands of Islam (either through mosques such as Finsbury Park, or via study/youth groups conducted in private homes or community centres) and potential recruitment for jihad.

Radical preachers have also targeted British universities in an effort to recruit a cadre of well-educated followers for ideological support, and professional support.[6] Student Islamic groups were increasingly penetrated in the early 1990s, and were continuously used as recruiting centres for ease of distributing leaflets and showing politically sensitive documentaries showing atrocities against Muslim populations worldwide. The group Al-Muhajiroun (see below), for example, has claimed that it sent as many as 700 undergraduates from British universities to fight abroad.[7]

Along with asylum seekers and immigrants who are resident in the UK, second generation immigrants have also been targeted for support and recruitment by radical Islamist preachers. The primary vulnerability of these individuals has been a perceived rising identity crisis exacerbated by increased racial tensions between Muslim and non-Muslim segments of the community. There have been several accounts presented by second generation Muslims suggesting that they find it difficult to identify with their ethnic background, yet are not completely accepted as British. As a result, some individuals within this small group have found solace in pan-Islamic causes.

Finally, Muslim radicals have also found it beneficial to focus on the UK prison system as another source of recruitment. The Muslim prison population has doubled between 1993 and 2000, according to Home Office reports, and therefore would have served as a major base of resentment creating an environment characterised by individuals resenting the British authorities and system, ultimately creating conditions conducive to recruitment. One recent example that illustrates attempts to recruit or convert inmates into following a radical interpretation of Islam is the case of Richard Reid, the infamous shoe bomber, who converted to Islam while he was serving a prison sentence. In response to the potential threat this specific case revealed, the UK prison service suspended a number of Muslim clerics from prisons for making 'inappropriate comments' regarding the 11 September attacks.

Communications and financial network

Given its geographical location, and the fact that the UK has become increasingly multinational and multi-denominational over the last few decades, it is of no surprise to find that it has become essential to international communications and financial systems/networks worldwide. Taken advantage of by licit channels such as international business and banking, these networks have also been harnessed by illicit groups – such as terrorism and organised crime.

Described in further detail with reference to specific terrorist groups in Appendix 2, the UK has served as an important communications centre from which radical propaganda has been collected and distributed. As a result, over the years several websites and publications associated with foreign-based terrorist groups have operated from within British territory. For example, several of Osama bin Laden's original fatwahs were first published in London; and UK-based websites are known to have published the virtues of jihad. Furthermore, the Advice and

Reformation Committee, established in 1994 by Khaled Al-Fawwaz in London to campaign for Islamic law in Saudi Arabia, also acted (knowingly or unknowingly) as a centre that redistributed messages, information and finances around the Al-Qaeda network.

As noted earlier, the UK is also of particular interest because it provides access to an intricate international network of commerce and finance – thus allowing terrorist groups to engage in numerous profitable endeavours, including fraud and money laundering.[8] Although the criminal threat from foreign-based terrorist groups to the UK will be covered later in this chapter, it is important to make early reference to this relationship as, unlike direct threats of violence posed to the UK by foreign-based groups, criminal and associated support activities appear to pose the greatest single threat to Britain from many of these groups.

The persistent dilemma

Although this section has only provided a brief overview of the benefits offered to terrorist groups who are able to successfully penetrate British society, it has fulfilled its main purpose of highlighting some dilemmas, which liberal democracies persistently face. The UK, like other democracies, is faced with the problem of devising counter-terrorist policies and legislation that can deal with the terrorist threat without demeaning the civil liberties that democratic states seek to uphold – such as the rule of law and respect for human rights.

It is this very dilemma that represents the greatest obstacle for the UK as it seeks to balance its liberal democratic nature with its counter-terrorist initiatives, and matching its counter-terrorism policy with an accurate assessment of the level of threat it faces. Paul Wilkinson concisely summarises the sensitive nature of this dilemma in his seminal study on liberal democracies and terrorism when he writes:

> On the one hand, the democratic government and its agencies of law enforcement must avoid the heavy handed overreaction which many terrorist groups deliberately seek to provoke: such a response would only help to alienate the public from the government and could ultimately destroy democracy more swiftly and completely than any small terrorist group ever could. On the other hand, if government, judiciary and police prove incapable of upholding the law and protecting life and property, then their whole credibility and authority will be undermined.[9]

Based on the specific threat assessment provided in the following two sections, compared with the UK terrorism response in the post-11 September environment, it becomes evident that British authorities have placed themselves in an uncertain predicament wherein a host of reactions to an inaccurately perceived threat may provoke greater long-term instability.

For a list of the Home Office list of proscribed organisations under the Terrorism Act 2000, see Appendix 2.

Other related threats to the UK

Groups of potential concern

Potentially, the greatest direct threat to the UK posed by foreign terrorist groups, are, in fact, groups established on British territory by first, second and third generation immigrants connected to international terrorist networks; and by radical Muslim converts. Prior to 11 September 2001, these groups largely focused on recruiting British youth to take part in a global jihad, and also to secure financial and operational support for the operations of affiliated terrorist groups abroad. In many ways, the framework of radical groups that emerged in the UK has provided an entry point for terrorist groups, including Al-Qaeda, to establish a British base of operations. However, even before the aftermath of 11 September – primarily resulting in intense investigations into terrorist networks – it was evident that these groups espoused a militant Islamist view. As a result, they have finally become the focus of investigations in the UK. The problem with this is that British concerns and policy, instead of alleviating tensions, may exacerbate the discontent and injustice perceived by the membership of these groups and movements. This predicament has the potential of creating a self-fulfilling prophecy with respect to the level of threat realistically posed to the UK from foreign and foreign-based terrorist groups.

Al-Muhajiroun (The Emigrants)

Al-Muhajiroun was founded by Sheikh Omar Bakri Mohammed, co-founder of the UK branch of Hizb ut-Tahrir (see below) in 1996. The primary aim of Al-Muhajiroun was to recruit students and provide funding for Islamic groups abroad. The group, boasting a network of contacts throughout the world, is allegedly composed of two distinct wings: the da'wah and the jihad. Da'wah (propagation) networks spread radical Islamist messages via the distribution of propaganda, whereas the jihad network seeks to recruit volunteers to join militant groups abroad by directing interested individuals to intermediaries capable of organising travel to training routes.[10] Sheikh Bakri has admitted in the aftermath of the 11 September attacks that he was responsible for recruiting for jihad,[11] and that he himself issued a fatwah in 2000 calling for a jihad against Israel on the al-Muhajiroun website and email list.

The actual goal of al-Muhajiroun is to have Sharia law implemented in the UK, going so far as to call Trafalgar Square the Mecca of Muhajiroun, and England the capital of the Islamic world. Holding gatherings at the Eton Road Community Centre in Ilford, Bakri has successfully attracted a following – apparently appealing to widespread feelings of 'not belonging' among Asian and non-Asian youth. The pan-Islamism advocated by Bakri has appeared to give a sense of identity to the members of Al-Muhajiroun, potentially helping explain why recruitment to the group is believed to have increased since 11 September 2001. Bakri is reported as saying that the group receives an average of seven recruits daily, most of whom are second-generation immigrants who are seeking to find their place within British society.

In addition to recruiting potential militants to take part in terrorist activity and guerrilla warfare abroad, and distributing radical propaganda, al-Muhajiroun has also explicitly incited hatred against the UK and the West amongst its followers. Supporting these feelings of discontent, Bakri has regularly released fatwahs; for example, specifically calling for all Muslims to conduct acts of terrorism against American targets in February 1998, in a fatwah entitled 'World Islamic Front's Statement Urging Jihad Against Jews and Crusaders', directing all Muslims to kill Americans and their allies in order to liberate the al-Aqsa Mosque and Mecca, and oust all foreign armies from the 'lands of Islam'.

Further highlighting this sense of discontent with the West were the warnings issued by Bakri in 2002–3 stating that should Britain follow the USA into war with Iraq, then terrorist acts in the UK would undoubtedly follow. Although it is unlikely that Bakri and his al-Muhajiroun have the operational capability to conduct acts of terrorism on British territory, the fact that they are evidently plugged into an international network of militants suggests that capability would not be difficult to acquire – so long as they have the will to turn their political and logistic role into an operational one. In order to be effective and cause great concern within the British public, members of al-Muhajiroun (working alone or as an organised group) would only have to be responsible for a relatively small attack.

Abu Hamza, the supporters of Sharia and 'other' radical preachers

When investigating militant Islamic groups based in London it is difficult to ignore the work and presence of Abu Hamza al-Masri. Notoriously identified as a radical preacher at the Finsbury Mosque (North London Central Mosque, Finsbury Park) in London, Hamza has ties with Omar Bakri Mohammed, and allegedly plays an important role in the group Al-Takfir wal-Hijrah (Anathema and Exile), which is believed to operate from Finsbury Park. More specifically, however, Hamza leads the Supporters of Sharia.

Believed to have fought in Afghanistan and Bosnia, Hamza is wanted by the government of Yemen for his alleged role in perpetrating acts of terrorism in Yemen, and also for his alleged connection to the Islamic Army of Aden. Yemeni authorities have accused Hamza of his involvement in a series of kidnappings of tourists in Yemen in 1998. Yemeni authorities have tied Hamza to a cell whose members were arrested in December 2001, including five British citizens[12] who were in possession of weapons and explosives and were accused of planning to carry out acts of terrorism. Despite Yemeni intelligence and official requests to the UK to extradite Abu Hamza (an Egyptian national), British authorities blocked this request because he held asylum status. Since 1998, it is believed that Hamza has, on several occasions, voiced his discontent against the government of Yemen, and has stated that he supports the goal of using violence to replace the Yemeni government with an Islamic Republic. Furthermore, as recently as the summer of

2002, US authorities accused Hamza of organising terrorist training camps at a remote ranch in Oregon.

In the aftermath of the 11 September 2001 terrorist attacks in America, Abu Hamza and his extreme outbursts have resulted in increased public and UK government attention. For example, following a year-long investigation by the Charities Commission, Hamza was suspended from preaching at Finsbury Park Mosque because of his radical statements. Hamza, however, persistently defied this order. Following intelligence gathered, British authorities conducted a raid on the Finsbury Park Mosque in January 2003. Although law enforcement officials noted that the raid had nothing specifically to do with Hamza, they did announce that the raid was conducted because they had reason to believe that the mosque was being used for recruiting terrorists and supporting terrorism. During the course of the raid police officers confiscated a CS gas canister, an electric stun gun, fake passports, stolen or counterfeit credit cards, and CBRN suits, and seven individuals (six of North African origin and one East European) were subsequently arrested.

Although it is evident that the Finsbury Park Mosque has been used to recruit individuals to train and fight in ongoing jihads abroad, and to spread radical and militant Islamist propaganda, it has been difficult for the British authorities to prove that the mosque, and Abu Hamza, are directly involved in terrorism.[13] The dilemma therefore facing the UK is at least twofold. First, authorities must balance their response to allegations emerging from the activities conducted through the mosque with an effective response that is not perceived by the public (or Muslim community) as inadequate. Included within this equation is the question of whether or not British authorities base their decision on a political 'fear' calculation; that is, they decide not to arrest senior figures (such as Abu Hamza) regardless of whether they have the evidence to do so because they fear an ensuing backlash from Hamza followers (see also 'Manipulating British rights and freedoms' above). Second, in conjunction with the previous dilemma, UK authorities must ensure that any decisions they make for short-term results do not interfere with investigations that may lead to further uncovering of the extent of the radical Islamist network that exists in the UK. Both dilemmas are extremely fragile.

The case of Abu Hamza and Finsbury Park Mosque, therefore, will likely serve as a framework for how British authorities deal with radical preachers (or group representatives) in the future. Unfortunately, the fact that the UK has been relatively unprepared to respond to the potential threat posed by radical preachers inciting hatred and the use of violence, despite evidence supporting these allegations, such as links to international terrorism (even if limited to recruitment and ideological support), means the country has placed itself at a disadvantage because it has already faltered in its response to other radical figures, including Abu Qatada (Sheikh Omar Abu Omar), Abdullah al-Faisal, Abu Doha, and Sheikh ur-Rehman.

Hizb ut-Tahrir al-Islami

Hizb ut-Tahrir al-Islami (HTI), also known as the Islamic Liberation Party, originated in Saudi Arabia, however is now a transnational network that extends from the Middle East, throughout Europe, and into Central Asia. Official declarations of the group strongly note that it is against the use of violence, and therefore seeks the creation of an international Islamic caliphate through peaceful, political and educational means. Despite the fact that the majority of the group does appear peaceful in nature, evidence indicates that factions have developed within HTI that entertain the use of violence, or support the use of violence by other groups with similar aims. Apart from facing widespread suppression in Central Asia and the Middle East (some of which may be justified, however much of which has been regarded as human rights abuses, thus potentially fuelling future interests to engage in violence), the group is also being looked at with suspicion in Europe. For example, after banning HTI at the end of 2001, German authorities were quick to conduct raids on buildings linked to the group and subsequently questioned 25 alleged HTI members under the auspices of the new German counter-terrorism legislation.

Sheikh Omar Bakri Mohammed founded the UK branch of HTI before establishing Al-Muhajiroun. Although Bakri is now the leader of Al-Muhajiroun, it is still believed that he continues to play a role in HTI (UK). For example, Bakri – not the current HTI (UK) leader, Jalal Uddin Patel – was the first person to deny allegations that four individuals detained in Egypt in April 2002 on charges of terrorism were members of the group.[14] Two of the detained members were British citizens and directors of an international internet company E-magine.net that provided services to companies including British Airways, and a US defence company.[15]

In light of official HTI activities conducted worldwide, it is extremely difficult to make the argument that the group incites the use of violence, or that the group is directly involved in any international terrorist networks. On the contrary, the group has taken considerable efforts to maintain its profile of 'non-violence'. However, increasingly over the past two years, there have been indications – at least on the group's website – that it does condone jihad in specific circumstances. It is this hidden attitude amongst the leadership of HTI that is of rising concern to security and intelligence officials throughout Western Europe. Furthermore, as happens with many legitimate non-state political actors, there are indications that violent factions within HTI are emerging in response to severe suppression of the group in many countries. As a result, it is essential that British authorities follow the lead of countries like Germany which remain vigilant in light of this potential threat.

The Takfiri movement

The Takfiri movement began in Egypt in 1971 as *Jama'at al'Muslimin* (The Society of the Muslims). It was established by Shukri Mustafa, a former member of the

Muslim Brotherhood who spent time in prison and joined the radical followers of Qutb. Press coverage surrounding *Jama'at al'Muslimin* in the late 1970s created an impetus to rename the group to *Al Takfir wa'l-Hijra*.

Established as a peaceful apolitical proselytising movement, the Takfiris were drawn into conflict with rival groups and the authorities, and thus responded to the pressure by resorting to violence. In 1977 and 1978 the group attacked two government ministers, for which Mustafa was apprehended and hanged. His death ushered in the emergence of two wings within *Al Takfir*: one under the leadership of Abbud al-Zammut (considered one of the original founders), and one under the leadership of Dr Ayman al-Zawahiri (now Al-Qaeda's second in command). Ultimately it was the beliefs of al-Zawahiri's *Al Jihad* that came to dominate Takfiri themes; he is therefore regarded as a Takfir ideologue.

Al Takfir wa'l-Hijra grew substantially through the 1990s as Takfiri militants returned to their respective homes in the Middle East and North Africa from Afghanistan. Their experiences were subsequently shared to younger generations, thus creating the foundation for the establishment of cells scattered throughout Algeria, Jordan, Lebanon, Libya, Morocco, Pakistan and Sudan. Furthermore, some Takfiri Mujahideen settled in Western Europe (including the UK), where they continued to propagate their radical form of militant Islam throughout their newly adopted communities.

The growth of *Al Takfir wa'l-Hijra* was not centralised, but focused on establishing a decentralised network of believers. As a result, in the contemporary operating environment, the group is best described as a movement seeking to create centres engaged in proselytising and recruiting for militant jihad. As a movement, *Al Takfir* activists generally pursue one central objective: re-educating and recruiting individuals to subscribe to their radical ideological view of Islam; thus contributing to the re-introduction of a caliphate that would not stop at traditional Muslim lands, but would extend throughout the Western world as well. British-based radical Islamists including Abu Hamza al-Masri and Abu Qatada have both been tied to the Takfiri Movement that has grown from the original *Al Takfir wa'l-Hijra*.

In Western Europe, Takfiri leaders are focusing their efforts on attracting first, second, and third generation Muslims to the movement by manipulating feelings of alienation and disorientation.

First-generation immigrants consist of two groups of individuals. First, this group consists of radical Islamists who purposely find a way to move to a Western country to distribute propaganda and actively recruit individuals for global jihad. Second are 'aliens' who have moved to Western Europe either as students or asylum seekers. After attempting to integrate within their newly adopted society, some first generation immigrants become 'born again' Muslims as a reaction to their experiences with Western practices (e.g. Mohammad Atta).

Second and third generation immigrants who have been successfully recruited into the Takfiri movement are integrated citizens who are normally downwardly mobile and have experienced discrimination. Many of these individuals subsequently become involved in criminal gangs, and thus find themselves in the prison system. It is at this point that they have commonly become vulnerable to recruitment: indirectly by radical imams and directly through appointed recruiters. Based on the fact that these recruits are often 'white' and culturally integrated within society (that is, not the stereotypical Arab male associated with terrorism), they are considered the most dangerous recruits because of the disassociation they feel with society. The biography and activities of Richard Reid typically exemplify this group of recruits These trends are exacerbated by the fact that the Takfiri movement continues actively to convert women.

The greatest present danger emerging from the recruitment strategy of the Takfiri Movement emerges in the potential for mixing between first generation and second/third generation recruits. In this scenario, as played out in the 9/11 attacks, Westernised operatives (that is, the student pilots from the Hamburg sleeper cell) are mixed with active 'musclemen' brought in from active terrorist hotbeds (that is, Saudi tribal areas).

It is becoming increasingly apparent that the Takfiri movement has harnessed a new type of recruitment that is centred in the Western world – a recruitment that is characterised by the battle over new generations. Thus in addition to mosques and community centres, recruitment strategies have simultaneously focused on university-based student groups where carefully selected members are confronted with harsh propaganda in the form of leaflets, videos and speakers, focusing on intolerance and injustices perpetrated against Muslim communities in various geographic hotspots (that is, Afghanistan, Bosnia, Chechnya, Iraq).

Although mosques remain an important recruitment target, it is important to differentiate between radical mosques and mosques that are preyed on by radical Islamist recruiters. For the most part, mosques only act as the common point of initial contact; recruitment seldomly takes place within a mosque. Instead, it is believed that recruiters observe the mosque environment, operating on the margins to spot isolated and vulnerable youths, especially those who appear to respond to the promise of adventure. Once an individual is spotted, they are drawn into a more radical-focused environment in the guise of study groups, youth clubs, or after-hour groups. It is in these environments that indoctrination can take place.

Militancy has thus become a vehicle of protest against socio-economic conditions faced by Muslim communities in the West, including problems of access to employment and housing, discrimination, and the deteriorating image of Islam in public opinion. In the post-9/11 environment the Takfiris of Western Europe appear to have met greater success in winning the battle over second and third generation 'teenage Islamic minds' seeking acceptance and an adventurous life that has meaning.

French scholar, Olivier Roy, has repeatedly noted that Western recruits have been attracted to militant Islam because they have undergone a 'triple rupture' – from family, native country and Islam. These recruits thus voluntarily reject what they perceive to be the failing society of their origin, and become seduced by the benefits accorded to them through jihad.

The UK is strongly believed to be the new transit point for *Takfiri* recruits because it has been regarded as an open distribution point for the 'revolutionary message of jihad'. Furthermore, the UK was a popular destination for Algerian, Egyptian and Afghan-Arab militants (some of whom were under sentence in their native countries for terrorism) because of relatively lax asylum procedures. These individuals subsequently began to propagate their radical views within Muslim communities. The case of Abu Hamza al-Masri (born Mustafa Kamel Mustafa) is illustrative of this predicament.

Abu Hamza has been directly tied to the original *Al Takfiri* group under the leadership of Mustafa in Egypt in the 1970s. His introduction to the UK allowed him to begin his own recruitment drive through the notorious Finsbury Park Mosque in London, and through the establishment of *Supporters of Sharia* (estimated membership of 200). Through his work, Abu Hamza has not remained quiet about his desire to contribute to the establishment of a caliphate, and has commonly voiced his radical and militant views. For example, in an interview he gave to the British Broadcasting Corporation, he was quoted as saying 'Bin Laden is a good guy. Everyone likes him in the Muslim world; there is nothing wrong with the man and his beliefs'.[16]

Since the late 1990s, attendees at Finsbury Park Mosque included:

- Dgamel Beghal (assigned by Osama bin Laden to establish European cells). By 1998 Beghal was responsible for recruiting three would-be suicide bombers: Richard Reid, Nizar Trabelsi and Zacarious Moussaoui
- Ahmed Ressam (Millennium plot)
- Anas al-Liby
- Abu Doha
- James Ugaama
- Rashid Ramda
- Allegedly several of the eight British citizens detained in Guantanamo Bay.

What is worth noting is that Abu Hamza has maintained a network that has held tight contacts to a larger militant Islamist community. These ties have been proved to cause concern in the UK, but have also been proved to have an impact on the USA. This became evident in 2002 when the US authorities froze his assets, and claimed that Abu Hamza attempted to establish a jihad training camp at a remote ranch in Oregon.

Comparable with the recruitment wave of second and third generation Muslims in other Western European states, the *Takfiris* in the UK have also manipulated social discrimination and poor job opportunities to pull vulnerable individuals towards extremism. In a sense, radical Islamism has given these 'new recruits' identity and faith that they have never previously possessed.

Algerian connection

As indicated in the background descriptions of Algerian-based terrorist groups, including the Groupe Islamique Armée (Armed Islamic Group) GIA, Algeria has waged a serious and violent terrorist campaign since 1992 after the military cancelled national elections. During this terror campaign, an estimated 150,000 people have died, and thousands of others have been uprooted from their homes. Although the de facto civil war being waged in Algeria does not directly affect the security of the UK, persistent violence in the country has had a significant indirect impact on Britain largely because of its reputation as a haven for dissidents. The UK government has welcomed a large wave of Algerian asylum-seekers since 1989. Although the majority of these individuals were unlikely to have been connected to terrorism, it is alleged that several Algerian terrorists did gain entry to the UK as asylum-seekers. There appears to have been two waves of militant Algerians penetrating Britain: the first wave appeared between 1989 and 1994, and the second wave began to seek entry to Britain in the late 1990s.

The first wave of immigration manipulated by militant Algerian Islamists began in 1989 shortly after the Soviet Union pulled out of Afghanistan. Soviet military withdrawal from Afghanistan resulted in many militants returning to their countries of origin where, in the case of Algeria, they continued their plight at home. Faced with security crackdowns (and death sentences for their involvement in terrorist crimes) several of these militants are believed to have sought safe havens in Western Europe, including the UK The fact that extreme propaganda[17] was being distributed more readily throughout Muslim communities should have warned authorities that militants had penetrated British territory. In retrospect, it is believed that this initial distribution of propaganda acted as a precursor to the collection of funds and eventual recruitment of young Islamists volunteering to train abroad for jihad.

Although this first wave of asylum-seekers can be partially blamed for introducing and spreading radical Islamist ideology throughout the Algerian community in Britain, it was the second wave of 'immigration' that has led to rising concerns that Algerian terrorists are interested in turning the UK into an operational theatre. There are several reasons explaining this turn of events. First, for those Algerian militants who are primarily concerned about the political situation in Algeria, the change in British policy towards Algeria since 11 September 2001 may provoke frustration within segments of the British-based Algerian community who have maintained ties to Algerian terrorist groups such as the Groupe Salafiste pour la Prédication et le Combat (Salafist Group for Preaching and Combat) (GSPC). More specifically, this situation refers to the UK decision to end a de facto arms embargo on the Algerian government for alleged human rights abuses, and finalising a deal to sell military equipment and arms to be used 'against Islamic insurgents'.[18] Second, considering that the GIA (with its considerable European network in place) merged its organisational structure with Al-Qaeda, there is a potential that British-based Algerian terrorists[19] can be mobilised to strike within the UK on behalf of Al-Qaeda. Third, just as Algerian terrorists continued their jihad in Algeria after leaving the Afghan theatre in 1989, the argument can be made that Algerian terrorists would consider extending their duty for jihad in the UK as a reprisal for British involvement in the 'War on Terrorism' and their participation in the ensuing war on Iraq.

Thus not only can the argument for an 'Algerian connection' to the UK be made, and the subsequent possibility that Algerian terrorists may embark on campaigns of terror on British territory can be rationalised, but evidence already reveals that this predicament already exists. For example, the majority of the individuals arrested since 2002 in various raids on alleged terrorist cells have been generally described by law enforcement as 'North African'; however, surveying media reports indicate that most of those arrested were, in fact, Algerian. Furthermore, investigations pursued by British authorities have also uncovered several Algerian networks accused of raising funds for terrorism (including Al-Qaeda), distributing propaganda (including speeches of Osama bin Laden, and videos espousing the honour of martyrdom and the art of suicide bombings), and being party to criminal activity (possession of false passports, credit cards and bank cards are among the most common), and engaging in crime (most notably credit card fraud).

The 'lone' terrorist and suicide attacks

One of the two most concerning developments with respect to foreign-based terrorism in the UK is that these groups, or loyal members of these groups, may embark on 'lone' terrorism or suicide attacks. Although these phenomena exist in what are often regarded as less stable terrorist theatres, such as the Middle East, they would almost undoubtedly create widespread fear through the British public. Used to 'dealing' with terrorism as perpetrated by Irish groups, it is unlikely that the British public would react complacently to suicide attacks or the lone terrorist.

The estimates of numbers of militants given by the Security Service to Parliament's Intelligence and Security Committee inquiry into the 7 July bombings suggest that there has been a dramatic rise in the number of militants believed to be involved and in the number of terrorist plots being hatched. In reports released in January 2003 by the Jane's Information Group, it was estimated that there could be as many as 100 suicide bombers resident in the UK – many of whom are likely to be Al-Qaeda supporters. Leading Muslim moderates have backed these figures.

Chemical, biological, radiological and nuclear weapons

There is no credible evidence, to date, which would indicate that foreign-based terrorist groups are seeking to use CBRN weapons in the UK. However, based on rising concerns that terrorist groups throughout the world have increasingly sought to attain a CBRN capability, combined with growing hostility towards the UK among the international Islamic militant population, the potential for foreign-based terrorist groups to perpetrate a CBRN attack on British territory has risen considerably. Even if foreign groups with a British presence do not have the resources to acquire a sophisticated capability, there is nothing precluding them from developing an improvised weapon (especially chemical) and delivery system.

Since 11 September 2001, there have been several episodes in the UK that allegedly threatened the use of CBRN weapons in planned acts of terrorism. Although it would be an exaggeration to suggest that these incidents posed serious threats to the UK, they highlight the rising risks presented to the UK from foreign groups. Furthermore, they simultaneously highlight the fact (primarily through the media frenzy that followed these developments) that the UK is not entirely prepared to respond to a CBRN attack should it occur.

Authorities uncovered the first CBRN plot in November 2002, culminating in the arrest of six North African[20] men who allegedly planned to release cyanide in the London underground. Despite not finding chemical or bomb-making equipment, authorities charged the men under the Terrorism Act 2000 with 'possessing articles for the preparation, instigation and commission of terrorism'. Of equal interest (and indicative of one of the greatest threats posed by foreign-based terrorist groups in the UK as discussed in 'The criminal factor' below), these men were also found to be in possession of false passports.

The ricin plot uncovered in London in January 2003 is a second example that illustrates the possibility that terrorists are becoming increasingly interested in perpetrating a CBRN attack in the UK. Although the ricin incident cannot (should not) be used as a definitive example of CBRN terrorism[21] organised by a foreign-based terrorist group, it does highlight several important factors. First, it revealed that groups present in the UK are interested in using unconventional weapons. Second, given that this was the first case in the UK wherein a chemical or biological agent was to be used in a terrorist attack on British territory, it drew notice to the level of UK preparedness in the event of a CBRN attack. Third, the discovery of ricin, and the subsequent media frenzy that followed, revealed the importance of the media in helping terrorist groups spread their message of fear and violent intent, thus underlining the dilemma faced by the media in the terrorism context between reporting the news and the need for public vigilance, and exaggerating the threat (or equally dangerous, misreporting the threat).

Finally, and potentially most telling of the potential threats posed by radical Islamic militants to the UK was the discovery of CBRN protection suits during a raid of the Finsbury Mosque at the end of January 2003. Assessments following these findings suggest that the raid confirmed fears that chemical attacks were/ are being planned by supporters (indirect) of Al-Qaeda.[22] This conclusion, however, may be somewhat premature as no evidence of chemicals was found according to official police statements. Regardless, this does highlight the threat posed by Abu Hamza and his radical following as initially described above. The discovery of an interest in chemical and biological weapons by radicals at the Finsbury Park Mosque, however, was not an entirely new phenomenon. Press reports published following the incident indicated that British and French security services paid an Algerian journalist to infiltrate the mosque in 1999 and 2000. It is alleged that the journalist forwarded reports to the security services in which he noted reports of conversations by radical militants expressing an interest in chemical and biological attacks, and even in using a 'dirty bomb'.

It was concluded that the UK authorities dismissed these findings as over-exaggerations.[23]

Recent evidence of UK-based radical Islamist interests in acquiring a CBRN capability (regardless of the level of sophistication), undoubtedly creates a need to analyse the threat this poses to the UK more cautiously. The most important analytical component that needs to be continuously investigated is the ties that have developed (or may be emerging) between UK-based radical Islamists and terrorist groups with a proven CBRN capability.

In the absence of such ties, an argument can be made that radical Islamist militants seeking to perpetrate a CBRN terrorist act in the UK have two alternative options. First, they may acquire an unsophisticated chemical or biological capability that can be used in simultaneously low-level, low-casualty attacks – thus potentially creating widespread panic and fear amongst the British population. Alternatively, groups willing to part with finances, and which have established relations with criminal organisations, may seek to use criminal groups as intermediaries for CBRN weapons, components or expertise. However, despite facilitating CBRN smuggling in other parts of the world, it is unlikely that criminal groups with a presence in the UK (physical and/or economic) would supply a terrorist group with weapons that have the potential to create havoc. This is especially true for criminal groups (very large proportion) that use the British economy and banking system to launder money, or to invest laundered money.

The criminal factor

Terrorist groups seeking to plan and perpetrate acts of terrorism evidently require financial backing in order to travel, and purchase supplies and related services. Prior to 1991, most terrorist groups enjoyed state support (financial and supplies). However, with the end of the Cold War, many states previously willing to siphon funding to terrorist groups were no longer capable to do so – either for economic or political justifications. As a result, terrorist groups became largely responsible to fund their own activities if they were to survive the post-Cold War environment. Over the past 12 years, most terrorist groups have thus secured avenues of funding through various criminal activities. Some groups have limited their criminal involvement to petty crime (theft) and low-level fraud (benefit fraud); however, others have become increasingly well versed at more lucrative criminal enterprises such as arms, drugs and human trafficking.

Most illicit criminal operations conducted by terrorist groups are focused in unstable regions where access to narcotics or weapons is relatively unhindered. However, considering the nature of criminal activities, it is equally evident that terrorist groups have used the stable nature of liberal democratic communities in order to gain maximum proceeds from their criminal enterprise. As a result, the UK may be considered a major haven for the crime-terror nexus for two predominant reasons. First, foreign-based terrorist groups with a diaspora located in the UK have targeted their communities as a source of revenue. In addition to voluntary contributions, diaspora communities (notably the Tamil and Kurdish communities) have been faced with extortion demands. Second, foreign-based terrorist groups have used Britain as an important conduit to launder money.

Evidence of foreign-based terrorist groups using the UK to conduct relatively low-level criminal operations has been abundant. Crimes most commonly attributed to terrorist groups are identity theft, credit card and bank fraud, and benefits fraud. For example, members of *Supporters of Sharia* (led by Abu Hamza) were arrested in November 2001 for running a benefits fraud ring, which included social security fraud. Counterfeiting factories[24] have also been uncovered in the UK as a result of intensified investigations conducted by British authorities in the aftermath of the 11 September attacks. As noted in the British media, a counterfeiting factory run from family homes allegedly operated in Leicester since 1998 (locations which were also believed to be used by senior Al-Qaeda lieutenants as a base). These 'factories' were found to produce fake credit cards and passports.[25] Immediate profits with low risks have allowed these activities to flourish significantly over the past decade. In addition to a constant supply of funding, these 'common' crimes are likely used by some foreign-based terrorist groups as a way of testing the loyalty of potential recruits to the group before they are brought in any further.[26]

Although low-scale criminality perpetrated by foreign-based terrorist groups poses an evident threat to the UK, of greater concern is the participation of these groups in serious crimes such as drug, human and arms smuggling.[27]

In addition to utilising criminal networks as a source of funding, there are concerns among police and security authorities that foreign-based terrorist groups could establish 'cells' in the UK on the back of the significant problem of organised immigration crime. Intelligence compiled by the National Crime Squad (NCS) has revealed that increasingly organised immigration crime groups will deal with anybody, and not just people from their own ethnic or national backgrounds. NCS reports have indicated that larger gangs are making up to £1 million a week through smuggling people into the UK. The unit says: 'You have to bear in mind that these people may be picked up in Pakistan, Iraq, Afghanistan, wherever, and shipped through and there is hard evidence that they are often "sold on" to a number of networks'.[28]

Notes

1 The UK, however, has been operationally targeted by international terrorism, as evident in the 1988 Lockerbie bombing which resulted in the death of 259 passengers aboard Pan Am flight 103 over Lockerbie, Scotland.

2 The Terrorism Act 2000 proscribed 21 foreign-based terrorist groups. This list was extended to 25 groups in the aftermath of 11 September and the Terrorism, Crime and Security Act 2001. These groups are listed and briefly described in Appendix 2 of this volume.

3 The attacks that Abu Hamza was connected to led to the incarceration of his son and nephew – both of whom were recently released from Yemeni prison.

4 Abu Qatada is also wanted by American and French authorities for his role in plotting the Millennium eve attack in Los Angeles airport, and for his role in plotting to bomb the G7 Summit in Lille in 1996.

5 Rehman, an imam at a mosque in Oldham, allegedly raised money and recruits for Lashar e-Tayyaba. Despite Home Secretary David Blunkett winning a ruling in the House of Commons for Rehman to be deported in 2001, the ruling was overturned for lack of evidence, thus granting Rehman the right to remain in the UK until 2005.

6 There is a short history of radical/extremist groups establishing student organisations at various universities. For example, the London School of Economics (LSE) had been especially singled out for allowing such groups to operate. Even when banned, these groups have generally reorganised themselves under an alternate name. A leading figure of Harakat ul-Mujahideen, Ahmed Omar Sheikh, was himself a former student at the LSE, who also volunteered at the Convoy of Mercy charity. Omar Sheikh was also found guilty in Pakistan of killing *Wall Street Journal* reporter Daniel Pearl.

7 Corera, G. (2002) 'How Militant Islam Found a Home in London', *Jane's Intelligence Review*, 15(8), August.

8 Immediately following the 11 September attacks, evidence uncovering the use of UK foreign currency exchange bureaus became a subject of contentious debate, leading British authorities to focus more attention on money laundering in the domestic framework.

9 Wilkinson, P. (2001) *Terrorism and Liberal Democracy*, London: Frank Cass Publishers, p. 214.

10 Corera (2002).

11 In addition to Richard Reid, who was associated with Bakri, several British prisoners held at Guantanamo and in Kandahar have allegedly admitted to affiliations to Al-Muhajiroun in the UK.

12 Among the British citizens arrested was Abu Hamza's son, Mohammed Mustafa.

13 For a good media account of Finsbury Park Mosque and the terrorists and extremists that have passed through its doors, see McGrory, D. (2003) 'A haven for faithful hijacked by extremists', *The Times*, 21 January, p. 4.

14 In separate statements, HIT (UK) representative, Dr Imran Waheed, acknowledged that the two British citizens detained in Egypt were, in fact, recognised members of the organisation.

15 The two British citizens were Reza Pankhurst and Ian Nisbet.

16 (2004) 'Profile Abu Hamza', www.bbc.co.uk, 17 January.

17 In addition to literature, videos showing violent attacks against Muslims in several regions of the world (Bosnia, Chechnya, Kashmir) were being circulated – especially among youths who were regarded as ideal targets for extremist ideology.

18 Phillips, J. (2003) 'Algiers arms sales on', *The Times*, 27 January, p. 12.

19 The GIA leadership claims that only 600 militants remain active in Algeria, whereas an estimated 27,000 militants have been dispatched throughout Algerian diaspora communities worldwide – a considerable percentage of whom are believed to have settled in Western Europe, especially the UK. For details, see Burke, J. (2003) 'All eyes on Britain as terror war accelerates', *The Observer*, 26 January, p. 7.

20 Articles published in *The Sunday Times* following this incident suggested that the men arrested could be affiliated with Al-Qaeda through their group, the North African Front. Despite these media allegations, there is no compelling evidence to suggest this to be the case.

21 This is due to several practical points surrounding the case. First, although the six people apprehended (and subsequently charged under the UK Chemical Weapons Act 1996) in the ricin plot were North African, there is no available evidence making a clear link between them and a foreign-based terrorist group. Thus there is no clear indication that they were part of a larger plot connected to the global operations of Al-Qaeda. As a result, it is most likely that they were operating as independent entities (even if influenced by the radical militant ideologies of terrorist groups like Al-Qaeda). Furthermore, the fact that ricin was the chemical agent in question – considered a moderate threat by the Centre for Disease Control and Prevention – indicates that

the intention of this plot was not to create mass casualties, but likely to target an individual, or several individuals. The latent intention of this type of tactic would be to attempt to create widespread panic.

22 Following the raid, six North African and one East European men were arrested under the Terrorism Act 2000.

23 (2003) *The Times*, 26 January.

24 Although some terrorist groups are believed to have the resources and expertise to counterfeit, such as the Algerian groups, it is also likely that terrorist groups have formed relationships with criminal groups operating in the British theatre in order to gain access to counterfeit documentation. For example, in addition to Algerian criminal rings, Serbian gangs have also sold stolen and forged passports on the European black market.

25 Authorities questioned 17 people on 18 January 2002 about their involvement in these counterfeiting 'factories' – the majority of which were reported to be Algerian. It is also worth noting that evidence collected by British law enforcement authorities revealed that Abu Doha acted as a 'gatekeeper' of passports flowing to and from London.

26 Recruits are initially invited to study-groups and dinners where their reactions to discussions focusing on violence and hatred for the West are assessed.

27 A report in the *Guardian*, 14 January 2003, notes that arms smuggling to the UK has increased. Confiscated arms over the past two years have commonly included hand grenades, machine guns, and Semtex explosives.

28 Unattributed interview with NCS source.

4 The chemical, biological, radiological and nuclear weapons threat

Jez Littlewood and John Simpson

Providing an accurate, timely, and verifiable assessment of the threat posed by possible terrorist use of CBRN weapons is an impossible task. It would require not only access to information held by the intelligence and counter-terrorism communities, but also detailed knowledge of the capabilities, intentions and motivations of a wide variety of terrorist groups. It would, in addition, also necessitate a comprehensive historical and scientific knowledge of CBRN weapons. In the public domain only the latter is available, and even in this area knowledge is incomplete. As a consequence, the variables involved in what actually constitutes the CBRN threat are too many for those outside the government machinery and/or those without access to intelligence information (complete with its caveats and context(s)) to make any claims with authority.

The potential CBRN threat has become too politicised. Of equal import the knowledge available in the public domain about the CBRN threat is too unspecific, often inaccurate in terms of the impact of certain weapons, and too often focused on the worst-case scenario. A threat assessment in terms of either 'the UK will be attacked with chemical weapons in 2006' or 'the threat posed by CBRN weapons is extremely limited and an attack is highly unlikely to occur in the next three years' cannot be conveyed with any confidence based on the available information.

In this chapter the CBRN threat is analysed using available information and the past as an indicator of possible future threats. Only then does the chapter proceed to draw a conclusion and make a heavily caveated assessment of the potential CBRN threat. The analysis relies heavily on past trends as a guide to future possibilities and it attempts to put the threat into a context the reader can understand. Through this approach it is hoped the reader can move away from an understanding clouded by fear about the worst-case scenarios involving CBRN and begin to approach this subject with greater clarity.

Guesstimates and chemical, biological, radiological and nuclear weapons

Five years on from 9/11 the CBRN threat has yet to manifest itself in a manner many politicians, commentators, or journalists imagined, that is, mass destruction and high casualties in major Western cities. Not only prior to 9/11, but also after it, there has been no mass destruction using CBRN weapons perpetrated by terrorists. Indeed, the use by terrorists of nuclear weapons or devices has never occurred and radiological dispersion devices have also not been used. Chemical weapons have been used in the past – but not since 9/11 – and terrorist use of biological weapons remains exceptional. Casualties resulting from CBRN weapons are few and far between. One analysis notes that of the 11,992 terrorist attacks between 1997 and 2004, 11,884 involved conventional weapons. Of the 108 incidents not involving conventional weapons, 15 involved biological materials, over 45 involved chemical substances, 11 related to contamination of food or water, and fewer than 10 people were killed as a result of these attacks.[1]

The lack of CBRN attacks should lead policy-makers, politicians, scholars, and governments to ask penetrating questions. Why have so few CBRN attacks occurred? What is the actual threat posed by CBRN? What is the perceived threat posed by these weapons? And, aside from what is real, what is supposition, and what is evidence concerning CBRN weapons, what does all this mean for future policy towards the domestic management of terrorist attacks?

Difficult as it may be to admit, those outside the intelligence and counter-terrorism community or without access to such information are in many cases simply guessing at the CBRN threat. Analysis and threat assessments that emerge from those guesses are influenced by subjective beliefs, perceptions, and opinions on the utility of existing government policy at the time. Some threat assessments may even be part of a concerted effort to ensure resources are channelled in certain directions. Such an approach does not produce accurate threat assessments: it produces opinions, of which some are informed and some are not.

Furthermore, real expertise on the scientific and technical aspects of CBRN weapons is in very short supply. Most scientific experts in this area know one type of weapon, not all four. They are able to make relatively informed opinions about the other weapons but are not experts in them. Second, most non-scientists rely on the opinions and assessments of others. Third, if we add to that mix the paucity of real historical knowledge about how these weapons have been developed, produced, and used in the past; which kinds of actors have succeeded in developing and using such weapons; which kinds of actors have attempted and failed to produce or use such weapons; and, our ignorance of the precise motivations for any actor – state, non-state, or individual – to develop and use nuclear, chemical or biological weapons, then it (should) become clear that any threat assessment is only of limited value.

Chemical, biological, radiological and nuclear weapons, not weapons of mass destruction

CBRN weapons can be defined in a variety of ways. The acronym WMD (weapons of mass destruction) has been in common usage in the international relations and diplomatic community for over half a century.[2] In the run up to the Iraq War (2003) the term 'WMD' entered the public lexicon. Such weapons have also long been termed 'unconventional' weapons.[3] The key point about such weapons is that they are different. That difference has a significant impact on perceptions about such weapons, how they are developed, produced, and used, the impact of their use, and the consequences of any use for both the attacked and the perpetrators.

CBRN is an addition to the discourse to take into account the terrorist threat using CBRN weapons might not cause actual mass destruction. As Carus notes, 'CBRN' has its own history[4] but has now been appropriated for use in the terrorist threat context denoting, principally, the distinction between a weapon which would be of military quality and employed to achieve its intended aim, which may be mass destruction, and a device such as the plastic bags filled with sarin released on the Tokyo subway in 1985. Although it is tempting to suggest, for example, that a chemical device is a chemical weapon, the type of chemical used, how much is used, how it has been weaponised, how it is dispersed or disseminated, where the target is, whether or not the intended targeted population has access to protective equipment or is familiar with chemical weapons, the immediacy and competence of any response to an attack, and meteorological and other conditions all affect its actual impact. Caveats abound and they should not be ignored: not all chemical weapons are equal, and similarly not all biological, radiological, or nuclear weapons are equal. When discussing terrorism and unconventional weapons we refer to CBRN: not WMD. In simple terms, this is to distinguish between state-led WMD programmes and interest of non-state actors in CBRN. Other terms have also emerged, including super-terrorism, weapon of mass effect, weapon of mass disruption, and mass casualty terrorism. The different discourse and its implications are important because the use of CBRN weapons will not necessarily result in mass destruction or mass casualties.

Indeed, 'WMD terrorism' may well turn out to be the 'missile gap' of the Global War on Terrorism (GWOT).[5] It has not yet occurred. Based on what is known in the public domain about actual capabilities, mass destruction using CBRN weapons is also not likely in the immediate future.

Interests, capabilities, and threats

There is sufficient evidence in the public domain to indicate that terrorist groups such as Al-Qaeda are *interested* in developing, acquiring, and using CBRN weapons.[6] An interest, however, does not constitute an actual *capability*. And, it is important to note that a *capability* does not automatically equate to an *intent* to use such weapons. While it is safe to assume that if terrorists of the ilk of the most hardened members of Al-Qaeda circa 2001 had CBRN weapons they would likely have used them,[7] as is explored below, as far as we know from publicly available information terrorists do not possess sophisticated CBRN capabilities. Flowing from that we can surmise that the threat is limited and, more importantly, can be managed. That assessment relates to the first half of 2006 and may hold for another few months or years.

This is not to say that there is no CBRN threat. There is, but a balance needs to be struck between apathy and hyperbole.[8] In 1995 Ron Purver, of the Canadian Security Intelligence Service (CSIS), published a survey of the chemical and biological weapons threat posed by terrorists.[9] Purver's 1995 study provided a typology of five types of threat. That typology can be usefully revised to assess the interests, capabilities, and threats posed by CBRN and terrorists at this juncture:

1   threats to use CBRN weapons without any evidence of actual capabilities;
2   unsuccessful attempts to acquire CBRN weapons;
3   actual possession of CBRN weapons;
4   attempted, unsuccessful use of CBRN weapons;
5   successful use of CBRN weapons.

Taking this typology, together with what is actually known about the current capabilities of various terrorist groups, and the past as an indicator of the future threat, it is possible to make a contextualised CBRN threat assessment.

Interest in chemical, biological, radiological and nuclear

Terrorist and other non-state actor interest in CBRN precedes the current paradigm of Islamic jihadists. Within the academic and policy-making community there is a substantial body of literature on the likely interest of terrorists in acquiring WMD.[10] In addition, there is a long history of criminal use of CBRN.[11] Criminal use of CBRN has contemporaneously been added to the terrorist threat assessment to an extent that criminal and terrorist interest has been conflated. The consequences of such conflation need further consideration beyond the scope of this chapter, but there is a distinction between the 1982 contamination of Tylenol with cyanide which resulted in seven fatalities, or the delivery of contaminated soil containing anthrax spores to the Chemical Defence Establishment (CDE) at Porton Down in 1981 by the 'Dark Harvest Commandos',[12] and the use of sarin by Aum Shinrikyo in 1995 or the anthrax attacks in the USA in 2001.

Nuclear and radiological weapons

A nuclear weapon may be either an atomic or fission one or a thermonuclear (fusion) or hydrogen one. The development and production of a thermonuclear device is beyond the wherewithal of most states and a terrorist group is so unlikely to be able to develop such a weapon that the scenario can be dismissed from the current threat assessment. That is not to say measures which have reduced, and will continue to retard, proliferation should be ignored or weakened. Such measures should be strengthened.

There has been continued speculation that the theft of a thermonuclear weapon from one of the seven states known to possess such weapons – China, France, Russian Federation, UK, USA, India, Pakistan – or Israel (a state with a high probability of possessing such weapons) is possible. This, again, remains an extremely remote possibility, but one that does need to be carefully, and continually, assessed. However, even if theft occurred, (re)configuring the weapon to detonate at a time and place of the terrorist's choosing, or successfully triggering an explosion by other, external, means (for example, exploding conventional explosives alongside it) remains very difficult. As a result, only terrorist development, acquisition or manufacture of basic atomic devices is considered likely, but even this remains much more difficult than many observers believe. Many states have tried and failed to develop nuclear weapons. States have sovereignty, territory, a scientific base of skilled individuals, and resources at their disposal in which to conduct nuclear weapons development. Few terrorist groups have any of these factors available to them, never mind all of them. State failure in the nuclear weapons area is a significant contextual factor in considering the nuclear weapons threat from terrorists.

Access to key fissile materials required to develop a nuclear weapon, uranium highly enriched in its isotope 235 and/or plutonium with a high content of its isotope 239, is the principal factor. Fissionable material must be manufactured and these processes are complex and require knowledge, time, resources, and a safe haven. Although certain components necessary for a weapon are more readily available, they remain restricted in their uses. Access to such materials, and thus their manufacture and distribution, is controlled nationally and internationally. Such mechanisms are not a guarantor of security, but taken together as a collective requirement for development of a nuclear weapon the obstacles are not insignificant, easily breached, or circumvented by States or non-state actors. States as diverse as Argentina, Brazil, Iraq, Libya, and Iran can testify to such realities.

While the knowledge of certain aspects of nuclear weapon manufacture has disseminated, developing a fully deliverable weapon – never mind a reliable one – is widely considered beyond the reach of even the most sophisticated group.[13] As a result of these scientific, technological, logistical, and security difficulties, nuclear weapons have become conflated in media reporting with improvised devices and radiological weapons or radiological dispersion devices (RDDs): the latter is something entirely different from a nuclear weapon.

It is useful, however, to consider the range of possibilities for acquisition of nuclear and/or radioactive weapons. The range has been identified as:[14]

- theft and detonation of an intact nuclear weapon;
- theft or purchase of fissile material leading to an improvised nuclear device (IND) or crude nuclear weapon;
- attacks and/or sabotage of nuclear facilities; and
- unauthorised acquisition of radioactive materials contributing to an RDD.

Recent analysis points to a continued possibility of a 'nuclear 9/11'[15] but unless assisted, any theft, capture or purchase of a nuclear weapon would have to overcome numerous obstacles.[16] Nevertheless, the idea of 'loose nukes' is a popular one and there are analysts who believe theft and capture to be a realistic, but not inevitable, risk.[17]

These technical-logistical difficulties exist regardless of whether or not a terrorist group has the financial and motivational commitment to nuclear weapons acquisition and use. A terrorist may have an *interest*, but that does not mean there is either a *capability* or a real *intention* to acquire, develop and use nuclear weapons. These latter factors cannot be dismissed. A full 'chain of causation' incorporating all the necessary sequential steps would involve: motivational objectives; a decision to engage in nuclear terrorism; acquisition of the necessary materials through gift, purchase, theft, or diversion; an ability to transport and deliver the weapon to the target; and, an ability to carry out the attack.[18]

Assuming terrorist interest in nuclear devices (that is, weapons and improvised devices) is real, understanding the risk *and* threat then involves an assessment of security related to nuclear materials that could be used to manufacture a rudimentary device. In contrast to a fully operational nuclear weapon the fissile or useable sources are much wider. Unrecorded caches of fissile material are widely believed to exist in the states of the former Soviet Union and radioactive materials are regularly lost,[19] but accurate judgements are stymied by the unavailability of reliable data.[20]

As of the end of December 2004 the International Atomic Energy Agency's Illicit Trafficking Database (ITDB) lists 650 illicit trafficking incidents 'confirmed to the Agency'. Of these the International Atomic Energy Agency (IAEA) indicates 'about 30% of the incidents involved nuclear materials and about 60% other radioactive materials … [with] … [e]ighteen confirmed incidents involved trafficking in high enriched uranium and plutonium. A few of these incidents involved kilogram quantities of weapons-usable nuclear material, but most featured very small quantities'.[21] The trend, based on this data, does appear to be upward, indicating concerns about nuclear terrorism and attempted acquisition of materials are justified. Whether or not the upward trend reflects increased illicit activity over the last five years (particularly in 2003 and 2004) or more comprehensive reporting of known losses and interdiction of illicit trafficking is unknown at this time. However, certain types of weapon design may be within the reach of highly motivated terrorist groups that could buy or acquire the necessary materials and technical capabilities to develop such weapons. The same analysis noted, however:[22]

> this would require enormous efforts. … The organisation would need shelter for several years, where they can work undisturbed and carry out the necessary experiments.

Many interpret Al-Qaeda or associates supported by as compromising such a group.[23] In addition to these observations three studies from the 1960s, 1970s, and this century indicate a non-state actor could develop a nuclear device. Indeed, one report notes that the US Nuclear Laboratories built a gun-type device 'using only components that, except for the nuclear material, were off the shelf and commercially available without breaking any laws'.[24]

There is general agreement that a nuclear attack would be a high consequence event, but it is one of low probability and 'the least likely to occur'.[25] Returning to Purver's revised typology, there has been no successful use of nuclear weapons, no attempted unsuccessful use, and no known actual possession of nuclear weapons by terrorists. Whether or not there has been an unsuccessful attempt to acquire a nuclear weapon or the fissionable materials to develop one is open to debate. However, caution should be the key guide. Based on the ITDB of the IAEA it would be prudent to assume, at this stage, unsuccessful attempts at acquisition have been made. Various threats to use nuclear weapons without any evidence of any capability can be gleaned from the public domain. On balance, there is certainly evidence of an interest in nuclear weapons. Verifiable evidence relating to actual capabilities is extremely scant. The key observation, in terms of the domestic management of attacks, may be ensuring the security and access to nuclear (fissile) materials.

Radiological weapons or radiological dispersal device

RDDs – commonly referred to as 'dirty bombs' – deny the use of territory. They disseminate radioactive materials inflicting contamination and (limited) human casualties. The April 2005 *US National Planning Scenario* for an RDD estimated 180 fatalities and over 250 casualties in an RDD using cesium-137 developed over years.[26] Such devices are expected to involve conventional high explosive in combination with a radioactive material. Both conventional explosives and radioactive material are more accessible than fissile materials. Radioactive materials could originate from a variety of sources including a nuclear reactor – in the form of used fuel rods or the waste produced within a reactor from its operation – from hospitals, agricultural uses stemming from sterilisation of pests and preservation of food, or from other industrial, medical and power-generating locations.[27]

Radioactive sources exist across the globe. The sheer number of sources, as well as their distribution, makes it difficult to prevent unauthorised acquisition. Returning to the ITDB, there have been 'numerous cases of discoveries of uncontrolled radioactive sources'.[28] This includes a significant amount of lost, abandoned, or inappropriately disposed of radioactive sources across the globe, including in Europe and the USA. Certain radiological sources may be accessible, relatively small and safe, and consequently of greater portability when placed in a shielded container. The largest missing radioactive sources are Radioisotope Thermoelectric Generators (RTGs), which were used to power mountain-top radio transmitters or remote lighthouses in the Soviet Union. It has been estimated by the Bellona Foundation (Norway) that up to 1,000 RTGs are unguarded or unaccounted for – the so-called orphan sources.[29] Although thieves or terrorists attempting to steal an RTG would likely succumb to the radioactive material if the protective shields were removed, the risk posed by what are regarded as portable and 'available' radioactive sources is sobering. Attempting to get former Soviet states to account for such sources is difficult.[30]

Used fuel is not a likely source of such material. While it is easily accessible because it is usually located in underwater storage ponds, its make-up and weight and its greater radioactivity make it difficult to shield when removed from a pond. A caveat, however, is that this source may be less secure than the materials used in nuclear weapons. Furthermore, it is often stored either at power stations or research reactors, or moved to a central location for storage and reprocessing.

Evidence does exist of interest in radiological weapons.[31] A variety of RDDs can be envisaged, but three predominate: wrapping the source material around a conventional explosive, such as that envisaged in the US planning scenario; passive distribution to spread the material, although it should be noted that this method borders on being a suicide activity; and, a scenario which gained a lot of attention in the immediate aftermath of 9/11, namely, an attempt to breach the containment shields of a nuclear power station, a used nuclear fuel cooling pond, or a high active waste storage facility. Although the most likely attack would be a direct assault or the use of explosives, post-9/11 the use of kinetic energy such as flying an aircraft into the facility, has gained notoriety. An attack of this kind would generate long-term effects, as the Chernobyl experience indicated. However, attacking a nuclear power plant with a ground-based force of terrorists in a commando-style operation in the UK would be difficult and unlikely to succeed. An air attack would require very skilled piloting of a large aircraft to generate a fuel-air explosive. It would require an accurate impact on the designated target.

Deliberate or sabotage attacks could result in considerable damage to non-power reactors, such as research reactors. One study in 2003 suggested that the 'consequences of a successful sabotage attack could be significant radioactive release and contamination of an area near the reactor site'. Furthermore, because 'many research reactors, unlike most power reactors, are located within or close to populated areas, they may present a greater threat of disruption to the public from a sabotage attack than do most power reactors'.[32]

In Australia, 18 men were arrested in early November 2005 on suspicion of planning an attack and, even though the target was not identified, headlines indicated that the Lucas Heights nuclear reactor was a possible target.[33] Again, however, technical impediments and obstacles to manufacture of an RDD and disseminating radioactivity to a target exist. In the latter case, the nature of the source material, the heat generating propensities of the radioactive substance, the type of physical environment in which the RDD is initiated, and the climatic conditions at the time all have an impact on the consequences of its use. The most commonly cited scenario, an attack in a built-up area, would present difficulties because buildings absorb radiation. One scenario using an RDD led to the conclusion that '[f]urther than a few blocks from the detonation site, the blast exposure dose would not exceed the level of everyday environmental background exposure'.[34]

Thus, the actual physical impact of an RDD would depend, *inter alia*, on the radioactivity of the material dispersed, the quantity of material involved, and the concentration of the material achieved by the distributing device. Unless large quantities of highly radioactive material were involved – which presents significant problems in terms of acquisition, handling, and transporting the materials – a lack of concentration of the material would limit the immediate deaths: RDDs do not result in mass destruction. Certainly, the explosion of an RDD in a city, as television dramatisations have implied, would result in significant social, economic and political consequences[35] Both the Homeland Security scenarios and the former US radiological weapons programme point less to destruction and more to contamination and area denial, as well as terrorizing a population[36] Such weapons are, as a consequence, better characterised as mass disruptive, rather than mass destructive. A critical factor is unfamiliarity with these weapons, particularly public fear of radiation, and uncertainty, all coupled with widespread misreporting on likely effects. These non-weapon aspects of the RDD threat are part of the problem of dirty bombs. Finally, the first use of RDDs could stimulate interest among terrorist groups (and greater reactions from governments) if mass disruption, but not major loss of life, resulted.[37]

Biological weapons

As with nuclear weapons the apparent 'ease' with which a biological weapon can be made has been grossly overstated. Over the last decade biological weapons have taken on an almost mythical status. To illustrate the potential threat of terrorists, if a nuclear weapon is not cited, then a biological weapon almost certainly will be. As Gearson remarked:[38]

> in a notorious interview on prime-time television in 1997, the US Secretary of Defense William Cohen held up a five-pound bag of sugar to demonstrate how much anthrax it would take to kill the population of Washington DC. The result was to focus attention on the low-probability end of the spectrum of threat …

The potential of biological weapons, the biotechnology revolution, and mass casualty attacks by terrorists using conventional weapons have been conflated in recent times to construct the bioterrorist ready to use a genetically engineered biological weapon to attack Western cities. This end of the spectrum is a myth and will most likely remain so in the short term.

Biological warfare or terrorism is essentially the deliberate use of disease. Any biological agent (for example, bacteria, virus, fungi) may be used, but only some pathogens are of real utility.[39] The scope of the threat also includes incapacitating pathogens, and anti-animal and anti-plant pathogens. The latter, agricultural terrorism, includes among its targets crops and animal husbandry. The US planning scenario used Foot and Mouth Disease in its April 2005 assessment, a possibility the UK is familiar with, given its recent experience with the natural outbreak of the Foot and Mouth virus (FMV) in 2001.[40]

Unlike fissile material for nuclear weapons the basic component of a biological weapon – a pathogen – exists across the world in culture collections, laboratories, civil and military facilities, and naturally in the environment. As a consequence, access to pathogens is theoretically high. Nevertheless, while there are legitimate concerns about the potentially devastating consequences of bioterrorism a number of caveats need to be considered.

The potential of biological weapons is based on extensive studies of the *military quantity* and *military quality* of particular pathogens. Terrorists are unlikely to develop either the quantity or the quality of a weaponised pathogen developed in sophisticated state-level programmes. There is also no large-scale deliberate use of biological weapons documented in history that has produced hundreds of thousands of casualties. Naturally occurring outbreaks of disease have, however, produced high numbers of casualties. The means of delivery is also important: effective aerosol dissemination of a biological weapon would be necessary to cause mass casualties in terms of thousands, and aerosolisation poses significant technical problems that many states have failed to overcome. Finally, as with naturally occurring outbreaks of disease, not everyone exposed to the pathogen will become infected, all infected will not necessarily progress to the disease, and not all those with the disease will necessarily die. These caveats are not interpreted as discounting the threat posed by bioterrorism. Scenarios involving sophisticated weapons using military quantities and military quality of a pathogen are, however, poor indicators of possible future trends.[41]

To illustrate, and necessarily underline these points, it is worth quoting in detail an assessment from the USA under testimony in 2002:[42]

> ... all the experts we met with agreed that while a laboratory scientist may be able to grow cultures of some bio-agents, the production and use of most biological warfare agents would require a relatively high degree of sophistication in terms of expertise and equipment.
>
> According to technical experts in the many fields associated with biological agents including those formerly with State-sponsored offensive biological weapons programs, it would be very difficult for a terrorist to overcome major technical and operational challenges to effectively weaponize and deliver a biological warfare agent to cause mass casualties. If terrorists could overcome these obstacles, experts believe that those without a prior knowledge of these agents would have to conduct extensive experimentation to perfect their skills, which would result in their increased risk of discovery. Specialized knowledge is needed to acquire the right biological warfare agent, process it, improvise a weapon or device, and effectively deliver it to cause mass casualties.

In March 2003 – a point when much more was known about *actual* Al-Qaeda activity in Afghanistan – a Congressional Research Report on terrorist motivations for chemical and biological weapons noted:[43]

> Projections of tens of thousands of casualties are theoretically possible, but many such estimates are worst-case scenarios likely to occur in hard-to-achieve circumstances, with ideal weather conditions, temperature conditions, dispersion rate, concentration of agent, and so on.

More recent work critiquing the bioterrorism bandwagon that has gathered pace in the last decade is unforgiving in its dissembling of the threats apparently posed by terrorists armed with biological agents.[44] Historical evidence together with what is known about current capabilities point not to technically adept bioterrorists but to a low incidence of real biological events. Of those events, two successes and two failures stand out. On the one hand the failure of Aum Shinrikyo in Japan between 1990 and 1994 to develop either an anthrax or botulinum toxin despite time, money, and a largely undisturbed effort, and the failure of Al-Qaeda between 1999 and November 2001 to obtain anthrax and prepare a facility to undertake microbiological work point to how difficult developing a biological weapon actually is. On the other hand, the use of Salmonella by the Rajneeshee cult in Oregon in 1984 (undiscovered at the time) and the unresolved October–November 2001 anthrax letter attacks in the USA point to dangerous possibilities.[45]

The US anthrax attacks in 2001 are the anomalous incident in the bioterrorism category to date. Considerable speculation that the perpetrator was a US biological defence insider remains but, of greater import, the quality of the anthrax used in the attack was, and remains, by order of magnitude more sophisticated than anything discovered or hinted at by other terrorists, including Al-Qaeda or those inspired by the latter's ideology.

As Leitenberg notes, excluding the US anthrax attacks, no other terrorist group to date has 'yet shown the ability to master the microbiological A, B, Cs in the real world', yet, nearly all terrorists have been 'endowed with the prospective ability to genetically engineer pathogens'.[46] The public's perception of the threat assessment for biological weapons is perhaps the most overblown of the CBRN assessments: to date it has been hyped out of all proportion.

Delivery via non-airborne means, such as water supplies or the food supply present a greater number of historical examples of bioterrorism and has recently come back into focus. Rather than genetically engineered attacks, it is at the simple end of the spectrum where bioterrorism may pose the principal dangers. Successful examples of attacks include the Rajneeshee cult attack on salad bars in Oregon, USA, in 1984 with *Salmonella Typhimurium*, resulting in 751 casualties. Whether or not this actually was terrorism, rather than the criminal act intended to influence local elections for which it was conceived, has been lost in the current environment. There have also been numerous extortion attempts against supermarkets or companies. While contamination of such sources precedes the current terrorist threat, the risk posed by contamination of water and food supply has to be put into perspective. Attacking the food supply at the point of delivery to the general population limits the numbers at risk or targeted. As in the Rajneeshee cult example, which serves as a better example of the likely threat, 750 casualties is not mass fatalities or mass destruction. Even a recent example, such as the 'toxic milk' farrago during June 2005, is open to actual speculation about the number of infected individuals likely to result in any contamination.[47] That assessment underplayed the extensive difficulties of actually producing a toxin from clostridium botulinum, which, again, a known terrorist group (Aum Shinrikyo) with no limits on time, resource, or effort, failed to do.

Attacking the food supply at the processing and manufacturing plant would require the perpetrator to circumvent existing food safety and management procedures within any facility. The global food industry remains highly regulated and food safety management is of significant importance to the manufacturers themselves, not least in terms of product branding and public confidence. While such an attack is not impossible, carrying it out without anyone noticing or the contamination being picked up in the quality control and safety checks is difficult.

A similar qualification is required when considering threats to the water supply. Mandatory water treatment procedures would locate many contaminants as part of the day-to-day safety checks. In addition, high expectations in the public act as a major sentinel in water safety. Furthermore, the task of contaminating millions of gallons of water, the natural dilution effect, and the quantity of contaminant required should not be underestimated. Nevertheless, as the World Health Organization (WHO) study in 1970 demonstrated, attacks on the water supply could result in considerable disruption and deaths in a large city (between 200 and 4,500 for the typhoid example).[48] While there are a number of new challenges posed by the terrorist threat, many basic procedures through which to prevent, detect, and respond to an attack are already in place.[49] Such measures are essential counters to the biological (and chemical) weapons threat, and as the more recent WHO publication on biological and chemical weapons noted elimination of all risk of contamination is impossible. As the study went on to note, '[t]he goal must be to reduce this risk to the greatest possible extent and to respond rapidly when contamination and disruption do occur'.[50]

The biological weapons threat from terrorists is therefore mixed. The worst case scenarios are just that. In the real world, as Leitenberg points out, the perpetrator of the anthrax attacks in the USA is the anomaly compared to the efforts of Aum in Japan and what is known (publicly) about Al-Qaeda. The (bio)terrorist armed with genetically engineered strains of smallpox is a myth. Despite the hyperbole, however, there are a range of agents and toxins, which could be used to conduct a bioterrorist attack. In addition, there is plenty of evidence of criminal activity in terms of deliberate contamination which, while not mass destruction, could be a cause for major concern if a terrorist group announced an attack on a water supply or food product, or even a building or geographic area. As Dando notes, '[t]here are many opportunities for an attacker to wreak havoc that fall short of what one might consider "mass destruction"'.[51]

Chemical weapons

In the UK, investigation of the use of toxic chemicals in criminal cases has been a regular law enforcement issue.[52] Other emergency services have also dealt with numerous chemical incidents caused by either accidents or contamination. Like biological weapons the threat spectrum is extensive because all toxic chemicals pose a risk. Under the 1993 Chemical Weapons Convention, 'toxic chemical' means:

Any chemical which through its chemical action on life processes can cause death, temporary incapacitation or permanent harm to humans or animals. This includes all such chemicals, regardless of their origin or of their method of production, and regardless of whether they are produced in facilities, in munitions or elsewhere.

Therefore, the threat spectrum is not restricted to classic chemical weapons such as mustard, chlorine, or cyanide. For example, recent studies have identified the chemical agent most commonly used in deliberate releases in the USA 'has been not some deadly nerve gas, but butyric acid, which is a malodorant'.[53] More recent studies have concentrated not on classic chemical warfare agents but on commonly available chemicals.[54]

As with attacks on nuclear power plants or reactors, attacks on industrial chemical plants pose an altogether different type of threat. The risk in this area is actually much greater than that posed by classic chemical weapons or nerve agents such as VX or Tabun. Toxic industrial chemicals and toxin industrial materials were ranked by NATO's International Task Force-25 (ITF-25) in 1998 in a hazard index. On the high hazard list are chemicals such as chlorine, formaldehyde, hydrogen cyanide, and nitric acid. One hundred and fifty tonnes of chlorine contained in 6,000 cylinders spread over a four-mile front was used in April 1915 by Germany on the Western Front, initiating the use of modern chemical weapons. On the medium hazard list of ITF-25 was the chemical methyl isocyanate: the chemical responsible for at least 2,500 deaths in December 1984 in Bhopal, India.[55] Many chemical plants and the chemicals within them are not fully protected against potential terrorist attacks. Indeed, during workshops held in the UK in 2003 and 2004, security of chemicals and chemical storage facilities was a recurring theme. The UK is not the sole problem: in the USA, for example, one report stated that:[56]

Across the country, each of 123 plants could endanger more than 1 million people if a terrorist attack released toxic clouds. Another 700 plants could threaten 100,000 people each. Another 3,000 plants could threaten 10,000 people each.

The basis of that report has subsequently been revised in the USA, but the original data is indicative of the scale of the problem. In 1983 the then Greater London Council was required to draw up civil defence plans and commissioned the *Greater London Area War Risk Study* (GLAWARS) published in 1986. Chemical and biological weapons featured in the six-volume report of GLAWARS, but in the subsequent book chemical and biological weapons were considered not to 'involve major consequences for London as a whole'.[57] Notwithstanding that GLAWARS was examining the issue from a perspective of war with the Soviet Union, the report offers some intriguing assessments. For example, attacking the two reservoirs at the head of the Lea Valley would require at least 60 tonnes of nerve agent to make the contamination effective.[58]

The GLAWARS report also noted that the (then) main chemical depots in the London area each held more than 50 tonnes of chlorine gas, and 'breaching a 50-tonne chlorine store would produce a 50 per cent death rate up to 1.4 km from the store, if weather conditions were optimum for windborne dispersion'.[59] Attacks on agriculture with chemical weapons are a possibility but their effect would be extremely limited.

Low-level and relatively unsophisticated attacks using chemical weapons have occurred. In addition to the activities of Aum, recent focus in the UK has been on the threat posed by ricin and the alleged existence of the al-Mubtakkar device to disperse hydrogen cyanide.[60] There has been a sufficient number of incidents to take the chemical terrorist threat seriously, ranging from the alleged al-Mubtakkar device, the ricin incident of 2003, and the alleged discovery in February 2001 of 'detailed instructions on how to manufacture and deploy sarin'[61] following the arrest of six Algerians in London. In the MV Nisha incident, 21 December 2001, a ship heading to the UK was alleged to be carrying terrorist materials. While MV Nisha was subsequently found to contain no such materials and was released following an extensive search, there are indications that at the time the personnel boarding the ship and those commanding the operation believed there was a possibility of a CBRN connection. Following the arrest of three men on 9 November 2002 and press speculation that chemical weapon attacks on the London Underground were planned, both the Foreign Secretary and the Deputy Prime Minister indicated there was no evidence relating to such an attack revealed during the arrests.[62]

The ricin incident and trial in the UK over the period 2003 to 2005 is illustrative of both terrorist interest *and* the media's approach to the subject. The 'chemical weapons factory' uncovered in Wood Green, London, resulted in the arrest of six men and a woman and, initially, positive tests for the presence of ricin. Found in the flat were castor beans, cherry stones, and other recipes. Intelligence indicated, and many observers believed, that 'the occupants of the flat were planning to mix ricin into jars of face-cream and smear it on the doors of tube trains and restaurants, in the hope of causing deaths and spreading panic'.[63] Two jars of cream remain unaccounted for according to the former Metropolitan Police Commissioner. Prior to this, under Operation Springbourne, others had been arrested in the UK and one suspect was later picked up in Norfolk. Here the police found, 'recipes for making ricin, cyanide and other lethal poisons'.[64]

It is clear that the individuals apprehended at Wood Green in London had an *interest* in producing ricin and perhaps using it as a weapon. While a legitimate cause for concern, this is, by no stretch of the threat assessment, sophisticated biological or chemical terrorism or evidence for it. Moreover, that ricin recipe 'would very likely not produce ricin or extremely little of it'.[65] Whether or not these individuals had a *capability* beyond their *interest*, is subject to ongoing debate.

As with all other aspects of the CBRN threat, understanding the chemical terrorism threat requires caveats and contextual information. Despite its pre-9/11 date, or perhaps because of it, the conclusion of the 1999 study by the US General

Accounting Office, *Combating Terrorism: Need for Comprehensive Threat and Risk Assessments of Chemical and Biological Attacks* with regard to chemical weapons remains largely valid. It noted, *inter alia*, that 'toxic industrial chemicals can cause mass casualties and require little if any expertise or sophisticated methods. Most chemical nerve agents, however, are technically challenging for terrorists to acquire, manufacture, and produce'.[66]

Threat assessment

If one (subjectively) believes that terrorist use of CBRN is highly likely and only a matter of time, or that Western states are ill-prepared to deal with that threat (never mind counter it) then a range of sources to substantiate the claims can be drawn upon from testimony of government officials, speeches from government Ministers, commentary – on and off-record – from intelligence officials, declarations from intergovernmental summits, and the espoused views of experts. As an example, Ron Noble, Secretary-General of Interpol, noted in 2005 that 'the threat of bioterrorism is real because the threat of terrorism is real'[67] and went on to note that 'the danger of a biological attack is not only from Al-Qaeda; it is from any individual or group that wishes to support Al-Qaeda by striking at us anywhere and everywhere they choose. We must thus be concerned by Al-Qaeda, Al-Qaeda-like groups and Al-Qaeda supporters'.[68]

Likewise, if one is (subjectively) sceptical of the ability of terrorists to develop, produce, and use CBRN or considers Western states are fairly well prepared to deal with the threat, then a range of sources can also be collected to support such a line of argument. As Freedman noted in 2002:[69]

> There was evidence of an interest in chemical and biological weapons, and a reasonable assumption that if these weapons were acquired they would be used, but there was no reason to suppose that this was a high-probability threat. Even when a scare was raised over a suspected plot to explode a radiation bomb, something which had clearly interested al-Qaeda from 1993, reports suggested that this was at an elementary stage and that, even if some device were constructed, the effects would be modest, becoming severe only if panic ensued.

Returning to Purver's revised typology, there is evidence of a threat in each of the five categories for each of the different types of weapons, with the exception of nuclear weapons.

Nuclear weapons

Nuclear weapons have been used twice in history by the USA against Japan in the closing stages of the Second World War. No other state has used nuclear weapons. No non-state actor or terrorist group has used nuclear weapons and there are no known cases of attempted unsuccessful use of nuclear weapons by terrorists, nor actual possession of such weapons by them. It would be prudent to assume that attempts have been made to acquire nuclear weapons, even though the evidence in the public domain is scant and open to some interpretation. There have, however, certainly been threats to use nuclear weapons without any evidence of actual capability; bin Laden in 2001 is reported as saying Al-Qaeda has nuclear weapons and is prepared to use them.[70] The threat assessment would, based on this evidence, appear to be in the realms of threats and possible attempts to acquire nuclear weapons.

Radiological weapons

As with nuclear weapons there has been no reported successful or unsuccessful use of an RDD. Possession of an RDD is difficult to gauge, but UK intelligence has claimed Al-Qaeda should be considered 'RDD-capable' following a small RDD allegedly uncovered in Afghanistan.[71] Furthermore, possession would have to include the incident whereby a container with a small amount of cesium-137 was placed in a Moscow park in 1995.[72] The IAEA ITDB presents the most reliable public data on which to assess theft, loss, trade, and illicit access to nuclear and radioactive materials. Although the period 1993 to 2004 indicated a downward trend in the number of incidents, 2004 itself witnessed an increase in illicit trafficking incidents. Anecdotally, individuals consulted during the research on the domestic management of terrorist attacks suggested heightened concern in the UK about radiological threats. The IAEA ITDB would suggest to the cautious analyst that at least some of these incidents involve attempts by terrorists, or black market intermediaries, to access radioactive materials. Here, therefore, using the revised Purver typology, it would appear the threat assessment is in the realm of threats without evidence of capabilities, unsuccessful attempts to acquire RDDs, and possible, but limited, actual possession of radiological devices.

Biological weapons

The biological weapons threat assessment is an altogether different picture to that of nuclear or radiological weapons. There is evidence of successful use of biological weapons from the 'Amerithrax' attacks of Autumn 2001 through to the UK-based Dark Harvest Commandos deposit of soil containing anthrax from Gruinard Island (the Second World War UK testing ground for the development of biological weapons) at Porton Down in 1981. Use, in this context, has to be considered as a broad spectrum of possibilities as the two incidents noted above illustrate. Aum Shinrikyo's attempts to use biological weapons fulfil the attempted, unsuccessful use of biological weapons in our revised typology. Clearly, the above also fulfil the possession and, in the case of Aum, unsuccessful attempts at acquisition categories of the typology. Furthermore, the sheer number of hoaxes involving 'white powder' mainly perpetrated by US anti-abortionists indicate the fulfilment of the threat without evidence of capability category of the revised typology. Such hoaxes are spreading to non-traditional targets, such as construction workers, and it may only be a matter of time before other groups opposed to certain issues such as abortion or animal testing begin to employ such means in the UK.[73]

The biological weapons threat assessment must acknowledge that sophisticated biological weapons have been developed, as in the US anthrax attacks. Yet, if the information on Al-Qaeda and its supporters is correct, terrorists inspired by its ideology have so far failed to acquire, develop, or use biological weapons. The threat posed by biological weapons use from non-state actors is probably increasing, but this may be a result of new interest stimulated by fear of, and vulnerabilities exposed by, potential biological weapons threats through repeated statements of Western governments, analysts, and experts.

Chemical weapons

Like biological weapons, a threat assessment based on the revised typology illustrates incidents in all five categories. Aum Shinrikyo's activities fulfil both the successful use (Matsumoto, Tokyo subway) and unsuccessful use of chemical weapons. Aum also fulfils the actual possession criterion. Of greater relevance to the UK, the Wood Green 'chemical weapons factory' indicates an unsuccessful attempt to acquire a chemical weapon, whereas that incident and the more recent investigation at Forest Gate suggest a threat to use chemical weapons exists. Statements from Al-Qaeda, as indicated above, also point to a threat to use without evidence of actual capabilities. In addition, recent reports from both the Middle East and South Asia point to increased concern about chemical weapons, with Palestinian groups threatening to use chemical weapons against Israel and Sri Lankan forces concerned about possible chemical weapons attacks from the Tamil Tigers.[74]

A broader picture

Overall, threats to use CBRN weapons without any evidence of actual capabilities have increased in recent times. Unsuccessful attempts to acquire CBRN weapons can be readily documented, not least through Aum's attempts to develop biological weapons in the early 1990s and activities of Al-Qaeda in general. Actual possession of CBRN weapons would, anecdotally, indicate a rise in recent times at least in relation to ricin, but much of this may be criminal rather than terrorist activities and more akin to the classic poisoning of individuals. However, possession of low-level and rudimentary CBRN weapons appears, albeit slowly, to be increasing. Attempted, unsuccessful, use of CBRN weapons would also include Aum Shinrikyo, whereas successful use of CBRN weapons would include both the 1995 Tokyo chemical weapon (Sarin) attacks and the anthrax attacks in the USA in 2001.

Based on this assessment, the most likely attack would appear to be based on the use of a toxin, namely ricin, or easily accessible and/or household chemicals. Such use would be at the low-technology end of the spectrum. Following that, it is toxic industrial chemicals which present if not the most likely weapon perhaps the most attractive target to terrorists. Again, evidence collected during the period 2002 to 2004 would suggest the UK, and others, need to undertake a significant amount of work in the area of chemical security of toxic industrial chemicals (TICs) which appear to present a much greater threat than nerve agents such as VX. Indeed, the focus on classic chemical weapons and highly toxic nerve agents may well have distracted attention away from a much more vulnerable set of chemicals which pose a constant safety, and therefore security, threat to most states and their respective populations. If policy-makers need to be reminded of the threat posed by 'normal' chemicals then the Bhopal incident in 1984 should serve as an adequate reminder to even the most sceptical politician.

Nuclear weapons constitute a category on their own: the high consequence– low probability status of potential nuclear weapons use coupled with the fact that such weapons exist in the arsenals of very few states reinforce their special status. The mass destruction nuclear weapons use threatens is mitigated by the technical complexities of developing a usable weapon. In contrast, the threat posed by chemical and biological weapons covers the basics of kitchen chemistry and bathtub biology through to the sophisticated chemical and biological weapons developed in state-led programmes. Differentiating the threat spectrum of chemical and biological weapons should include a recognition that sophisticated chemical or biological weapons are difficult to produce and use.[75] It has been done, as the anthrax attacks demonstrate, but whether or not that is a true indication of the future threat or an outlier is a subjective judgement.

Comforting and disconcerting lessons emerge from the last decade and, more importantly, in the five years since 9/11. Aum's failure in the biological weapons area – at least nine failed biological weapon attacks are now known to be documented – is perceived as one of the prime reasons for the shift to attacks with chemical weapons. Perhaps, like states, as terrorists fail in one type of CBRN weapon, they move to the 'easier' ones. Chemical weapons provide a very broad spectrum of possibilities, a great number of risks, and, possibly, are the 'easiest' of the CBRN weapons to develop and use. As stated at the beginning of this section, somewhere between hyperbole and scepticism on CBRN terrorism is a realistic threat assessment, but what is it?

Worst case scenarios, including nuclear weapons, cannot be discounted, but any use of a worst case scenario to illustrate a threat assessment must include numerous caveats. Equally, past trends of low or little interest in CBRN among terrorists and/or low or limited actual use of CBRN by terrorists must equally be subject to caveats. What is evident over the last decade is an increase in the interest of non-state actors in CBRN as a method of attack. Added to this is an alarming tendency in Western states – particularly the USA and the UK – to identify or imply vulnerabilities within states to CBRN weapons. As others have remarked, the very fear and vulnerability CBRN has evoked may well fuel terrorist interest in such weapons. CBRN threat assessments may become self-fulfilling.

Based on the evidence available to date there is evidence of *interest* in CBRN to various degrees but there is extremely limited evidence of a terrorist group *acquiring* a CBRN capability beyond the most basic means. The sole incident that stands out in this area is the 2001 anthrax attacks in the USA. The key question is whether that incident is treated as anomalous compared to other terrorist incidents involving CBRN, or as an indicator of all other future threats. It has important portents but it cannot be considered as representative of other terrorist activities in this area.

As the WHO guidance on chemical and biological weapons noted – and here it can be extended to cover all CBRN – a spectrum of threat can be envisaged ranging between the extremes of relative insignificance at one end to mass destruction or mass casualties at the other end of the spectrum.[76]

A further change over the last five years is a slow shift away from hyperbole. Sober voices are increasingly berating the 'endless exaggeration of low-probability events [that] continues diverting limited attention and resources away from real weapons real terrorists use …'.[77] In addition, there is recognition that:[78]

> preaching the 'inevitability' of an attack, as the Metropolitan police commissioner did on March 16 [2004], is a dangerous message. It suggests that we cannot so arrange our security affairs as to stand a good chance of thwarting catastrophic attacks. … Assigning inevitability to Islamist terror attacks risks aggrandising the terrorist in his own mind as well as that of the public.

Furthermore, behind the headlines and the media portrayal of the threat, testimony in 2005 in the USA acknowledges that 'we still assess that a mass casualty attack using relatively low-tech methods will be their [Al-Qaeda] most likely approach'.[79] In conclusion, it is both dangerous and foolish to discount entirely the threat posed by the terrorist use of CBRN weapons. There is certainly a sufficient amount of information to warrant serious concern about terrorist interest and desire to use such weapons, even if some of this may have been a self-generated threat. Those seeking to guard against the use of CBRN must not fall into apathy about its actual threat simply because little has occurred since 11 September 2001. However, responding to the threat must not be driven by hyperbole or worst case scenarios. The response requires a broad, measured, and clear-headed approach to manage the threat, and any use, of such weapons. Any CBRN response must be part of an overall threat assessment and be managed as part of an all-disasters plan.[80]

Notes

1　Smithson, A.E. (2005) 'Observations on the Nature of the Terrorist Threat', in Purcell, J.S. and Weintraub, J.D. (eds) *Topics in Terrorism: Towards a Transatlantic Consensus on the Nature of the Threat*, a compendium of papers presented at a conference on 'Topics in Terrorism', 29 and 30 November 2004, Washington, DC: The Atlantic Council, pp. 56–61.
2　Carus, W.S. (2006) 'Defining "weapons of mass destruction"', *Center for the Study of Weapons of Mass Destruction*, Occasional Paper No. 4, Washington, DC: National

Defense University Press, available at www.ndu.edu/WMDCenter/docUploaded// OP4Carus.pdf.

3   The accepted definition of 'weapons of mass destruction' stems from a 1947 United Nations Security Council document defining such weapons as 'atomic explosive weapons, radioactive material weapons, lethal chemical and biological weapons, and any weapons developed in the future which have characteristics comparable in destructive effect to those of the atomic bomb or other weapons mentioned above', United Nations Security Council document S/C.3/SC.3/7/Rev.1 8, September 1947.

4   Carus, W.S. (2006) 'Defining "weapons of mass destruction"', *Center for the Study of Weapons of Mass Destruction, Occasional Paper No. 4*, Washington DC: National Defense University Press.

5   We owe this observation to a very senior former diplomat with extensive experience of WMD negotiations throughout the Cold War period. (The 'Missile Gap' referred to an early Cold War scare during the early 1960s when during the US presidential election candidate Kennedy referred to a 'missile gap' between the USA and the Soviet Union, with the Soviet Union forging ahead of the USA in missile deployments. Upon election, Kennedy found there was a 'missile gap', but it was heavily in the favour of the US.)

6   See, for example, Salma, S. and Hansell, L. (2005) 'Does intent equal capability? Al-Qaeda and weapons of mass destruction', *Nonproliferation Review*, 12(3), November, pp. 615–53.

7   Wilkinson, P. (2003) 'Implications of attacks of 9/11 for the future of terrorism', in Buckley, M. and Fawn, R. (eds) *Global Responses to Terrorism*, London: Routledge, p. 34.

8   Howlett, D. and Littlewood, J. (2005) 'Future terrorist weapons', in Purcell, J. and Weintraub, J.D. (eds) *Topics in Terrorism: Toward a Transatlantic Consensus of the Nature of the Threat*, The Atlantic Council of the United States, compendium of papers presented at a conference on 'Topics in Terrorism', 29 and 30 November 2004, available at www.acus.org/docs/0507-Topics_Terrorism_Transatlantic_Consensus_ Threat.pdf, p. 52.

9   Purver, R. (1995) *Chemical and Biological Terrorism: The Threat According to Open Literature*, Ottawa: Canadian Security Intelligence Service 1995, unclassified.

10 See, for example, Beres, L.R. (1979) *Terrorism and Global Security: The Nuclear Threat*, Boulder, CO: Westview Press; Leventhal, P. and Alexander, Y. (1987) *Preventing Nuclear Terrorism*, Lexington, MA and Toronto: Lexington Books; Clutterbuck, R. (1990) *Terrorism and Guerrilla Warfare*, London: Routledge, pp. 50– 2; Cameron, G. (1999) *Nuclear Terrorism: A Threat Assessment for the 21st Century*, Basingstoke: Palgrave Macmillan; Stern, J. (2000) 'Getting and using weapons', in Howard, R.D. and Sawyer, R.L. (eds) *Terrorism and Counterterrorism*, Guildford: McGraw-Hill/Dushkin, pp. 158–71; Tucker, J.B. (ed.) (2001) *Toxic Terror: Assessing Terrorist Use of Chemical and Biological Weapons*, Cambridge, MA: MIT Press.

11 Watson, K. (2003) *Poisoned Lives: English Poisoners and Their Victims*, London: Hambledon & London.

12 *Globalization, Biosecurity and the Future of the Life Sciences*, p. 44 (pre-pub e-edition); Wiggins, P.H. (1982) 'Tylenol recall expense is put at $100 million', *New York Times*, 29 October.

13 Kelle, A. and Schaper, A. (2003) 'Terrorism using biological and nuclear weapons: a critical analysis of risks after 11 September 2001', *PRIF Research Report No. 64*, Frankfurt: Peace Research Institute Frankfurt, p. 18.

14 Ferguson, C.D., Potter, W.C., with Sands, A., Spector, L.S. and Wihling, F.L. (2004) *The Four Faces of Nuclear Terrorism*, Monterey, CA: Center for Nonproliferation Studies, p. 3.

15 Bunn, M. and Weir, A. (2006) 'Securing the bomb 2006', Project on Managing the Atom, Belfer Center for Science and International Affairs, John F. Kennedy School

of Government, Harvard University. Commissioned by the Nuclear Threat Initiative, July 2006, www.nti.org/securingthebomb.

16 Stern, J. (2000) 'Getting and using weapons', in Howard, R.D. and Sawyer, R.L. (eds) *Terrorism and Counterterrorism*, Guildford: McGraw-Hill/Dushkin, p. 164.

17 Etzioni, A. (2004) *Pre-empting Nuclear Terrorism in a New Global Order*, The Foreign Policy Centre, October, http://fpc.org.uk/fsblob/314.pdf.

18 Ferguson, C.D. and Potter, W.C. (2004) 'Improvised nuclear devices and nuclear terrorism', Paper No. 2, Stockholm: Weapons of Mass Destruction Commission, www.wmdcommission.org/.

19 See www.iaea.org/NewsCenter/Features/RadSources/orphaned20040219.html.

20 Potter, W.C. and Sokova, E. (2002) 'Illicit nuclear trafficking in the nis: what's new? What's true?', *Nonproliferation Review*, Summer, p. 16.

21 International Atomic Energy Agency, 'IAEA Illicit Trafficking Database (ITDB) Fact Sheet for 1993–2004', available at www.iaea.org/NewsCenter/Features/RadSources/ fact_figures2004.pdf. See also the International Atomic Energy Agency, 'IAEA Illicit Trafficking Database (ITDB) 1993–2003', available at www.iaea.org/NewsCenter/ Features/RadSources/PDF/itdb_31122003.pdf.

22 Kelle and Schaper, op. cit., p. 19.

23 Ferguson *et al.*, *The Four Faces of Nuclear Terrorism*, op. cit., p.37.

24 Bunn, M. and Weir, A. (2005) 'The seven myths of nuclear terrorism', *Current History*, April, p. 156.

25 Ferguson *et al.*, *The Four Faces of Nuclear Terrorism*, op. cit., p. 5.

26 US, National Planning Scenarios Created for the Use of National, Federal, State, and Local Homeland Security Preparedness Activities, April 2005, version 20.1 DRAFT p. 11-1.

27 Putnam, T.L. (2002) 'Communicating nuclear risk: informing the public about the risks and realities of nuclear terrorism', Workshop Report, 20 May, pp. 7–10, available at http://iis-db.stanford.edu/pubs/20063/NuclearRisk.pdf. See, also, Schaper, A. (2003) 'Nuclear terrorism: risk analysis after 11 September 2001', *Disarmament Forum*, 2, p. 13.

28 IAEA (2004) www.iaea.org/NewsCenter/Features/RadSources/fact_figures2004.pdf.

29 Alimov, R. (2003) 'Radioisotope thermoelectric generators', available at http://bellona. org/english_import_area/international/russia/navy/northern_fleet/incidents/37598. See also, Alimov, R. and Digges, C. (2005) 'Status report: RTGs still an underestimated foe in securing loose nukes in Russia', 02 April, available at http://bellona.org/english_ import_area/international/russia/navy/northern_fleet/incidents/37566.

30 Broomby, R. (2005) 'Kyrgyz hunt for radioactive matter', *BBC News*, 7 October, available at http://news.bbc.co.uk/go/pr/fr/-/2/hi/asia-pacific/4315928.stm.

31 Oppenheimer, A. (2002) 'Weapons of mass destruction: radiological devices', *Jane's Terrorism and Security Monitor*, May.

32 Bunn, G., Braun, C., Glaser, A., Lyman, E. and Steinhausler, F. (2003) 'Research reactor vulnerability to sabotage by terrorists', *Science and Global Security*, 11, p. 103.

33 BBC News (date) 'Nuclear link to terror suspects', available at http://news.bbc.co.uk/ go/pr/fr/-/1/hi/asia-pacific/4434270.stm. Bonner, R. (2005) 'Australian reactor is called possible terror target', *International Herald Tribune*, 14 November.

34 Putnam, I., 'Communicating nuclear risk: informing the public about the risks and realities of nuclear terrorism', op. cit., p. 7. See also, Stern, J. (2000) 'Getting and using weapons', in Howard, R.D. and Sawyer, R.L. (eds) *Terrorism and Counterterrorism*, Guildford: McGraw-Hill/Dushkin, pp. 162–3.

35 See also, Barnaby, F. (2005) *Dirty Bombs and Primitive Nuclear Weapons*, Oxford: Oxford Research Group, April.

36 (1995) 'News chronology, 27 December 1994', *Chemical Weapons Convention Bulletin*, 27, March, p. 27.

37 For a discussion see Ferguson, C.D., Kazi, T. and Perera, J. (2003) *Commercial Radioactive Sources: Surveying the Security Risks, Center for Nonproliferation Studies*, Occasional Paper No. 11, January; Ferguson *et al.*, *The Four Faces of Nuclear Terrorism*, op. cit.

38 Gearson, J. (2002) 'The nature of modern terrorism', in Freedman, L. (ed.) *Superterrorism: Policy Responses*, Malden, MA: Blackwell, p. 22.

39 In the UK the 'Category A' agents, those deemed of particular risk, are: anthrax, smallpox, botulism, plague, tularaemia, and viral haemorrhagic fevers (VHF) such as lassa, marburg, and ebola. See http://hpa.org.uk/infections/topics_az/deliberate_ release/categoryaagentsmatrix.asp.

40 Gewin, V. (2003) 'Agricultural shock', *Nature*, 421, 9 January, pp. 106–8; Townsend, M. (2003) 'Bioterrorists may mount foot and mouth attack', *The Observer*, 5 January, p. 8.

41 Leitenberg, M. (2004) *The Problem of Biological Weapons*, Stockholm: Swedish National Defence College, p. 120; Cookson, C. (2003) 'Scientists play down risk of bioterrorism', *Financial Times*, 30 January, p. 6; (2003) 'CIA: small al-Qaida attacks more likely', *Associated Press*, 3 June, 12.23.

42 US Government Accounting Office, Testimony Before the Select Committee on Intelligence, US Senate, and the Permanent Select Committee on Intelligence, House of Representatives (2002) 'Diffuse security threats information on U.S. domestic anthrax attacks', Statement for the Record by Keith Rhodes, Chief Technologist, Center for Technology and Engineering, 10 December 2002, GAO-03-323T.

43 Cronin, A.K. (2003) *Terrorist Motivations for Chemical and Biological Weapons Use: Placing the Threat in Context*, Report for Congress, CRS-RL31831, 28 March.

44 Leitenberg, M. (2005) 'Assessing the biological weapons and bioterrorism threat', December, available at www.StrategicStudiesInstitute.army.mil/pubs/display.cfm? PubID=639.

45 Ibid., pp. 21–2.

46 Ibid., p. 44.

47 Wein, L.M. and Liu, Y. (2005) 'Analyzing a bioterror attack on the food supply: the case of botulinum toxin in milk', *Proceedings of the National Academy of Sciences*, 102(28), July, pp. 9984–9.

48 World Health Organization (1970) *Health Aspects of Chemical and Biological Weapons*, Report of a WHO Group of Consultants, Geneva: WHO, see Annex 5, pp. 113–15.

49 Seefried, V. (2003/4) 'Keeping our drinking water safe', *Homeland Security & Resilience Monitor*, 2(9), December/January, pp. 12–15. See also World Health Organization (2004) *Public Health Response to Biological and Chemical Weapons: WHO Guidance*, Annex 5 'Precautions against the sabotage of drinking-water, food, and other products', Geneva: WHO, pp. 294–319.

50 World Health Organization (2004) *Public Health Response to Biological and Chemical Weapons: WHO Guidance*, ibid. World Health Organization (2004) *Public Health Response to Biological and Chemical Weapons*: report of a WHO Group of Consultants (2nd edn), Geneva: WHO, pp. 317–18.

51 Dando, M. (2005) 'The bioterrorist cookbook', *Bulletin of the Atomic Scientists*, 61(6), November/December, p. 36.

52 Watson, K. (2003) *Poisoned Lives: English Poisoners and Their Victims*, London: Hambledon & London.

53 World Health Organization (2004) *Public Health Response to Biological and Chemical Weapons: WHO Guidance*, Geneva: WHO, p. 19.

54 Kosal, M.E. (2006) 'Near term threats of chemical weapons terrorism', *Strategic Insights*, V(6), July.

55 Lindstrom, G. (2004) 'Protecting the European homeland: the CBR dimension', *Chaillot Paper*, No. 69, July, EU Institute for Security Studies, p. 22.

56 (2003) 'Chemical terrorism', *The Charlotte Observer* (online edition), 9 June.
57 (1986) The Report of the Greater London Area War Risk Study Commission, 'London under attack', Oxford: Basil Blackwell, p. 37.
58 Ibid.
59 Ibid.
60 For the 2006 incident in Forest Green (London), see Alderson, A., Rayment, S. and Hennessy, P. (2006) 'Terror cell "was planning nerve gas attack on capital"', Telegraph.co.uk, 4 June, available at www.telegraph.co.uk/news/main.jhtml?xml=/news/2006/06/04/nterr04.xml. WMD Insights (2006) 'Special report: manual for producing chemical weapon to be used in the New York subway plot available on Al-Qaeda websites since late 2005', available at www.wmdinsights.com/I7/I7_ME1_SP_MaunualFor.htm.
61 (2001) 'News chronology, 17 February 2001', *CBW Conventions Bulletin*, 52, June, p.39.
62 (2002) 'News chronology, 9 November 2002', *CBW Conventions Bulletin*, 59, March, p. 12.
63 Stevens, J. (2005) *Not for the Faint-Hearted: My Life Fighting Crime*, London: Weidenfeld & Nicolson, pp. 304–7.
64 Ibid., p. 306.
65 Leitenberg, 'Assessing the biological weapons and bioterrorism threat', op.cit., p. 27.
66 (1999) 'News chronology, 7 September 1999', *CBW Conventions Bulletin*, 46, December, p. 26.
67 Interpol (2005) 'Interpol African regional workshop in the prevention of bio-terrorism', speech by Interpol Secretary-General Ronald K. Noble, 21 November, available at www.interpol.int/Public/ICPO/speeches/SG20051125.asp?hml.
68 Ibid.
69 Freedman, L. (2002) 'The coming war on terrorism', in Freedman, L. (ed.) *Superterrorism: Policy Responses*, Malden, MA: Blackwell, p. 41.
70 Salma, S. and Hansell, L. (2005) 'Does intent equal capability? Al-Qaeda and weapons of mass destruction', *Nonproliferation Review*, 12(3), p. 618.
71 Mayer, J. (2003) 'Al Qaeda feared to have "dirty bombs"', *Los Angeles Times*, 8 February.
72 Specter, M. (1995) 'Chechen insurgents take their struggle to Moscow park', *New York Times*, 24 November.
73 (2006) 'Barratt receives poison-package threat', *Contract Journal*, 16 August, available at www.contractjournal.com/Articles/2006/08/16/51884/Barratt+receives+posion-package+threat.html.
74 For Sri Lanka, see (2006) 'Potential LTTE chemical weapon attack', 12 July, available at www.defence.lk/new.asp?fname=20060712_02. For the claims from Palestinian groups, see (2006) 'Chem warfare claimed in showdown at Gaza: Palestinian terrorists say they fired rocket tipped with WMD at Israel', 28 June, available at http://worldnetdaily.com/news/article.asp?ARTICLE_ID=50841, (2006) 'Al-Aqsa Martyrs' Brigades will declare chemical warfare', 26 June, available at www.israeltoday.co.il/default.aspx?tabid=178&nid=8303.
75 (1999) 'News chronology, 27 August 1999', *CBW Conventions Bulletin*, 46, December, p. 25.
76 World Health Organization (2004) *Public Health Response to Biological and Chemical Weapons*, ibid. World Health Organization (2004) *Health Aspects of Chemical and Biological Weapons*: report of a WHO Group of Consultants (2nd edn), Geneva: WHO, p. 10.
77 Reynolds, A. (2005) 'WMD doomsday distractions', *Washington Times*, 10 April. See also, Norton-Taylor, R. (2005) 'Scaremongering', *Guardian*, 8 March; Burke, J. (2005) 'Be afraid, perhaps. But very afraid? No', *The Observer*, 13 March; Leitenberg, M. (2004) *The Problem of Biological Weapons*, Stockholm: Swedish National Defence

College, p. 120; Cookson, C. (2003) 'Scientists play down risk of bioterrorism', *Financial Times*, 30 January; (2003) 'CIA: small al-Qaida attacks more likely', *Associated Press*, 3 June, 12.23.

78 Black, C. (2004) 'Never say inevitable', *Guardian*, 7 April.

79 US, Testimony of Robert S. Mueller, III Director Federal Bureau of Investigation before the Senate Committee on Intelligence of the United States Senate, 16 February 2005.

80 Willis, H. (2005) 'Analyzing terrorism risk', Testimony before the Committee on Homeland Security, Subcommittee on Intelligence, Information Sharing, and Terrorism Risk Assessment United States House of Representatives, 17 November.

5   The domestic threat

The cases of Northern Ireland and animal rights extremism

Anthony Richards

NORTHERN IRELAND

The political context

At the time of writing, the Good Friday Agreement institutions remain in a state of suspension following the October 2002 Sinn Fein 'spying scandal' at Stormont. Ever since, the British and Irish administrations have endeavoured to restore devolved government in the province but, with little trust, the continuing existence and alleged activity of the IRA, and unionist frustration, the task has not been an easy one, particularly after the success of the anti-agreement Democratic Unionist Party in eclipsing the pro-agreement Ulster Unionist Party in the November 2003 Assembly election (following the breakdown in negotiations). Talks aimed at restoring devolution broke down once more in November 2004. On 28 July 2005 the IRA issued a statement announcing the end of its armed campaign, that IRA units had been ordered to dump arms, that it was to pursue the struggle through purely democratic and peaceful means and that 'volunteers must not engage in any other activities whatsoever'. This has raised hopes that devolution may once again be restored but, with little trust from unionists, the institutions have yet to be resurrected. It is in the context of the 'political vacuum' that has developed since October 2002 that one needs to fully assess the security threat from terrorist groups in Northern Ireland.

The groups

The IRA (or PIRA)

History and ideology

The IRA's ideology emanates from the 1916 Easter proclamation of an Irish Republic and the establishment of the 1919 Dail (not recognised by the British government) when Sinn Fein won 73 out of a possible 175 seats. The IRA and Sinn Fein were bitterly opposed to the 1922 treaty that brought about the partition of the island. It has therefore viewed Westminster rule, any Northern Ireland assembly and the Dublin administration as illegitimate. The IRA Army Council is seen as the legitimate government of the whole of a united Ireland, inheriting the legacy of the 1919 Dail. The organisation's stated aim is a united socialist Republic of Ireland, but in the first instance its primary objective is to end partition and rid the British from the island. It is an absolutist ideology with no room for compromise on complete independence, with the use of 'physical force' seen as the means to achieve its political objectives.

Underpinned by this uncompromising ideology, the IRA launched a bombing campaign in 1939, and also the 'Border Campaign' of 1956–62, but it gained its reputation as the most dangerous terrorist organisation during the tumultous years of the 'Troubles' from 1969. A number of developments prompted the group to call a ceasefire in August 1994 but it ended in February 1996 with a massive bomb attack on the Canary Wharf building in London, killing two people and causing severe damage. The ceasefire was reinstated in July 1997 and, officially at least, it has held since then.[1]

The current peace process, sometimes referred to by Irish republicans as a 'historic compromise', has seen the IRA dilute some of its most cherished principles. In fact, its history has often been characterised by a more pragmatic approach than the absolutism of its ideology might suggest.[2] More lately, driven by an acknowledgment that popular support was crucial to its struggle, it engaged in electoral politics and ended its policy of abstention from the Irish Dail in 1986. The IRA then declared its ceasefire in 1994 (and again in 1997), its political front sat in the 'partitionist' institutions of the new Northern Ireland Assembly and executive (when it was in operation), it has accepted the Irish Republic's renouncement of its territorial claim to the province,[3] and it has seemingly accepted the principle of consent.[4] Indeed, most lately the Independent Monitoring Commission (in its April 2006 report) believed that 'there was a clear strategic intent to eschew terrorism and follow a political path' on the part of the IRA.[5]

This has not always been obvious to some despite continuous claims from Irish republicans (since the ceasefire of 1997) that the organisation has not represented a threat to the peace process. The apparent persistence of its alleged activity has undermined the Good Friday Agreement and has shaken unionist confidence in the accord. Such activity included the alleged training of FARC guerrillas in urban warfare in Colombia, the suspected IRA involvement in the theft of sensitive security documents from the Castlereagh police complex in March 2002, the apparent orchestration of street violence in the disturbances in North and East Belfast in the Summer and Autumn of 2002, and alleged spying in Castle Buildings at Stormont that led to the collapse of the institutions in 2002 (after the Ulster Unionist Party threatened to walk out).

More recently, the IRA was heavily criticised for its alleged involvement in the £26.5 million Northern Bank heist[6] and for the involvement of some of its members in the murder of Robert McCartney outside a pub in Belfast. McCartney's partner and sisters embarked on an international campaign for justice, including visits to the White House and Strasbourg. Under pressure at home and ostracised abroad (by the White House and many senior US politicians during the St Patrick's Day celebrations) it was in that context that Gerry Adams publicly called upon the IRA to embrace democratic means to achieve its political goals. The latter's response was a statement in July 2005 announcing that it was ending its armed campaign, followed by an act of 'significant' decommissioning confirmed by the Independent International Commission on Decommissioning in September of the same year. Many, particularly unionists, however, remain sceptical and doubt that the IRA will actually match its words with actions. There have been, however, a number of potential reasons for the endurance of IRA activity, not least that to keep the mainstream movement as united as possible some continuation of such practices may have been inevitable.

Capability

It is believed that membership of the IRA has stood at around 400–500[7] although there has also been a 'large support network consisting of thousands'.[8] 'Non operational members' have engaged in hiding, moving and storing weapons, providing safe houses and perhaps financial provision.[9]

As far as the IRA's weaponry is concerned estimates suggest that, prior to the unknown quantity of weapons decommissioned so far, the group's arsenal consisted of:

> 588 Kalashnikov assault rifles, 400 other rifles, including Armalites, and one or two Barret Light .50 long range sniper weapons, 12 general purpose machine guns and 17 DShK heavy-duty machine guns capable of bringing down helicopters, eight rocket launchers, six surface-to-air (SAM) missiles, 100 pistols, 60 revolvers, two or three flame throwers and an unknown quantity – perhaps a ton – of Semtex military explosives.[10]

Tactics

When the IRA was not on ceasefire its tactics ranged from assassinations and sniper attacks to bombings (including car bombs), mainly targeting security force personnel and their associated contractors and suppliers, prison staff and politicians, although many civilians have also died at the hands of the group. It also targeted city centres and transport links to cause maximum disruption and damage to the British economy.

Organised crime

A parliamentary report released in July 2002 suggested that the IRA has raised between £5 million and £8 million a year through organised crime.[11] 'Traditional' activities include extortion, smuggling, and robberies. The latest (tenth) IMC report, however, suggests that the leadership of the IRA has instructed its members to refrain from engaging in organised crime, although there are apparently still some members (including senior ones) who are involved in it.[12]

Assessment

On 28 July 2005 the IRA issued a statement that included the following:

> All IRA units have been ordered to dump arms. All Volunteers have been instructed to assist the development of purely political and democratic programmes through exclusively peaceful means. Volunteers must not engage in any other activities whatsoever.
>
> The IRA leadership has also authorised our representative to engage with the IICD (Independent International Commission on Decommissioning) to complete the process to verifiably put its arms beyond use in a way which will further enhance public confidence and to conclude this as quickly as possible.[13]

There is no doubt that this statement and what it promised to deliver has had a significant impact on the peace process but the key, especially as far as many unionists were concerned, was to see 'action' as well as words. In September 2005 the IRA carried out a further act of decommissioning and the IMC (in its latest, tenth, report) believes that the IRA is committed to a political path and has left terrorism behind it. If this is the case it represents a major boost for the peace process.

The significance of the IMC, set up to monitor the paramilitary ceasefires, is that it was the first time since the Good Friday Agreement was signed that an *independent* body has assessed the extent of paramilitary activity and, at a time when there have been no institutions to protect, there has been no effort to influence or water down the Commission's very frank findings. The following assessment of the groups in Northern Ireland has therefore drawn considerably from the very useful series of reports that the Commission has produced since April 2004. It stated in its first report (in April 2004) that although 'PIRA is not presently involved in attacks on security forces' it 'nevertheless remains active and in a high state of readiness' including 'undertaking training in the early part of this year [2004]' and is therefore 'maintaining its capacity to undertake acts of violence or to participate in a terrorist campaign if that seemed necessary to it'.[14] It also found that 'in addition to its involvement in other criminal activities, PIRA is engaged in the use of serious violence which we believe is under the control of its most senior leadership, whose members must therefore bear responsibility for it'.[15]

The IMC's third report published in November 2004 noted that although 'it [appeared] to have suspended action against those it believed to be behaving anti-socially' there were 'no signs of PIRA winding down its capability. It continued to recruit, though in small numbers, and to gather intelligence'. The report also expressed the view that the IRA was responsible for a 'major theft' earlier in the year that 'would have been sanctioned at leadership level'. Although it stated that there was 'no fundamental change in the capacity of the organisation or its maintenance of a state of preparedness' it did find, however, 'no evidence of activity that might presage a return to a paramilitary campaign'.[16]

The IMC in its fourth report, specially commissioned in light of the Northern Bank robbery, was of the view that the IRA was responsible for the December 2004 heist,[17] while its fifth report (February 2005) stated that the IRA 'remains a highly active organisation' and that it is 'at present determined to maintain its effectiveness, both in terms of organised crime, control in republican areas, and its potential for terrorism'. The report re-affirmed, however, that it had no evidence that the IRA 'intends to resume a campaign of violence'.[18]

Indeed, although the possibility that the IRA could have returned to 'war' at this time should not have been dismissed out of hand, it was unlikely for a number of reasons. First, Gerry Adams' 'peace strategy' continued to pay dividends for the republican movement, both in terms of Sinn Fein's electoral performance and through 'concessions' from the British government, which was determined to keep the movement on board the process. Second, the Irish republican leadership, one could have assumed, would have been too shrewd to risk the ire of the American establishment who initially cajoled the British government into accepting the apparent peaceful bona fides of the republican movement in the first place. Third, the US 'War on Terrorism' in the aftermath of the events of 11 September 2001 meant that the White House would presumably have given short shrift to any return to 'war' by the IRA.

It was nevertheless vital that the political process progressed so that, to use Sinn Fein's words, republicans 'can see that politics works'. If the process faltered then it was possible that mainstream republicans may have become disillusioned with it. Whatever the arguments for or against 'placating' the IRA and Sinn Fein, the fact was that mainstream republicans' own views of the results of the negotiations would have had a direct impact on their faith in the peace process which in turn may have led to IRA 'volunteers' returning to 'action' by joining dissident groups.

A major security concern, then, as far as the IRA has been concerned, has been the possibility of defections from its ranks into those of dissident groups. In this regard the peace process has represented something of a double-edged sword. If greater momentum is generated in the peace process, and this has entailed republican 'concessions' (for example, the IRA statement of July 2005, or if Sinn Fein joined the new Policing Board), the potential for defections to the anti-agreement dissidents who are not on ceasefire could increase.[19] Hugh Orde, the Chief Constable of the Police Service of Northern Ireland, stated on 9 January 2003 that if the IRA stood down and/or Sinn Fein joined the Police Board the dissident threat was likely to increase in the short term.[20] Indeed, reports in November 2004 suggested that 'disgruntled Provisionals' from East Tyrone, South Down and County Antrim were ready to split from the IRA in protest over further decommissioning.[21] Yet, conversely, if the process is in limbo and appears to be faltering (that is, politics is not seen to be working) this may also potentially lead to defections from the IRA. These fears appear to have been allayed for the time being, however, because according to the IMC:

The [IRA] leadership sets high store on unity and on avoiding the movement of people to dissident republican groups – which we do not think has happened in any significant way. It appears generally though not universally to have maintained authority over its members.[22]

The second security concern in relation to the IRA is the extent that the organisation matches, or is able to match, its words in its July 2005 statement, that is, that it was to pursue the struggle through purely democratic and peaceful means and that 'volunteers must not engage in any other activities whatsoever'. Will it, for example, cease to exercise 'social control' in its communities using violence or the threat of violence (time and time again security sources have expressed the view that dissident republicanism has hitherto not been able to present a significant threat to the peace process because mainstream republicanism has not allowed it to do so)? Will it risk ceding control of its areas to other groups by relinquishing the use of violence? Will 'exiles' be allowed to return unhindered?

In its latest (tenth) report the IMC noted that 'there has now been a substantial erosion in PIRA's capacity to return to a military campaign without a significant period of build-up' and that senior IRA figures have tried to stop members engaging in criminal activity although 'there are indications that some members, including some senior ones, (as distinct from the organisation itself) are still involved in crime, including offences such as fuel laundering, money laundering, extortion, tax evasion and smuggling'.[23] The leadership has also apparently instructed its members not to engage in rioting and street disturbances. The possibility that there are members who step out of line from the leadership's wishes should not be overlooked as 'some members continue to be engaged in significant crime and occasional unauthorised assaults'.[24] Nevertheless, in general, the findings of the IMC in relation to the threat that the IRA now presents are very encouraging and the assurances contained in IRA and Sinn Fein statements appear in large part as though they are being realised.

Gerry Adams stated in the party's Ard Fheis of 2006 that the 'war' was over[25] and, although organised crime is rife in the province (and the IRA, like the other paramilitaries have been deeply embedded in it), he has apparently argued in support of 'the pursuit of criminal assets and said that anybody involved in criminality should face the full rigours of the law'.[26] Criminal activity undertaken by members of the IRA (as with any other paramilitary members or groups) remains a key challenge. Nevertheless, in general, the positive developments noted above appear to represent another step in what hopefully has been, and continues to be, a gradual evolution away from the use of violence and illegal activity in the province.

The Real IRA

Brief history and ideology

The Real IRA was formed in 1997 as a result of a split within the IRA over its engagement with the peace process, and particularly over Senator Mitchell's principles of non-violence. It advocates traditional republican ideology – that for as long as the British presence remains in the North then it should be removed by force of arms. It began its campaign of violence with car bomb and mortar attacks in Counties Down and Armagh. The group is most notorious, however, for the August 1998 Omagh bomb that killed 29 people and two unborn twins. Following the public outrage at the atrocity the organisation called a temporary ceasefire.

It was not long before it re-launched its campaign and up to June 2002 it is estimated to have carried out at least a further 80 attacks.[27] Security sources believe that the group was behind a series of attacks on security personnel and facilities in Northern Ireland[28] as well as operations on the mainland. Targets in England included Hammersmith Bridge, a railway line near Ealing Broadway and a Post Office depot in Hendon. The group was also responsible for a bomb that exploded outside the BBC and an audacious mortar attack on the MI6 headquarters in London. Tactics seemed to take a sinister turn, however, when a car bomb exploded outside busy pubs at closing time in Ealing Broadway in August 2001, and when a device planted near a busy nightlife spot in Birmingham city centre in November 2001 could have caused severe casualties (had it detonated properly). The group was responsible for its first death since the Omagh bomb when it placed a device in the sandwich box of a civilian contractor, David Caldwell, at a Territorial Army base in Londonderry in August 2002. The organisation continues to target security force bases and personnel in Northern Ireland as well as members of the new District Policing Partnerships (DPPs).[29]

It is believed that there was a split within the Real IRA in 2002 over whether or not the organisation should be stood down. Towards the end of 2002 the fault line was believed to lie between the group outside prison and nearly all of those within prison. The old leadership 'inside' was of the view that the Real IRA 'outside' had lost sight of traditional republican objectives and had become more interested in organised crime and financial gain. This was denied, however, by the new leadership which had declared its intention to continue its terrorist campaign. The threat from the Real IRA has since continued.

Capability

The Real IRA is said to have around 100 members with approximately 30 or so hardcore activists. It is unclear as to how much weaponry the group possesses. One RIRA member, arrested after attempting to buy weapons from an undercover MI6 agent in Slovakia, is quoted as saying that the organisation had to start from scratch following its split from the IRA in 1997.[30] Another source suggests that most of the group's armoury 'came with group members following their split from the PIRA' and that 'the inventory is primarily comprised of light weapons imported from Eastern Europe, assault rifles and rocket propelled grenades'.[31] Certainly, the audacious attacks on the mainland in 2000 and 2001 suggest that the group had a degree of firepower at that time, while its financial standing through organised crime would have put it in the market for arms procurement. More lately (April 2004) the first IMC report stated that 'RIRA has access to a significant quantity of arms and equipment'.[32] In addition, it is understood the group has considerable bomb-making skills that were acquired when its members belonged to the mainstream IRA.

Organised crime

The Real IRA has been extensively involved in organised crime. The parliamentary report alluded to above estimated that the group's annual income from illegal activity amounted to £5 million, with 'running costs' that amount to just a tenth of this. From a financial point of view, therefore, it appears to be in a position to purchase weapons if it was able to establish channels for this purpose. It has profited from armed robbery, fraud, smuggling, and racketeering. The group is believed to be particularly heavily engaged in the production of counterfeit goods as well as cross border fuel smuggling and cigarette smuggling. The Real IRA's organised criminal activity is not just restricted to Northern Ireland. Former Assistant Commissioner David Veness reportedly estimated in late 2002 that '80%' of Real IRA activity on the mainland is linked to ordinary crime.[33]

Tactics

These include bombs, car bombs, under car booby trap bombs (one was used in an attack on a new Catholic recruit to the Police Service of Northern Ireland), other booby trap bombs (such as the one that killed David Caldwell), mortar attacks and assassinations.

Security force response

The security forces on both sides of the border have had a string of notable successes against the Real IRA. This has largely been due to the successful infiltration of the group that led to a number of failed operations and arrests up to the time of the Omagh bomb. This success has continued with a series of arrests on both sides of the border as well as in England, thanks to 'good intelligence and a lot of luck'.[34] In May 2002, three prominent RIRA members were each jailed for 30 years after trying to purchase weapons from MI6 agents posing as Iraqi arms dealers in the summer of 2001. Others convicted include the perpetrators of the mainland London and Birmingham bombs of 2001. With such successful penetration by the security forces it was perhaps frustrating for them that a judge (in May 2004) felt obliged to clear four dissident republicans for membership of the Real IRA on the grounds that legislation does not list the Real IRA as a proscribed organisation.[35]

Perhaps the most notable success for the authorities was the conviction of the alleged former Real IRA leader, Michael McKevitt, for directing terrorism and being a member of the group (leading to a 26-year sentence in total),[36] while the decision by the British government to grant the relatives of the victims of the 1998 Omagh bomb £800,000 in support of their civil action against those that were allegedly involved in carrying out the atrocity has also given the impression that there has been a new determination to take on dissident republicans. More lately, in June 2006, 10 suspected dissident republicans were arrested which may have prevented 'a major terrorist conspiracy'.[37] On the international front the organisation has been designated a terrorist group since May 2001 by the USA with its assets there frozen and a ban imposed on its fundraising activities.

Assessment

Despite the security force successes against the group, the Real IRA continues to pose a serious threat for a number of reasons. First, it appears that its criminal activity has placed the group on a sound financial footing. Second, as the peace process doggedly continues, the organisation appears to be determined to ensure that traditional IRA ideology has not been forgotten and that physical force republicanism is very much alive. The group will be even more determined to make this point if the institutions are restored and the peace process recovers. Third, given that the former leadership in prison stated that the Real IRA 'outside' no longer represented a 'credible military threat',[38] it might be reasonable to assume that it would want to illustrate unequivocally that it is not thinking of disbanding and to prove that it can carry on effectively without the backing of the former leadership in prison, and, by doing so, to continue to be the focus for defectors from mainstream republicanism. Four years after the signing of the Good Friday Agreement the group stated that 'the war goes on'.[39]

Of particular concern are reports that the group has increased its level of cooperation with another anti-agreement republican group, the Continuity IRA. Collaboration between the two is not something new. The two are said to have worked together to carry out the Omagh atrocity. Apparently 'the bomb was fused by the Real IRA but ... the Continuity IRA had picked the target and delivered it'.[40] The only man to have been convicted in connection with the attack, Colm Murphy, has Continuity IRA connections.[41] Moreover, it was reported in September 2002 that 'an increasingly active CIRA cell' had been testing mortars with RIRA members in Ballyhornan, County Down.[42] Following the security force successes against the Real IRA in 2002 it had apparently regrouped and was 'working closely with the Continuity IRA'.[43]

There are two other reasons why the group represents a serious security threat. The first is related to its level of intent. The extensive shopping list of arms that it requested in the Slovakian sting operation, including 5,000 kilos of semtex, indicated that the group was in the business of giving itself considerable fire power and, given its ideological orientation, there is no reason to believe that it would not want to utilise such a capability. The IMC report's finding that the group has 'access to a significant quantity of arms and equipment' is therefore of serious concern.[44] The second issue of concern is that the Birmingham and second Ealing bombs of 2001 were planted in the vicinity of civilians, apparently indicating a willingness to target more heavily populated areas.

Finally, the peace process itself could boost the Real IRA's membership – if Sinn Fein signs up to the Policing Board, for example, then it is possible that there will be further defections by those for whom such 'concessions' might be the last straw. Yet if the peace process continues to falter, some mainstream republicans may defect over disillusionment with the lack of political progress.

One factor that is often overlooked when assessing the threat from dissident republicans is the impact of the mainstream IRA. As noted above, security sources have intimated that mainstream republicanism would simply not allow dissidents to present a serious threat to the peace process in which it has invested so much. Nevertheless, one should take note of the IMC's third report which concluded that the Real IRA 'continues to attract new members and its senior members are committed to launching attacks on security forces' and that 'RIRA remains a considerable threat'.[45] The IMC's fifth report stated that the Real IRA continued to be the most active of the dissident republican groups and 'has been responsible both for brutal attacks and for robbery', including sending explosive packages to District Policing Partnership members in September 2004 and January and February 2005, and shooting attacks against Police Service of Northern Ireland stations.[46]

Subsequent IMC reports make it clear that the Real IRA continues to pose a threat, having targeted police officers and apparently having planted a number of incendiary devices at shopping centres in March 2005 as well as being responsible for a number of hoaxes and bombs later in the year.[47] More lately, it apparently claimed responsibility for firebombing shops in Newry.[48] Existing in the form of two factions (between whom there is 'a good deal of infighting') it has also continued to train and recruit.[49]

The Continuity IRA

Brief history and ideology

The Continuity IRA was formed in 1986 after IRA members split from mainstream republicanism in protest at the decision to allow Sinn Fein to take up seats in the Irish Dail. They were opposed to the dilution of the sacred republican tradition of abstention from the Westminster, Dublin and (when it has existed) Stormont parliaments. Apparently 'ineffective and riddled with informers' the group has generally been regarded as less of a threat than the Real IRA.[50] Nevertheless, it 'has technical expertise sufficient to construct improvised explosive devices' that have enabled it to carry out successful attacks.[51]

Capability

The Continuity IRA is said to be less organised than the Real IRA and its membership is believed to be in the 'dozens'. According to the 'Cain' website the group 'probably has access to a few dozen rifles, machine guns, and pistols; a small amount of Semtex (commercial high explosive); and a few dozen detonators'.[52]

Tactics

The group primarily uses bomb explosions, car bombs and firebombs.

Organised crime

It is not clear how much income the Continuity IRA generates from organised crime but the Northern Ireland Select Committee report cited above suggests that its running costs are approximately £25,000 to £30,000 . It is likely, however, that, given the cooperation that has existed in joint operations with the Real IRA,[53] the group is either involved with the Real IRA's organised criminal exploits or has access to at least some of the proceeds.

Assessment

The Continuity IRA is thought to have been less of a threat than the Real IRA in recent years. In light of the security force successes against the latter, however, the Continuity IRA was seen to be the potential rallying point for recruits and defectors in 2002. Although the group has yet to pull off a 'spectacular' it has still represented a threat in its own right – evident in its bomb attack on the Garneville police training college in April 2002, its attack on the County Fermanagh estate of Viscount Brookeborough in July 2002 and the placing of a firebomb outside a Dugannon Supermarket in January 2003. In February 2003 six police officers were injured when a bomb it is believed to have planted exploded in Enniskillen. As the first IMC report stated, attacks have continued – living up to the group's threat in February 2003 of more attacks to come.[54] It has also 'recently been involved in setting up new active service units'.[55] The third IMC report concluded that the Continuity IRA 'has increased its level of activity' and 'remains capable of making effective attacks'.[56]

The IMC's fifth report warned that the organisation has made a number of threats to District Policing Partnerships and stated that it 'is taking on new members, has continued to train ... and it makes efforts to improve its engineering capacity ... we believe it is a dangerous organisation capable of serious if sporadic attacks'.[57] The Continuity IRA continues to target on and off duty police officers and, despite some internal feuding, a lack of coherent organisation, and an apparent inability to mount a sustained campaign, it remains a dangerous and active organisation[58] that 'will continue to mount real and hoax attacks'.[59] It was believed to be behind the planting of explosive devices outside police stations in Belfast and East Tyrone in April 2006.[60] In the same month the IMC confirmed that 'CIRA remains committed to terrorism'.[61]

As dissident republicanism is often personality driven, indications suggest that the two dissident groups often cooperate closely, especially at a local level[62] – in some cases security sources suggest that the different labels have now become almost academic. It is in this context – in partnership with the Real IRA – that the Continuity IRA represents a more serious threat. If dissident republicans manage to present more of a united front then potential IRA defectors might be more persuaded to join them. As with the Real IRA, however, much of what the Continuity IRA is able to achieve might depend on the response of the mainstream IRA.

Finally, in relation to the general dissident republican threat, the Director General of MI5 was quite right to recall (prior to the 7 July 2005 attacks) that the last bomb attack on the UK mainland was carried out by the Real IRA and that dissident groups continue to be 'a substantial cause for concern'.[63] Indeed, police claim to have foiled a major bomb plot after discovering explosives in Lurgan, County Armagh in April 2006.[64] This was followed by the discovery of a partially detonated 70 pound device in August 2006.[65] While they continue with attacks on security force personnel in Northern Ireland they both also 'recognise the propaganda value of a successful attack on the UK mainland'.[66]

The INLA

Brief history and ideology

The INLA came into existence after a split in the official IRA (from which the Provisional IRA split in 1969) in 1974. Its Irish nationalist ideology is merged with a left wing dogma that finds its roots in the tradition of James Connolly and that of republican socialism. Among its most notorious operations was the killing of MP Airey Neave in 1979 in a car bomb and the murder of 17 people in the 'Droppin' Well' pub bomb in Ballykelly in December 1982. In the 1980s the group suffered a damaging split when members broke away to form the Irish People's Liberation Organisation. In the following decade the INLA was engaged in 'low level' activity but in August 1998 it called a ceasefire. It has, however, continued with vigilante activity and is opposed to the Good Friday Agreement, although its ceasefire is still intact.

Capability

The INLA is said to have no more than a few dozen activists.[67] It has, however, been heavily engaged in organised crime which has put it on a sound financial footing. It is believed that the group has 'a limited arsenal of rifles, hand-guns and home-made explosive devices'.[68]

Tactics

When not on ceasefire the INLA used gun and bomb attacks.

Organised crime

It is estimated in the parliamentary report cited above that the INLA annually raises £500,000 with running costs of just 25,000 to 30,000.

Assessment

The INLA has a history of unpredictable and volatile behaviour and is heavily involved in organised crime and vigilantism. It has a heavy vigilante presence in parts of Belfast and is said to have been taking over some 'community policing' from the IRA in some areas of the city. In January 2002, following the murder of Catholic postal worker Daniel McColgan by the UDA, the INLA threatened revenge killings. It apparently stated that 'we warn that such attacks put an almost impossible strain on republicans. Unless there is a halt, then a response is inevitable'.[69] Although this statement was made over four years ago, the possibility that the INLA could end its ceasefire and/or cooperate with the other dissident groups should not be discounted, particularly if Sinn Fein becomes 'more constitutional' and if any loyalist feuding broadens into sectarian killings. The first IMC report noted that it is still 'a significant terrorist group' and 'remains active' and the third IMC report stated that the 'INLA's potential remains essentially unchanged',[70] while more lately the IMC concluded that 'the threat of the organisation's more active involvement remains high although its present capacity for a sustained campaign is not high'.[71]

New Republican groups

It is also worth noting the IMC's observation (in its eighth report) that two new groupings have emerged, one calling itself Oglaigh na Eireann (ONH), which was formed by members who split from the Continuity IRA, and the other labelling itself as Saoirse na hEireann (SNH).[72] To date they have been responsible for an assault, a Post Office robbery and two hoax devices.[73]

The UDA

Brief history and ideology

The UDA emerged from a number of Defence Associations that were established to counter armed republicanism in the early years of the Troubles. Opposed to a united Ireland and any dilution of the 'Britishness' of the province, the UDA has very much been a mass organisation and was heavily involved in the Ulster Workers Strike of 1974 that brought down the 'Sunningdale' power-sharing executive. The UFF is the name it has used to take responsibility for the murders of Catholics, a tactic that helped to ensure that the UDA was not declared an illegal organisation until 1992. Under the aegis of the Combined Loyalist Military Command, the group declared a ceasefire in 1994 and initially supported the Good Friday Agreement in 1998, through its political front the Ulster Democratic Party. It soon, however, became disillusioned with the peace process, withdrawing its support from the agreement and dissolving the UDP in November 2001. In October 2001 John Reid, the then Northern Ireland Secretary, declared the group's ceasefire to be over after it was alleged to be involved in violence and intimidation in Belfast.

After the Good Friday Agreement was signed, the organisation continued to carry out the occasional sectarian assassination of Catholics. A building worker, Gary Moore, was murdered for his religion in December 2000; Gavin Brett, a Protestant mistaken for a Catholic, was killed in July 2001; and Danny McColgan was shot dead on his way to work in January 2002.

The UDA has gained a reputation for being heavily involved in organised crime and its 'brigades' are said to be more concerned with maintaining their illegal fiefdoms and turf control than any political ideology or the peace process. With a loose decentralised structure and its various criminal enterprises, the UDA has been prone to involvement in internal loyalist feuding. It was involved in a bitter feud with the UVF in 2000 that left seven men dead, and internal differences in 2002–3 led to the deaths of four more. After this last feud its new political front (the Ulster Political Research Group) stated that the UDA was going to 'clean up its act' and support the peace process, though how much these sentiments are genuine or designed to deflect attention away from the group's criminal activity is open to question. Nevertheless, Paul Murphy, the then Secretary of State for Northern Ireland, made the decision to recognise the UDA ceasefire in November 2004.

Capability

The UDA is said to have a membership in the high hundreds, though of a 'lower grade' than the IRA. According to Jane's Intelligence the group is said to have in its arsenal several hundred AKM/AK47 assault rifles, Uzi sub-machine guns and several hundred handguns as well as a 'substantial quantity' of Powergel explosive and some rocket propelled grenades.[74]

Organised crime

Along with the Loyalist Volunteer Force (LVF), the organisation is probably the most notorious for its involvement with organised crime, not because it generates the most income from such activity in comparison with some of the other groups but because, like the LVF, its political *raison d'être* has been virtually non-existent. The parliamentary report noted above estimates that the organisation raises anything between £500,000 and £1 million annually, while its running costs are said to be around £500,000.

Tactics

Its tactics range from assassinations (mainly of innocent Catholics) to pipe bombs. Sometimes the organisation (usually the former West Belfast Brigade's 'C Company') has used the name Red Hand Defenders to take responsibility for them.

Security response

Hugh Orde, the Chief Constable of the Police Service of Northern Ireland, has made no secret of the fact that he is determined to crack down on the loyalist paramilitaries and their organised criminal activities. To date, he has lived up to his commitment with a number of arrests of loyalists. In a speech to US politicians in January 2003 he disclosed that more troops were on the streets of Northern Ireland than at any time over the past five years to combat the loyalist paramilitaries involved in the internal UDA feud.[75] Following an assessment from the Police Service of Northern Ireland, Johnny Adair, the notorious former leader of West Belfast's 'C' Company (who was said to be behind much of the feuding), was returned to prison by the Secretary of State, Paul Murphy, for revoking his license under the terms of the Good Friday Agreement early release scheme.

Assessment

As far as the peace process is concerned there has been general disillusionment amongst loyalists. The widespread view is that republicans have managed to negotiate an endless stream of concessions while the loyalist groups have been sidelined. In the case of the UDA, however, this should not divert observers from the fact that its main *raison d'être* has been organised crime, power and turf control rather than any genuine political agenda. In fact the peace process has served to expose these activities which had hitherto been given the 'cover' of the political conflict.

Quite apart from the threat that organised crime and its competing fiefdoms represent, Hugh Orde warned in January 2003 (during the internal UDA feud) that the warring loyalists would soon 'resort to what they do best, which is more random and disorganised violence against the Catholic community'[76] a development that could have had serious implications for the level of threat from the republican groups and their roles as 'protectors' of their communities.

As noted above, the Secretary of State for Northern Ireland recognised the UDA ceasefire in November 2004 stating that 'I am persuaded that the UDA is now prepared to go down a different road, moving away from its paramilitary past',[77] while the Ulster Political Research Group stated that the UDA had agreed to enter 'a process that will see the eradication of all paramilitary activity' and that its strategy 'will become one of community development, job creation, social inclusion and community politics'.[78] When the political credentials of the organisation have been so suspect in the past, however, it will take actions rather than words to convince many, particularly in the Catholic community, that these sentiments are genuine. The third IMC report, for example, found that in the six months between March and August 2004, although the UDA had 'not been responsible for any murders' it did 'undertake shootings and assaults' including 'a vicious sectarian attack against three Catholic men'.[79] The report also found that 'the UDA remains heavily involved in many kinds of organised crime'.[80]

Since then, the organisation has allegedly been responsible for four murders[81] and at least two bank robberies leading the IMC to conclude that 'it is not clear if the UDA will achieve the transition [envisaged in November 2004]'.[82] In its Seventh report the IMC reiterated that 'the organisation is involved in violent and other serious crime and that it remains an active threat to the rule of law in Northern Ireland'.[83] This remains the case, despite the apparent efforts of some affiliated to the group to steer the organisation away from violence and organised crime.[84] More recently (end of July 2006), the organisation was said to be on the verge of another internal feud.[85]

The LVF

Brief history

The LVF was formed in 1997 after an internal dispute within the UVF over the determination of Billy Wright, the mid Ulster Brigade Commander, to carry out 'operations' without the sanction of the leadership, for which he was expelled. In the same year the LVF was proscribed by the then Northern Ireland Secretary, Mo Mowlam. The group is suspected of being behind the murder of Catholic solicitor Rosemary Nelson and it claimed responsibility for the killing of journalist Martin O'Hagan in 2001. Until the feuding within the UDA, the LVF had close links with the West Belfast 'C' Company of the group originating from the close friendship of Adair (head of C Company) and Wright, who was murdered in prison by members of the INLA. In 2000 the LVF (along with the UDA) was involved in a feud with the UVF that led to seven deaths and in July/August 2005 another feud between the two organisations led to four more killings.

Capability

Estimates of the size of the LVF vary from 'dozens'[86] to around 150 members and the group is said to possess 'a limited arsenal of rifles including AK-47s, sub-machine guns, hand-guns and shotguns'.[87] It is 'also believed that the group attained a quantity of the explosive Powergel, through its close ties to the UDA'.[88]

Tactics

The group has used gun and bomb attacks. It has targeted innocent Catholics, loyalist rivals and the journalist Martin O'Hagan (who was killed for exposing the group's activities).

Organised crime

The parliamentary report noted above suggests that the LVF raises £2 million a year and yet its running costs are just £50,000. This might indicate why Adair was so keen to link up with the LVF.

Assessment

The LVF continues to represent a threat. It is highly prone to feuding, largely because its main preoccupation is with protecting its 'turf' or territory against other groups rather than any political agenda. Indeed, the third IMC report noted that 'the organisation remains involved in virtually every form of organised crime'.[89] Although in its first report the IMC stated that it had 'continued to carry out paramilitary shootings and assaults in 2004'[90] it concluded in November 2004 'that the LVF is less active than it has been, with the exception of organised crime'.[91] This was reiterated in the IMC's fifth report.[92] As noted above, however, it was engaged in a violent feud with the UVF which led to the deaths of four men in July and August 2005.[93] In October 2005 the group announced that it would stand down (apparently in response to the IRA decommissioning of the previous month) and that this would take effect from October. The IMC, however, has stated that it has not seen any evidence of this and that 'there has therefore been no change to the earlier conclusion about its essentially criminal nature'.[94] The group therefore remains a threat for as long as it maintains the capacity to use violence to protect its hugely profitable criminal exploits.

The UVF

Brief history

The modern UVF was formed in 1966 in response to the liberal policies of Terence O'Neill and in the belief that there would be a resurgence of the IRA to commemorate the fiftieth anniversary of the Easter Rising. It is the second largest loyalist paramilitary group and was a ruthless killer during the course of the Troubles, targeting innocent Catholics. It was part of the Combined Loyalist Military Command that signed the ceasefire of 1994. It has been the most 'political' of the loyalist paramilitary groups through its political front, the Progressive Unionist Party (PUP), which, until the November 2003 Assembly election, was entitled to two Assembly seats but currently would have only one if the political institutions were to be restored. The UVF was reportedly about to dissolve in February 2006[95] but as yet this has not been confirmed by the IMC which stated in April 2006 that the group still remained an active and violent organisation.[96]

Capability

The UVF is believed to be a few hundred strong with 'a smaller number being 'active' members'.[97] It is said to have in its armoury approximately 200 AK-47 rifles, in addition to Uzi machine guns, machine pistols, home made sub-machine guns, along with 'dozens of pistols and revolvers'.[98] The group is also said to possess a 'small number' of RPG-7 rocket launchers and a 'small amount of Powergel'.[99]

Organised crime

The UVF is heavily steeped in organised crime and was said to reap an annual income of £1.5 million from it, with estimated running costs of £1 million to £2 million.[100]

Assessment

There is no doubt that the UVF does represent a security threat. It has been a more centralised, disciplined and politically orientated group than either the UDA or the LVF and so, while all the groups are steeped in organised crime in Northern Ireland, the UVF does have more of a political *raison d'être* than either the UDA or the LVF. As a result, developments in the peace process have been of more interest to the UVF and the PUP and therefore the feeling that loyalists have been sidelined from the negotiations could have, and indeed has had, an effect on the level of threat that the group has posed. In August 2002 David Ervine, the PUP spokesman, warned that the UVF was becoming increasingly disillusioned with the way the process was developing.[101] Reports suggested that the UVF was rearming[102] and this appeared to be evident when one of its units was caught attempting to transport explosives for pipe bombs from Glasgow in May 2002.

The IMC has reported that it believes that the group has been responsible for a number of murders, including those related to feuding with another loyalist group, the LVF. The UVF was said to be responsible for four murders in July/August during its feud with the latter (it also apparently attempted to commit nine others).[103] The IMC stated that 'the UVF and RHC[104] are ruthless and reasonably well controlled organisations, heavily engaged in major crime and punishment attacks. They retain a capacity for more widespread violence in which they would not hesitate to engage if they judged the circumstances made it appropriate'.[105] Despite the ending of the feud (and reports in February 2006 that the UVF was about to disband), the IMC stated in April 2006 that the group still remained 'active, violent and ruthless'.[106]

The threat from organised crime

Organised crime has soared in Northern Ireland. One theory is that such activity has increased because it provides a substitute activity for those adhering to a ceasefire. Paramilitary organised crime has also become more transparent – now that the political conflict is receding these nefarious activities no longer have the cover of an ostensible political goal. This is particularly the case with the UDA and LVF. The culture of organised crime in Northern Ireland is a huge problem for the police to have to deal with in the years ahead. Gangs and groups vying for control of territory in which to practise their racketeering and sell their smuggled or counterfeit goods represents a serious security threat in itself – epitomised by internal loyalist feuding. Table 5.1 is a chart (from which some of the above information is taken) from the Northern Ireland Select Committee report on

Table 5.1 Northern Ireland organised crime groups – running costs and fundraising capacity

Organisation*	Estimated running costs (per year)	Estimated fundraising capacity (per year)
Provisional IRA (PIRA)	£1.5 million	£5 million to £8 million
Real IRA (RIRA)	£500,000	£5 million
Continuity IRA (CIRA)	£25,000 to £30,000	[107]
INLA	£25,000 to £30,000	£500,000
UDA	£500,000	Between £500,000 and £1 million
UFF	£250,000	
UVF	£1 million to £2 million	£1.5 million
LVF	£50,000	£2 million

Source: Northern Ireland Select Committee, July 2002.

organised crime in the province (July 2002), highlighting the extent to which the groups have been immersed in it.

In September 2000 the government announced the creation of an Organised Crime Task Force (OCTF) to provide 'the strategic direction' for 'a new multi-agency approach to tackling organised crime in Northern Ireland'.[108] In its first report it stated that such activity 'threatened the development of a normal society' in Northern Ireland although it claimed to have scored some notable successes against fuel fraud and cigarette smuggling.[109] The government's new Serious Organised Crime Agency (SOCA) was launched in April 2006 and is linked in to the OCTF.[110]

The establishment of the Assets Recovery Agency, the equivalent of the Criminal Assets Bureau in the Irish Republic, has been another step designed to tackle organised crime in the province. From February 2003 the new agency has had powers to investigate the bank accounts and tax returns of suspects, and the onus has been and will be placed on the latter to justify and explain their wealth.[111] On a national level, as well as the creation of the SOCA, the government is planning to create a new department that will combine the roles of Customs and the Inland Revenue including 'Customs' investigative and intelligence capabilities for tackling fiscal fraud and related criminal finances'.[112] It is also considering proposals for a national witness protection programme.[113]

Meanwhile, in the province, internal restructuring of the Police Service of Northern Ireland has led to the creation of the Crime Operations Department designed to 'focus on top-level organised criminals who continue to engage in serious illegal activity'.[114] Plans have also been put in place to introduce a pilot of the 'Independent Private Sector Inspector General programme'[115] which has been used in the USA to 'ensure compliance with relevant law and regulations to deter, prevent, uncover and report unethical and illegal conduct by, within, and against the organisation'.[116] Finally, in September 2004 the Chief Constable of the Police Service of Northern Ireland and the Garda Commissioner launched the first ever cross-border organised crime assessment as part of the effort to enhance arrangements for cooperation against organised crime on the island.[117] This effort has also included improving procedures 'relating to the transfer of evidence for use in prosecutions in either jurisdiction' and the consideration of establishing Joint Investigation Teams.[118]

It is too early to tell what effect these initiatives might have in curtailing the deep-seated problem of organised crime in Northern Ireland but the challenge is indeed a formidable one. The 2004 OCTF assessment report noted that there were 230 organised crime gangs in the province. Of paramilitary related crime it stated that in general paramilitary groups are very heavily involved in counterfeiting, that 'republican groups are heavily involved in Oils Fraud (smuggling, laundering and misuse of rebated fuel)', that '70% of reported incidents of extortion in 2003 were attributable to Loyalist Paramilitaries', that '70% of Republican groups and 60% of Loyalist groups are involved in the illegal tobacco trade', and that 'Dissident Republican Groups are involved in large-scale and highly lucrative smuggling operations'.[119]

In its latest report (*Annual Report and Threat Assessment 2006*) the OCTF noted that:

> Loyalist groups remain involved in drugs supply, intellectual property crime, importation and distribution of contraband goods, extortion, money lending and armed robbery. They are also known to use legitimate businesses, notably pubs, clubs and taxi firms as cover for their illegal operation .... The dissident republican groups (Continuity IRA (CIRA) and Real IRA (RIRA)) are heavily involved in robberies, smuggling contraband goods and intellectual property crime ... The Irish National Liberation Army (INLA) continues to engage in robbery, intellectual property crime and extortion.[120]

In relation to the IRA (and in light of the IMC's tenth report), although some members (including senior ones) seem to be still involved in organised crime, it appears that the organisation itself is trying to distance itself from such activity. Nevertheless, in general, organised crime in the province is one legacy of the 'Troubles' that will take many years, if not decades, to eradicate. As the first IMC report stated it 'may present the biggest long-term threat to the rule of law in Northern Ireland'.[121]

ANIMAL RIGHTS EXTREMISM

History

Animal rights extremism has represented the cutting edge of a very broad animal rights movement that includes a plethora of legitimate organisations opposed to animal experiments and hunting. Although the impression is that there have been a number of different animal rights organisations that have engaged in illegal activities it is believed that there are no more than 30 hardcore animal rights activists who have used different labels in order to try to confuse the police authorities and to give the impression that they have, in fact, been more numerous than has actually been the case. In addition, as the Animal Liberation Front (ALF) has a public strategy of non-violence against any 'sentient'[122] beings, 'the ALF policy is that any attacks which either cause or threaten to cause violence against people should be claimed under another name, so that the name of the ALF does not attract the public condemnation which the use of violence would bring … However, in every case where the identities of the perpetrators of these attacks are known, they are leading ALF activists'.[123]

The different noms de guerre

In 1973 Ronnie Lee, a member of the Hunt Saboteurs' Association, set up an organisation called the Band of Mercy. He was arrested and jailed for arson but upon his release he formed the ALF (in 1976). Ever since, the organisation has been something of:

> a flag of convenience. … The organisations which have claimed responsibility for attacks include the Justice Department and the Animal Rights Militia. The extremists are surrounded by a support network of about 200 sympathisers who are prepared to lend cars or give help. There may be another 2,000 supporters prepared to take part in demonstrations and give cash.[124]

The 'Justice Department' was 'formed' in 1993 and it launched a new campaign the following year. The 'Hunt Retribution Squad' is believed to be another label used by the same group from the early 1990s.[125] The hardcore of animal rights activists are said to be very dedicated to their cause and fully accept that they are likely to have to spend a degree of time in jail.

Tactics

The tactics of animal rights extremists have varied enormously. The activities of the Band of Mercy included the 'liberation' of animals from laboratory animal breeders and arson attacks on pharmaceutical laboratories.[126] The ALF began with arson attacks in the 1970s. In the following decade it carried out raids on laboratories that used animals and in 1982 sent letter bombs to scientists and other targets (one was sent to each of the four leaders of the main political parties in the UK). In 1984 it began a product contamination campaign (such as the Mars Bars case) and in 1990 explosive devices were placed under the cars of two vets in Bristol and Salisbury.[127] In 1994 the 'Justice Department' sent six letter bombs to companies involved in animal exports, for which Gurj Aujla was jailed for six years. On 28 July 2001 Glynn Harding, apparently a 'paranoid schizophrenic' with links to the organisation, was found guilty of sending 15 letter bombs to people 'perceived to have links with animal cruelty'.[128] The group is also said to have despatched letters containing razor blades coated in rat poison.[129]

In October 2000 the 'Hunt Retribution Squad' was responsible for planting explosive devices under vehicles belonging to two members of the Old Surrey Burstow and West Kent Hunt. The group has also issued threats to Prince Charles and Prince William, both of whom ride on hunts.

In summary, animal rights extremists have used a variety of tactics – from death threats, abuse, intimidation, vandalism, email 'bombs' to crash computers, requesting mail-order goods under false pretences and even arranging for undertakers to collect the bodies of living people',[130] to product contamination, 'animal liberation' raids, arson attacks, letter bombs and car bombs (in the period 1986–8 nine such devices were planted).[131] More lately tactics reached a new macabre level with four animal rights activists convicted for the digging up of the remains of a relative of a guinea pig breeder in Staffordshire.[132]

To give some idea of the unrelenting nature and intensity of the attention that has been meted out to targets the last case is worth exploring further. Prior to the desecration of the grave it was reported that the Hall family (who ran the guinea pig farm) sold their dairy herd after tankers that collected their milk were attacked, that harvesting of corn on their farm was disrupted after metal bars had been placed in the ground, that a fuel supplier was forced to stop supplying them with diesel, that their local publican was threatened and 'forced out' for serving them, and that a golf course that they played at was vandalised – in addition to '30 or 40 abusive calls a day', bricks thrown through their lounge window at night, tyres slashed, and so on.[133] After a long struggle against intimidation the Hall family were finally forced to close the farm, reportedly in the hope that the remains of their relative would be returned.[134] The determination of such extremists is also evident in the account of Dr Mark Matfield, the former executive director of the Research Defence Society, who stated that he had '[given] up counting the death threats many, many years ago' and that he 'had a letter bomb sent to my office, my car smashed up a couple of times, windows broken, car tyres slashed, paint poured over it, and I have had protests – sometimes quite violent ones – at my office and home'.[135]

Huntingdon Life Sciences

In the late 1990s the ALF began to engage in aggressive targeting of those establishments that it deemed had been violating animal rights. In 1997 it managed to close down a company in Hereford that bred dogs for research and did likewise to a cat-breeding company in Oxfordshire. Animal rights extremism really came to the fore in British public life, however, when activists tried to close the Huntingdon Life Sciences (HLS) Laboratory from 2000.

Stop Huntingdon Animal Cruelty (SHAC) organised numerous protests outside the laboratory with the objective of harassing and intimidating staff. A statement from the organisation, however, asserted that 'we unreservedly condemn any act of violence be it against animals or humans' and it argued that it ran a legal campaign.[136] It is clear, however, that there have been elements that have used a variety of extra legal means to intimidate the company's staff and its financial backers.

The onslaught surrounding HLS began with a brick being thrown through an employee's window in December 1999. It then developed into demonstrations outside the company that included threats and intimidation against staff members. Tactics took on a more sinister tone with approximately 500 threatening calls made a day, as well as hate mail delivered to employees' home addresses. Threats were not just limited to HLS staff but were also meted out to staff of the financial backers of the company, 'which led the firm's bankers, auditors and insurers to withdraw their services'.[137] In August 2000 five cars were burnt outside the HLS site while police also had to cope with the tactic of 'flying squads' of protesters. Brian Cass, the managing director of HLS, needed stitches after being wounded by a blow to the head inflicted by an extremist in February 2001.

SHAC has also been engaged with targeting the suppliers of HLS. One of these was the British Oxygen Company (BOC) which provided the nitrate oxide that companies like HLS need to carry out its research and so SHAC organised protests outside BOC premises. The company finally withdrew its services in November 2004 stating that 'BOC's contract with Huntington is no longer commercially viable'.[138] In all, 80 companies are said to have 'severed their ties' with HLS.[139]

The Cambridge and Oxford sites

The proposed laboratory site at Girton, Cambridge was abandoned in early 2004 due to increased costs for building it, largely due to security considerations in the face of animal rights protests. One source argued that 'we can't afford to build and run Fort Knox'.[140] The intimidation has now focused on Oxford where the proposed Cambridge work is to be carried out. SPEAC (Stop Primate Experiments at Cambridge) was set up in July 2003 to target the Cambridge site but changed its name to SPEAK (as a voice to 'speak' for the animals). Tactics have followed similar lines to those used against HLS by SHAC. Critical suppliers and contractors in particular have been targeted, beginning with a polite letter before escalating into intimidating behaviour and protests. The strategy is very much to 'identify and pick off suppliers and contractors one by one'.[141] One of these was the building company Montpellier plc which pulled out of the project. Another is the Ready Mixed Concrete group which suffered £150,000 worth of damage at one of its sites at the hands of animal rights extremists.

The construction of the Oxford laboratory was severely delayed when the building contractor pulled out of the project following intimidation from animal rights extremists, although work has since recommenced. Activists then warned (in early 2006) that all those connected to the university (including students) would be targeted for intimidation, a move that prompted students to respond with the formation of the group PRO-Test which organised a protest march against the extremists.

Unlike some of the extremist tactics of previous decades, however, the activists are not using bombs. While there have been incendiary devices delivered there have not been petrol bombs placed underneath vehicles and there have been no serious assaults (with the exception of the attack on Brian Cass). This may be for two reasons. First, the 'main bomber' (David Blenkinsop) is currently serving a prison sentence for planting explosives on lorries at a Mutchmeat livestock plant in Oxfordshire. Second, the strategy of targeting and intimidating suppliers appears to be an effective one with some contractors finding it 'hard to stay in the game'.[142]

State response

The UK Animal Rights National Index, established in 1985, has provided the police with a vital intelligence tool – by listing animal rights activists and accumulating information relating to their activities. It has been instrumental in leading to the arrest and conviction of a number of extremists. According to security sources the police have been able to cope with the more serious crimes quite well but the lower level type crimes are more difficult to deal with. For example, in the overall scheme of things serious resources are not going to be directed towards an incident where a brick has been thrown through a window. Nor is it going to be picked up by the National Crime Squad. Yet, cumulatively, such incidents do represent a serious problem.[143]

The government's response to the HLS episode was seen as somewhat belated. Indeed, it was even reported that the Labour party instructed Phillips and Drew to sell its £70,000 pension stake in the firm[144] – hardly an endorsement for the laboratory or an example to other financial backers not to give in to threats and intimidation. Both the Royal Bank of Scotland and Barclays withdrew financial support for HLS, actions that the then Home Secretary Jack Straw apparently (and perhaps ironically) condemned as 'cowardly'.[145]

In the short term staff were advised to register their cars at the company address rather than their home one. The government also gave the Cambridgeshire police a £1 million grant to deal with the demonstrations[146] while a new police squad was developed under the National Crime Squad to respond to the activists' 'flying columns'.[147] An important development has been the creation of a national unit to counter animal rights extremism. Funded by the Home Office, the National Extremism Tactical Coordination Unit (NETCU) has been set up to provide a more national and joined up approach to single issue extremism as well as to give advice on the use of legislation, the policing of injunctions and to act as a liaison point for industry.[148] It reports to the Association of Chief Police Officers Council Committee on Terrorism and Allied Matters (ACPO TAM). The government has further confirmed its commitment to tackling the problem of animal rights extremism through the Department of Trade and Industry's bankrolling of HLS' insurance and accountancy needs.[149]

There are currently a plethora of different Acts that are used to deal with the wide variety of extremist tactics – including the Public Order Act 1986, the Malicious Communications Act 1988, the Protection from Harassment Act 1997, the Criminal and Public Order Act 1994, the Criminal Justice and Police Act 2001 and the Terrorism Act 2000. There have also been legislative changes and amendments that have taken particular account of the problems faced in dealing with animal rights extremism. The Criminal Justice and Police Act 2001, for example, has been amended to include the offence of demonstrating outside targets' homes and to permit the restriction of access to Company Directors' and Company Secretaries' addresses. Another example is the amendment to the Malicious Communication Act 1988, where the defence of 'reasonable grounds' for sending hate mail can no longer be used,[150] and where it has been extended to include electronic communications. Harassment laws have also been strengthened to deal with campaigns of harassment aimed at groups of people working for the same company,[151] while the Public Order Act was amended by changing the definition of what constitutes a public assembly from 20 people to two because demonstrators were ensuring that they were no more than 19 in number.

While such measures have been welcomed by researchers, an organisation called Victims of Animal Rights Extremism (VARE) has called for the groups organising the campaigns of harassment to be proscribed under the Terrorism Act 2000.[152] As things stand it is not illegal for anyone to be a member of the ALF nor is it against the law to raise money for it.[153] These would become offences under proscription, along with arranging and/or addressing meetings in support of a proscribed organisation.[154]

The government has so far resisted proscribing the 'group', perhaps because it has not represented the same degree of threat posed, for example, by some of the Northern Irish groups.[155] One Home Office source was quoted as saying that 'we are not going down the road of proscription. It is a public order question rather than a terrorist issue at the moment'.[156] A further point for consideration is that one could hardly reduce animal rights extremists to 'a group'. Indeed, although there are believed to be around 30 or so hardcore activists, there appears to be no hierarchical organisational structure but more of a decentralised network of almost self-appointed activists, and so membership of a group would be difficult to prove. As ALF guidelines have stated 'any group of people who are vegetarians or vegans and who carry out actions according to ALF guidelines have the right to regard themselves as part of the ALF'.[157]

There have also been calls to introduce a single piece of legislation that would specifically deal with the problem of animal rights extremism rather than tinkering with existing laws every time activists are able to find and exploit a loophole. The Research Defence Society and VARE have been proponents of this but to date the government has used the alternative avenue of amending existing legislation.[158] There is also the view that a separate piece of legislation to deal with animal rights extremists specifically (rather than amending existing laws) 'could restrict the use of powers in other situations such as anti-abortionists protesting outside the homes of doctors'.[159]

In November 2004 the government did, however, announce its intention to introduce 'economic sabotage' as a criminal offence in a further development designed to counter the threat from animal rights extremists (and this came into force in July 2005 as part of the Serious Organised Crime and Police Act). The Prime Minister stated that:

> Our ambition is for the UK to become the science capital of the world, to become a world leader in exploiting knowledge, to become the most open and supportive environment in the World [sic.]. A place where scientists everywhere in the world want to come and work. We are well on the way. But I believe we can do better. Stem cell research is just one example of a new area of science which has tremendous potential to improve quality of life and where the UK can lead the world ... If we are to achieve this vision we must redouble our efforts to tackle Animal Rights Extremism.[160]

In relation to the protests, one option that has been successfully pursued by those targeted for intimidation has been to issue civil injunctions (Anti-Social Behaviour Orders or ASBOs) against the activists which has led to the imposition of exclusion zones around work premises and employees' home addresses so that protesters are not permitted to harass or intimidate in these designated areas. In November 2004 Oxford University successfully renewed such an injunction against activists, with a 'no harassment' zone extending to 45 metres around the laboratory.[161] A 91 metre 'no go' area was also imposed 'around the homes of the university's members, employees and their families, its shareholders, its contractor employees, shareholders and their families, and anyone who visits the research laboratory'.[162] This was shortly followed by a whole village applying for an injunction against extremists.[163] Police sources have stated that the 'ASBOs' have provided clarity to the protestors as to what is acceptable and what isn't though it has also led to an increase in criminal activity overnight, such as defacing employees' properties. It has been very difficult to make arrests because 'you actually have to catch them at it'.[164]

As with all sound strategies intended to counter extremism the security and legislative response is only half the battle. The other half in the case of animal rights extremism is to ensure that the legitimate concerns of animal welfare groups are properly addressed, hence reducing the motivation for legal campaigners to become illegal extremists. The government has repeatedly argued that it has the most tightly regulated regime governing animal experiments in the world, where companies have to go through a 'rigorous process' to obtain a license to conduct animal experiments, and which will only be granted if there is no alternative to the use of animal experiments.[165] Also, included in the Queen's Speech of November 2004 were measures to introduce new penalties against animal cruelty.[166]

The government has also developed a 'refine, reduce and replace' agenda. Its purpose is to promote best practice and to look at ways where the use of animals in experiments can be reduced. This includes assessing alternatives such as computer modelling, which can apparently mimic systems inside the body, and mathematical models, and, where animal testing is unavoidable, ways that suffering can be reduced.[167] In 2004 a national centre was established designed to develop a strategy for the implementation of the '3 Rs'.[168]

Assessment

A combination of police and legislative action has helped to quell the intimidation that surrounded the HLS episode. It is important to remember, however, that the dedication of a small number of activists is unlikely to have been dimmed and when one considers that animal experiments are set to continue then it is fair to assume that animal rights extremism is here to stay. It is likely that the same hardcore of activists who have been at the heart of animal rights extremism in the past few decades were also behind the organisation of the protests against HLS. For example, the man convicted for the firebomb attacks on lorries at Mutchmeats meat factory in May 2000 under the name of the ALF was the same man who attacked the managing director of HLS.[169] Also, Robin Webb, the official spokesman for the ALF, has been a main speaker at the HLS protests.[170] Thus, the modus operandi of these extremists can vary from bomb attacks to harassment and intimidation.

It was therefore possible that, having failed to close HLS, this hardcore of activists would resort to more extreme measures when it came to other targets, a possibility acknowledged by police sources in 2003.[171] In the meantime, however, the decision was taken to abandon plans for a new laboratory site at Girton, Cambridge, due to the expected high levels of protest. This has undoubtedly given a boost to the extremists who may now believe that if their protests are intimidating enough they will achieve their objectives. They will have been further encouraged by the closure of the Hall's guinea pig farm in Newchurch. In addition, the harassment campaigns have prompted a number of suppliers to withdraw their services. The alleged founder of SHAC was reported as saying in September 2004 that 'the movement was more successful now than at any stage in its history'.[172] A real problem for the authorities, then, is that animal rights extremists appear to have grown in confidence. Elsewhere, the SHAC founder was quoted as saying:

> When Huntingdon closes we won't just go on to another company. We will go on to a whole area of animal abuse. And look to knock out big chunks – puppy farming, factory farming, circuses and zoos. All these could be finished. We're becoming bigger, even more intelligent and even more determined not just to take companies down but to finish whole areas of animal abuse.[173]

The activists are not, however, able to muster the large scale demonstrations that were mobilised against HLS and there are still only a small number of core activists – no more than 30 people. HLS has not been forced to close down but is still going strong (in fact its business has increased since the protests began). Moreover, injunctions carried out against the protesters have curtailed the latter's day-to-day activity. Finally, in spite of government figures indicating that attacks had increased during the first six months of 2004 (with '140 animal rights activists either arrested or reported compared with only 34 over the same period in 2003'[174]), statistics from the Association of the British Pharmaceutical Agency show a dramatic decrease in attacks in the first six months of 2006 which 'it attributes to a three-pronged strategy of new legislation; enhanced policing with co-ordinated enquiries; and working with stakeholders to combat attacks'.[175]

Nevertheless, animal rights extremism is still a serious issue to be dealt with, especially as the core of activists are very determined, very surveillance and security aware, and legally well briefed.[176] Also of concern was the establishment of a three-day animal rights extremist 'training camp' in September 2004 (widely reported in the British media), which apparently 'offered workshops on strategy and tactics'.[177] The government, under pressure from drugs manufacturers and the pharmaceutical industry does appear to be taking a firmer line against animal rights extremists by attempting to curtail their ability to intimidate. However, given that at least some of the hardcore activists that have been behind the more violent protests are the same people that have been at the heart of animal rights extremism in the last few decades (when bombs were planted and letter bombs were despatched), and if the government proves to be successful in preventing extremists from intimidating those that they target, the danger is that more extreme tactics will be adopted.

Notes

1 Notwithstanding subsequent Independent Monitoring Commission (IMC) reports that stated that IRA activity was continuing.
2 See, for example, Patterson, H. (1997) *Political History of The IRA*, London: Serif.
3 Although ideologically there should not have been a problem with this as it was, presumably, an 'illegitimate' claim anyway.
4 That is as long as the majority of the people of Northern Ireland wish to remain within the UK then the province's constitutional status should not change.
5 (2006) *Tenth Report of the Independent Monitoring Commission*, April, London: The Stationery Office, available at www.independentmonitoringcommission.org/ documents/uploads/ACFEF3.pdf.
6 The IMC believed that the IRA was responsible: (2004) *Fourth Report of the Independent Monitoring Commission*, February, London: The Stationery Office, available at www.independentmonitoringcommission.org/documents/uploads/HC% 20308.pdf.
7 Police Service of Northern Ireland Special Branch source, interview.
8 Horgan, J. and Taylor, M. (1997) 'The Provisional Irish Republican Army: command and functional structure', *Terrorism and Political Violence*, 9(3), Autumn, p. 3.
9 Ibid.
10 Clarke, L. (2004) 'IRA set to destroy guns by new year', *The Sunday Times*, 5 December.
11 Northern Ireland Affairs Select Committee report (2002) *The Financing of Terrorism in Northern Ireland*, 2 July, available at www.parliament.the-stationery-office.co.uk/ pa/cm200102/cmselect/cmniaf/cmniaf.htm.
12 Tenth IMC report (n. 5).
13 See www.timesonline.co.uk/article/0,,2-1711752,00.html.

14 (2004) *First Report of the Independent Monitoring Commission*, April, London: The Stationery Office, available at www.independentmonitoringcommission.org/documents/uploads/First%20Report.doc.

15 Ibid.

16 (2004) *Third Report of the Independent Monitoring Commission*, November, London: The Stationery Office, available at www.independentmonitoringcommission.org/documents/uploads/Third%20Report.pdf.

17 Fourth IMC report (n. 6).

18 (2005) *Fifth Report of the Independent Monitoring Commission*, May, London: The Stationery Office, available at www.independentmonitoringcommission.org/documents/uploads/IMC_Report.pdf.

19 Indeed, the IMC noted in its seventh report that dissident republicans approached IRA members who they thought may have been disillusioned after the 28 July statement in an attempt to obtain weapons, though it also stated that there was no evidence to suggest that they were successful. (2005) *Seventh Report of the Independent Monitoring Commission*, October, London: The Stationery Office, p. 12, available at www.independentmonitoringcommission.org/documents/uploads/7th%20%20IMC%20%20Report.pdf.

20 (2003) 'Some Orde officers "want him to fail"', UTV, in nuzhound.com, 9 January, available at www.u.tv/newsroom/indepth.asp?id=27566&pt=n.

21 See, for example, McDonald, H. (2004) 'IRA rift set to derail power sharing', *Guardian Unlimited*, 28 November, available at www.guardian.co.uk/Northern_Ireland/Story/0,2763,1361391,00.html.

22 (2006) *Eighth Report of the Independent Monitoring Commission*, February, London: The Stationery Office, available at www.independentmonitoringcommission.org/documents/uploads/8th%20IMC%20Report.pdf.

23 Tenth IMC report (n. 5).

24 Eighth IMC report (n. 22).

25 See www.ardfheis.com/elections.

26 Tenth IMC report (n. 5).

27 Sheehan, M. (2002) 'Embattled Real IRA barters with Dublin for release of prisoners', *The Sunday Times*, 9 June.

28 Evans, R. (2002) 'Real IRA indicates willingness to intensify terror campaign', *Jane's Intelligence Review*, 1 December.

29 The DPPs are part of the new policing dispensation arising from the Patten report.

30 See (2002) 'Real IRA trio are jailed for 30 years after MI5 "sting"', *The Times*, 8 May.

31 (2002) 'Real IRA', Group Profile, *Jane's Intelligence Review*, 14 November.

32 First IMC report (n. 14).

33 Veness, D. quoted in Evans, R. (2002) 'Down but not out? The threat from the Real IRA', *Jane's Intelligence Review*, 25 October.

34 Quoting a Police Service of Northern Ireland security source.

35 The IRA is listed as a proscribed organisation but the Real IRA is not. Rather than list the dissident republican groups separately as proscribed organisations, no explicit distinction in legislation has to date been made between the groups, although they are clearly different entities in their own right with different views and strategies. Nevertheless, there is still scope to convict for membership as legislation does allow for the inclusion of any other terrorist groups not included in the proscribed list.

36 The former charge was made an offence by law in the Irish Republic in response to the Omagh atrocity and McKevitt was the first person to be charged under it.

37 Bowcott, O. (2006) 'Ten arrested as Ulster police "foil terror plot"', *Guardian Unlimited*, 20 June, available at www.guardian.co.uk/Northern_Ireland/Story/0,,1801484,00.html. See also Bowcott, O. (2006) 'Bomb was for major

attacks say police', *Guardian Unlimited*, 20 April, available at www.guardian.co.uk/Northern_Ireland/Story/0,,1757183,00.html.

38 (2003) 'Real IRA will keep waging war', UTV, nuzhound.com, available at www.u.tv/newsroom/indepth.asp?id=28361&pt=n.

39 See Walsh, L. and Okado-Gough, D. (2003) 'War goes on says new leadership of the Real IRA', *Irish Independent*, 31 January.

40 Lister, D. (2002) 'Real IRA plotted to kill Blair', *The Times*, 9 October.

41 Although another man, Sean Hoey, is currently facing charges in connection with the Omagh attack.

42 Lister, D. (2002) 'Terrorism takes root in tranquil seaside hideaway', *The Times*, 7 September.

43 (2003) *Sunday Life*, 26 January.

44 First IMC report (n. 14).

45 Third IMC report (n. 16).

46 Fifth IMC report (n. 18).

47 Seventh IMC report (n. 19).

48 Bowcott, O. (2006) 'Real IRA says it firebombed shops', *Guardian Unlimted*, 12 August, available at www.guardian.co.uk/Northern_Ireland/Story/0,,1843079,00. html .

49 Tenth IMC report (n. 5).

50 (2002) 'Continuity group "now main threat"', *The Times*, 2 July.

51 First IMC report (n. 14).

52 Cain, available at http://cain.ulst.ac.uk/othelem/organ/corgan.htm#cira.

53 Such as over attempts to establish an arms supply route from the Balkans, which was apparently at least partly financed by cigarette smuggling. See (2000) 'Real IRA arms purchasing in Croatia indicates a change of tactics', *Jane's Intelligence Review*, 23 August.

54 See (2003) 'More bombs, says Continuity IRA', *Daily Telegraph*, 12 February.

55 First IMC report (n. 14).

56 Third IMC report (n. 16).

57 Fifth IMC report (n. 18).

58 Seventh IMC report (n. 19).

59 Eighth IMC report (n. 22).

60 See Bowcott, O. (2006) 'Bomb was for major attacks say police', *Guardian Unlimited*, 20 April, available at www.guardian.co.uk/Northern_Ireland/Story/0,,1757183,00. html.

61 Tenth IMC report (n. 5).

62 Eighth IMC Report (n. 22).

63 Director General's keynote address, 'Countering Terrorism. An International Blueprint', The Royal United Services Institute Conference, 17 June 2003.

64 See Bowcott, O. (2006) 'Bomb was for major attacks say police', *Guardian Unlimited*, 20 April, available at www.guardian.co.uk/Northern_Ireland/Story/0,,1757183,00. html.

65 Bowcott, O. (2006) 'Bomb discovery fuels fears of dissident republican revival', *Guardian Unlimited*, 17 August, available at www.guardian.co.uk/Northern_Ireland/Story/0,,1851817,00.html.

66 Director General's keynote address, 'Countering terrorism. An international blueprint', The Royal United Services Institute Conference, 17 June 2003.

67 (2002) 'Irish National Liberation Army', Group Profile, *Jane's Intelligence Review*, 21 November.

68 Ibid.

69 Quoted in (2002) 'Belfast revenge fear as Catholic is shot', *The Sunday Times*, 13 January.

70 First and third IMC reports (n. 14 and n. 16). This was also confirmed by the fifth IMC report (n. 18).
71 Eighth IMC report (n. 22).
72 Ibid.
73 Ibid.
74 (2003) 'Ulster Defence Association', Group Profile, *Jane's Intelligence Review*, 8 January.
75 (2003) 'Some Orde officers "want him to fail"', UTV, nuzhound.com, available at www.u.tv/newsroom/indepth.asp?id=27566&pt=n.
76 Ibid., 'Some Orde officers "want him to fail"'.
77 Paul Murphy, quoted in (2004) 'Government brings UDA in from the cold', *Guardian Unlimited*, 13 November, available at www.guardian.co.uk/Northern_Ireland.
78 Tommy Kirkham, quoted in (2004) 'UDA pledges end to violence', *Guardian Unlimited*, 15 November, available at www.guardian.co.uk/Northern_Ireland.
79 Third IMC report (n. 16).
80 Ibid.
81 See tenth IMC report (n. 5).
82 Fifth IMC report (n. 18).
83 Seventh IMC report (n. 19).
84 See eighth and tenth IMC reports (n. 22 and n. 5).
85 McDonald, H. (2006) 'New feud rips apart the UDA', *Guardian Unlimited*, 30 July, available at www.guardian.co.uk/Northern_Ireland/Story/0,,1833493,00.html.
86 Cain, available at http://cain.ulst.ac.uk/.
87 (2003) 'Loyalist Volunteer Force', Group Profile, *Jane's Intelligence Review*, 8 January.
88 Ibid.
89 Third IMC report (n. 16).
90 First IMC report (n. 14).
91 Third IMC report (n. 16).
92 Fifth IMC report (n. 18).
93 See Cowan, R. (2005) 'Fourth man shot dead in loyalist turf war', *Guardian Unlimited*, available at www.guardian.co.uk/Northern_Ireland/Story/0,2763,1549749,00.html.
94 Eighth IMC report (n. 22).
95 See McDonald, H. (2006) 'UVF says the war is over at last', *Guardian Unlimited*, 12 February, available at www.guardian.co.uk/Northern_Ireland/Story/0,,1708098,00.html.
96 Tenth IMC report (n. 5).
97 Cain website (n. 52).
98 Ibid.
99 Ibid.
100 Parliamentary report (n. 11).
101 (2002) 'UVF on brink of returning to violence, loyalist chief warns', *The Times*, 12 August.
102 (2002) 'Ulster loyalists admit breach of ceasefire', *The Times*, 1 August.
103 Seventh IMC report (n. 19).
104 The Red Hand Commando is a smaller group with close links to the UVF.
105 First IMC report (n. 14).
106 Tenth IMC report (n. 5).
107 No figure was entered here in the report. The assumption is that either it is not clear how much the Continuity IRA is engaged in organised crime or that it is not itself heavily engaged in it, but given security force assessments of cooperation between the Real IRA and the Continuity IRA one might assume that the latter has access to at least some of the proceeds of the former.
108 OCTF, see www.octf.gov.uk/background.cfm.

109 See (2002) 'More Success For Northern Ireland Organised Crime Task Force', Press Release, 6 March, available at www.britain-info.org/nireland. Also see Northern Ireland Information Service, available at www2.nio.gov.uk/010323a-nio.htm.

110 OCTF, *Threat Assessment and Strategy 2004–5*, available at www.octf.gov.uk/Publications.cfm.

111 The OCTF 2006 report for 2005–6 noted that between them the PSNI (Police Service of Northern Ireland), the HMRC (HM Revenue and Customs) and the ARA restrained or confiscated assets worth over £30 million (*Organised Crime Task Force Annual Report and Threat Assessment 2006*, available at www.octf.gov.uk/publications/PDF/OCTF%20Annual%20Report%20and%20Threat%20Assessment%202006.pdf.

112 OCTF, *Threat Assessment and Strategy 2004–5* (n. 110).

113 Government response to Professor Goldstock report, *Organised Crime in Northern Ireland, a Report for the Secretary of State*, available at www.nio.gov.uk/government_response_to_goldstock_report.pdf.

114 OCTF, *Threat Assessment and Strategy 2004–5* (n. 110).

115 A recommendation made by Professor Ronald Goldstock in his report commissioned by the government, *Organised Crime in Northern Ireland, a Report for the Secretary of State*, available at www.octf.gov.uk/pdfs/goldstockorgrep.pdf.

116 OCTF, *Threat Assessment and Strategy 2004–5* (n. 110). For a fuller definition see Professor Goldstock's report (n. 115).

117 *A Cross Border Organised Crime Assessment 2004*, available at www.octf.gov.uk/Publications.cfm .

118 Ibid.

119 OCTF, *Threat Assessment and Strategy 2004–5* (n. 110).

120 OCTF, *Annual Report and Threat Assessment 2006*, available at www.octf.gov.uk/publications/PDF/OCTF%20Annual%20Report%20and%20Threat%20Assessment%202006.pdf.

121 First IMC report (n. 14).

122 For the rationale behind this strategy see Monaghan, R. (1997) 'Animal rights and violent protest', *Terrorism and Political Violence*, 9(4), Winter, pp. 109–11.

123 Matfield, M. (1997) 'The Animal Liberation Front', *Jane's Intelligence Review*, 1 May.

124 (2002) 'Tiny secret army where prison is badge of commitment', *The Times*, 5 April.

125 Matfield (n. 123).

126 Ibid.

127 See (2001) 'Drugs firms say violence could cost UK billions', *The Times*, 5 April.

128 (2001) 'Letter bomb man', *The Times*, 28 July.

129 See, for example, (2001) 'Death risk as animal rights war hots up', *The Observer*, 11 March.

130 (2001) 'Animal protest law too weak, say scientists', *The Times*, 29 January.

131 Matfield (n. 123).

132 See, for example, 'Protest "link" to desecrated grave', BBC News online, available at http://news.bbc.co.uk/1/hi/england/staffordshire/3725702.stm . The remains were eventually discovered and re-buried (see (2006) 'Woman whose remains were stolen reburied in same grave', *Guardian Unlimited*, 1 June, available at www.guardian.co.uk/animalrights/story/0,,1787324,00.html).

133 (2004) 'Desecrated, how animal rights extremists are holding a community under siege', *The Sunday Times*, 17 October.

134 (2005) 'Targeted guinea pig farm closes', BBC News online, 23 August, available at http://news.bbc.co.uk/1/hi/england/staffordshire/4176094.stm.

135 (2004) 'I no longer count death threats', BBC News online, 30 July, available at http://news.bbc.co.uk/1/hi/uk/3939211.stm.

136 Quoted from (2001) 'Drugs-test chief is clubbed by masked gang', *The Times*, 24 February.
137 (2004) 'Pharma firms take on the extremists', BBC News online, available at http://news.bbc.co.uk/1/hi/business/3933939.stm.
138 Merrell, C. (2004) 'Gas firm ends supply deal after staff threats', *The Times*, 1 December.
139 Cox, S. and Vadon, R. (2004) 'How animal rights took on the world', BBC News online, available at http://news.bbc.co.uk/1/hi/magazine/4020235.stm.
140 (2004) 'Primate research plans axed', BBC News online, available at http://news.bbc.co.uk/1/hi/business/3933939.stm, 30 July.
141 Police source.
142 Police source.
143 Police source.
144 (2000) 'Labour pension fund sells animal research lab shares', *The Daily Telegraph*, 30 January. Also confirmed by police source.
145 See (2001) 'Straw attacks "cowardly" banks', *The Times*, 13 March.
146 (2001) 'Drugs-test chief is clubbed by masked gang', *The Times*, 24 February.
147 (2001) 'New police squad for animal rights extremists', *The Times*, 27 April.
148 Police source.
149 Police source.
150 (2001) 'Straw to curb animal activists with union laws', *The Times*, 18 January.
151 Ibid. See also www.homeoffice.gov.uk/n_story.asp?item_id=1046.
152 'I no longer count death threats', BBC News online, available at http://news.bbc.co.uk/1/hi/uk/3939211.stm.
153 One report has suggested that activists are raising £500,000 a year in donations from the public, with some of it used for 'direct action'. (See Fielding, N. (2004) 'Fears as animal rights funds soar', *The Sunday Times*, 14 November.)
154 Walker, C. (2002) *Blackstone's Guide to the Anti-Terrorism Legislation*, Oxford: Oxford University Press.
155 As intimated by Clive Walker in 2002 (n. 154, p. 40).
156 Travis, A. (2004) 'New legal powers to trap animal rights militants', *Education Guardian*, available at http://education.guardian.co.uk/higher/research/story/0,9865,1270691,00.html.
157 ALF guidelines, quoted in Monaghan (n. 122, p. 112).
158 Home Office document (2004) *Animal Rights – Human Rights: Protecting People from Animal Rights Extremists*, July, available at www.homeoffice.gov.uk/docs3/humanrights.pdf.
159 Travis, A. (2006) 'New legal powers to trap animal rights militants', *Education Guardian* (n. 156).
160 Prime Minister Tony Blair, www.number-10.gov.uk/output/Page6596.asp.
161 'University wins animal rights bid', BBC News online, available at http://news.bbc.co.uk/1/hi/england/oxfordshire/3997835.stm.
162 Ibid.
163 Woolcock, N. (2004) 'Village demands exclusion zone to keep animal rights terrorists at bay', *The Times*, 1 December.
164 Police source.
165 Prime Minister Tony Blair (n. 160). See also Home Office document (2004) *Animal Rights – Human Rights: Protecting People from Animal Rights Extremists*, July (n. 158).
166 See, for example, 'Animal welfare laws toughened', available at http://news.bbc.co.uk/1/hi/uk_politics/4034739.stm.
167 (2002) 'Reduce animal testing, Lords urge', BBC News online, 24 July, available at http://news.bbc.co.uk/1/hi/uk_politics/2148065.stm.

168   The establishment of the national centre was a recommendation made by the former House of Lords Committee on Animals in Scientific Procedures in its report of 24 July 2002, available at www.publications.parliament.uk/pa/ld/ldanimal.htm.
169   Police source.
170   Police source.
171   Police source.
172   (2004) 'Animal rights activists hit training camp to sharpen up battle plans', *Guardian Unlimited*, available at www.guardian.co.uk/animalrights/story/0,11917,1297859,00. html.
173   Cox, S. and Vadon, R. (2004) 'How animal rights took on the world', BBC News online, available at http://news.bbc.co.uk/1/hi/magazine/4020235.stm.
174   Home Office document (2004) *Animal Welfare – Human Rights: Protecting People from Animal Rights Extremists*, July (n. 158).
175   See (2006) 'Sea change in level of attacks by animal extremists', 26 July, ABPI online, available at www.abpi.org.uk/press/press_releases_06/060726.asp.
176   Police source.
177   (2004) 'Animal rights activists hit training camp to sharpen up battle plans', *Guardian Unlimited*, available at www.guardian.co.uk/animalrights/story/0,11917,1297859,00. html. See also Nugent, H. (2001) 'Animal fanatics give lessons in death', *The Times*, 6 September.

Part III

UK efforts to enhance preparedness since 9/11

6 National governance structures to manage the response to terrorist threats and attacks

A cross-national comparative analysis with special reference to the UK 'lead department' response structure and UK counter-terrorism strategy

Frank Gregory

Introduction

In the UK, the very proper public debates on the governance capacity[1] to respond to terrorism post-9/11 has often been polarised around arguments for and against the UK variable 'lead department' model versus the US centralised Department of Homeland Security (DHS) established after 9/11. Any engagement with this debate has to reflect that terrorism only forms part of a spectrum of 'contingencies' covering what Sir David Omand has called '... a predicted future threat or hazard and a materialised risk now'.[2] Or as the 2004 EU Constitution Treaty put it: the threats to society from natural or manmade disasters or a terrorist attack.[3] However, the polarisation of the debate on the optimum homeland security system is mistaken on five grounds. First, the UK system is actually a more complex mixed model of centralised and decentralised systems. Second, the debate tends to neglect consideration of the comparable systems in other EU States. If comparison is made within the EU and the Commonwealth, then it will be found that whilst most other EU states have a response system which is similar to that in the UK there are signs of more centralised direction, on a smaller scale, in both Canada and The Netherlands. Third, account needs to be taken of the inherent problems in the establishment and construction of the DHS in the USA. Fourth, other than in an extreme form of catastrophic terrorism, all response systems are ultimately dependent upon the efficient functioning of some form of localised response capacity, a point recognised by both Sir David Omand, the UK's first Security and Intelligence Coordinator, in his observation that '... it is certainly the case that the overwhelming likelihood is that the challenges that local responders will be called upon to face are the everyday hazards of modern life, not terrorism' and by the

Secretary of the US DHS, Mr Michael Chertoff who referred to security as being '... built upon a network of systems that span all levels of government and the private sector'.[4] Sir David's comments are well borne out by the UK Emergency Planning College's listings of major incidents (air, rail, sea, pollution, severe weather, hazardous materials (HAZMATS), fire, terrorism and others), globally. In the period from 1990 to summer 2004 the UK experienced 262 major incidents of which only 3.8 per cent were due to terrorism plus one further which was a siege/hijack incident.[5] Lastly, the USA actually considered more than one model and its final choice is in fact an amalgamation of two models. Carter identifies four models that were considered in the USA: command and control (as proposed by the Clinton administration), the lead agency approach, establishing a homeland security department and creating the post of White House coordinator or 'czar' which was tried for a short while.[6]

In fact the Bush administration merged the last two by the upgrading of Governor Ridge's coordinator position to that of the first head or Secretary of the new DHS. Moreover, this decision was not as simple as it may appear, Szylcowicz refers to '... the Bush administration's reluctant decision to yield to outside pressures and create a Department of Homeland Security ...'.[7] As will be shown later both Canada and The Netherlands have also moved towards more centralised control structures, in the case of The Netherlands, belatedly, following domestic evidence of Muslim extremists' activities and in the case of Canada in a more evolutionary manner.[8] This chapter will commence with an outline of the UK homeland security system, provide some comparative analysis with the USA, other EU countries and Commonwealth countries and conclude with a critical review of the 'lead department' approach.

The UK counter-terrorism and civil contingencies system

In this section, the British system will be considered in descending hierarchical order from the Cabinet downwards. At the apex of the structure are the main coordinating committees which provide the specialised frameworks for the discharge of government responsibility for tackling terrorism: DOP (IT), which is a Cabinet Committee, chaired by the Prime Minister with the Home Secretary as Deputy Chair. This oversees the work of: DOP (IT) (PSR), which is chaired by the Home Secretary and coordinates policy on protect and prepare strategy. Lastly, the Civil Contingencies Committee, which is also chaired by the Home Secretary and is tasked with ensuring essential supplies and services.

This top level structure is supported by the Defence and Overseas Secretariat within which is located the Civil Contingencies Secretariat (CCS). The principle objectives of the CCS are[9] horizon scanning and overseeing the departmental responses to the threat assessments produced by the Joint Terrorism Analysis Centre (JTAC), in this context, the CCS '... is responsible for developing and maintaining the Planning Assumptions that underpin the UK Resilience Capabilities Programme',[10] policy development, ensuring that those responsible for crisis management and operational matters properly discharge their duties and promulgating doctrine, development of key skills and issue awareness through the Emergency Planning College.

The actual response to any civil contingency/emergency can be divided into two stages:

1   Anticipation, prevention and planning. Here, a lead government department (LGD) would have responsibility supported by DOP (IT) committees, CCS and regional and local structures.
2   Response and recovery. Again, an LGD would have principle responsibility, supported by the Civil Contingencies Committee, with the Home Secretary in the Chair, the CCS and regional and local structures. If the contingency/ emergency is caused by terrorism, then both the lead department role, and of course the lead coordination role, will fall to the Home Office.

In the UK model, the aim is to bring to bear on any contingency or emergency the best available expertise in the shortest possible time. For example, in the case of the Foot and Mouth Disease epidemic, the lead department was the ministry of agriculture. However, a weakness of this system is that the scale and nature of a particular contingency/emergency may overwhelm a lead department, which is why reforms such as the establishment of the CCS were instituted even before the events of 9/1.[11] It has been argued that the establishment of CCS builds on the UK tradition of inter-departmental coordination via the Cabinet Office.[12] However, 'coordination' is a contested term within academic analyses of governance. As Professor Stoker pointed out,[13] any reliance on a 'coordination' approach to management requires careful consideration of: structural questions, system questions (for example, information flows), staff sharing via cross-posting and developing a shared culture. He also drew attention to the key question concerning what is being coordinated. Is it policy, implementation or outcomes or all three?

A good example of the reflective development of a lead department's capabilities is provided by the Department for Transport (DfT). In its area of responsibility, the DfT '... is the security regulator and as such provides support in relation to counter measures for the full range of terrorist and other threats to the transport industries'.[14] Because of this role, the DfT instituted in 1990, with the impetus of Lockerbie, a post of Chief Inspector of Security; this post was expanded in remit in October 1991 to that of Director and Coordinator of Transport Security. It became known as TRANSEC and had a rapid initial expansion of staff from 13 in 1990 to 117 in 1993 and has grown further since that time. Another example of this Department's response evolution occurred in February 2003 when the DfT gained responsibility for the security regulatory role on London Underground. This role was introduced in order to bring legal force to security measures for the Underground and to provide a better focus for communications between the parties in London Underground and its security.

As has been said earlier, the Home Office is the lead department for the government's overall response to the threat from terrorism within the UK. Included in this role is the Home Office's responsibility to provide a focal point with respect to the specific threat from CBRN terrorism. Although, in a typically British manner, the appointment of Sir David Omand, at Permanent Secretary level, as the first Security and Intelligence Coordinator and accounting officer for the Single Intelligence Account has also led to Sir David, from outside the Home Office, taking '... a leading role in developing the integrated national counter-terrorism strategy'.[15] Moreover the Cabinet Secretary, Sir Andrew Turnbull, specifically referred to the post of Security and Intelligence Coordinator as additionally filling '... a gap around what Americans call "homeland Security"'.[16] Sir David was succeeded, in 2005, by Mr Bill Jeffrey, formerly Director-General of the Home Office's Immigration and Nationality Department. In the context of Mr Jeffrey's responsibilities, the Intelligence and Security Committee demonstrated how the post covered 'homeland security' in a comprehensive bureaucratic role with the post-holder being, *inter alia*, chair of the Permanent Secretaries' Committee on the Intelligence Services, chair of the Official committee to deliver CONTEST the UK's five-year counter-terrorism strategy, Deputy Chair of the Civil Contingencies Committee and Chair of the Official Committee on Security.[17]

Although, notwithstanding the key role of the Security and Intelligence Coordinator, as the actual terrorism 'lead department', the Home Office itself does seem a little uncertain about the ministerial handling of the 'terrorism portfolio' within the Department. The Home Secretary obviously has it as a priority area, among many. At the junior minister level, not long after Home Office Minister Beverley Hughes responded to a parliamentary question, in late 2003, about why she held three demanding portfolios, immigration, asylum and terrorism by saying she provided '... in-depth support and scrutiny'.[18] Beverley Hughes was later forced to resign because of failures to tackle an identified immigration scam. Interestingly, these portfolios were separated out for her successor, Hazel Blears, who had a more focused portfolio comprising crime reduction, policing, community safety and terrorism. Even so, these areas of responsibility are very considerable in terms of their policy area coverage. There has, so far, been resistance to the idea of a 'terrorism minister', although it may be questioned as to whether even the necessary bureaucratic focus on terrorism, within the Home Office, is really ideally established by the location of the terrorism expertise within the very broad 'Crime Reduction and Community Safety Group'. Obviously all of these arrangements are rather far removed from the apparent simplicity of the US DHS, with its single Secretary in charge with the mission statement 'We will lead the unified national effort to secure America'.[19] Although criticisms of the DHS response to Hurricane Katrina has led to major questions being raised concerning its actual competency.

The government recognises that major cross-departmental emergencies need to be more centrally managed through the DOP (IT) and COBR structures. In this context, it is pertinent to note the comment of a former member of the CCS that '... what we have found since 11 September is that the plans for one particular department may well be sound, but the problem is that they are not synchronised with other departments'.[20] The government's own caveat with regard to the lead department response principle, involving a single lead department, is that it is most '... appropriate to smaller, more local emergencies'.[21]. Moreover it may well be the case where a department has multiple key responsibilities, as does the Home Office, areas of relative issue neglect may occur. For example, the Home Office accepted that in regard to its important CBRN responsibilities, especially over research '... a clear lead had not been established'.[22] A similar point arose concerning the need to improve the coordination, across departments, of counter-terrorism research. In its 2003 Report on *The Scientific Response to Terrorism* the House of Commons Select Committee on Science and Technology suggested that the government consider the establishment of a dedicated Centre for Homeland Defence. In its response to the Committee the government conceded that such a centre '... could have some advantages ...'.[23] However, in the government's view such an innovation would have two disadvantages: first, the lead time necessary for its establishment and, second, that it would necessarily draw away scarce skilled resources from where they were already in high demand. The government made a similar response in reply to a recommendation in the Royal Society's report, *Making the UK Safer: Detecting and Decontaminating Chemical and Biological Agents.*[24] In this report, the Royal Society advocated the establishment of a dedicated centre for Home Defence. In a reply, Home Office Counter-Terrorism Minister, Hazel Blears, said 'The Government already has a crosscutting resilience programme to continue improving the coordination of civil counter-terrorism research. I believe this adds more value than a stand alone centre for home defence'. In the specific case of CBRN the government also pointed out that the CBRN Resilience Programme, established in 2001, was '... overseen by a Home Office led cross-government Programme Board'.[25] This was described by Home Office Minister Hazel Blears as operating a '... "virtual centre" approach'.[26]

However, the government does not have a consistent line with regard to over-arching centralised bodies. They have been established post-9/11, at least at subordinate levels, where the government and/or senior officials feel it is necessary as evidenced by the establishment of JTAC, the Health Protection Agency (HPA), the National Security Advisory Centre (NSAC*), the Government Decontamination Service and two 'smaller police services', the Police International Counter Terrorism Unit (PICTU) and the police National Counter-Terrorism Security Office (NaCTSO).

With regard to the actual operation of the 'lead department' principle in respect of counter-terrorism it can better be understood by reference to how the government classifies emergencies, other than 'local emergencies'.[27] The classification uses three levels to reflect degrees of emergency. Level 3 is a 'catastrophic emergency', such as a 9/11 scale of terrorist attack. This would be run by the Cabinet Office Briefing Rooms (COBR) with considerable Prime Ministerial involvement as well as the Home Secretary playing a key role and with the Cabinet Office chairing preparatory meetings of officials. Level 2 is a 'serious emergency' and a major terrorist attack, like the London incidents of 7 and 21 July and 2005, would come

---

* As of February 2006, The NSAC and NISCC have been merged to form the Centre for the Protection of National Infrastructure (CPNI).

into this category. At this level COBR would still lead the central government response but the 'lead department', here obviously the Home Office, would normally chair the meetings of officials. Lastly, at Level 1 comes a 'significant emergency'; a single terrorist incident would come under this level. In a terrorist incident, at this level, COBR is unlikely to be involved and the Home Office's role would probably be more in support of a locally directed response. In the cases of actual or suspected terrorist incidents the specific response procedures are set out in the national Counter-Terrorist Contingency Manual.

A more debateable point in the UK structure is the role and value of the regional tier of response which the present government has highlighted in the Civil Contingencies Act 2004.[28] Part 2 of the Act details the actual emergency powers that are proposed and includes a new regional element in contingency management in subsection 24. This subsection allows for the appointment of an emergency coordinator for Wales and Scotland and for a regional nominated coordinator for each English and Welsh region. This innovation reflects the importance that the government attaches to the relatively new regional government tier. Under the latest published arrangements, March 2005, it will be up to COBR and/or the lead department to determine whether to convene the appropriate regional resilience tier.[29] If the nature of a terrorist incident requires liaison between COBR and a local Strategic Coordination Group the Government Liaison Officer will be a senior Home Office official supported by a multi-disciplinary team.[30]

However, some questions have been raised about the 'value added' of the regional level in contingency management. Partly this is because the regional offices' roles are limited to planning facilitation, support and aiding linkages to central government. Additionally, there is concern that the government's regional boundaries do not always reflect actual working or even infrastructure linkages. For example, Deputy Chief Constable Alan Goldsmith of the Lincolnshire Police pointed out, in Oral Evidence to the Joint Committee on the Civil Contingencies Bill, that in the East Midlands Region there were no linkages between Lincolnshire and Northhamptonshire.[31] Although Sir David Omand has suggested that there has been a serious effort to develop a regional structure in the counter-terrorism/ civil contingencies context. He told MPs that 'As a result of hard work over the last few years we now have a set of boundaries for the various services, including the Armed Forces, which are coterminous so that police areas do now nest within government regions and the military structure now fits alongside that. Compared to the situation that existed a few years ago it is now much simpler'.[32] Indeed there is evidence of the strengthening of the regional level with the development of Security Service regional offices and police forces looking at the notion 'brigading' certain capabilities as a virtual regional pool. Any moves to further amalgamate police forces might also produce more of a regional structure to the police; however, the proposed police force mergers were all postponed, by the Home Office, in July 2006 without a date set for re-visiting the issue.[33] This chapter will next consider the 'homeland security' systems in the USA and other EU states and then return to a further consideration of the UK's position on the basis of the comparative study.

The United States response system

In the USA, one of the most visible features of that country's response to 9/11 has been the creation of the DHS. As of 2004, a total of 180,000 people in 22 agencies were employed by the DHS, a figure which represented about one out of 12 federal[34] civilian employees. The majority of those employed by the DHS are in the categories of 'watchers' or 'investigators' of various categories. The total number of federal government employees has risen since 9/11 by circa 4.5 per cent and circa 4 per cent of that rise is accounted for the 96,266 employees hired by the Transportation Security Administration (TSA).[35] Not surprisingly, this major bureaucratic innovation has attracted much interest and comment. In the UK, the DHS has often been considered by parliamentarians and other commentators as an alternative response model to that of the UK, as described earlier. Although it should be noted that the DHS still, like UK lead departments, has to work with other powerful bureaucracies such as the Treasury Department, Department of Defence and the Transportation Department.

However, the creation of this new department has been designated by the US Government Accountability Office (GAO) as '... high risk ...' response in terms of the problems of '... implementation and transformation ...' with regard to its missions and constituent agencies.[36] In essence, the DHS is a large umbrella department, formed by the inclusion of previously separate federal agencies. For example, the new Bureau of Customs and Border Protection (BCBP) was formed from the Inspections component of the US Customs Service, the Border Patrol and Inspections component of the Immigration and Nationality Service and the Animal and Plant Health Inspection Service (APHIS) of the department of Agriculture. As the DHS has drawn its employees from a variety of different agencies it is this diversity of components that has caused concern to the GAO. In Testimony to Congress, the GAO has justified its warning of a high risk in the creation of the DHS on three grounds: the size of the undertaking, the individual, unresolved challenges that were facing agencies brought into DHS, which still have to be tackled. For example, there remains the extensive fleet modernisation requirement of the US Coast Guard and because with DHS's all-embracing remit, any failures would expose the nation to serious danger. The GAO concluded that '... not since the creation of the DoD more than 50 years ago has the Government sought integration and transformation of this magnitude'.[37] Although it must be recognised that giving the DHS a proper departmental budgetary status does overcome the inherent weaknesses of a mere homeland security 'czar' (Carter quotes a Washington saying on federal 'czars' – 'The barons ignore them and eventually the peasants kill them'[38]) as was the initial status of Governor Ridge.

One issue that is common to both the UK and the USA is the question of how to sensitively and to positive effect, involve citizens in homeland security. An important matter when Dory has shown, first, that with regard to Cold War US Civil Defence, '... the vast majority of the US population did little or nothing, responding to civil defense with a mixture of indifference, fear, anger, and occasional support' and, second, that 'A recent study [USA, 2003] revealed that, if directed to do so, 90 percent of respondents nationwide would not comply with a directive to evacuate immediately'.[39] Moreover, Dory further points out that the key DHS 'pillars' which could support a civil security programme: the ready terrorism preparedness campaign, the Citizen's Corps initiative, the Emergency Alert System (EAS) and the Strategic National Stockpiles (SNS) are '... currently managed by different parts of DHS and the Centers for Disease Control and Prevention (CDC) with little vision of how they interrelate from the public's perspective'.[40] Indeed, the GAO has also been generally critical of the decentralised information sharing system within the DHS sphere.

DHS Secretary Chertoff has recognised some of these concerns by carrying out what he called a 'Second Stage Review', the first stage obviously was the establishment of the DHS. This Review's conclusions are now being acted upon in bureaucratic goal terms that are familiar in the UK's own current approach to counter-terrorism and civil contingencies. The Review has emphasised prioritisation based upon risk analysis, urgency in making improvements, effective stewardship of public resources and having a clear national strategy to clarify the roles and responsibilities of all levels of government and the private sector.[41] The organisational changes, prompted by the Review, may be seen as the natural development of central management structures necessary to manage effectively a very disparate bureaucratic conglomerate. Thus Secretary Chertoff has established: a central policy staff under a Deputy Secretary, better management of intelligence flows from the 10 intelligence generating parts of DHS through a strengthened division under the assistant secretary for Information Analysis, who is designated the DHS Chief Intelligence Officer, and brought all preparedness efforts in a Preparedness division under an Under Secretary (Preparedness) in order to better support the Federal Emergency Management Agency (FEMA). Therefore the DHS is not a static comparator model but rather an evolving structure and it remained largely untested until Hurricane Katrina struck Louisiana, Mississippi and Alabama on 29 August 2005. The overall US response, including that of the DHS, has been severely criticised. The criticism has been accepted by President Bush. On the DHS's performance, Clark Kent Ervi, the former DHS Inspector-General, is reported as commenting that responding to disasters was 'what the department was supposed to be all about. ...[and]... It raises serious questions about whether the Government would be prepared if this were a terrorist attack. It's a devastating indictment of the department's performance'.[42]

On the basis of such concerns and revisions, it is necessary to examine very carefully proposals for comparable centralised structures in other countries' responses. For example, there is consideration, in the UK, of the creation of a new unified border control service, which might bring together the police, ports and airports units, the entry controls division of HM Revenue and Customs and the entry controls division of the Immigration and Nationality Department. Each of those parts of any proposed UK unified border service would also have a number of current unresolved problems to tackle.[43]

Response systems in other EU member states[44]

France

The French system is very similar to the British one, in that the Home Office equivalent ministry, the Ministry of the Interior, has the central internal coordinating role and manages the national rescue services, supported, as required, by other ministries such as Defence and Health. Similarly, France has its equivalent to the UK top Cabinet Committees in the Council for National Security, chaired by the Prime Minister with the Ministers of the Interior, Justice, Defence, Foreign Affairs and Finance. It evaluates threats to France and can make changes in anti-terrorism policy and policy instruments. Local responses are coordinated by a powerful group of officials, the Prefects. There is no British civil service equivalent to the Prefects, except where emergency legislation might establish the posts of Regional Commissioner. At Cabinet level, there is a similar coordinating committee structure – CILAT. Within the Ministry of the Interior, an important police and military coordination function is provided by a special coordination unit – UCLAT. The French equivalent to the UK's COBR is provided by the inter-ministerial crisis management centre (COGIC) and the joint operations centre of the Defence Ministry (COIA). The French only made limited civil and military response changes post-9/11 partly because, in the military case, restructuring to more flexible forces had been underway since 1996. In the civil side case, whilst President Chirac did appoint an ex-prefect a 'terrorist supremo' [Philippe Massoni] this could not alter the fact that UCLAT remained responsible through the Interior Minister to the Prime Minister and not the President.[45]

Germany

As a federal state, the primary location of response will be within the sixteen Länder, and the Federal Government complements their resources in terms of police (BGS), fire protection, health, welfare and NBC protection. At the federal level, there are similar coordinating bodies to those found in the UK, principally the Federal Security Council and the Security Commission. Like Britain, Germany also relies heavily on private sector–public sector cooperation. In Germany many private organisations are recognised by the state as significant contributors to major incident management, for example, the Deutsches Rote Kreuz.

The Netherlands

This country also had, until January 2005, a similar response structure to the UK and, if anything, had an even looser coordinating framework. A RAND Europe Report of 2002 commented, on the pre-2005 period, that 'There is not one centralised specific responsibility and authority for combating terrorism in the Netherlands'.[46] The Ministry of Justice is the lead counter-terrorism ministry and the Ministry of the Interior has the lead responsibility for managing disasters not caused by criminal activity or terrorism. However, at the central government level, the Netherlands does have comparable coordinating bodies to those found in the UK. At the top, there is a Ministerial Steering Group supported at senior civil servant level by an Inter-Departmental Commission. In addition, ministerial Task Forces have been set up to look at particular problems such as the NBC threat and health protection. Also, the Netherlands has taken similar steps to improve its intelligence coordination to that represented in the UK by the establishment of JTAC. The Dutch system provides an 'evaluation triangle' which links AVID (Civilian Intelligence Service) to the Ministries of Justice and Interior together with advisory inputs from the Ministries of Defence and Foreign Affairs and also from 'scenarios' provided by the Council of Police Chiefs (RHC). This evaluation triangle is also assisted by a Technical Evaluation Committee. The Netherlands also, like the UK, recognises the key roles to be played by 'first' or 'local' responders.

The Netherlands system has, however, now changed quite significantly following growing awareness of radicalised elements within the Dutch Muslim communities, and high-profile incidents such as the murder of Theo van Gogh. As a step towards better centralised management of internal security, not, of course, of civil contingencies overall, the Dutch Government appointed, in April 2004, a National Counter-Terrorism Coordinator, the NCTb. The NCTb and his staff (drawn from the Ministries of the Interior and Justice) have been coordinating, since becoming operational in January 2005, the work of the relevant sections of the Ministries of the Interior and Justice, the intelligence agencies and the immigration and nationality service. In total, the work of approximately 20 organisations has to be coordinated in the counter-terrorism field. One of the NCTb's tasks is to develop a single national and internationally aligned counter-terrorism framework.[47] In so doing the NCTb has articulated a similar counter-terrorism strategy to the UK 'Contest' strategy: 'prevention' of radicalisation, 'repression' or averting attacks, 'preparedness' (security measures) and 'response and preparedness' or crisis management. An important difference between the new Dutch system and that in the UK is that the NCTb holds the responsibility for civil aviation security whereas in the UK the responsibility is held by the DfT's TRANSEC. Professor Monica den Boer sees the NCTb as very much providing a central commanding authority because the Minister of Justice can order other ministers to comply with the requirements set by the NCTb.[48] Thus the NCTb is, potentially, in a stronger position than the UK's Security and Intelligence Coordinator.

The response system in comparable Commonwealth countries[49]

Here the picture is a little different from the EU examples. New Zealand, certainly on what it calls 'civil defence', looks more towards the US model. New Zealand enacted a new Civil Defence Management Act in 2002 and has appointed a Director of Civil Defence Emergency Management (CDEM) who advises the

Ministry of Civil Defence and Emergency Management. The Director CDEM is also responsible for the National CDEM Plan and its technical standards and guidelines. Canada's system seemed to lie somewhere between the UK and New Zealand in having an office of Critical Infrastructure Protection and Emergency Preparedness (OCIPEP) and a designated Minister responsible for Emergency Preparedness with contingency planning still being primarily the responsibility of each Federal Ministry, as is the case in the UK. However, since 2003 Canada appears to have been moving towards its own version of a DHS. In 2004 legislation was introduced to establish a Department of Public Safety and Emergency Preparedness. The Department is charged with delivering the policy known as Public Safety and Emergency Preparedness Canada (PSEPC) which is defined as covering threats to personal safety from: natural disasters, criminal activities and terrorism. The responsibilities combine the core activities of the Solicitor-General's Department, the Office of Critical Infrastructure and Emergency Preparedness and the National Crime Prevention Portfolio. Thus the Department's remit covers most of the work of the UK Home Office plus wider civil contingencies responsibilities. The policy portfolio covers a total of 52,000+ employees and has a budget of $4.9 billion. The RCMP, the Canadian Security and Intelligence Services (CSIS), the Canadian Border Services Agency (CBSA), the Correctional Service of Canada (CSC) and the National Parole Board (NPB) all report to the new Department.[50]

In summary, therefore, it can be suggested that the UK's 'homeland security' system is, certainly in terms of its EU counterparts, quite comparable and that, indeed, the US new model does not have any parallel in the EU area although Canada now seems to have a version of DHS. However, that does not mean the UK's 'lead department' model necessarily addresses, fully, all the range of problems in the domestic management of the spectrum of 'contingencies' of which terrorism is seen as the current major challenge. The new stress on a real central executive authority in the counter-terrorism area in the Netherlands may be something the UK needs to further reflect upon.

The 'lead department' debate revisited

The Cabinet Office Minister, Mr Alexander, responded robustly to questions, in the context of the Civil Contingencies Bill, about whether the government should have actually provided for a UK Department of Homeland Security by re-emphasising the Home Secretary's primary responsibility for the safety and security of the population, the action coordinating role of the Cabinet Office, CCS, and the value of relying upon the expertise of particular 'lead departments', as required by particular emergencies. However, opinion outside government is still divided over adequacy of those arrangements. The House of Commons Defence Select Committee reflected on these issues in 2002 in its hearings and report on 'Defence and Security in the UK'.[51] Its conclusions seemed to propose an organisational change that went towards a US DHS/FEMA format but not quite as far. In essence, the Defence Committee recommended, first, that the

CCS should be in effect upgraded from a 'secretariat', which the Committee felt '… conjures up images of *Yes Minister* …',[52] to a renamed Emergency Planning Agency or Centre with '… adequate resources and authority to carry out its terms of reference'.[53] Second, in terms of civil contingencies leadership, the Defence Committee was not convinced that the Home Secretary '… given his many other responsibilities, is best placed to deliver it[leadership].[54] The Committee recommended that another Cabinet Minister be specifically charged with that task, leaving the Home Secretary, quite properly with the terrorism lead. The Committee cited the precedent of placing the President of the Council in charge of the millennium bug preparations. The government rejected these proposals although it did accept that CCS could do more to raise its profile and role and underlined the Committee's view that the appointment of Sir David Omand as Security and Intelligence Coordinator and Permanent Secretary, Cabinet Office, should help '… to reinvigorate the central government machinery for co-ordinating and directing national security and consequence management functions'.[55] Moreover it was stressed by the Home Secretary that Security and Intelligence Coordinator's remit is very comprehensive covering '… the whole range of counter-terrorism, including the preventive elements of security intelligence plus the international elements'.[56] The government's case for leaving the Home Secretary with both civil contingencies and counter-terrorism responsibility rested, as stated earlier, upon the Home Secretary's '… responsibility for the security of the citizens of the UK' and his ability to call upon the '… collective support of Ministers from all Departments'.[57] One Home Secretary quantified his counter-terrorism role to Parliament by stating that he would '… normally spend about 20% of … [his] … time on a regular basis on resilience and counter-terrorism because the two go hand in hand'.[58] Moreover this counter-terrorism lead role for the Home Secretary was '… reinforced by … experience in the fuel crisis where it was important to establish that there was somebody who could pull the security and policing elements together without engaging in prolonged discussions with those who did not have responsibility for those areas'.[59]

In another example, the 2003 Report of the Commons' Science and Technology Select Committee, whilst accepting that the UK did not need an actual Department for Homeland Security, did '… recommend the creation of a Centre for Home Defence as a Government agency' under the Home Office.[60] This was because the Committee did not feel that the Home Office, as the 'lead' counter-terrorist department had sufficient oversight expertise to direct efforts to counter potential CBRN terrorist threats. Whilst the Joint Committee on the Bill was unable to comment on this proposal in its Report it did put forward its own strong recommendation that a Civil Contingencies Agency should be set up, reporting to the Home Office and Parliament, to provide a source of contingency management expertise and to audit the outcomes of the contingency planning required in the Bill.

It was not until March 2004 that the government, through the Cabinet Office, set out clearly and in public, its understandings about the parameters within which the LGD would operate in response to emergencies/civil contingencies.[61] This document on 'Guidance and Best Practice' is rightly prefaced by the recognition that: 'Most emergencies in the United Kingdom are handled at a local level and by the emergency services and by the appropriate local authority or authorities, with no direct involvement by Central Government'.[62] The guidance then sets out the definition of and criteria for the involvement of an LGD:

- Generally an LGD is '... that [Department] which has day-to-day policy oversight of the sector(s) of the national infrastructure that may be affected in an emergency'.
- An LGD will be involved '... where the scale or complexity of an incident is such that some degree of Central Government co-ordination or support becomes necessary'.

The involvement system reflects three levels of emergency (catastrophic, serious and significant) discussed earlier. As a consequence of LGD responsibilities an LGD must '... incorporate an assurance on contingency planning within the annual assurance and risk control mechanism for Central Government corporate governance. In each LGD senior officials need to be assured by some form of validation that '... the contingency planning process and plan content' are '... adequate ...'. However, the term 'adequate' is not defined in the document. Although it is later stated in relation to 'adequacy' that validation is achieved by both regular exercises and 'benchmarking' against local, national and international experience and specialist/scientific knowledge. Moreover, it is recognised that '... some Departments' planning activities (such as the Department of Trade and Industry, DfT and Department for Food and Rural Affairs) are largely dependent upon the environment, relationships and management structures existing mainly in the private sector. Other departments, the Home Office and Department of Health, by contrast '... have large public sector planning constituencies ...'.

At the basic task level all LGDs must:

- Carry out Risk Assessments for those risks which the LGD '... should be capable of responding ...' and identified in the LGD's Resilience Capability Framework (RCF).
- Based on the Risk Assessments the LGD must carry out Capability Assessments to assess '... the current state of preparedness of the component capabilities required ... to fulfil its remit'.

As part of its response LGDs' Planning and Crisis Management Teams are required to:

- Maintain '... well resourced and resilient Emergency Operations/ Co-ordination Centres'.
- Provide good, regular training and motivation.
- Have a sound public information and media strategy.

The terms used above, 'good' and 'sound' are, like 'adequacy', used previously, not defined in the document.

Thus far the guidance document has mainly dealt with organisational, managerial and audit issues. However, Chapter 1 on 'Core Responsibilities' does at least identify the 'how' issues by reference to:

- Building up an LGD's resilience to shocks and its capacity to lead the response.
- An LGD identifying the capabilities available to local responders and responses at each level on contingency management.
- An LGD '... planning for and leading negotiations with the Treasury for any necessary additional funds ...'

Chapter 2 'The Centre and Assurance' also identifies the need for all LGDs to be able to deliver their responses to a common level of competence. This is expressed in the format that:

- The Home Secretary with the Permanent Secretary at the Cabinet Office, in his role as the Security and Intelligence Coordinator wishes to see all Government Departments with lead responsibilities for contingency planning working to common guidance and best practice in planning for responses to emergencies.

The LGDs' ability to deliver this response to common standards will, in the case of terrorism, now also be aided by the promulgation in April 2004 of the latest version of the government's counter-terrorism strategy (Contest) against which departments can clarify their specific roles in the strategy in relation to the '4Ps' against the government's strategic aim for the next five years of '... reducing the risk from terrorism ... so that our people can go about their business freely and with confidence'.[63] Moreover, departments should be aided, to some extent, in delivering their obligations by the 2004 Spending Review announcement of rising allocations to meet requirements of the response to global terrorism in the defence, civil contingencies and anti-terrorism sections of various Votes.[64] However, an important budgetary issue arises within the 'lead' department approach where departments may hesitate to accept a particular 'lead' role as that role's costs would need to be funded from within their budget. This problem arose, initially, in respect of 'ownership' of 'lead' department responsibilities for any counter-terrorism aspects of controlling the availability of ammonium nitrate.[65] At the local level the Audit Commission has developed a very detailed, 27-page, *Self Assessment Tool: Local Authority Emergency Planning and Business Continuity.*[66] This can also be used at the local level for an authority to measure its performance and resource needs against its role in the '4Ps' strategy.

Indeed, the Chancellor was quite 'bullish', on the point of enhanced budgetary allocations, in his speech to the British Council on 8 July 2004 when he said, on the 2004 Spending Review, '... I will make available those resources needed to strengthen security at home and take action to counter the terrorist threat at home and abroad. Those who wish to cut in real terms the budget even for security will need to answer to the British people. We will spend what it takes on security to safeguard the British people'.[67] Did he mean that? Surely other Ministers can argue that the range of government promises on service delivery to the British people must also have a 'spend what it takes tag'? Indeed, the Treasury's own draft document *Managing risks to the public: appraisal guidance* certainly does not offer a 'spend what it takes approach. A budgetary measure in potential fatalities avoided is provided by the DfT's valuation range for preventing road traffic accidents which is £1 million to £1.5 million/fatality potentially avoided.[68] At least an enhanced budget for security, as defined by the Chancellor, plus the 'Contest' strategy gives a little more power to departments, which can cite 'Contest' strategy objectives, as set out below, to be fulfilled in the detailed arguments with the Treasury.

From a speech by Home Office Permanent Secretary for Counter-Terrorism, Leigh Lewis, to the May 2004 Police Federation Conference and Home Office briefing papers of February 2005, the basic elements of the '4Ps' 'Contest' strategy, first articulated in only a classified version in early 2003 can be amplified and also now better understood through the July 2006 published review of 'Contest'.[69] As Mr Lewis said, this strategy is '... led by the Home Secretary' and it is based on the 'four Ps':

- Prevention – addressing underlying causes of terrorism here and overseas: that means, among other things, ensuring that our Muslim citizens enjoy the full protection of the law and are able to participate to the full in British society.
- Pursuit – using intelligence effectively to disrupt and apprehend the terrorists – the UK has increased joint working and intelligence sharing between governments and law enforcement agencies across the world. The government aims here: to make the UK borders more secure; to make identity theft harder and to curb terrorist access to financial sources.
- Protection – ensuring reasonable security precautions, including those needed to meet a CBRN threat, are in place ranging from physical measures at airports to establishing Counter-terrorism Security Advisers (CTSAs) in each police force.
- Preparedness – making sure that the UK has the people and resources in place to effectively respond to the consequences of a terrorist attack.

Moreover, the government recognises the need to, as Mr Lewis put it, '... broaden the range of stakeholders involved in counter-terrorism planning'. The government's planning horizon for its strategy looks towards an initial five-year threat horizon from Islamist extremist terrorists attempting mass effect attacks against UK targets at home and abroad.[70] The strategy, recognising that there is no 100 per cent protection for terrorism, emphasises 'risk management' and the prioritising of protection at home and of UK interests overseas. Mr Lewis' speech identified some of the major tasks that remain to be accomplished. He referred to, *inter alia*, ensuring that emergency services have adequate and inter-operable communications equipment for all scenarios, that the ambulance service can provide casualty assessments as early as possible and that the UK must not underestimate the personnel numbers and equipment scales required for major emergencies. Looking back over the period since 9/11 it can be suggested that the UK's response has several identifiable stages:

*   Responding to immediate pressures '... such as the need to improve protective security at embassies and the need for the emergency services to enhance their search and rescue capabilities ... [and enabling] departments to reprioritise resources to respond to the threat from international terrorism ...'.[71]
*   Medium- to longer-term planning – including the Civil Contingencies Act and the development of government's counter-terrorism 'Contest' Strategy (the 4Ps) – to '... focus on the work needed across all departments ...'.
*   Funding the necessary expenditure on items such as the Fire Service's New Dimension project, enhanced CBRN capability for the police, HM Revenue and Customs improving port security, Foreign and Commonwealth Office Embassy protection work and Home Office enhanced border controls work – this provision was set out in a more defined manner in the Treasury's 2004 Spending Review which shows what is called 'Counter-Terrorism/ Resilience spending since 2001–2' and the expenditure rise from £923 million in 2001–2 to £2,115 billion in 2007–0.[72] However, even by 2007–8 this allocation only represents 0.65 per cent of total departmental spending although that does not take account of possible local authority allocations after reviewing their civil contingencies needs and allocations within other departmental budgets, for example, the Home Office and the Ministry of Defence.

Issues arising

The government has put considerable effort into organisational systems, managerial lines and quality assurance procedures in relation to contingency planning and response. However, the appearance is still more of a 'skeleton' response structure than a fully 'fleshed-out' response, especially as key terms like 'adequacy', 'good' and 'sound' have yet to be defined. Sir David Omand recognised some of these difficulties in respect of the Critical National Infrastructure (CNI) (telecoms, energy, finance, health, water and sewerage, food, transport, emergency services, government services and the hazard and public safety management sectors) where '... the commercial competitive pressures that now control most of our [CNI] that in years gone by would have been in public sector control or at least subject to influence in the public interest'.[73] However, notwithstanding '... the potential scale of the threat from international terrorism' the UK still seeks to resolve some of the issues surrounding sectors of the CNI 'delivering' on counter-terrorism response by '... a dialogue with the industry or sector bodies, companies or trade associations to discuss vulnerabilities'.[74] Is 'dialogue' rather than 'requirement' an approach that matches the stated urgency of the problem? In the USA the GAO has pointed to similar issues relating to the implementation of agreed cargo security measures in respect of the absence of '… deadlines and performance targets … federal decision-makers cannot know whether resources are being deployed as effectively and efficiently as possible'.[75] There are also a number of other linked reasons for advancing this contention.

1   Ministers long hesitated over implementing quite simple public awareness measures, for example, the long promised pamphlet for all households which only came out in Summer 2004, and the release of a suicide bomber precautions CD -rom for businesses is still awaited notwithstanding the July 2005 London bombing incidents.

2   Equipment procurement processes are at 'peacetime' timescales rather than 'War on Terrorism' timescales.

3   Identified necessary expenditure can be 'deferred' for a variety of reasons; for example, costs of the Iraq conflict, assumptions about project costs being met from assumed savings from an organisation's restructuring.

4   The problem of securing enduring commitments at the public/private interface; for example, the funding of 16 specialist CBRN-trained British Transport Police (BTP) officers – Extended Duration Breathing Apparatus (EDBA) trained in BTP terms. This unit initially had only one-year funding from DfT on the presumption by the DfT that it was the rail industry's responsibility.[76] However, the 2004–5 Annual Report of the BTP seems to suggest that these issues were eventually addressed as it refers to DfT funding enhancements to BTPs counter-terrorist capability with 26 officers now having been EDBA trained.[77]

5   The most significant recent example is the long delay in providing interagency communications on the underground in London which was a weakness first recognised in 1988 after the King's Cross Fire and described by the current Metropolitan Police Commissioner as 'a significant problem for London'. The problem is supposed to be rectified by the end of 2007.[78]

6   A similar case has been identified by Lord Carlile in both his 2002–3 and 2004 Reviews of the Terrorism Act 2000 where he commented 'In summary the adequacy of accommodation for police at seaports and airports remains a matter of less than universal contentment – I am still concerned enough to report that continuing attention needs to be given to the accommodation issue to ensure that the working of the act is in no way compromised'.[79] However, he still recommended a negotiated solution to this matter but notes that powers of compliance on port managers exist under para. 14(1)(b) of Schedule 7.[80]

7   The true extent of capabilities needed cannot really be known until an assessment of the implementation requirements of the Civil Contingencies Act are known through measures such as the National Capabilities Survey which was launched in February 2006.

Moreover there will be no new specific auditing body, established in respect of the Civil Contingencies Act. The government has said that monitoring will be through existing bodies and that although the Government does have more specific monitoring powers available under the Act, it has stated that it '... does not intend to use these monitoring powers on a regular basis to assess responders performance'.[81]

Although there is an annual cycle of emergency response exercises:

(a) There is *no* overall annual assessment of the exercise outcomes for an overall awareness of 'gaps' and best practice.

(b) Even some of the individual exercise assessments that have been done have been criticised as avoiding a robust approach to shortcomings.

(c) The anti- terrorist chemical attack exercise at the Birmingham NEC (18 July 2004) apparently still required lessons to be learnt, in terms of speed of response and cordon controls, and it was reported that 'Talks to decide whether a multi-agency team designed specifically to deal with major incidents would improve response time are expected to be held with the Home Office ...'.[82]

The major incident of the Glasgow factory explosion, in May 2004, provided good illustrations of some of the above contentions. Government has budgeted £132 million for tackling the aftermath of a major terrorist attack and this programme will eventually include 15 high-tech urban search and rescue vehicles deployed nationwide. However, the current state of this procurement was that the nearest available vehicle of this group was in London and had to be sent to Glasgow from London with its attendant team. While the Commissioner for fire and emergency planning in London, Mr Ken Knight rightly said: 'This highlights the value of the national arrangements ...'[83] the issue that arises is, quite simply, what would be the impact in London of a major terrorist incident happening in parallel with the Glasgow incident if the London based equipment and team were in Glasgow? Some amelioration of this sort of problem may come from Cabinet Office Parliamentary Secretary Jim Murphy's reference, in 2005, to the national exercise series, '... which for the first time, co-ordinates the range of exercises which have always taken place across government'. This process he expects will ensure that lessons are learnt but he does not say how this will occur.[84]

Finally, the issue of the effectiveness of the counter-terrorism LGD role of the Home Office is clearly back on the political agenda. First, it was rumoured, amongst Labour Party reflections on a post-Blair government structure, that the Home Office could well be split into two departments: one for Homeland Security and one for Immigration and Asylum responsibilities.[85] These proposals seemed to reflect recent evidence of role overload in the case of the resignation of the Home Office Minister Beverley Hughes who had both immigration and terrorism portfolios. Her successors have had the terrorism responsibility separated out from the immigration and asylum responsibilities, as noted earlier. Second, Home Secretary John Reid, who replaced Charles Clarke in 2006 after the foreign offenders' deportation debacle, has very clearly expressed his dissatisfaction with the functional efficiency of the Home Office. Indeed, the Home Office now admits, as this research project found by anecdote through interviews, that 'Policy and operations across immigration, crime, counter-terrorism and offender management have too often been fragmented. All this needs to change'.[86]

Can the government have an adequate counter-terrorism strategy without a 'homeland security' department?

The answer to that question is a cautious 'yes' because many policy areas are, as the government's preferred term puts it, 'cross-cutting' across several departments areas of responsibility. Moreover, as in the UK we don't have the equivalent of US 'Presidential Decision' documents, we are used to looking for 'strategy' in legislation and white papers. In the case of the global terrorism problem definitions and responses are set out in legislative terms primarily in: the Terrorism Act 2000, the Anti-crime Terrorism and Security Act 2001, the Civil Contingencies Act 2004, the Terrorism Acts 2005 and 2006. In non-legislative terms, problem definitions and responses are to be found in the 'Contest' strategy, CCS documents and on the Home Office 'terrorism', 'ukresilience' and MI5 websites. Of particular note is the public review of the 'Contest' strategy published in July 2006, especially welcome as the last such public review was in 2002.

Although there may be a tension between the role of the Cabinet Office CCS and the position of the Security and Intelligence Coordinator on the one hand and the Home Office as the 'lead department' on terrorism. Certainly comments encountered in this research have suggested that, outside the 'higher circles' of Whitehall (at super–TIDO level), some confusion exists about lines of demarcation. Moreover, Professor Clive Walker has argued that as *Dealing with Disaster* (Cabinet Office, 2003, paras 1.8, 1.12) describes the CCS's role as 'pivotal' then '… the rule of law surely demands legal authority and clarity, especially at a time of crisis'.[87]

Both the domestic and overseas elements of the counter-terrorism strategy are significant long-term commitments in terms of personnel and resources. The example of the funding assumptions made regarding BTP CBRN trained officers, referred to earlier, illustrates the problem that although under our 'lead department' system the Home Secretary does, indeed, 'lead' on counter-terrorism, he does *not* actually control the delivery of much of the response. A key part of this project's research focuses on this question of the *adequacy* of resource provision, in the widest sense, in the domestic management of terrorism in the UK. In that context there is an important statement in the Chapter 6 'Global Security and Prosperity' of the Treasury's 2004 Spending Review, namely that 'The Home Secretary will agree with ministers across departments what resources they will allocate from their 2004 Spending Review settlements to deliver the UK's Counter-terrorism Strategy before they finalise their budgets'.[88] This is a potentially important step in the Home Office exercising a real leadership role on counter-terrorism. Although of course the Home Secretary is not in authority over other ministries.

In discussions around the Whitehall counter-terrorism community there does seem to be a view that some other structure for general directional oversight could be a valuable enhancement for the current arrangements.[89] It is difficult to express this in organisation terms. However, the key participating elements are clearly the Home Office, Defence Ministry, the new Department for Communities and Local Government (DCLG) – which replaced the ODPM's portfolio in this area in 2006 – and the Cabinet Office CCS. It is also possible to specify the key functions as being:

- Annual audit of activities focusing on implementation of agreed objectives.
- Enforcement of implementation of agreed targets where necessary.
- Capacity for lateral thinking in addition to carrying out established tasks.

A step in this direction might be to set up an inter-departmental group with the counter-terrorism remit as set out above, certainly for the next few years as the Civil Contingencies Act 2004 is being implemented, under a Home Office Minister of State with *only* a terrorism/homeland security portfolio. Just after he left the post of Security and Intelligence Coordinator, Sir David Omand contended that '… the UK system has advantages, and the Government was right to resist calls for the creation of a super-Department of Homeland Security that would have taken key security and resilience tasks away from the portfolios of line Departments and centralized them and risked the distraction of bureaucratic institution building'. However, he added the very important rider, regarding the delivery, by departments, of resilience and counter-terrorism objectives that '… there must be unambiguous political accountability for the result, through the Home Secretary and ultimately the Prime Minister'.[90] But where will the public see evidence of this unambiguous political accountability? This is a particularly relevant question because the Prime Minister's Delivery Unit *Capability Review of the Home Office* illustrates not only a range of poor performance indicators for the Home Office, it also draws our attention to the fact that, of the seven Public Service Agreement targets set for the Home Office in the 2004 Spending Review, not one actually mentions terrorism.[91] Given that the new Home Office reform plans have a timescale running out to 2010 it is to be hoped that the Home Office's terrorism role will be made to feature more visibly within the deliverables of those plans.

The broad conclusions of this chapter now seem to be reflected in the reports of government plans to split the Home Office by transferring some functions to a new Ministry of Justice.[92] As reported, these plans are indicating that the Home Office remit will retain responsibility for policing, immigration and nationality matters and oversight of MI5 and SOCA. Moreover, it is proposed that the Home Secretary may be better enabled to discharge the 'lead department' role in counter-terrorism by chairing a top-level committee which will meet weekly and have authority over counter-terrorism priorities. However, this reform will still need to be under-pinned by collective Cabinet agreement to deliver the resources to meet those priorities, as appropriate, wherever the specific departmental responsibility is to be found.

Notes

1 On the concept of governance as applied to the response to terrorism see Kamarck, E. (2000) *Applying 21st Century Government to the Challenge of Homeland Security*, New Ways to Manage Series, Cambridge, MA: Harvard University, Kennedy School of Government.

2 Sir David Omand, Keynote Speech to RUSI Homeland Security and Resilience Programme, 1 July 2004, available at www.ukresilience.info/contingencies/rusi.htm, accessed 6 July 2004.

3 European Convention Secretariat, Draft Treaty establishing a Constitution for Europe, Docs CONV 820/03 and CONV 725/03, Brussels: European Convention Secretariat May–June 2003.

4 Sir David Omand, Keynote Speech to RUSI Homeland Security and Resilience Programme, 1 July 2004, available at www.ukresilience.info/contingencies/rusi.htm, accessed 6 July 2004, and Chertoff, Secretary Michael (2005) *Second Stage Review Remarks,* 13 July, available at www.dhs.gov/dhspublic/display?theme=44&content=4 597vprint=true, accessed 25 August 2005.

5 Emergency Planning College, *Major Hazards Database*, available at www.epcollege. gov.uk/, accessed 20 July 2004.

6 Carter, A.B. (2001–2002) 'The architecture of government in the face of terrorism', *International Security*, 26(3), Winter, p. 10.

7 Syzylcowicz, J. (2004) 'Aviation security: promise or reality?', *Studies in Conflict and Terrorism*, 27, p. 51.

8 The information on current developments in the Netherlands draws, with permission, partly on an unpublished paper by Professor Dr Monica den Boer, Free University of Amsterdam and Director of Research at The Netherlands Police Academy given at a PICTU/Southampton University Workshop on 29 June 2005.

9 Susan Scholefield, Head of Civil Contingencies Secretariat, Cabinet Office, 'National Resilience and Central Government', Paper presented to ESRC Project Workshop, April 2003.

10 Government Reply to the Eighth Report from the House of Commons Science & Technology Select Committee, Session 2002–2003, HC 415-I, *The Scientific Response to Terrorism*, Cm. 6108, January 2004, para. 16.

11 Cabinet Office (2002) *The UK and the Campaign against International Terrorism – Progress Report*, 9 September.

12 Presentation at ESRC Project Workshop, April 2003, by Ms Susan Scholefield, CMG, Head of CCS.

13 Presentation at ESRC Project Workshop, April 2003, by Professor Gerry Stoker, University of Manchester.

14 Cm. 6108, op. cit., paras 93–5.

15 Intelligence and Security Committee (2004) *Annual Report 2003–2004*, Cm. 6240, London: The Stationery Office, June, p. 32, para. 110. Sir David was succeeded, in 2005, by Mr Bill Jeffrey, formerly with the Home Office's Immigration and Nationality Department.

16 Intelligence and Security Committee (2005) *Annual Report 2004–2005*, Cm. 6510, April, para. 11, p. 7.

17 Ibid., para. 13, p. 8.

18 House of Commons, *Hansard*, Answer by Home Office Minister Beverley Hughes, 10 December 2003, vol. 415, col. 498W.

19 See www.dhs.gov/dhspublic, as cited in Cm. 6240, op. cit., p. 6, para. 5.

20 Ibid., para. 175.

21 Sixth Report of the House of Commons Select Committee on Defence, Session 2001–2002, *Defence and Security in the UK*, HC 518-I, para. 173.

22 Cm. 6108, op. cit., para. 23.

23 Ibid., para. 44.
24 Home Office (2004) *Government Response to Royal Society's Report: 'Making the UK Safer; Detecting and Decontaminating Chemical and Biological Agents'*, Stat 018/2004, 26 May.
25 Home Office Speech 'Terrorism – policing the unknown', by Leigh Lewis, Home Office Permanent Secretary for Counter-Terrorism, to the Police Federation Annual Conference, Bournemouth, 20 May 2004, available at www.homeoffice.gov.uk/docs3/speech_policefed.html, accessed 3 June 2004.
26 Home Office, Stat018/2004, op. cit.
27 (2005) *Central Government Arrangements for Responding to an Emergency*, 31 March, para. 5.
28 See Gregory, F. (2004) *Jane's Intelligence Review*, January.
29 *Central Government arrangements for Responding to an Emergency*, op. cit., para. 12(vi).
30 Ibid., para. 20.
31 Deputy Chief Constable Alan Goldsmith, Lincolnshire Police, Chair of the ACPO Emergency Planning Committee, Oral Evidence to the Joint Committee on the Bill, HL 184/HC 1074, 9 September 2003.
32 Oral Evidence before the Defence and Home Affairs Committees' inquiry into 'Homeland Security', HC 417-I, 2 March 2004, Q.19.
33 See ACPO, Latest News, Ref: 58/06, 12 July 2006, Police Merger Programme.
34 Department of Homeland Security, 'Budget in brief fiscal year 2005', Secretary's Message.
35 TRAC (2003) *Special TRAC Study of DHS Payroll*, Syracuse, NY and Washington, DC: TRAC Reports Inc., available at www.trac.syr.edu, accessed 25 August.
36 Testimony before the Subcommittee on Infrastructure and Border Security, Select Committee on Homeland Security, House of Representatives – 'Homeland Security – Challenges Facing the Department of Homeland Security in Balancing its Border Security and Trade Facilitation Missions' – Statement of Richard M. Stone, Director Homeland Security and Justice Issues, General Accounting Office, GAO-03-902T, 16 June 2003.
37 Ibid.
38 Carter, op. cit., p. 12.
39 Dory, A.J. (2003–2004) 'American civil security: the U.S. public and homeland security', *The Washington Quarterly*, 27(1), Winter, pp. 39 and 41.
40 Ibid., p. 48.
41 Secretary Chertoff, July 2005, op. cit.
42 As quoted in (2005) *The Times*, 5 September.
43 See the discussions of UK border control services in Gregory, F. (1991) 'Border controls and border controllers – a case study of the British police response', *Public Policy and Administration*, 6(1); House of Commons Select Committee on Home Affairs, Session 1999–2000, *Border Controls – Special Report*, HC 375, and Session 1999–2000, *Border Controls – Report and Evidence*, HC 163-I and II, and see also (2003) 'Police chiefs want 5,000 frontier guards', *The Times*, 29 September.
44 This section is partly based on the 'Quick scan of post 9/11 national counter terrorist policy making and implementation in selected European countries', RAND-Europe Paper No. MR-1950 (RAND-Europe: 2002), see also Eleventh Report of the House of Commons Public Accounts Committee, Session 2002–2003, *NHS Emergency Planning*, HC 545, March 2003, Appendix 1, Supplementary Memo from the Department of Health and the national reports to the UN Counter Terrorism Committee as required by UNSCR 1373, available at www.un.org/Docs/sc/committees/1373.
45 Gregory, S. (2003) 'France and the War on Terrorism', *Terrorism and Political Violence*, 15(1), Spring, pp. 140–1, and see also Shapiro, J. and Suzan, B. (2003) 'The French experience of counter-terrorism', *Survival*, 45(1), Spring, pp. 67–98.

46 RAND – Europe Paper No. MR-1950, op. cit.

47 'Start of recruitment campaign for staff of the national coordinator for combating terrorism', NCTb, available at www.justitie.nl/english/press/press_releases/archive_ 2004/301204coord..., accessed 17 August 2005.

48 den Boer, op. cit.

49 The details on Canada and New Zealand are partly taken from Clive Walker, *Joint Committee on the Draft Civil Contingencies Bill – Draft Report on Constitutional Issues*, School of Law, University of Leeds, September 2003.

50 See (2005) 'An Interview with Anne McLellan', *Emergency Management Canada*, 1(2), Summer, pp. 32–3, and 'Legislation to establish Department of Public Safety and Emergency Preparedness Introduced', October 2004, Bill C-6, available at www. psepc.gc.ca/publications/news/20041008-2_e.asp, accessed 17 August 2005.

51 House of Commons Defence Committee, Sixth Report of Session 2001–2002 (2002) *Defence and Security in the UK*, vol. 1, HC 518-I, London: The Stationery Office, July, and see also House of Commons Defence Committee, Seventh Special Report of Session 2001–2002 (2002) *Defence and Security in the UK: Government Response*, HC 1230, London: The Stationery Office, October.

52 HC 518-I, op. cit., para. 181.

53 Ibid.

54 Ibid., para. 182.

55 HC 1203, op. cit., paras 35–6.

56 Oral Evidence before the Defence and Home Affairs Committees' inquiry into 'Homeland Security', HC 417-I, 2 March 2004, Q.11.

57 Ibid., para 34.

58 Oral Evidence before the Defence and Home Affairs Committees inquiry into 'Homeland Security', HC 417-I, 2 March 2004, Q.9.

59 Ibid., Q.15.

60 Eighth Report of the Commons Science and Technology Select Committee (2003) *The Scientific Response to Terrorism*, HC 415-I, Session 2002–2003, London: The Stationery Office, November, p. 77, and see also HL 184/HC 1074, op. cit., para. 256.

61 Cabinet Office, CCS (2004) *The Lead Government Department and its Role – Guidance and Best Practice*, March, and see also HM Government (2005) *Emergency Preparedness* (Pt 1 Guidance re Civil Contingencies Act 2004), and HM Government (2005) *Emergency Response and Recovery – Non Statutory Guidance to Complement Preparedness*.

62 Ibid.

63 Sir David Omand, Keynote Speech to RUSI Homeland Security and Resilience Programme, 1 July 2004, available at www.ukresilience.info/contingencies/rusi.htm, accessed 6 July 2004.

64 HM Treasury, 2004 Spending Review (2004) *Stability, Security and Opportunities for All: Investing in Britain's Long Term Future*, New Public Spending Plans 2005–2008, July, Chapter 1.

65 Interview, Home Office, 22 July 2004.

66 Audit Commission, *Self Assessment Tool: Local Authority Emergency Planning and Business Continuity*, available at www.ukresilience.info/whats_new.htm, accessed 2 July 2004.

67 (2004) *Guardian*, 8 July, available at www.politics.guardian.co.uk/labour/story/ 0,9061,1256548,00.html, accessed 8 July 2004.

68 See HM Treasury (2004) *Draft for Consultation. Managing Risks to the Public: Appraisal Guidance*, October, para. 5.25, p. 25.

69 Home Office, Speech 'Terrorism – policing the unknown', by Leigh Lewis, 20 May 2004, available at www.homeoffice.gov.uk/docs3/speech_policefed.html, accessed 3 June 2004, and see also (2004) *The Sunday Times*, 30 May, and HM Government

(2006) *Countering International Terrorism: The United Kingdom's Strategy*, Cm. 6888, London: The Stationery Office, July.

70 Information on five-year planning horizon from briefing by Sir David Omand to St Andrews team, 2004.

71 HM Treasury, 2004 Spending Review, Chapter 6 'Global Security and Prosperity', paras 6.9–6.10, available at www.ukresilience.info/whats_new.htm, accessed 19 July 2004.

72 Ibid.

73 Omand, Keynote Speech to RUSI, 1 July 2004, op. cit.

74 Ibid.

75 GAO Report, 2002, as cited in Szylcowicz, op. cit., p. 56.

76 Twelfth Report House of Commons Transport Committee, Session 2003–2004 (2004) *British Transport Police*, HC 488, London: The Stationery Office, June, Ev.5, Q.33, answer by BTP Chief Constable, Mr Ian Johnston.

77 British Transport Police (2005) *Annual Report 2004/05*, p. 3.

78 London Assembly (2006) *Report of the 7 July Review Committee*, June, paras 2.24–2.27.

79 Lord Carlile of Berriew (2004) *Report on the Operation in 2002 and 2003 of the Terrorism Act 2000*, April, p. 18, para. 96, and (2005) *Report on the Operation in 2004 of the Terrorism Act 2000*, April, para. 119, p. 32.

80 The dialogue solution was also referred to by Mr Robert Whalley of the Home Office in Oral Evidence, HC 417-I, Q.52.

81 HM Government (2005) *Emergency Preparedness* (Pt. 1 Guidance re Civil Contingencies Act 2004), p. 147.

82 (2004) *The Times*, 19 July.

83 (2004) *The Times*, 13 May.

84 Mr Jim Murphy, MP, Cabinet Office Parliamentary Secretary (2005) *Taking the Lead in Civil Contingencies*, 27 September, available at www.ukresilience.info/murphy. htm, accessed 10 October 2005.

85 (2004) *The Sunday Times*, 16 May.

86 Home Office (2006) *From Improvement to Transformation – An Action Plan to reform the Home Office so it meets public expectations and delivers its core purpose of protecting the public*, July, Chapter 4, para. 18.

87 Walker (2003), op. cit.

88 HM Treasury, 2004 Spending Review, Chapter 6, op. cit., Box 6.1.

89 Interviews with the Home Office, 22 July 2004.

90 Omand, Sir David (2005) 'Developing National Resilience', *RUSI Journal*, 150(4), August, p. 15.

91 Civil Service Capability Reviews, Cabinet Secretary (2006) *Capability Review of the Home Office*, July, p. 9.

92 (2007), *The Times*, 29 March.

7 Reducing the chemical, biological, radiological and nuclear weapons threat

The role of counter-proliferation, arms control and disarmament

John Simpson and Jez Littlewood

The philosopher Edmund Burke wrote that 'no passion, so effectually robs the mind of all its powers of acting and reasoning as fear'.[1] The threat of WMD terrorism – or more accurately CBRN terrorism – appears to have had a similar effect on certain governments in relation to the role of arms control and counter-proliferation within a broader framework of managing terrorist attacks. As a concrete example, in 2002 representatives from the US Government Accountability Office (GAO) were discussing the role of the Biological Weapons Convention 1972 (BWC) in the UK. Efforts to strengthen the BWC through an additional legally binding agreement (the BWC Protocol) collapsed in August 2001. GAO officials indicated that strengthening the BWC was not important in the new terrorist-led threat environment because 'the Protocol would not have stopped the anthrax attacks in the US'. Those non-governmental experts discussing the issue with GAO officials avoided the obvious retort that US domestic law had also failed to stop the anthrax attacks but no one was thinking about abandoning domestic measures to reduce the risk of terrorism. The example illustrates a short-sightedness in some circles about the full range of measures required to address the CBRN threat.

There is a tendency to think of arms control and disarmament as a state-to-state issue. Dual-use issues – whereby the equipment, materials, and knowledge can be used for legitimate peaceful purposes or for hostile purposes – inherent to CBRN technologies and knowledge, however, mean that disarmament and counter-proliferation mechanisms have to embrace both military and civil authorities, state and non-state actors. This has long been evident in all areas of WMD controls. All these actors have a role in preventing access to CBRN weapons and the technologies required to develop and produce them. In the US National Strategy to Combat Terrorism it was noted that, '[a] central goal must be to prevent terrorists from acquiring or manufacturing the WMD that would enable them to act on their worst ambitions'.[2] The nexus of terrorism and CBRN is therefore one part of the proliferation problem. To counter it, as the US WMD Strategy outlines, '[w]e must enhance traditional measures – diplomacy, arms control, multilateral agreements, threat reduction assistance, and export controls

– that seek to dissuade or impede proliferant states and terrorist networks, as well as to slow and make more costly their access to sensitive technologies, material, and expertise'.[3]

Arms control, disarmament, non-proliferation and counter-proliferation all have some role to play in countering the terrorist threat from CBRN. Such agreements play a normative and a legal role. The WMD regimes – Treaty on the Non-Proliferation of Nuclear Weapons 1968 (NPT), Chemical Weapons Convention 1993 (CWC), and BWC – and their supplemental governance elements related to technologies and knowledge, all contribute to that objective. As noted in chapter two, sophisticated WMD remains, at present, beyond the actual capabilities of non-state actors of the ilk of Al-Qaeda. Through a number of arms control and counter-proliferation mechanisms the WMD regimes have not only contributed to that fact, but also will continue to play a principal role in preventing future acquisition of such weapons.

In this chapter we outline the role of traditional mechanisms of disarmament, arms control, and non-proliferation in the management of terrorist attacks, examine how more recent developments such as CTR and counter-proliferation contribute in preventing access by non-state actors to CBRN, and consider the role of the weapons and technology governance architectures in the broader domestic management of terrorist attacks.

Disarmament, arms control, and non-proliferation

In April 2006 the United Nations Secretary-General launched his report *Uniting against terrorism: recommendations for a global counter-terrorism strategy*.[4] The proposed strategy noted that several terrorist groups had expressed their determination to acquire and use WMD, and the Secretary-General stated that denying such groups access to the materials to develop such weapons 'must be a serious part of the international effort'.[5] That approach – non-proliferation and legal proscriptions on certain types of weapons – has been central to the disarmament, arms control, and non-proliferation agenda of the last half-decade.

In simple terms the global approach to WMD is no chemical weapons, no biological weapons, and no new nuclear weapons. There are, of course, states which refuse to be bound by the global WMD treaties and regimes, states that either violate them or are in non-compliance with their international obligations assumed under the agreements to which they are party, and legal loopholes and diplomatic nuances in the broader anti-WMD architecture. Yet, taken as a whole the global regime against WMD is comprehensive in its scope: the use of chemical and biological weapons is prohibited by the 1925 Geneva Protocol; chemical and biological disarmament are mandated by two international conventions. And, only five states should possess nuclear weapons and those five should be moving towards disarmament. Many observers consider the Geneva Protocol part of customary international law, binding on all states whether or not they are party to it.[6] The BWC prohibits the development, production, stockpiling, acquisition, and transfer of biological and toxin weapons. The CWC prohibits the development, production, stockpiling, and use of chemical weapons (including toxins) as well as their acquisition and transfer. And, the NPT identifies five states – China, France, Soviet Union (now Russian Federation), the UK and the USA – as the recognised nuclear weapons states. All other states parties to the NPT are legally bound to remain non-nuclear weapons states. Today, only India, Israel, and Pakistan are not states parties to the NPT, although the status of the Democratic People's Republic of Korea (DPRK) *vis-à-vis* the NPT is under question. Together with other agreements such as the Convention on the Physical Protection of Nuclear Material 1980 and the International Convention on the Suppression of Acts of Nuclear Terrorism 2005, the scope of the legal prohibitions against WMD is broad.

As with many states the visible component of UK actions to address WMD threats has until recently been focused on the three treaty-based WMD regimes, together with national, regional, and like-minded action in fora such as the United Nations, the export control regimes, CTR, and, more recently, the Proliferation Security Initiative.

The WMD treaties were developed to address states acquiring WMD. While there is strong evidence that meetings of states parties under these treaties and conventions were aware of the role such agreements had in contributing to the prevention of terrorist access to such weapons, long before the terrorists and WMD were linked in the public mind, their main focus was, and remains, states. Transnational terrorist groups operating from a safe haven within a state, such as Al-Qaeda pre-9/11, were not a focus of these regimes. All international agreements require, however, implementation at the national level. One example of how the WMD treaties and conventions are relevant to the threat if implemented correctly is the example of Aum Shinrikyo in Japan. As detailed in preceding chapters, Aum Shinrikyo developed an extensive interest in chemical and biological weapons in the early 1990s prior to the attack on the Tokyo subway in 1995. To the surprise of many, until Aum actually used these weapons against the Japanese population it was not breaching Japanese law: while the use of chemical weapons to attempt to poison and kill people was illegal (that is, attempted murder), the development, production, and stockpiling of chemical weapons by an individual, cult, or other sub-national organisation within Japan was not illegal under Japanese legislation until the mid-1990s. The example is illustrative because the CWC did not enter into force until 1997 – after the Aum attacks – but that agreement did require implementing legislation to prohibit and prevent nationals of each state party undertaking acts which were prohibited by the CWC. Nevertheless, the role of arms control in countering terrorism was illustrated by the debate in Washington over ratification of the CWC. With reference to the sarin attacks in Tokyo, the Director of the US Arms Control and Disarmament Agency, John Holum, noted that enactment of the CWC – and the implementation legislation required – would 'make it much easier for law enforcement officials to investigate and punish chemical terrorists early, before chemical weapons are used'.[7] The US Biological Weapons Anti-Terrorism Act of 1989 – which implements the BWC in US domestic law – had already proven its worth in this area, with the pursuit and indictment of members of the

Minnesota Patriot's Council relating to the production of ricin.[8] Such oversights may seem naive in the current climate but were – and in some cases still are – common prior to 9/11.

For radiological materials there was no international legal regime to handle these matters, as the existing nuclear-weapon states saw no cost-effective military role for radiological devices, and thus regarded weapons which were of little military utility as being undesirable to all actors. Such undesirability, it was assumed would reduce the need for international controls. To bolster the international prohibitions against WMD the UK, and other states, have become involved in three sets of initiatives to address these deficiencies: enhanced national and international controls over CBRN materials and equipment; activity in the United Nations; and work in other international organisations.

CBRN controls

The main area of activity has involved strengthening or establishing arrangements whereby trade and transfers of WMD and CBRN materials between and within states may be controlled, licensed, and monitored more effectively. Export controls have a long history: controlling the export of chemicals was considered in the development of the 1925 Geneva Protocol, but shelved because of the difficulties of distinguishing between legitimate peaceful uses in the dye industry and for weapons development, production, and use of chemical weapons. Although this early effort at coordinated international control failed in the 1920s, export controls were developed and maintained on a national basis. In fact, until 2002 and the passage of the Export Control Act 2002 UK export controls remained rooted in the Export and Customs (Powers) Act 1939.

Export controls on nuclear weapons-related materials, equipment, technology, and knowledge were in place from the end of the Second World War in some form or other. The creation of the Zangger Committee and Nuclear Suppliers Group (NSG) formalised these controls for nuclear weapons. Export controls were, and are, implicit in the NPT, BWC, and post-Cold War an explicit import–export mechanism exists within the CWC. In addition, the Coordinating Committee for Multilateral Export Controls (CoCom) and its successor, the Wassenaar Arrangement of 1996, all contributed to export controls being normalised as part of Western non-proliferation and security policy. Historically, however, export controls were tainted politically as being discriminatory to non-Western States because of the perception that such controls were a cartel on dual use technologies with applications to nuclear, chemical, and biological weapons. The new security environment has altered perceptions about export controls.

The principal development since 9/11 is the mandatory internalisation of controls to encompass accountability on the materials, equipment, technology, and knowledge for the development of CBRN weapons. United Nations Security Council Resolution 1540 (2004) reaffirms that the proliferation of nuclear, chemical, and biological weapons 'constitutes a threat to international peace and security' and the Council affirmed 'its resolve to take appropriate and effective actions against any threat to international peace and security caused by the proliferation of nuclear, chemical and biological weapons and their means of delivery', noting the grave concern that non-state actors 'may acquire, develop, traffic in or use nuclear, chemical and biological weapons and their means of delivery' and that illicit trafficking networks pose an additional and new dimension to the threat posed by proliferation. The resolution required all states to refrain from providing 'any form of support' to non-state actors attempting to develop, acquire, manufacture, possess, transport, transfer or use nuclear, chemical, and biological weapons, and their means of delivery.[9] Under the resolution all states were required to ensure effective national controls were in place to prevent non-state actors from undertaking such activities.

With the passing of Security Council Resolution 1540 (2004) under Chapter VII of the United Nations Charter internal controls on CBRN materials and export controls became a requirement for all member states of the United Nations. Such controls are no longer an option in the non-proliferation toolbox; they are a requirement, for every state, and for all nuclear, chemical, biological weapons and their means of delivery. That a United Nations Security Council resolution under Chapter VII was required to mandate such controls in 2004 spoke volumes about the actual implementation of international and national obligations to control the proliferation of WMD. In essence, Security Council Resolution 1540 (2004) internalised and internationalised CBRN controls. The internationalisation of export controls will, in due course, remove many of the political difficulties that surrounded the existence and application of export controls under the NSG, the Australia Group, and under the Missile Technology Control Regime. In addition, with the emergence of the Proliferation Security Initiative (PSI), the growth in CTR activities under the Global Partnership and activity by the World Customs Organization (WCO), the post-9/11 environment has had a major impact on import-export controls for CBRN materials and technology.

Resolution 1540 (2004) builds on the export controls in place for states of concern. These arrangements have traditionally been between like-minded states or 'coalitions of the willing' and have been interpreted as exclusive, rather than inclusive, in their nature. The nuclear 'coalition of the willing' is the NSG, first convened in London in 1974 to harmonise the then nuclear-supplying states export control lists and activities.[10] The UK has consistently supported this body, and a similar entity for chemical and biological precursors, the Australia Group.[11] In the chemical and biological weapons area, the principal export control coordination body, the Australia Group, agreed to an initiative following the Tokyo subway attacks to ensure the control lists and the information-sharing aspect of the Australia Group's activities addressed the issues of CBW terrorism. Similar endorsements for action and tighter controls were made at the December 1995 meeting of the G7 plus Russia in Ottawa.[12] In 2004, the Group of 8 (G8) established a more comprehensive Action Plan on Non-Proliferation, although it contained no new developments *per se* and reiterated the commitment of these states to existing mechanisms and efforts against WMD proliferation.[13] A further addition to the efforts to control CBRN materials and proliferation was the development of the

PSI in 2003. This initiative was designed to enhance the ability of states to interdict clandestine shipments of WMD materials by sea, air or land.[14]

All these elements increase the potential effectiveness of existing arms control agreements and add a significant implementation focus that is also important in a counter-terrorist context.

International organisations

The United Nations, as against the WMD regimes and their linked verification agencies, has not played a significant role in the past in preventing the dissemination of WMD materials. It has provided an important normative role to counter the proliferation of WMD, but after 9/11 the UK, and others, saw it as a forum where an inclusive policy had to be pursued to combat weapons proliferation. As in the case of Resolution 1540 (2004) this entailed persuading all states to achieve minimal standards of oversight and control over WMD-related manufacturing and other activities within their borders. As with the creation of a Security Council Committee to address terrorism, Resolution 1540 (2004) created a committee to assess the measures in place to prevent proliferation to terrorists. Working through a small group of international consultants, this committee has been evaluating information provided by states on their current arrangements in these areas. Its mandate was renewed for a further two years under resolution 1673 (2006) together with a commitment to develop a work programme and assistance measures to enhance the implementation of Resolution 1540 (2004).[15]

A further development within the United Nations is the completion of the Convention outlawing nuclear terrorism, now agreed through the United Nations's General Assembly's Fifth Committee.[16] In the case of control of radioactive sources and materials, it was the IAEA which was encouraged to take ownership of this issue, and attempt to establish minimum standards of security and accountancy for them. The result was a legal convention through which it is hoped to account for all relevant radioactive sources within states, as well as establish standards for their security.

The UK is also involved with efforts by two European-based organisations to play an effective role in the campaign to prevent WMD reaching terrorist groups. One of these is NATO, the other the EU. The latter has been the most active, as well as inclusive in developing initiatives in this area. Indeed, at the same time as the balance in UK counter-proliferation policy appeared to be tilting away from strengthening the global WMD institutions towards more direct action through US-led coalitions of the willing, it has also been integrating itself more closely into EU defence and foreign policy, and thus WMD policy, from which the US was excluded.

This integration has occurred through the EU policy coordination framework. Member states are bound legally to adhere to these common positions. As one example, France and the UK could not (re)start nuclear testing without being in breach of EU law. At the end of 2003 under the Greek presidency, the EU sought to play a more independent role in WMD politics by creating its own strategy against the proliferation of WMD.[17]

The examples cited above are illustrative of the role played by arms control and counter-proliferation against terrorism with CBRN weapons. The practice of disarmament and arms control has undergone change since 9/11. Some of these developments, such as United Nations Security Council Resolution 1540 (2004) can be traced as direct consequences of 9/11. Other developments, such as the establishment of supplemental implementation arrangements in the form of export controls or their nascent enforcement arm, the PSI, have their origins in the Cold War and post-Cold War practice. The range of actions that encompass activities from disarmament through to counter-proliferation was recognised by experts following 9/11. In a United Nations symposium on terrorism in New York, Paul Wilkinson noted that adaptation of the arms control agreements such as the BWC in order to prevent the proliferation of materials in the hands of terrorists was a better policy than abandoning the arms control agreements.[18]

It is, however, easier to envisage the role played by arms control and counter-proliferation through a specific example drawn from the nuclear area. In Chapter 2 it was noted that nuclear terrorism was a low probability–high consequence event, with one assessment characterising the implications of this:[19]

> Preventing nuclear terrorism will require a comprehensive strategy: one that denies access to weapons and materials at their source, defends every route by which a weapon could be delivered, and addresses motives as well as means. … The centrepiece of a serious campaign to prevent nuclear terrorism – a strategy based on three no's (no loose nukes, no new nascent nukes, and no new nuclear weapons states) – should be denying terrorists access to weapons and their components.

The principal issue is preventing access to High-Enriched Uranium (HEU), Plutonium, and the materials required for a nuclear device. Ferguson and Potter advocated a similar approach with four steps to reduce such threats in the form of specific priorities for action based on the risk posed by particular materials and its geographic location. Potter and Ferguson suggested efforts to prevent nuclear terrorism should begin with the security of HEU through efforts in Russia, and then globally, to secure, consolidate, and eliminate HEU. Such a strategy would then turn its attention to South and Central Asia as the zone where Islamic militant groups are most active and access to nuclear materials in parts of Pakistan, Kazakhstan, and Uzbekistan poses the highest risk. Finally, such an approach would promote robust global security standards for the physical protection of nuclear material.[20] Similarly, Bunn and Bunn have argued for a multilateral initiative to make the protection and accounting of weapons-usable nuclear materials as rigorous 'as the nuclear weapons states protect and account for nuclear weapons themselves'.[21] Leaving aside the actual threat at this juncture, if a policy to counter nuclear terrorism was to be developed from nothing then it would need to contain certain essential elements.

At the international level it would be necessary to mount an effort to reduce, or limit, the number of states in possession of nuclear weapons. To bolster that, the materials and technology required to develop a nuclear weapon should be controlled as much as possible, particularly by the principal suppliers, even if it curtails the activities of civilian industry. Notwithstanding such regulatory measures, mechanisms for interdicting any illegal supply of technology would be required, and sanctions and punishments should be sought against those in breach of the legal obligations and regulations that give effect to such law. Given the dual-use nature of some materials, some kind of material accounting system to ensure legitimate uses were not covering attempts to acquire materials and technology for illegitimate purposes would be required. And, to shift beyond the legal realm, nuclear weapons, or at least their use, would themselves be subject to some kind of taboo or normative restraint.

At the national level, a state in possession of nuclear weapons would seek to ensure the security and safety of its own stockpile. The materials and equipment necessary for the manufacture and development of a nuclear weapon would be controlled, access to such materials would be limited, restrictions would be placed on the acquisition of such materials by those without legitimate requirements to use such materials, and the law applied in cases where breaches of regulations occurred.

Such an approach is recognisable: it is, in many respects, exactly the kind of disarmament, arms control, non-proliferation, and counter-proliferation system for nuclear weapons that has developed over the last 50 years.

Threat reduction

Cooperative threat reduction (CTR) was developed at the end of the Cold War following the emergence of concerns about 'loose nukes' in Russia and the New Independent States (NIS) of the former Soviet Union and the prospect of 'brain drain' from former Soviet nuclear, chemical, and biological weapons programmes. As Russia declined economically and the state of its security infrastructure became apparent, the USA became increasingly concerned that the theft or sale of WMD from Russia or the NIS would permit 'rogue states' hostile to US policy, such as the DPRK, Iran, Iraq, and Libya, to acquire WMD. Equally, as former weapons scientists and technicians became unemployed, concern about a brain drain of individuals with the expertise to overcome the complex technical problems required to weaponise nuclear devices or chemical and biological agents emerged as an important security issue.

From these concerns a US-led initiative with Russia and certain NIS states from the mid-1990s has morphed into what is now known as CTR. Since 1991 CTR has 'proven to be the most effective tool of nonproliferation policy to emerge since the end of the Cold War'.[22] The USA carried the burden of this effort throughout the 1990s, but following 9/11 as concern about terrorist acquisition of CBRN increased, the US partners in the G8 decided to act in concert with each other. At the Kananaskis summit in 2002 the G8 established 'a new G8 Global Partnership against the Spread of Weapons and Materials of Mass Destruction … [to] support specific cooperation projects, initially in Russia, to address non-proliferation, disarmament, counter-terrorism and nuclear safety issues'. The Global Partnership established as its priority concerns 'the destruction of chemical weapons, the dismantlement of decommissioned nuclear submarines, the disposition of fissile materials and the employment of former weapons scientists'. The members of the Partnership committed to raise $20 billion over 10 years to implement these projects, with $10 billion coming from the USA and $10 billion coming from the other Global Partnership members.[23]

The Global Partnership and other CTR activities are not a panacea for the risks posed by insecure weapons facilities or unemployed former scientists and technicians. Yet, as the Foreign Affairs Committee of the House of Commons (UK) noted in its 2005 report, the work is of 'critical importance'.[24] In its most recent report, June 2006, the Committee noted that the work of the Global Partnership remains important to the objective of preventing insecure materials and weapons from being lost or stolen, but the slow progress on plutonium and chemical weapons destruction was a serious concern.[25] Due to various bureaucratic difficulties and the re-emergence of a stronger and more assertive Russia, the pace of developments under the Global Partnership has stalled. However, on the positive side, the Global Partnership now includes over 20 states (and the EU), indicating that support for CTR among Western states is growing even though Russia is now economically and politically more able to maintain security of its own weapons infrastructure.

The Global Partnership will continue until at least 2012 under current arrangements. In addition, similar CTR approaches have been mooted for Iraq, Libya, and possibly the DPRK and Iran in the future. While Iraq and Libya may acknowledge former weapons scientists and WMD programmes, other states are unwilling to increase transparency about their WMD activities.

Counter-proliferation

In the UK the 'counter-proliferation toolbox' encompasses all of the above aspects, that is, arms control and disarmament, multilateral agreements and treaties, export controls, and CTR. In certain cases the UK also undertakes direct action against proliferation threats. Such activities, according to the Foreign and Commonwealth Office, include interception of illegal shipments of WMD-sensitive items, defence against nuclear, biological and chemical weapons, including civil defence, and, 'as a last resort, the government does not rule out direct action, including military action in accordance with international law'.[26]

UK participation in the military interventions in both Afghanistan and Iraq was the most visible indicator of this evolving policy of neutralising terrorist and WMD threats at source. In the case of Afghanistan, the relationship between Al-Qaeda and the Taliban government suggested there was no alternative to intervention if the terrorist network was to be disrupted. Regime overthrow by force appeared to be the only effective method of resolving the problem in a definitive manner. This deployment of UK forces to contribute to the removal of the Taliban, and thus Al-Qaeda, was accepted. In contrast, using the military option in this way generated major domestic disharmony within both Parliament and the country at large in relation to Iraq. The US-led move into Iraq exposed the limitations and risks of intelligence-led policies of neutralising WMD threats at source in this way. By contrast, the case of Libya in late 2003 illustrated the ability of the UK intelligence system to play a pivotal role in such policies. It succeeded in infiltrating the A.Q. Khan network, and precipitated the UK/US-led process for neutralising Libya's WMD capabilities and eliminating the risk of it being a source of materials and technology for terrorist organisations.[27]

The lessons from the three experiences of Afghanistan, Iraq, and Libya have thus been radically different from a UK perspective, and the results contradictory. On the one hand a nascent threat in Afghanistan was ignored until it was too late (9/11). In contrast, Iraq was an intelligence failure that demonstrated the perils of using intelligence information (or the lack of it) as a basis for interventionist counter-proliferation policies.[28] Yet, on the other hand the intelligence services appear to have played the major role in securing Libyan WMD disarmament and in so doing exposing publicly the A.Q. Khan network and its potential as a source of supply for terrorists. Effective intelligence capabilities targeted on clandestine WMD proliferation networks have thus moved to the heart of UK security policy, demonstrated among other things by the expansion of the numbers of those working in these organisations since 9/11.[29]

Changing threat perceptions and intelligence-led policy-making

In the US discussions on WMD counter-proliferation strategies and terrorist threats had started in the early 1990s. It was not until after 9/11 that these issues entered the mainstream of public debate and became fully transparent to UK audiences. While the issue of dealing with Iraq's WMD capabilities remained a central theme of UK public decision-making over proliferation from 1991 onwards, it took a series of events including 9/11, the intervention in Afghanistan, and the revelations about the Pakistan-based 'commercial' nuclear-weapon procurement network of A.Q. Khan to align UK public perceptions of the new WMD threats with those already held in the USA.[30]

Perceptions of the relative importance of the different WMD threats held by officials moved towards those held in the USA at a much earlier date. Walker points to a desire to 'keep in step with Washington' as one explanation for the shift at the politico-military levels[31] though the main driver appears to have been intelligence information. UK and US intelligence services had been monitoring the activities of both Al-Qaeda and the A.Q. Khan procurement network for some time, though a comprehensive understanding of the latter's activities took years to evolve.[32]

Intelligence has thus become central to both UK anti-terrorism and anti-proliferation policies. Intelligence sharing and cooperation has been a core element of UK counter-proliferation policy, as well as an important element in its international capabilities.[33] Pakistan's negative role as a nuclear proliferator and its later positive role as a base for anti-Al-Qaeda operations was public knowledge, but the activities of A.Q. Khan remained hidden until Libya decided to disarm. If nothing else, the different positive and negative roles Pakistan has played in countering proliferation and countering terrorism illustrate that complete coherence within a complex policy environment is rare. The necessity to act at certain times requires trade-offs and compromise on other, equally important, issues. Intelligence, and actions based on the information it provides, is part of a larger multilayered approach to countering CBRN terrorism. The UK strategy of multilateral, bilateral and unilateral indirect and direct action when confronted by the new proliferation threats was a natural continuation of existing policies for officials: by contrast, those outside government had tended to focus on the more visible and accessible WMD Treaty regimes. This gap closed as more information emerged about clandestine proliferators and international terrorists networks, though the UK government 'remained deeply uneasy ... with the aggressive and unilateral approach taken by the Bush administration'.[34]

After 9/11 the terrorist proliferation threat became a central driver of Western WMD counter-proliferation policies. Even if not all states bought into the policy shift they recognised that existing ambivalence to multilateral arms control within the USA prior to 9/11 had now sharpened. The opportunity to engage the USA on the multilateral arms control and disarmament agenda was now through the lens of counter-terrorism, and terrorist interest in WMD and policy followed the new reality. When information emerged from Afghanistan that some elements of Al-Qaeda had been exploring methods of using CBRN for terrorist purposes and attempting to acquire WMD precursors and technology through clandestine A.Q. Khan-type procurement channels, there was increased emphasis on countering threats at source and via interventionist counter-proliferation policies and export controls.[35] Many observers perceived a change in the name of the relevant sections of both the Foreign and Commonwealth Office and the MoD to the Counter-Proliferation Department (CPD) and Counter-Proliferation and Arms Control Secretariat (CPACS) and being evidence of new policy approaches.[36] In reality, the name changes may have reflected more bureaucratic reasons, not least the need to increase recruitment to this area of the Foreign and Commonwealth Office.

The upshot of the changed threat environment and the dominance of terrorism as the principal security threat facing the UK is, as a result, both substantive and somewhat superficial. As reflected in the UK's international priorities of both 2003 and 2006, the threat posed by terrorism has affected UK policy-making and activities. There has not, however, been a wholesale re-ordering of priorities. Five years on from 9/11 many of the issues that demanded attention mid-2001 still require attention mid-2006: WMD proliferation; the Middle East peace process; relations between nuclear-armed India and Pakistan; the nuclear weapons programmes of the DPRK and Iran; China's rise to superpower status; and ensuring the WMD regime architecture remains equal to the emerging threats from various actors. Global chemical and biological disarmament remain UK priorities; non-proliferation of nuclear weapons remains a UK priority; and, working with a variety of allies, states and organisations in a number of ways remains the UK *modus operandi* to address these issues. Perhaps the greatest change is not in what is being done, but how objectives are being pursued. The range of actors involved in countering the threat posed by CBRN terrorism requires coherence and a policy approach beyond that traditionally cast as 'arms control' or 'non-proliferation' in the UK.

Governance and technology management

Arms control – broadly conceived to encompass the full range of activities that encompass disarmament through to counter-proliferation – has long grappled with the issues surrounding dual-use materials and equipment. Although the nature of possible CBRN terrorist threats to the UK involves a much wider and more complex set of activities than those of terrorism using conventional explosives or car and lorry bombs or pre-9/11 airline hijacking, it is erroneous to suggest that a completely new set of policies needs to be devised and implemented to manage this threat. While it is certainly true that terrorist interest in CBRN weapons raises new and different challenges to state-led proliferation of WMD, the policy responses developed over the last 50 years to prevent the proliferation of nuclear, chemical and biological weapons are, in many cases, valid in addressing newer threats.

This inevitably means working both inside and outside the UK, and utilising many of the mechanisms that already exist for addressing clandestine trading and/or state-to-state trading in materials, equipment, and technology. It involves addressing the 'enemy within' by strengthening the security and safety of materials and equipment in the UK, and access to them, and requires a regional (EU) and international dimension to addressing such threats.

Just as proliferation is a global problem it is also true that CBRN weapons and the management of terrorism are a multi-agency, cross-government, public-private, and civil-military issue. Rather than considering the management of terrorism involving CBRN weapons as either a counter-terrorist issue or a counter-proliferation issue, or considering it as an international issue or a national responsibility, the connections between all these different approaches had to be bridged to develop more effective policy responses. In short, arms control – broadly conceived – is now an issue of governance. Governance in a security context has been defined as:[37] the coordinated management and regulation of issues by multiple and separate authorities, the interventions of both public and private actors (depending upon the issue), formal and informal arrangements, in turn structured by discourse and norms, and purposefully directed toward particular policy outcomes.

Governance, it has been argued, has an important role to play in the War on Terrorism because the 'multifaceted phenomenon in which power, rules, ideas, norms, culture, regimes, and institutions feature prominently' that constituted governance (for Makinda) encompasses the wide range of actors and forms of power and influence actually required to play a role in defeating terrorism.[38] US security expert Ashton Carter has also pointed out that a successful strategy against terrorism at the national level rests with an effective governance system that cuts across all agencies of the federal government, state, local, and private sector.[39]

Makinda's approach is based on the belief that if the War on Terrorism becomes only a blunt and brutal use of force, coercion, power, and influence by the USA and its allies, then the use of these means to achieve their objectives – and security – at the expense of other norms, rules, and means of order in the international system, the latter will be undermined. Instead of enhancing the security of the world, the response may invoke less sympathy, less support, and greater antipathy to the USA and the Western world. Iraq is a case in point. In 2003 Stern argued that 'America has created – not through malevolence but through negligence – precisely the situation the Bush administration has described as a breeding ground for terrorists: a state unable to control its borders or provide for its citizens' rudimentary needs'.[40] The use of force alone is an insufficient response to terrorism, whether state-sponsored or not. Likewise, the use of force and direct intervention against WMD and CBRN threats cannot remove, or reduce, the threat to manageable proportions. Hence, a WMD governance architecture can support the War on Terrorism by being strengthened as long as the USA and others remain within the 'rules' established over the last 50 years: no chemical weapons, no biological weapons, and no nuclear proliferation. However imperfect the existing global WMD regimes may be it is evident that governments alone cannot, nationally or internationally, manage the problems and threats on their own. No government – and no state – is omnipotent. To manage WMD and CBRN threats requires a governance approach based on all actors: states; international organisations; national bodies; sub-national actors; and public, private, civil, and military sectors all playing a role.

This holds true in managing an actual attack: it is even more so when one takes the approach that the domestic management of terrorist attacks, including preventing CBRN attacks, involves a strategy aimed at deterring and preventing such an attack as part of the overall management plan.[41] The health maxim that prevention is better than cure fits neatly with the security approach which seeks to fight and combat threats outside the UK wherever possible. It is now taken as read that 'domestic management of attacks' incorporates a broad definition of the issue and is not only concerned with the mitigation of the consequences of an actual attack.

The end of the Cold War witnessed an increase in the number of multilateral and bilateral agreements intended to reduce the threat posed by WMD. These included: the Strategic Arms Reduction Treaty (START) in 1991 between the US and the then Soviet Union; the Cartegena Declaration on renunciation of WMD in Latin America (1991); the Protocol to START I that ensured Ukraine, Kazakhstan, and Belarus became non-nuclear weapons states (1992); the CWC (1993); the Agreed Framework between the US and the DPRK (1994); the NPT Review and Extension Conference decision on strengthening the review process of the NPT (1995); the South East Asia Nuclear Weapons Free Zone (1995) and the Treaty on the African Nuclear Weapons Free Zone (1995); the Wassenaar Arrangement on export controls for conventional arms and dual-use goods and technologies (1996); the Comprehensive Nuclear Test-Ban Treaty (1996); and the Model Additional Safeguards Protocol of the IAEA (1997). If these agreements represented arms control as traditionally understood, other arrangements were equally as important. This included the emergence of newer mechanisms such as CTR, action by the United Nations in the form of the United Nations Special Commission (UNSCOM) and later the United Nations Monitoring, Verification, and Inspection Commission (UNMOVIC), the Hague Code of Conduct on Ballistic Missiles, the G8 Global Partnership, and the PSI. In the eyes of many states these other mechanisms were not viewed as significant: they were viewed as discrete agreements and mechanisms intended to address specific issues. After 9/11 the changing threat resulted in these discrete mechanisms moving from the periphery to the centre of efforts to counter WMD threats. This is not to say that they replaced the WMD treaties of regimes; rather they complemented them in specific ways. As the former UK Ambassador noted in the area of biological weapons: these types of 'newer' arrangements and discrete mechanisms serve important functions that add to national and international capabilities to counter WMD.[42]

Countering WMD and CBRN threats requires a layered and integrated approach. Despite claims that countering CBRN terrorism required new approaches and the sidelining of traditional mechanisms, the approach to CBRN has been similar to the state-to-state one familiar to defence and security specialists: deterrence, detection, pre-emption, interdiction, defence, prevention, and consequence management.[43] The layered approach is central to the US National Strategy for Combating Terrorism to defeat, deny, diminish, and defend against 'terrorist organizations of global reach through the direct or indirect use of diplomatic, economic, information, law enforcement, military, financial, intelligence, and other instruments of power'.[44, 45] At more concrete level the layered strategy which uses all available tools is central to the US Joint Doctrine for Combating Weapons of Mass Destruction and emphasis on non-proliferation, counter-proliferation, and consequence management.[46] The UK, also, has a layered strategy in its previous, and recently revised, Counter-Terrorism Strategy (CONTEST). Its four principal strands – prevent, pursue, protect, and prepare – are as equally applicable to CBRN terrorism as to terrorism more generally.[47]

In simple terms, whatever label is used, such as governance, the approach is based on the management of the problem posed by terrorism at all levels with a set of policies that includes arms control and counter-proliferation, but which in fact goes much further and is outside the Foreign and Commonwealth Office, the MoD, the DTI or the Home Office. Prevention includes upholding the moral, normative, and legal prohibitions related to WMD such as the 1925 Geneva Protocol, the NPT, BWC, CWC and other Treaties. Terrorists must not only be prevented from acquiring the materials to develop a weapon in the UK, but from abroad also, underlining the necessity of export controls and enforcement of non-proliferation obligations and activities such as the PSI. The security and safety of laboratories and scientists abroad has to be supported where controls are sub-standard, as in the CTR activities under the G8 Global Partnership. And, nationally, the security of pathogens and other dangerous materials needs to be ensured, as required under the Anti-Terrorism, Crime and Security Act 2001. Hence, in the domestic management of terrorist attacks, the role of the Foreign and Commonwealth Office is important. When enforcement of international norms or treaties becomes necessary, the MoD and the armed forces play a clear role. In controlling the export of substances and materials, the DTI has the lead. Intelligence and law enforcement agencies have a role in all such aspects as well.

Clearly this is not a single policy or strategy which is wholly integrated or linear in its creation. It has grown organically, and has been pieced together in recognition of the problem. Despite the shock of 9/11, wise heads realised there was no need to reinvent the wheel to counter CBRN threats: what was required was holistic thinking and joined up government.

As Parachini noted, '[e]liminating all possibility of terrorist groups or individuals using CBRN weapons is impossible'.[48] Differentiation between conventional and CBRN terrorism at a strategic level or emphasis on a particular type of terrorism while neglecting others is potentially dangerous, resulting in '[i]nordinate attention on the comparatively unique challenges of coping with unconventional weapons [that] draws scarce resources away from the more basic but essential activities of law enforcement, intelligence, border and customs control, diplomacy, and military action'.[49] The WHO also underlined the importance of using existing systems for consequence management and emphasised the need to 'resist the temptation to create special systems for terrorism, and … instead integrate counterterrorism and preparedness programs into the existing all-hazard systems for emergency management and disaster response. … This emphasis on dual-use assistance can help ensure that capabilities created by the domestic preparedness program remain strong'.[50, 51]

Since 9/11 the UK has maintained its attachment to the international order of the WMD regimes. They have not been abandoned. Rather, integrating existing mechanisms with new approaches has been the UK approach to CBRN counter-terrorism. Others, including many of the UK's European partners have followed similar strategies.

As terrorism becomes more diffuse, amorphous, less centralised, and with more opaque command and control relationships[52] a number of factors may delay or prevent certain types of CBRN acquisition occurring. The safe havens, time, networks, freedom to operate, access to technologies, and surprise required to develop sophisticated CBRN have diminished compared to the situation pre-9/11. Efforts since 9/11 across a range of areas – proliferation, finance, state-support, etc. – do appear to have reduced the terrorist CBRN threat. All the evidence points to such an approach being the foundation of UK management policy: arms control, disarmament, and counter-proliferation remain central to the overall approach to managing and reducing the CBRN terrorist threat.

Notes

1 Burke, E. (1756) *A Philosophical Inquiry into the Origin of Our Ideas and of the Sublime and Beautiful.*
2 (2003) *US National Strategy for Combating Terrorism*, February, p. 10.
3 (2002) *US National Strategy to Combat Weapons of Mass Destruction*, December, p. 2.
4 United Nations (2006) *Uniting against Terrorism: Recommendations for a Global Counter-terrorism Strategy*, Report of the Secretary-General, United Nations General Assembly A/60/825, 27 April.
5 Ibid., para. 43, p. 9.
6 Goldblat, J. (2002) *Arms Control: A New Guide to Negotiations and Agreements*, London: SAGE Publications, p. 137.
7 (1995) 'New chronology, 25 May 1995', *Chemical Weapons Convention Bulletin*, 29, September, p. 18.
8 (1995) 'New chronology, 4 August 1995', *Chemical Weapons Convention Bulletin*, 29, September, p. 31.
9 United Nations (2004) United Nations Security Council Resolution 1540, S/Res/1540 (2004), 28 April.
10 Information on the NSG is available at www.nuclearsuppliersgroup.org/.
11 Information on the Australia Group is available at www.australiagroup.net/index_en.htm.
12 (1995) 'New chronology, 16–19 October 1995', *Chemical Weapons Convention Bulletin*, 30, December, p. 24. (1996) 'New chronology, 12 December 1995', *Chemical Weapons Convention Bulletin*, 31, March, p. 19.
13 (2004) *G8 Action Plan on Nonproliferation*, Sea Island, 9 June, available at www.g7.utoronto.ca/summit/2004seaisland/nonproliferation.html.
14 The PSI is not an 'organisation' although the US Department of State maintains a website for the PSI, www.state.gov/t/np/c10390.htm.
15 United Nations (2006) United Nations Security Council Resolution 1673, S/Res/1673 (2006), 27 April.
16 The text of the Convention is available at http://untreaty.un.org/English/Terrorism/English_18_15.pdf.
17 See, Portela, C. (2003) *The Role of the EU in the Non-Proliferation of Nuclear Weapons: The Way to Thessaloniki and Beyond*, PRIF Reports No. 65, available at www.hsfk.de/downloads/prifrep65.pdf.
18 (2001) 'News chronology, 25 October 2001', *The CBW Conventions Bulletin*, 54, December, p. 55.
19 Allison, G. (2004) 'How to stop nuclear terror', *Foreign Affairs*, 83(1), January/February, pp. 68–9.
20 Ferguson, C.D. and Potter, W.C. (undated) *Improvised Nuclear Devices and Nuclear Terrorism*, Paper No. 2, Stockholm: Weapons of Mass Destruction Commission, available at www.wmdcommission.org/.
21 Bunn, M. and Bunn, G. (undated) *Reducing the Threat of Nuclear Theft and Sabotage*, IAEA-SM-367/4/08, p. 15, available at www.iaea.org/NewsCenter/Features/Nuclear_Terrorism/bunn02.pdf.
22 Gottemoeller, R. (2005) 'Cooperative threat reduction beyond Russia', *The Washington Quarterly*, 28(2), Spring, p. 151.
23 The G8 Global Partnership Against the Spread of Weapons and Materials of Mass Destruction, Statement by the G8 Leaders, Kananaskis, Canada, 27 June 2002.
24 House of Commons, Foreign Affairs Committee (2005) *Foreign Policy Aspects of the War Against Terrorism*, Sixth Report of Session 2004–2005, HC 36-I, 5 April, p. 124.

25 House of Commons, Foreign Affairs Committee (2006) *Foreign Policy Aspects of the War Against Terrorism*, Fourth Report of Session 2005–2006, HC 573, incorporating HC-904-I, 2 July, p. 150.

26 See the Foreign and Commonwealth Office website on counter-proliferation. Counter-proliferation remains one of the international priorities of the UK, www.fco.gov.uk/servlet/Front?pagename=OpenMarket/Xcelerate/ShowPage&c=Page&cid=1065432 164878.

27 See, Beaumont, P., Ahmed, K. and Bright, M. (2003) 'The meeting that brought Libya in from the cold', *The Observer*, 21 December.

28 Although the Iraq case is often seen as an intelligence failure, the Butler Report indicated that the British 'Government's conclusion in the spring of 2002 that stronger action (although not necessarily military action) needed to be taken to enforce Iraqi disarmament was not based on any new development in the current intelligence picture on Iraq', Report of a Committee of Privy Counsellors, Chairman: The Rt Hon. The Lord Butler of Brockwell KG GCB CVO (2004) *Review of Intelligence on Weapons of Mass Destruction*, 14 July, HC 898, London: HMSO, p. 105, para. 427, available at www.official-documents.co.uk/document/deps/hc/hc898/898.pdf.

29 See, Huband, M. (2003) 'MI6 steps up spy recruits to cold war levels', *Financial Times*, 5 May.

30 The Butler report specifically mentions the effect of 9/11 on British policy towards Iraq. 'In his evidence to us, the Prime Minister endorsed the view expressed at the time that what had changed was not the pace of Iraq's prohibited weapons programmes, which had not been dramatically stepped up, but tolerance of them following the attacks of 11 September 2001'. (2004) *Review of Intelligence on Weapons of Mass Destruction*, 14 July, HC 898, London: HMSO, p. 105, para. 427, available at www.official-documents.co.uk/document/deps/hc/hc898/898.pdf.

31 Walker, W. (2005) 'Caught in the middle: the United Kingdom and the 2005 NPT Review Conference', *Arms Control Today*, 35(1), p. 17.

32 See, for example, Langewiesche, W. (2004) 'The point of no return', *The Atlantic Monthly*, January/February, pp. 96–118.

33 The Foreign and Commonwealth Office emphasised the importance of international cooperation and intelligence sharing in a December 2003 and, revised, March 2006 document outlining its international priorities. International terrorism and the proliferation of WMD were stated as having 'emerged as potentially the most catastrophic dangers to our (UK's) national security in the early twenty-first century' in December 2003, whereas by March 2006, preventing terrorist acquisition of or access to CBRN weapons was considered a 'key task'. (2006) *Active Diplomacy for a Changing World: the UK's International Priorities*, Cm. 6762, March.

34 Op. cit., Walker, p. 17.

35 The Foreign and Commonwealth Office clearly states that as 'there is no panacea' or 'one-size-fits-all' policy to counter WMD threats, 'the Government uses the tools that it judges will be most effective in each case'. See Counter-Proliferation Strategy, available at www.fco.gov.uk/servlet/Front?pagename=OpenMarket/Xcelerate/Show Page&c=Page&cid=1065432164878.

36 Op. cit., Walker, p. 17.

37 Webber, M., Croft, S., Howorth, J., Terriff, T. and Krahmann, E. (2004) 'The governance of European security', *Review of International Studies*, 30(1), p. 4.

38 Makinda, S.M. (2003) 'Global governance and terrorism', *Global Change*, 15(1), February, pp. 43–58.

39 Carter, A.B. (2001/2002) 'The architecture of government in the face of terrorism', *International Security*, 26(1), p. 22.

40 Stern, J. (2003) 'How America created a terrorist haven', *New York Times*, 20 August.

41 Falkenrath, R.A. (2000) 'Problems of preparedness: U.S. readiness for a domestic terrorist attack', *International Security,* 25(4), Spring, pp. 147–86.

42 Freeman, J. (2005) 'The biological and toxin weapons convention review process: what more can it contribute?', *The CBW Conventions Bulletin,* 69 and 70, September–December, p. 2.

43 Simpson, J. and Littlewood, J. (2003) 'A framework for assessing UK responses to CBRN terrorism', paper presented to BISA 28th Annual Conference University of Birmingham, 17 December.

44 *US National Strategy for Combating Terrorism,* p. 15.

45 *US National Strategy for Combating Terrorism,* p. 2, available at www.whitehouse. gov/news/releases/2003/02/counter_terrorism/counter_terrorism_strategy.pdf.

46 (2004) *US Joint Doctrine for Combating Weapons of Mass Destruction,* 8 July, available at www.fas.org/irp/doddir/dod/jp3_40.pdf.

47 HM Government (2006) *Countering International Terrorism: The United Kingdom's Strategy,* July, Cm. 6888.

48 Parachini, J. (2003) 'Putting WMD terrorism into perspective', *The Washington Quarterly,* 26(4), Autumn, p. 47.

49 Ibid., pp. 47–8.

50 World Health Organization (2004) *Public Health Response to Biological and Chemical Weapons: WHO Guidance,* Geneva: WHO.

51 Falkenrath, R.A. (2000) 'Problems of preparedness: U.S. readiness for a domestic terrorist attack', *International Security,* 25(4), Spring, p. 182.

52 Hoffman, B. (2004) 'The changing face of Al Qaeda and the global war on terrorism', *Studies in Conflict & Terrorism,* 27(6), November–December, p. 556.

8 The UK and the threat of nuclear terrorism

A case study of organisational responses

John Simpson

Introduction

The threat of attacks on nuclear facilities in the UK, from the land, sea and air, has been a constant concern of UK governments since they were first built in the UK from the late 1940s onwards and since nuclear weapons were first deployed on its territory in 1953. For decades the threat of such actions was seen to arise from attacks of Warsaw Pact special forces, its air forces and 'sneak boats'. As a consequence, contingency plans were made to deal with such attacks on a 'military on military' basis, and nuclear power stations were designed and built with such possibilities in mind. As the Irish Republican Terrorism (IRT) threat on the UK mainland developed, this also led to measures being put in place to mitigate a terrorist attack using conventional explosives.

In parallel, the recognition that nuclear power stations and other facilities could be subject to accidents and misuse led to an evolving system of physical security regulations and the implementation of common standards for their safety arrangements. As all nuclear facilities were initially owned by the state, the UK Atomic Energy Authority (UKAEA) which managed them created its own regulatory bodies to handle safety and security issues, as well as its own police force, the UKAEA Constabulary. Over time, however, the power, size and functions of the UKAEA decreased as its military, fuel cycle and medical divisions were hived off to the Ministry of Defence (MoD), British Nuclear Fuels Ltd (BNFL) and private enterprise. At the same time, decisions were made to try to privatise the nuclear power stations operated by the state Electricity Generating Boards. The result was a slow, incremental and somewhat confusing transfer of statutory regulatory responsibility for the safety of nuclear sites from the UKAEA to the Health and Safety Executive's Nuclear Installations Inspectorate (NII). Issues of security, however, remained the responsibility of the UKAEA's Directorate of Civil Nuclear Security (DCNSy).

Military facilities were subject to different arrangements, though civil standards of 'best practice' in safety matters were slowly adopted by the MoD for some of its military facilities, such as Aldermaston, after they were made subject to civil standards of safety and to inspections by the NII. Security at these facilities remained the responsibility of the MoD. The most visible sign of this difference was that policing of MoD sites was (and is) the responsibility of the MoD's police force. In addition to the MoD Police Force (MDP), sites holding operational nuclear weapons also have armed military guards.

After the collapse of first the WTO and then the USSR, contingency plans for 'military-on-military' attacks were revised as such events seemed increasingly unlikely. At the same time these events and the subsequent reduction in the numbers and type of UK and US nuclear weapons on UK soil ameliorated concerns about attacks on their storage and other facilities. By contrast, attempts by the Thatcher government and its successors to privatise the civil nuclear industry stimulated a need to strengthen and verify the implementation of more intrusive and rigorous safety and physical protection standards. However, the split between the regulatory bodies dealing with safety and physical protection was retained, and while the NII was strengthened following public concerns over accidents at civil plants, resources allocated for the security function remained static at best.

While safety was vested in the independent national Health and Safety Executive and its specialist NII, regulatory responsibility for physical protection and security of licensed civil sites remained with the UKAEA and its DCNSy. In 1998, however, the Trade and Industry Committee of the House of Commons produced a report on its inquiry into security and safety at the UKAEA's Dounreay plant in Scotland, which found these wanting. One cause of this was identified as the UKAEA starving DCNSy of resources: another that it was acting as its own regulatory body for the plant. It therefore recommended that in future management of plants and regulatory activities in the security area should be clearly divorced and independent from each other, and that the licensed nuclear industry should collectively pay for its regulation. As a consequence, the staff of the DCNSy was transferred in 2000 from the UKAEA to a new Office for Civil Nuclear Security (OCNS) within the Department of Trade and Industry (DTI), though it remained headquartered at the UKAEA headquarters site at Harwell.

The threats of nuclear terrorism

The types of threat posed by global terrorist networks to nuclear targets in the UK can be divided into five broad categories:

- Theft of nuclear weapons, fissile materials or radiological materials from sites within the UK. Also from transport activities both within the UK and involving UK companies operating outside the UK.
- Smuggling of nuclear weapons, their components or radiological materials into the UK and its territorial sea.
- Use of nuclear weapons, improvised nuclear explosive devices and improvised radiological contamination devices.
- Attacks on nuclear facilities that result in the spread of radiological materials.
- Attacks against nuclear submarines or an SSBN (that is, an armed Trident submarine) in transit.

As the UK is a nuclear-weapon state, its nuclear holdings and facilities are divided between those under the control of the military (including the US Air Force) and those under some type of civil regulation. One key difference between the two is that little is known in detail about the security aspects of military capabilities and facilities, and thus the responses of the MoD to the threat of nuclear terrorism after 9/11 are opaque at best. By contrast, there has been much more openness and transparency about responses in the civil sphere, though this is for reasons unconnected with the events of 9/11. Indeed those 40-plus civil servants responsible for security within the overall civil nuclear regulatory regime have gone out of their way to address publicly a key policy issue involved in this, namely how to strike the right balance between providing information to the population to assure them that active steps are being taken to safeguard their nuclear security, while not providing potential terrorists with the data to mount an attack. This has resulted in them producing a publication offering an argued case why certain information has to remain secret under the Freedom of Information Act, while other data can be released.[1]

Finally, the distinction between threat prevention and consequence management is relevant to all UK sites. While military arrangements remain obscure, on the civil side prevention is the responsibility of the OCNS while consequence management appears to be handled by the Home Office, local arrangements, the Civil Contingencies Unit of the Cabinet Office and a variety of other government departments and units.

Since it has to be assumed that the military responses have been roughly in line with those in the civil area, the latter will be addressed in detail first, followed by some observations on the military situation and on consequence management.

Security regulation in the civil sector and the immediate impact of 9/11

When OCNS was established on 1 October 2000, it was tasked solely with regulating physical security arrangements at nuclear power stations and licensed civil nuclear sites. Later its role broadened to include all civil nuclear sites, the transport of nuclear materials, and protection of sensitive information.[2] The statutory basis upon which OCNS was created resided in delegated powers granted to the Secretary of State for Trade and Industry under the Atomic Energy Act 1954, the Nuclear Installations Act 1965, and the Nuclear Generating Stations (Security) Regulations 1996. OCNS was stated to be 'an independent unit with operational and regulatory autonomy' within the DTI. Due to the parliamentary inquiry which had stimulated its creation, its Director was required to report annually on the state of security in the civil nuclear industry and on the effectiveness of its regulation to the Secretary of State. At its inception it had 35 staff and a budget of £1.6 million.[3]

The relevant IAEA guidelines for 'best practice' in such security matters emphasised that measures to safeguard nuclear facilities against sabotage should involve close consultation between specialists in both the safety and security areas. However, the UK chose not to create a new combined agency, but left it to the civil service to make appropriate arrangements to ensure effective cooperation between the OCNS and NII. They signed a 'Memorandum of Understanding' in 2001 committing themselves to collaborate on matters having implications for both safety and security.

From its inception, OCNS sought to focus on four key areas of regulatory activity: site security, transport security, personnel security, and information security. In doing so, it was seeking to address all of the nuclear threats confronting the UK, including attacks on nuclear facilities and materials in transit; theft of nuclear or radiological materials; and access to sensitive nuclear information. All four regulatory activities contributed to confronting these three threats.

Site security

One of the first tasks undertaken by OCNS was to develop a new procedure for assessing security threats, based on a standard planning tool, the Design Base Threat (DBT). This was a classified document which sought to provide 'a definitive statement of the possible scale and methods of attack that could be faced at civil sites, or when nuclear material is being transported' and 'takes account of the availability of countermeasures and contingency arrangements provided by the police, the Ministry of Defence and other agencies'. The DBT was the basis for the 'design, implementation and management of security measures and systems by the regulated civil nuclear companies'[4] (that is, BNFL, UKAEA, Urenco and British Energy), and was claimed to be regarded by the IAEA as an example of 'best practice'. This criteria-based approach was to be supplemented by communicating specific threat assessments and alerts to operating companies, which could respond by instituting agreed tailored measures following changes in alert levels. OCNS also started to act as a conduit between the UK security services and the operators in such matters.

The security standards and procedures specified by OCNS were confidential and were influenced by the guidance on *Physical Protection of Nuclear Material and Nuclear Facilities* issued by the IAEA. A team of UK inspectors, initially five strong but later doubled in size, was tasked with tracking international developments in these policies, as well as inspecting civil nuclear sites and reviewing their security plans. A wide range of security improvements were recommended as a consequence of these initial inspections, and a database of reports on security arrangements at sites was created, which included work completed or in hand to remedy deficiencies. These were also made available to site licensees and the NII. A Standing Committee on Police Establishments (SCOPE) was inherited from DCNSy and tasked with discussing ways of integrating, and possibly trading off, improvements in physical security arrangements against patrolling and guarding requirements at specific sites.[5]

Individual inspectors were given a specific range of sites to monitor, to enable them to have better knowledge of the sites they were inspecting and advising and of key company and site police personnel, and to develop closer working links with NII site inspectors who operated on a similar basis. At the same time, the companies involved started to employ specialist security personnel at both site and corporate headquarters level to undertake internal audits of required enhancements in site security, and to implement effective security arrangements.

The intention at this stage was that the inspection process would slowly shift the responsibility for auditing security arrangements against the OCNS's quality standards to the companies, with OCNS inspectors moderating those audits.[6] It was also envisaged that the existing prescriptive regime of standards and regulation could evolve into one with greater emphasis on companies making proposals for alternative arrangements for security, taking into account both the policies of individual companies and local circumstances.[7]

The immediate response of OCNS to 9/11 was to suspend the annual programme of site visits, and thus interrupt the monitoring of progress in implementing earlier recommendations. Instead, its inspectors were tasked with examining the additional security measures that appeared necessary to prevent or limit the consequences of similar attacks on UK nuclear facilities. They worked closely on this with staff from the NII, with several joint audits being conducted of the ability of sites to withstand both attacks from the ground and the air. The result was a series of recommendations for immediate action.

In the case of the ground attack threat, arrangements were already in place to combat the possible activities of Irish republican terror groups. However, the creation of additional chicanes, or where they already existed their strengthening, was recommended, as well as other measures to combat possible vehicle or truck bombs. The arrangements for the security of sensitive areas within sites were also reviewed and strengthened, given the possibilities of attack by individual suicide bombers. Measures were also taken to protect sites, and in particular Sellafield, against attacks by aircraft. This involved strengthened warning procedures and interdiction by Royal Air Force interceptor aircraft. However, implementation of these was not the responsibility of the OCNS, but of officials within the DTI Nuclear Industries Directorate, who had responsibility for reviewing emergency planning arrangements.[8]

The UKAEA Constabulary

The UKAEA Constabulary was a core component of the 1990s civil physical nuclear security regime. One of its main functions was to provide an armed response capability at designated nuclear sites in the event of a terrorist attack. It also provided perimeter and internal patrols, a police presence at all open perimeter gates and certain sensitive buildings and areas within sites, and armed escorts for the transport of sensitive nuclear material. In the wake of a public dispute in 1998 over police numbers at Dounreay, which was partly responsible for the creation of OCNS, the SCOPE had been created to ensure that policing levels would be set according to security, rather than commercial, criteria. This resulted in an increase in numbers of 27 per cent over the following three years, which in turn enabled it to respond more effectively to the new demands placed upon it following 9/11.

One response to 9/11 in this context was that on 28 November 2001 it was decided in principle to detach the Constabulary entirely from the UKAEA, and introduce legislation to make it into a stand-alone force by becoming a statutory Police Authority, while OCNS created a new inspectorate post specifically to strengthen its oversight of policing, guarding and security management issues.[9] However, as will be seen below, providing the legislative backing for this decision took some years to implement.

Transport security

OCNS also acted as the designated national authority under the international *Convention on the Physical Protection of Nuclear Material* for nuclear shipments to and from overseas destinations. It was also responsible for regulating arrangements for the secure transport of sensitive nuclear materials within the UK by civil operators. The former task included managing shipments of French and UK manufactured MOX fuel to Japan, and the return of sensitive material from it for reprocessing, as well as the movement of weapon grade plutonium between the USA and France for conversion into MOX fuel and its return to the USA. These shipments took place on a UK-registered vessel, carrying deck-mounted naval guns and having an armed escort of UKAEA police. They were reviewed in cooperation with the Japanese and US governments after 9/11, and judged sufficiently robust to handle any possible terrorist attack.

In the case of transport of material within the UK, this mostly involved the delivery of fresh fuel to nuclear power stations and the transport of used fuel to Sellafield for storage and reprocessing. This was the responsibility of the companies involved, who again had a variety of rules and regulations to control and ensure the safety of these activities.[10]

Personnel security

The UKAEA had its own security vetting system, which was transferred from DCNSy to OCNS on its inception. Latterly, its basis had been the Prime Minister's statement to Parliament on 15 December 1994 in which the continuation and expansion of this security vetting system had been justified as an element in controlling access to sites and nuclear materials, as well as sensitive information. The intention was to safeguard against those within the industry assisting terrorists to plan attacks on nuclear facilities or steal materials that could be used in weapons. OCNS thus inherited the task of supervising a comprehensive system of security vetting for those working in the nuclear industry, including deciding what clearance levels were necessary for specific posts and tasks.[11]

When DCNSy was part of the UKAEA, it inhibited the responsible authorities from providing a full service of intelligence reporting. These difficulties ceased to exist following the transfer of its staff to OCNS, while its authority over security standards was greatly strengthened by it having delegated authority to exercise the Secretary of State's statutory powers on all matters affecting civil nuclear security. Also, the transfer permitted more effective collaboration with the Nuclear Industries Directorate over the security aspects of the future of the nuclear industry.

Information security and other issues

OCNS was also given responsibility for supervising arrangements within the civil nuclear industry to protect sensitive information, other than through security vetting, as well as investigating any loss or compromise of information. This involved implementing the government's protective marking and classification system for such information, and validating the information security arrangements of individual companies or organisations working in the civil nuclear industry. OCNS also constituted the UK security authority for Urenco under the terms of the Almelo Treaty, and on its inception became the direct regulatory authority over the nuclear power stations operated by BNFL and British Energy, a role previously performed indirectly by DTI policy officials.

The legislative consequences of 9/11

The existing framework for security regulation in the civil nuclear industry had grown up in an *ad hoc* fashion, with different parts of the industry being governed by different and often incompatible regimes and in some cases small sites had no formal regulation at all. The events of 9/11 provided the necessary impetus to legislate quickly to address many of these issues, in the shape of the Anti-terrorism, Crime and Security Act 2001 (ACSA 2001). This contained within it powers to promulgate new statutory regulations applicable throughout the nuclear industry. New powers were also granted to the UKAEA Constabulary to protect any designated civil nuclear site, and exercise full police powers within 5 km of such sites. It also became a criminal offence to disclose information intentionally or recklessly about a nuclear site or nuclear materials.

The provisions in the 2001 Act enabled new regulations to be drawn-up to address both existing and post-9/11 security concerns. The core concept was that operators had to submit to OCNS a Site Security Plan (SSP), structured around the DBT, for approval. This set out the proposed security arrangements and committed them to observe the provisions of the plan once approved. The area where the most change was to occur was in the regulation of the transport of nuclear material, where the existing system of indirect regulation was to be replaced by a direct one. Under the existing system, nuclear operators had a duty to ensure that their contracts with carriers required that the latter took adequate security measures. Under the new regulations, transporters of sensitive nuclear material had to be directly approved by OCNS. To obtain this approval, they had to submit a statement on their security systems and arrangements again based on a DBT.

Arrangements for the regulation of transport were based on using internationally agreed categories of the types of nuclear material that presented a security risk.

This was the basis for deciding what types of guarding and other arrangements should be implemented. After 9/11 consideration was given to including within the UK regulatory framework nuclear materials in lower risk categories, such as those used for research, industrial or medical purposes – and which might have a role to play in the construction of improvised radiological devices. However, as these were already covered by the Radiological Substances Act 1993 (RSA), which regulated their access and storage, any OCNS regulations would have duplicated the existing powers, and it was decided not to do this immediately. It was agreed in principle, however, that OCNS would strengthen its cooperation with the Environmental Agency, which administers the RSA, to ensure that the RSA regime took due account of security concerns.[12]

The follow through after 9/11

The four annual reports produced by OCNS since its establishment on 1 October 2000 offer a unique series of moving snapshots of how this remit has been implemented, and the UK responses to 9/11 in this area. As a result the UK's responses to 9/11 in this area have been highly transparent.

Legislative activities

Until 9/11 the UK, in common with many other states such as Japan, had legislation in place covering acts of espionage or sabotage by individuals acting on behalf of another state, but not acts by individuals on behalf of themselves alone or non-state entities. One of the main aims of the UK ACSA 2001, enacted in the aftermath of the New York and Washington attacks, was to close these loopholes. It did this in four main areas:

- Section 47 of the Act made it an offence for anyone to explode, develop, produce, possess, transfer or prepare to use a nuclear weapon.
- Section 76 of the Act extended the powers of the UKAEA Police.
- Section 77 gave the Secretary of State powers to make regulations to ensure the security of (licensed) nuclear sites or other nuclear premises, the security of nuclear and radioactive material and related equipment or software, the security of nuclear material in transit, and the security of sensitive nuclear information. It also had a catch-all clause covering any information relating to these items by prohibiting any development, production, transfer or possession of nuclear weapons by individuals or groups or their use.
- Section 79 prohibited disclosure of any information or thing which might prejudice the security of any nuclear site or nuclear material.
- Section 80 prohibited the disclosure of uranium enrichment technology.

The focus of much OCNS activity after the end of 2001 was to first convert the powers available under sections 76, 77, 79 and 80 of ACSA 2001 into a set of Nuclear Industries Security Regulations (NISR),[13] promulgated in 2003, and then to ensure that they were being implemented. Although the Energy Act 2004[14] was principally concerned with separating off part of BNFL to create the Nuclear Decommissioning Authority (NDA), which has responsibility for the dismantlement of nuclear plant, it also provided enhanced powers to OCNS to ensure that its dismantling activities would not generate any security risks. In addition, it gave it powers to enhance security over the holding and transport of sensitive uranium enrichment equipment outside licensed nuclear sites. The latter allowed the existing regulations under NISR 2003, arising from section 80 of ACSA 2001, to be expanded and strengthened.

In addition to the provisions of ACSA 2001, the Terrorism Act 2006[15] contains a more recent legislative response to possible nuclear terrorist threats. It contains provisions 'involving radioactive devices and materials and nuclear facilities and sites'.[16] Its provisions also cover the 'making and possession of devices and materials',[17] the 'misuse of devices or material and misuse and damage of facilities',[18] 'terrorist threats relating to devices, materials or facilities',[19] and 'trespassing, etc. on nuclear sites'.[20] These provisions are rather exhaustive and expanded the scope of what constituted an offence, as well as containing many 'catch-all' elements.[21]

Site security

Regulations based on section 77 of the ACSA 2001 came into effect on 22 March 2003 making it mandatory for an operator to submit an SSP for sites under their control. All the sites, including the six additional ones now covered by these regulations, met the guidelines; four of these were managed by Amersham Plc and involved medical isotopes, while two were university research reactors, making 43 in all (about the same number as the total of OCNS staff – staffing numbers rose to 45 by March 2004, but had fallen to 42 by March 2005).

All companies met the deadline of 22 June 2003 for the submission of SSPs under their control. Most had to be returned after review and, by December 2004, all had been approved.[22] Approved SSPs were the operative instrument against which compliance with the regulations was to be determined and prosecutions for non-compliance brought. It was argued that this process ensured that all security plans would be fully scrutinised, and their existence and implementation would guarantee that the industry had reached a high standard of compliance with comprehensive, up-to-date security standards. It was also hoped that the comprehensive review of safety standards that was involved, linked to regular inspections and internal security audits, would make it unnecessary to repeat the process.[23]

An updated version of the DBT was issued in 2003. This was stated to be based on intelligence about the motives, intentions and capabilities of potential adversaries and sought to provide a definitive statement of the possible scale and methods of attack that could be faced at civilian nuclear sites, or when nuclear material was being transported, as well as taking account of availability of countermeasures and contingency arrangements provided by the police, the MoD and other Agencies. As the DBT evolved, it made clear to the nuclear operating companies what forms of possible nuclear attack they were expected to guard against and which type was the responsibility of the Government. In the latter case, it also specified what mitigating or preventive measures the companies were to take.[24]

All sites were expected to have 'baseline measures', which were permanent structural, technical and administrative security defences. OCNS was also working closely with NSAC on the security standards and equipment which should be used within the nuclear industry. OCNS was also involved in a Cabinet Office led initiative to adapt the government colour-coded alert system to reflect the changing nature of the terrorist threat.[25]

In parallel, the civil nuclear sites were classified into three new risk categories and the additional security measures that were to be taken in each category at different levels of alert were revised. OCNS was also working with NII and the operating companies to provide additional measures against risk of a large aircraft deliberately crashing on a civil nuclear site. Two sites having the most rigorous security measures – Sellafield and Dounreay – were classified as *high* risk, all other sites were classified as *medium*, and a few small sites *low*. In addition, Magnox sites had moved to the standard government colour-coded system of alert levels from their pervious non-standard one. Steps were also taken to extend or strengthen searching of vehicles and personnel entering sites, and all sites had been resurveyed and in some instances given additional anti-crash features. Further measures were also reported to have been taken against suicide bombers.[26]

As a consequence of a 2003 security review, additional pat-down body searches were introduced for all personnel at Sellafield and Dounreay, as well as visitors, whenever access was needed to protected areas. This was to safeguard against individual suicide bombers, among other things. Those conducting the searches were to be protected by armed police. No one was to be permitted to work unaccompanied on hazardous material, and all such work was to be monitored at all times by CCTV. In addition, the plutonium separation area within the Sellafield used-fuel reprocessing plant was to be given additional security fencing and to be protected by a dedicated armed police patrol. Additional measures introduced to counter risks from large aircraft included the building of substantial concrete barriers at two locations around the periphery of Sellafield.[27]

A programme had also started at Sellafield to examine security and safety arrangements at what were termed 'vital areas' in a cooperative programme with the NII. These were areas outside the site or sensitive locations containing equipment, systems and devices whose failure could result in serious consequences. One objective was to fully understand the interaction between existing security, safety and operational features. Another was to evaluate the extent to which proactive measures might prevent or mitigate a serious radioactive release following a sabotage attack. Yet another was to demonstrate that safety controls would continue to operate effectively in the event of a sabotage attack, as against an accident. After applying this methodology to sites within Sellafield, it was extended to other secondary facilities outside inner security zones, such as reactor coolant systems at nuclear generating stations. As a consequence, recommendations were developed in some cases for additional controls to be added to existing safety and security systems.[28] While this was regarded as an insurance programme, it was one being conducted at a level of sophistication beyond conventional counter-terrorist security arrangements.

This was associated with a wider effort of systematically monitoring the effectiveness and resilience of the operating companies' security management systems. It was hoped that this would inform future decisions on which companies might in future be given greater autonomy in managing and auditing their own security arrangements.

One consequence of OCNS's activities in promoting the development of internal audits by the operating companies was that BNFL's Security, Safeguards and International Affairs Division emerged as the largest security organisation within the nuclear industry. It employed 700 of its own security staff, and regularly submitted its internal security assessment reports to OCNS, as well as annual assurance statements. Moreover, it had become clear that the threat of OCNS using its statutory powers was a powerful tool that an operating company's internal security staff could use when asking their Board for more resources. In short, the operating company internal security regulators and auditors were starting to regard OCNS as valuable allies when seeking to do their job.

By 2005, the focus of OCNS inspections had started to move from trying to expose shortcomings in existing security arrangements to one of developing SSPs collaboratively in order to enhance mutual trust and respect between the regulator and site licensees. In addition, OCNS had been working with the NDA in mapping out its future activity at individual sites, so that security requirements could be incorporated at an early stage in its planning. Temporary Site Plans (TSPs) had also been introduced to cover the situation when building work threatened to invalidate elements of SSPs. In addition, it was moving in the direction of reducing the number of full inspections in favour of shorter visits to address specific issues and develop Schedules of Improvements. In addition, a system of six-monthly senior managers (nuclear) security briefings lasting three days had been introduced, jointly sponsored by OCNS and the security service and held at Porton Down.[29]

OCNS was also involved in the 2003 decision to establish JTAC. This was expected to enhance the quality and focus of intelligence reporting. The OCNS Director was a member of its oversight board and as a participating organisation, it provided JTAC with insights into, and expertise on, nuclear security issues. JTAC rapidly became regarded as a very effective body for facilitating an intelligence-led civil nuclear security operation, and some thought was given to bidding to have a member of OCNS staff permanently seconded to it.[30] It was clear that the interface of OCNS with the security services had improved significantly since 9/11, in part because OCNS was receiving JTAC reports electronically via an encrypted data-link.[31]

In that context of changing the focus of regulation, a new OCNS inspector post was created in 2004 to supervise compliance with guidelines on companies' commitment to security at Board level, the quality, training and accountability of company security managers, funding provision and involvement of heads of sites and other budget holders. These issues were the key ones in determining the extent to which companies might in future be permitted to exercise greater autonomy in managing security arrangements, including variations in security provision. A Nuclear Industry Security Forum was also created in 2003 to enable companies to meet with security services and OCNS officials at six-month intervals to coordinate and review site and transport security arrangements.

The UKAEA Constabulary

Between 1998 and 2004, UKAEA police numbers increased by 30 per cent. The Constabulary had been given additional powers by the Terrorism Act 2000, and the authority to undertake special investigations, or participate with other forces in doing so, under the Regulation of Investigative Powers Act of the same year. ACSA 2001 expanded its powers still further. At the same time, its status as the UKAEA's police force had become increasingly anomalous as the OCNS superseded the DCNSy and became an independent entity, and from 2001 onwards plans were slowly developed and implemented to break the link with the UKAEA and create a stand-alone force.

These plans eventually came to fruition through the Energy Act 2004. This detached the Constabulary from the UKAEA, ostensibly on the grounds of the possible conflict of interest created by the UKAEA that might arise if it were to bid for decommissioning contracts from the NDA. The new stand-alone force, known as the Civil Nuclear Constabulary (CNC) was to be managed by its own statutory Police Authority. This was to avoid any suggestion that its size and operations were being influenced by any inbuilt interest in minimising costs inherent in one of its commercial funding bodies.[32] This Civil Nuclear Police Authority (CNPA), which came into existence on 1 April 2005, was to be responsible for maintaining an efficient and effective CNC. However, the Director of OCNS was to continue to lay down the security standards that CNC was to work to, and the Chief Constable was to be responsible for implementing them. Sites to be protected and security tasks undertaken continued to be specified by OCNS, while the SCOPE would continue to determine police numbers required. Through the 2004 Act, CNC officers would for the first time have powers to stop and search analogous to those given to the civil police by the Terrorism Act 2000.

One of the prime responsibilities of the new CNC was to provide an armed policing service for selected civil nuclear sites and sensitive nuclear materials in transit (and on the high seas). Training standards were based on the same 'Home Office Code of Practice' applied to Authorised Firearms Officers in all UK police forces. The effect was to change what had been a small force of Special Constables with limited jurisdiction into a duly constituted, well-resourced and well-armed police force with full powers to combat terrorist attacks.[33]

In parallel with the creation of the CNC, OCNS consulted with the operating companies about the best means to strengthen the deployment of armed UKAEA/ CNC police officers at the generating stations, to reinforce the protection already provided by the companies' own unarmed civilian guards. Powers to do so were already in existence through ACSA 2001. Contingency arrangements already existed for local police forces to provide an off-site armed response in the event of a terrorist attack, but it was felt that the terrorist threat also required an on-site response. CNC-authorised firearms officers started to be deployed to designated nuclear power stations in 2004. Until permanent support units for individual stations had been recruited and trained, OCNS tasked the UKAEA police to establish two mobile tactical response units to provide mobile on-site cover on an interim basis.

Facilitating these arrangements was a project to equip the UKAEA Constabulary/CNC with the new encrypted radio communications system used by the other emergency services, thus facilitating coordinated responses to any terrorist incident. It appears that there also exist arrangements under which the armed forces could assist the police to protect civil facilities in the event of a threat or actual armed attack, while armed civil police could also be called upon in emergencies to reinforce site security.

Transport security

For the first time, the NISR 2003 extended direct regulation of security to companies transporting nuclear material within the UK and territorial waters and UK-registered shipping anywhere in the world. They were based on section 77 of ACSA 2001, and came into effect on 22 September 2003. Twenty-one organisations applied to OCNS for approved carrier status by submitting a Transport Security Statement (comparable to an SSP) under regulation 14. Eighteen of the organisations which applied were given approved carrier status. Within this listing, carriers were divided into two categories, A and B, with only class A carriers able to handle all types of nuclear material.[34]

The practical effect of the new regulations was to bring the 18 companies approved to transport nuclear materials within the scope of OCNS's powers of direct regulation. Previously, nuclear operators had found it difficult to ensure that effective security had been maintained after contracts had been signed as they had no authority to do this. The new arrangements closed this gap. The basis for the new system was again evaluation of the transport security plans, associated intelligence information and monitoring of compliance with the plans.

More specifically, OCNS instituted action to step up the number of security inspections undertaken at ports, railheads and other transhipment points, and to facilitate this its Transport Security Branch was allocated an additional inspector. Arrangements for transporting spent fuel from power stations in the south-east passing through outer London were examined, and when an inspection at Willesden revealed deficiencies in carrying out approved guarding arrangements, shipments were stopped until deficiencies were corrected. Shipments were only restarted when BNFL took them under direct BNFL supervision. In addition, formal inspections of carriers' transport facilities were instituted.[35]

Measures to counter attempts to board vessels carrying nuclear fuel and prevent unauthorised interference were focused upon the case of MOX shipments by sea. It was planned to transport them from their place of manufacture to the port of embarkation in special high-security vehicles (HSVs) under armed police escort at all times. Other (secret) security measures also were planned. OCNS was also responsible for certifying the security measures to be taken on UK-flagged PNTL ships used to transport plutonium from Los Alamos to Cherbourg for manufacture into MOX fuel for power stations, as part of a US–Russian agreement to degrade surplus weapon grade fissile materials.[36]

The Energy Act 2004 also contained revised powers over those holding and transporting sensitive uranium enrichment equipment outside licensed sites. Additional regulations had to be drafted for these, and covered the need to maintain necessary security standards to protect this equipment.[37]

Personnel security

OCNS gained new powers to develop its security vetting activities through regulations 19, 17(3) and 22(3) of the NISR 2003.[38] These apply to all permanent employees and contractors working in the civil nuclear power industry. There are four rising levels of clearance: enhanced basic, counter-terrorist, security and developed vetting. Clearance levels differed according to an individual's level of access to nuclear material and sensitive nuclear information. Revalidations were also to take place at regular intervals.

In the year March 2004–5, 12,500 clearances were issued, 10,000 of which were basic checks. Numbers have been rising steadily since 9/11, and a continuing practical problem is the backlog of vetting applications and revalidations. At Sellafield this was up to 10 months in March 2003, while revalidations were 12 months behind. One cause appears to be contractors requesting higher level clearances than were actually needed.[39]

Information security

Section 79 of ACSA 2001 made the intention to recklessly disclose nuclear information a criminal offence. The previous statutory provisions, including the Official Secrets Act, had only partially covered transfer of information to an individual, as against a state. The new provisions applied to both individuals and to operating companies. The initial work on this focused on deciding what information should and should not be disclosed, in order to translate the NISR 2003 into revised guidelines to companies on what information was covered by the Act. Sensitive information was deemed to be information relating to defence, national security or nuclear proliferation. Regulatory actions included ensuring the use by all those involved in the industry of the national protective marking system for documents and electronic media, approval of the physical and electronic measures taken to store, transmit and retrieve sensitive nuclear information, and investigating the loss or compromising of such information.

The Uranium Enrichment Technology (Prohibition on Disclosure) Regulations 2004,[40] another legislative response to perceived threats from nuclear terrorism, formally criminalised unauthorised disclosures of uranium enrichment technology. They also consolidated the provisions relating to disclosure in ACSA 2001.[41] From August 2004, these regulations applied to both intentional and reckless disclosures of equipment, software and information relating to uranium enrichment technology. Regulation 2(2) sought to define in detail what constituted 'reckless' disclosure. In addition, the regulation detailed the duties of all other persons who had access to sensitive nuclear information other than those located on licensed nuclear sites or working for carriers. This was needed to ensure that with the formation of the NDA and the resultant reorganisation of the civil industry, all persons keeping sensitive information on any premises were obliged to maintain the necessary security to protect it.[42]

OCNS inspections also started of companies' IT security arrangements. Three of these took place in the year March 2004–5. One was in the main offices of the British Energy Group plc, which for the first time had become subject to such regulation. Nine breaches of information security were reported during this period. Accreditation of systems was also ongoing, including the core data network of British Energy Group plc and four of its smaller systems. Work was also in progress on the accreditation of Wide Area Systems for two URENCO Group subsidiaries and the NDA. In the latter case, OCNS worked closely with the contractor designing and installing the NDA's core data network, both to grant accreditation and facilitate the connection to the Government's Secure Intranet (GSI). Daily interaction between the two organisations was governed by a Memorandum of Understanding between them. A major concern of OCNS was how to safeguard information subject to UK security caveats while not frustrating the NDA's obligations to create greater competition in the nuclear industry.[43] To encourage a dialogue with industry on this and other related natters, in 2004 OCNS instituted an annual forum for company staff responsible for information security to discuss these parameters. This included observers from Aldermaston.

In addition, a project had been instituted with the NII prior to 9/11 to explore methods of guarding against unauthorised interference in the working of IT safety and other systems. Pilot joint inspections of computer based systems important to safety (CBSIS) took place in 2001–2, and raised a number of issues. These proved very complex to resolve, and it was April 2005 before joint inspections restarted, including one at a major generating station. Arrangements were also made with the US Nuclear Regulatory Commission (NRC) to exchange and protect sensitive information. Similar arrangements were negotiated with the Canadians.

Other OCNS issues and responsibilities

Organisational matters and diversification of regulatory structures

When OCNS was being created, it had been intended to establish it as an Executive Agency with its own administrative structure to underpin its independent status.

This idea was rejected at a late stage, nominally on economic grounds, and instead its administration was given to the Nuclear Industry Directorate of DTI. However, in a reorganisation of DTI in 2003 it was transferred to a new Energy, Innovation and Business Unit, and in 2004 a further reorganisation led to OCNS being grouped within the DTI's Energy Group, together with the Export Control and Non-Proliferation Divisions.

While these changes may have been logical and desirable from a DTI perspective, they did beg the question of whether OCNS should have greater formal independence, as its legal advisers had confirmed that it had no statutory or administrative regulatory autonomy in law, even though in practice no one has so far challenged its assumed powers in the courts. The fear was that at some point the DTI's nuclear security and energy policy interests might conflict, and security would be the loser. As the retiring Director of OCNS put it bluntly in his valedictory report, 'it is desirable to entrench the independence of OCNS. Remaining an autonomous unit within the DTI's mainstream policy and administrative structures does not appear to be a viable long-term solution'.[44]

The UK is unusual in that regulatory responsibility for the civil nuclear industry is dispersed among several government departments and agencies. By contrast, responsibility for nuclear safety, security, safeguards, transport, environmental issues and radioactive materials in many other countries is centralised in one, or at most two, regulatory bodies. It has been argued that while those involved in the UK collaborate closely, it would be more efficient to concentrate these activities in fewer bodies, as IAEA guidance on good practice suggests.[45]

One area of close collaboration, and also an area where regulatory fusion might be argued to be desirable, is between OCNS and NII. On the one hand contacts between the two inspectorates are well established, with their senior management meeting formally twice a year, and inspectors and other staff attending each other's training courses. Moreover an NII inspector was seconded to OCNS to fill its inspector (Decommissioning Security) post in anticipation of the creation of the NDA. An OCNS inspector was to be seconded to NII in return to coordinate work on safety projects with security implications. The NII has five times the staff of OCNS, leading to suggestions that they merge as a genuinely independent body. This has merits, but it also poses problems. NII regulates safety at some MoD facilities operated by contractors, most obviously Aldermaston, but OCNS has no comparable responsibilities. NII's parent organisation, the Health and Safety Executive, may also have difficulties in incorporating the OCNS vetting programme and security focus into its safety culture, though it has had to do this to some extent when it is dealing with Aldermaston and other sensitive sites. There are also obvious problems of maintaining the confidentiality of the sensitive information which is OCNS's stock in trade.[46]

Legal status of intruders on civil nuclear sites

By 2005, many of the existing loopholes in the legislation on security regulation at UK civil nuclear sites appeared to have been addressed. However, one major one remained: the absence of legal sanction in the event of unauthorised entry into licensed sites. While this was an offence of trespass under civil law, it was not a criminal offence. As a consequence, Ministers were asked to legislate urgently to make unauthorised entry into licensed nuclear sites illegal.

Politically this posed some difficulties, as many anti-nuclear protestors had used invasions of sites as a method of protest against nuclear power and to demonstrate the weaknesses of plant security.[47] The gap was intended to be closed by amending the Serious Organised Crime and Police Act to make it an offence under paragraph 128 to trespass on a designated site, including a nuclear one. This was done by including the amendment in the Terrorism Act 2006 (c.11).[48] This amendment clarifies what constitutes the premises of a nuclear site and therefore what would be considered trespassing of such a site. This clarification was apparently designed to combat terrorist activities, but it will also apply to others who trespass on nuclear sites such as anti-nuclear protestors.

Regulation of radiological materials

One practical issue that has raised the profile of these organisational questions has been regulatory responsibility for the security of radioactive materials outside licensed nuclear sites. This has been an issue driven by both intelligence concerns over the creation by terrorists of 'dirty bombs' from low grade radioactive materials, and the attempts through the IAEA to account for, and secure, radioactive sources globally. At the creation of OCNS, regulatory responsibility for these materials was in the hands of the Department of the Environment. In 2003 an interdepartmental study was started to recommend how best to strengthen security arrangements for radioactive material held outside of licensed sites. OCNS's position on this issue was that statutory regulation by a competent security authority was the way forward.

One consequence was a decision to amend NISR 2003 to ensure that due concern would be addressed to the security of all classes of nuclear material, including low-risk materials outside nuclear sites.[49] It was hoped to do this by 2006 through an extension of the regulatory regime embodied in NISR 2003 to cover lower-risk material employed for industrial or research purposes in use, storage or transportation. Amendments to the international Convention of Physical Protection of Nuclear Material suggest the UK will have an obligation to protect this material prudently. More specifically, international standards will require that all except 'exempted packages' containing nuclear material require the imposition of the security provisions applicable to dangerous goods in transit. The remit of OCNS is thus being extended to include this further role.[50]

OCNS as a player on the international stage

After 9/11, exchanges started informally on problems they were facing, alternative solutions and 'best practice' among bodies dealing with nuclear security in several European states, including Belgium, France, Germany, Spain, Sweden,

Switzerland and the UK. By 2004 this group had formalised into the European Nuclear Security Regulators Association (ENSRA).[51]

On the global level, OCNS has worked with the IAEA Office of Nuclear Security on proposals to revise the international Convention on Physical Protection of Nuclear Material. It also was instrumental in creating in 2003 the IAEA's Revised Code of Conduct on the Safety and Security of Radioactive Sources, as well as developing its revised guidance on Physical Protection of Nuclear Material and Nuclear facilities (INFCIRC/225/Rev.4). It played a significant role in the IAEA Nuclear Security Conference held in London in March 2005 and in the work of the IAEA Advisory Group on Nuclear Security (AdSec). It is also participating in the shaping and implementation in the UK of the nuclear security obligations arisen from United Nations Security Council Resolution 1540 of 2004 and the Convention on the Suppression of Acts of Nuclear Terrorism of 2005. This process has involved both shaping these international regulations to reflect UK security experiences and practices, and amending UK legislation and regulations to reflect its new international commitments.[52]

Security regimes at military facilities and the impact of 9/11

By 2001, the number of military facilities holding nuclear weapons and materials had been reduced significantly from its peak in the 1960s. Only eight sites remained: the atomic weapon research and production facilities at Aldermaston and Burghfield Common; the weapon storage, submarine maintenance and missile facilities at Coulport and Faslane; the USAF base at Lakenheath; and the submarine reactor facilities at Barrow, Ansty, and Devonport. One significant difference between security arrangements at military and civil sites prior to 9/11 was that it had been anticipated that the former might be subject to attack by all possible methods, while the same expectation did not apply to the latter. Some of the former were subject to safety regulation by the NII, but not security regulation by the OCNS.

Military nuclear facilities are categorised as 'military key points' but there is scant information available in the public domain on the security arrangements relevant to them. However, it is known that the methodology used by those responsible for security at the military sites starts with a DBT document, and presumably includes SSPs. In addition, it is known that nuclear submarines, for example, are regulated by the Naval Nuclear Regulatory Panel, an 'independent' body within the MoD. Guarding of military facilities is also the responsibility of the MDP, while special forces provide rapid response units to safeguard both nuclear sites and transport of materials and artefacts between them.[53]

Consequence management following nuclear terrorism

The consequences of a terrorist attack on a nuclear facility, or with a nuclear or radiological weapon, will differ greatly depending on location. Although the sources of a nuclear accident and a terrorist attack may differ significantly, its consequences may not, and thus emergency plans for deliberate releases of radioactive material from civilian nuclear sites are based on plans for accidental releases. The Home Office would initially take the lead in coordinating the response at a national level for an incident at the UK nuclear site or during the transport of nuclear materials. In addition there is a Nuclear Emergency Planning Liaison Group (NEPLG) within the DTI which aims to bring together different groups with interests in off-site emergency planning.[54]

Under the Radiation Emergency Preparedness and Public Information Regulations 2001 (REPPIR),[55] the production and implementation of off-site emergency plans and the provision of information to the public in the event of an emergency is the responsibility of the local authority in which the nuclear site is situated. Detailed emergency plans exist for areas within a few kilometres of nuclear sites. It has, however, been argued that the extent of these areas and the scope of these plans should be significantly increased. CBRN emergencies involve many players, as the CCS, the MoD, the Office of Science and Technology, the Department of Health and the DTI, to name but a few, could all be involved. One aim of the Civil Contingencies Act was to clarify the responsibility of this plethora of agencies and place statutory obligations on certain agencies at local level.

Consequence management of radiological or nuclear attacks away from sites would be managed in the normal civil contingencies/terrorism manner with help from nuclear experts.[56] In addition, longer-term issues of organising recovery and decontamination after an attack are now the responsibility of the newly created Government Contamination Service.[57]

Responses to nuclear terrorism after 9/11 in the UK: some conclusions

After 9/11, it is clear that a major effort has been made both to strengthen the security surrounding the civil nuclear industry and to ensure that these improvements are sustained, despite significant structural changes in that industry in the meantime. The main instrument for this has been new security methodology and regulations based on several differing pieces of legislation. The process now in place starts with assessment of design-based threats to plants and transport operations, infused with intelligence information on actual threats, and the subsequent development of SSPs or Transport Security Plans. Initial responsibility is then placed on the plant operators and their security organisations to implement these plans, backed up by OCNS inspections and the legislative authority to prosecute those in non-compliance. Yet there has been a certain amount of serendipity about these developments. Many were already in train for very different reasons prior to 2001, although 9/11 gave them more momentum and financial and legislative priority than would probably otherwise have been the case.

The evidence in the public domain suggests that the overall planning of a regulatory-based security system for UK nuclear sites has been both comprehensive and incisive. At the same time, it has been constrained by existing bureaucratic limitations and the process has evolved in an uneven manner. Legislation, and its implementation through regulations, has occurred in a somewhat piecemeal manner, suggesting it has encountered problems over prioritisation. This is illustrated by the lateness of the decision to legislate on making unauthorised entry into a civil nuclear site a criminal offence. There have also been limitations on resources arising in part from the contradictions inherent in the independent funding of OCNS' regulatory role and the central management and regulation of the human resources to fulfil it by the DTI.

The outcome of this activity, chronicled transparently in four annual reports, has been impressive, but the real question is how much has changed on the ground, and what alternative actions would have strengthened the situation. Given that the regulators of the past became the regulators of the present when OCNS was created out of DCNSy, and the number of inspectors involved (no more than a dozen) to cover 49 sites and 18 transport contractors, the main criteria can only be whether the approach to security has changed at the grass roots in the operating companies. Recent OCNS reports have claimed that it has, and that the company security personnel now see the Office as an ally in their fight to secure more attention and resources for security within the operating companies, including at the board level. Security procedures have also changed and been made more stringent, while new physical structures have been created to seek to ameliorate the consequences of a terrorist attack. Yet both the human and physical factors involved in these changes are very difficult, if not impossible, to evaluate unless an event occurs. There can be little doubt, however, that they must have had a deterrent effect by making terrorist planning more complex and difficult.

There also exist some obvious criticisms of the UK model for enhancing security, which those implementing it appear fully aware of. The prime one is that legal and regulative responsibility for civil nuclear site security is spread among several departments and agencies, when it might be more effective concentrated in one or two. There also exists the question of whether the OCNS should have a role in regulating the separate system of military nuclear site security, given that its inspectors already have a high security clearance. Moreover, as OCNS evolves from a standard setting organisation into a standard monitoring and moderating one, will it and the operating companies' security staffs become complacent? One advantage of having to tackle the ongoing issues of site security during dismantlement of nuclear facilities is that this may provide inadvertently the type of ongoing challenges which would assist in preventing this and in continuing to recruit staff of the right calibre. Finally, nuclear security regulation has now been made independent of all other nuclear activity and apparently divorced from resource issues by being funded by industry. However, OCNS' lack of formal independence granted through statute, rather than on the basis of devolved powers, and thus its inability to fully exploit its ability to raise its own operating costs and fund the establishment it regards as appropriate, may yet come to haunt it at some point in the future. In short, great progress has been made in a short period of time from a very low starting point, but can it be sustained?

Notes

1 OCNS (2005) *Finding a Balance: Guidance on the Sensitivity of Nuclear and Related Information and its Disclosure*, Issue No. 2, April, Harwell: OCNS.
2 Parliamentary Office of Science and Technology (2004) *Assessing the Risk of Terrorist Attacks on Nuclear Facilities* (hereafter cited as POST Report 222), July, available at www.parliament.uk/documents/upload/POSTpr222.pdf, p.20, Box 3-3.
3 OCNS (2000–2002) *The State of Security in the Civil Nuclear Industry and The Effectiveness of Security Regulation* (hereafter cited as OCNS report 2000–2002), October 2000–March 2002, para. 8.
4 OCNS report 2000–2002, para. 12.
5 Ibid., paras 2 and 14.
6 A similar arrangement already existed at the international level in Europe, where Euratom inspectors audited the implementation of IAEA safeguards at plant level and the IAEA audited the Euratom inspectors' activities.
7 OCNS report 2000–2002, paras 20–6.
8 Ibid., paras 39–42.
9 Ibid., paras 47–50.
10 Ibid., paras 29–31.
11 Ibid., paras 14–17.
12 Ibid., para. 76.
13 The Nuclear Industries Security Regulations 2003, SI 2003, No. 403, available at www.opsi.gov.uk/si/si2003/20030403.htm.
14 Energy Act 2004 (c.20), available at www.opsi.gov.uk/acts/acts2004/20040020.htm.
15 Terrorism Act 2006 (c.11), available at www.opsi.gov.uk/acts/acts2006/ukpga_20060011_en.pdf.
16 Ibid., Part 1, ss. 9–12.
17 Ibid., Part 1, s. 9.
18 Ibid., Part 1, s. 10.
19 Ibid., Part 1, s. 11.
20 Ibid., Part 1, s. 12.
21 For instance, s. 11.2(b) indicates that an offence is committed 'if the circumstances and manner of the threat are such that is reasonable for the person to whom it is made to assume that there is real risk that the threat will be carried out, or would be carried out if demands made in association with the threat are not met'. This definition allows for a very broad coverage of what qualifies as an offence, and may be open to multiple interpretations, depending on what criteria are used to define 'reasonable'. The responsibility thus rests upon who judges what is 'reasonable' (and how this judgement is made) to determine whether an offence has been committed.
22 OCNS (2004–2005) *The State of Security in the Civil Nuclear Industry and The Effectiveness of Security Regulation* (hereafter cited as OCNS report 2004–2005), April 2004 to March 2005, para. 7, available at www.dti.gov.uk/files/file23299.pdf2004–2005.
23 OCNS (2003–2004) *The State of Security in the Civil Nuclear Industry and The Effectiveness of Security Regulation* (hereafter cited as OCNS report 2003–2004), April 2003 to March 2004, para. 46, available at www.dti.gov.uk/files/file23300.pdf?pubpdfdload=04%2F4182003–2004.
24 OCNS report 2003–2004, para. 14.
25 Ibid., paras 16–18.
26 Ibid.
27 Ibid., paras 49 and 51.
28 Ibid., para. 50.
29 OCNS report 2004–2005, paras 9–12.
30 OCNS report 2003–2004, para. 13.

31   Ibid., para. 11.
32   Ibid., para. 91.
33   Ibid., and OCNS report 2004–2005, paras 15–16.
34   OCNS report 2004–2005, para. 18.
35   Ibid., para. 23.
36   OCNS report 2003–2004, paras 58 and 62.
37   OCNS report 2004–2005, para. 43.
38   OCNS report 2003–2004, para. 19.
39   OCNS report 2004–2005, paras 35–9.
40   The Uranium Enrichment Technology (Prohibition on Disclosure) Regulations 2004,
     SI 2004, No. 1818, available atwww.opsi.gov.uk/si/si2004/20041818.htm.
41   Section 80(7) of ACSA 2001.
42   OCNS report 2004–2005, para. 43.
43   Ibid., paras 24–31.
44   OCNS report 2003–2004, para. 143.
45   Ibid., paras 135–7.
46   Ibid., paras 101–3.
47   OCNS report 2004–2005, paras 42 and 63.
48   Terrorism Act 2006 (c.11) amends s. 128(1), (4), (7) and s. 129(1), (4), (6) of the
     Serious Organised Crime and Police Act 2005 (c.15). See www.opsi.gov.uk/acts/
     acts2005/50015--1.htm#128.
49   OCNS report 2003–2004, para. 12.
50   OCNS report 2004–2005, para. 43.
51   OCNS report 2003–2004, para. 108.
52   Ibid., paras 109–13 and OCNS report 2004–2005, paras 45–8.
53   POST Report 222, July 2004. Assessing the risk of terrorist attacks on nuclear
     facilities, p. 19, para. 3.9.
54   Ibid., p. 109.
55   Radiation Emergency Preparedness and Public Information Regulations 2001, SI
     2001, No. 2975, available at www.opsi.gov.uk/SI/si2001/20012975.htm.
56   POST Report 222 op.cit., pp. 104–5, Chapters 11.1 and 2.
57   For details on this new organisation, see www.gds.gov.uk.

9 An assessment of the contribution of intelligence-led counter-terrorism to UK homeland security post-9/11 within the 'contest' strategy

Frank Gregory

Introduction[1]

The significance of intelligence in counter-terrorism stems from three main drivers: its role in, ideally, pre-emption and disruption of terrorist activity, its role in post-incident investigations, and the priority given to the maximisation of the efficient use of counter-terrorism resources through *intelligence-led* counter-terrorism. This is not a new aspiration but it is given current emphasis within the performance-related public service culture and the priority assigned to preventing and pre-empting a 9/11 type of attack in the UK. Consequently, the role of intelligence in counter-terrorism needs to be fully understood and appreciated, both in its possibilities and its limitations. Four examples will serve to illustrate the range of problems that need to be managed.

1   9/11 – US intelligence agencies had received some relevant information pre-9/11 and at the least had either failed to appreciate its significance or failed to share information.
2   Deployment of 400 troops and armoured vehicles to Heathrow in an alert in February 2003 because of intelligence indicating a possible attack – Prime Minister Blair was later to comment over the deployment of troops that '… To this day we don't know if it was correct and we foiled it or if it was wrong'.[2] Although the intelligence source was regarded as a strong one.[3]
3   Madrid March 2004 – a large-scale multi-location attack without any apparent prior signs of terrorist activity but with some relevant intelligence available but not fully shared.[4]
4   The suicide bomb attacks on the London tube system and a London bus on 7 July 2005 and the further bomb attacks, but with main charges not exploding, on the tube system on 21 July 2005 were both attacks for which there was no warning available from the then running prioritised intelligence operations and which came after a decision by Joint Terrorism Analysis Centre (JTAC) (created in June 2003), in June 2005, to 're-calibrate' downwards the threat level facing the UK from 'severe general' to 'substantial'. The 're-calibration' was on an assessment that there was no intelligence of a specific plot. After

7 July the threat assessment was raised to 'severe specific', meaning a further attack was anticipated.[5] However, it should also be noted, as stated by the Home Secretary that the downward assessment did not lead to any '... significant diminution to specific protective measures'. Such measures being connected to the separate public sector alert status system.[6]

In developing these introductory points, it is helpful to refer to the 2004 Royal United Services Institute (RUSI) article by Col. Hughes-Wilson, who has provided a very sound basic introduction to intelligence work and to the Home Office paper on strategic intelligence by James Sheptycki.[7] Sheptycki, referring to Willmer (1970) provides a basic definition of the intelligence function as consisting of '... the acquisition of knowledge and the processing of that knowledge into meaningful "bits" which lead to action'.[8] Although as the Butler Report cautioned 'Intelligence is not only – like many other sources – incomplete, it can be incomplete in undetectable ways'.[9] A point underlined by Dame Eliza Manningham-Buller, after the July London bombings, when she noted '... that intelligence rarely tells you all you want to know'.[10]

Hughes-Wilson's breakdown of the 'Intelligence Cycle' is well worth quoting in full, as it helps to identify issues that run through this chapter. The cycle should start with:

1   Statement of end-user[s] *requirements*. These should lead to:
2   Planned *collection*.
3   *Collation* of all collected information.
4   *Interpretation* by trained *analysts* for *relevance, reliability, credibility* and *accuracy*.
5   Timely *dissemination* to end-user[s].

Thus, in the British context, we can pose five questions regarding 9/11, its aftermath and the July 2005 London bombings.

1   When, how and with what levels of resources did the UK start its process of considering the wider international terrorist threat with its emphasis on Islamic groups?
2   What changes, if any, did the UK make to its collection, collation and interpretation systems?
3   What changes, if any, did the UK make to its dissemination system?
4   Has the failure to find WMD in Iraq, the existence of which was reported in intelligence assessments in the USA, the UK and elsewhere, raised questions about intelligence reliability and the political use of intelligence?[11]
5   If, as seems likely, the July 2005 London bombings reveal intelligence 'gaps', what were those 'gaps'? How can the 'gaps' be reduced?

Taking the penultimate question first of all, this does need some reflection. The Hutton Inquiry and its aftermath provides some evidence that perhaps not all the expert views were properly reflected in the Joint Intelligence Committee (JIC) analysis. This was a point particularly raised in relation to Defence Intelligence Staff (DIS) experts. More seriously, it does appear that the JIC allowed too much weight to be given to Number 10's presentational concerns. As Hughes-Wilson reminds us: 'The job of the JIC is to go to Downing Street, thrust an impartial, objective assessment through its iron gates and walk briskly away to let the elected policy makers do with it as they will'.[12] Indeed, the Government now accepts this point and has said that 'Any future presentation of intelligence will separate the Government case from the JIC assessment'.[13] Indeed, Home Secretary John Reid further admitted, regarding official assessments of the terrorist threat that 'There is no doubt that the whole story of WMD undermined the confidence and, therefore, trust in the assessment of the Government in these matters; and that for me, as Home Secretary, has to be a central problem and issue'.[14]

Although, in the domestic management of terrorism the JIC does, in practice, play a less contentious role. Sir David Omand saw JIC providing the comprehensive assessment of security risks to '… illuminate policy decisions' working alongside the domestic Strategy Unit's remit to carry out 'in-depth strategic' examinations of major policy issues over a 10 year or more timeframe.[15] Moreover, the inter-agency, JTAC, has been assigned the primary responsibility for producing threat assessments relating to terrorism. Thus the JIC would be working within a threat framework set by JTAC. Moreover, before he moved to head MI6, John Scarlett, as JIC Chairman, recognised that '… recent developments and above all the new techniques and skills required to combat international terrorism, have introduced a new meaning to 'Joint Working'. These we must now exploit, and be seen to exploit, to the full'.[16] This chapter's research base has been developed within the parameters of the St Andrews/Southampton ESRC-funded project on 'The Domestic Management of Terrorism in the UK post 9/11' and its focus reflects those parameters.[17]

Scoping the issues

In a recent study, Paul R. Pillar has provided an important general contemporary critique of the intelligence function that can help us to understand the current situation in the UK.[18] As Pillar aptly points out: 'The bull's eye of this intelligence target – an individual terrorist plot – lacks the size and signatures of most other targets, from nuclear weapons programs to political instability'. Moreover, as he further notes '… intelligence specific to terrorist plots is often unattainable'.[19] One UK intelligence officer is quoted as offering the metaphor that counter-terrorism intelligence activity is about 'tracing threads and weaving patterns'.[20] Therefore, a counter-terrorism response system that relies too much on ratcheting up security only on receipt of actual tactical warnings can be badly caught out, as the UK found in Istanbul in 2003. Although the Foreign and Commonwealth Office had an understandable dilemma in seeking to maintain both a visible and approachable diplomatic presence and maximising the security of staff and the local population in the vicinity of a post. The Foreign and Commonwealth Office's recent security review has sought to arrive at the correct balance between approachability and security. A similar dilemma is present in the response to the London bombings of July 2005 where a huge overt counter-terrorism police presence (estimates of around 6,000 police), with Special Forces back-up, was subsequently deployed, on certain days, for public re-assurance and preventive reasons *without* any specific threat intelligence. Such a response is acknowledged to be unsustainable over prolonged periods.

Much of counter-terrorism intelligence has to focus on the relatively small intelligence footprint of suspect individuals but to reach this focus the analytical work has to manage a geographically dispersed, large volume of information. This is a resource-intensive process, in terms of: humint, sigint, imint (photography/imagery) and intercept sources. It is also an extremely complex task in relation to the Islamic groups and their supporters, which are made up of a mixture of nationals, non-nationals, unknown illegals, false identities (anything up to around 200 for one person) and apparently law abiding persons with no criminal records. In the case of some of the suspects in the 21 July London incidents, false identities have already been revealed as an issue. For example, Muktar Said-Ibrahim is said to have used six aliases and Hussain Osman used five names and variously claimed to be from Eritrea or Somalia when in fact he was Ethiopian.[21] As one UK intelligence source observed, the more stones that are turned over, the more suspects we uncover. In this context Dame Eliza Manningham-Buller pointed to the dilemma in intelligence work of '... balancing investigation and monitoring of those whom we know present a threat, with work to discover and nullify previously unknown threats'.[22] In terms of possible intelligence 'gaps' and the London bombings of 7 July 2005 an issue may exist in respect of one of the dead bomb suspects, Mohammad Sidique Khan. It has been reported that Khan did come to the attention of MI5 before 2005, in relation to the ammonium nitrate seizures and other matters, but at the time he was not thought to be a priority target for surveillance. This clearly suggests that the priority parameters need to be rather more widely drawn in terms of when counter-terrorism resources are assigned to a person appearing on the intelligence 'radar',[23] and, indeed, these target priority parameters have been reformulated following intelligence services' post-London bombings reviews.[24] Another important part of counter-terrorism intelligence is that which looks at organisations in terms of whether they should be added to the list of proscribed organisations. If this does not happen, suspects may have to be released but, of course, 'groups' may circumvent proscription by starting new organisations. Proscription considerations have formed part of the response to the July 2005 London incidents as the Home Secretary has indicated to Parliament.[25] By mid-2006, 40 international and 14 domestic terrorist organisations were proscribed with the list having been expanded by Order in 2005.[26]

Currently, a key element of counter-terrorism intelligence is that which assesses the intentions and capabilities of terrorists related to the spectrum of 'deadly and determined' threats, particularly identified post-9/11. For example, to what extent do terrorists seek to add on to the common improvised explosive device (IED) a CBRN component to, first, cause more casualties and longer lasting effects and, second, to complicate the counter-terrorism response? In this important sub-set of counter-terrorism intelligence activities, counter-terrorism intelligence specialists most emphatically do not see themselves as looking for the military intelligence equivalent footprint of WMD. They have to operate in the much more low intelligence visibility arena of who is receiving, for example, a Western university training in chemistry or biological sciences and for what purposes, purchases of chemical precursors, those which are both officially designated and ordinary household cleaning agents or horticultural chemicals, and online websites on how to make bombs, etc.

This is an arena which is often both literally and metaphorically described as 'kitchen chemistry'. One current preoccupation, among intelligence agencies, is not so much with accounting for all former Soviet Union (FSU) stockpiles of CBRN materials but knowing where all key FSU defence scientific personnel are currently located.[27] Moreover, some of the CBRN building blocks are to be found in remarkably common-place locations. One of our Workshop speakers recounted the story of a souvenir bead necklace, bought in Central America for his young daughter, which, on closer examination, contained castor oil seeds (the plant basis for ricin) among the beads.

As Herman has pointed out, counter-terrorism intelligence is not a new intelligence activity but as he notes, '… its importance now warrants regarding it as an intelligence discipline in its own right, with equal standing to the accepted 'political', 'military' and 'economic' categories of collection and products'.[28] He also underlines the fact that although counter-terrorism intelligence's '… most important and direct value is in providing pre-emptive tactical warning of a terrorist action … this may not result in immediately observable action such as arresting terrorists or capturing their *materiel*'.[29] In this context, because of the UK's long experience with Irish terrorist campaigns in both Northern Ireland and on the mainland, it has not suffered to anything like the same extent as the USA in terms of information-sharing problems between intelligence and law enforcement agencies. Gregory Treverton, former Vice-Chair of the US National Intelligence Committee (NIC), has referred to the situation from the mid-1970s where 'The domestic intelligence activities of the Federal Bureau of Investigation were sharply restrained and the Chinese wall separating intelligence from law enforcement was built higher'.[30] This chapter seeks to demonstrate the various ways that the UK has been trying to avoid a 'Chinese Wall', 'silo thinking' (UK term) or 'stovepiping' (US term) effect from hindering effective and timely counter-terrorism responses.[31] This will be illustrated by reference to MI5's much more public role, institutional innovations, the emphasis on inter-agency cooperation and availability of much more widely disseminated intelligence-based threat information to the private sector and public. The chapter continues with an overview of the British intelligence system which is followed by an examination of the intelligence aspect of the domestic management of terrorism in the UK. The chapter concludes with a consideration of the issues related to the dissemination of intelligence and this section covers both pre-emptive operational activities and protective security work. Overall, this chapter seeks to provide focus on those of the broad questions, identified earlier, which most closely relate to the St Andrews/ Southampton ESRC project, namely, those of:

- The intelligence role in, ideally, pre-emption and disruption of terrorist activity.
- The priority given to the maximisation of the efficient use of counter-terrorism resources through intelligence-led counter-terrorism.with their linkages to the questions of:
  - When, how and with what levels of resources did the UK start its process of considering the wider international terrorist threat with its emphasis on Islamic groups?
  - What changes, if any, did the UK make to its collection, collation and interpretation systems?
  - What changes, if any, did the UK make to its dissemination system?

Britain's domestic intelligence system

This can be described as a layered, pyramidal structure. In the top layer are the security service (MI5) – domestic counter-terrorism, counter-espionage, the limited role in countering organised crime was dropped in 2006; the secret intelligence service (MI6) – foreign intelligence; GCHQ Cheltenham – elint and sigint; and the DIS – military intelligence including aspects of counter-terrorism. The most important change in this top layer came in 1992 when, after prolonged discussions, MI5 added to its responsibility for the collation, assessment and collation of all intelligence on international terrorism the same responsibility for Irish terrorism affecting the UK mainland, a responsibility previously belonging solely to the Metropolitan Police Special Branch (MPSB).[32] More recently, in February 2005, MI5 also took over responsibility for national security tasks in Northern Ireland. A responsibility that Dame Eliza Manningham-Buller noted as '… challenging to implement at a time of more general expansion and change for the Service'.[33] However, the MPSB still receives copies of all intelligence on Irish republican terrorism in the UK as the MPSB retains a national responsibility in this area under the lead responsibility of the Security Service. New Guidelines on the work of the police Special Branches were issued in March 2004 and these make it clear that '… counter terrorism remains the key priority for Special Branch…' and that 'All intelligence about terrorism obtained by Special Branch is provided to the Security Service … [as the lead agency] .. [and] … The Security Service sets the priorities for the gathering of counter terrorist and other national security intelligence by Special Branch'.[34] In the second layer are the provincial police forces' special branches, working with MI5 and other agencies as necessary (for example, SOCA and HM Revenue and Customs). MI5 took account of the variable size and resources of the Special Branches, before the introduction of the Special Branch Regional Intelligence Cells, by negotiating annual Statements of Joint Working Objectives with individual force Special Branches.[35] Although it should be noted that the introduction of the Special Branch Regional Intelligence Cells

(RICs)[36] does represent quite a low-level compromise with the more significant reform options suggested by HM Inspectorate of Constabulary (HMIC) because of the very variable capability of force SBs. Following the introduction of the Special Branch RICs, MI5 has been developing 'regional offices' to promote even closer cooperation between itself and the police.[37]

The linkages between anti-terrorist work and tackling serious and organised crime will be strengthened by the recent appointment of former-MI5 head Sir Stephen Lander as Chair of the Service Authority for the new SOCA which will commence working from April 2006 and incorporate the National Criminal Intelligence Service (NCIS), the NCS, elements from the investigative side of HM Revenue and Customs and other agencies. At present a long standing specialist input has come from the Terrorist Finance Team at NCIS and similar expertise in other agencies, such as the MPSB, and from long experience from the Northern Ireland anti-corruption and terrorist finance units.

Feeding into both the first and second layers are a number of specialist agencies such as DfT's Transportation Security Directorate (TRANSEC) which was established in 1990, the OCNS and the HPA. The CBRN threat has also led to a number of other specialists becoming involved in this second layer. For example, health service personnel concerned with epidemiology and toxicology.

Prior to 9/11, domestic intelligence work in the UK, the primary preserve of MI5 and police special branches, can be described as reflecting both an understandable pre-occupation with Irish terrorism and an initial scaling down of counter-espionage operations post 1989. Counter-extremism intelligence, for example, on animal rights protesters remained a police responsibility but MI5 was taking on a small amount of work in support of police operations against serious and organised crime.[38] Indeed, MI5's new headquarters at Thames House had been specifically planned on the assumption that, after the Cold War, a smaller domestic intelligence service would be required. Irish-related counter-terrorism operations were also generally regarded as having reached a success plateau after the IRA announced its cease-fire in 1996. After 20 years of efforts to penetrate Irish terrorist groups, these groups were thought to be quite well constrained by intelligence operations.[39] However, some events before 9/11 do have some significance for current intelligence pre-occupations. The 1996 Manchester bombing by the Provisional IRA alerted counter-terrorism agencies to the potential scale of effects that domestic terrorism on the mainland could produce. UK intelligence agencies identified the growth of extremist Islamic terrorism from the 1980s, and from the mid-1990s were beginning to look more carefully at Islamic groups and individuals, particularly with regard to their CBRN aspirations. Although as Stella Rimington noted, whilst '… resource is devoted to assessing likely new threats but before an investigation can be mounted … it has to be demonstrated that a serious threat to national security exists'.[40] This slow process of recognising new forms of terrorist threats has been well documented in the Butler Report in its presentation of JIC terrorist threat analyses from the late 1980s.[41] The first JIC assessment which specifically examined a potential CBRN threat from terrorists was in 1992 but the linking of 'suicide' tactics with CBRN aspirations by Islamist extremists is not identified by the JIC until 1999. Although the general terrorist threat from Islamic groups to areas outside the Middle East was identified by the JIC in 1995. However, as Sir David Omand has pointed out, MI5 actually 'under-estimated the extent to which there were radicalised individuals here in the UK'.[42] One part of that underestimation related to a relative lack of appreciation of the radicalisation impact of the conflict in Bosnia. The presence of the Bosnian factor is illustrated in the September 2005 Old Bailey trial, on four charges under the Terrorism Act 2000 relating to the possession of items relating to the commission, preparation or instigation of acts of terrorism, of a British national, former drug dealer and Muslim convert, Andrew Rowe. In court Rowe is reported to have said, after travelling to Bosnia in 1995 as a volunteer aid-worker, 'I wanted to participate and help people defend themselves against an aggressive force'. He admitted that he was prepared to act as a courier carrying military equipment and ordnance, however, he denies the terrorism related charges.[43]

Assessing the intelligence aspect of the domestic management of terrorist attacks in the UK

One can distinguish between active MI5 and MI6 efforts to disrupt and dismantle terrorist groups or terrorist activities and keeping a general watching brief on potential terrorist threats. In this context, until 1996, the bulk of MI5's counter-terrorism effort was, naturally, directed against Irish terrorism both on the mainland and in Northern Ireland. The Service estimated that by 1996, it had achieved a significant disruption rate of active service unit (ASU) activities although even in that year the London Docklands bombing and the bombing of the centre of Manchester do provide stark examples of what happens '... when intelligence fails to prevent an incident ...'.[44] However, as has been said earlier, it took nearly 20 years to achieve this degree of penetration of a geographically proximate and ethnically linked threat. [45]

From the mid-1990s, MI5 and MI6 were devoting more resources to monitoring Islamic groups and individuals. Their basic interpretation of this threat used a three-level model: the Al-Qaeda network itself; groups with variable 'linkages' to Al-Qaeda, for example, Algerian, Moroccan and Chechen; and lone individuals and *ad hoc* groupings or cells, though as the JIC commented in 2001 '... the networks associated with UBL are changeable and ad hoc groupings of individuals who share his agenda, and who may come together only for a particular operation. Nevertheless, 'groups' is used as a short form for want of another available term'.[46] The overall intelligence assessment as of July 2006 was that the '... principal terrorist threat is currently from radicalised individuals ...'.[47] Although, of course, account is taken of common experiences and knowledge derived from overseas 'training camps', websites and other forms of radicalising fora.

The two London bomb incidents in July 2005 starkly illustrate the key counter-terrorism intelligence problem of the 'clean' terrorist. That is to say a person, usually a national or established resident, who has either not been noticed from routine intelligence work of all kinds or whose presence in an intelligence database appears peripheral to the extent that surveillance of some kind is not deemed to be a justifiable use of resources. This was not an unrecognised problem because, as the Intelligence and Security Committee (ISC) commented in April 2005, the '... need to address the threat from these individuals is the primary reason why the Security Service is currently expanding significantly'.[48] There will be a 50 per cent expansion in MI5's operational capability between 2004 and 2008.

It was also well-understood that some of these groups or networks have had a clear CBRN ambition from the early 1990s. Further evidence of these intentions came from materials gathered from the camps in Afghanistan after Operation Enduring Freedom. In this area of work Stella Rimington pointed out that whilst traditional investigations were still necessary to understand and counter the groups '... they were difficult to monitor, being often a long way away and usually in countries which were sympathetic to them. ... [therefore] ... we also had to develop the ability to take rapid action, to react quickly to events as they unfolded'.[49] She also identifies the crucial role of the networks of trusted international contacts between security and intelligence services such as the heads of European Security Services group and CAZAB (Commonwealth) to '... increase the chances of success in this difficult field'.[50] Moreover, as is well known the UK benefits from its close US intelligence links as 'Britain is one of the few American allies regularly in receipt of this intelligence in its raw form, affording it the chance to conduct an independent analysis'.[51] Interviewees in the UK have often commented on the range and variety of the US material and Aldrich has referred to the UK being '... firmly orientated towards the United States, in part because it provides the UK with intelligence as a "loss leader" ...'.[52] A recent innovation, again linking anti-terrorism to countering serious and organised crime has been that the G8 Lyon meetings on crime have been at the same time as the G8 meetings on intelligence and have had shared agendas. It is obvious from the many accounts in the press of circumstances leading to arrests and from court evidence that the sigint work of GCHQ, MI5 and MI6 is making a major contribution to disruption and dismantling operations against those suspected of terrorist offences. Older, traditional methods of penetration and the management of human intelligence sources are also being used although of course one cannot expect to find confirmed details of these. However, Home Secretary Charles Clarke did note that, relating to arrests and detentions of terrorist suspects, '... in many of these issues intelligence is brought not through intercept, not through phone tapping, but by the existence of individuals within organisations we are talking about who are giving information about what is taking place'.[53]

Naturally, MI5 and MI6 are reticent about the level of detail on their work that they place in the public domain. However, Stella Rimington states that as far back as 1990, when she moved from the post of Director of the Counter-terrorism Branch that the '... level of terrorist activity in both Irish and international arenas had increased to the point where ... we decided to split the branch in half and two directors were appointed ...' to cover the work of the Branch.[54] Since 1994, the reports of the ISC do provide some quantitative indicators for MI5 as set out below.[55]

Table 9.1 MI5's counter-terrorism work as resource allocation percentage of total MI5 activities

	International terrorism	*Irish terrorism*	*Protective security*
2001–2	25%	32%	10%
2002–3	32%	29%	11%
2003–4	41%	25%	*c.*11.9%
2004–5	44%	23%	13%

MI5's budget for research and development for areas such as surveillance technology and protective security also increased over this period and by the Autumn of 2003 the MI5 DG was stating that '… approaching 70% of our effort is devoted to [terrorism in] all its manifestations'.[56] No comparable quantitative data is available for MI6 but this Service was reported as having increased its counter-terrorism work in the period 2001–3 and by 2004–5 its '… direct allocation of operational effort to counter-terrorism .. [was] … over three times the 2000–2001 figure',[57] including rises in resources devoted to the Middle East, North Africa and counter-proliferation. This was an important adjustment because the Butler Report found the strains on MI6's resources because of the, externally generated, need to make staff savings, meant that MI6's resources '… were too thin to support [its] responsibilities …'[58] in the Near and Middle East.

Over the period 2001–6, the total declared budgets for MI5 and MI6 will have risen by about 31 per cent.[59] However, it may be argued that these resources are only really keeping pace with the new terrorist challenges. For example, currently, the 24/7 surveillance capabilities of MI5, police Special Branches and other police resources are fully stretched keeping track of the current number of identified person targets. There is, post the July 2005 London bomb incidents, an even greater strain on surveillance and investigation resources. For the MPSB, Assistant Commissioner Tarique Ghaffur, who was responsible for Serious Crime operations, has said that 300–470 of his serious crime investigating officers were posted to the post-incident investigations.[60] As a rough quantitative measure of the problem, a senior police officer has indicated that around a 40-person strong surveillance team is required to keep 24/7 surveillance on one target individual and the Home Secretary stated, in September 2005, that there are '… certainly hundreds of individuals who we have been watching very closely and continue to watch closely …'.[61] Therefore, even the fact that MI5 will be able to recruit an extra 1,000 staff (current staff level is around 2,000) over the next few years needs to be placed in a context.[62] First, it will take time to recruit, vet and train this increase in personnel, assuming that sufficient recruits of the right calibre can be found. Second, MI5 has also recently admitted that, despite the ending of the Cold War, it has not only a continuing but also a rising need for resources to be devoted to counter-espionage.[63] Given the significance of electronic intelligence gathering in counter-terrorism through the monitoring of communications, the role of GCHQ is of great significance and by 2003–4 'counter-terrorism work was GCHQ's single largest collection effort ... and was due to increase by half as much again in 2004–2005 ...'.[64] As a consequence of this, GCHQ has had to reduce its collection activities in many non-priority geographical areas and even proportionately reduce its '... allocation of resources to counter-proliferation and weapons systems'.[65] This latter changed allocation seems somewhat unfortunate given the current emphasis in the counter-terrorism threat on the CBRN aspect. Moreover, GCHQ, like MI5, now finds that its new building also has insufficient accommodation because of the increased counter-terrorism work.

Another feature of the priority given to countering Islamic terrorism is the unprecedented heightened public profile of the Director-General of MI5 and the resulting increased workload on that post. Dame Eliza Manningham-Buller has given about four public speeches, for example, one to the Dutch security service, the AVID, on 1 September 2005, about the terrorist threat and is much involved with the development of both the general domestic and international counter-terrorism responses. Amongst her innovative actions has been to hold a publicly reported meeting at Thames House with Mr Iqbal Sacranie the Secretary-General of the Muslim Council of Britain. This meeting was in the context of concerns in the Muslim community about police activities in respect of Muslims, as Home Office statistics were then showing that between October 2000 and October 2004 some 700 people from possibly Muslim backgrounds had been arrested, 100 charged with various offences but only six actually tried and convicted.[66]

Collection and analysis

Not surprisingly, all those working in the intelligence field have become very wary of neglecting some, apparently or possibly, low significance item, in case it was later found to have had potential significance for the pre-emption of an actual terrorist incident. Consequently, the collection threshold has been lowered since 9/11.[67] This, in turn, produces a greater flow of information that the analysts have to manage. In the UK's case, this is magnified by the volume of information passed on from US sources, which comprises both processed and unprocessed data. A key skills base 'gap' that is being tackled is the recruitment of Arabic-speaking personnel, a gap that was also present in the US agencies pre-9/11. For example, pre-9/11, the international division of the MPSB had only one Arabic-speaking officer in post. In another example, as of 2003–4, the Foreign and Commonwealth Office had only 80 staff with a qualification in Arabic from the Diplomatic Service Language Centre.[68]

The most significant development in the analytical element of the UK's management of terrorism was the establishment of JTAC.[69] In part, this was a response to criticisms of its more limited membership predecessor, CTAC (essentially MI5), especially in the aftermath of issues related to prior warnings in the context of the Bali bombings. JTAC operates under the authority of the Director-General of MI5, but has autonomy in its workings; and its Director, currently from the MoD, reports to an inter-agency management board. It represents a specific move to break down institutional barriers between intelligence agencies by the processes of co-locating the analysts and creating a new shared identity through JTAC membership. The personnel are drawn from MI5, MI6, GCHQ, MoD, and TRANSEC. The Foreign and Commonwealth Office, the Home Office, the OCNS and the HPA also participate in its work. JTAC's remit, as stated by the government, is to provide:

- long-term studies of international terrorism, for example, on the suicide bomber problem;
- immediate assessments of current threats.

This remit actually breaks down into three components: the provision of country-based threat analyses and sector or location specific threat analyses for the UK which, from the available evidence, are used to set the security alert states for the UK; analyses of terrorist groupings and networks, including studies of key individuals; and terrorism trends analyses. The Government conceives of JTAC as '... the UK's centre of excellence and expertise on the threat from international terrorism ...'.[70] Since the Autumn of 2003 JTAC has been '... dealing with an average of 100 pieces of threat intelligence worldwide every week ... [i.e.] ... intelligence related to a plan or intention to mount a terrorist attack'.[71] Sir David Omand described the threat assessments as a means to inform 'risk management judgements. [because] We cannot give absolute guarantees of security'.[72]

From field work interviews, it has been possible to glean some initial perspectives on JTAC in operation.[73] A sense of a positive new collective JTAC identity is said to be evident from the staff from the participating agencies. It is hoped that this collective identity will help remove barriers to inter-agency intelligence sharing. Top-level representatives of the 'user groups' are also said to have positive views on the value of JTAC's products. In part this is because JTAC senior staff take seriously the requirement to liaise forwards in the intelligence cycle with 'user-groups' and backwards to the collection sections in order to be certain that the collection and the product, in terms of JTAC analyses, meet the key end-use requirements of prevention and pre-emption. A point supported by the comment of the OCNS Director who stated in his 2002–3 Report that 'As well as receiving intelligence, we aim to provide JTAC with insights into nuclear security issues to aid reporting on these topics'.[74] This positive approach has been endorsed by the ISC in its 2004 Report where it concludes that JTAC '... has significantly improved the UK intelligence community's ability to warn of terrorist attacks'.[75] In support of this contention the ISC cited the comment of the Transport Secretary, who said he found the JTAC reports '... useful'[76] and the comment of Sir David Omand who felt that the work of JTAC was '... of a very high quality ...'.[77] However, in some instances, it has been suggested, during the course of the research for this project, that initially some of JTAC's products may not always have met the needs of some 'users' in specific circumstances. Although, in this context, it must be remembered that there is a corollary stage, for which the users must take the responsibility. As the Government has commented, JTAC's '... threat assessments are used by customer departments to inform their own risk assessments, which inform strategic spending decisions…'.[78] Although, as the ISC has pointed out, notwithstanding all the increased focus on international terrorism by MI5, MI6 and GCHQ it is still necessary to comprehend that 'Obtaining and understanding the actual intelligence remains difficult'.[79] Of great concern to the ISC is that there is now a lack of intelligence resources available for deployment in counter-espionage work. MI5's Director-General said she had reported to the Home Secretary that '… we are carrying some risk here' especially as she also had to note that '… if we don't do it nobody does'.[80] The ISC concluded that in fact '… significant risks are inevitably being taken in the area of counter-espionage'.[81]

Dissemination of intelligence

The UK's counter-terrorism intelligence products are disseminated at several levels and formats. At the Cabinet level, through the JIC, JIC Papers are produced on topics requested by Ministers and departments and as part of a rolling programme, for example, terrorism threat assessment updates. However, the ISC commented that, 'The JIC Chairman, in his review of performance 2001–2, noted the need to produce starker papers, which could then aid ministerial decision-making'.[82] In this context, a major JIC weakness was the small size of the Assessments Staff (around 30) in the Cabinet Office. Indeed the Butler Report commented forcibly that 'The cost of the Assessments Staff is minimal in relation to the amounts the nation spends on the collection of intelligence. It is a false economy to skimp on the machinery through which expensively collected intelligence passes to decision makers'.[83] After the Butler Report the government established a Butler Implementation Group and, after receiving its review, has published a Command Paper outlining its response plans and implementation programme.[84] As part of the implementation process the Assessments Staff will increase in size by about one-third.[85]

From the available terrorism threat-related intelligence, JTAC sets the general alert state for the UK, which was for much of 2004 to June 2005 at the second highest alert level. Just prior to the July London bombings JTAC had in fact 're-calibrated' the threat level to the next lower state of threat because of its assessment of the threat intelligence that was available. It was quickly revised upwards after the London bombings.[86] The Cabinet would be involved in responding to specific assessments if, say, there was intelligence of a possible CBRN attack and, if in the case of an aviation related threat, troops were required for airport deployments. Responding to criticisms about lack of transparency and clarity regarding 'threat states' the government published in July 2006 both revised threat states and their associated response levels.[87]

At the next level, intelligence might be passed to a specific department for a response. For example, the DfT's TRANSEC has received a number of JTAC assessments, and on four occasions in February 2004 transatlantic flights from the UK were cancelled.[88] In the case of the decision to deploy troops to Heathrow in 2003, the MI5 assessment formed the basis of a report from the then Assistant Commissioner (Specialist Operations), David Veness, to the Prime Minister and

Home Secretary on which ministerial authority was granted for troops to be called upon as required by the head of SO13.[89] An even wider dissemination is also planned; Sir David Omand refers to '... seeking to develop our arrangements for alerting key sectors to relevant threat information, such as aviation, the CNI, in the City of London and other areas based on assessments of threat level from JTAC'.[90] More counter-terrorism operationally related intelligence would be passed from MI5 via the Special Branches to their operations departments as required or needed. Here the innovation of the establishment of PICTU as a new 'smaller police service' in 2002 has been an additional help by providing an interlocutory service between MI5 and the police forces through PICTU's specific remit and close working relationship with MI5.[91] In the more operationally related aspects of the management of intelligence, the intelligence services are conscious of the need to prevent communication 'gaps' as happened on some previous occasions. A key issue is when, in the development of the chain of information through intelligence to evidence usable in court proceedings, might the decision be taken to intervene by carrying out arrests? The answer, from operational examples since 9/11, is as early as necessary to protect the public; and the inter-agency group that takes such decisions is chaired by the National Coordinator for Terrorist Investigations, Deputy Assistant Commissioner Peter Clarke, which reflects the emphasis placed on public protection. Indeed in some instances, because of this protective emphasis, the usable weight of evidence for charging purposes was only, finally, uncovered just before the custody period ended.

Protective security advice also flows from intelligence assessments and is provided through two sources.[92] MI5's protective security departments (T4 and T3) provide advice to the 'government estate' and to list 'X' companies involved with work in sensitive areas. T4 has been expanded, in terms of personnel and resources, in the aftermath of 9/11 and it and parts of T3, following internal branch amalgamations have merged and together with NaCTSO, discussed next, now come under the umbrella of MI5's National Security Advice Centre (NSAC) which is both multi-agency in personnel and has a wider private sector outreach through an enhanced number of Security Advisers. NSAC's work in providing counter-terrorism security advice for the wider business and public sector community is assisted by the London-based smaller police service – NaCTSO – which, in early 2006, was under the line management of the National Coordinator Special Branch and NSAC. NaCTSO carries out this task through a network of police officers in post in each force who act as local counter-terrorism security advisers (CTSAs), by running country-wide workshops and providing help through the distribution of advice documents and CD-roms.[93] Finally, in terms of dissemination bodies under the aegis of MI5, there is the National Infrastructure Security Coordination Centre (NISCC) which covers communications and cyberspace matters. In one area, MI5 expertise has moved much more centre-stage into actual facilities security management with the report of the appointment of a senior MI5 officer, Peter Mason, as security-coordinator for the Houses of Parliament.[94]

A particular security advice dissemination issue arises in this context. For some years, the security service has produced a low security classified (restricted) series of terrorism threat assessments called 'Vellums'.[95] These have been made available to those private sector bodies, whose security management staffs contain former police or military personnel. The Vellums have not been available, for example, to public sector local authority emergency planning officers. Clearly, this has not been a helpful situation, when government is trying to raise counter-terrorism awareness and response levels. However, the wider dissemination and development of vellum-type intelligence products has been the subject of discussions between the security service and the Cabinet Office.[96] As a result of these discussions, there are now moves to put local authority emergency planning officers through the vetting procedures, so that they may be cleared to receive such classified information as is necessary for the proper performance of their duties under the new civil contingencies legislation.[97] Moreover, the new MI5 website is usable for both the dissemination of counter-terrorism advice and guidance and for receiving suspicious activities reports from members of the public.

The direct usability of intelligence in relation to response requirements is a very variable factor. Obviously, if terrorist groups provide, as did the Provisional IRA, coded threats giving some timing and location details or if similar details are provided from suspects, then emergency services can be fairly specific in their response strategies. However, as CIA Director, George Tenet, said to the Independent Commission in America, there were many indications of a major terrorist attack pre-9/11 but the warnings were '... maddeningly short on actionable details'.[98] In the case of the interception and search of the MV Nisha, off the Isle of Wight, the intelligence was not 'ship specific' and the Nisha was one of several vessels that happened to have a profile in terms of route background and time of arrival into UK waters, but the Nisha's cargo (sugar) and destination (the Port of London) seemed the best 'fit' with the limited intelligence available. The decision to intercept was based upon the priority given to ensuring public safety by pre-emptive action, wherever possible. As the Prime Minister said '... even if the possibility of such a threat is remote we act'.[99] This approach to the use of counter-terrorism intelligence was underlined by Mr Michael Todd, Chief Constable of Greater Manchester, when he told the Home Affairs Committee Inquiry into 'Anti-Terrorism Powers' that although in a Greater Manchester Police (GMP) counter-terrorism operation all those arrested were released '... I am convinced, the security services are convinced, the anti-terrorist squad are convinced that there was no alternative but to arrest those individuals'.[100] Underlining the impact of post-9/11 public inquiries in the USA on UK counter-terrorism decision-making, Mr Todd also said '... if there had been a terrorist outrage on that particular date at that particular location I do not think I would have to wait for the Home Secretary to ask me to resign; I think I would be resigning'.[101] Sometimes, fortunately, a failed terrorist attack provides usable data that can lead intelligence agencies to other results. For example, Richard Reid's nervousness about his IED suggested that he was not the bomb maker and therefore not a complete 'loner'. Eventually, this understanding was to lead to the arrest (in Gloucester), charge and conviction of Saajid Badat.[102] Similar follow-ups are being carried out after the 21 July 2005 attacks.

In other instances, the gap between suspicions, usable evidence and also proportionality may be quite wide. The Court of Appeal gave judgement on 18 March 2004 against the Home Secretary's appeal against the decision by the Special Immigration Appeal Court (SIAC) that there were no valid grounds for the continued detention without trial of 'M' under section 21 of the ATCSA 2001 as a suspected international terrorist. Their Lordships agreed with SIAC that '... the fact that there were suspicious circumstances did not mean that, when all the circumstances were looked at, the suspicious circumstances established that there was a reasonable suspicion'.[103] This case came before the House of Lords and on 16 December 2004 the Lords of Appeal ruled against the Home Office and upheld the Appeal Court judgement. Amongst the Law Lords' comments was that the ATCSA, Pt 4 allows '... both for the detention of those presenting no direct threat to the UK and for the release of those of whom it is alleged that they do. Such a paradoxical conclusion is hard to reconcile with the strict exigencies of the situation'.[104] In another case, a man arrested in Eastbourne and charged with possessing bomb-making equipment was acquitted. At the Central Criminal Court the charge of having articles for use in terrorism laid against Noureddine Mouleff for possession of batteries and wire was dropped as the articles were later deemed not capable of making an IED.[105] These evidential issues, especially over the use of the Part IV powers in the ATCSA 2001 have led the Parliamentary Joint Committee on Human Rights to suggest that the publicly available threat information is '... insufficient for Parliament to make an assessment of the necessity or proportionality of specific measures designed to deal with an emergency when it is asked to renew them'.[106]

Even where a conviction is secured, the trial record can illustrate just how difficult it can be to, first, acquire intelligence, second, have sufficient data to give grounds for an arrest and, third, produce the requisite evidential materials. In March 2003, two Algerians, Baghdad Meziane and Brahim Benmerzouga, were given 11-year prison sentences for terrorist activities and concurrent 7-year sentences for fraud.[107] They were involved in credit card fraud, which yielded about £100,000 for terrorist purposes. They appeared to have developed terrorist-group links from the mid-1990s onwards. Although they spent several of the years between about 1996 to September 2001 (when they were arrested) in the UK, they carried out classic intelligence-evasion tactics. First, their '... use of multiple false identities and bank accounts allowed them to remain below the intelligence screen for much of their time in the UK'.[108] As Sir David Omand commented, 'More than in the past, terrorists and facilitators are operating under multiple identities that are hard to validate – thus weakening one of the traditional security "tools", the "dossier" or filing system'.[109] Second, they kept a low profile within local Islamic community affairs in Leicester, whilst they were actively committing fraud. Both these problem points about multiple identities and low profiles can be related to those involved in the London July 2005 incidents. One development that may be forthcoming to aid the provision of more evidence in court proceedings, is a change in the UK law to allow use of intercept material but this is not expected to have a major impact on proceedings. Although it will still be necessary to heed Dame Eliza Manningham-Buller's comments that information from intelligence 'All too often falls short of evidence to support criminal charges …'.[110]

As an example to illustrate both successful disruption and dismantling work by the use of intelligence, the arrests in late March 2004 of eight men, British nationals of Pakistani origin, in relation to the seizure of half a tonne of ammonium nitrate followed an extensive and intensive surveillance operation by the security service and the police. Assistance was also received from the Royal Canadian Mounted Police, who arrested one suspect in Ottawa.[111] An important aspect of the British end of this operation was that non-British nationals did not feature in the arrests. It has been speculated that this might have been for a vehicle-borne IED targeting an entertainment location.

Conclusions

Because the current form of threat from international terrorism is regarded as 'long-term', with the Director-General of MI5 considering, as do her colleagues overseas, that the threat is '… serious and sustained, with a proven lethality and the potential to continue for years to come'[112], the Joint Committee on Human Rights has posed two quite important questions to the government which have significant implications for the intelligence services. These are:

1 '… could not more be done to provide both Parliament and the public with more of the gist of the intelligence on which the Government's assessment of the threat is based, without prejudicing legitimate security interests'?
2 That Parliamentary scrutiny and hence accountability could be strengthened if the government gave '… careful consideration to whether there is a role for the Intelligence and Security Committee to scrutinise the material on which the Government's assertions about the level of the threat are based'.[113]

Given the extra resources now going into the intelligence and security services and the much enhanced domestic role of the Director-General of MI5, the Joint Committee's second proposition seems entirely appropriate. However, the example of the MV Nisha fits very well within Pillar's comment, cited earlier, that '… intelligence specific to terrorist plots is often unattainable'[114] suggesting that '… more of the gist' may simply not be available. The optimum use of counter-terrorism intelligence has been well described in terms of a three-fold usage:

1 *Public information* – '… provided so that we have an informed and supportive public …'.
2 *Alerting information* – '… aimed at specific sectors and those who carry responsibilities for public safety'.
3 *Public warnings* – '… which we should only give when we are clear what advice we accompany a warning with so that the public can help put themselves out of the way of danger'.[115]

It may be suggested that the current use of intelligence in the UK with regard to the domestic management of terrorism in the UK does now, in general, fulfil the alerting and public warning role as far as is feasible. However, perhaps under 'public information' more could be done in explaining the intelligence-led disruption strategy and how early interventions, whilst producing headline-grabbing features on large-scale police raids, may in fact be inconclusive in terms of criminal justice system outcomes. As Assistant Chief Constable Beckley said, regarding the Terrorism Act 2000, '… it was specifically understood that it was about disruption as opposed to detection'.[116] The government confirmed, in July 2006, that '… the police and the security and intelligence agencies have disrupted many attacks against the UK since November 2000, including four since last July alone'.[117]

The crucial problem, with regard to intelligence, appears to be the adequacy in terms of numbers, of the human resources elements in both MI5 and MI6 as noted in the official reports on the services. Increased recruiting has been budgeted for, but given the acknowledged relative neglect of counter-espionage and the need to track a rising number of international terrorism person targets, will even these increased staffing levels, once recruited and trained, be sufficient resources in terms of intelligence risk management? This seems to be a particularly pertinent question as the Director-General of MI5 stated in November 2006 that the service and the police were contending with '… some 200 groupings or networks, totalling over 1600 identified individuals … [with an] … 80% rise in casework since January [2006]'.[118]

Notes

1   This chapter has benefited from the participation, under Chatham House rules, of members of a range of counter-terrorism agencies in the series of St Andrews/ Southampton ESRC Project Workshops.
2   (2004) *The Sunday Times*, 29 March.
3   Interview with Senior Anti-Terrorist Branch Officer, 6 September 2004.
4   Information from Project Workshop.
5   See the reports in *The Times* (2005) 11 July and 20 July.
6   Home Secretary, Charles Clarke, Home Affairs Select Committee, Minutes of Evidence (2005) *Counter-Terrorism and Community Relations in the Aftermath of the London Bombings*, September, HC 462-I, Qs 1 and 13, available at www. publications.parliament.uk/pa/cm200506/cmselect/cmhaff/uc462-i/uc462, accessed 14 September 2005.
7   Hughes-Wilson, Col. J. (2004) 'Pre-war intelligence and Iraq's WMD threat', *RUSI Journal*, 149(1), February, pp. 10–15; Sheptycki, J. (2004) *Review of the Influence of Strategic Intelligence on Organised Crime Policy and Practice*, Special Interest Paper 14, Crime and Policing Group, Home Office.
8   Sheptycki, op. cit., p. 5.
9   Report of a Committee of Privy Counsellors (2004) *Review of Intelligence on Weapons of Mass Destruction*, Chairman Lord Butler (hereafter cited as 'Butler Report'), HC 898, London: The Stationery Office, July, para. 50.
10 Dame Eliza Manningham-Buller, 'The International Terrorist Threat and the Dilemmas in Countering it', Speech to The Netherlands security service (AVID),

1 September 2005, available at www.mi5.gov.uk/output/Page387.html, accessed 14 September 2005.

11 A point acknowledged by Home Secretary Charles Clarke, although he felt the scepticism was '… not justified'. See Minutes of Evidence (2005) *Terrorism and other Home Office Matters*, Home Affairs Select Committee, 8 February, HC 321-I, Q.3.

12 Hughes-Wilson, op. cit.

13 Foreign and Commonwealth Office (2005) *Review of Intelligence on Weapons of Mass Destruction: Implementation of its Conclusions*, Cm 6492, April, para. 13.

14 House of Commons, Home Affairs Committee, 4th Report, Session 2005–06 (2006) *Terrorism Detention Powers*, Vol. II, HC 910-II, London: The Stationery Office, June, Ev.59, Q.295.

15 Sir David Omand, Keynote Speech to RUSI Homeland Security and Resilience Programme, 1 July 2004, available at www.ukresilience.info/contingencies/rusi.htm, accessed 6 July 2004.

16 Scarlett, John (2005) *Annual Report by the JIC Chairman: 2004–05*, as quoted in Intelligence and Security Committee (2005) *Annual Report 2004–2005*, Cm. 6510, April, para. 44, pp. 18–19.

17 The author acknowledges the ESRC Funding support provided by Grant No. L 147251004.

18 Pillar, P.R. (2004) 'Intelligence', in Cronin, A.K. and Lendes, J.M. (eds) *Attacking Terrorism – Elements of a Grand Strategy*, Washington, DC: Georgetown University Press, pp. 115–39.

19 Ibid.

20 Herman, M. (2003) 'Counter-Terrorism, Information Technology and Intelligence Change', *Intelligence and National Security*, 18(4), p. 43, quoting from the RUSI Security Monitor, 2002.

21 See the reports in *The Times* (2005) 6 August.

22 Manningham-Buller, Speech, 1 September 2005, op. cit.

23 *The Times* (2005) 17 and 18 July, and *The Independent* (2005) 18 July.

24 Intelligence and Security Committee (2006) *Report into the London Terrorist Attacks on 7 July 2005*, Cm. 6785, London: The Stationery Office, May, p. 8.

25 HC 462-I, op. cit., Qs 11 and 12.

26 HM Government (2006) *Countering International Terrorism: The United Kingdom's Strategy*, Cm. 6888, London: The Stationery Office, July, para. 83.

27 Information from Project Workshop.

28 Herman, op. cit., p. 42.

29 Ibid., p. 43.

30 Treverton, G.F. (2003) 'Terrorism, intelligence and law enforcement: learning the right lessons', *Intelligence and National Security*, 18(4), Winter, p. 121.

31 Herman, op. cit., describes 'stovepiping' occurring where '… single-source intelligence is passed up to the top without sufficient all-source integration and without sufficient cooperation in the steerage of collection', pp. 45–6.

32 Rimington, S. (2001) *Open Secret*, London: Arrow, pp. 218–21.

33 Cm. 6510, op. cit., para. 28, pp. 14–15.

34 Home Office, Scottish Executive, Northern Ireland Office (2004) *Guidelines on Special Branch Work in the United Kingdom*, March, paras 20–1.

35 HMIC (2003) *HMIC Thematic Inspection of Special Branch and Ports Policing – A Need to Know*, Home Office Communications Directorate, p. 20, para. 2.20.

36 Ibid.

37 Cm. 6888, op. cit., para. 105.

38 See MI5 website www.mi5.gov.uk.

39 Information from Project Workshop.

40 Rimington, op. cit., p. 105.

41 Butler Report, op. cit., Chapter 3.
42 Omand, Sir David, as cited in Intelligence and Security Committee (2004) *Annual Report 2003–2004 re the Intelligence Services Act 1994 ch.13*, Cm. 6240, June, London: The Stationery Office, p. 38, para. 137.
43 *The Times* (2005) 15 September.
44 Ibid., p. 263.
45   Information from Project Workshop.
46 Butler Report, op. cit., para. 123, fn 5.
47 Cm. 6888, op. cit., para. 25.
48 Cm. 6510, op. cit., para. 23, p. 12.
49 Rimington, op. cit., p. 213.
50   Ibid., and pp. 206–7.
51 Ryan, M. (2002) 'Inventing the axis of evil: the myth and reality of US intelligence and policy-making after 9/11', *Intelligence and National Security*, 17(4), Winter, p. 66.
52 Aldrich, R.J. (2004) 'Transatlantic intelligence and security', *International Affairs*, 80(4), July, p. 737.
53 HC 321-I, op. cit., Q.15.
54 Rimington, op. cit. p. 222.
55 Intelligence and Security Committee (2003) *Annual Report 2002–2003 re the Intelligence Services Act 1994 ch.13*, Cm. 5837, London: The Stationery Office, June, pp. 8–10, Intelligence and Security Committee (2004) *Annual Report 2003–2004 re the Intelligence Services Act 1994 ch.13*, Cm. 6240, London: The Stationery Office, June, and see also (2002) *National Intelligence Machinery*, London: The Stationery Office.
56 Eliza Manningham-Buller, DG MI5, James Smart Lecture 2003, 'Global Terrorism; Are we meeting the challenge?', 16 October 2003, available at www.mi5.gov.uk/output/Page172.html, accessed 30 April 2004.
57 Cm. 6240, op. cit., p. 14, para. 42.
58 Butler Report, op. cit., para. 415.
59 Manningham-Buller, James Smart Lecture, op. cit.
60 See the report in *The Times*: (2005) *The Times*, 3 August.
61 HC 462-I, op. cit., Q.5.
62 MI5 Staffing increases announced: *The Times* (2004) 23 February and 2 March. By comparison the Central Intelligence Agency has around 16,000 personnel and a budget in 2004 of around \$40 billion, see Goodman, M.A. (2003) '9/11: The Failure of Strategic Intelligence', *Intelligence and National Security* 18(40), Winter, pp. 66–8.
63 See the report in *The Times* (2004) 7 March.
64 Cm. 6240, op. cit., p. 16, para. 49.
65 Ibid.
66 See the report in *The Times* (2004) 19 April.
67 Information from Project Workshop.
68 The details on Arabic speakers are taken from Third Report House of Commons Defence Committee, Session 2003–2004 (2004) *Lessons of Iraq*, HC 57, London: The Stationery Office, March, Ev.441 'Further Memo from MOD'.
69 On JTAC see Cm. 5837, op. cit., p. 18, Cm. 6492, op. cit., para. 7, and also the Government's Reply to the House of Commons Select Committee on Science and Technology's Report on *The Scientific Response to Terrorism*, Cm. 6108, London: The Stationery Office, 2004, para. 16, and information from Project Workshop.
70 Cm. 6108, op. cit., and see also the commendation of JTAC in the Butler Report, op. cit., para. 134.
71 Manningham-Buller, James Smart Lecture 2003, op. cit.

72   Oral Evidence to the Defence and Home Affairs Committee inquiry into Homeland Security, HC 417-I, 2 March 2004, Q.62, and Manningham-Buller, Speech, 1 September 2005, op. cit.
73   Interviews with PICTU and MPSB Anti-Terrorist Branch Officer.
74   Report to the Secretary of State for Trade and Industry by the Director of Civil Nuclear Security (2003) *The State of Security in the Civil Nuclear Industry and the Effectiveness of Security Regulations April 2002–March 2003*, OCNS, para. 16.
75   Cm. 6240, op. cit., p. 22, para. 76.
76   Ibid., p. 27, para. 95.
77   Ibid., p. 28, para. 97.
78   Cm. 6108, op. cit., para. 16.
79   Ibid.
80   Cm. 6240, op. cit., p. 30, para. 104.
81   Ibid., para. 106.
82   Cm. 5837, op. cit., p. 18.
83   Butler Report, op. cit., para. 600.
84   Cm. 6510, op. cit., paras 65–9, and Cm. 6492, op. cit.
85   Cm. 6492, op. cit., para. 23.
86   See the reports in *The Times* (2005) 11 July and 20 July.
87   Home Office (2006) *Threat Levels: The System to Assess the Threat from International Terrorism*, July.
88   See the BBC News report (2004) 'Terror threat to airlines queried', February, available at www.news.bbc.co.uk/1/hi/uk/3449903.stm, accessed 28 July 2004.
89   Oral Evidence by the Home Secretary to the Defence and Home Affairs Committee inquiry into Homeland Security, HC 417-I, 2 March 2004, Q.26.
90   Sir David Omand, Keynote Speech to RUSI Homeland Security and Resilience Programme, 1 July 2004, available at www.ukresilience.info/contingencies/rusi.htm, accessed 6 July 2004.
91   Interview with Head of PICTU.
92   On the role of T4 see Cm. 6108, op. cit., para. 103, and interview.
93   Interview with NaCTSO officers, 1 April 2004, and on NSAC see www.mi5.gov.uk.
94   (2004) *The Sunday Times*, 19 December.
95   HC 518-I, para. 85.
96   Information from Project Workshop and see also HC 57-II, op. cit., Q.1675.
97   Interview with a local authority emergency planning officer, 26 April 2004.
98   (2004) *The Times*, 25 March.
99   Interview with the SIO for the MV Nisha operation, 11 August 2004, and BBC TV news extract.
100 Oral Evidence, Home Affairs Committee inquiry into 'Anti-Terrorism Powers', HC 886-I, 8 July 2004, Q.67.
101 Ibid., Q.68.
102 (2003) *The Times*, 4 December.
103 (2004) *The Times*, 24 March.
104 House of Lords, Opinions of the Lords of Appeal in the case *A 7 Another, X and Another v. Home Secretary* [2004] UKHL 56, 16 December 2004, p. 21.
105 (2004) *The Times*, 27 March.
106 Joint Committee on Human Rights, Eighteenth Report, HC 158, Session 2003–04, para. 19.
107 Evans, R. (2003) 'News', *Jane's Intelligence Review*, May.
108 Ibid.
109 Sir David Omand, Keynote Speech to RUSI Homeland Security and Resilience Programme, 1 July 2004, available at www.ukresilience.info/contingencies/rusi.htm, accessed 6/7/04.
110 Manningham-Buller, Speech, 1 September 2005, op. cit.

111 *The Times* (2004) 31 March, 1 and 2 April.
112 Manningham-Buller, Speech, 1 September 2005, op. cit.
113 HC 158, op. cit., para. 23.
114 See n. 11.
115 HC 417-I, op. cit., Q.75.
116 ACC Robert Beckley, ACPO-TAM, Oral Evidence, Minutes of Evidence (2005) *Terrorism and Community Affairs*, Home Affairs Select Committee, 25 January, HC 165-II, Q.342. Cm. 6888, op. cit., is a useful public source in this respect.
117 Cm. 6888, op. cit., para. 68.
118 Dame Eliza Manningham-Buller, DG MI5, 'The International Terrorist Threat to the UK', Speech at Queen Mary's College, London, 9 November 2006.

10 Police and counter-terrorism in the UK

A study of 'one of the highest and most challenging priorities for police forces nationally'

Frank Gregory

Introduction

Because of the recent long period of Irish terrorist activity from 1969 to 2001, the British police have developed a well-regarded competency in counter-terrorism in partnership with MI5, MI6 and military special forces. Indeed, the police expertise was used to assist the Greek authorities in dismantling the 17 November Group. This chapter will provide an overview of UK counter-terrorism policing, review the impact of 9/11, discuss the major changes and issues that have arisen in the overall context of the domestic management of terrorism in the UK and reflect on the implications of the London bombings of July 2005.

The counter-terrorism strategy used in England, Scotland and Wales is centred on the law enforcement model of response to terrorism. That is to say, that terrorism is essentially a criminal activity and therefore the primary and lead responders are the police in terms of both the national role of the MPSB (SO12) and the Anti-Terrorist Branch (SO13), who take a national lead in investigations, in England and Wales, and that of the comparable elements in the other police forces.[1] A recent change is that during 2005–6 Metropolitan Police Commissioner, Sir Ian Blair, has created a single Metropolitan Police Counter-Terrorism Command by merging the investigative side of SO12 with SO13.

In Scotland, each Chief Constable still remains solely responsible for counter-terrorism policing in the force area but can and does involve the Metropolitan Police (SO12 and SO13) and the National Coordinator for Terrorist Investigations (NCTI) as required. In Northern Ireland the model was somewhat modified by special legislation because of the pre-1996 levels of terrorism and the wider roles for the military in the province, including the use of military personnel in the terrorist suspect surveillance role. This surveillance role is only carried out by the military on the mainland where the police and security service need extra personnel support.[2] Such support has been reported as having been used in response to the UK's first post-9/11 international terrorism attacks, the July 2005 London bombings.[3]

This chapter, in its examination of the police response, raises the issue of 'parallel agendas'. This issue is defined to cover a situation where a public or private sector agency, within the governance mode of counter-terrorism response, finds itself facing potentially separate and possibly conflicting policy agendas. In the case of the police, at the same time as the government is placing a priority on their counter-terrorism preparedness and response, the government also expects the police to give priority to meeting targets it has set in other crime control policy areas, to take on new responsibilities with regard to tacking anti-social behaviour, and to provide public 'reassurance' while taking steps to improve the confidence in particular of minority ethnic communities.

The police service was trying to fulfil these policies at a time when it also faced the challenges of proposals for major structural reforms including police force amalgamations and the formation of new law enforcement bodies. Currently, the government has proceeded with the planned merger of the NCIS, National Crime Squad and other agencies into the new SOCA, which became operational in April 2006. There are also ongoing studies concerning the possibility of forming a unified UK Border Control Agency under the Border Management Programme (BMP).[4]

Whilst the move to set up SOCA may be a long overdue and logical amalgamation it does raise a potential problem in the counter-terrorism area. There is evidence from the Northern Ireland experience and, in the case of recent arrests in the UK and in other EU member states, that terrorists operate at the interface of terrorist activity/organised crime/low-level crime. For example, Richard Reid was also known as a 'Peckham mugger', some of those involved in the Madrid railway bombings were involved in low-level drug dealing and some of those suspected of involvement in the 'ricin plot' were fund raising via stolen credit card purchases.[5] The concern here is that this aspect of the problem of 'parallel agendas' might reinforce barriers to inter-agency cooperation, often expressed to this project as the 'silo' thinking problem. This concern can be linked to the vital need to maintain what the HMIC thematic inspection of Special Branches called the 'golden thread' of information flows linking communities to counter-terrorism policing in the UK.[6]

The issue of police restructuring was a significant issue during this research. For example, the Police Superintendents' Association proposed, to the Home Secretary, a three-tier system based on 270 local police divisions and 10 regional controllers with regional police units for public order and major investigations and, presumably, the national units and agencies like SOCA. They also envisaged the police side to be headed by a national police director with a national headquarters, altogether quite a radical proposal, but one that echoes previous ideas.[7] Another reform variant was suggested by former Metropolitan Police Commissioner, Sir John Stevens, who has proposed that no provincial police force should be less than 3,000 strong or more than 7,000 strong.[8] Within the police counter-terrorism specialisation, there have also been proposals for the radical reform of Special Branches, by the HMIC, and for a National Counter-Terrorism Police force. Lastly, former Home Secretary, Charles Clarke, demanded, in Autumn 2005, a new round of police force amalgamations, following the September 2005 HMIC Report, *Closing the Gap*.[9] Initially, Home Secretary Clarke wanted the proposals completed by the end of 2005. However, there was significant resistance within police forces and police authorities and cost implications also arose. These factors and the existence of more pressing Home Office problems caused the Home Secretary and Police Minister to announce, in statements in June and July 2006, that these aspirations for police force amalgamations no longer had any active implementation timetable.[10]

Thus the general background for the current study of counter-terrorism policing in the UK remains, as it always has done, that of a tension between an essentially hybrid policing system with its mix of decentralised and centralised bodies and pressures for provincial police force rationalisation and national organisational modes in order to deliver policy objectives. This chapter will address the background to counter-terrorism policing in the UK, the legal framework, police organisational response to 9/11, the police response to particular forms of terrorist threat not previously experienced in the UK and an assessment, to date, of the outcomes of the policing of counter-terrorism post-9/11. This analysis must also be considered as reflecting linkages with the Security Service's lead role in the development of counter-terrorism intelligence which, of course, forms the basis for pre-emptive interventions by the police and their protective security work.

The background to counter-terrorism policing in the UK

This has its origins in the late nineteenth century with the establishment in the Metropolitan Police of the Special Irish Office, the fore-runner of today's Special Branch, to tackle the mainland manifestations of the Irish problem of the period. The present system comprises a number of central police services, the specific Anti-Terrorist Branch and the MPSB plus their associated special units, the provincial police forces' Special Branches and those other provincial police force assets that may be deployed, from time to time, in counter-terrorism operations. To date, only a few police forces, for example, North Yorkshire, West Midlands, City of London and Greater Manchester Police, have brought all the relevant specialist sections together in a single counter-terrorism unit or other form of centralised structure.[11] The MPSB continues to play its leading role in anti-terrorist operations in London, nationwide and internationally, especially through the role of the NCTI, currently Deputy Assistant Commissioner Peter Clarke. The Anti-Terrorist Branch has also been developing anti-terrorist investigation skills nationwide through its courses for National Senior Investigating Officers, the three courses run up to 2004 trained 42 Senior Investigating Officers in the anti-terrorism field.[12]

At the outset, it is important to set out the range of incidents that the police in mainland UK faced, before 9/11, from international, Irish-related groups, extremist groups and individual 'bombers'. The range of incidents covered the use of IEDs, for example, the Brighton Hotel and Manchester Shopping Centre Provisional IRA bombings, the Provisional IRA mortar attack on Downing Street, letter bombs, the nail bombing of the minority communities in London, the Lockerbie incident and one recent aerial hijack. Therefore, it can be seen that the police experience and thus their practised response was quite extensive in the period before 9/11. For the general public, probably the most symbolic police counter-terrorism response was the deployment of armed police and, on occasion, troops and armoured vehicles, to Heathrow, Gatwick and Edinburgh Airports.

It is also necessary to remember that although there is now some 'nostalgia' for the era of Irish bomb threat messages, these actually could be much less than helpful. For example, there was a partial IED detonation at Smallbrook, Queensway in Birmingham in the late evening of Saturday, 3 November 2001. In this incident 'police were only given 30 minutes to respond [by the Real IRA] to imprecise and inaccurate coded warnings and ... severe loss of life and major damage to buildings would have been caused if the device had been detonated fully'.[13] This incident and the police post-incident investigation also provides an important example of the problem of the scale of resources required for counter-terrorism, which will feature as one of the key themes of this chapter. Eventually, in January 2003, five men were sentenced for the Smallbrook bombing and other offences at the Central Criminal Court. Operation 'Heartsett', the West Midlands Police and MPSB post-incident investigation necessitated the taking of, *inter alia*, 4,500 witness statements and the collection of 11,000 documents in the incident room.[14]

What additional counter-terrorism planning assumptions and planning challenges, therefore, did the British police face after 9/11? First, a potentially catastrophic event defined, partly, by reference to scale of casualties caused by deliberate terrorist actions. Second, an attack, without threat warning, by a suicide bomber or bombers, using IEDs, as occurred in London on 7 July 2005. Third, the variant that is called the 'deadly and determined' (DADA)[15] terrorist attack (for example, Riyadh), which combines assault with automatic weapons, car/truck bombs and suicide or sacrifice bombers. Fourth, there might be an attempt to mount an attack against aviation targets using MANPADS. Finally, there is the generally accepted ambition of the Al-Qaeda network to try and add either a CBRN component to an IED or to directly use a CBRN 'weapon' as in the Sarin attack on the Tokyo Underground.

No incidents of any of the above types had previously occurred in the UK.[16] Therefore, the response had to assess, plan and provide the personnel and equipment to meet these challenges. Nearly five years after 9/11, one can distinguish between the necessary immediate responses and the medium- and longer-term responses.[17]

The evaluation of the police response needs to be set within the context of the government's 'Contest' counter-terrorism strategy, the 'four Ps' which is set out, in brief, below:

- Prevent – addressing underlying causes of terrorism in the UK and overseas, especially issues relating to Muslim citizens.
- Pursue – using intelligence effectively to disrupt and apprehend the terrorists – where the UK has increased joint working and intelligence sharing between

governments and law enforcement agencies across the world and the government also aims to make the UK borders more secure; to make identity theft harder and to curb terrorist access to financial sources.

- Protect – ensuring reasonable security precautions, including those needed to meet a CBRN threat, are in place ranging from physical measures at airports to establishing CTSAs in each police force.
- Prepare – making sure that the UK has the people and resources in place to effectively respond to the consequences of a terrorist attack.[18]

It is evident that the police have identifiable roles in respect of all the 'Ps' and particularly 'Pursue' and 'Protection'. However, there was something of a 'gap' between ministerial warnings on the threat from international terrorism and the terms of the actual annual policing priorities set by the Home Secretary. From 1999–2000 to 2001–2 the two priorities were to reduce local problems of crime and disorder in partnership with local authorities, other local agencies and the public, and to increase trust and confidence in policing amongst minority ethnic communities.[19] Neither of the above mentions terrorism because they were set before 9/11 but they did continue into 2002–3.

Even the first National Policing Plan (NPP) for 2003–6, published in November 2002, pursuant to section 1 of the Police Reform Act 2002, does not include 'counter-terrorism' as a specific police priority to be reflected in local force plans.[20] In the 2003–6 NPP 'counter-terrorism' is listed among 'Other policing responsibilities' and only highlights the need to regularly review local terrorist contingency plans and the need to maintain contact with the MPSB and national agencies.[21] However, it does add the imperative 'will' to the requirement for provincial forces to maintain this contact. However, the first NPP did also give priority to the effective implementation, across all forces, of the National Intelligence Model (NIM) which should contribute to better standards of intelligence gathering and evaluation. The NIM could be an important factor in supporting the 'Pursue' counter-terrorism objective. However, the Bichard Inquiry, into the Soham murders, has raised the significant, linked issue of the delayed introduction of a single national police intelligence computer system.[22] Terrorism does, however, enter the second NPP, 2004–7 in a more visible manner. In the 2004–7 NPP it is entered, however, not as a 'key priority' but as the second of two 'underpinning themes', the first being 'community engagement and civil renewal'.[23]

The Home Office identified five 'key elements' in achieving the goal of 'countering terrorism and the threat of terrorism' which are set out as follows: robust local contingency plans, within the national guidance (including tackling chemical, biological and radiological materials), specialist chemical, biological and radiological training for the police, the provision of intelligence and operational support to the national counter-terrorism effort, proportionate and consistent application of counter-terrorism legislative powers to prevent and disrupt acts of terrorism and terrorists, and effective links with other frontline agencies and members of the public to raise awareness of the threat from terrorism and to improve resilience against that threat.[24]

In terms of the mechanisms for assessing police performance in respect of this 'underpinning' theme, as of November 2003 all the Home Office could say was that for '... 2004/05, assessment of counter-terrorism activity and performance will be informed by HM Inspectorate of Constabulary's professional opinion'. In parallel, the Home Office said it will work with 'key partners' to decide how to '... include this critical area of police work in the Policing Performance Assessment Framework in the longer term'.[25] The work on counter-terrorism police performance indicators was still in the preparatory stages in the Summer of 2006.

In his 2002–3 Annual Report the Chief HMIC refers to 'Terrorism' in the 'Significant Cases' section of his Report and he commences by noting '... how valiantly the Police Service has risen to this particular challenge and how quickly it adopted new ways of working to counter these threats'. However, he ended the section rather prophetically, in the light of the policing demands of the July 2005 incidents, by commenting '... it is a fact that these requirements to respond to such intelligence and incidents, and as a result reassure the public, *are expensive and take place at a time when resources are already desperately needed to tackle more fundamental crime reduction problems*' (emphasis added).[26] Apart from the obviously counter-terrorism policing related HMIC thematic inspection of Special Branches in 2003, none of the recent force-based focused inspections even remotely looked at a counter-terrorism policing-related issue. Moreover although none of the current police Performance Indicators (PIs) specifically refers to counter-terrorism policing, some of the PIs can be interpreted as offering some useful counter-terrorism related PIs. Consequently, in this chapter, data on the police capacity for the domestic management of terrorism in the UK has to be found by looking for evidence of the police response to the 'four Ps' which stemmed from their own post-9/11 counter-terrorism review, Operation Fairway. Operation Fairway promoted a five-strand strategy covering the elements of preparatory activity, preventive measures, proactive operations, post-incident investigations and consequence management with community involvement underpinning all the previous strands;[27] especially the police seeking to use intelligence, effectively, to disrupt and apprehend suspect terrorists.

The legal framework and policing by consent issues

As the duties of the police service are particularly grounded in statute and common law, the analysis will commence with a brief review of legal framework, some of which pre-dated 9/11. The most important pre-9/11 piece of legislation was the Terrorism Act 2000. The Terrorism Act 2000 contained quite a wide definition of terrorism which covered political, ideological and religious motivations for acts of terrorism and the Act also made provision for the proscription of terrorist groups, thus making it an offence to be a member of such a group. It was designed to provide permanent, as opposed to the previous temporary anti-terrorism legislation, and to cover all forms of terrorism both domestic and international. Amongst its new provisions were the creation of a new offence of inciting terrorism abroad, an expanded offence of providing or receiving weapons training, and powers to allow the police to set up cordons for limited periods in designated areas for the purposes of terrorist investigations.[28] After 9/11, a significant, controversial and swiftly drafted piece of legislation was enacted – the ATCS 2001. It was a particularly controversial piece of legislation because anti-terrorism powers were concluded in a general crime-control act and these powers also included (section 4) the power to detain, without trial under special immigration controls, those non-UK nationals suspected of terrorism for whom insufficient evidence was available for court proceedings and who could not be deported under European Convention on Human Rights (ECHR) grounds; they could of course leave the country voluntarily.[29] The government indicated that the legislation had nine main anti-terrorism objectives: to cut off terrorist funding, to promote counter-terrorism information sharing, to streamline relevant immigration procedures (Part 4 covering detention without trial of non-UK nationals suspected of being international terrorists), to tackle those who seek to stir up religious and racial hatred and violence, to ensure the security of nuclear and aviation industries, to improve the security of dangerous substances that may be targeted or used by terrorists (Part 7, control of pathogens and toxins), to extend police powers to the relevant non-Home Office police forces (BTP, MDP), to ensure that the UK could meet all EU Justice and Home Affairs (JHA) obligations and all international obligations relating to countering bribery and corruption and to update parts of the UK's anti-terrorist powers.[30]

When asked how useful the provisions of the ATCSA 2001 had proved, Home Secretary Blunkett provided some rather limited forms of indicators to Parliament relating to the period up to January 2004: over 100 disclosures, 18 seizures of terrorist funds and 24 arrests for religiously aggravated crime.[31] The total funds seized between 2001 and 2006 (excluding assets frozen in relation to the Taliban) was around £1.46 million.[32] Additionally, the former Home Secretary Charles Clarke noted, in September 2005, that the Treasury had taken a total of 30 administrative actions, 28 of which were in 2001, involving freezing funds, financial assets and economic resources against groups proscribed under the Terrorism Act 2000.[33] In the case of terrorist finances, whilst the sums involved may not be large, for example, the total costs of the Madrid bombing is estimated at around £8,500 and the cost of the 7 July London bombings is estimated at around £8,000 raised by the bombers themselves, the investigation of money trails is a useful tool in disruption and the identification of suspects and suspect companies and organisations.[34] Use of the powers of the Terrorism Act 2000 has also been increasing, as Lord Carlile of Berriew's Reports show.[35]

Part IV of ATCSA 2001 was controversial from the outset and the detention without trial of non-UK nationals under special immigration procedures was eventually challenged by the Law Lords in December 2004.[36] After very considerable public and parliamentary debate it was replaced, temporarily, by the Prevention of Terrorism Act 2005. This established a regime of control orders that could be applied to UK as well as non-UK nationals. These required judicial approval, were limited to 12-month periods and covered a range of restraints and did not necessarily include house arrest.[37] However, a number of these new control orders were ruled by the Appeal Court, in August 2006, to be contrary to Article 5 of ECHR.[38] Consequently, the Home Secretary has to think again about how suspects thought to pose a serious risk to the public but for whom there is inadequate evidence for court proceedings are treated.

After the two bombing incidents in London in July 2005 one of the major responses was a consultation process on the issue of possible legislative changes that would further aid the counter-terrorism response. The changes proposed were not solely related to the incidents but rather reflected ongoing studies and lessons from previous operations. In particular a high level meeting was held in 10 Downing Street between the Prime Minister, Home Secretary senior counter-terrorism figures, including the Director-General of MI5 and the Chairman of the Association of Chief Police Officers Terrorism and Allied Matters Committee (ACPO TAM), Chief Constable Ken Jones from the Sussex Police. Mr Jones presented an ACPO TAM paper, based upon operational experiences and workshops, which proposed, *inter alia*, that the law should be changed to allow for the detention of terrorist suspects, after arrest, for up to 90 days before charges were brought and that further thought should be given to the organisation of the UK's border control services. The extended detention period was proposed in order to facilitate evidence gathering in the UK and overseas where, for example, early arrest was necessary for public protection or evidence might have to be obtained through the lengthy process of accessing encrypted computer files.[39] Ministers were also making public statements about the changes in the law they would like to bring before Parliament. On 20 July the Home Secretary made a statement to the House of Commons proposing three new offences: acts preparatory to terrorism, indirect incitement, and training or receiving training for terrorist purposes involving hazardous substances.[40] The latter proposal was seen as reflecting 'gaps' in existing related legislation.[41] On 5 August the Prime Minister produced a list of further proposals. He proposed an offence of glorifying terrorism, an examination of the merits of longer post-arrest pre-charge detention periods, proscription of the group Hizb ut Tahir and consultations on ways of closing down radical 'mosques'.[42] Subsequent public debate suggested that offences such as 'glorifying terrorism' were probably unworkable in practice.

In October 2005 the Home Secretary brought forward a new Terrorism Bill. It had been preceded by a three-month consultation process in which the consensus of judicial opinion was certainly not persuaded of the need for long pre-charge detention periods and even the Attorney-General was reported as being not fully convinced.[43] However, the case continued to be urged by senior counter-terrorism officials. On 6 October the Assistant Commissioner (Specialist Operations) (AC (SO)), Mr Andy Hayman, wrote to the Home Secretary outlining, in detail, the police case for extending the maximum period of detention without charge to three months. In support of the case he attached an Anti-Terrorist Branch (SO13) briefing note. The briefing note compared post-9/11 international terrorism with the UK experience of Irish terrorism and noted that '... we can no longer wait until the point of attack before intervening. The threat to the public is simply too great to run that risk'. The briefing note advanced eight points in support of a longer pre-charge detention period, for example, the time needed to conduct the international aspects of an investigation, the problem of establishing an accurate identity of a suspect and the complexity of forensic work. Referring to the 'bomb factory', found in Yorkshire after the 7 July attack, the briefing noted that it took '… over 2 weeks before safe access could be gained for the examination to begin. It took a further six weeks to complete the examination'.[44]

The Terrorism Bill, as presented to Parliament in October 2005, contained three sections on offences in Part I, including: encouragement of terrorism (section 1), dissemination of terrorism publications (section 2) and preparation of terrorist acts (section 5). It also includes offences involving radioactive devices and materials, nuclear facilities and site (sections 9 and 10). The provisions to extend pre-charge, post-arrest detention for periods up to three months on the application of a Crown Prosecutor or police officer of at least superintendent rank and under judicial authority are set out in Part II. These amended Schedule 8 to the Terrorism Act 2000.[45] The Act as eventually passed, the Terrorism Act 2006, only extended detention provisions to 28 days in recognition of the extensive parliamentary opposition to the original proposal.[46]

With regard to the debate (discussed later) about the relationship between numbers of arrests and numbers eventually charged it is important to remember that the legal framework actually performs several different functions.[47] It can be seen to provide:

- political symbolism – response to a problem
- defining activities as unlawful
- providing an investigative tool through the assembly of 'grounds for arrest'
- providing the parameters in which the available evidence is considered with regard to presenting cases to answer before the courts.

In using these legal provisions the police are guided by three principles of response in terms of anti-terrorist policing: first, and primarily, public safety, second, gathering evidence and, third, maintaining public support.[48]

Consequently, given the priority of public safety, early arrest interventions resulting from an anti-terrorist surveillance operation may be inconclusive on evidential grounds and thus lead to smaller numbers charged or charges under legislation other than the Terrorism Act 2000. Moreover, in respect of the prevention of terrorism the maintenance of public support amongst sections of the community who may feel singled out for anti-terrorist policing attention is absolutely vital and forms a key element in the Home Office and police response. An ACPO committee has special responsibility for police initiatives in this respect. Important contributions to this work have been made by the placing of the police National Communities Tension Team on a permanent footing and by the creation of the Muslim Safety Forum.

Police response options to 9/11

These can be divided into two groups. The first group represents a form of revisiting the option of creating a national police force, as suggested in the 1964 Royal Commission Minority Report on the Police and revisited periodically, when frustrations emerge concerning the performance of the decentralised police system. The second group of options involves the, by now, quite familiar format of introducing new 'central police services' alongside more traditional methods of coordinating common responses through the Home Office, ACPO and its committees and other agencies such as MI5 and the promotion of provincial police force amalgamations.

Central to counter-terrorism policing is the established role of Special Branches in carrying out their part of the counter-terrorism intelligence-gathering and investigative role under the parameters set by the Director-General of MI5. Originally, only the Metropolitan Police had a Special Branch, which in mid-1960s was about 300 strong. Gradually, the provincial police forces established their own Special Branches with similar duties of intelligence-gathering and sea and airport watch. Estimates suggest that in 1978, the total strength of the Special Branches was 1,638 and by 2003 the strength had risen to 4,247 with 600 in the MPSB.[49]

In January 2003, HMIC published a thematic inspection Report on special branch and ports policing under the heading *A Need to Know.*[50] This Report merits a full discussion because its import is very germane to the issues of the domestic management of terrorism. As the Report's introduction said, 'Whilst this inspection had been planned for some time, before 11 September 2001, that day's events underlined the need to review Special Branch and to assess the effectiveness of its contribution to the national structure of this country'.[51] At the time of the Report, the Special Branches were working under 1994 guidelines and were tasked to gather intelligence '... to meet national security requirements as well as to support other policing priorities such as the prevention of disorder'.[52]

One of the first points that the Report made and one which reflected the varied sizes of provincial police forces, was the variable size of Special Branch units, ranging from just a few officers, headed by a detective sergeant to around 500 in the MPSB, headed by a commander. The impact of this dispersion and diversity was, first, the range of levels of interface that MI5 had to engage with. Second, the fact that '... the operational capability of individual units depended very much on their size, the smaller units having neither the officers nor the resources to meet the full range of operational requirements'.[53] Additionally, the HMIC noted that in some forces '... Special Branch personnel were routinely diverted to tasks outside the normal remit of the Branch'.[54]

A further major set of issues related to the border control capabilities of the Special Branch ports units (SBPUs). The issues identified were: the low status of SBPUs in the Special Branch and the often accompanying '... poor standards of accommodation and resources found at several ports'.[55] This latter problem was also raised by Sir John Wheeler in his Report on airport security and has been raised by Lord Carlile of Berriew in his Reports on the operation of the Terrorism Act 2000.[56] The SBPU's resource gaps also raised a general concern by HMIC on the need for a '… secure locally and nationally networked IT'.[57]

In terms of the coordination and oversight of Special Branches, the HMIC Report made two significant criticisms:

- The current regional groupings of Special Branch, which were primarily based around quarterly meetings of HSBs chaired by ACPO regional representatives varied in their effectiveness.
- There was no single organisation which had overall responsibility for the coordination of Special Branch.

Of the Report's five main recommendations, one was controversial and the others somewhat overdue. These were, first, the creation of regional Special Branch units based on ACPO regions '… *Under the executive control of regional directors answerable to relevant chief constables' management committee*'[58] (controversial proposal). Second, it was proposed to create the appointment, at Deputy Chief Constable (DCC) level, of a National Coordinator of Special Branch – non-executive but with responsibility for ports policing, policy, training and issues common to Special Branch nationally. Third, providing dedicated security-post funding. Fourth, requiring chief constables to ensure that Special Branches and SBPUs are '… appropriately staffed and adequately resourced to meet the continuing and developing threats to us'.[59] Finally, recognising the need to identify and fund national Special Branch IT requirements.

Behind these recommendations lay three significant post-9/11 concerns:[60] that the 1994 guidelines had created a tension with its statement that chief constables can use Special Branches '… on any duties flowing from their [chief constables'] responsibilities …', and the statement that Special Branches '… exist primarily to acquire intelligence … to meet both local policing needs and also to assist the Security Service; the fact that '… prior to 11 September 2001 some forces were downsizing their special branches on the basis of a perceived reduction in the overall threat to national security';[61] and the variable provision for and recognition of '… counter-terrorism as a core police responsibility'.[62]

One obvious consequence of this diversity of provision was the fact that all Special Branches received the same number of operational messages from ACPO TAM and, until recently, the same statement of MI5 requirements. Another consequence was the fact that some Special Branches would struggle severely to staff some levels of surveillance operations and indeed might have very limited access to surveillance resources. These consequences formed important parts of the driver for some proposal to rationalise Special Branch provision.

Regarding SBPUs, the Report pointed to the distinction between the designated sea ports and airports, including the nine major airports (which are designated under the Policing of Airports Act 1974) and the rest of the ports and airports. The designated category has a dedicated local Special Branch presence, which is nationally funded by the Home Office Dedicated Security Posts (DSP) scheme.

The remainder, which may be regionally significant or just small recreational facilities, will have a variable coverage. At some ports, the various border agencies – Special Branch, HM Customs and Excise (HMCE) and the UK Immigration Service (UKIS) – have formed Joint Intelligence Cells.

In its strategic overview sections, the Report made some highly pertinent general comments relating to the domestic management of terrorism in the UK.[63] It related the placing of the Report in the public domain under the title *A Need to Know* to what it called the 'golden thread' of the linkage between the local police and their Special Branches to their communities and onward to the national security levels, a linkage '... noticeably absent from the national security structures of some countries ...'. Moreover, this Special Branch local coverage was deemed vital to national security and to be retained '... at all costs ...'.[64]

Both these points were made in the context of the fact that '... one of the key lessons to emerge from the investigation into the 11 September attacks has been the vital importance of extending the reach of the national security agencies by further utilising the close links between local police and the communities ...'.[65] These points can be linked to the importance of surveillance as a counter-terrorism tool.

Surveillance

As pointed out in the intelligence section, this is a key resource in the domestic management of the terrorist threat in the UK and HMIC noted that it is '... an expensive and resource-intensive tool and the capacity of Special Branches to mount surveillance operations varies widely ... and is largely related to the size of Special Branch'.[66] The following examples from the Report will illustrate this point:

- The large Metropolitan forces have '... dedicated full-time surveillance teams and rarely need to call on force surveillance resources'.[67]
- Medium and small Special Branches maintain an ac hoc surveillance capability forming teams from trained officers as required.
- The smallest Special Branch units '... have no dedicated surveillance capability and may even be too small to field an ad hoc team ...'.[68]

In these latter two cases, the force Special Branch would be able to call on assistance from forces in its ACPO region via mutual aid or from an MPSB team or Security Service surveillance team if the operation met the Security Service threshold for deployment. Importantly, the Report stated that '... recent intelligence-led operations have pointed the need for a more consistent surveillance capability and improved response times across the country'.[69] This issue was also linked to the related problem of the uneven distribution of the technical resources for surveillance.

Outcomes of the report

The main structural change proposed by HMIC, that chief constables should lose force Special Branches in favour of regional Special Branch units under executive regional Special Branch directors, was, at that time, strongly resisted by the majority of chief constables. They obviously felt it was yet another move to radically change the UK's de-centralised police system in favour of some mix of local police commands, regional and national units. These measures were perceived as a means of allowing for increased central control of policing through the Home Office.

This *impasse* was resolved by ACPO TAM tasking the Head of the newly established Police International Counter Terrorism Unit (PICTU) to consult and propose an alternative restructuring. However, the task's parameters excluded the options of 'do nothing' and 'create a national SB'.[70] The compromise solution, that was accepted, was the proposal to develop and formalise regional Special Branch cooperation into eight new Regional Intelligence Cells (RICs) with central funding support of £3 million per year. The proposed post of National Coordinator for Special Branch was established and is regarded by the Home Office as an important element of the national policing response, especially in the development of the RICs as '... clearing houses for intelligence in their regions'.[71] In its 2005–6 Report the ISC commented, in relation to RICs, that it had visited an MI5 regional station and '... saw examples of how the Service was working with the police to share information and best practice on investigative and intelligence-gathering methods, and to co-ordinate rapid response to threats'.[72]

On one aspect of Special Branch work, the ports and airports policing, Lord Carlile of Berriew, in his Terrorism Act 2000 review for 2002–3 commented that, whilst he had concerns over small ports and airports, 'Nevertheless I have received plenty of evidence to support the view that pilots of small aircraft and operators of small facilities are very vigilant ...'. Moreover, he noted that 'A high level of community policing has been developed by many forces in this context. I am impressed by the way in which expertise is being shared between police forces in this context ... perhaps one of the benefits of the regional structures now operated routinely by special branches'.[73] All the staffing and funding for the RICs is now in place. There is evidence of better cross-force coordination of intelligence operations and the promotion of 'best practice' through meetings of RIC managers. However, the pace of development of the RICs is variable depending upon the circumstances of the contributing forces.[74]

The then Home Office Minister, John Denham, welcomed the Special Branch Report and referred, *inter alia*, to the initiation of a funding review to see how dedicated funding was actually allocated to support the policing of sites with '... significant national security implications'.[75] The Minister also noted that counter-terrorism now featured as a policing responsibility more visibly with its place in the NPP and thus counter-terrorism would have to be reflected in local policing plans. In addition, the Minister referred to the 6.2 per cent rise in the overall police budget settlement for 2003–4, a cash rise of £534 million. Of that, £59 million was specifically for counter-terrorism measures, of which £47 million was for the MPSB, with £12 million for '… other forces …'. The latter is not a large sum and as it is spread out over 42 forces, it does not amount to a generous provision although by 2004–5 the terrorism related allocation had risen to £84 million and may well be partly used to offset 'counter-terrorism extras' which come on top of normal policing duties.[76] Nonetheless, the issues of the availability and continuity of central funding support for DSPs remains a concern to police forces.[77] Although there is some misunderstanding about DSPs in that whilst money is 'top-sliced' from the police budget for these purposes and is available to police forces it is an un-hypothecated allocation and thus actual usage is still within the discretion of chief officers. Some alleviation of the funding issues may come from the Chancellor's increased allocations in the 2004 spending review.[78] It is hoped that some of these funds will be allocated to provision enhanced IT facilities for the Special Branches, as proposed in the HMIC Report, and now developed under the National Special Branch Technical Unit's iMAST strategy (Special Branch Information Management and Supporting Technology strategy).[79]

PICTU (re counter-terrorism strategy 'pursue' objective)

In the preceding sections, the chapter has raised the problem of the variability of Special Branch counter-terrorism response capability with regard to surveillance and border controls as a matter of significance in the domestic management of terrorism in the UK. Reference was also made to the important response management change of the establishment of Special Branch RICs.

Intimately linked to these issues was the establishment in April 2002 of PICTU. PICTU is a smaller Police Service. The police officers are drawn from UK police forces and a Detective Chief Superintendent from the Anti-Terrorist Branch was the first head of the unit. Its basic task is to:

> … add value to and strengthen the existing partnership between the police service and the Security Service, in relation to the threat from International Terrorism …

PICTU's establishment is a good example of both the enhancement of MI5's profile in 'outreach' terms and the role of key decision makers within the UK domestic management of terrorism response. In this case, the initiative was developed by the current Director-General of the Security Service, former Assistant Commissioner David Veness and former Chief Constable Ben Gunn, through an ACPO TAM initiative following 9/11. In June 2002 ACPO TAM formally agreed PICTU's remit as: promoting the dissemination of assessed intelligence regarding intelligence of value to the National Coordinator and the police service and promoting the efficient coordination of police action before, during and after joint Security Service/police investigations.

PICTU achieved these objectives by conducting environmental scanning to identify gaps, real or perceived, between expectations at the local level and delivery from the centre. PICTU staff regularly visit police forces across the UK they have also organised and participated in counter-terrorist workshops and seminars. A recent ACPO TAM review of PICTU placed it, initially, under the line management of the National Coordinator of Special Branch (subsequently PICTU has come directly under the ACPO Advisory Group) with the following terms of reference: '... To develop and strengthen existing partnership work between the police service and the Security Service in countering international terrorism'. This will be achieved by working with the Security Service, ACPO Advisory Group and JTAC to ensure: the effective dissemination of assessed intelligence, relating to international terrorism, of value to the National Coordinator for Terrorist Investigations and the National Coordinator for Special Branch and all UK police forces, and the efficient co-ordination of the national police counter terrorist strategy that supports the joint police/Security Service response to international terrorism ...'.[80]

As part of PICTU's work, close contact is maintained with a variety of external sources. New links have been established with counter-terrorist experts and leading academics from a wide range of institutions. These links have contributed to a greater understanding of the nature of the threat, the scale of the threat and the enduring nature of the threat posed by international terrorism.

The value of international police cooperation against terrorism has long been recognised and it is still proving valuable in respect of the current priority of tackling the Islamic network/group threat. In Europe the Police Working Group on terrorism network of CTELOs (Counter Terrorism and Extremism Liaison Officers) has been expanded and is an important and swift source of help. The UK intelligence services and police input has helped the UK become '... one of the biggest providers of information to [EU] SitCen papers'.[81] One of the valuable forms of information sharing for the UK police, alongside the tracking of suspects, is the sharing of forensic information from terrorist crime sites. Thus, for example, Anti-Terrorist Branch officers have been able to gather valuable data from site visits and cooperation with: the Turkish police after the bombings of the British Consulate and HSBC in Istanbul, the Spanish police after the Madrid railway bombing and from the Russian police, and FSB after the Chechen bomb attacks on the Moscow Underground.[82]

National Counter Terrorism Security Office (NaCTSO) and the counter-terrorism strategy objectives of 'protect' and 'prepare'[83]

This smaller Police Service with local force outreach was set up in 1998 as one of the responses to the 1996 Provisional IRA bombing of Manchester city centre. One of the post-incident conclusions was that the police did not have a mechanism for providing protective security advice to the general and high street business community. Initially, some advice was provided through local forces crime prevention officers. When the unit was set up, in January 1998, as the National Terrorist Crime Prevention Unit, it only had two officers, who were co-located with MI5's T4. They acted as a channel for 'best practise' advice, mostly from T4 (now the NSAC), to police forces through their Special Branches. In October 2001, a further two officers were added to the unit and their remit was extended to include extremism and animal rights issues. Following 9/11, the unit's strength was further increased. A national programme was put into place, under which, by April 2003, all police forces had at least one CTSA in post and the unit was re-titled NaCTSO. The CTSAs are responsible to their chief constables and some CTSAs may also be allocated to the duties set out under Part 7 of ACSA 2001. Under these provisions for the 'control of pathogens and toxins', '... managers of laboratories and other premises holding stocks of specified disease causing micro-organisms and toxins [must] notify their holdings, to comply with any reasonable security requirements which the police may impose, and to furnish the police with details of people with access to the dangerous substances'.[84] By 2004 there were 100 CTSAs in post in all police forces in the UK, Home Office and non-Home Office with, not surprisingly, the largest concentration of CTSAs (13) in the areas covered by the MPSB and City of London forces.[85] In 2003 the MPSB CTSAs carried out 200 security surveys for businesses operating in the MPSB area.[86]

The lead body for protective security is now NSAC and NaCTSO works within its response framework for protective security as set out on the MI5 website. The CTSAs' potential clients can range through clearing bank branches, branches of chains/franchises to very locally established commercial enterprises. Additionally, clients are also drawn from other potential target sites, such as universities and communications providers. In the public sector, the natural partners for the CTSAs are their relevant local government Emergency Planning Officers. NaCTSO and the CTSAs are also making links with growing networks of resilience fora, such as London First.

The outreach of NaCTSO and the CTSAs has been based upon a very rapid initial and ongoing training programme. It has also benefited from the very active support of ACPO TAM and the various National Coordinators. NaCTSO has been particularly involved with projects to develop public–private counter-terrorism partnerships. In this context, NaCTSO has a programme of regional workshops to involve national and local businesses in developing continuity and resilience strategies. The ESRC Project worked as a partner to NaCTSO in the running of two of the workshops in February and April 2004. Some 50 corporate and local government bodies were represented, in total, at these two events. The commercial sectors covered included banking and finance, fast food outlets, food and retails chains, road transport and utilities. UK public sector governance tiers were represented at devolved administration, regional and local levels. Participants were invited to complete a short questionnaire and about 25 per cent of participants completed these questionnaires. Two comments were common from the discussions with both full groups on workshop days. These were, first, the warnings by people like the Home Secretary and the Director-General of MI5 were heard *but* they were felt to be difficult to translate through individual corporate risk assessment processes into contingency planning as these warnings were couched in very general terms. Second, even where those responsible for security, broadly defined, tried to raise issues further up the management chain, they faced reluctance at board level to commit resources, because boards were looking for threat information which was more narrowly focused on their specific geographical area or field of operations.

Responding to particular forms of terrorist threat – counter-terrorism strategy objectives of 'prevent' and 'prepare'

In the introduction to this section, reference was made to five specific current priority forms of terrorist threat:

1   the catastrophic event – 9/11
2   the suicide bomber attack
3   the 'deadly and determined' attack
4   the threat from MANPADS
5   the threat from terrorists using a CBRN element with or without an IED.

Within the UK police service, it is often said that the usual response to a new problem is to form a specialist squad. In some ways, that has been the response to some or all parts of the threats, except that, for 'form squad' the response was, very sensibly, to set up multi-agency working groups. These groups work to a formal agenda and with a clear timetable for the progression of tasks to 'in-service'. Additionally, some senior officers have been given particular lead roles with small support teams to carry out in depth studies of particular threats with reporting lines up to ACPO level.[87]

The catastrophic event

As the police have long experience of planning for, exercising and handling natural, manmade and terrorist incidents, it is necessary to establish how different the example of 9/11 is felt to be to previous experience. The differences may be summarised as: scale – in terms of numbers of potential casualties, a multi-site incident with geographical separation of the component incidents, as in the case of 9/11 and the London July 2005 incidents and the successful use of commercial aircraft, vessels or vehicles as suicide attack weapons. Added to these factors was the concern, since the mid-1990s, that on the actual evidence of the Sarin attack on the Tokyo Underground and from evidence of CBRN-use planning by international terrorist groups, that some terrorists had discernible ambitions to use CBRN in some way, perhaps in conjunction with an IED. An example of a response to such fears was the MPSB anti-terrorism raid on a house in Lansdown Road, Forest Gate, London on 6 June 2006 where intelligence had suggested that some kind of 'chemical' materials or weapon device might be found. In this case, the raid uncovered nothing suspicious despite very intensive searches.

If attacks of the magnitude of 9/11 cannot be pre-empted or prevented, and making the necessary assumption that a terrorist group would, if it could, seek to use a CBRN element, then the following incident and consequence management issues arise: the crucial need for risk assessments and emergency planning (see the updated requirements in the Civil Contingencies Act 2004)[88] and the maintenance or development mutual aid between emergency services and other emergency responders. Additionally, for the police, there are four specific requirements: a well trained and practiced capability to exercise overall command and control at an incident – 'gold' level; similar capabilities at the more tactical 'silver' and 'bronze' levels of command using Police Support Units and other specialist units to secure the location(s) and maintain public order. The counter-terrorism response requirement includes: Special Branch, the Anti-Terrorist Branch, fire arms units plus additional assets, as required, for example, Security Service Technical Teams, explosive ordnance disposal (EOD) personnel (possibly from 11 EOD Regiment), specialist scientific support from the Defence Science and Technology Laboratory (Dstl), if CBRN is suspected, and, lastly, military special forces (SAS/SBS) on standby. Finally, the police have to provide for the securing, as and when possible, the location(s) as a 'crime scene' which requires the presence of a Criminal Investigation Department, Senior Investigating Officer (CID SIO) and team.

Not only are all the above needed in a particular incident(s) but they will also be required to be deployed 'just in case' in relation to events such as party political conferences, state visits and world summits. The scale of the deployment will depend upon the prevailing threat analysis and resulting risk assessment. For example, the London element of President Bush's visit in November 2003 cost an estimated £14 million and necessitated the deployment of around 14,000 police; President Bush's visit to the Prime Minister's Sedgefield constituency required the deployment of 1,300 police. Such planned events require a considerable amount of preparatory work led by a senior police officer, who is designated the SECO (security coordinator) for the event.

The new incident management requirements that have arisen, post-9/11 are: the training and equipping of police CBRN teams, preparations to maintain a secure cordon if people have or are suspected of exposure to chemical, biological or radiological weapons, overseeing potentially large-scale evacuations, planning for multi-incident scenarios (where mutual aid may be either delayed or unavailable because it is already fully committed elsewhere), recognising that some potential forms of attack using chemical, biological or radiological agents may only be known at a later stage through Health Service agencies' collation of patient data and dealing with a suicide bomber(s). Moreover, in the case of the 'deadly and determined' attack, terrorists overseas, as drug traffickers already have in the UK, may use automatic weapons. The UK police currently do not deploy officers with small arms able to operate in the fully automatic mode. If that response was required, then military aid would have to be sought.

The nature of the military aid available for the counter-terrorism element of homeland defence has actually not changed very greatly post-9/11.[89] The Defence Secretary has stated that as the Home Office has the 'lead' responsibility it remains the task of the MoD to '… provide appropriate support to the civil authorities …', with reconfigurations, where necessary.[90] The MoD has refocused its commitment to defend key national targets from a Cold War level of 160 sites down to the most essential, in contemporary terms, 56 sites and to regard the SAS/SBS as interchangeable Special Forces assets 'on call' to the police. The recent Defence Review has also indicated that the Special Forces will be augmented, perhaps by an additional SAS 'sabre' squadron.[91] Moreover, the regular forces are still regarded as the most likely immediate military responders with the 14 regionally deployed Civil Contingencies Reaction Force (CCRF) units regarded as only a '... very short term rapid response'.[92] The MoD is also trying to enhance the value of its regional military civil contingencies liaison officers.

However, their effectiveness will partly depend on bids with other departments to the current spending round for improved communications equipment. In one respect, the MoD is caught in a rather 'catch 22' situation with regard to its variable presence in the police force areas. The Defence Secretary said, in 2003, that MoD needs '... to look at the footprint of our Armed Forces in the United Kingdom ... and also to spread that footprint more evenly across the United Kingdom'.[93] However, will that not run counter to demands for economies of scale with large military bases in Wiltshire and Yorkshire? Indeed a very realistic view of MACC (Military Aid to the Civil Community) has been provided by the Cabinet Office CCS which has commented that 'Neither the production of contingency plans nor the participation in civil exercises guarantees the provision of MACC support, it is therefore essential that responding agencies do not base plans upon assumptions of military assistance'. Furthermore, the CCRFs '... require mobilisation before deployment. They are not, therefore, well placed to provide immediate MACC support ...'.[94]

The CBRN threat and the police response

Prior to 9/11, there was an emerging view that the police needed to provide selected personnel across the country with a level of CBRN training. Some training had already been given to MPSB officers.[95] Thus 9/11 acted as an impetus to get the Police National CBRN Training Centre at Winterbourne Gunner up and running and, by 2003, the plan was for each police force to have at least one CBRN-trained PSU by May 2003. In parallel with these new training requirements, came a joint police and fire services project for specially developed CBRN protective suits to replace the initial use of military protective suits.[96] Moreover, the assessed requirement for police CBRN-trained personnel has been upgraded from an initial requirement of about 2,500 (a target of 2.5 per cent of total police strength CBRN-trained) to about 6,500 (a revised target of 5 per cent of total strength trained).[97] The actual current number of trained personnel is over 7,000 and the Police National CBRN Centre and the MPSB have produced a CBRN awareness CD-Rom to be used within the training of the remaining 95 per cent of police. The Centre received extra resources in 2006 and from Autumn 2006 will be located near Coventry, alongside the new National Policing Improvements Agency.

For the police, this very much enhanced CBRN commitment raises four new ongoing requirements. Protective equipment will have to be procured and maintained at a cost of about £1,000 per suit. A continuous training programme has to be maintained for both commanders and Police Support Unit (PSU) members. Both the procurement of protective suits and the training programme has to take account of an anticipated 10 per cent turnover in CBRN-trained personnel per year. All the associated instructional and operational manuals will also require continuous updating.

At a confirmed CBRN incident, it is the Fire Service and other specialist teams, for example, from the police (SO13 forensic teams and possibly Authorised Firearms Officers), from Dstl or the military, who will operate in the 'hot zone'. The key police role at the incident is the preservation of life and property which will include provision of the cordon between the identified 'hot zone' and the outer 'cold zone'. This may require, as will be discussed later, the potential need to use firearms to maintain the integrity of the cordon. The counter-terrorism exercise, Black Knight, in Hampshire in early 2003, also encountered the problem of persons 'missed out' from the decontamination process.

Maintaining a secure cordon and overseeing evacuations

This is a police personnel-intensive requirement because of the need effectively to secure a contaminated area and contaminated people until the appropriated decontamination/treatment procedures are complete. Mutual aid will be vital in this response to guard what may be an extensive perimeter. The aid may also need to involve the support of both the regular armed forces and the recently formed, reserve manned, CCRFs. One CCRF unit is maintained in each military region. However, the CCRF units may only be available after quite a lengthy call-out period.[98] Moreover, other operations may drastically affect availability. The Defence Committee found that '... during a period when the British consulate in Istanbul was bombed and Madrid suffered its worst terror attacks ever, the capital's flagship reinforcement unit, the London District CCRF had deployed over a third of its trained strength to Iraq'.[99] Although intelligence may allow for some element of pre-deployment, there is still likely to be a worrying 'gap' period while numbers of cordon personnel are built up and first resort will be to nearby regular military units from any service under MAC(P) (Military Aid to the Civil Power).

A publicly important question that has to be addressed relates to the powers of the police, if necessary, to use force, including lethal force, to maintain the integrity of the cordon in the event of a CBRN attack and the consequent risk of wider contamination of people and locations. It has been considered that police powers and duties under common law to protect life and property provide one source of authority.[100] These powers could be supplemented by emergency powers enacted under the new Civil Contingencies Act. However, this issue does raise a very real human response situation – would police officers, if non-lethal force failed, actually fire on ordinary members of the public naturally seeking to flee from a disaster location? After all, the Prime Minister, Ministers and ordinary

MPs showed a very poor example of civic discipline, when faced with the powder incident in the Commons Chamber in May 2004.[101] These sorts of problems are recognised, as Ms Cheryl Plumridge of the Cabinet Office CCS noted '… mass evacuation is one of the things that we plan for but it is not a panacea in itself. We have to aim, also, for the circumstances in which mass evacuation may not be recommended but perhaps people start to self-evacuate. It is something we are very aware of and do plan for but it is fraught with difficulties'.[102]

This potential response management issue is not raised because people in the UK normally seek to cross police incident barriers. In fact, the public generally obeys the restrictions quite well. However, research from the USA has suggested that there is potentially quite a problem of people trying to ignore official orders after a catastrophic event. Indeed the UK exercise at the Birmingham NEC in July 2004 had the same experience with 'role-playing' members of the public trying to evade the cordons.[103]

The response to other new forms of terrorist threats to the UK

Some preliminary remarks need to be set out at this stage. The US post-9/11 political rhetoric has tended to use the term 'War on Terror'. Whilst this is a contested term, it does have some implications in response terms. British ministerial rhetoric and, indeed, the import of the measured statements of key figures like MI5 Director-General Eliza Manningham-Buller and others, have underlined the *when* rather than the *if* nature of the threat. Remarks which were sadly prophetic and well founded in the light of the July 2005 attacks on London. If these statements are correctly interpreted as conveying a sense of the urgency of the problem, then one could reasonably argue that the search for counter-measures should be equally urgent. Sir David Omand, the former Security Coordinator, indicated that the overall matrix of current response measures are expected to have a five-year time-scale to full implementation. In which case, it seems to be fair to suggest that the UK will not be fully ready to tackle even the current threats until about 2009. The appropriateness or otherwise of the time-scale of this response resource programme may need to be re-examined in the context of the post-incident assessments on the July 2005 London bombings.

However, there are a number of arguments that can be made for a measured response, in some areas, while recognising that some aspects of the threat will have an urgency that may require, initially, 'quick fix' solutions. For example, concrete block barriers may well be an appropriate obstacle to vehicle-borne IEDs but, in the event of an explosion, the populace in the vicinity of the protective target will suffer death and injury from concrete barrier shrapnel as well as from normal explosion fragments. This problem was recognised and more refined barrier structures have been procured.

In a measured response, there are a number of important considerations: *discovering, defining and understanding* new problems and evaluating responses tried in other countries in the UK context, carefully considering the operational performance required from new techniques and technology – *qualitative issues* and considering the scale of the requirement and its cost – *quantitative issues and budgetary issues.*

The suicide attack

This was the first post-9/11 specific new threat study carried out by the UK police as distinct from the more general studies of response to catastrophic events. The initial work was carried out by the ACPO TAM Working Group on Suicide Bombers led by a superintendent of the MPSB Anti-Terrorist Branch.[104] The initial work consisted of an open source study of suicide attacks worldwide supplemented by field work visits to locations where such attacks were experienced, for example, Israel, Sri Lanka and Russia. Field work visits were also made to countries without prior experience of suicide terrorist attacks in order to compare UK response plans to those in this group of countries, such as the USA.

This research work covered areas such as typologies of suicide bombers, the psychology of the suicide bomber, commonly-encountered suicide IEDs and their methods of delivery whether by person or vehicle, the 'lone' bomber problem and the bomber with a support, supply and command and control network. This research resulted in a valuable analytical study for use in issue-awareness briefings and training and it was also used as the basis for developing strategic and tactical responses. *En passant*, the project research revealed, in this threat area, an example of the British response problem of 'silo' thinking. By early 2004, three separate agencies had been carrying out, in isolation, three separate studies of the suicide terrorism threat; the police service, JTAC and MoD. Whilst each will undoubtedly have some unique organisational slant, it might have made more efficient use of resources and promoted a coordinated response if the work could have been carried out, at least in part, as a joint effort.

Why does the threat of a suicide bomber(s) pose a separate set of challenges to those present where terrorists or extremists simply plant an IED? First, the element of control over the IED may allow a more precise form of targeting. Second, the suicide bomber using an aircraft, vehicle or boat may be able to reach target locations in a way and on a scale not available by simply planting an IED as 9/11 showed so dramatically. Third, the suicide bomber gains publicity through the shock value of a human being blowing themselves up, leaving a legacy in the public's mind that it could be the passenger/shopper next to them. Fourth, tactically, a suicide bomber poses four sets of problems for the police:

- Can intelligence help to identify at an early stage a suicide bomb threat and the bomber(s)?
- Can technology or sniffer dogs identify the bomber(s) if earlier disruption operations are either not feasible or are unsuccessful?
- How will the IED be triggered? The options are self-detonation, automatic timer or remote detonation by a third party.
- How do you tackle an identified bomber(s)?

The police team reflected on both the knowledge that they had gained from their research period and the issues, set out above, raised by the research and channelled their findings into response projects. Operation Clydesdale was a project which considered the implications of a response, where intelligence had identified both target and potential perpetrator. Here, the issues related to whether the police would have time to make a suspect identification and carry out an intercept operation at a point where damage could be limited in the event of the device being triggered during interception. Operation Kratos was a linked project, which considered what was called a spontaneous incident in which the police would have no prior intelligence warning but may receive just a 'suspicious behaviour' report from sources ranging from CCTV, a private security guard, a member of the public or a police patrol. Moreover, in this case, they might face the additional uncertainty about whether the suspect person is the bomb transporter or the actual bomber. In this case, the police have to prepare to tackle a situation without any previous information and where other possible indicators – such as bulky clothing or a wire coming from a shoulder bag – may be indicators of nothing more sinister than that the suspect person feels the cold and has also just bought some garden wire. Furthermore, unlike the situation of facing a person with a firearm, in the suicide bomber case, there may be no realistic option of getting closer and negotiating unless the bomber, in some way, 'gives up'. Therefore, the Silver Commander must prepare to authorise an armed response involving the lethal force option.[105]

As the suicide bomber threat was not covered in the Provisional IRA-orientated *Bombs, Police, Response* operational guidance manual, the Working Party produced training and operational command and control documents, as the first element of the response. The second element of the response was to consider, in parallel, the development of new operational aids such as explosives detection-trained sniffer dogs and special detection devices.

Normally, our knowledge about special detection devices would, under-standably, be limited. However, in December 2003, interviews with the then Metropolitan Police Commissioner, Sir John Stevens, put some information into the public domain.[106] The reports referred to the development and deployment of a portable scanner device based on millimetre-wave technology. It was said that this device can detect objects, such as a bomb, through a suspect's clothes and that information can be relayed to a police control location. Sir John Stevens had referred to the threat of a suicide attack as having taken a 'quantum leap' since the attacks in Saudi Arabia, Morocco, Russia and Iraq.

Five conclusions can be drawn from this analysis of the response to the suicide bomber threat:

1   Good intelligence remains the fundamental requirement for pre-empting or preventing a suicide bomb attack and this needs to operate in parallel with appropriate preventive security measures.
2   Technical solutions' value depends upon their reliability and their availability in sufficient numbers for rapid emergency response.

3   The suicide bomber response has to become an ongoing component of training.

4   It raises a particular training requirement for AFOs, in that they may be instructed to shoot a suspect in a situation where the visibility of the threat is markedly less than where an armed suspect is visibly pointing a firearm.

5   Any local evacuation orders, which may be considered in the short time likely to be available in the face of a spontaneous event, will need to be well informed by an understanding of the varied effects of explosions depending on the position of the IED, when detonated.

Because of the ongoing de Menezes case arising out of the aftermath of the 21 July London bombing, attempts at further comment on the suicide bomber policies must necessarily be restricted. However, first, the Home Secretary has indicated that after the Independent Police Complaints Commission has reported that he would look at the issue of a public debate on '… lethal policies …' and suggested that the House of Commons' Home Affairs Committee might also want to look at the issues.[107] Second, Metropolitan Police Commissioner, Sir Ian Blair, has pointed out that the policy was based on '… a development of existing law …' and based upon '… section 3 of the Criminal Justice Act, the use of reasonable force, which has to be "proportionate and necessary" to the threat'.[108] Moreover, Sir Ian Blair pointed out that the policy had been developed through the normal official consultations process and approved by ACPO in January 2003. He said '… Home Office officials, the CPS, the Treasury, councils [legal counsel], independent advisers were aware of the policy …'.[109] ACPO, in its post-event review of the suicide bomber policy, endorsed the policy as it had been promulgated but note, *inter alia*, the need for: a review of police C3I procedures, the suicide bomber policy to be articulated in a public document, and for the police to engage with communities in developing suicide terrorism policies.[110] Currently, the Metropolitan Police is being prosecuted by the Crown Prosecution Service, under sections 3 and 33 of the Health and Safety Act 1974, for failing in its duty of care to Mr de Menezes.

The deadly and determined attack

Following the attacks on Riyadh and Casablanca, a new threat variant to the UK was identified and named DADA. ACPO TAM responded by forming a DADA Committee to explore the response requirements and to set in train the appropriate procurement, planning and training actions. The DADA Committee had to cover three areas: the continuing Irish problem, suicide bombing, and sacrifice bombing. The latter category covers an incident where an attacker is prepared to die, if necessary, but does not have the initial intention of martyrdom. The DADA Committee worked through seven specialist sub-committees covering: intelligence; technology, police and detection tactics; prevention and physical security; police resources, deterrent and responses; business, commerce and community; media and post-incident. A very important feature of this multi-strand response, in the context of the domestic management of terrorism, is that it is an inter-agency approach, albeit under the ACPO TAM umbrella. Thus, the sub-committees' membership was drawn from the police, other government departments and agencies, the military and private sector bodies as appropriate. Of equal importance was the fact that the committees were working to well-defined goals with clear implementation timetables.[111]

In summary, the main issues that the DADA Committee had to consider, in terms of response, are attacks that would result in significant casualties, could be aimed at a wide range of hard and soft targets, would be well planned and possibly planned as simultaneous events. Whilst the DADA Committee was working on the detailed development of the response, police forces continued to exercise for extreme contingencies with their current resources. Lord Carlile of Berriew refers to the example of a large-scale exercise '… to ensure the best possible outcome for the public in the extreme circumstances that could arise from a terrorist attack in a place of mass public aggregation'. He also referred to a Kent Police table-top exercise on controlling public movements into and within a designated area.[112]

Assessing outcomes

In general, assessing the outcomes of policing has long been a contested area within the study of the police with debates over rises and falls in reported crime figures, clear-up rates and victim surveys.[113] In the counter-terrorism field, this is also true especially when analyses must start from the premise that no counter-terrorism policy can give 100 per cent protection and that the 2005 London bombings occurred without there being any apparent prior usable intelligence indicators available. Moreover, currently and fortunately, in terms of catastrophic events like 9/11, we can mainly consider, in the UK, police actions in terms of pre-emptive and preventive measures such as the August 2006 arrests and charges connected with alleged transatlantic passenger aircraft bomb plots. However, the July 2005 London bombings do provide an example of a level 2 terrorist incident and therefore some comments on actual incident and consequence management issues can be made.

In respect of police performance in counter-terrorism, it is necessary to restate certain factors which underline the policing of terrorism. First, it must take place within the framework of law and the current rules of evidence and give priority to public safety. Second, it is a multi-agency activity, where the police are partnered in various ways by the security and intelligence services, HM Revenue and Customs, the Immigration and Nationality Directorate, and SOCA. Third, the policing of terrorism has, as its primary objective, the protection of life and property. Therefore, a priority is given to the pre-emption and disruption of terrorism in order to minimise the risk to public safety which is consistent with the 'pursue' element of the government's 'four Ps' counter-terrorism strategy. An important consequence of this strategy is that arrests to cause disruption may be seen to be of almost equal importance in counter-terrorism as the eventual securing of convictions. However a disruption strategy has to be balanced against the possible consequence of aggravating radicalisation in an ethnic minority community.[114] This matter has been taken very seriously in two ACPO TAM work streams with police forces and by the National Communities Tensions Team. Moreover three forces are formally measuring Islamophobic incidents. Overall, the police view is that '… we do not see a significant rise in tension nationally. [but] We get reported incidents and reported concerns'.[115] One way of managing potential community tensions, pre-operations, being discussed by the police is '… the idea of panels of independent advisers who might be able to look at intelligence and give a community context and assessment, not necessarily on its veracity but its impact on communities'.[116]

The police and other agencies are fully aware that reliance cannot solely be placed on pre-emption and disruption. It is equally important to have regard for preventative measures and measures to enhance incident and consequence management. In this area, the UK has been able to build upon its long experience of Irish terrorism and adapt that, where necessary, in the light of the new threats. Here, it is more difficult to provide 'outcomes' evidence, because, to date, there is, fortunately, only the two London bombing incidents to draw upon. Other forms of outcomes information can be derived from lessons learnt and responded to from counter-terrorism exercises, the funding and implementation of agreed capability enhancements, such as the provision of CBRN-trained personnel and the provision of DSPs in police forces and evidence of police force planning actually incorporating counter-terrorism within force annual plans. As the counter-terrorism response is a dynamic process and is subject to the problem, identified earlier, of 'parallel agendas', it is sometimes difficult to know precisely whether a proposal is in response to a counter-terrorism priority or merely reflects an 'opportunistic' linkage of other agendas.

Some proposals clearly relate to a Home Office goal of controlling expenditure on the police by looking for personnel categories which need not be paid at full police officer rates and such a proposal has also been mentioned by Sir Ian Blair. The Commissioner referred, in a speech to superintendents in Warwickshire in September 2005, to the possible introduction of a new category of '… partially warranted' police officers.[117] For example, where primarily an armed response or presence was needed he speculated '… could we bring staff in directly from the armed services, give them a certain amount of basic training … on a fixed term contract to undertake only those duties?'.[118] Second, the Home Office has proposed expanding the numbers and powers of CSOs over the next few years. CSOs could certainly add to the 'eyes and ears' capacity, in terms of information flows from particular areas and communities. They could also help in some aspects of an incident management system, for example, helping with cordons and crowd control. However, for these categories of police support personnel there does arise important questions concerning selection, training and equipment.

Outcomes from established data sources[119]

Police forces are required to record anti-terrorist 'stops and searches' under section 44(1) and 44(2) of the Terrorism Act 2000. It is from this data and consequent arrests that one can begin to identify outcomes issues in respect of counter-terrorism policing. Because of the marginal variability between statistics taken from different sources at different times this section will draw primarily upon the official data as presented, in April 2005, in the House of Commons Home Affairs Committee's Sixth Report of Session 2004–05 into *Terrorism and Community Relations* (see Table 10.1).[120]

Of the total for 'stops and arrests' figures for 2002–3, the vast majority of these figures were accounted for by 8 police forces: Metropolitan Police Service, City of London, Thames Valley, Gloucestershire, Cheshire, Greater Manchester, Hampshire and Sussex. In 2003–4, 77.5 per cent (83 per cent in 2002–3) of all Terrorism Act 2000 'stops and searches' were carried out by the Metropolitan Police and the City of London Police. Useful contextual information in respect of the Greater Manchester Police (GMP) area was provided by Mr Todd, the Chief Constable, when he told MPs that 95 per cent of the use of section 44 powers in the GMP area related to their use at Manchester Airport. He said that in the previous year, 828 people were stopped at the airport out of the 20 million who passed through. So clearly in the GMP area there is no large-scale use of section 44 powers among the GMP population at large.[122]

The Home Office figures showing the breakdown by ethnic origin category are set out below However, as Professor Marian FitzGerald has pointed out '... the system used from 1996 until last year [2003] simply depended on police officers recording the ethnic *appearance* of people they searched according to four very crude categories – white, black, Asian and other'.[123] The *Stop and Search Manual* which was published in March 2005 reflects concerns over ethnic issues but Professor Marian FitzGerald further commented that 'Your chances of being an innocent member of the Asian community going about your lawful business and being stopped and searched by the police are infinitely higher than a white person'.[124] The Chief Inspector of Constabulary's 2003–4 Report also showed a steady rise in the percentage of persons stopped and searched who were of ethnic minority origin, rising from 14 per cent in 1999–00 to 25 per cent in 2003–4.[125]

Table 10.1 Stops and searches by ethnic classification recorded under section 44(1) and 44(2) of the Terrorism Act 2000 – and resulting outcomes[121]

Ethnic group	2001–2	2002–3	2003–4
White	6,629	14,429	20,637
Black	529	1,745	2,704
Asian	744	2,989	3,668
Other/not recorded	618	2,414	2.398
Total	8,550	21,577	29,407

However, the crude nature of these recording categories was further amplified by the comment of Mr Sadiq Khan, Chair, Legal Affairs Committee of Muslim Council of Britain, to the Home Affairs Committee when he pointed out that '… the statistics are broken down by ethnicity and not by religion. … [and] … Those alleged to be involved in 9/11, Madrid and Istanbul are of Middle-Eastern appearance'.[126]

People of Asian origin certainly feature more in percentage terms in these figures but possibly not out of line with the ethnicity of the regions of the world from where the international terrorist threat is most expected; although evidence to the Home Affairs Select Committee pointed out that the 'ethnicity' category gives no clear picture of the religious background of those arrested or stopped.[127] Moreover, ethnicity data is inconclusive. In the Metropolitan Police Service area more Asian people were stopped in 2001–2 than Black people but this position was reversed in 2002–3.[128]

A frequent criticism of police counter-terrorism activity is the low arrest rate resulting from 'stops' under the Terrorism Act 2000 powers and this criticism is often linked to the low arrest and conviction rate (see Table 10.2). The Home Affairs Committee pointed out that, in 2003–4 '… fewer than 1.5% of stops and searches of pedestrians under the Terrorism Act resulted in an arrest'.[129] Another perspective, with a useful comparative element, was provided by the Director of Public Prosecutions to the Home Affairs Select Committee. Mr Macdonald told the Committee in January 2005, that '… around 50% of the people arrested under the Terrorism Act later go on to be charged with some form of offence which is about right for serious crime'.[130] Twenty-three separate categories of offence under

Table 10.2 Outcomes of arrests under Terrorism Act 2000 between 11 September 2001 and December 2004

Total arrests under Terrorism Act 2000	702
Charged under Terrorism Act 2000	119 (of whom 45 were also charged under other Acts as well)
Charged under legislation other than Terrorism Act 2000 but with terrorist offences covered by these Acts	135
Convictions under Terrorism Act 2000	17*
Transferred to immigration authorities	59
On bail to return	22
Cautioned	7
Dealt with under mental health legislation	7
Awaiting extradition	1
Returned to Prison Service custody	1
Released without charge	351

* These figures do not include three convictions in 2005 of Saajid Badat, Kemal Bourgass and Andrew Rowe

the Terrorism Act 2000 were listed in the charging process. In trying to relate 'outcomes' to counter-terrorism policy priorities, we should look for significant correlations between objectives and outcomes. From the 23 offence categories used, the following aggregations are evident. The largest group of offences was 59 citations for 'possessing an article in circumstances which give rise to a reasonable suspicion that its possession is for a purpose connected with the commission, preparation or instigation of an act of terrorism' (section 57(1)). The second largest group of offences was 28 citations for 'belonging or professing to belong to a proscribed organisation' (section 17). The third largest category totalled 16 citations, validating the prominence given to the CBRN/IED/DADA threats. Ten offences are recorded under section 54(2) of '*Receiving* instruction in the making or use of firearms, explosives or chemical, biological or nuclear weapons' and six offences are recorded under section 54(1) of '*Providing* instruction of training in the use of firearms, explosives or chemical, biological or nuclear weapons'. The fourth largest group of offences was seven citations for 'receiving money or other property intending that it should be used, or has reasonable cause to suspect that it may be used, for the purposes of terrorism' (section 15(2)).

As UK counter-terrorism agencies have, over the last few years, been focusing more on international terrorism, and given the existence of the UK's relatively strict laws on firearms, explosives, dangerous substances and money laundering, it would actually be more worrying if a larger number of chargeable offences and arrests were being recorded. It may be postulated that these figures reflect the publicly stated current parameters of the UK's threat from international terrorist groups and supporters. [131] That is to say, the probable existence of several groups plus numbers of persons with varied levels of association, the estimated number of suspects by 2005 had risen to around 800 from around 250 in 2001. However, as we are also being told that more suspects are being identified, it will be interesting to see if the figures for arrests and charges move further upwards.

A further correlation that should be expected is that non-national or British nationals of North or East African, Middle Eastern and Asian origin, who may also be Muslims, should feature more significantly in the figures, if the main current threat is from Islamic terrorist groups and supporters. This background in terms of geographical area of family origin is also seen in respect of the July 2005 London bombers. However, the actual available statistical evidence is not comprehensive and the Home Secretary informed the Parliament that the nationality and immigration status of those arrested in connection with terrorist offences was not available for the period 1999–2004. [132] Although the Metropolitan Police Service statistics on 'stop and search' do record ethnic group origin and do show a slight rise in the number of Asians being subject to 'stop and search' and the Home Office issued a new guidance document on this matter in March 2005 (see Table 10.3).

A better correlation of the identified threat with the most likely group of perpetrators comes from press reports of the ethnicity of those arrested and brought to trial, following counter-terrorism operations. North Africans feature significantly among the arrestees, as do people possessing British nationality but

Table 10.3 Metropolitan Police statistics of the ethnic origin of persons 'stopped and searched'

Year	Asians as % of total stopped
2000–1	9.9%
2001–2	11.8%
2002–3	12.2%
2003–March 2004	11.7%

having Asian, North African or Middle Eastern ethnic origins. The arrestees also do seem to correlate with the 'Al-Qaeda' typology presented in the intelligence section. They represent both long-term terrorist activists and younger, previously unknown sympathisers. Another correlation is between the arrests and the level of resources deployed to effect the arrests. These should be at a high level to reflect the potential threat and the potential risk to the police and other agencies from the target suspects. This correlation does seem to be found both from reports of arrests and from presentations on operations at Project Workshops and data on the 2005 July London bombings. The ISC noted, in the context of the London bombings, that 'An intensive operation, for example, into imminent attack planning, can consume almost half of the Security Services' operational and investigative resources'.[133]

As an example, Operation Scotia, an operation headed by the Lothian and Borders Police in 2002, had to deploy seven surveillance teams (around 350 personnel), two drawn from its own resources with teams from MPSB, GMP and Strathclyde Police plus teams from other agencies for about 20 suspects, and gathered a total of about 6,500 pieces of evidence.[134] Although no persons were eventually charged in connection with this operation, some were in connection with operations in 2003. Lord Carlile of Berriew commented on both years' operations in Scotland that the investigations '… justified the conclusion that the potential for public harm was towards the extreme'.[135] However, he also pointed to problems in cross-border cooperation between England and Wales and Scotland over the flexibility of warrants and the differing roles of the Crown Prosecution Service and Procurators-Fiscal.[136]

In an operation in late March/early April 2004, in London and the South east, eight men, ranging in age from 17 to 32, were arrested in connection with a range of offences involving half a tonne of ammonium nitrate. These arrests were described as '… a massive police and MI5 operation …'.[137] A total of around 700 officers from the Metropolitan Police Service, Home Counties forces (Bedfordshire, Surrey, Sussex and Thames Valley) and MI5 were deployed in that operation which carried out 24 searches under Terrorism Act 2000 powers in Uxbridge, Ilford, Colindale, Crawley, Slough, Luton, Horley and Reading.[138] The arrests followed an extensive and intensive surveillance operation by the security service and the police. Assistance was also received from the Royal Canadian Mounted Police, who arrested one suspect in Ottawa.[139] The cases following these arrests are still before the courts so comment is necessarily limited. However, it has been suggested in the press that the arrests might be linked with intelligence suggesting a possible plan to explode a large vehicle-borne IED near a London night club.[140]

Another series of arrests in early August 2004 stemmed from data found in a computer belonging to a Mohammed Naeem Noor Khan, described as an Al-Qaeda computer specialist, who was detained in Pakistan and whose computer data indicated plans and persons possibly planning major actions in the UK such as an attack on Heathrow. Thus on 3 August police from the Anti-Terrorist Branch arrested 13 males, many of Pakistani origin but British born, aged between 19 and 32 under Terrorism Act 2000 powers on suspicion of planning terrorist attacks in raids in Blackburn (two), Watford, Luton, and London (five in Willesden, one in Wembley, one in Sudbury and two in Paddington). The operation stemmed from intelligence sharing between Britain, Pakistan and the USA. One man was quickly released but among the detainees is one suspect who is regarded by the Metropolitan Police Service as '… a significant figure …'; however, because of the publicity from the Pakistan arrest it is believed that five further suspects evaded capture.[141]

This 2004 case and the August 2006 suspected aircraft bombing plots would appear to be among the most significant disruption operations against international terrorism in the UK since 9/11 because of both the numbers of arrestees actually charged and the gravity of the charges including the specific use charges under the Terrorism Act 2000. Of the 13 arrested on 3 August, two were freed without charge, two are no longer subject to Terrorism Act 2000 procedures but have been re-arrested for forgery related offences and one man has been charged with possessing a prohibited weapon. The remaining eight (Dhiren Barot, Qaisar Shaffi, Mohammed Naveed Bhatti, Abdul Aziz Jalil, Omar Abdul Rehman, Junade Feroze, Zia ul Huq and Nadeem Tarmohammed) have been jointly charged (both conspiracy charges were under section 1(1) of the Criminal Law Act 1977) with conspiracy to plot murder and conspiracy to commit a public nuisance involving radioactive toxic gas, chemicals or explosives. Dhiren Barot is also charged (section 58 of the Terrorism Act 2000) with possessing '… reconnaissance plans of the US financial buildings and having notebooks with information on explosives, poisons, chemicals and related matters'. Nadeem Tarmohammed has also been further charged under section 58 of the Terrorism Act 2000. Qaisar Shaffi is also charged (section 58 of the Terrorism Act 2000) with owning an extract from a terrorist's handbook which explains the use of chemicals and explosive devices'.[142] The use of a 'public nuisance' charge suggests some possible issues of actual evidence in relation to the non-use of Terrorism Act 2000 powers in that context.[143]

A feature of all these intelligence led operations is the great care that is taken in deciding to proceed with an operation. Witnesses before the Home Affairs Committee from the Campaign for Racial Equality and the Muslim Council of Britain were concerned that the small numbers of persons charged and prosecuted after arrest under Terrorism Act 2000 powers represented either 'fishing trips' by the police of use of Terrorism Act 2000 powers to tackle other forms of crime. In his evidence Chief Constable Todd of the GMP provided a detailed explanation of these operations. First, he pointed to the basic aim of protecting the public by disrupting and preventing acts of terrorism. Second, he drew attention to the important difference between intelligence and evidence. Intelligence may provide the first step in gathering evidence. Third, he stressed that in his force the quality of the intelligence available before an operational decision was made would be reviewed by the ACC (Crime) and even, in a potentially high profile case, by the Chief Constable himself, with similar practices in other forces. Fourth, he pointed out that no force acted on its own but within the framework of '… Counter-terrorism plc for the UK', that is to say with the involvement of MI5 and the Metropolitan Police Service Anti-Terrorism Branch.[144]

The demands on the Metropolitan Police Service Anti-Terrorism Branch, SO13, has been described by the former Metropolitan Police Commissioner, Sir John Stevens, as involving a workload which is two to three times that required for the IRA bombing campaigns of the 1970s to 1990s. Consequently, because of the Metropolitan Police Service's national counter-terrorism responsibilities Sir John had allocated, from April 2004, an extra £1.5 million to employ 100 extra experienced officers from other forces in SO13 to bring its strength to 350, its largest ever total strength.[145] Pre-9/11 the strength of SO13 was approximately 100 officers.[146] In evidence to Parliament, following the London bombings, the ACSO, Mr Andy Hayman provided details of the scale of those police operations and referred to the storing of 38,000 exhibits, 1,400 fingerprints, over 160 crime scenes and the investigation of 54 murders and other crimes.[147] These points were reinforced by the Commissioner, Sir Ian Blair, stating that it was '… the first time in living memory that the Metropolitan Police has declared something called "mutual aid", which means that we are paying hundreds of officers from other forces to work with us'.[148] The 2006 operation in connection with suspected plots to bomb transatlantic passenger aircraft is already showing similarities of scale to the response to the July 2005 London bombings. On 22 August, 11 suspects made their first court appearances facing charges that included conspiracy to murder (section 1 of the Criminal Law Act 1977), preparing to smuggle IED components onto aircraft (section 5(1) of the Terrorism Act 2006) and possession of items connected with terrorism (section 58(1)(b) of the Terrorism Act 2000). The police anti-terrorist operation has involved the 69 site specific searches (including houses), the seizure of 400 computers, the examination of 200 mobile phones and the seizure of 8,000 removable storage devices like memory sticks for further examination. In total 6,000 gigabytes of data had to be accessed and assessed for evidential value.[149]

Trial outcomes are also a significant way of assessing outcomes because, if the accused are found guilty, then, *prima facie*, there was a weight of evidence 'beyond all reasonable doubt'. In what may be termed high profile CBRN-linked new terror threat cases, the ricin case was concluded in April 2005 though with only one suspect, Kamal Bourgass, being convicted and sentenced to 17 years' imprisonment for conspiracy to cause a public nuisance by the use of poisons and/ or explosives to cause disruption, fear or injury. Bourgass was already in prison on a life sentence for the murder of Detective Constable Oake in Manchester in 2003.

Four other defendants were cleared of conspiracy charges and a second related trial was abandoned. Some of these suspects were later detained on national security grounds. Commenting on the trial outcomes, an Anti-Terrorism Branch Briefing Note said that if there had been an opportunity for a longer pre-charge investigative process then 'The quality of the original charging decisions would also have been higher, and it is probable that the suspect who fled the country while on bail and who eventually proved to have been a prime conspirator, would have stood trial in this country. If that had happened, the outcome of the trial process might have been very different'.[150] In his overall assessment the NCTI, Deputy Assistant Commissioner Peter Clarke, said a 'real and deadly threat' was prevented.[151]

This case had its origins in police and intelligence service work going back to September 2002 which was focusing warnings of low-level criminality among '… a network of Algerians in this country [who] were raising funds for terrorism …'.[152] This work led to the identification of three to four groups in the UK totalling about 80 people in all. The police Operation Springbourne concentrated on one of the groups based in London and among 15 arrests was that of David Khalif in Norfolk where recipes for making ricin, cyanide and other poisons were found. Khalif had at one time been employed in food factories. It was the discovery of these recipes that '… led directly to the raid on Finsbury Park [Mosque] later in January [2003]'.[153] The raid, carried out by about 1,000 police, stemmed from the mosque's address being found on documents seized in the arrest of Khalif. That raid in turn led to the arrest, among others, of two men from the 'most wanted' list.[154]

Sometimes, fortunately, a failed terrorist attack provides usable data that can lead, by intelligence work, to other results. For example, Richard Reid's nervousness about his IED suggested that he was not the bomb-maker and therefore not a complete 'loner'. Eventually, this understanding was to lead to the arrest, in Gloucester in 2003, and charge of Saajid Badat who subsequently pleaded guilty to conspiracy to place a device on an aircraft in service and was sentenced in March 2005.[155] In commenting on the outcome the NCTI, DAC Peter Clarke, referred to the fact that the case had involved 'Three years of intensive and painstaking international investigation' and said further 'We must ask how a young Briton was transformed from an intelligent, articulate person who was well respected, into a person who has pleaded guilty to one of the most serious crimes you can think of'.[156] This, of course, is one of the current key issues being addressed by the UK counter-terrorism agencies.

Even where a conviction is secured, the trial record can illustrate just how difficult it can be to, first, acquire intelligence, second, have sufficient data to give grounds for an arrest and, thirdly, produce the requisite evidential materials. In March 2003, two Algerians, Baghdad Meziane and Brahim Benmerzouga, were given 11-year prison sentences for terrorist activities and concurrent seven-year sentences for fraud.[157] They were involved in credit card fraud, which yielded about £100,000 for terrorist purposes. They appeared to have developed terrorist-group links from the mid-1990s onwards. Although they spent several of the years between about 1996 to September 2001 (when they were arrested) in the

UK, they carried out classic intelligence-evasion tactics. First, their '... use of multiple false identities and bank accounts allowed them to remain below the intelligence screen for much of their time in the UK'.[158] The use of false identities is a major problem in tracking and properly identifying terrorist suspects. The Home Secretary told Parliament that it was estimated that at least 35 per cent of those involved in terrorist activities were using false identities.[159] Second, these particular individuals kept a low profile within local Muslim community affairs in Leicester, whilst they were actively committing fraud.

After some of the defendants were found not guilty in the ricin trial, although some were subsequently detained again on national security grounds, the issue of available evidence to convince a jury clearly remained a substantive issue. However, there is satisfaction at the conviction of Andrew Rowe on 25 September 2005 on two counts of possessing articles useful for terrorist purposes and his sentence to 15 years' imprisonment. The Director of Public Prosecutions, Ken Macdonald, commented that 'This was the first trial prosecuted by the CPS Counter-Terrorism Division set up in May [2005] ... The challenge we successfully met was to prove to a jury that although there was no direct link between Andrew Rowe and a particular terrorist act, the possession of these items together with other supporting evidence was sufficient for a jury to conclude that he had them for the purpose of terrorism'.[160] Among the interesting features of the Rowe case were the facts that he was a British national, of non-European origin, who converted to Islam in the early 1990s, using the name Yusef Abdullah and had been under surveillance for some time. Furthermore, Rowe had fought in the Bosnian conflict in 1995 and the radicalising influence of that conflict is regarded, within the UK counter-terrorism agencies, as having been less well understood than should have been the case.

The following example is illustrative of a disruption operation based upon intelligence indicating a level of threat that, in the professional judgement of intelligence service and police officers, simply could not be ignored. In late April 2004 premises in Staffordshire, South Yorkshire and houses in central Manchester used by Iraqi Kurd asylum seekers were raided by armed police in connection with a possible plot to stage a suicide bomb attack at a major public event location in the area. In total nine men and one woman were arrested but by the end of April none remained in custody on suspicion of the commission and preparation of acts of terrorism but one of the suspects who was released was immediately re-arrested by the Immigration and Nationality Directorate.[161]

An important issue for the domestic management of terrorism in the UK arises from a mapping of arrest locations which clearly shows the wide geographical spread of arrests across the country. By contrast, monitoring of person movements related to Irish terrorism could be somewhat more concentrated along the urban and transport corridor between Holyhead and London. However, the recent pattern of international terrorism arrests and incidents means that *no* police force can assume that its location insulates it from the possibility of being the location for some form of international terrorist activity. This underlines the importance of the fact that counter-terrorism training is being further developed, with PICTU assisting in producing packages for trainers. Currently, there is a general 'counter-terrorism training slot' at the following career stages: recruit, probationer, BCU course, Senior Command Course and post-Senior Command Course for ACPO rank aspirants. This is supplemented as required by, for example, specialist training for Special Branch and Anti-Terrorism Branch officers, CBRN training and training in the handling of suicide bomber situations. Also a specialist cadre of SIOs are being trained by the Anti-Terrorism Branch to take account of the geographical spread of operations.[162]

Therefore, we need to look for evidence that terrorism-awareness exists across a wide spectrum of force areas. In a survey carried out by NaCTSO in 2004, it was of some reassurance to learn that 85.45 per cent of police forces did actually identify counter-terrorism as an objective within their annual policing plan. However, only some 45.46 per cent of forces had then implemented that objective down to the level of their crime reduction partnership plan.[163] A good example of the police reaching out into the wider public for counter-terrorism help is provided by Operation Rainbow, in the London area, which is described as the '... longest running operation in police history'.[164] Operation Rainbow contains a 'menu of options' aimed at detecting, deterring or disrupting terrorism. An example of this operation is provided by the exercise to collect data on the location of as many CCTVs as possible cited on homes, offices, shops, schools, public houses, etc. so that the police can seek access to the tapes for anti-terrorist operations and general crime prevention. Chief Constables' Annual Reports provide some detailed commentary for particular forces. The 2002–3 Reports have been used simply as an indicative set of examples.

The forces selected in Table 10.4 have been chosen because they represent a wide geographical spread of locations, types of force area and overall performance, as assessed by HMIC. Whatever the performance rating there is some evidence, below, across a spectrum of forces of varied but appropriate forms of counter-terrorism awareness and response.

In a 2004 overall assessment of police performance in England and Wales, covering 16 key areas of police work, the Home Office/HMIC survey obtained the following results, as set out below in Tables 10.5, 10.6 and 10.7, regarding 'Handling Major Incidents' and 'Tackling Serious Crime'.[170] There is, as yet, no specific performance indicator on counter-terrorism work *per se*.

Overall, this picture is a reasonable profile, in available performance indicators, on aspects of performance linked to counter-terrorism, except for the forces only graded fair/poor in terms of handling major incidents. Although clearly, the HMIC Report ('Closing the Gap') of September 2005 shows that there still remain significant concerns about the ability of the current structure of provincial police forces to meet some aspects of terrorism policing challenges.[171] For example, the Report notes that '... almost none of the forces assessed have planned, tested or practised for a chaotic, distributed event'.[172] The London incidents of 7 and 21 October 2005 would fall into this category of event. Moreover the problems for smaller forces are evident in the Report's comments about reliance, in those forces, on both '... multi-tasking for individuals ...' and on assistance from other forces '... for fairly modest operations ...'.[173]

Table 10.4 Performance of police forces 2002–3

Cambridgeshire 2002–3 overall performance score = 8	This force records reviewing its counter-terrorism capacity in respect of the increased level of threat facing the UK from international terrorism and focusing on its '… capability to search a large ocean-going vessel should the need arise'. This capability was tested during an anti-smuggling operation by the deployment of a multi-agency team from Cambridgeshire Special Branch, the Hertfordshire Police and Royal Air Force personnel from Cambridgeshire RAF stations. It was reported that the operation '… gave valuable experience in coping with the difficulties of searching a large vessel thoroughly and safely'.[165]
Gloucestershire 2002–3 overall performance score = 31	This force reported the enhancement of training for Major Incidents '… following the rewrite the county's multi-agency Major Incident Manual' and 80 officers, ranking from sergeant (bronze) to Chief Inspector (silver) will undertake these courses.[166]
Derbyshire 2002–3 overall performance score = 31	The Report refers to the force's 22-strong Uniform Task Force, who are '… trained in counter-terrorism search techniques and policing large-scale public order'. The force now also has 24-hour mobile cover from its new dedicated Armed Response Unit of six sergeants and 38 constables.[167]
West Midlands 2002–3 overall performance score = 33	Not surprisingly, as a large metropolitan force, West Midlands records a range of counter-terrorism activities and describes its Special Branch as '… the pivotal partner in the force's anti-terrorist strategy'. The contribution of Special Branch is linked with the running of Operation 'First Fleet' as '… the [strategic] mechanism to co-ordinate all counter-terrorism activity and monitor tension throughout the force [area]'. Among what are called '… a number of high profile AT operations …', reference is made to armed Automatic Number Plate Recognition (ANPR) checks and investigations into possible terrorist money supply routes.[168]
North Yorkshire 2002–3 overall performance score = 17	This force has taken the radical step of establishing a unified anti-terrorist unit along the lines of the 'guardian force' model from the London area. In addition to the structural changes, supported by 20 DSPs, the force has also carried out a very detailed risk assessment over the entire force area. It is also developing local level multi-agency counter-terrorism partnerships.[169]

Table 10.5 Handling major incidents

Categories	% of forces (total 43) in each category
Excellent	25.58%
Good	58.13%
Fair	13.95%**
Poor	2.30%*

*Actually only one force in this category – Cambridgeshire
** Some forces in important population areas were in the 'fair' category
– West Midlands, Surrey and South Wales (6 in total)

Table 10.6 Tackling serious crime

Categories	% of forces (total 43) in each category
Excellent	–
Good	23.25%
Fair	76.74%
Poor	–

Table 10.7 Working with other agencies to cut crime

Categories	% of forces (total 43) in each category
Excellent	20.93%
Good	67.44%
Fair	11.62%
Poor	–

Conclusions

The police seem to be managing the disruption aspect ('pursue') of the domestic management of terrorism quite well within the parameters of the available intelligence. In this aspect of counter-terrorism a major resource issue is the availability of sufficient trained surveillance personnel and other officers to carry out the actions arising from extensive surveillance, this is a matter that needs to be monitored together with its opportunity costs in terms of addressing other NPP priorities. The investigative element is also resource intensive and may, in the end, not even lead to court appearances or only to trials on relatively minor offences. However, this will still meet the UK counter-terrorism strategy objective of 'pursue' and some of these problems may be resolved through the provisions of the Terrorism Act 2006. Although it may be necessary for these forms of non-trial outcomes to be specially recognised within performance assessment criteria, such as those being developed by the Home Office and HMIC. It is very difficult to draw definitive conclusions about the incident and consequence management capability of the police as, fortunately, these capabilities have, as yet, mainly only been tested either in exercises or in the well-practised scenarios of major event management and enhanced airport security operations. However, the London bombing incidents of July 2005 do provide clear evidence, that even the largest force in the country can become seriously stretched in responding to multi-site attacks, both in the incident management and in the post-incident investigative phases. Moreover, these attacks only used IEDs with conventional forms of explosive components and did not involve any CBRN element.

There is certainly evidence of police forces engaging with the other parts of the public sector and also the private sector in the kind of multi-agency contingency planning envisaged in the current NPP and in the Civil Contingencies Act 2004. One issue that has emerged from several project sources and from parliamentary inquiry which relates to the 'prevent' and 'prepare' components of the 'four Ps' has been the adequacy of funding arrangements to meet some police counter-terrorism security needs. Finally, if one considers the police performance data in the periodic surveys by HMIC which give 'best' and 'worst' performing forces over many performance categories and the occasional controversial operational decisions,[174] such as that by Thames Valley Police in June 2004 in a fatal shootings incident and in the July 2005 de Menezes case, then one can postulate that the police may still show a rather varied response capacity to 'spontaneous' or 'surprise' terrorist attacks depending on the random factors of where an event takes place and the functioning of the response command structure in an emergency.

The new head of ACPO TAM, ACSO Andy Hayman, instigated a review of police counter-terrorism strategy after the July 2005 London bombings. As of July 2006 the final report of the outcome of the review has yet to be published. A delaying factor has, of course, been the promulgation and now abandonment of plans for police force mergers. For the present all that can be noted is that: the DADA inter-agency committee work was suddenly curtailed in Summer 2005, the future of the smaller police services, PICTU and NaCTSO is a little uncertain and so also is the future of some of the National Coordinator posts. Therefore the UK police counter-terrorism response seems most likely to remain with its present mix of national roles for some Metropolitan Police Service assets and the variable capabilities of the provincial police forces. ACSO Hayman was very candid regarding provincial capabilities, speaking of his former post of Chief Constable of Norfolk, when he said 'I have worked in a smaller force alongside two other smaller forces and the extent to which I, as the chief there, could meet some of the demands not just of terrorism, but of serious crime, it was just impossible'.[175] However, it is probable that the police will build on the past practice of regionalising specialist assets so that wherever an incident might be anticipated or occur, effective and planned support could be available. This could clearly link in well with the new MI5 regional offices. The terms currently used to describe such police asset grouping in the counter-terrorism field are: 'brigading', 'hubs' and 'corralling'. More generally, ACSO Hayman spoke of the need, during 2006, 'to get the gearing right in terms of terrorist investigations between intelligence gathering and investigation and what we call "protective security"'.[176]

Both the July 2005 London bombings and the August 2006 suspected transatlantic aircraft bombing plots clearly demonstrate the scale of the demands on police resources and the disruption capacity that this form of terrorism can cause. If Islamist terrorist activity in the UK or threatening the UK was ever at the level of a sustained campaign necessitating prolonged use of the 'critical' alert status then the adequacy of current levels of UK counter-terrorism resources would become a serious issue.

Notes

1 See the comments on this point in Clutterbuck, L. (2004) 'Law Enforcement', in Cronin, A.K. and Ludes, J.M. (eds) *Attacking Terrorism – Elements of a Grand Strategy*, Washington, DC: Georgetown University Press, pp. 142–3.
2 Reference here is made to the counter-terrorism surveillance role of 14 Int Coy in Northern Ireland – but there are now reports of the formation of a new counter-terrorism unit combining some Special Forces with 14 Int Coy personnel and intelligence services personnel with 14 Int Coy surveillance personnel deployable on UK mainland on surveillance duties, see (2004) *The Sunday Times*, 25 July and (2004) *The Times*, 26 July. Although this may simply refer to a longer standing practice of Special Forces and 14 Int personnel operating under Security Service control as required.
3 (2005) *The Times*, 18 July and 31 July.
4 See Home Office (2004) *One Step Ahead – A 21st Century Strategy to Defeat Organised Crime*, Cm. 6167, London: The Stationery Office. See also the Home Secretary's comments on enhancing the border agencies' effectiveness in his Oral Evidence to the Defence Committee and Home Affairs Committee joint inquiry into 'Homeland Security', HC 417-I, 2 March 2004, Q.51, and HM Government (2006) *Countering International Terrorism: The United Kingdom's Strategy*, Cm. 6888, London: The Stationery Office, July, para. 91.
5 Presentation at PICTU/ESRC Project Workshop, June 2004, and see also Stevens, J. (2005) *Not for the Faint-hearted*, London: Weidenfeld and Nicoloson, p. 304.
6 HMIC (2003) *A Need to Know: HMIC Thematic Inspection of Special Branch and Ports Policing*, Communications Directorate, Home Office, January.
7 (2004) *The Times*, 21 June.
8 Sir John Stevens, Police Review, 2004.
9 See the comments of Commissioner Sir Ian Blair to the Home Affairs Select Committee, Minutes of Evidence (2005) *Counter-terrorism and Community Relations*, 13 September, HC462-I, Q.47.
10 ACPO, Latest News, Ref: 58/06, 12 July 2006, *Police Merger Programme*, available at www.acpo.police.uk/pressrelease.asp?PR_GUID={249F8AA8-EBOC-4DF5_B5, accessed 28 July 2006.
11 North Yorkshire Police Presentation at PICTU/ESRC Project Workshop, 9–10 June 2004, and see HMIC, *Closing the Gap*, op. cit., para. 9.3. Updated as at Spring 2005 from Survey carried out by the Project for Assistant Commissioner (SO), Sir David Veness during 2004–5.
12 Metropolitan Police and Metropolitan Police Authority (2004) *Joint Annual Report for 2003–2004*.
13 *West Midlands Chief Constable's Annual Report 2002–2003*.
14 Ibid.

15 The DADA phrase was introduced by the former Assistant Commissioner (SO) Sir David Veness in an ACPO briefing paper. (Interview with an Anti-Terrorist Branch officer and various discussion with Sir David Veness.)

16 These new challenges have been well set out in public lectures by MI5 Director-General, Eliza Manningham-Buller. See her James Smart Lecture on the MI5 website and by Acting Commissioner (SO) David Veness. See his article (2004) 'The Fight Against Terrorism: Achieving a New Balanced Normality', *RUSI Journal*, June.

17 An excellent source on the initial responses and issues are the House of Commons Defence Committee Reports: *The Threat from Terrorism*, HC 348, Session 2001–2002, and *Defence and Security in the UK*, HC 518-I and II, Session 2001–2002.

18 Home Office, Speech 'Terrorism – policing the unknown', by Leigh Lewis, Home Office Permanent Secretary for Counter-Terrorism, 20 May 2004, and see also HM Government (2006) *Countering International Terrorism: The United Kingdom's Strategy*, Cm. 6888, July.

19 *Annual Report of HM Chief Inspector of Constabulary for 2001–2002*, HC 59, p. 8.

20 (2002) *National Policing Plan 2003–2006*, The Home Office, November.

21 Ibid., p. 17.

22 'An independent inquiry arising from the Soham murders', established by the Home Secretary and carried out by Sir Michael Bichard, reported in November 2004.

23 (2003) *National Policing Plan 2004–2007*, The Home Office, November, p. 3.

24 Ibid., p. 20.

25 Ibid.

26 *Annual Report of HM Chief Inspector of Constabulary for 2002–2003*, HC 34, p. 6. Later Reports of the Chief HMIC barely mention terrorism, the 2004–2005 Report (HC 842, February 2006) mentions the July 2005 London bombings but describes them as 'falling strictly out of the scope of this Report', p. 9.

27 Presentations by PICTU to Project workshops.

28 Baber, M. (1999) *The Terrorism Bill, Bill 10 of 1999–2000*, House of Commons Library Research Paper 99/101, December.

29 Broadbridge, S. (2001) *The Anti-Terrorism Crime and Security Bill: Introduction and Summary, Bill 49 of 2001–02*, House of Commons Library Research Paper 01/101, November.

30 Ibid., pp. 22–5, and see also Garton Grimwood, G., Oakes, M. and Carling, P. (2001) *The Anti-Terrorism Crime and Security Bill: Part X: Police Powers*, House of Commons Library Research Paper 01/97, November, and see also Payne, S. (2002) 'Britain's new anti-terrorist legal framework', *RUSI Journal*, 147(3), June, pp. 44–52.

31 House of Commons, *Hansard*, Written Answer by Home Secretary David Blunkett, 28 January 2004, vol. 417, col. 437–8W, NB Lord Carlile of Berriew gives a figure of 22 for terrorist cash seizures 2002–3.

32 Cm. 6888, op. cit., paras 81–2.

33 *Hansard*, Written Answers, 12 September 2005, col. 2616W.

34 Information from PICTU/ESRC Project Workshop June 2004, and see also Raphaeli, N. (2003) 'Financing of terrorism: sources, methods and channels', *Terrorism and Political Violence*, 15(4), pp. 59–82, and (2006) *Report of the Official Account of the Bombings in London on 7th July 2005*, HC 1087, London: The Stationery Office, p. 23.

35 Lord Carlile of Berriew (2004) *Report on the Operation in 2002 and 2003 of the Terrorism Act 2000*, April, p. 38, Annex F.

36 *A (FC) and others (FC) (Appellants) v. Secretary of State for the Home Department (Respondent)* (2004) UKHL 56, on appeal from [2002] EWCA Civ 1502, 16 December 2004.

37 Prevention of Terrorism Act 2005, available at www.homeoffice.gov.uk/security/terrorism-and-the-law/prevention-of-terrorism/, accessed 10 October 2005.

38 Case No T1/2006/9502 *Secretary of State for the Home Department v. JJ and Others* [2006] EWCA Civ 1141, 1 August 2006.
39 (2005) *The Times*, 22 July, and PICTU Workshop 13 May 2005.
40 Home Secretary Commons Statement, 20 July 2005, available at www.homeoffice. gov.uk/security/terrorism-and-the-law/prevention-of-terrorism/, accessed 10 October 2005.
41 Home Secretary Commons statement, *Hansard Debates*, col. 1254, 21 July 2005.
42 Ibid.
43 (2005) *The Times*, 11 October.
44 Letter from Assistant Commissioner (SO) Andy Hayman to the Home Secretary, 5 October 2005, available at www.statewatch.org/news/2005/oct/met-letter-law.p, accessed 12 October 2005.
45 Terrorism Bill, 55, 54/1 and the Explanatory Notes, available at www.parliament.uk, accessed 13 October 2005.
46 See the extensive discussions of these issues in House of Commons, Home Affairs Committee, Fourth Report of Session 2005–06, *Terrorism Detention Powers*, vols I and II, HC 910-I and II, London: The Stationery Office, June 2006.
47 For a full discussion of current anti-terrorist legislation see Walker, C. (2002) *Blackstone's Guide to the Anti-Terrorism Legislation*, Oxford: Oxford University Press.
48 Interview with Senior Anti-Terrorist Branch Officer, 6 September 2004.
49 (2004) 'Special Branch more than doubles its size', Statewatch News Online, available at www.statewatch.org/news/203/sep/01specialbranch.htm, accessed 23 April 2004, and see also *The Times*, 16 April 2004.
50 HMIC, *A Need to Know*, op. cit., and see also ISC, *Annual report 2002–2003*, Cm. 5837, para. 68, p. 21, and HC 518-I, pp. 21–7.
51 *A Need to Know*, op. cit. p. 7.
52 Ibid., p. 10.
53 Ibid.
54 Ibid.
55 Ibid., p. 11.
56 *Airport Security*, Report by the Rt. Hon. Sir John Wheeler, JP, DL, October 2002.
57 *A Need to Know*, p. 11.
58 Ibid.
59 Ibid.
60 Ibid.
61 Ibid.
62 Ibid.
63 Ibid.
64 Ibid.
65 Ibid.
66 Ibid.
67 Ibid.
68 Ibid.
69 Ibid.
70 Interview with PICTU officers, 11 September 2004.
71 Home Office (2004) *One Step Ahead – A 21st Century Strategy to defeat Organised Crime*, Cm. 6167.
72 ISC (2006) *Annual Report 2005–2006*, Cm. 6864, July, para. 40.
73 Lord Carlile of Berriew (2004) *Report on the Operation in 2002 and 2003 of the Terrorism Act 2000*, April, p. 20, para. 105.
74 Interview with PICTU, 11 August 2004.
75 Home Office, Press Release 020/2003, *Government Response to HMIC Review on Special Branch and Ports Policing*, 23 January 2003.

76 House of Commons, *Hansard*, Answer by Home Office Minister Hazel Blears, 30 April 2004, vol. 420, col. 359W.

77 This point emerged from the NaCTSO survey of police forces and from the North Yorkshire Police Presentation at PICTU/ESRC Project Workshop, 9–10 June 2004 where 20 DSP posts vital to the new Anti-Terrorism Unit are only centrally funded for a year at a time.

78 See the spending review reports: (2004) *The Independent*, 7 July, and (2004) *Guardian*, 8 July.

79 Interview with MPSB SO12 Officer, 7 July 2004.

80 Information supplied by the Head of PICTU, 12 August 2004.

81 Intelligence and Security Committee (2006) *Annual Report 2005–2006*, Cm 6864, July, para. 102.

82 Interview with Anti-Terrorist Branch Officer, Presentation at PICTU/ESRC Project Workshop June 2004, and see also Gregory, F. (2003) *Jane's Intelligence Review*, January.

83 The detailed discussion of the work of NaCTSO is taken from several interviews with NaCTSO officers in 2002–3.

84 Broadbridge, op. cit., p. 23.

85 Data from NaCTSO Survey of CTSAs, 2004.

86 Metropolitan Police and Metropolitan Police Authority (2004) *Joint Annual Report for 2003–2004*.

87 This Project has been particularly fortunate in being able to gain a considerable depth of knowledge of this aspect of the domestic management of terrorism in the UK, through its workshops, regular contact with lead officers and by participating in an ACPO TAM committee on explosives detection. Further appreciation of the counter-terrorism management problems was also gained by one Project Team member attending as, an invited observer, at the Hampshire Police-run Home Office sponsored national counter-terrorism exercise 'Black Knight' in February 2002.

88 See Walker, C. and Broderick, J. (2006) *The Civil Contingencies Act 2004*, Oxford: Oxford University Press.

89 Interview with MoD Staff Officer, May 2004.

90 House of Commons Defence Committee, Fifth Report, Session 2003–04, *Defence White Paper 2003*, HC 465-I and II, London: The Stationery Office, 2004, HC 465-II, Q.115.

91 Ministry of Defence, para. 2.4, p. 7, July 2004, *The Times*, 21 July 2004.

92 HC 415-II, op. cit., Q.115.

93 Ibid.

94 Cabinet Office, CCS (2004) *Responding to Emergencies, Draft Guidance*, paras 3.38–3.39, p. 14.

95 Interview with MPS SO 12 officer, 7 July 2004.

96 Such suits were evident in exercise Black Knight in February 2003.

97 Home Office, Speech, 'Terrorism – policing the unknown', by Leigh Lewis, 20 May 2004.

98 Interview with MoD Staff Officer, May 2004.

99 HC 465-I, op. cit., para. 150.

100 Discussions during exercise Black Knight, February 2003.

101 See the reports in *The Times*, 20 May 2004.

102 Oral Evidence to the Defence Committee and the Home Affairs Committee inquiry into 'Homeland Security', HC 417-I, 2 March 2004, Q.72.

103 (2004) *The Times*, 19 July.

104 Interviews with Working Group leader 2003, 2004 and 2005.

105 (2003) *The Times*, 7 December.

106 (2003) *The Times*, 23 December.

107 Oral Evidence by the Rt. Hon. Charles Clarke to the Home Affairs Committee, 'Counter-terrorism and Community Relations', HC 462-I, 13 September 2005, Q.23.

108 Ibid., Q.59.

109 Ibid.

110 *The Police Service Response to the Threat Posed by Suicide Terrorism*, Review by the Association of Chief Police Officers Use of Firearms Committee, ACPO, March 2006.

111 The Project has gained valuable insights into DADA response planning through one of the team becoming a co-opted member of a DADA sub-committee. This structure of response through ACPO DADA committees was subject to review in the summer of 2005 and a new scheme is planned to replace the DADA committees.

112 Lord Carlile of Berriew (2004) *Report on the Operation in 2002 and 2003 of the Terrorism Act 2000*, April, p. 21, para. 112.

113 The Statistics Commission is currently examining this issue. I am grateful to Professor Marian FitzGerald of Kent University for drawing this to my attention.

114 Information from Project Workshop.

115 Minutes of Evidence, 'Terrorism and Community Affairs', Home Affairs Select Committee, 25 January 2005, HC 165-II, Q.333 answer by ACC Robert Beckley.

116 Ibid., Q.355.

117 Commissioner Sir Ian Blair, Speech to Superintendents in Warwickshire, 21 September 2005, available at www.Timesonline.co.uk/article/0,,2-1791105,00.html, accessed 6 October 2005.

118 Ibid.

119 Statewatch and see also these figures as listed in House of Commons, *Hansard*, Written Answer by Home Secretary David Blunkett, 27 January 2004, vol. 417, col. 268–9W.

120 House of Commons, Home Affairs Committee (2005) *Terrorism and Community Relations*, Sixth Report, Session 2004–05, HC165-I, London: The Stationery Office, April, paras 47–58.

121 HC 165-I, op. cit., para. 50, Lord Carlile of Berriew (2004) *Report on the Operation in 2002 and 2003 of the Terrorism Act 2000*, April, and *Hansard*, Written Answer, 21 December 2004, col. 1555W.

122 Oral Evidence, Home Affairs Committee Inquiry into 'Anti-Terrorism Powers', HC 886-I, 8 July 2004, Q.96.

123 FitzGerald, op. cit.

124 See Home Office Minister Hazel Blears, *Hansard*, Written Answer, 12 September 2005, col. 2615W, and Dodd, Vikram (2005) 'Asian men targeted in stop and search', *Guardian*, 17 August.

125 (2004) *Report of HM Chief Inspector of Constabulary 2003–2004*, London: The Stationery Office, December, p. 25.

126 Oral Evidence, Home Affairs Committee Inquiry into 'Anti-Terrorism Powers', HC 886-I, 8 July 2004, Q.19.

127 Oral Evidence, Home Affairs Committee Inquiry into 'Anti-Terrorism Powers', HC 886-I, 8 July 2004.

128 'Statistics on Race and the Criminal Justice System', collected pursuant to s. 95 of the Criminal Justice Act 1991, Home Office, June 2004, p. 28, Table 4.5.

129 HC 165-1, op. cit., para. 53.

130 Minutes of Evidence, 'Terrorism and Community Affairs', Home Affairs Select Committee, 25 January 2005, HC 165-II, Q.368.

131 As set out in Cm. 6888, op. cit.

132 House of Commons, *Hansard*, Written Answer by Home Secretary David Blunkett, 5 May 2004, vol. 420, col. 1554–5W.

133 ISC (2006) *Report into the London Terrorist Attacks on 7 July 2005*, Cm. 6785, London: The Stationery Office, May, pp. 7–8.
134 Presentation at PICTU/ESRC Project Workshop, June 2004.
135 Lord Carlile of Berriew, *Report on the Operation in 2002 and 2003 of the Terrorism Act 2000*, April 2004, p. 29, para. 148.
136 Ibid., para. 149.
137 (2004) *The Times*, 2 April.
138 Statement by DAC Peter Clarke, Head of the Metropolitan Police Service Anti-Terrorist Branch and National Coordinator of Terrorist Investigations, Metropolitan Police Service Bulletin 2004/0041, 30 March 2004, available at www.met.police.uk/pns/DisplayPN.cgi?pn_id=2004_0041, accessed 6/7/04, and see also Metropolitan Police and Metropolitan Police Authority (2004) *Joint Annual Report for 2003–2004*.
139 (2004) *The Times*, 31 March, 1 and 2 April.
140 See reports: (2005) *The Times*, 17 July, and (2005) *The Independent*, 18 July.
141 See the reports: (2004) *The Times*, 4 and 5 August, and Metropolitan Police Service Press Bulletin 2004/0102.
142 (2004) *The Times*, 18 August.
143 (2004) *The Times*, 19 August.
144 Oral Evidence, Home Affairs Committee Inquiry into 'Anti-Terrorism Powers', HC 886-I, 8 July 2004, Qs 48, 53 and 62.
145 (2004) *The Times*, 16 April.
146 Stevens, op. cit., p. 273.
147 HC 462-I, op. cit., Q.47.
148 Ibid., Q.51.
149 (2006) *The Times*, 22 and 23 August.
150 Anti Terrorist Branch (SO13), 'Three Month pre-charge Detention', 5 October 2005, op. cit.
151 BBC News online, available at news.bbc.co.uk/1/hi/uk/4433709.stm, accessed 4 October 2005.
152 Stevens, op. cit., p. 304.
153 Ibid., pp. 304–6.
154 Ibid.
155 (2003) *The Times*, 4 December.
156 BBC News online, 28 February 2005, available at news.bbc.co.uk/1/hi/england/gloucestershire/4304223.stm, accessed 4 October 2005.
157 Evans, R. (2003) 'News', *Jane's Intelligence Review*, May.
158 Ibid.
159 House of Commons, *Hansard*, Written Answer by Home Secretary David Blunkett, 19 May 2004, vol. 421, col. 1037–8W.
160 Crown Prosecution Service Press Release, 23 September 2005, available at www.cps.gov.uk/news/pressreleaes/146_05.html, accessed 4 October 2005, and see also '"Warrior" gets 15 years for terrorism', available at uk.news.yahoo.com/23092005/325/warrior-gets-15-years-terrorism-offences.html, accessed 4 October 2005.
161 (2004) *The Times*, 22, 27, 28 and 29 April, and interview with senior Metropolitan Police Service Officer.
162 Interview with PICTU, 11 August 2004.
163 NaCTSO Survey of police forces and CTSAs, 2004.
164 Barnet Police, Metropolitan Police Service, *Anti-terrorism in Barnet*, available at www.met.police.uk/barnet/anti_terrorism.htm, accessed 6 July 2004.
165 *Cambridgeshire Police Chief Constable's Annual Report 2002–3.*
166 *Gloucestershire Police Chief Constable's Annual Report 2002–3.*
167 *Derbyshire Police Chief Constable's Annual Report 2002–3.*

168 *West Midlands Police Chief Constable's Annual Report 2002–3.*
169 Presentation to PICTU/ESRC Project Workshop, June 2004.
170 (2004) *The Times*, 14 June.
171 *Closing the Gap*, op. cit.
172 Ibid., para. 5.38.
173 Ibid., para. 5.42.
174 (2004) *The Times*, 14 June.
175 HC 910-II, op. cit., Ev.54, Q.274.
176 Ibid.

11 Immigration and asylum issues

Tamara Makarenko

Introduction

In the aftermath of the 11 September 2001 terrorist attacks on the USA, and subsequent counter-terrorist operations in the UK, the relationship between the threat of international terrorism, immigration, and asylum more specifically, has received significant interest. Fuelling what appears to be growing public fear that these issues are inextricably linked has been a plethora of stories printed in the tabloid media over the past two and a half years, publishing articles with bleak titles including: 'Murder, terrorism, theft and violence: how asylum crisis affects life in Britain',[1] 'Stop the 'asylum' killers getting into our country',[2] 'Terror suspects safe in Britain'.[3] The conclusion made in many of these articles was simply that the UK had become a *de facto* safe haven for terrorists because of lax immigration policies. Although there are indications that certain individuals have manipulated immigration laws to secure residence in the UK, there is no available evidence indicating that terrorists favour any specific form of entry onto British territory.

Evidence available in open-source resources suggests that some individuals arrested in counter-terrorism operations throughout the UK gained entry as asylum seekers. However, based on an overview of known terrorists who have penetrated Western European countries in general, it may be concluded that most of these individuals seek entry to a country, including the UK, through legitimate channels (that is, education or on a work permit). As a result, it would be especially inaccurate to conclude that asylum and terrorism are connected in any way apart from circumstantially. Failure to debunk what has become a widespread 'terrorism myth' may have significant implications for race relations, and ultimately for domestic security. Taking the race riots of 2001 in Bradford, Burnley and Oldham as an example of how community relations can deteriorate into violence – without public education about the terrorist threat, an act of terrorism successfully perpetrated by Islamic militants has the possibility of reproducing a comparable scenario.

Although terrorists and criminals have manipulated the immigration system in the past, it is not the only avenue through which illicit actors can enter Britain. In fact, another worrying trend is the apparently growing number of British-born youths 'going through an identity crisis' that 'extremists are quick to exploit'.[4]

This threat was reflected in the March arrests of 'eight young men of Pakistani descent alleged to have been planning a bombing campaign'.[5] Not necessarily associated with any specific terrorist group, such as Al-Qaeda, these individuals reflect how the ideology of Al-Qaeda has spawned individuals to commit to a radical and militant agenda that they are willing to perpetrate at home. Of greater significance, this dynamic played an important role in the recruitment and motivation of the 7/7 bombers.

The emergence of an asylum–terrorism connection

Despite seeking to dissipate fears that UK immigration policies, specifically those on asylum, have been manipulated by terrorists, several examples have emerged illustrating the asylum–terrorist relationship. Most evidence of this link is tied to a contemporary history of the UK granting Algerians asylum, including several alleged terrorists with suspected links to the GIA – which has been linked to Al-Qaeda. Although there is no direct threat associated with allowing Algerian nationals refuge from the violence they have sustained during years of internal violence, the fact that UK immigration officials have reportedly lost track of hundreds of Algerian asylum seekers raises serious issues for the prevailing perception of national security. As quoted in *The Times*, 'More than 9,000 Algerians are still in Britain years after having their asylum claims refused'.[6]

Based on the link between Algerian terrorism and Al-Qaeda, and evidence that many Algerian asylum seekers are unaccounted for, the dangers of an asylum-terrorism link – even if limited – warrant consideration. The need to assess the extent of this threat is merely highlighted after reports that apprehended terrorists are asylum seekers. For example, concerns about British asylum procedures peaked after 15 of 18 Algerians arrested in Edinburgh, Leicester, Bournemouth, Manchester and London – following the January 2003 discovery of a terrorist cell manufacturing ricin in London – were believed to be asylum seekers. This was further heightened after statements from the Algerian Refugee Council noted that hundreds of Algerians that sought asylum in the UK had a violent past. A similar peak in concerns about British asylum occurred following media reports that Omar Saiki – an Islamic militant jailed for his part in a plot to bomb the 1998 World Cup in France – sought asylum in Britain.[7] It was further discovered that after arriving in the UK in September 2002, Saiki allegedly stayed at the Finsbury Park Mosque, and was secretly filmed in January 2003 by a French journalist while staying in the Muslim Welfare House, describing himself as a representative of the Salafist Group for Preaching and Combat.

Sporadic examples of the asylum–terrorism relationship in the UK, although not necessarily reflective of a wider trend, are reflective of the ways in which terrorists can manipulate an immigration policy that is ill-defined, or well-defined but not functional because of insufficient manpower and resources. Considering the significant rise in migration to the UK since 1997, it would be naïve to conclude that illicit actors have not sought to enter the UK through these population movements. According to Home Office statistics, between 1993 and

1998 net migration[8] into Britain averaged approximately 50,000 a year; this grew to an average of 158,000 per year between 1998 and 2002.[9] This is supplemented by asylum-specific statistics, with Home Office bulletins reporting that asylum applications[10] trebled between 1996 and 2002 from approximately 30,000 to 80,000. Furthermore, of the applicants refused asylum during this period, it is believed that only one-fifth have left the UK.[11] Compared to the rest of the world, the UK has absorbed a significant percentage of asylum seekers (see Figure 11.1). As reported by the United Nations High Commissioner for Refugees (UNHCR), Ireland and the UK received as many asylum seekers per capita as the EU as a whole. Based on statistics from 36 countries, the distribution of asylum claims in 2003 has been divided as follows: UK: 13.2 per cent, USA: 13.1 per cent, France: 11.1 per cent, Germany: 10.9 per cent, Austria: 7.0 per cent, Canada: 6.9 per cent, Sweden: 6.8 per cent, Switzerland: 4.5 per cent, Belgium: 3.7 per cent, Norway: 3.4 per cent, Other: 19.5 per cent.[12]

Exacerbating the potential problems of this situation is the fact that the numbers of illegal immigrants are largely unknown. However, those discovered by customs and immigrations officers have increased significantly, from 3,300 in 1990 to over 48,000 in 2002.[13]

As previously noted, these statistics do not point to the certain manipulation of the British immigration system by terrorists, as the supporting evidence is limited. However, based on immigration flows, combined with evidence of scandals within the Immigration and Nationalities Directorate of the Home Office, this suggests that British efforts to secure its territorial integrity have been undermined from within. For example, allegations that immigration staff were ordered to avoid arresting illegal immigrants, even those suspected of criminal activity, because it 'was feared that the immigrants would apply for asylum if detained and would therefore undermine the Prime Minister's pledge to reduce the number of asylum seekers by half'.[14] According to a written statement provided to *The Times*

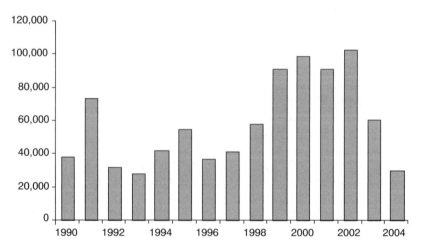

Figure 11.1 Asylum applications to the UK[15]

newspaper by an immigration official, enforcement staff were told 'not to conduct visits to arrest illegal immigrants unless they were absolutely certain that they were failed asylum seekers, lest any hitherto undetected illegal immigrants encountered claimed asylum and thereby boosted the number of asylum claims'.[16] Adding this factor to the equation, it may be concluded that although most migrants are genuine and skilled workers, 'thousands of people, including possible terrorists, have been allowed to enter and stay in Britain without proper checks'.[17]

The Immigration and Nationality Directorate's counter-terrorism role

The Immigration and Nationality Directorate, part of the Home Office, explicitly exists to 'regulate entry to, and settlement in, the UK effectively in the interests of sustainable growth, and social inclusion'.[18] Although considered to be an essential component of ensuring the integrity of national security, the role of Immigration and Nationality Directorate has received extraordinary attention since 9/11. In many respects, rising public concerns (fed by the media) about acts of terrorism perpetrated by foreign nationals on UK territory has resulted in unprecedented debates about the relationship between asylum and immigration and national security.[19]

Government concerns about the connection between asylum, immigration and security are outlined in the Home Office White Paper *Secure Borders, Safe Haven: Integration with Diversity in Modern Britain*, Cm. 5387 (February 2002). This chapter outlines the key challenges faced by the UK government in developing an effective and efficient nationality, immigration and asylum policy that balances the benefits of immigration with any potential tensions (such as the disturbances in Bradford, Oldham and Burnley) that they may bring.

The *Secure Borders, Safe Havens* White Paper is divided into seven chapters, each attempting to outline the benefits of the UK immigration and naturalisation process. Chapter 2, for example, explains how the UK government seeks to promote the importance of British naturalisation, and chapter three describes how the government intends to enhance current legitimate routes of entry into the UK (to detract people seeking entry through illegitimate routes) while tightening procedures to ensure that migration policies complement policies for the labour market, integration and international development.[20] The keys to further asylum changes, according to the White Paper, include: developing a system that is primarily based on recognising who is and is not in need of protection; and, developing a more managed asylum system that would track each applicant throughout the entire asylum process.

Chapter 4 of the White Paper focuses on providing recommendations for asylum system reform. Suggestions presented include:

* preparing a resettlement programme with UNHCR;
* introducing a managed system of induction, accommodation, reporting and removal centres;

- introducing an Application Registration Card to provide more certain evidence of nationality and identity;
- phasing-out voucher support;
- providing better assistance to unaccompanied children;
- streamlining the asylum appeals system to minimise delays;
- developing a strategy to increase the number of removals of people with no claim to remain in the UK; and,
- enhancing opportunities of accepted refugees so that they can play a full role in society through the Refugee Integration Programme.

In conjunction with recommended improvements to the UK asylum system, the White Paper makes it clear that an essential component of any reforms must include reducing illegal people trafficking, illegal entry into the UK and illegal migrant workers. The primary ways in which this could be facilitated would be to strengthen the law to increase the penalties for facilitating illegal entry into the UK and trafficking for the purposes of sexual exploitation; and to target criminals involved in people trafficking through intelligence and enforcement operations. The latter would necessitate increased cooperation with EU and international partners; and encourage and support prevention strategies in source and transit countries. Illegal migrant workers, on the other hand, could only be tackled through improved enforcement action, and cooperation with business and trades union.

The need for increased international cooperation in reducing people-trafficking is an element that is built on in Chapter 6 – which is focused on strengthening border protection. In addition to strengthening domestic border control arrangements, such as using technology to improve control and security of passengers, and help locate people seeking illegal entry (for example, through the use of CCTV), recommendations to improve UK border security by focusing on international initiatives are discussed. These include the following suggestions:

- The deployment of Airline Protection Officers overseas to help prevent improperly documented passengers to travel to the UK.
- Employing visa regimes for countries where there is evidence of systematic abuse of UK controls.
- Placing immigration officers abroad, and where deemed necessary, to check passengers before they travel to the UK.
- Maintain operational arrangements for UK immigration officers to conduct passport control checks in France, and develop a new concept of screening passengers before they travel to the UK.
- Strengthening cooperation with EU partners, and others, to strengthen EU common borders and strengthen border controls along transit routes.

Finally, the White Paper concludes by noting the importance of measures to prevent war criminals from entering the UK. The key to ensuring that this does not happen, according to the document, is by strengthening the relevant nationality and immigration policy, and by cooperating with other government departments and agencies. However, this latter strategy – inter-departmental cooperation – is the key to any efforts to secure immigration policy.

Considering the recommendations outlined in the *Secure Borders, Safe Havens* White Paper released in February 2002, it appears as though this document may have acted as an impetus to the Nationality, Immigration and Asylum Act 2002[21] which received Royal Assent on 7 November 2002. According to Beverley Hughes, former Minister for Citizenship and Immigration:

This Act is the most radical and far-reaching reform of the UK's immigration, asylum and nationality systems for many years and provides us with a foundation on which to build confidence and trust in the integrity of our systems. The task facing all of us is to take this opportunity to deliver real and lasting change.

The Act will enable us to ensure that our borders are secure, to put in place an effective end-to-end asylum system and to make the acquisition of British citizenship more meaningful and celebratory for new citizens. At the same time however, we are continuing to honour our international obligations to protect those who are fleeing from persecution, including opening up a new gateway, with UNHCR, for genuine refugees to come here.

The key provisions of the Asylum Act 2002[22] include:

- The establishment of an effective and efficient end-to-end asylum process with a system of induction, accommodation and removal centres.
- Speeding up the asylum process, improve contact management and reduce opportunities for abuse of the system.
- Strengthen the integrity of UK borders by ensuring that immigration controls exclude individuals who are an immigration or security risk while responding to legitimate immigration requests in a timely manner.
- Tackle illegal working, people trafficking and fraud.
- Update nationality law and enhance the importance of citizenship to strengthen social inclusion.

More specifically, there are four powers exercised by Immigration and Nationality Directorate that have direct relevance for counter-terrorism operations in the UK. These are: exclusion to the UK, deportation from the UK, refusing asylum, and extradition.

Under British immigration control mechanisms, people may be excluded from entrance to the UK by the personal power of the Home Secretary. Although this power is rarely exercised, there are three justifications under which it may be called upon: national security (including people suspected of having ties to or involvement in terrorism), public order, and foreign relations. Between 1990 and 2001, 273 individuals were excluded from the UK on grounds of national security.[23]

In addition to being excluded from the UK, individuals who successfully enter British territory may be deported if their presence is deemed 'not to be conducive to the public good'.[24] Justifications for deportation are outlined in the Immigration Act 1971 (as amended) – however, it is important to note that the right to appeal does exist. The difficulty with deportation, as recognised by the UK government, relates to the removal of Article 3 of the ECHR, which prevents removal of individuals to countries where there is a real risk of human rights abuses. As such, where removal from the UK is not possible, individuals involved in terrorism may be detained indefinitely in the UK. Indefinite detention is also enabled by the Anti-Terrorism, Crime and Security Act.

In the event that it is uncovered that an individual has ties to terrorism during an asylum application process – either through intelligence, interview, or fingerprinting – they may legally be excluded from protection of the 1951 Convention and can be removed from British territory. This safeguard is highlighted in the Anti-Terrorism, Crime and Security Act.

Finally, in the event that an individual successfully enters the UK and is granted asylum, should they later be tied to terrorism, they may be extradited from the UK as stipulated in the Extradition Act 1989.[25] One of the most controversial exceptions to extradition is that, according to section 6, Schedule 1, paragraph 1(2) of the 1989 Act, individuals will not be extradited from the UK for an 'offence of a political character'.[26] This provision is qualified in several ways, which are outlined in the 2001 UK Resolution 1373 submission to the United Nations Counter Terrorism Committee. The 'political rule', however, does not apply to serious crimes (for example, murder, kidnapping, arson), various offences against the person (for example, abduction, hostage taking, explosive and firearm offences), and specific offences against property (including offences in relation to ships, aircraft, oil rigs and the Channel Tunnel).[27]

The UK has special extradition arrangements with designated Commonwealth partners (outlined in Schedule 3 to the 1989 Act), the Hong Kong Special Administrative Region, the Republic of Ireland, and foreign states designated by an order in council (Schedule 4 to the 1989 Act). Other than states specifically referred to in the Extradition Act, the UK is entitled to make special extradition arrangements upon a request from any state.

Notes

1 (2003) *The Sun*, 29 August.
2 (2003) *The Sun*, 17 January.
3 (2001) *Daily Mail*, 19 October.
4 (2004) 'Hardline youths divide Muslims', *The Observer*, 4 April.
5 Norton-Taylor, Richard (2004) 'Arrests point to radical new threat', *Guardian*, 1 April.
6 McGrory, Daniel (2003) 'Hundreds of terror suspects on the loose', *The Times*, 17 January.
7 Grey, Stephen and Hamzic, Edin (2003) 'World Cup bomb plotter seeks asylum in Britain', *The Sunday Times*, 30 March.

8 Net migration refers to the difference between the total number of migrants entering Britain, minus the total number of people leaving Britain during a specified period.

9 (2004) 'Net immigration reaches a new peak under Blair', *The Sunday Times*, 4 April.

10 During the first three quarters of 2003, the top 10 countries represented among asylum seekers were: Somalia, Iraq, Zimbabwe, Chad, Iran, Afghanistan, India, Turkey, Pakistan, and Congo. UNHCR (2004) *Asylum Levels and Trends in Industrialised Countries, January–September 2003*, Geneva: Population and Data Unit, Division of Operational Support, UNHCR, February.

11 *Asylum Statistics: UK 1997–2002*, cited under the 'statistics' section of the Migration Watch UK website www.migrationwatchuk.org.

12 UNHCR (2004) *Asylum Levels and Trends: Europe and Non-European Industrialised Countries, 2003*, Geneva: Population Data Unit/PGDS, Division of Operational Support, UNHCR, February.

13 *Control of Immigration Statistics: UK 2002*, Section 7.

14 (2004) 'Coming or going? Ministers lose control of Britain's borders', *The Sunday Times*, 4 April.

15 Figures for 2004 available as of 1 February 2005 were limited to the third quarter – retrieved from the UNHCR website at www.unhcr.ch.

16 Ibid.

17 Ibid.

18 This is Aim Six of the Home Office.

19 This was exacerbated by reports that asylum applications to the UK had risen 20% between 2002 and 2003. Travis, A. (2003) 'Blunkett pushes for refugee safe havens', *Guardian*, 1 March.

20 Even prior to the events and aftermath of 11 September 2001, the UK government introduced numerous improvements to the asylum system through the Immigration and Asylum Act 1999. These improvements included: the introduction of a national asylum support system and an electronic fingerprint system to deter multiple applications and for identification; the strengthening of immigration enforcement powers; the introduction of an intelligence-led approach to improve the use of resources; and a one-stop appeals system (which, unfortunately, still remains open to fraud).

21 The text of the Nationality, Immigration and Asylum Act 2002 can be downloaded at www.hmso.gov.uk/acts/acts2002/20020041.htm.

22 As outlined on the website http://194.203.40.90/default.asp?PageID=3784.

23 As reported in the UK Report to the United Nations Counter-Terrorism Committee pursuant to paragraph 6 of Security Council resolution 1373 (2001) of 28 September 2001, document S/2001/1232.

24 Ibid.

25 See www.legislation.hmso.gov/United Kingdom/acts/acts1989.

26 Ibid.

27 UK Report to the United Nations Counter-Terrorism Committee pursuant to paragraph 6 of Security Council Resolution 1373 (2001) of 28 September 2001, document S/2002/787.

12 Enhancing UK aviation security post-9/11

Paul Wilkinson

The UK's civil aviation industry is an important part of the National Critical Infrastructure. As a means of transportation it is inherently vulnerable to attack. When a bomb explodes on an airliner at an altitude of over 30,000 feet, the passengers and crew have no chance whatsoever of survival. It is mass murder in the skies. The huge payloads of modern jumbo jets maximise the carnage and because air travel is also inherently international, major attacks of this kind receive instant worldwide publicity.

The 9/11 attacks demonstrated that terrorists could cause severe damage to the economy as well as the mass murder of thousands of civilians because Al-Qaeda showed how hijacked airliners could be turned into 'cruise missiles' and crashed into highly populated buildings.

What lessons has the UK aviation industry learnt from 9/11 and subsequent Al-Qaeda-linked conspiracies to use attacks on civil aviation? What needs to be done to increase our preparedness for new and emerging threats?

The most dramatic and tragic evidence of Al-Qaeda's interest in civil aviation terrorism as a method and a target was the 9/11 suicide hijackings.[1] It would be a serious mistake to assume that this exploitation of the vulnerability of aviation was a one off, a unique departure from their normal pattern of tactics and targeting. In the eyes of Al-Qaeda, 9/11 was a huge victory, a blow struck at the solar plexus of the US economy and the headquarters of the US military. It proved to itself and to the world that it could turn airliners filled with aviation fuel into the equivalent of cruise missiles capable of killing thousands of people and causing mass destruction on the ground. For an estimated cost of around $500,000 it inflicted damage and disruption costing many trillions of dollars, not counting the billions of dollars expended by the USA and the coalition allies on the war in Iraq and the ensuing occupation, all in the name of fighting the War on Terrorism. The suicide-hijacking tactic enabled Al-Qaeda to carry its jihad into the heartland of America, to kill thousands of Americans (an explicit objective of the terrorist movement), and to gain unprecedented global publicity.[2] Moreover, long before 9/11 the 'new terrorists' had already clearly demonstrated their fascination with civil aviation as both a method and a target. Ramzi Yousef, a terrorist master bomb maker who was closely linked to Al-Qaeda's leadership, bombed a Philippine Airlines plane in midair as a dry run for his 'Bojinka' plan to blow up a dozen US carriers in the Pacific region, a plan which would have cost thousands of innocent lives and which was only prevented by the accidental discovery of the plan on Yousef's computer in a Manila apartment. We also know that Al-Qaeda was involved in a plan to cause an explosion at Los Angeles International Airport at the time of the Millennium celebrations.[3]

Al-Qaeda's continuing interest in targeting civil aviation and using airliners as weapons

Nor is there any evidence that post-9/11 Al-Qaeda has lost interest in civil aviation as a method and a target in its global terrorist campaign. On the contrary, there is abundant evidence that it continues to recognise that aviation terrorism can still provide a low cost, potentially high yield means of achieving its tactical objectives.

In August 2006 New Scotland Yard and the Home Secretary announced details of an alleged conspiracy to blow up nine or possibly 10 airliners in mid-air en route from Heathrow to destinations in the USA. The UK security authorities believe that they disrupted the plot just in time. However, because they could not be sure that they had identified all the alleged participants in the conspiracy they acted swiftly to introduce new aviation security measures. As the plot was believed to involve terrorists taking liquids on board airliners in their hand luggage and the constructing of improvised bombs using liquid explosives on board the aircraft, the emergency measures were designed to severely restrict the hand luggage passengers were allowed to carry on board and to ensure that hand luggage did not contain liquids which could be used in this way. There measures were swiftly implemented and most UK airports staff and passengers adapted to the new regulations without much difficulty. Heathrow, with its huge daily flow of passengers had real difficulties, many flights were delayed or cancelled and some airlines complained vociferously to the media about the chaos caused at Heathrow. What the emergency measures revealed was the need for major airports to have contingency plans ready for problems of this kind, including the vitally important recruitment of additional security staff to reduce the delays and to ensure that new measures are implemented efficiently. However, the police are convinced that they disrupted a plot that would have led to mass carnage in the air and probably on the ground as well if the planes had been blown up over heavily populated areas. If the police are correct in their view that at least nine airliners were to be targeted we are looking at an alleged conspiracy which would have been at least as deadly as the 9/11 attacks. Hence, the major lesson of this alleged conspiracy is that Al-Qaeda still regards attacks on civil aviation as an attractive tactic because of their potential for mass-killing and major damage to the National Critical Infrastructure.

We know that Al-Qaeda was behind Richard Reid's attempt at the suicide bombing of an American Airlines jet using a bomb hidden in his shoe.[4] It is also clear that the Al-Qaeda network was behind the attempt to shoot down a charter aircraft full of Israeli terrorists when it was taking off from Mombasa Airport in

Kenya. The missiles, of Soviet manufacture, narrowly missed the aircraft.[5] We also know that the intelligence services in the USA, the UK and other EU countries, and in the Middle East, continue to be concerned at the amount of intelligence they have gathered which suggests that Al-Qaeda is continuing to plan suicide bombings, suicide hijackings, and the use of MANPADs as a method of attacking civil aviation. It is clear that, despite the best efforts of the USA and its allies to curtail Al-Qaeda funding and block its funds held in the Western banking system, the terrorist network is still capable of circumventing these controls and certainly has sufficient assets to acquire additional supplies of surface-to-air missiles.

To sum up, the threat of international terrorist attack against civil aviation, not only against UK airliners but also against other carriers using British airport facilities and carrying British passengers, remains very real. Indeed since 9/11, which Al-Qaeda sees as a great victory, the threat has been considerably heightened. We know from Al-Qaeda's track record that it not only favours no-warning coordinated suicide attacks; it also tends to repeat the same tactics and return to the same targets once it is convinced that this will bring it success in its 'holy war' against the USA and its allies.

Statistics on the annual totals of terrorist incidents may therefore become dangerously misleading and must not be allowed to create complacency. There is no doubt that aviation security measures and standards have been greatly improved in the USA, and that EU countries' aviation security, which was already well ahead of US standards prior to 9/11, has continued to improve incrementally. However, many other countries, especially the poorest countries of the Global South, have pathetically inadequate airport security measures to deal with the suicide hijacker or suicide sabotage bombers threats. It is clear to the author that the Al-Qaeda terrorist network has the resources, sophistication and ruthlessness to find the weaknesses in UK and international aviation security and to commit mass murder on the airways on a scale we have not seen before. One of the key lessons we should have learnt from the 9/11 attacks is that *qualitative* changes in terrorists' *modus operandi* can lead to a massive increase in the lethality of attacks. Although the author of this study found ample evidence that the UK Government, the Security Service, the Metropolitan Police and TRANSEC, were fully aware of the heightened level of threat, he was somewhat surprised to find some senior staff in the aviation industry, including some members of the International Air Line Pilots Association (IALPA) and some senior commercial managers, ill-informed about the changed nature of the threat, reluctant to adopt any additional security measures and, in some cases, anxious to discard or suspend some of the measures introduced or proposed in the wake of 9/11.

Need for greater awareness of the threat to civil aviation

Hence, one of our key recommendations for the enhancement of civil aviation security in UK airports and airlines is that a much higher priority be given to the dissemination of basic security awareness and better security education across the branches and sectors of the civil aviation industry, public and private. There should be a significant upgrading in the security education of all categories of aircrew and ground staff, including technical and air traffic control staff, and the UK authorities should take proactive steps to promote similar improvements in the security component in the training of airline and airport staff internationally, prioritising efforts to promote these improvements in countries and airlines with direct services to and from the UK.

A second key recommendation is that the UK authorities should ensure that the government, working through the most appropriate lead department should permanently retain responsibility of the shaping of all aspects of aviation security policy and for the monitoring of standards of implementation throughout the industry, with the vital power of utilising Maritime and Aviation Security Act and other relevant legislation to ensure proper implementation by all sectors and to ensure sanctions against those who fail to meet the requirements, and that companies are, if necessary, suspended for serious breaches of security rules. We know that in theory this is what is supposed to happen now: in reality we believe TRANSEC is suffering from a severe shortage of inspection staff as a result of budgetary constraints. The author believes that such constraints on such a key element of the UK's aviation security structures are a false economy.

Why government should take the lead role in aviation security

The author is aware of the frequent complaints of Chief Executive Officers and other figures in the commercial world of aviation that they are subject to too much oversight and 'interference' by government Ministers and officials in security matters. (I recall the loud complaints over the efforts to introduce a UK 'sky marshal' programme to enhance in-flight security, for example.) I would draw readers' attention to the latest academic research by Hainmuller and Lemnitzer who have concluded:

> … we have shown that the different performance of the American and German security regimes before September 11 can be largely attributed to institutional factors. In the US, responsibility for airport security was assigned to airlines whose cost cutting efforts resulted in low performance and lax controls. In Germany, in contrast, responsibility was delegated to the government, which shielded the provision of airport security from market pressures and led to high performance. Drawing upon the in-depth study of both cases, experience from other European countries and the theoretical arguments developed above we claim that the delegation of responsibility for airport security to government is a necessary condition for a satisfactory security performance.[6]

These findings are confirmed by my study of the UK experience. The policy implications are very clear. I note that members of the US 9/11 Commission concluded that, despite some continuing weaknesses, US airport security has been greatly enhanced since the Federal authorities took over responsibility for its implementation in all major airports. This adds further weight to the Hainmuller-Lemnitzer thesis and strengthens this author's case for recommending that HM Government should not relinquish or diminish its key regulatory role in aviation security matters.

Another powerful argument for ensuring that HM Government and its relevant security and counter-terrorism agencies maintain their lead role in preventing and combating aviation terrorism is of course the vital requirement for efficient overall strategic direction and oversight, a case made by Frank Gregory in an early chapter of this study (see Chapter 6, pp. 117–40). One of the most important reasons for maintaining the government's lead role in the field of aviation security is the need to fund and conduct top-calibre scientific and technological development in fields such as the detection of IEDs, the bomb-proofing or strengthening of airliners, airport terminals and other potential terrorist targets, perimeter and access control, computerisation of passenger profiling data, enhancing cyber-security to help prevent sabotage and disruption of air traffic control systems, etc.[7] Research and development of this kind is extremely expensive but nevertheless essential if we are to keep ahead of increasingly sophisticated ruthless and fanatically dedicated international terrorists who have already demonstrated their capacity for technical and tactical innovation.

The need to keep ahead of the terrorists' tactics and technology

Aviation authorities should have learned this lesson in the 1980s, especially in the wake of the Air India flight 122 and Pan Am flight 103 sabotage bombings, which together caused the death of almost 600 people. The civil aviation authorities and the industry in the 1980s were still dependent on boarding-gate search technology that was capable of detecting guns and other metallic weaponry of the kind used by hijackers but was incapable of detecting explosives hidden in passenger or hold luggage. We paid a heavy price for our failure to introduce appropriate measures and technology to protect civil aviation from the sabotage bomb threat.[8]

The vital role of international cooperation

There are a number of current and emerging threats to aviation security, which call for a concerted response by the UK aviation security authorities working in close cooperation with the USA and other allies within the international Coalition Against Terrorism. International cooperation is, as argued earlier in this study *of the essence* here because unless there are *reciprocal* improvements in aviation security and other related counter-terrorism measures in countries whose airlines fly to and from the UK, the UK is going to be vulnerable not only to attacks on our homeland, for example, by a foreign registered aircraft bringing a terrorist bomb or other weaponry and or terrorists into the UK's airspace, but also to our airliners, passengers and crew becoming targets in foreign airspace/airports.

One important area of emerging terrorist innovation is in the choice of explosives. In recent years terrorists have favoured the use of powerful military explosives such as PETN, RDX and TNT, easily obtainable by means of theft, purchase or supply through illegal arms market or by a state sponsor. But as the explosives detection technology currently deployed in most airports is geared to detecting these well-known military explosives, so the terrorists have a strong incentive to try switching to non-nitrogenous agents or pyrotechnics which do not conform to the classic formulas for military explosives and which can be taken on board aircraft disguised as innocent liquids (for example, contact lens solution or cosmetics). For example, peroxides can be used as stand alone explosives or as oxidisers in composite explosives, triacetone triperoxide (TATP) can be synthesised from acetone, as is believed to have been used in a number of terrorist incidents. The methods for making this and a wide range of nitrogen-free explosives are easily accessible in do-it-yourself explosives manuals and from the internet.

1   Aviation security authorities and personnel need to be fully aware of the growing interest being shown by terrorist groups in a wide range of non-detectable home explosives. *I recommend that the necessary research and development resources be provided to develop, test and deploy detection technologies capable of identifying non-nitrogenous explosives* and other 'exotic' explosives. In addition to using nitrogen-free explosives, terrorists could make use of a wide variety of incendiary devises, self-igniting materials, hydrides and phosphorus. Nor should it be assumed that it is only the 'new' terrorist groups, which are aware of the possibilities of non-nitrogenous explosives. (For example, Hamas has used TATP in its bombing campaign against Israel.)

2   In addition to the terrorist search for 'non-detectable' and exotic explosives, there is worrying evidence that some terrorists, particularly the Al-Qaeda network and its affiliated groups, are seriously interested in acquiring and using CBRN weapons. As explained in the threat assessment in Chapter 2 of this study, Al-Qaeda, unlike most of the 'traditional' terrorist groups, explicitly aims at mass killing. It does not observe any humanitarian limits to its 'holy war' terror. It totally ignores the Hague and Geneva Conventions and does not recognise any distinction between combatants and non-combatants. Nor does it appear to be persuaded by any particular arguments for restraint in attacks on the civilian population. It is not constrained by any concern that the use of WMD might endanger the lives of their operatives as it believes in suicide attacks and it seems convinced that it has a limitless supply of potential volunteers for 'self-sacrifice' for the jihad. Hence, aviation security authorities need to prepare for the possibility of attacks using chemical, biological or radiological weapons. Even if the terrorists only succeed in improvising very crude devices of this kind, we should be aware that their deployment in the enclosed space of, for example, a busy airport terminal building or subway system or on board a jumbo jet could have extremely serious consequences,

including the loss of large numbers of lives. In light of the above dangers and threats referred to in Chapter 2 of this study that indicates that some form of CBRN attack by 'new terrorists' is no longer simply a low-probability event, it should be a major consideration for contingency planning by aviation security authorities. This must involve closest possible coordination with the emergency services and the NHS Trusts. A key requirement is for rapid detection and identification of any CBRN agent that may have been used. Without adequate and rapid means to do this it is impossible to make appropriate decisions about how to deal with treatment of casualties, and how to mitigate the scale of lethality. The experience of the Japanese authorities dealing with the 1995 Sarin gas attack on the Tokyo subway system showed the value of calling on the expertise in the defence forces.[9] Training exercises to practice civil military coordination in such emergencies are vital and should be held in all major airports. Where there are known antidotes to specific chemical or biological weapons, it is important to ensure that NHS Trust hospitals in all regions of the UK can call on local stocks to deal with a mass casualty terrorist emergency. Similarly, it should be an urgent priority to equip hospitals and ambulance services for all regions with supplies of decontamination units sufficient to provide rapid processing in a mass-casualty attack and that there is a proper training and exercise programme to ensure that the coordination of all services involved works effectively and smoothly, and that not only paramedics but *all* emergency personnel know how to use the equipment and the appropriate antidote, if one is available. In view of the interest shown by Al-Qaeda in civil aviation target airports and airline staff should be regularly offered briefings and training on this type of threat and provided with regular opportunities to participate in appropriate exercises with the emergency services.

All experts in civil aviation we have consulted in the course of this research agree that another rapidly emerging threat to the civil aviation industry stems from 'cyber-terrorism' or the use of information technology to cause great damage and disruption, including possibly mass killing of passengers and crews in multiple coordinated cyber-sabotage attacks on the aviation computer systems. For a discussion of possible measures to help to give some protection against the threat see Chapter 15 in this study, 'Cyber security and the critical national infrastructure' by my colleague, Dr Darryl Howlett.

However, taking full account of these threats, it is clear that the four most serious current threats to civil aviation are MANPADS, suicide hijacking, and bomb attacks on passenger terminals in the check-in areas, and suicide sabotage bombing. These will be dealt with in the ensuing discussion. The UK, like other major aviation countries, is still searching for more effective counter-measures against these types of threat – all of which have been posed by Al-Qaeda.

Post-Lockerbie improvements of UK aviation security

The bombing of Pan Am flight 103 in December 1998 over Lockerbie, Scotland, causing the loss of 270 lives in the air and on the ground acted as a catalyst for a major review and enhancement of British aviation security.[10] The combination of measures implemented in the wake of Lockerbie led to the UK becoming one of the best-protected countries in the world as far as aviation security is concerned. Action was taken to provide a strong legislative framework, the Maritime and Aviation Security Act, which authorised the DfT to suspend the activities of any airline airport company for breaches of the Act, and for an inspectorate, TRANSEC, to ensure industry compliance. 100 per cent checked baggage screening using multi-layered integrated technology was initiated. 100 per cent staff screening, using pre-employment background checks and a security electronic access control system, was introduced. And, in 1993 a system of air cargo screening, the Regulated Agent and Annual Known Consignor validation scheme was introduced.[11] The UK aviation security system is by no means 100 per cent reliable. Errors and weaknesses have been discovered by the government inspectors, by the media and by observant members of the travelling public. Nevertheless, the combination of the above measures has greatly enhanced UK civil aviation security and made it a world leader in this field. (The USA, despite its huge resources and major scientific contribution to the development of new security technologies, did not institute an equivalent security regime until after 9/11.)

New and emerging threats

The UK, in common with all major aviation countries, now faces a range of new or emerging threats, all of which are extremely difficult to counter. The first and most challenging of these is the MANPADS threat,[12] the use of man-portable air defence systems, or shoulder launch surface-to-air missiles. This type of weapon has been used for many years against primarily military targets. Annually since 1996 there have been several attacks on civilian aircraft and 19 civilians have been killed per year. However, the Al-Qaeda network, which is, as we know, waging a 'holy war' involving mass killing, has access to surface-to-air missiles and has used them in attempts to down aircraft in Saudi Arabia and Kenya. It has been estimated that up to 700,000 such weapons are in circulation, in the hands of various regimes and terrorist and insurgent movements around the world, including Al-Qaeda and its affiliates. What are the main options for countering this threat?

1   First, there is the possibility of installing anti-missile defence systems on all airliners. El Al is reported, in 2004, to be fitting the Flight Guard systems to all its passenger aircraft. The system works by automatically releasing diversionary flares if an on-board sensor detects a heat-seeking missile approaching.[13] To adopt this measure for all UK passenger aircraft would be prohibitively expensive. The UK has far greater numbers of aircraft and flights than Israel and the airlines have made it clear that, in their present

rather fragile financial position with the cost of fuel escalating rapidly, they could not afford to adopt the El Al policy. It is estimated that it would cost billions to adopt the measure for all the passenger fleets and would take six to 10 years to install.

2   A far cheaper, though more uncertain, protection is greatly to enhance the intelligence efforts to gain advance warning of a conspiracy to use MANPADS weapons and to intercept the perpetrators before they can launch their attack. The most practicable countermeasure is to combine this intelligence effort with intensive surveillance and monitoring of the vulnerable areas around major airports, which provide the most likely points for launching MANPADS weapons. It is known that the British authorities have completed MANPADS defence plans of this kind for Heathrow Airport. Unfortunately, as the result of a serious security lapse, documents outlining the anti-missile defence plan were mislaid close to the perimeter of Heathrow Airport in 2004: it is to be devoutly hoped that these plans have not been obtained or seen by a terrorist group for they would provide invaluable data for anyone planning a missile attack.[14]

3   What of the suicide hijacking threat? It might be assumed that in the wake of the devastation and loss of life caused by the 9/11 hijackers the UK authorities would have acted swiftly and effectively to block the threat of this type of attack.

The suicide hijacking threat is a product of the 'new terrorism' of Al-Qaeda and its affiliates, though there had been earlier plans and threats by extreme Islamist terrorist groups to crash aircraft onto urban targets, for example, the GIA group which threatened to force an Airbus they had hijacked in Algeria to fly to Paris where they would crash the plane onto the city.[15] However, it was the 19 Al-Qaeda suicide hijackers who brought this idea to reality by crashing airliners into the World Trade Center and the Pentagon. The details of these attacks, how the terrorists planned and prepared for them, why the US authorities failed to obtain advance warning and how the US responded are authoritatively covered in the 9/11 Report[16] and it is not our purpose to re-examine these matters here. However, it is of vital importance for the UK and the international community to learn from the tragic experience of the US attacks, in order to enhance our strategies, policies and measures to prevent or protect against this form of mass casualty terrorism. (As noted in our Introduction to the present study, one of the aims of the St Andrews/Southampton Project has been to learn lessons from the experience of the USA and other major democratic countries.) The first key area requiring examination is the intelligence facilities, which in large part explain why the US authorities did not have advance warning and why they lacked any effective counter-measures. Some counter-terrorism and intelligence officials had enough indications to know that a very big Al-Qaeda attack was about to happen but they did not know in what form it would take. Their political masters did not attach a high enough priority to the problem of combating the Al-Qaeda threat, and were thus caught completely off guard, and the US public had been generally oblivious to the threat and were therefore shocked and stunned by the magnitude and severity of the attacks.[17]

The 9/11 Report concluded that:

> During the spring and summer of 2001, US intelligence agencies received a stream of warnings that Al-Qaeda planned, or as one report put it, 'something very, very, very big'. Director of Central Intelligence George Tenet told us, 'The system was blinking red'.[18]
>
> Although Bin Ladin was determined to strike in the United States as President Clinton has been told and President Bush was reminded in a Presidential Daily Brief article briefing him in August 2001, the specific threat information pointed overseas. Numerous precautions were taken overseas. Domestic agencies were not effectively mobilized. The threat did not receive national media attention comparable with the millennium alert.

Intelligence failures

The 9/11 Report and the Senate Intelligence Committee Report on the intelligence failures agree that there were points of vulnerability in the 9/11 plot and there were opportunities to disrupt the plot, which, tragically, were missed. These missed opportunities included: failing to put two terrorist suspects on the watch-list, failing to trail them after they travelled the Bangkok and failing to inform the Federal Bureau of Investigation (FBI) about one suspect's US visa or his companion's journey to the USA; failing to take adequate measures to track the two suspects in the USA; failing to connect the arrest of Moussaoui, described as being interested in flying training simply to use the plane for an act of terrorism; failing to give adequate attention to clues of an impending major Al-Qaeda attack; and failures to discover manipulation of passports and false statements on visa applications.[19]

Moreover, in addition to the specific 'missed opportunities' listed above, there were more fundamental weaknesses in the US intelligence community, which contributed to the overall failure to anticipate 9/11 attacks. There was an acute shortage of high-quality intelligence on Al-Qaeda. HUMINT, which is the best means of learning about terrorist plans and intentions, had been neglected at the expense of reliance on electronic intelligence. The efforts of the plethora of intelligence organisations, including the major agencies, the CIA and the FBI, were inadequately coordinated and there was no proper inter-agency review of National Intelligence Estimate on terrorism through the whole period from 1995 to 9/11. Meanwhile the FBI, which is primarily a Federal law enforcement agency rather than intelligence organisation, had become increasingly worried about the threat of terrorism from Islamic extremist groups, but its efforts were primarily case-specific and aimed at bringing prosecutions of individuals rather than aimed at preventing terrorist attacks. The FBI had very limited capabilities for intelligence collection and strategic analysis, and for sharing intelligence with domestic and friendly overseas agencies. It also had to cope with a shortage of funds and inadequate training for the counter-terrorism role. Some of these endemic weaknesses have been addressed by the Bush administration. The FBI and CIA have now been directed by the President to closely coordinate their counter-terrorism efforts. The FBI has been given more resources and improved training. In response to the 9/11 Report the President has appointed a National Director and a National Counter-terrorism Centre. (However, the National Director is not apparently being provided with a budget, and the first appointee was a Republican Congressman with only very limited and junior experience as a CIA employee in the 1970s who was widely regarded as a *political* appointee rather than as an intelligence professional.)

The establishment of a National Counter-terrorism Center is clearly a highly encouraging development. As the 9/11 Commission explains in its Report, '… the problems of coordination have multiplied … and a new National Center would help to break "the older mould of organization stovepiped purely in executive agencies'.[20]

It is to be hoped that an effective and well resourced National Center will overcome the major weaknesses which the establishment of the DHS failed to address, that is, the lack of coordination between the CIA and the FBI which has been the subject of criticism both by the Senate investigation and the 9/11 Commission.

Crisis management and military options

Just as successive US administrations prior to 9/11 had always seen terrorism as a threat to American personnel and facilities overseas rather than in the American homeland, so the US crisis managers and military planners prepared a variety of strike options for attacking bin Laden and his movement overseas. Prior to 9/11 the only case where military action was taken was on 20 August 1998 when the USA used missile strikes to hit Al-Qaeda targets in Afghanistan and a factory in the Sudan which US officials alleged made precursors of chemical weapons, though this was never proved. Following this action, which was the Clinton administration's response to the Al-Qaeda bomb attacks on US embassies in Kenya and Tanzania, it was claimed that there was no sufficiently actionable intelligence to justify further military attacks. The use of the military to protect the US homeland against terrorist attack was not even considered as a serious issue.

As the 9/11 Report explains, officials were completely unprepared to respond to the 9/11 attacks. As the Commission states:

> On the morning of 9/11 the existing protocol was unsuited in every respect for what was about to happen … What ensued was the hurried attempt to create an improvised defence by officials who had never encountered or trained against the situation they faced.[21]

Time and again air traffic controllers lost the hijacked planes. One airliner (the one heading for the Pentagon) was lost track of for over half an hour. US Air Force jets were ultimately scrambled, but they believed that the Pentagon had been hit by Russian missiles, and were heading away from Washington. Communications among those supposedly responsible for handling the crisis were appallingly bad. By the time Vice President Cheney's order to shoot down the airliner was received by the US Air Force, three of the hijacked planes had already been crashed into their targets, and apparently for a time, Cheney was under the impression that two of the planes had been shot down by US forces. One of the major problems had been that civilian officials were far too late in alerting the military to the developing attack.

In other words, the immediate response of the US authorities shows an appalling weakness in crisis management, communications and coordination.

Suicide hijacking as acts of war: the dilemmas posed for crisis managers

9/11 inaugurated a new and infinitely more dangerous era of aviation terrorism. The traditional hijacking is naturally still of concern and has, on occasion, led to deaths and injuries among passengers and crews. However, there are tried and tested means of dealing with such events. In cases of traditional hijacking which are politically motivated, the hijackers' aim is generally to obtain international publicity for their cause and to wrest concessions from the authorities they are targeting. Most hijackings of this type end peacefully with the majority of passengers and crew physically unharmed.[22] The aim of the suicide hijackers is entirely different. They want to turn the aircraft into a missile and crash it into a target on the ground, causing destruction, disruption and, in the case of Al-Qaeda and its affiliates, mass killing of the target population. They know that such attacks will help to create a climate of fear in the targeted population, but, in essence, they are turning the tactic of hijacking into a weapon of asymmetrical warfare. Prior to 9/11, aviation security measures around the world were based on the assumption that the terrorists would not wish to sacrifice their own lives if they could avoid this. Al-Qaeda's suicide hijackers are indoctrinated to prepare them for 'voluntary self-martyrdom' and they believe they will go to paradise for striking a blow in what they believe is a 'holy war' against the infidels. It is for obvious reasons very difficult, especially in open societies, to prevent and combat this form of terror warfare.

Obviously, the best form of prevention is to intercept and pre-empt the would-be suicide hijackers' conspiracy through high quality and timely intelligence on the terrorists' intentions and plans. Yet, as was seen on 9/11 the intelligence may be lacking. Airport boarding-gate security becomes a key final opportunity to prevent the suicide hijackers from boarding the plane. CAPPS (Computer Assisted Passenger Profiling System) is one tool that may be useful here: this would be particularly useful in cases where would-be hijackers are found to be travelling with forged or stolen passports under false identities. The standard process of screening passengers, their hand luggage and hold luggage, for weapons and explosive may also play a key role in such cases, provided that screeners conduct their duties with maximum diligence and vigilance. However, although there have been big improvements in standards of airport boarding-gate security in the USA and other countries since the disastrous failures of airport security on 9/11, it is clear that there are weaknesses and gaps in airport security which can still result in hijackers getting aboard with items that can be used as effective weapons to seize control of an airliner. One obvious reason for this is human fallibility. It only needs one airport/airline security screener to be distracted or lax in their task to allow the hijacker access to boarding. Moreover, there are still many airports around the world where the authorities are complacent, where they believe they are immune from attack, and may therefore allow would-be suicide hijackers on board an airliner which could then be turned into a missile for use against a target country's homeland or against a designated strategic, diplomatic, business or symbolic facility of the target country located overseas. Moreover, the level of airport security around the world is extremely variable, and terrorist movements such as Al-Qaeda and its affiliates are known to undertake careful reconnaissance to find loopholes in security, including airport security, which they can exploit. In other words, it would be foolish to regard airport security as a guaranteed method of preventing hijackers from boarding airliners.

For this very reason, it is particularly foolish to dismiss or neglect measures to maximise in-flight security. In-flight security is literally the last line of defence from preventing hijackers from seizing control of an airliner. Two measures now introduced into UK airlines, despite some fierce opposition within BALPA, make very good sense in the light of 9/11. The installation of intrusion-proof doors dividing the pilot's cockpit from the passengers' cabin is a sensible protective and deterrent measure. If the would-be suicide hijackers are unable to gain access to the cockpit this effectively blocks their efforts to turn the airliner into a weapon. Of course, this does not prevent would-be hijackers from threatening the lives of passengers and cabin crew. For this reason, and to help forestall the would-be suicide sabotage bomber who aims to blow up the airliner in mid-air, the deployment of armed, highly trained sky marshals on board airliners is also a sensible additional in-flight security measure. It is obviously impracticable to provide sky marshals for every flight, but the knowledge that they are being employed on a wide range of flights can act as a deterrent against suicide hijacking attempts.[23] The reason for this is that Al-Qaeda and similar organisations want their attacks to succeed. There is no point in wasting the lives of 'martyrs' for the cause if they are simply going to die in a shoot out with sky marshals and fail in the real objective of taking control of the airliner. Provided the sky marshals are trained to a very high standard, and that the protocols on their precise role and their relationship to the Captain of the aircraft are clear, the new measure is certainly a logical enhancement of in-flight security. The opposition to this measure expressed by some members of the British Air Line Pilots Association was, one suspects, partly the result of lack of awareness of the severity of the threat and the general lack of up-to-date knowledge of counter-terrorism developments overseas. There are two practical arguments in favour of the new measures, which should suffice to quash the opposition. First, opponents of intrusion-proof doors and sky marshals should be aware that if boarding gate and in-flight security fail in the face of a suicide hijacking attempt the crew and their passengers will end up *either* crashing into a building on the ground *or* being shot down by Air Force jets or by surface-to-air missiles to prevent them crashing into a building. Either way they will probably all end up dead. If this practical strategic argument fails, there is a stark commercial reality: if they do not employ proper in-flight security measures the US authorities will act to deny them landing rights in US airports. Given the vital importance of transatlantic routes to all the major British carriers, this argument is likely to prevail at the end of the day.

The crisis manager's dilemma: what to do if the suicide hijackers are in control?

If the suicide hijackers gain control of an aircraft it is vital that the information regarding the flight path and possible target/s is conveyed as rapidly as possible to the crisis decision-makers and that air traffic control, civilian aviation authorities and the military authorities coordinate all emergency action as swiftly as possible. The terrorists may be heading for a major target literally only minutes away from the airport where the hijackers boarded. The aircraft is likely to be fully loaded with fuel. The impact of crashing the airliner into a building or over a heavily habited area would be likely to lead to the deaths of hundreds of civilians. Clearly, the lesser evil would be to shoot down the hijacked plane, knowing that this will be likely to cause fewer total deaths than allowing the aircraft to proceed to its target. However, the need for speedy response is made all the more vital by the fact that if the hijacked plane is aimed at an urban target the shoot down should be carried out well before it reaches the built-up area. However, we may be talking of minutes in trying to calculate the time available to prevent the possibly huge loss of life that could ensue. For these reasons, some security experts, notably in France, have favoured the deployment of surface-to-air missiles around potential targets to provide a swifter response than is possible with interception by fighter aircraft. In calculating the extremely limited opportunity for preventing the hijacked plane from proceeding to its target, the argument for the use of surface-to-air missiles is certainly more persuasive. Whichever method is used, however, one needs to ensure that air traffic control is carefully and accurately monitoring the seized aircraft *throughout* the crisis, and that there is a well prepared plan for dealing with all the likely suicide hijack and suicide sabotage bombing scenarios.

The establishment of strictly policed air exclusion zones over major cities and potential targets limiting access to authorised passenger, cargo and military flights is a valuable measure, because if the air traffic control authorities monitor the zones constantly and report any unauthorised flight immediately to the security authorities there should be more opportunity for a swift response to deal with the threat. The UK system aims to use a combination of air exclusion zones regimes and Air Force fighter aircraft interception to deal with such challenges. However, with a high level of both boarding-gate and in-flight security, one hopes these plans will never have to be put to the test.

The 'Robolander' device

In its constant search for technologies which enhance aviation security, the aerospace industry has come up with an interesting and novel device, which is currently in the stage of development and could be adopted and built into the next generation of air traffic control systems. The system, called 'Robolander', is designed to allow air traffic controllers to take control of aircraft and land them remotely. The device also includes a 'refuse to crash' computer program designed to steer the airliner away from high buildings if the pilots fail to respond to audible warnings.[24]

A senior US aerospace industries chief executive has indicated that the next logical development should be a computerised system that allows air traffic control to take control of a plane in an emergency. The pilot sending an encrypted signal to air traffic control the moment he became aware of the hijackers breaking through the cockpit door would trigger the system.

One major obstacle to the adoption of this type of remote control technology is its sheer expense. However, costs could considerably reduce if the system were to be incorporated into the next generation of air traffic control systems and airliners. Hence, this technology does not offer a 'quick fix' to the suicide hijacker threat, but it does offer a potentially valuable tool for future generations of airliners and air traffic control systems which could save the lives of passengers and crews in a wide range of emergency situations, such as intrusion into the cockpit by a mentally disturbed passenger attempting to grab the controls, or a pilot experiencing a heart attack or severe stroke. As one would anticipate, IALPA tends to be strongly opposed to remote control technologies. They are reluctant to accept any system where they would have to surrender command of the aircraft to a computer system. One senior executive of IALPA has been quoted recently as objecting: 'What would happen if the terrorists took over the air traffic control tower and hacked the codes? They would have a dozen flying bombs'.

It is clear that there is not at present any generally accepted remote control technology which would be a guaranteed effective counter to the suicide hijacker, though one aerospace company has patented a device which requires a code before the aircraft can be operated. There are, of course, serious problems about all remote control technologies.

The suicide sabotage bomber threat

The attempt by Richard Reid to blow up an American Airlines plane using a bomb hidden in his shoe, thwarted only by the vigilance and speedy intervention of the cabin crew and other passengers, was a sharp reminder that we now have to face the suicide sabotage bomber threat, a threat that was dismissed as too improbable by those who planned the response to sabotage bombings of airliners in the 1980s.

The threat to passenger terminals

From the terrorists' point of view one of the most accessible targets in the civil aviation industry is the passenger terminal crowded with passengers and staff in the check-in areas. These facilities have been the targets of particularly bloody attacks in the history of aviation terrorism. For example, Japanese Red Army terrorists indiscriminately shot down passengers in Lod Airport on 30 May 1972, including Puerto Rican pilgrims who happened to be in the area of the terminal when the terrorists opened fire. And the Abu Nidal group murdered passengers in Rome and Vienna airports in 1985.

Al-Qaeda has no compunction about killing hundreds of civilians. Security at airport terminals needs major enhancement in view of the danger of the Al-Qaeda-linked groups posing the suicide bombings threat. Intelligence to disrupt or thwart such attacks may not, alas, always be available. Hence we need to consider access control at a barrier point outside the terminal buildings.

The emergence of the suicide sabotage bomber greatly strengthens the case for maximising boarding-gate and in-flight security. The task at the boarding-gate is now greatly complicated by the fact that more sophisticated terrorist organisations have now mastered the technique of carrying small components of bombs on board rather than an entire IED, thus making it far more difficult to identify the bomber. Ramzi Yousef, the terrorist master bomb designer, pioneered this method. For example, he used liquid explosive, which was hidden in an apparently innocent contact lenses solution container. The bomber then assembled the bomb in the toilet.

A bomb detonated at any altitude over 30,000 feet is likely to cause the aircraft to crash with the loss of all lives on board. The emergence of Al-Qaeda-linked suicide sabotage bombing is therefore a serious challenge. The only effective means of prevention are enhanced intelligence enabling the would-be bomber to be caught before boarding the plane, and greatly improved and extra vigilant boarding-gate and in-flight security.

Conclusion

What general conclusions can be drawn from this research study regarding the degree and quality of domestic preparedness of the civil aviation industry and the relevant security agencies for future terrorist attack?

There are a number of very positive findings:

- Pre-9/11 the UK had already developed one of the most effective and comprehensive civil aviation security systems in the world. The trigger for the major improvements made from the late 1980s to the mid-1990s was the Pan Am flight 103 bombing over Lockerbie in December 1988, the largest act of mass murder within the UK's jurisdiction in modern history, causing 259 fatalities of passengers and crew and 11 deaths on the ground. In the wake of Lockerbie the government made a thorough review of existing security and initiated the following reforms: enhanced access control, staff search, 100 per cent checked baggage screening, a new methodology of screening, 100 per cent staff screening, staff pre-employment background checks, training for security staff and the introduction of the Maritime and Aviation Security Act to help establish a legal framework of legal obligations for the aviation industry. A system of inspection to ensure full implementation and the power to suspend companies found to be in breach of the regulations were introduced.

- Problems and weaknesses, for example, failures to carry out effective employment background checks for airport and airline ground staff have been identified, and no vigilant aviation security expert from TRANSEC would ever claim that the UK has eliminated all the loopholes and weaknesses in the system UK-wide. Nevertheless, by comparison with the USA and our EU neighbours, the UK's airport security prior to 9/11 was widely regarded as one of the best among the first world countries.

- 9/11, however, and the continuing Al-Qaeda threat of suicide hijackings, suicide sabotage bombings, and MANPADS attacks, raise new and much more severe challenges. Recent intelligence derived from terrorist plans captured from a terrorist suspect's computer in Pakistan has confirmed that Al-Qaeda has plans to attack Heathrow. The threat is real and very severe.

- The major means of prevention of attacks on UK aviation targets is our counter-terrorism intelligence secured with the cooperation of the Security Service, MI6, GCHQ, Special Branch, the MPSB and the military, all of which share intelligence with their counterparts overseas.

- However, because both proactive intelligence efforts and airport boarding-gate security may fail to pre-empt an Al-Qaeda-style attack, we need to consider fresh ways of enhancing in flight security, including new technologies of remote control, and we need to win over the aviation professions, especially the airline pilots, to acceptance of some radical innovations to strengthen our defences against these new and emerging threats.

- Lastly, but most urgent of all, the study concludes that the UK authorities need to improve radically their strategic planning and crisis management capabilities to face the challenge of having to deal with a situation in which terrorist suicide hijackers have seized control of one or more airliners and are heading for their targets.

Notes

1 For valuable insights and information on the 9/11 attacks, see (2005) *The 9/11 Commission Report*, New York: W. W. Norton & Co. Hereafter 9/11 Report.

2 For a chilling insight into the motives and beliefs of the suicide hijackers see 'September 11, the letter left behind', available at www.ict.orl.il/articles.

3 Ahmed Ressam was arrested on 14 December 1999 when en route to carry out a bombing of Los Angeles International (LAX) Airport, having spent a week in Vancouver obtaining materials for the bomb he was planning to use. Customs officers found the explosives hidden in the spare tyre well of his rental car. See 9/11 Report, op. cit., pp. 178–9.

4 AP Report, December 2001. It was an American Airlines Flight from Paris to Miami. Reid had UK citizenship.

5 The missiles used were Strela, Soviet-made weapons, more accurate than the early types, SA 7a and SA 7b.

6 See Hainmuller, J. and Lemnitzer, J.M. (2003) 'Why do Europeans fly safer? The politics of airport security in Europe and the US', *Terrorism and Political Violence*, 15(4), p. 28.

7 See Wilkinson, P. and Jenkins, B. (eds) (1999) *Aviation Terrorism and Security*, London: Frank Cass.

8 See Wilkinson, P. (1989) *The Lessons of Lockerbie*, London: RISCT.

9 For an interesting analysis of the Aum Shinrikyo, see Campbell, J.K. (1997) *Weapons of Mass Destruction in Terrorism*, Seminole, FL: Interpact Press.

10 See Wilkinson, *The Lessons of Lockerbie*, op. cit.

11 See Wallis, R. (1993) *Combating Air Terrorism*, Washington, DC and New York, NY: Brassey's (US). (Wallis is a former director of security for IATA and made a major contribution to enhancing international aviation security against the sabotage bombing threat.)

12 See Schaffer, M.B. (1999) 'The missile threat to civil aviation', in Wilkinson, P. and Jenkins, B.M. (eds) *Aviation Terrorism and Security*, London: Frank Cass, pp. 70–82.

13 Ibid., pp. 70–80.

14 Ibid., p. 81.

15 Wilkinson and Jenkins, op. cit., p. 155.

16 9/11 Report, 'The system was blinking red', op. cit., pp. 254–77.

17 Ibid.

18 Ibid.

19 Ibid., pp. 272–6.

20 Ibid., pp. 400–3.

21 Ibid.

22 See Wilkinson, P. (1996) 'The hijacking problem', in Wilkinson, P. (ed.) *Terrorism and the Liberal State*, Basingstoke: Macmillan Education, pp. 223–58, and St John, P. (1991) *Air Piracy, Airport Security and International Terrorism*, New York: Quorum Books.

23 On deterrence, see the useful analysis by Jenkins, B.M. and Davis, P.K. (2002) *Deterrence and Influence in Counterterrorism*, Santa Monica, CA: RAND.

24 See Harlow, J. (2004) '"Robolander" to combat terror hijacks', *The Sunday Times*, 22 August.

13 Port security in the UK

The spectre of maritime terrorism

Peter Lehr

Introduction

The events around 9/11 contain many a lesson for us. The most important one in my point of view is that now we have to face a new global group of terrorists willing to disrupt our ways of life and perfectly capable to do so. Contrary to previous terrorist groups like, for example, the Abu Nidal Organization, which also operated worldwide, Al-Qaeda or the International Islamic Front (IIF) with all their associate groups do not restrict themselves to symbolic acts of terror as a way to communicate, they want to kill as many people as possible, and they want to destroy the very fabric of our lifestyle, of our societies. They frequently target Western tourists at various destinations, for example in Luxor/Egypt in 1997, in Djerba/Tunisia in 2001, in Bali in 2002 and in Taba/Egypt in 2004. Such tourist spots are very difficult to protect. They frequently target Western symbols of power, like embassies or armed forces installations. They also target air traffic, since airports are also very difficult to protect. And now they have an eye on the sea. The best known examples are the suicide attacks on the USS The Sullivans in January 2000 and on the USS Cole on 16 October 2000, the first one botched, the second one successful; and the suicide attack by a two-man crew on board an explosive-laden boat on the French tanker Limburg on 6 October 2002. Less well known, but potentially much more dangerous, are attempts by Al-Qaeda mastermind Khalid Shaikh Mohammed (KSM) to get regular access to the shipping containers of the Pakistan-based International Merchandise Group (IMG) simply by investing US$200,000. IMG is a company shipping rugs and clothing for US customers to Port Newark in the New York Harbor complex. This special attempt failed since KSM was arrested before the plan could be realized. But the Tamil Tigers' shipping operations show how this connection[1] would have been used by Al-Qaeda: most of the time, their ships – at least 10 freighters sailing under Honduran, Liberian or Panamanian flags and 'equipped with sophisticated radar and Inmarsat communication technology' – make money carrying legitimate cargo, but in some cases, they 'played a vital role in supplying explosives, weapons, ammunition and other war-related material to the LTTE in Sri Lanka'.[2] Very probably, IMG containers would have been used in a similar fashion.

Of course, there are rumours that Al-Qaeda already operates as many as 300 ships, but as we know from the Nisha affair in December 2001, these ships remain elusive. As a senior US government official rightly pointed out in regard of registering ships under flags of convenience: 'This industry is a shadowy underworld'.[3] We do not really know whether these ships exist, and the figure may be grossly overstated. The attempt to take over IMG, however, is a fact, and it can be taken as proof that sooner or later, Al-Qaeda-affiliated terrorists will attack our ships in our ports in one way or another. Sooner or later, they will attack our own waterfront, and not only our assets in far-away places like Aden or Basra.

Threat perceptions

We do not need too much imagination to realise that in a post-9/11 world, ships pose a potential threat to our security – they could either be the targets of acts of maritime terrorism or they could be the instruments of such attacks.

Currently the undisputed number one of the maritime terrorism nightmare charts is an attack with a WMD launched by sea against a major port, either of the USA or of one of the USA's allies – especially the UK as the USA's staunchest ally. The usual scenario, as superbly described by Stephen Flynn,[4] revolves around one or more RDDs or so-called 'dirty bombs' hidden in cargo containers on board of a large container ship bound for a major Western port. The bombs could easily be fitted out with GPS systems and, therefore, could be triggered by remote control when having reached a location where they can do as much damage as possible, which means a location from where they can contaminate key parts of the port including industrial parks and suburbs surrounding it.

Number two on the list is a similar attack conducted by a hijacked Liquefied Natural Gas (LNG) tanker being driven into a major port and exploded there, also with the intent of disrupting seaborne global trade. However, the opinion of experts is quite divided in regard of the possibility of triggering such an explosion: while one half of the experts warn that such an explosion would have the force of a small nuclear war head, the other half asserts that in 99 of 100 cases, liquefied gas would not even burn. Of course, law enforcement agencies prefer to err on the safe side, which is why currently a veritable armada of US Coast Guard cutters, police launches and helicopters escorts such tankers inbound for a US port.

Another way of reaping havoc in a major port is by using a large ship like an oil tanker or a chemical tanker as a momentum weapon – currently number three on the hit list. In such a case, the terrorists would attempt to drive such a ship into the harbor at high speed, to ram either other ships with vulnerable cargoes, or oil terminals and the like, and then detonate the ship. Such a scenario has been developed for the Port of Singapore, home of Southeast Asia's largest oil refineries.[5]

Then there is the flourishing cruise liner business: hundreds of cruise ships filled with rather wealthy Western or East Asian tourists are journeying through the seven seas. Many of them originate from ports in the USA, the UK, or other Western countries. So, if I were an Al-Qaeda operative with an interest in maritime terrorism, I would have an eye on a ship like the new Queen Mary II – hijacking such a ship with the threat of turning it into a modern-day version of the Titanic would give me worldwide media coverage, exactly what terrorists want. So would ramming it with a small boat laden with explosives, and that is fairly easy to accomplish, as the cases of the USS Cole and the Limburg show: modern ports are literally 'littered' with small boats, launched from dozens of jetties. Keeping track of all these small, fast movers is well-nigh impossible, even for the best organised maritime police forces.

Apart from the cruise liners, there are literally hundreds of ferries, large and small, running on a tight schedule between two or more harbours. One should just take a look at the ports of Calais and Dover to get an idea how difficult or easy it would be for terrorists to get on board of these vessels – either by car, or even by truck – and then think of the Herald of Free Enterprise or the Estonia disasters. Terror attacks against ferries did happen quite frequently in the Philippines, by the way. The most devastating so far was the 2004 attack against the Super Ferry 14, in which more than 100 passengers and crew lost their lives. Far away, may be, but these terror attacks may give us a glimpse at the shape of things to come. After transport by air had been attacked on 9/11 and after that transport by rail in March 2004 in Madrid as well as in July 2005 in London, transport by sea may be next. To prevent such acts from happening or to at least prevent the worst scenarios from coming true, a flurry of new maritime security initiatives have been introduced in the wake of 9/11. Let us turn to them now.

Counter measures: an overview

On 1 July 2004, several (maritime) security initiatives focusing on enhancing what is usually known as 'supply chain security' came into force. The most important of them are:

- the International Ships and Port Security Code (ISPS);
- the Container Security Initiative (CSI); and
- the Customs-Trade Partnership Against Terrorism (C-TPAT).

The most important of all is the International Maritime Organization's (IMO) ISPS Code, which will be described in more detail below. The second security measure, the CSI, comes from the USA. As part of the United States Maritime Transportation Act of 2002 and basically catering for US security, it is not mandatory outside the USA. However, ports which are not members of the CSI initiative will sooner or later find themselves locked out of business with the USA. CSI consists of four core elements:

1   the use of intelligence and automated information to identify and target high-risk containers;

2   the pre-screening of containers identified as high-risk, at the port of departure, before they arrive at US ports by US Customs and Border Protection officials;

3   the use of detection technology to quickly pre-screen high-risk containers;

4   the utilisation of smarter, tamper-proof container seals.[6]

Up to now, all of the world's top 20 mega ports have agreed to join the initiative and are at various stages of implementation.[7] As a quid-pro-quo, participating states may also send officers to US ports to ensure the safety of containers bound for their respective ports. Within the EU, CSI first had to overcome a typical EU legal hurdle: while eight EU member states – UK, Belgium, France, Germany, Italy, The Netherlands, Spain and Sweden – individually reached an agreement with the USA concerning their participation in the initiative, the European Commission (EC) was of the opinion that it was the EU's prerogative to sign customs agreements – CSI being one in the eyes of the EC – with any non-EU country. In November 2003, this hurdle was finally removed when the EC signed an agreement concerning its participation in CSI. Quite interestingly, as Michael Richardson pointed out, the EC ultimately even expanded the scope of CSI in a significant way:

> [The] EC said that the [EU–US] agreement would ensure not only the security of container cargo trade between the EU and the US but also the security of containers from all locations that are imported into, trans-shipped through, or transit the EU and US.[8]

This interesting and consequent enlargement of CSI meant to render the so-called supply chain more secure fills a certain gap between CSI and C-TPAT, often described to be the 'companion piece to CSI'. The C-TPAT, also a US initiative, addresses companies and carriers involved in importing goods into the USA, and encourages them to (a) assess the vulnerabilities of their supply chains, and (b) to devise measures to close any security gaps they discover. Companies joining C-TPAT will be treated as low-risk shippers by US officials. That means their shipments will not be subjected to routine examinations too often, thus saving them time and money.

An impressive array, no doubt about that. But what is even more important than these initiatives and all the technical solutions proposed, is a gradual development of a much better understanding of what is going on at sea through piecing together information from a variety of sources, such as the Automatic Identification System (AIS) or the potentially global-range Long Range Identification and Tracking (LRIT) System.[9] In short, what is required now is a Maritime Domain Awareness (MDA), comparable in a sense to our awareness of what is going on in our airspace. It can no longer be that for port authorities, ships appear and disappear somewhat surprisingly on the not-so-far horizon. And after that remark, it is time to take a look at what I would like to call the centre piece of MDA, the ISPS Code.

The International Ships and Port Security Code

The ISPS Code as an amendment to the 1974 Safety of Life at Sea Convention (SOLAS) is a mandatory initiative from the IMO. ISPS has been described as a 'tough mandatory security code for ports and ships including contingency arrangements, computer systems, surveillance equipment and manual patrols'.[10] ISPS contains detailed security-related requirements for governments, port authorities and shipping companies, including the appointment of security officers, conducting risk assessments, devising security plans and enhancing the overall security through technical devices of both ships and ports. The cost estimate for the implementation is US$1.3 billion, and then there is an annual cost of US$750 million for ships alone.

Seen from a legal perspective, the ISPS Code is basically part of a set of amendments to Chapters V 'Safety of Navigation' and XI 'Special Measures to Enhance Maritime Safety' of SOLAS, meant to enhance maritime security in a post-9/11 environment. These new regulations have been adopted by the IMO's Diplomatic Conference which was held in December 2002. ISPS itself went into force on 1 July 2004.

Chapter V contains regulations regarding the mandatory carriage of voice data recorders and AIS, which are meant (a) to enhance maritime safety by providing accurate manoeuvring information including the ship's course and speed, and (b) to enhance maritime security by allowing ports and maritime security authorities to identify, track and monitor vessels approaching.[11] This Chapter was amended with a provision meant to accelerate its implementation.

The changes and amendments of Chapter XI were much more substantial. The previous Chapter XI, covering ship safety measures, was split into two parts, XI-1 and XI-2, and some additional amendments:

- Chapter XI-1 'Special Measures to Enhance Maritime Safety' contains additional safety requirements such as ship identification numbers (XI-1/3) and the carriage of a continuous synopsis report as an on-board record of the history of the ship (XI-1/5).
- Chapter XI-2 'Special Measures to Enhance Maritime Security' as the more important amendment in our context contains the ISPS itself (XI-2/3): a comprehensive set of measures to enhance the security of ships and port facilities as well as requirements for the implementation of and compliance with these measures (XI-2/6). The ISPS Code again is split into two parts, a mandatory one – mandatory for all 148 Contracting Parties (signatory states) to SOLAS – and a recommendatory one which contains guidance for the implementation of the mandatory part of ISPS.

All in all, the ISPS Code aims at enhancing maritime security in the age of global terrorism by:

- enabling the detection and deterrence of security threats;

- establishing roles and responsibilities in this regard;
- enabling the collection and the exchange of security information;
- providing a method for assessing ships and port facilities security; and
- ensuring that adequate security measures are in place.

The ISPS code requires ships and port officials to:

- gather and assess security-relevant information;
- maintain communication protocols;
- restrict assess and prevent the introduction of unauthorised weapons. etc.;
- put in place vessel and port security plans; and
- ensure that training and regular security drills are conducted.

IMO offers several model courses to assist ships and ports in implementing the ISPS provisions:

- Company Security Officer: this course aims at providing basic knowledge to personnel designated to perform the duties and responsibilities of a Company Security Officer.
- Port Facility Security Officer: this course aims at providing basic knowledge to personnel designated to perform the duties and responsibilities of a Port Facility Security Officer.
- Ship Security Officer: this course aims at providing basic knowledge to personnel designated to perform the duties and responsibilities of a Ship Security Officer.

For port facilities and shipping companies of the UK, the DfT's website contains much valuable information concerning frequently asked questions in regard of Port Facility Security Officers, Port Facility Security Plans, and Port Facility Security Assessments.[12] More general information can be found on the website of the IMO.[13]

ISPS implementation in the UK

We are living in an era of globalisation – an era in which news and ideas travel around the globe in near real time, an era in which people routinely travel to distant places in a matter of hours, and an era in which a farmer in New Zealand can ship his olives to the UK, while shrimps harvested at Scottish shores are transported to Thailand to be processed there before being shipped back again. The terms 'shores' and 'ship' have not been used coincidentally, quite the contrary. It is the experience of this author that, in a time of interconnectedness, a very obvious point needs to be driven home to the British citizens: the UK still is an island nation, and it still depends very heavily on seaborne trade and traffic. More than 90 per cent of all goods come or go by ship, the tunnel beneath the Channel or the new sub-sea gas pipeline from Norway notwithstanding. They arrive in bulk on board of oil tankers, gas tankers, chemical tankers, container ships or other general cargo ships. They arrive as freshly harvested or frozen fish and other sea food on board of industrial trawlers or coastal fisher vessels. And they arrive on trucks on board of Channel ferries, day by day.

How hard the UK would be hit by a disruption of seaborne traffic can be gleaned from the fact that, when an oil tanker bound for the UK was re-routed to the USA in the aftermath of Hurricane Katrina, long queues at British gas stations were the immediate result. That was only a psychological effect which was at work here, but imagine a terror attack at or near a major UK port, such as the sinking of an oil tanker or the bombing of a cross-Channel ferry. Port security obviously does matter, at least for the major ports of the UK. But how well are the British ports prepared for an attack? What has been done, and what is being done, to protect ports and to prevent terror attacks from happening? And what has been done to survive an attack and to go back to business as quickly as possible in case of a successful terror attack? These are the questions which will be addressed in the remainder of this paper, however, for obvious reasons, only in rather general terms.

High-risk UK ports: an overview

Of course, not every port in the UK faces an imminent terrorist threat. For a small fishery harbour or a harbour mainly exporting iron ore, for example, the new spectre of maritime terrorism is a rather abstract one. For a port like Dover or Felixstowe, however, there is a certain risk of a maritime terror attack sometime in the foreseeable future. According to the DfT, five categories of ports have been developed, of which four come under the scope of the ISPS Code.[14] These categories are:

- Category PAX: this category includes all passenger ports handling international passenger ships.
- Category PCG: this category includes all ports handling petrochemical shipments or LNG/LPG gas shipments.
- Category CRR: this category includes ports handling container traffic and/or roll-on, roll-off ferry traffic.
- Category OBC: this category includes ports handling any other bulk and general cargo.
- Category AOP: the category 'all other ports' describes all ports not taking part in international traffic, that is, fishery ports or leisure ports.

The most prominent of the high-risk ports falling under one of the first four categories are the ports of London, Milford Haven, Felixstowe, and Dover. The following facts are taken from these ports' official websites.

Port of London: city port

The Port of London describes itself as 'one of the top three ports in the UK and handles over 50 million tonnes of cargo each year. The Port of London comprises over 70 independently owned and operated terminals and port facilities, which handle a wide range of cargoes'.[15]

According to its own statistics, the port 'handles over 53 million tonnes of cargo, carried in 12,500 commercial vessels' and 'generates over 35,200 full time equivalent jobs and contributes more than £3.4 billion per annum to the London and South East regional economy'. Also, the Port of London is visited by roughly 2 million people per year, 'in pleasure boats, cruise ships and private boats'.[16]

Felixstowe: container port

The Port of Felixstowe is 'the largest container port in the UK and one of the largest in Europe'.[17] Its website states that 'with 14.5 metres below chart datum in the navigation channel and up to 15 metres alongside the quay, Felixstowe boasts deep water suitable to accommodate the world's latest generation of deep-draughted vessels'.[18] In 2003, Felixstowe completed a 270 metre deep-water berth with a continuous quay of 2.6km and 24 ship-to-shore gantry cranes in operation. 'This expansion programme has further enhanced Felixstowe's position as one of the world's leading container ports', its website says.[19]

Proof of the Port of Felixstowe's confidence in its future can be found in the fact that its facilities were capable of handling the first visit of Emma Maersk, the world's biggest container ship with an official capacity of about 11,000 TEU, in November 2006. The Emma Maersk has an overall length of 397 metres, and boasts a deadweight 40 per cent greater than its next-largest rival.[20]

Milford Haven: oil port

Milford Haven is both the fifth-largest commercial port of the UK and the largest port of Wales. Apart from being a passenger port – its Pembroke Port features a modern purpose-built roll-on, roll-off terminal frequented mainly by ferries to Ireland – Milford Haven also is a dedicated oil port, catering for no less than three oil refineries along its waterway. For these refineries, Milford Haven provides a deep-water berth and accommodates heavy lift operations.[21] At the time of writing, the port prepares for LNG traffic, which is expected to use this port and its new facilities from end of 2007 onward.

Regarding possible future acts of maritime terrorism, especially when it comes to scuttling big ships such as oil or LNG tankers, it is noteworthy that Milford Haven is situated 'in the heart of the only Coastal National Park in Great Britain',[22] and it is even more noteworthy to remind the reader that the approaches of the port have already been the scene of a major oil spill. In 1996, the oil tanker Sea Empress ran aground, initially spilling just 2,500 tonnes of oil. Efforts to refloat the tanker led to a second grounding, which resulted in a much more devastating oil spill of nearly 70,000 tonnes and a substantial pollution of the coast.[23]

Seen against this background, it is not very surprising when Milford Haven Port Authority emphasises that safety and security features very high on its agenda, manned security being present around the clock, and all operations being handled in full compliance with the Aviation and Maritime Security Act regulations and, of course, the ISPS Code regulations.[24]

Dover: passenger port

As the website of ports.uk.org points out, Dover is 'the busiest passenger ferry terminal in the world, the busiest cruise liner terminal in Britain and a major port for freight, particularly for fruit and other perishables imported via the massive reefer cargo ships'.[25] Since 1978, Dover even sports a dedicated Hover-Port at the port's Western Docks.

The importance of Dover as a ferry port can be gleaned from the fact that the roll-on, roll-off ferries frequenting it handle a total of around 1.8 million trucks a year.[26] In regard of Dover's importance as a cruise port, one can take a look at the forthcoming (at the time of print) 2007 cruise season. It will be one of the busiest ever and the longest at that 'with the first call in April running right through until the end of the year', as Kate O'Hara, head of Commercial and Marketing, stated.[27] Dover's cruise port expects no fewer than 135 calls by cruise ships from 22 operators during 2007.[28]

High risk ports: a comment

As the reader can see, these four ports feature general and special sets of vulnerabilities which could turn them into targets for acts of maritime terrorism: Felixstowe would be a convenient location for the 'dirty bomb' scenario described above, Milford Haven could be the scene of a 'momentum weapon' attack with the intent of either ramming another ship or a port facility and/or creating an oil spill, and Dover seems to be just perfect for a devastating bombing attack such as the one against the Super Ferry 14 in Manila Bay in April 2004. The Port of London would be a very special and, thus, very tempting target indeed: an attack would happen basically in the 'heart of the city', thus being highly visible and a major media event – apart from being potentially very costly in terms of lives lost and property damaged, depending on the type of attack. Therefore, it seems to be quite obvious that preventing such worst-case scenarios from becoming bitter reality by being able to protect one's port facilities and by being generally prepared to deal with an attack if it happens is the order of the day.

As was stated above, this article does not attempt to scrutinise individual port's security approaches and to point out loop-holes future maritime terrorists could exploit. However, what we can do now is to take a general look at how the ISPS Code is being implemented in the UK, from assessment to the final approval of a

Port Facility Security Plan, before we conclude this article with some examples and some general remarks on the UK ports' preparedness in regard of a maritime terrorist attack.

The UK's port facility security assessment procedure

The Port Facility Security Assessment (PFSA) leading to the issue of an approved Port Facility Security Plan (PFSP) is fairly straightforward. The first step towards developing security plans for all port facilities falling under the scope of ISPS consists of sending a security questionnaire to all UK port facilities identified from industry groups, port registers and other directories. The returning security questionnaires are then examined by TRANSEC, which (a) categorises the port facilities according to the type of traffic they primarily handle, and (b) prioritises the PFSA programme according to the risk the responding port facilities face.[29]

TRANSEC then sends a team of security inspectors to the port facility in question, who carry out the PFSA in cooperation with officials from the port facility's management. After the assessment, a 'site specific PFSA report' together with a Port Facility Security Instruction (PFSI) and a PFSP template are developed for and issued to this specific port facility. The port facility then has to develop a PFSP within two months. If the plan finds approval, the IMO is notified, which then starts its own process of verification and inspection.

The deadline of 1 July 2004 was met by the 'overwhelming majority of port facilities' falling 'within the scope of the ISPS Code'[30] – among them all high-risk ports. Only a comparatively small number of port facilities not identified as high risk did not meet the deadline due to either a late submission or a PFSP which did not meet TRANSEC standards. As of the time of writing (November 2006), all port facilities of the UK falling within the scope of the ISPS Code are compliant.

Preparedness of ports in the UK: some (general) observations

However, 'compliant' in this context means having an approved PFSP – no more and no less. The difficulty for the ports, not only within the UK, is how to fill these 'paper forms' with life. And that's exactly the point where it starts to get difficult. The IMO Secretary General, Efthimios Mitropoulos, recently quoted a report from the Lyndon B. Johnson School of Public Affairs, stating that:

> From country-specific research and site visits, it became clear just how inconsistent ISPS is from port to port and country to country. While the language of ISPS is uniform in each port and each country, it was as if [we] were seeing several different codes. Not only has ISPS been implemented in different ways and with varying levels of success, but overall opinions of ISPS among shippers, port workers and government officials fluctuate as well.[31]

One should assume that, while within the UK, the implementation of the ISPS Code is uniform indeed, the level of success does vary from port to port. While some ports are more or less 'going through the motions', usually due to a certain lack of funds available for implementation, other ports are more successful, even proactive, in regard of filling the security plans on paper with meaning – and action.

For example, a very important step forward in regard of security is the Port of Felixstowe's Road Haulier Identity System (RHIDES), which was introduced in November 2005. An article in the professional magazine *Cargo Security International* celebrates Felixstowe's pioneering initiative – the Port of Felixstowe being the first one in the UK to make identity cards for hauliers mandatory – in glowing terms:

> As a requirement of the [ISPS] Code, the Port has introduced a series of measures to enhance security and tighten access controls, particularly to the terminals. As hauliers represent the largest group of visitors, making up some 4,000 movements in and out each day, the Port decided upon biometric identity cards as a means of recording their comings and goings. The cards will not increase the time taken to process hauliers arriving at the Port's terminals. Importantly, there is no charge to hauliers for registering their drivers for RHIDES cards.[32]

Of course, this pioneering move remains incomplete as long as hauliers do not apply a rigorous system of vetting their drivers. But it is most definitely a step in the right direction. Another step in the right direction is the acquisition of modern scanner systems by several ports, which facilitate – and speed up – screening of cars and trucks. This is of special importance for a ferry terminals handling an ever-increasing number of vehicles and passengers crossing the Channel. The long queues at Dover's ferry terminals as a result of heightened security measures in the wake of the 7/7 bombings are indicative of the need for fast scanners. Such systems are, unfortunately but not surprisingly, expensive. So are modern CCTV systems with face-recognition features. So are modern, computer-controlled access systems. So are miles and miles of barbed wire. And last but most definitely not least, so are the officers on the beat – no matter whether we are talking about police forces or private security patrols. In a time when high-tech solutions are the talk of the town, it needs to be pointed out that the first line of defence still is the good old 'mark one eyeball'. All high-tech gizmos ultimately depend on a human operator making sense out of them. But unfortunately, here we can conclude with some British understatement that officers are 'spread a little thinly and that's not entirely satisfactory'.[33]

Conclusion: some open questions

The pressing question now is: how credible are the worst case scenarios? Or, how likely are acts of maritime terrorism of any kind to happen near British shores or in British ports? As we all know, merely being interested in doing something and actually being able to do something are two very different matters. Now, here, the opinion of security analysts is divided. Some security analysts argue that one of the objectives in the temporary hijacking of vessels in the Straits of Malacca by maritime raiders from 2003 onwards is to learn how to manoeuvre a big ship, thus acquiring the expertise necessary to 'mount a maritime attack'.[34] They also point out that several terrorist groups loosely affiliated with Al-Qaeda are interested in acquiring scuba diving skills – but not for recreational purposes: taking their cue from a successful, but not very well known, scuba diving attack of LTTE Sea Tigers against a Sri Lankan Navy vessel in their naval base at Trincomalee in 1994, they could attempt to do likewise. Other security experts are not so sure about an imminent threat posed by maritime terrorism. Brian Jenkins, for example, counselled in an attempt to separate facts from hype that 'assessing the real risk from maritime terrorism should not confuse threat assessment with vulnerability assessment'.[35]

Answering this crucial question is by no means merely an academic exercise. If in your perception the threat is an imminent one, you will put pressure on your respective authorities to harden your ports as quick as possible; if you do not think the threat is imminent you will take a much more relaxed attitude regarding port security. Personally, I think there was much more hype than fact around the spectre of maritime terrorism immediately after 9/11. But I also prefer to err on the safe side: acts of maritime terrorism may not be imminent, but they will come sooner or later. As of now, we seem to have a head start: terrorists are obviously still trying to get some maritime expertise, while we are already implementing new security mechanisms to protect our ports. But are we really making good use of this window of opportunity? Let us take a second look at CSI, ISPS and the problem posed by dirty bombs:

- in regard of CSI, many ports have ratified it but are just starting to think about implementation and how to get funds for that; and
- in regard of dirty bombs, many of our ports either (a) do not have radiation detection equipment, or (b) have them in a distant location, which means the container has first to be off-loaded and transported to that facility.

In the end, for the USA, the UK and everybody else it boils down to the question of how do we want to fight our war against terrorism? Do we allocate our scarce funds for a War on Terrorism far away from our shores in places such as Afghanistan, or do we reserve them for the protection of the home front by hardening our sea borders, including our ports? There is no easy answer to that, unfortunately, because whichever way you do it, it could be wrong, and trying to fight on both fronts at the same time is quite a costly affair, not only in terms of money. The choice is yours.

Notes

1 Richardson, M. (2004) *A Time Bomb for Global Trade: Maritime-related Terrorism in an Age of Weapons of Mass Destruction*, Singapore: ISEAS, p. 9.
2 OECD (2003) *Security in Maritime Transport: Risk Factors and Economic Impact*, July, pp. 14–15.
3 Mintz, J. (2002) '15 freighters believed to be linked to Al-Qaeda', *Washington Post*, 31 December.
4 Flynn, S. (2004) *America the Vulnerable. How Our Government is Failing to Protect Us from Terrorism*, New York, NY: Harper Perennial, especially Chapter 2, 'The Next Attack', pp. 17–35; reprint edition 2005.
5 LaMoshi, Gary (2004) 'How it could happen…', *Asia Times Online*, 11 August, see this and related articles at www.atimes.com, accessed 19 October 2006.
6 CalTrade (2006) *China Signs on to Container Security Initiative. Agreement Expands the CSI to the Ports of Shanghai and Shenzen*, available at www.caltradereport.com/eWebPages/front-page-1059593992.html, accessed 3 December.
7 Ibid.
8 Richardson, M. (2004) *A Time Bomb for Global Trade. Maritime-related Terrorism in an Age of Weapons of Mass Destruction*, Singapore: ISEAS, p. 78.
9 Both systems were extensively covered at the Lloyd's List Events Conference, *Vessel Tracking and Identification 2006*, 24–25 April 2006, Crowne Plaza, St James' Hotel, London.
10 Ország-Land, T. (2004) 'Waiving the flag of convenience', *Jane's Terrorism and Security Monitor*, 1 June, pp. 4–5.
11 On AIS, see for example Lehr, P. (2006) 'AIS: a convenient tool for pirates and maritime terrorists?', *Seaways*, June 2006.
12 See www.dft.gov.uk/stellent/groups/dft_transsec/documents/divisionhomepage/030860.hcsp, accessed 2 December 2006.
13 See the IMO website under 'Legal: maritime safety', at www.imo.org, accessed 2 December 2006.
14 DfT (2004) *ISPS Code Operational Guidance: Frequently Asked Questions 2004*, p. 3.
15 Information taken from the Port of London website, see www.portoflondon.co.uk/display_fixedpage.cfm/id/157/site/commercial, accessed 1 December 2006.
16 Ibid.
17 'Port of Felixstowe: Port Journal – Introduction', at www.portoffelixstowe.co.uk/publications/journal/frmintroduction.aspx, accessed 1 December 2006.
18 Ibid.
19 Ibid.
20 'World's Biggest Container Ship Calls at the Port of Felixstowe', *Press Releases*, 3 November 2006, at www.portoffelixstowe.co.uk/pressreleases/frmPress.aspx?pid=207, accessed 3 December 2006.
21 'Pembroke Port and Ferry Terminal', see the Port Authority's website at www.mpha.cu.uk/pp.php, accessed 2 December 2006.
22 'Ports and Harbours of the UK: Milford Haven', see www.ports.org.uk/port.asp?id=241, accessed 2 December 2006.
23 'Port Authority faces prosecution over *Sea Empress*', see www.bbc.co.uk/politics97/news/07/0716/empress.shtml, accessed 2 December 2006.
24 Ibid.
25 See 'Ports and Harbours of the UK: Dover', at www.ports.org.uk/port.asp?id=100, accessed 1 December 2006.
26 Ibid.
27 'Dover Cruise Port announces 2007 cruise schedule', *News Headlines*, 3 December 2006, see www.doverport.co.uk/news.asp?ckey=24, accessed 3 December 2006.

28 Ibid.

29 TRANSEC defines risk as threat × vulnerability × consequence, see DfT, op. cit., 'PFSA and PFSP Process' (PowerPoint slide).

30 DfT, op. cit., p. 1; and DfT (2005) *DfT Responses to FOI Requests > 2005 > March 2005.*

31 (2006) 'Mitropoulos Voices Fears over ISPS Code Inconsistencies', *Lloyd's List*, 1 December.

32 (2006) 'United Kingdom: Port of Felixstowe issues 1,000th RHIDES card', *CSI*, 8 November, available at www.cargosecurityinternational.com/channeldetail. asp?cid=4&caid=7736, accessed 23 November 2006.

33 Lord Carlile on BBC Radio 4's *File on 4*, 14 March 2006, quoted by BBC News, 'UK ports "are open to terrorists"'. A key government adviser on terrorism has warned there are not enough customs and immigration officers at many sea and airports', see http://news.bbc.co.uk/go/pr/fr/-/1/hi/uk/4804482.stm, accessed 9 November 2006.

34 (2003) 'Peril on the sea', *The Economist*, 4 October, pp. 61–2 (61).

35 In 'Maritime security: separating fact from hype', available at www.iccwbo.org/ccs/ news_archives/2004/ccs_conference.asp, accessed 25 September 2004.

14 Terrorism and public information

Anthony Richards

Introduction

There has been much discussion as to the degree to which the government should provide the public with information on the terrorist threat. It is generally agreed that a balance should be found between keeping the public as fully informed as possible without causing panic or spreading alarm – people should be alert but should also 'carry on as usual'. The main argument put forward in this short article is that the general public should be *better* informed about the nature of the terrorist threat and its possible consequences and that this will help us to be better prepared if a major attack takes place. Far from panicking the public, the National Steering Committee on Warning and Informing the Public has argued that people 'are better able to accept … risk if they understand the protective action they should take in the event of an emergency'.[1] More information (on both the nature of the threat and what action to take in the event of an attack) would also help to overcome the problem of apathy that prevails in many parts of our society (indeed most of it) towards the threat and will encourage greater numbers of people to take note of it.[2] [3]

What the government is doing

The government has made efforts to inform the public of the nature of the terrorist threat, what it is doing about it, how it is preparing for the possibility of a successful attack and what the public can do. One of the ways it has done this is through ministerial statements and through placing information on the websites of the Home Office, the Health Protection Agency, London Resilience, MI5 and the Metropolitan Police.[4] In 2004 the Home Office website put out a joint assessment of the threat from the JTAC. Also included was an outline of the government's position on public information:

> It remains the Government's policy to issue warnings when the public can take action in response to a specific threat. There are no such warnings currently in force. However, given the threat picture, members of the public should always remain alert to the danger.[5]

In August 2004 the government sent out to all UK households a booklet entitled *Preparing for Emergencies, What You Need to Know* which is meant to provide 'practical common sense advice on what to do in an emergency'.[6] Its advice at a time of emergency is to 'go in, stay in, tune in' and it states that 'there is an agreement with radio and TV companies that if there is a major emergency they will interrupt programming to give public safety advice and information about the incident'.[7] It also gives advice on how to treat casualties until the emergency services arrive, on what measures to take at home (such as turning off water, gas and electricity supplies) and what useful items to gather if necessary. The Home Office website also provides guidelines on the steps that members of the public can take at home, at work or on the way to work, as well as providing advice as to what to do if a terrorist attack takes place.[8] Further advice is available on the UK Resilience website 'Taking Sensible Precautions'.[9]

The *Preparing for Emergencies* booklet also emphasises the importance of public vigilance and includes an anti-terrorism hotline number. The Metropolitan Police, too, has called for greater public vigilance through, for example, its 'Who owns this bag?' poster campaign on the London Underground,[10] while the MI5 website includes a page that invites people to anonymously report suspicious activity.[11] Both of their websites provide advice and information on terrorism, including the current security position.[12]

Room for improvement

The government's booklet *Preparing for Emergencies* is to be welcomed especially when it is not a knee-jerk response to a specific threat that could indeed cause public anxiety. There is much to be done to prepare the public for the possibility of a major terrorist attack so that when a specific threat *is* identified we are all as psychologically prepared as possible, thus lessening the chance of panic, and this booklet is certainly a step in the right direction.

Public vigilance is a vital, but under-developed, aspect of our response to terrorism. It should be recalled that there was apparently very little 'chatter' on the airwaves that could have given an indication to the Madrid authorities that the 11 March attacks were about to happen. It was subsequently reported that a member of the public had noticed suspicious behaviour from the perpetrators before the bombs went off. Thus the emphasis on public vigilance in the booklet and on the government, MI5 and Metropolitan Police websites is to be welcomed.

The information that the government has provided is therefore available for those who are interested. The difficulty, however, is knowing how much of it has actually registered with the general public as a whole. To what extent has the booklet been treated as 'junk mail'? What needs to be done to raise the public consciousness of the threat without causing panic or without disrupting daily life? Is the government more concerned about being seen to be doing the right thing or is it genuinely trying to engage the public in this crucial area? The booklet, according to the government, was a response to research that showed 'that people want more information about what to do in an emergency and want to know what the Government and the emergency services are doing to prepare for an emergency'.[13] We suggest, however, that only a minority of people would have requested such information and that, in our view, the vast majority of citizens remain apathetic to the terrorist threat.

Public education

The main thrust of this short article is that there needs to be greater public awareness of the threat, greater public vigilance and greater awareness as to what to do in the event of a major terrorist attack. It is not, of course, wise to generate anxiety amongst the population. Doing so could actually increase the danger of mass panic that could be far more serious than an incident itself. One expert on crowd behaviour noted that a normal message like 'please leave the station as soon as possible' could lead to a stampede if people have become too anxious about the terrorist threat.[14] He argued that 'raising the anxiety of the general population can only exacerbate public reaction, and in some cases over-reaction, to a situation. This can be more life threatening in an emergency than the incident'.[15]

We do believe, however, that a public education programme can be advanced without causing unnecessary panic. The National Steering Committee on Warning and Informing the Public stated that 'NSCWIP is confident that a [public education] campaign could be designed in such a way that people become more informed and vigilant, without increasing anxiety or causing panic' and that such a programme would increase UK resilience.[16] The former chairman of the Emergency Planning Society argued that 'I think we should be more open to the public, to let them know what we're doing, but also what their part is ... What I'm saying is give the public the information. Familiarisation will give them the confidence, knowing they're in good hands'.[17]

The National Steering Committee also found that:

> The national policy ... needs to acknowledge current research which suggests that members of the public who have received warnings typically seek confirmation via consistent and multiple reliable sources before taking requested actions. The quality and rapid conveyance of the initial alert, therefore, is crucial to the receptiveness of the public to follow-up messages including safety advice. This underlines *the requirement for public education in order to develop a warning culture* to support the system.[18] (italics added)

The USA

The USA has a more developed public education programme on the terrorist threat and what the public can do about it. This is facilitated, at least to some extent, by the fact that there is a clear government department in charge of homeland security and so it is *the* major source of information on the terrorist threat and what the US government is doing about it.[19] Its public information website (www.

ready.gov) is comprehensive by comparison to that of the UK's, offering more detailed information on, for example, the biological, chemical, and nuclear threat and what the public should do if any of these types of attacks takes place.[20] It is also, perhaps understandably after 9/11, more hardhitting through headings such as 'Terrorism forces us to make a choice. We can be afraid. Or we can be ready' and 'Preparing Makes Sense. GET READY NOW'.[21]

Perhaps, whatever the merits or otherwise of having a lead agency like the US Homeland Security Department, one of the obstacles to the UK's ability to disseminate public information on the terrorist threat/emergency response effectively is that there is no central source, or central website, that covers all aspects. Public information dissemination, perhaps confusingly, is shared between various departments and agencies whether it be the Home Office, the Department of Health (Health Protection Agency), MI5, the Metropolitan Police and so on. Thus, there appears to be a strong case for centralising the whole process. Perhaps this will help to address the 'lack of a national culture of awareness amongst the public of how to respond to large-scale emergencies'.[22]

At the time of an incident

As noted above, for public information to be most effective at the time of an incident there needs to be a 'culture of awareness' already in place. There also needs to be trust in public pronouncements about an incident. Two striking examples of where public information released by government in relation to terrorist attacks undermined trust in the authorities was in the Spanish government's initial claims that the Madrid attacks were carried out by the Basque terrorist group ETA, and in the early reluctance of the Russian authorities to admit that the simultaneous destruction of two passenger jets that had taken off from Moscow airport in August 2004 could have been acts of terrorism.

The National Steering Committee noted above has recommended a 'broad strategy' including the following:

- The effective use of new technology, including mass telephony, the internet, digital television and radio, etc. in such a way that it maximises the menu of available options for the transmission of messages to a static and mobile population in the event of an emergency.
- The effective use of the media through the whole range of radio, television, online services including Ceefax, Teletext and websites. Plans should be developed by public information and warning partnerships such as Media Emergency Forums. In this way, we can maximise the capability to broadcast timely, unambiguous and coordinated information to the population in the event of an emergency.[23]

In the face of criticism that the government had inadequate plans for addressing the public in the event of an emergency,[24] it responded by stating that:

- If a specific terrorist threat becomes apparent the government and the appropriate authorities will, without hesitation, inform the public of what action to take.
- The government has agreed arrangements with the media to provide factual information quickly in a crisis. The public would be kept informed and updated on the situation via the television and radio.
- In the event of an attack, the advice of the government is to remain indoors and await further instructions from the emergency services or the local authorities.
- In addition other means of communication such as transport operators' and other public address systems, electronic message boards, etc. would be used.
- The emergency services would use loudhailers at street level.
- Most local authorities should have arrangements for communicating rapidly with the public in major shopping areas.
- The government is currently working on the most effective ways to enhance the information that is already in the public domain, whilst ensuring that the public remain alert but not alarmed.[25]

On the Emergency Information Procedures page of the Home Office Terrorism website the government states that it has emergency broadcasting systems and a Media Emergency Forum:

Emergency broadcasting systems

We have arrangements with the BBC and other broadcasters to ensure that, in the event of any incident, we can get the right information to those who need it, when they need it.

This emergency broadcasting system allows us to provide immediate information or warnings through the whole range of radio, television and online services, including Ceefax, Teletext and websites.

The Media Emergency Forum

The Media Emergency Forum is a group that was set up in the mid-90s as a voluntary arrangement between the media, government and the emergency services to develop best practice in getting the right information to the right people in an emergency. This work has included developing protocols and high level contacts for use in emergencies, planning for the millennium, and giving feedback after major incidents.

Recent developments include a network of regional Media Emergency Forums. These will bring together local news media and local emergency services so that area-specific information and advice can be quickly distributed in an emergency.

New technologies

We are also evaluating new technologies – such as the phone system, mobile phones, pagers, and digital technology – as methods to quickly disseminate information and advice.[26]

There are, however, issues of concern. In relation to the scene of an incident there is a real need to assess the public order implications of disseminating public information. For example, if people who have been contaminated need to be retained in the contaminated zone what information is to be imparted to them? If they are told precisely what has happened would there be the risk of a stampede to get out of the area to avoid further potential contamination? On the other hand 'lack of information can [also] turn a passive crowd into a stampede'.[27] We recommend, therefore, that a comprehensive assessment be made of the public order implications of public information disseminated at the time of a major emergency.

Another potential difficulty relates to the government's advice to 'go in, stay in, tune in'. If information was not immediately forthcoming and there were rumours of a radioactive, biological or chemical release nearby would people be prepared to stay at home? Or would there be mass self-evacuation that could create all kinds of problems for the emergency services and transport links?

Conclusion

The challenge for the government is to get the balance right. Creating a culture of excessive anxiety may lead to mass panic if and when incidents do occur, and this could lead to far greater numbers of casualties than the incidents themselves cause. On the other hand, the government must provide adequate information on the nature of the threat and what the British public can do to not only counter the threat but also to help themselves and others in the event of a major emergency. The government has to some extent done this. The key challenge, however, is to tackle the apathy of the vast majority of people without raising the anxiety of the minority that do actually take notice of the advice issued by government. We therefore recommend the following:

- That government place more emphasis on a national education programme to enhance the public's knowledge of the types of threat that we face. We believe that the public can be better prepared psychologically for a major terrorist attack without causing panic.
- That government endeavours to centralise the source and provision of information to limit the confusion that might arise from information being disseminated from multiple sources (that is, Home Office, MI5, Health Protection Agency, and so on).
- That government assesses the impact of public information dissemination at the time of an incident on: public order, the transport network and the emergency response.

Notes

1 National Steering Committee on Warning and Informing the Public (2003) *Third Report*, April, available at www.nscwip.info/thirdreport.htm.

2 One report concluded from its qualitative research that even soon after the attacks on 9/11 'most members of the public [in the UK] felt that given their perception of limited danger to themselves, there was little need for information about dealing with attacks'. It went on to state that 'some seemed unmoved by possible risks' and that 'a few said they would take advantage of the situation and seek cheap flights. These people tended to assume that there would be no attacks in the UK and/or that the country was well defended. Most had not given the issues careful consideration'. In general, 'among the mainstream white sample there is a widespread feeling that there is no need to be concerned about safety from further terrorism or retaliatory attacks; this stance seems to be founded on a blend of stoicism, complacency and news fatigue', Dawson, C.R. (2001) *Qualitative Research on Public Perceptions of The Current Situation*, November, available at www.ukresilience.info/contingencies/pubs/current_stg1.pdf.

3 This article is not primarily concerned with the role of the media nor with government advice to business (for the latter see the UK Resilience website at www.ukresilience.info/contingencies/cont_bus.htm).

4 See, for example, www.mi5.gov.uk/output/Page8.html, www.homeoffice.gov.uk/terrorism/protect/athome/index.html and www.homeoffice.gov.uk/terrorism/threat/face/index.html.

5 Home Office website www.homeoffice.gov.uk/terrorism/threat/index.html.

6 Preparing for Emergencies website www.pfe.gov.uk/introduction/index.htm.

7 *Preparing for Emergencies, What You Need to Know*.

8 See website www.homeoffice.gov.uk/terrorism/protect/index.html.

9 UK Resilience website www.ukresilience.info/package.htm.

10 See, for example (2004) *Police Renew Call for Vigilance Against Terrorists*, 15 March, available at www.met.police.uk/pns/DisplayPN.cgi?pn_id=2004_0031. For other Metropolitan Poster campaigns see www.homeoffice.gov.uk/terrorism/reports/campaigns.html.

11 MI5 website www.mi5.gov.uk/output/Page6.html.

12 Metropolitan Police, *Advice and Information on Terrorism*, available at www.met.police.uk/operationcalm/index.htm, and *Make London a Hostile Place for Terrorists – and Save Lives*, available at www.met.police.uk/campaigns/anti_terrorism/march.htm. MI5 website www.mi5.gov.uk/.

13 Preparing for Emergencies website www.pfe.gov.uk/introduction/index.htm.

14 Still, K. (2003) 'Lack of information can turn a passive crowd into a stampede', *Guardian*, 18 February, available at society.guardian.co.uk/publicvoices/emergencyplanning.

15 Ibid.

16 Ibid.

17 Brian Ward, chairman of the Emergency Planning Society (2003) 'I think we should be more open with the British public', *Guardian*, 28 February, available at http://society.guardian.co.uk/publicvoices/emergencyplanning/0,12872,893559,00.html.

18 National Steering Committee on Warning and Informing the Public, *Third Report*, op. cit., n. 1.

19 See website www.dhs.gov/dhspublic/index.jsp.

20 The Australian emergency response booklet (*Preparing for the Unexpected*) and the Canadian booklet (also called *Preparing for the Unexpected*) also contain advice and information in the event of a chemical, biological or nuclear/radioactive incident. Websites www.ema.gov.au/ and www.ocipep.gc.ca/info_pro/self_help_ad/general/unexpected_e.asp).

21 See website www.ready.gov.

22 The National Steering Committee on Warning and Informing the Public.

23 Website www.nscwip.info/index.htm.

24 See, for example, the BBC Panorama website http://news.bbc.co.uk/1/hi/programmes/panorama/3711829.stm.

25 UK Resilience www.londonprepared.gov.uk/antiterrorism/update.htm.

26 See www.homeoffice.gov.uk/terrorism/threat/info/index.html.

27 Ward, op. cit., n 17.

15 Cyber security and the critical national infrastructure[1]

Darryl Howlett

Introduction

Over the past decade there has been growing concern about the rise of cyber crime and the possibilities for new Information and Communications Technology (ICT) to assist terrorist networks in the recruitment, funding, planning and execution of their operations. The latter concerns were emphasised following the attacks on the London transport system on 7 July 2005 and the failed attempts two weeks later. These events have led to calls for further policing powers to combat the use of ICT for such purposes.

Shortly after the incidents in London ACPO requested that it should become an offence for those suspected of involvement in terrorist operations to withhold details of encryption keys used to store secret computer files.[2] Such an offence was later included in the Terrorism Act 2006, which states that the withholding of encrypted information on computer files should be subject to 'the appropriate maximum term' of five years in 'a national security case' and two years 'in any other case'.[3]

Additionally, in a briefing note of 5 October 2005 by the police in support of an increase in maximum detention powers to the House of Commons Home Affairs Committee, the following view was expressed:

> Terrorists are now highly capable in their use of technology. In recent cases, large numbers (hundreds) of computers and hard drives were seized. Much of the data was encrypted. The examination and decryption of such vast amounts of data takes time, and needs to be analysed before being incorporated into an interview strategy. This is not primarily a resourcing issue, but one of necessarily sequential activity of data capture, analysis and disclosure prior to interview.[4]

After reviewing the written and oral evidence, the Home Affairs Committee concluded that data encryption:

> does not appear, for the time being, to be the problem in practice that had been feared. However analysis of data on computers, both unencrypted

and decrypted, is time-consuming and resource-intensive. This will be an increasing problem for all types of investigations.[5]

Another development that has come to the fore since the mid-1990s is the potential for novel cyber-related forms of disruption or attack against the UK's CNI. The CNI is understood as:

> Those assets, services and systems that support the economic, political and social life of the UK whose importance is such that any entire or partial loss or compromise could: cause large scale loss of life; have a serious impact on the national economy; have other grave consequences for the community; (and) be of immediate concern to the national government.[6]

It is therefore important to be able to distinguish between a dedicated attack on the CNI and other types of disruption. In 2003 there were power blackouts in New York and Italy. While in these instances it was identified that the blackouts were not the result of malicious intent, analysts comment that such occurrences could be the result of malfunction, lightning storms or computer-generated attacks on the networks that control the electrical power grid.

As one study has characterised it, 'Intrusions into information and communication systems can be understood in terms of three "d"s: distortion, disruption, and destruction'.[7] The UK's view of an electronic attack is that it:

> usually involves using computers to gain unauthorised access to the data or control of software of systems in order to acquire or corrupt the data, or disrupt its functioning. Typical methods are hacking, the insertion of malicious software or hardware and denial of service.[8]

Additionally, the means for engaging in these attacks:

> are widely available and many can be downloaded from the internet. Sophisticated attacks are unlikely to be detected by routine security measures such as firewalls and intruder detection systems.[9]

And, at risk is any 'system connected directly or indirectly to the internet or public networks'.[10]

Concern about the impact of cyber-related disruption has been reinforced in the public consciousness by media attention devoted to virus outbreaks and hacking operations. In January 2004, for example, the extent of damage that can be caused to computer systems worldwide was emphasised by the arrival of the 'MyDoom' virus, which at its peak was estimated to have infected 55 million computers and generated one in 12 of all email messages.[11] At the same time, computer security specialists observed that in the first half of 2004 around 70 per cent of viral activity was traceable to one individual after that person released the NetSky and Sasser worms on to the internet.[12] Earlier, in October 2002, what is known as a distributed denial of service (DDoS) attack was reported to have occurred on the 13 'root servers' that form the basis of the domain names system governing internet addresses. The report suggested that seven of the 13 servers were forced offline because of the attacks, although it was considered to have had little effect on internet users as the other root servers were able to cope with the disruption.[13]

The analogies and metaphors used to highlight the impact of viruses and other malicious software can strike a collective psychological chord within society. These images depict undetected and sometimes catastrophic intrusions or attacks on a country's security and draw attention to situations where vulnerabilities have been exploited. These may be derived from well-known Greek legends, such as the calculated deception of the people of Troy by Greek warriors during the 'Trojan horse' episode or the weaknesses exposed in the story of 'Achilles' heel'. They may also stem from real events that have transformed a country's security thinking like the references in the USA to the possibilities of a 'digital Pearl Harbor'. Similarly, the notion of a 'virus' infecting a computer network is itself an analogy that resonates with the spread of disease within the human population.

The advent of the cyber revolution has consequently generated complex issues concerning our understanding of conflict and security.[14] As one research group has commented, there are 'new vulnerabilities' precipitated by society's increasing reliance on ICT and the impact these have '… for individuals (identity theft), corporations (industrial espionage), financial institutions (theft and extortion) and nations'.[15] Another study has highlighted the diversity of threats that may be present, ranging 'from the systematic and persistent, to the decentralized and dispersed, to the accidental and non-malevolent'.[16]

In a 2005 forecast of the issues and risks associated with electronic attack to 2010, the head of the NISCC's* Threat Investigation Team noted that the UK's CNI is already experiencing sophisticated electronic attacks, although thus far there are few signs that terrorist groups are using such attacks 'to disable or disrupt critical systems'.[17] As a caveat the analysis warns that this could change over the next few years as ICT skills develop and therefore the situation will require monitoring for indications of change. The current assessment, however, is that the principal method of these groups will continue to be physical rather than electronic attack.[18]

A balanced perspective may therefore be appropriate. This is an area where technological innovation has transformed communications and access to knowledge in many parts of the world, though not all as a global 'digital divide' exists, and measures have been taken to identify and where possible mitigate the risks involved. Equally, because this is a technologically dynamic area over the longer-term responses will be needed that are sustained and aimed at developing 'a culture of security' for ICT.[19] The initiatives underway already to develop a broader awareness of cyber-security issues at the individual, local, national, regional and global levels is consequently considered an important aspect of the UK's overall security perspective for the twenty-first century.

---

*   As of February 2006, The NSAC and NISCC have been merged to form the Centre for the Protection of National Infrastructure (CPNI).

ICT: drivers of change

There are at least four drivers of change that impact on the development of ICT and which are likely to feature in considerations for cyber security and the CNI. The first is the science and technology sector, which has been a catalyst for ICT innovations such as the cellular revolution, the world wide web (web) and computer connectivity.[20] Concomitant with this development has been what some commentators consider is the shrinking of time and space, resulting in the generation of a ubiquitous global communications and information network the consequences of which 'are still barely understood'.[21]

The internet has been described as 'a set of interconnected communications networks for the transfer of digital data'.[22] It originated in the USA in the 1960s as a result of a project known as ARPANET (Advanced Research Projects Agency Network) and since then the number of countries and host computers involved in this network has increased significantly.[23] Until recently the majority of host computers were in the USA although more countries and hosts have now been connected to the internet. Estimates put the growth of connectivity at '50–100 percent per year and much higher in some years in many countries'.[24] By 2006, an estimated 1,043,104,886 people were connected to the internet although, as noted, earlier analysts have pointed to a 'digital divide', meaning that the benefit of this technology is not a universal collective good.[25] Africa and many parts of Asia have limited access to the internet, although there are exceptions as both China and India have embarked on expansion programmes.[26] Assessments now suggest China may replace the USA in the coming decades as the country with the largest percentage of its population connected to the internet.

The advent of the web was a key computer-related development as it, 'shifted the emphasis from individually crafted islands of computing to a global utility that can be accessed, using common standards, by any networked computer anywhere'.[27] This trend towards a global utility is consequently enabling the realisation of an advanced infrastructure for computing, collaboration and communication.[28]

The infrastructure for this advanced web is now being referred to by several names such as metacomputing, seamless scalable computing, global computing and Grid computing.[29] The term Grid is chosen to suggest the idea of a 'power grid' because users can connect to this global computing infrastructure like plugging into the electrical power grid.[30] The Grid can provide access to geographically distributed resources such as computers, storage devices, mobile devices, instruments, sensors, databases, and software applications, conceived as a single powerful virtual computer.[31]

As a driver for change the science and technology sector is a key element of the future ICT environment, but human responses will also be important:

> The evidence of technology adoption so far suggests that there will be many people willing to move rapidly into this world, well ahead of understanding the issues it raises. Others will be very reluctant, and some will challenge the explicit or implicit agendas of the commercial or government interest that are driving the changes.[32]

A second driver of change is the role that the business and commercial sectors play as the 'first adopters of new technologies'.[33] This sector is a significant actor as ICT has 'increased the speed, quality, and ease of communications between business partners ... these technologies also enable higher levels of collaboration across the product-delivery chain.[34] The possibility for unauthorised access to, or corruption of, information and data is thus already an important aspect as there may be a greater potential in these circumstances for those within as well as outside the business or organisation to conduct such operations.

Similarly, many businesses are undergoing change with new organisational models being adopted that are more ICT intensive. Consequently, the notion of the virtual organisation where personnel may be more geographically dispersed and ICT-dependent than in traditional organisations makes the issue of responses to cyber security a principal element of this development.[35]

The third driver of change concerns the nature of globalisation and its impact on economics, politics and security.[36] Globalisation has been described as an historical process, which:

> transforms the spatial organization of social relations and transactions, generating transcontinental or inter-regional networks of interaction and the exercise of power ... Although contemporary globalization has elements in common with its past phases, it is distinguished by unique spatio-temporal and organization features, creating a world in which the extensive reach of global relations and networks is matched by their relative high intensity, high velocity and high impact propensity across many facets of social life, from the economic to the environmental.[37]

At the turn of the millennium Victor Cha identified what he termed a 'globalization-security' spectrum.[38] At one end of this spectrum Cha placed grand strategic options related to the ending of the East–West rivalry, because these were derived 'from the end of bipolar competition rather than from globalization'. At the other end were those aspects stemming from globalisation's security effects, which had heightened 'the salience of substate extremist groups or fundamentalist groups because their ability to organize transnationally, meet virtually, and utilize terrorist tactics has been substantially enhanced by the globalization of technology and information'.[39] As Cha characterised it:

> The most far-reaching security effect of globalization is its complication of the basic concept of 'threat' in international relations. This is in terms of both agency and scope. Agents of threat can be states but can also be non-state groups or individuals.[40]

Cha thus considered that ICT was 'the currency' of what he termed 'non-physical security'.[41]

A fourth driver, and related to the other processes, is generational change and the impact that ICT has on individual empowerment. The arrival of the internet is a recent phenomenon yet there are now generations of individuals who have grown up with this medium of information and communication. This is also a world of individual empowerment that is both global in scope and potentially unique in its implications for the dissemination of knowledge and the development of future society. Concomitantly, analyses suggest that empowerment may have negative consequences as computers have allowed individuals or groups to target large companies or states and cause disruption to economies and societies at a distance.

Coupled to this are issues related to privacy, civil liberties, identity theft and data security.[42] For example, at the turn of the millennium reports began identifying 'electronic identity theft' as the fastest growing crime in the USA.[43] This was paralleled by concern that 'digital impersonation' was becoming more prevalent in the UK and Europe generally.[44] Additionally, the entry cost to conduct these operations is relatively low compared to many previous technological innovations.[45] As Cha has commented, the advent of 'instantaneous communication and transportation, exchanges of information and technology, flow of capital – catalyse certain dangerous phenomena or empower certain groups in ways unimagined previously'.[46]

Conceptualising conflict and security in cyberspace

A 2005 report for the Congressional Research Service (CRS) in the USA noted that distinctions, 'between crime, terrorism and war tend to blur when attempting to describe a computer network attack (CAN) in ways that parallel the physical world'.[47] Another observation is that in the literature there is an 'important distinction … between the use of the internet in an ancillary role in furtherance of terrorism ("ancillary cyber-activities") and those uses which do themselves terrorise by using the internet as the mode or the object of attack ("cyber attack"). There is a strong line of literature which contends that only the latter fall within the definition of terrorism'.[48]

Since the early 1990s a number of conceptual ideas have been advanced to assist in understanding these complexities. John Arquilla and David Ronfeldt consider that 'the information revolution is altering the nature of conflict across the spectrum'.[49] They identify two related developments concerning both changes to organisational structures and how we understand conflict: first, 'network forms of organization' now have the advantage 'over hierarchical forms'; and second, as this 'revolution deepens, the conduct and outcome of conflicts increasingly depend on information and communication'.[50] Consequently, Arquilla and Ronfeldt consider that, 'information-age threats are likely to be more diffuse, dispersed, multi-dimensional nonlinear, and ambiguous than industrial-age threats'.[51]

These authors have also made a conceptual distinction between what they term 'cyberwar' and 'netwar':

> netwar is the lower-intensity, societal-level counterpart to our earlier, mostly military concept of cyberwar … what distinguishes netwar as a form of

conflict is the organizational structure of its practioners – with many groups actually being leaderless – and the suppleness in their ability to come together quickly in swarming attacks. The concepts of cyberwar and netwar encompass a new spectrum of conflict that is emerging in the wake of the information revolution.[52]

Additionally, Dorothy Denning distinguished between *activism, hacktivism* and *cyberterrorism* (although noting that the boundaries between these activities may not be defined clearly).[53] Activism, for Denning, 'refers to normal, nondisruptive use of the internet in support of an agenda or cause'.[54] Hacktivism, in contrast, 'refers to the marriage of hacking and activism' – '"hacking" is used here to refer to operations that exploit computers in ways that are unusual and often illegal, typically with the help of special software'.[55] Thus the aim of hacktivism is to disrupt normal operations while not causing serious damage.

Cyberterrorism is a term that appeared in the mid-1990s to describe the convergence of cyberspace and terrorism, and where the aim for the attacker is to cause serious damage in the political, economic or social spheres.[56] In this context, Barry Collin distinguished between the 'virtual world' and the 'physical world'.[57] For Collin, the former 'is symbolic – true, false, binary, metaphoric representations of information – that place in which computer programs function and data moves'; the latter, in contrast, is 'matter and energy ... that place in which we live and function'.[58]

Also, at this time, Matthew Littleton distinguished between 'technoterrorism' – using classic weapons to destroy infrastructure targets and cause disruption in cyberspace – and 'cyberterrorism' – operating new weapons-malicious software, electromagnetic and microwave weapons to destroy data in cyberspace to cause disruption in the physical world.[59] For Littleton, the potential of cyberterrorism to cause disruption and violence in cyberspace might be considered akin to the physical realm, although he considered 'the lessons learned from previous counter and anti-terrorism efforts might be of limited value'.[60]

Some analysts do consider there are parallels between traditional types of terrorism and those relating to cyberspace, including 'the diversity of actors involved, the reliance of at least some of them on networks, the broad range of motivations, the anonymity of the perpetrators of terrorist incidents ... and the enormous array of potential targets and weapons'.[61] Studies have also identified a trend between conflicts in physical space being replicated in cyberspace. Examples offered are the disputes between India and Pakistan, and in the context of the Middle East.[62]

The impact on threat perceptions

Threat perceptions are based on assumptions about the nature of the threat environment, the risks involved and the extent of any vulnerability. Such assessments can also be delineated at different levels of analysis and across many sectors.[63] Sector threat assessments 'focus on vulnerabilities and threats either in particular areas such as national infrastructure, or in particular sectors of the economy such as banking or e-commerce'.[64] Analyses of trends can 'highlight changes over time, and identify new challenges or departures from the norm'.[65] Similarly, analyses focusing on the potential for damage can make judgements about the effects of 'low level intrusions to what have been referred to as cascade events'.[66]

When considering the impact on ICT systems these can be attacked by the following methods, whether individually or in some combination: through corrupted system hardware or software; through electronic jamming devices; through the use of an insider; by means of an external hacker; and by physical attack.[67] One complicating factor in making such judgements is that cyberspace is global in context and evolving continually.[68]

Threat assessments of the impact of ICT on terrorist strategies have consequently generated a range of possible scenarios and policy options. For Richard Falkenrath 'terrorist methods appear to evolve with changes in weapons technology, the counterterrorist policies of individual states, and the international system'.[69] In the USA the issue that prompted the government to re-invigorate its policies for dealing with cyberspace was a 1997 military exercise called 'Eligible Receiver'. It was reported that this exercise involved a team of hackers who demonstrated that by downloading computer tools from the internet they could shut down parts of the US power grid and disrupt the functioning of the command and control system of the US Pacific Command in Honolulu.[70] A Canadian assessment around this period also highlighted the potential vulnerabilities of the emerging cyber environment:

> The potential for physical conflict to be replaced by attacks on information infrastructures has caused states to rethink their concepts of warfare, threats and national assets, at a time when information is recognized as a national asset. The adoption of new information technologies and the use of new communication media, such as the internet, create vulnerabilities that can be exploited by individuals, organisations and states.[71]

Other analysts point to the new forms of operational doctrine afforded to terrorist networks by information technology. One study concluded that the advent of ICT has allowed groups to collect information about targets, engage in propaganda and recruitment; and launch attacks from a distance at multiple targets to cause disruption.[72] As a qualification, it was noted that the latter 'have been relatively few and fairly unsophisticated—but they do seem to be increasing in frequency'.[73]

Not all are agreed on the nature of the threat, the degree of vulnerability and the extent of damage that may be caused.[74] Some consider there is little novel in the current context as attacks against civil infrastructures have been a central element of government thinking for decades and disruptions to power supplies and communications are a routine occurrence.[75] Consequently, there is a view that considers cyber attacks to be less damaging and disruptive than physical attacks.

The prospect that as technology develops a cyber attack might be conducted in connection with a physical attack has generated attention in the USA due to the potential disruption and/or destruction stemming from it.[76] The concern is that as the interdependencies between networks in the infrastructure increase then disruption in one sector could have ramifications in another, and if this occurred simultaneously with a physical attack it would amplify the seriousness of the situation due to the knock-on effects. By way of qualification, it is also noted that views are divided over both the feasibility of such an attack and whether this would be the objective sought.[77]

One factor when considering computer attack trends is that since 1988 not only has the technology changed but the volume of recorded incidents has also increased. The historical statistics produced by the Computer Emergency Response Team (CERT) Coordination Center in the USA reveal that the number of recorded incidents rose from six in 1988 to 137,529 in 2003 (the last year that such incidents were recorded).[78]

Similar trends have been identified in the UK. The DTI's Information Security Breaches survey for businesses in 2004 concluded that one in three had their websites attacked and the costs of security breaches were increasing.[79] The survey for 2006 observed that while security controls had been improved and confidence in these controls was growing, the overall cost of security breaches was up by 50 per cent since the 2004 survey and amounted to around £10 billion per annum.[80]

Analysts have also identified that computer attacks are becoming more automated and self-generating. Such attacks usually consist of four phases involving 'scanning for potential victims, compromising vulnerable systems, propagating the attack, and coordinated management of attack'.[81] Attack tools seek to exploit vulnerabilities and often generate new attack cycles, which can reach 'global saturation' in a matter of hours.[82] The Code Red worm attack in July 2001 was considered at the time to be an exemplar of this type of attack because it produced DDoS attacks, which overwhelmed computers with junk communications.[83] Such attacks, because they use 'public communication protocols (e.g. internet relay chat [irc] and instant messaging [im]) ... exploit anti-forensic techniques to obfuscate the nature of the attack; dynamic behaviour to vary patterns of attack; and are self-evolving', are 'likely to remain a high-impact, low effort modus operandi for attackers'.[84]

Because of these trends governments, businesses and other organisations have been faced with a major issue: at what point should an alert be given, who or what should do it and through what medium should it be conveyed? The question is complex because there is considerable communication traffic at any time and although sensors can identify anomalies, the problem of hoaxes and false alarms represents a limitation to what can be achieved. A related issue is how to distinguish between the multitude of untargeted and uncoordinated disruptions that are a commonplace occurrence in cyberspace and a dedicated, coordinated and directly targeted attack.[85]

The UK's cybersecurity policy and apparatus

For those with cybersecurity responsibilities, the task of matching the source or sources of threat with a particular attack or set of attacks, given the range possible is a complex one.[86] This is because electronic attack could originate from a range of sources including: terrorist; state sponsored; organised crime; activist; hackers/crackers; and individuals or groups (who develop malicious software such as viruses, known as malware, or conduct malicious computer operations in order to gain unauthorised access to specific sites).[87] Similarly, because there are several potential types of attack much effort is often required to match the attack with a particular source or sources (as it could originate from multiple sites).[88]

Developing appropriate responses to these situations is thus an activity where both traditional and innovative thinking has been required.[89] Where this has been particularly relevant is in relation to the potential for cyber disruption or attack on the CNI.[90] Attention has subsequently focused on establishing the nature and interdependencies inherent in this infrastructure. As outlined in 2004 by Sir David Omand, the person then responsible for overseeing policy in this area, at the heart of the 'UK government's counter-terrorism strategy is the "protection" of the public and the UK's CNI'.[91]

Official pronouncements indicate that the CNI has been redefined over the last few years.[92] Originally the CNI comprised six sectors, later the CNI was expanded to eight and then to 10 (communications, emergency services, energy, finance, food, government and public service, health, public safety, transport and water).[93] These 10 CNI sectors have subsequently been divided into 39 sub-sectors.[94]

Identifying the linkages between the CNI and any vulnerabilities, particularly the potential for acute failure that may cause disruption in a relatively short period of time, is helpful to those who have to devise appropriate policy responses.[95] The UK has consequently been on a learning curve in respect of the CNI in the context of the new security environment.[96] Concomitantly, an outreach programme has been devised to assist in this process:

> a dialogue is now underway with the industry or sector bodies, companies or trade associations to discuss vulnerabilities, resilience, and protective security issues. And security in this context means physical, personnel and information security.[97]

A key question in the outreach programme has been determining what constitutes 'national criticality'.[98] Two methods are used for making this judgement:

> in consultation with the organisation NISCC determines that it operates a nationally critical service that is supported by an information system; or

> the organisation has an information system that is a key dependency of a nationally critical service operated by another organisation.[99]

There are also varying degrees of criticality between the 10 CNI sectors and their constituent 39 sub-sectors.[100] In this context, NISCC makes a distinction between two kinds of information dependency. One kind is 'inter-sector', which is considered 'easier to identify' due to the inherent nature of the dependencies.

As an example, the communications used by the emergency services are nationally critical because if they are not in operation lives could be lost as a result of crime, fire or medical emergencies that are not responded to quickly enough. These emergency communications systems depend on electricity to operate, which in turn depends on fossil fuels to power the back-up generators. In short, the emergency services sector has key inter-sector dependencies on the electricity, gas and oil industries.[101]

The second kind of information dependency identified by NISCC is 'intra-sector'. This is considered more complex due to the variation between the sectors involved.

As an example, a finance sector payments system may depend on a closed financial network infrastructure, a key intra-sector dependency of the UK CNI. As a constrasting example, telecommunications providers will route traffic across each other's networks depending on cost, thus making it difficult to separate out telecommunications providers in terms of criticality.[102]

The broad outline of the UK's policy for CNI protection was announced in 1999. This policy was devised to provide strategic direction for the public and private sectors. In the public sector the objective has been to enhance protection by improving IT security and developing advice and response tools; in the private sector the task has been to improve coordination between this sector and government.[103]

Several agencies and government departments have become involved in developing policies for CNI protection. Under the auspices of the Cabinet Office, the Central Sponsor for Information Assurance (CSIA) was established to provide overall strategic guidance. Since its inception the CSIA has been involved in forging partnerships between the public and private sectors as well as providing security-related information to individual computer users.[104] The CSIA views its role as 'addressing the following five key areas in relation to protecting information systems, the information they carry and their users: combating hi-tech crime; increasing protection of information systems; promoting education and awareness of information security; addressing training and skills for professionals; and developing international co-operation'.[105]

In December 1999 the Home Secretary established NISCC to minimise the risks to the CNI from electronic attack.[106] Also, in March 2000 the Information Assurance Advisory Council (IAAC) was launched to act as a conduit for assessing the possibilities for information sharing between public and private organisations. As one study has characterised this arrangement:

> On the public side, the issues relate to what information the government can
> legally provide in view of its mission responsibilities. For the private sector,

the question is how far it is willing to go in sharing proprietary information and information on its vulnerabilities.[107]

NISCC has subsequently been engaged in threat assessments, outreach activities, warning and responding to threats and vulnerabilities, and research and development in methods and techniques designed to enhance its overall operation.[108] The Centre also draws on the expertise of the: Communications Electronic Security Group (CESG), a branch of GCHQ based in Cheltenham; Home Office; Cabinet Office; MoD; DTI; National Hi-Tech Crime Unit (NHTCU, which has now been embraced within SOCA); Dstl; and the Security Service.[109]

NISCC has responsibility for operating the Unified Incident Reporting and Alert Scheme (UNIRAS), the UK's CERT.[110] As described above, in conjunction with other government departments NISCC has been engaged in developing partnerships with UK business and industry as part of its outreach programme. An important aspect of this work is to respond to serious computer-related incidents affecting large organisations such as sabotage of data or networks, virus attacks, financial fraud, denial of service attacks, and theft of laptops. The outreach programme also involves business partnerships and information exchanges designed to promote trust and confidence in the sharing of confidential information.[111]

UNIRAS operates with support from the Central Incident Recording and Reporting and Alert System (CIRRAS) of the Central Computer and Telecommunications Agency (CCTA).[112] It also provides vulnerability advisory notices (VANs) related to vulnerabilities identified in information technology systems and, where possible, the provision of patch information for mitigating any effect stemming from them.[113] Additionally, NISCC produces Monthly Bulletins providing 'a compilation of open source material concerning electronic attack, significant malicious software infection, and the ... (CNI) it may affect'.[114]

NISCC has launched several initiatives as part of its remit. One is the enhancement of what are known as Warning, Advice and Reporting Points (WARPs) for local authorities and communities.[115] These are intended as a means for promoting exchanges of confidential information such as incident reporting, for dialogue on information technology security and promoting best practice. More recently a public website called ITSafe was established 'to provide both home users and small businesses with advice in plain English on protecting computers, mobile phones and other *devices* from *malicious attack*'.[116] Another aspect of NISCC's work is the international outreach effort to forge links with other countries operating CERTs under the auspices of the global Forum of Incident Response and Security Teams (FIRST).[117]

The DTI also plays a key role in ICT development and security by encouraging 'confidence in the use of new information and communication technologies' and by working with business 'to raise awareness of the importance of effective information security management and to encourage the adoption of security standards such as ISO/IEC 17799 and BS 7799'.[118] BS 7799 provides UK-wide standards for information security management, including data protection, the promotion of best practice, continuity management, and education and training.[119]

The DTI has launched the 'Foresight' initiative designed to consider the implications of cyber trust and crime prevention in relation to information technology and to assess developments over the longer term. This Project identified 'future societal risks' as an important aspect of the assessment. This is because such analysis involves the:

> consideration of a broad, integrated policy approach to risks to society over the long term (e.g. war, terrorism, crime, natural disasters, technological hazards), rather than the fragmented approach of traditional policymaking.[120]

In a report addressing these issues it says this broader policy method for considering 'societal risks' is one that is now being adopted in the UK as part of a 'government-wide approach to risk management'.[121]

Before becoming part of SOCA in 2006, the NHTCU was established in April 2001 with a remit to combat 'serious and organised hi-tech crime, both nationally and internationally'.[122] The work of this Unit has involved, in conjunction with UK businesses, the development of a strategy to prevent and respond to hi-tech crime. As part of the strategy an Industry Liaison Team works in partnership with business to develop relationships that allow for the mutual exchange of information.[123] Additionally, the NHTCU devised a reassurance approach to business in the conduct of their investigations.[124] Because there is an awareness that companies rely on reputation for their business, and that loss of confidence as a result of computer crime could impact on that reputation, the Unit has produced a Confidentiality Charter to allay concerns.[125] This Charter is 'designed to provide reassurance that business can report hi-tech activity and attacks without fear of causing unwelcome interference to their business'.[126] Finally, like the other agencies and departments the NHTCU has developed relationships with counterparts abroad as part of its mission to prevent and thwart cyber crime activities.[127]

Other measures have been launched to reinforce national and international coordination and cooperation. At the national level, the Security Service has established the National Security Advice Centre to coordinate links between the businesses and industries involved in the operation of the CNI and government departments and policing agencies.[128] Internationally, the UK has been involved with the G8 and the OECD in the development of guidelines and principles for cyberspace. The OECD guidelines encourage the promotion of greater awareness of cybersecurity issues by focusing 'on the need to develop a 'culture of security' in the development of information systems and networks ...'.[129] Additionally, the G8 has outlined a series of protective and response measures as well as stating that these efforts, 'should be undertaken with due regard for the security of information and applicable law concerning mutual legal assistance and privacy protection'.[130]

The future for cybersecurity?

In the section on conceptualising conflict and security in cyberspace the complexities associated with this area were identified, such as the difficulties in distinguishing between crime, cyberterrorism and war. Consequently, there remains disagreement among analysts on how to define cyberterrorism.

Some observers feel that the term 'cyberterrorism' is inappropriate, because a widespread cyberattack may simply produce annoyances, not terror, as would a bomb, or other CBRN weapon. However, others believe that the effects of a widespread computer network attack would be unpredictable and might cause enough economic disruption, fear, and civilian deaths, to qualify as terrorism. At least two views exist for defining the term cyberterrorism:

> **Effects-based**: cyberterrorism exists when a computer attack results in effects that are disruptive enough to generate fear comparable to a traditional act of terrorism, even if done by criminals.
> **Intent-based**: cyberterrorism exists when unlawful politically motivated computer attacks are done to intimidate or coerce a government or people to further a political objective, or to cause grave harm or severe economic damage.[131]

Many also consider that absolute security in cyberspace is unobtainable: but how much security in the ICT area will be enough? Analyses produced by the DTI and NISCC in the UK, and the CERT Centre in the USA indicate that the number of reported attacks on computer systems and the infrastructures they support has been increasing. This is paralleled with similar assessments that the attacks are becoming more sophisticated, automated and damaging to end-users.

One study of the UK and USA has identified five issues for protecting infrastructure systems:

> (a) Attempt to deter attacker – by demonstrating ability to inflict punishment, by promoting norms of behaviour which condemn attacks, and by pre-emption (b) thwart attack and try to prevent damage – individual owners can monitor activity surrounding its site, pool information about attacks, develop uniform standards of security, and build systems with a 'degree of intrusion-tolerance' ... (c) if unsuccessful, attempt to limit damage – by having a 'battle management strategy' (d) attempt to re-constitute the pre-attack position – by dealing with the urgent but short term threats to life and property and long-term stockpiling of essential or long-lead time items, plus planning for and insuring against risks (e) learn from failures – 'post-attack analysis of intrusion attempts, whether successful or unsuccessful, is critical'.[132]

This represents a comprehensive approach to infrastructure protection but it is also acknowledged there are limitations to what can be accomplished.[133] This is because in the near term 'preventing an attack is no more likely to be feasible in the UK than in the US'.[134] At the same time thwarting attacks is considered 'technically feasible'.[135] Firewalls can stop or slow much unwanted activity but in the case of a massive surge of intrusions prevention is considered beyond the realm of current technology although this could improve as intrusion detection and early warning capabilities are enhanced.[136]

Efforts to improve infrastructure protection have therefore been undertaken within acknowledged provisos. Additionally, much of the CNI is in private hands so 'improving its protection will be a matter for contract negotiation rather than direct government decision'.[137] One aspect that has received attention in recent years has been improvements in the operation of what are known as SCADA (supervisory control and data acquisition) systems. These are systems that are used to manage a range of industrial processes remotely from control rooms:

> The flow of gas and oil through pipes; the processing and distribution of water; the management of the electricity grid; the operation of chemical plants; and the signalling network for railways. These all use various forms of process control or 'supervisory control and data acquisition' SCADA technology.[138]

The SCADA programme run by NISCC has consequently been engaged in developing an understanding of the risks to these systems as well as devising appropriate methods for mitigating them.[139]

Analysts have noted that businesses are often the first to adopt new technology and suffer losses in the event of cyber disruption. The 2006 report for the DTI on security incidents noted the positive trend that many organisations were now implementing company-wide cybersecurity policies and some have gone further by operating their own CERT. At the same time, there remains concern that the basic standards for good information practice are not being adopted throughout the sector.[140] An earlier study for the DTI's Foresight project indicated that:

> although 93% of companies have anti-virus software, half were infected by a virus in the last year, reflecting the increasing trend for viruses to exploit vulnerabilities in operating systems, which companies do not keep up to date with the latest security patches. Although three-quarters of businesses with in-house websites have a firewall, for over half of these it is their sole defence. Contingency planning is not much better with fewer than one in ten businesses having tested their disaster recovery plans.[141]

It has also been reported that a study by the Communications Management Association (CMA) indicated that many organisations were ill-prepared:

> The CMA asked 172 of its senior personnel to report on incidences of cyberterrorism – 48% reported that the future of their organisation 'could be at risk by a major network-related security breach' – thirty-two percent admitted being the victim of cyber terrorism.[142]

In response the CMA has established the Institute for Communications Arbitration and Forensics to emphasise the importance of computer security among businesses.

As reliance on ICT increases and commercial organisations become what some call 'virtual organisations', changes in the context of business operations and cybersecurity will also occur. This will require 'new and evolving rules to deal with technology and personnel changes'.[143] Similarly, an important aspect is the need to 'involve all partners in the supply chain in the discussion of information security: so all implement uniform security practices'.[144] Finally, as business globalisation evolves, in addition to the advantages stemming from operating in a global marketplace the outsourcing and offshoring of data of all kinds could lead to this information becoming accessible to a range of actors who might use it to disrupt the computer systems on which the UK's CNI depends.[145]

Education and training innovation will also be a key factor in responding to the issues stemming from the driver of generational change. Many people have grown up and become accustomed to use of the internet, but there could be a shortage of specialists with knowledge of computer security and forensic analysis in both the commercial and policing sectors. This type of education and knowledge has two categories: 'training, marked by an emphasis on particular systems, situations, or environments rather than broad principles'; and 'scholarly (or scholarship), marked by an emphasis on underlying principles, concepts, and their application'. Good practice is said to involve two sets of principles.

The principle of least privilege – discussion of the creation of subordinate system management accounts so no system administrators can avoid using the omnipotent root account and means for limiting the number and power of network servers that the system runs. The principle of psychological acceptability – discussion of the suitability of various authentication mechanisms for different environments, as well as methods to provide users with timely assistance and finding ways of working without violating security policies.[146]

An emphasis on education and training could therefore produce a new generation with the necessary analytical and computer skills to contribute to the development of an emerging 'culture of security' in cyberspace.

The UK and human societies around the world are increasingly reliant on ICT. As Project Foresight has identified, these technologies are continuing to transform our ability to communicate, engage in commerce and address complex problems.[147] Individuals, groups, companies and governments can now communicate and conduct business transactions in ways unavailable to our predecessors, generating a vision of an emerging e-society and the business, educational, welfare and developmental opportunities presented by it.[148] ICT is essential to the people and economic future of the UK. The country is also considered to be in a good position to play a central part in the development of this sector of the economy.

The UK is in a strong position to exploit the advances being made in ICT. We have the world's second most productive science base in terms of volume and impact of scientific publications; 80 per cent of the UK population can access broadband; the UK is the second largest software consumer in the world; the third largest producer of ICT goods and is predicted to become the biggest market for ICT in Europe.[149]

Equally, the vision of the emerging e-society has generated uncertainties about what the long-term effects of dependence on these new information and communication technologies will be. This has raised questions about what it means for governments in this new era and for trust, civil liberties and the future of democracy. One aspect of developing a broader approach is consequently to engage with all sections of society, particularly in cyberspace, to encourage discussion on appropriate policies so these are not viewed as repressive of cultural identities.[150] Some have also noted the possibility of a different trend to the 'digital divide' where people that do have access to ICT become 'digital hermits' to avoid what they see as an unwarranted loss of privacy and civil liberty.[151]

The evolving context for ICT development is therefore one that has considerable implications for the government and population of the UK. Moore's law predicts computing power will double every 18 months, although some assessments consider this trend could tail off in the future, and new developments such as grid computing and mobile technologies will continue to transform the way of life in this country and elsewhere. Yet it is also recognised there are complex issues associated with the emerging global information and communication environment. Those working on the development of the Grid have observed that the 'specific problem that underlies the Grid concept is coordinated resource sharing and problem solving in dynamic, multi-institutional virtual organisations'.[152] Consequently, there is a need for greater understanding of how these trends will evolve. Because this development may involve individuals, virtual organisations and states operating in a global context, the issue of how this environment will be regulated and governed to ensure security and to minimise its mal-appropriation is thus an aspect for further consideration.

Work has already begun in thinking through some of these complexities. Those concentrating on applications for the Grid have developed inter-Grid protocols and sharing rules for the basis of collaboration in this emerging context, and where the 'organisation' is understood to be, 'A set of individuals and/institutions defined by such sharing rules'.[153] Inter-Grid protocols are designed to enable interoperability and security in a distributed computing environment and which allows for communications between multiple end points.[154]

Similarly, it has been observed that 'different cultures value security differently' and so ensuring that all users, irrespective of culture or region, understand the nature of their collaboration and agree to abide by the rules and protocols established is thus an important aspect of future ICT development.[155]

In the UK the work of Project Foresight has provided important insights into the implications of ICT 'in areas such as identity and authenticity, surveillance, system robustness, security and information assurance and the basis for effective interaction and trust between people and machines'.[156] An important feature of this research has been its focus on generating long-term inter-disciplinary knowledge in these crucial areas. The Project's work on cyber trust for example has indicated there are significant issues for the future of ICT development:

There is a commonly expressed concern both that failures in or attacks on cyber-dependent infrastructures will threaten public safety and that vulnerabilities in the wider information infrastructures will undermine trust and confidence in the information society.[157]

Much has been accomplished in responding to the threats and risks in the evolving environment of cyberspace, and in identifying the opportunities it presents. At the same time this is a dynamic arena where there is likely to be a continuing need to develop a consensus on the requirements of both government and citizens in the context of the emerging 'culture of security'.

Notes

1 The author would like to thank Alex Mcleod for research help with this chapter, Professor Mark Baker, University of Reading, for materials and knowledge on computer-related developments, and Dr Tony Moore for comments on an earlier draft.
2 (2005) *The Times*, 22 July, p. 15.
3 Terrorism Act 2006, Part 1 – Offences, Maximum penalty for contravening notice relating to encrypted information, section 15, '"a national security case" means a case in which the grounds specified in the notice to which the offence relates as the grounds for imposing a disclosure requirement were or included a belief that the imposition of the requirement was necessary in the interests of national security', www.parliament.uk.
4 Terrorism Detention Powers, House of Commons Home Affairs Committee, Fourth Report of Session 2005–2006, Volume 1, Report together with formal minutes and appendix, 3 July 2006, HC 910-1, London: The Stationery Office, para. 48.
5 Ibid., para. 63.
6 'What is the Critical National Infrastructure?', available at www.uniras.gov.uk/ nisccc/aboutCNI-en.html.
7 Williams, P., Shimeall, T. and Dunleavy, C. (2002) 'Intelligence analysis for internet security', *Contemporary Security Policy*, 23(2), August, p. 2.
8 *Threats*, available at www.uniras.gov.uk/niscc/threats-en.html, p. 1.
9 Ibid., p. 2.
10 Ibid., p. 2.
11 Central Sponsor for Information Assurance (CSIA) (2004) *Protecting our Information Systems. Working in Partnership for a Secure and Resilient UK Information Infrastructure*, CSIA, Cabinet Office, p. 7. The trend of virus attacks indicates the changes in speed and damage that has been caused over time. In the early 1990s, computer viruses and worms numbered in the hundreds, but by the mid-1990s the 10,000+ virus threshold was reached and there was also the first denial-of-service attack. By the time the 'melissa' virus arrived in March 1999, it was able to affect 150,000 computer systems in four days, and the 'I love you' virus in May 2000 is estimated to have damaged 500,000 systems in 24 hours. I thank Professor Mark Baker, University of Reading, for these figures.
12 Leyden, J. (2004) 'Sasser kid blamed for viral plague', *The Register*, 30 July. The Sasser worm spread worldwide very rapidly and reports indicate it hit, 'the South African government, Taiwan's national post office, Sampo (Finland's third largest bank), RailCorp in Australia and the UK's coastguard service', available at www. theregister.co.uk/2004/07/30/jaschanviralmenace/print.html.

13 (2002) 'FBI probe attack on the net', BBC News, Technology, 23 October, available at http://news.bbc.co.uk/1/hi/technology/2352667.stm.

14 In the USA this has generated an extensive literature, see, for example, Rattray, G.J. (2002) 'The cyberterrorism threat', in Howard, R.D. and Sawyer, R.L. (eds) *Terrorism and Counterterrorism. Understanding the New Security Environment*, Guildford, CT: Dushkin/McGraw Hill, pp. 221–45; Schwartzstein, S.J.D. (ed.) (1996) *The Information Revolution and National Security. Dimensions and Directions*, Washington, DC: The Center for Strategic and International Studies, and (1998) *Cybercrime, Cyberterorism and Cyberwarfare: Averting an Electronic Waterloo*, Washington, DC: The Center for Strategic and International Studies. One commentator has also suggested that what is required is an, 'unprecedented change in laws, policies, culture, and attitudes about cyber security', McConnell, M. (2002) 'Information assurance in the twenty-first century', *Security & Privacy*, available at http://computer.org/computer/sp/articles/mcc/index.htm.

15 Williams *et al.*, op. cit., p. 2.

16 Goldman, E.O. (2003) 'Introduction: security in the information technology age', in Goldman, E.O. (ed.) 'National Security in the Information Age', special issue, *Contemporary Security Policy*, 24(1), April, p. 1.

17 (2005) 'Emerging electronic Attack (eA) threats to 2010', *NISCCC Quarterly* 02/05, p. 6, available at www.uniras.gov.uk/niscc/docs/re_20050728-00635.pdf?lang=en.

18 Ibid.

19 The notion of a 'culture of security' is derived from the guidelines for the security of information systems and networks developed by the Organisation for Economic and Co-operation and Development (OECD). These are reproduced in Esterle, A., Ranck, H. and Schmitt, B. (Schmitt, B. (ed.)) (2005) *Information Security. A New Challenge for the EU*, Chaillot Paper No. 76, March, pp. 64–73.

20 Williams, *et al.*, op. cit.

21 Ibid., p. 1.

22 Ranck, H. and Schmitt, B. 'Threat assessment', in Esterle, A., Ranck, H. and Schmitt, B. (Schmitt, B. (ed.)), op. cit., p. 10.

23 Goodman, S.E. (2002) 'Preventing and responding to cybercrime and terrorism: some international dimensions', in *High-Impact Terrorism: Proceedings of a Russian-American Workshop*, Washington, DC: National Academy Press, pp. 198–9.

24 Ibid.

25 The figures are taken from the World Internet Usage and Population Statistics table for 2006, available at www.internetworldstats.com/stats.htm.

26 Franda, M. (2002) *Launching into Cyberspace. Internet Development and Politics in Five World Regions*, Boulder, CO: Lynne Rienner Publishers. See also (2004) *Millennium*, special issue.

27 Sharpe, B. and Zaba, S. (2004) *Technology Forward Look: User Guide. Part 2, 'Pervasive Computing'*, 12 February, Foresight Cyber Trust & Crime Prevention Project, Office of Science and Technology, DTI, p. 9, available at www.foresight. gov.uk.

28 For a discussion of the issues see Anderson, D.P. and Kubiatowicz, J. (2002) 'The worldwide computer', *Scientific American*, 286(3), March, pp. 28–35.

29 Foster, I. and Kesselman, C. (eds) (1998) *The Grid: Blueprint for a New Computing Infrastructure*, San Francisco, CA: Morgan Kaufman Publishers.

30 Ibid.

31 De Roure, D., Jennings, N., Shadbolt, N. and Baker, M.A. 'Research agenda for the semantic grid: a future e-science infrastructure', submitted to the *International Journal Computation and Currency: Practice and Experience*, February 2002.

32 *Technology Look Forward*, op. cit., p. 14.

33 Cremonini, L., Rathmell, A. and Wagner, C. (2003) *Cyber Trust & Crime Prevention: Foresight Overview*, Rand Europe, p. 41.

34 McConnell, op. cit.
35 Foster, I., Kesselman, C. and Tuecke, S. (2001) 'The anatomy of the grid: enabling scalable virtual organizations', *International Journal of Supercomputer Applications*.
36 Baylis, J. and Smith, S. (eds) (2005) *The Globalization of World Politics: An Introduction to International Relations* (3rd edn), Oxford: Oxford University Press.
37 Held, D. and McGrew, A. (2003) 'Introduction', in Held, D. and McGrew, A. (eds) *Governing Globalization: Power, Authority and Global Governance*, Cambridge: Polity Press, p. 2.
38 Cha, V.D. (2000) 'Globalization and the study of international security', *Journal of Peace Research*, 37(3), pp. 391–403.
39 Ibid., p. 392. See also, Kurth Cronin, A. (2002/03) 'Behind the curve: globalization and international terrorism', *International Security*, 27(3), Winter, pp. 30–58, especially pp. 46–8.
40 Cha, op. cit., p. 393.
41 Ibid., p. 396.
42 Aronson, J.D. 'The communications and internet revolution', in Baylis, J. and Smith, op. cit., pp. 621–43; and Walden, I. (2005) 'Crime and security in cyberspace', *Cambridge Review of International Affairs*, 18(1), April, p. 67.
43 Robinson, N. (2001) 'Stealing identity – the rise of personal data theft', *Jane's Intelligence Review*, May, 13(5), pp. 54–5.
44 Ibid. See also, Valeri, L. (2001) 'Europe tackles cyber-crime', *Jane's Intelligence Review*, 13(4), April, p. 52.
45 Williams *et al.*, op. cit., p. 4.
46 Op. cit., p. 394.
47 Rollins, J. and Wilson, C. (2005) 'Terrorist capabilities for cyberattack: overview and policy issues', *CRS Report for Congress*, received through the CRS Web, Order Code RL33123, 20 October, p. CRS-2.
48 Walker, C. (2006) 'Cyber terrorism: legal principle and law in the United Kingdom', *Penn State Law Review*, 110(3), p. 633.
49 'The Advent of Netwar (Revisited)' in Arquilla, J. and Ronfeldt, D. (eds) *Networks and Netwars: The Future of Terror, Crime, and Militancy*, Santa Monica, CA: Rand, vol. 1, p. 1, available at www.rand.org/publications/MR/MR1382/. See also, Karatzogianni, A. (2004) 'The politics of "cyberconflict"', *Politics. Surveys, Debates and Controversies in Politics*, 24(1), February, pp. 46–55.
50 Arquilla and Ronfeldt, op. cit., p. 1.
51 Ibid., p. 2. There is also said to be a spectrum of actors in netwar, ranging from those with peaceful objectives to those with criminal or terrorist intent.
52 Ibid., 'summary', p. ix
53 'Activism, hacktivism, and cyberterrorism: the internet as a tool for influencing foreign policy', in Arquilla and Ronfeldt, op. cit., vol. 2, pp. 239–88.
54 Ibid., p. 241.
55 Ibid., p. 263.
56 Ibid., p. 241.
57 Collin, B.C. (1997) 'The future of cyberterrorism: where the physical and virtual worlds converge', Eleventh annual international symposium on criminal justice issues proceedings, 27 March, www.acsp.uic.edu/01cj/confs/terror02.html.
58 Ibid. See also Kadner, S., Rees, B. and Turpen, E. (1998) 'The internet information infrastructure: terrorist tool or architecture for information defense?', in Brown, J. (ed.) *New Horizons and New Strategies in Arms Control*, Alberquerque, NM: Sandia National Laboratories, pp. 269–88.
59 Littleton, M.J. (1995) *Information Age Terrorism: Toward Cyberterror*, Monterey, CA: Naval Postgraduate School, December, abstract, Director of the Institute for

Security Technology Studies at Dartmouth College on Cyber Terrorism: The State of US Preparedness.

60   Ibid., pp. 5–6.

61   Williams *et al.*, op. cit., p. 13.

62   Research by the Institute for Security Technology Studies at Dartmouth College in the USA for example has observed this trend to be occurring. See, Statement for the Record of Michael A. Vatis, Director of the Institute for Security Technology Studies at Dartmouth College on Cyber Terrorism: The State of US Preparedness, Before the House Committee on Government Reform Subcommittee on Government Efficiency, Financial Management and Intergovernmental Relations, 26 September 2001.

63   Williams *et al.*, op. cit.

64   Ibid., p. 9.

65   Ibid., p. 10.

66   Ibid. In the context of the USA, for example, Michael A. Vatis comments that, 'Serious cyber attacks against infrastructures, through unauthorized intrusions, ddos attacks, worms, or trojan horse programs, or malicious insiders, have been the subject of speculation for several years. Vulnerabilities in the nation's power distribution grid were first exposed during the joint chiefs of staff exercise "eligible receiver" … the specter of an unanticipated and massive attack on critical infrastructures that disables core functions such as telecommunications, electrical power systems, government services, and emergency services, has been raised in a number of reports on national security and by the NIPC. The degrees to which these infrastructures are dependent on information systems, and interrelated to one another, are still not well understood. Neither is the extent to which these information systems are exposed to outside entry from the internet', Vatis, M.A. (2001) *Cyber Attacks During the War on Terrorism: A Predictive Analysis*, Institute for Security Technology Studies at Dartmouth College, 22 September, p. 17.

67   Stark, R. (undated) *Cyber Terrorism: Rethinking New Technology*, p. 6, available at www.infowar.com/MIL—C41/stark/Cy…rrorism-Rethinking—New—Technology1.html.

68   Williams *et al.*, op. cit.

69   Falkenrath, R. (2001) 'Problems of preparedness. U.S. readiness for a domestic terrorist attack', *International Security*, Spring, p. 150.

70   For an overview of US policy initiatives see Lukasik *et al.*, op. cit., pp. 49–54; and Rogers, P. (2001) 'Protecting America against cyberterrorism', *U.S. Foreign Policy Agenda*, 6(3), November (electronic). The re-assessment of US policy led to Presidential Directive 63 (PDD-63), which stated that the USA should be prepared for the possible imminence of a cyber-attack. PDD-63 established the National Plan for Information Systems Protection. This was later updated by Executive Order 13231, which seeks to ensure minimal disruption and damage to the CNI. On 14 February 2003, the US President issued a new strategic plan, setting five priorities: 'A national cyberspace security response system; a national cyberspace security threat and vulnerability reduction programme; a national cyberspace security awareness and training programme; securing government cyberspace; and national security and international cyberspace security cooperation' (Lukasik *et al.*, op. cit., pp. 60–1).

71   Canadian Security Intelligence Service (1996) *1996 Public Report, part iv, Information Technology*, available at www.csis-scrs.gc.ca/eng/publicrp/publ1996 e.html, quoted in Whine, M. (1999) *Cyberspace: A New Medium for Communication, Command and Control by Extremists*, April, available at www.ict.org.il/articles/cyberspace.htm.

72   Zanini, M. and Edwards, S.J.A. 'The networking of terror in the information age', in Arquilla and Ronfeldt (eds), op. cit., p. 44. See also Soo Hoo, K., Goodman, S. and Greenberg, L. (1997) 'Information technology and the terrorist threat', *Survival*, 39(3), Autumn, pp. 135–55.

73 Zanini and Edwards, op. cit., p. 44.

74 One analysis has commented that, 'although it is possible for electronic intrusions to damage infrastructure and threaten physical danger, taking control of those systems from the outside is extremely difficult, requires a great deal of specialised knowledge and must overcome non-computerised fail-safe measures', Lemos, R. (2002) 'Cyberterrorism: the real risks', 27 August, CNET news.com, available at http://news.com.com/.

75 'Control-system attacks attempt to disable or take power over operations used to maintain physical infrastructure, such as "distributed control systems; that regulate water supplies, electrical transmission networks and railroads. While remote access to many control systems have previously required an attacker to dial in with a modem, these operations are increasingly using the internet to transmit data or are connected to a company's local network – a system protected with firewalls that, in some cases, could be penetrated ... but damage would be measured in loss of data not loss of life"', Lemos, Robert, op. cit.

76 (2002) *Making the Nation Safer: The Role of Science and Technology in Countering Terrorism*, Washington, DC: National Academy Press.

77 Rollins and Wilson, 'Terrorist capabilities for cyberattack: overview and policy issues', op. cit., pp. CRS-3-4.

78 See www.cert.org/stats/cert_stats.html. 2003 was the last year that these statistics were recorded. A note attached to the statistics explains that, 'Given the widespread use of automated attack tools, attacks against internet-connected systems have become so commonplace that counts of the number of incidents reported provide little information with regard to assessing the scope and impact of attacks. Therefore, as of 2004, we will no longer publish the number of incidents reported. Instead, we will be working with others in the community to develop and report on more meaningful metrics'.

79 See www.dti.gov.uk/cii/datasecurity/index.shtml

80 (2006) *Information Security Breaches Survey 2006*, technical report, managed by PricewaterhouseCoopers for the Department of Trade and Industry, April, URN 06/803, p. 2.

81 Householder, A., Houle, K. and Dougherty, C. (undated) 'Computer attack trends challenge internet security', *Security & Privacy*, available at computer org/computer/sp/articles/hou/inex.htm.

82 Ibid.

83 Meinel, C. (2001) 'Code red for the web', *Scientific American*, October, pp. 36–43.

84 Householder *et al.*, op. cit.

85 These observations stem from presentations at a Workshop on Cyber crime and Cyber terrorism, Chilworth Manor, November 2003 (hereafter, Workshop, November 2003).

86 Presentation at Workshop, November 2003.

87 Ibid.

88 Ibid.

89 Ibid.

90 Lukasik *et al.*, op. cit.

91 Sir David Omand, Keynote speech, 1 July 2004, at launch of RUSI Homeland Resilience Programme (8 July 2004), available at www.ukresilience.info/contingencies/rusi.htm.

92 Omand, ibid., p. 6.

93 'What is the critical national infrastructure?', op. cit., pp. 1–2.

94 (2005) 'What is national criticality?', *NISCC Quarterly*, 04/05, p. 2, available at www.uniras.gov.uk/niscc/docs/re-20051230-01143.pdf?lang=en.

95 Lukasik *et al.*, op. cit.

96 Omand, op. cit., p. 6.

97   Ibid., pp. 6–7.
98   'What is national criticality?', op. cit., p. 2, available at www.uniras.gov.uk/niscc/docs/re-20051230-01143.pdf?lang=en.
99   Ibid.
100 Ibid.
101 Ibid., p. 3.
102 Ibid.
103 Presentation at Workshop, November 2003.
104 (2004) *Protecting our information systems. Working in Partnership for a Secure and Resilient UK Information Infrastructure*, available at www.cabinet-office.gov.uk/CSIA.
105 'Central sponsor for information assurance', available at www.knowledgenetwork.gov.uk/CO/KIMSCSIA.nsf/0/7922576C7B1FC67E80.
106 Lukasik *et al.*, op. cit., pp. 67–8; and (2004) 'Security threats in a networked world', para. 6, speech by Beverley Hughes to The Royal Institute of International Affairs, 22 March, available at www.homeoffice.gov.uk/docs3/dft-speech.html, published 23 March 2004; and (2004) *NISCC Good Practice Guide. Telecommunications Resilience*, May, p. 4.
107 Lukasik *et al.*, op. cit., p. 69.
108 'Frequently Asked Questions', available at uniras.gov.uk/niscc/faq-en.html, pp. 1–2.
109 Ibid., p. 2.
110 'UNIRAS…provides government and CNI organisations with support in responding to electronic attack incidents', available at www.uniras.gov.uk/niscc/respToIncidents-en.html, p. 1.
111 'Information exchanges', available at www.uniras.gov.uk/niscc/infoEx-en.html.
112 Lukasik *et al.*, op.cit, p. 68.
113 'NISCC vulnerability advisory notices', available at www.uniras.gov.uk/vuls/.
114 A disclaimer is also included in these Bulletins wherein NISCC states that it, 'takes no responsibility for the accuracy of the original reporting and only incidents of special interest are reported', *NISCC Monthly Bulletin*, June 2004, document reference: MB0604, issued 2 July 2004.
115 Global Secure Systems Ltd 'UK government plans new cyber-security initiatives', available at www.gsec.co.uk/news/news.php?id+814; and Ensom, J. (2004) 'UK local authorities launch warning system', available at www.globalcontinuity.com/article/articleprint/10254/-1/30/.
116 'IT security awareness for everyone', available at www.itsafe.gov.uk.
117 'NISCC glossary', available at uniras.gov.uk/niscc/glossary-en.html, p. 2.
118 Central Sponsor for Information Assurance, available at www.knowdgenetwork.gov.uk/co/kimscsia.nsf/0/5F168F61AAAEB27D8025, accessed 8 July 2004.
119 Lukasik *et al.*, op.cit, pp. 68–9.
120 Rand CTCP, p. 15. The study identified Sweden's total defence and emergency management doctrine and the US DHS as examples of this approach.
121 Ibid. The Foresight Project has undertaken research on potential 'risks to cyber trust (which are also opportunities for cyber crime)'. Three sets of vulnerabilities have been identified in this context: 'technical; economic and societal (e.g risk perceptions and perceptions of trust, legislation)', whereas, 'in relation to threats, there is an emerging consensus on the importance of addressing both accidents and malicious activities', ibid., pp. 19–20.
122 'Protecting our information systems', op. cit., p. 9.
123 Ibid., p. 12.
124 Workshop, November 2003.
125 Ibid.
126 Ibid.
127 'Protecting our information systems', op. cit., p. 20.

128 Omand, op. cit., p. 7.

129 'Protecting our information systems', op. cit., p. 20.

130 G8 Principles for Protecting Critical Information Infrastructures, Meeting of the Ministers of Justice and Home Affairs, Paris, 5 May 2003.

131 Rollins and Wilson, 'Terrorist capabilities for cyberattack: overview and policy issues', op. cit., p. CRS-3. See also Wilson, C. (2003) *Computer Attack and Cyber Terrorism: Vulnerabilities and Policy Issues for Congress*, CRS Report for Congress, Received through the CRS Web, Order Code RL32114, 17 October.

132 Lukasik *et al.*, op. cit., pp. 15–22.

133 Ibid., p. 15.

134 Ibid.

135 Ibid., p. 55.

136 For a discussion of the evolution of intrusion detection technologies, see Kemmerer, R.A. and Vigna, G. (2002) 'Intrusion detection: a brief history', available at computer. org/computer/sp/articles/kem/index.htm.

137 Lukasik *et al.*, op. cit., p. 57.

138 'SCADA Security', available at www.uniras.gov.uk/niscc/scada-en.html, p. 1. In the USA, a CRS report on this stated that these systems, 'are often used for remote monitoring over a large geographic area and transmitting commands to remote assets, such as valves and switches ... they may be vulnerable to implantation of faulty data and to remote access through dial-up modems used for maintenance'. *CRS Report*, p. 2 Distributed control systems, on the other hand, 'are process control systems, commonly deployed in a single manufacturing or production complex, characterized by a network of computers. DCS generally provide processed information to a series of commands ... an attack targeting DCS might cause extensive damage at a single facility, but might not affect more than the single site'.

139 'SCADA Security', op. cit., p. 1. The NISCC SCADA programme involves annual conferences, vulnerability and protection research, a confidential forum with industry to discuss threats and responses, and exchanges with SCADA programmes in the USA, Canada, Europe and Australia.

140 Rathmell, A. and Valeri, L. (2002) 'New methods needed to counter cybercrime', *Jane's Intelligence Review*, 14(8), August, p. 52.

141 Op. cit., p. 13.

142 Hopkins, N. (2003) 'Cyber terror threatens UK's biggest companies', *Guardian*, 3 April, available at www.guardian.co.uk/print/0,3858,4164109-103690,00.html.

143 McConnell, M. (undated) 'Information assurance in the twenty-first century', *Security & Privacy*, available at computer.org/computer/sp/articles/mcc/index.htm.

144 Ibid.

145 'We define outsourcing as purchasing or subcontracting a business capability, product or service from or to a third party; and offshoring as transferring all or part of the functions of a business to a centre located in another country'. 'What does the future hold? Emerging electronic attack threats to 2010 (01/05A), op. cit., p. 7.

146 Bishop, M. (2002) 'Computer security education: training, scholarship, and research', *Security & Privacy*, available at computer.org/computer/sp/articles/bis/index.htm.

147 Cyber Trust and Crime Prevention Project, Executive Summary, DTI, available at www.foresight.gov.uk.

148 Ibid.

149 Blears, H., ibid., pp. 11–12.

150 Walker, 'Cyber-terrorism: legal principle and law in the United Kingdom', op. cit., p. 665.

151 *Technology Look Forward*, op. cit., p. 31. The term 'digital hermit' was coined by Brian Collins.

152 Foster, I., Kesselman, C., Tsudik, G. and Tuecke, S. (1998) 'A security architecture for computational grids', Proceedings of the Fifth ACM Conference on Computer and Communications Security Conference, pp. 83–92.
153 Ibid.
154 Ibid.
155 Soo Hoo, K., Malpass, K.B., Harrington, K., Elliott, D.D. and Goodman, S.E. (1997) 'Workshop on protecting and assuring critical national infrastructure: setting the research and policy agenda', CISAC, Stanford University.
156 Foresight Directorate, Office of Science & Technology launched *Cyber Trust & Crime Prevention: Foresight Overview*, Rand Europe, mr-1786-ost, July 2003, p. 8.
157 Summary, p. 5. 'Cyber trust is a confident expectation in the reliability and value of the internet and related ICTs, such as the equipment, people and techniques essential to the use of online services', Dutton and Shepherd (2003) *The Social Dynamics of Cybertrust*, CTCP Foresight paper, p. 14..

16 Private sector roles in counter-terrorism

Frank Gregory

Introduction

Even before 9/11, non-terrorist emergencies, such as the Foot and Mouth Disease epidemic, the wide-spread flooding and the fuel tax protests, had made government aware that responding to emergencies necessitated the involvement of the wider public. These crises, together with the growing awareness of the vulnerability of IT, on which so many activities depend, led to recognition of the need for both the public and private sectors to adopt strategies for what is variously called business continuity or resilience. Home Office Permanent Secretary for Counter-Terrorism, Leigh Lewis, reaffirmed this lesson, in respect of counter-terrorism, in a speech to the Police Federation Annual Conference in May 2004. He said, referring to a counter-terrorism exercise that:

> We have also recognised since 9/11 that we needed to broaden the range of stake-holders involved in counter-terrorism planning.[1]

Within the specific arena of counter-terrorism, as one aspect of emergency or contingency planning, it has long been recognised by government that policies of privatisation together with post-Cold War and post-colonial cut-backs in the armed forces have meant that both much of the critical national infrastructure and the means to support it in emergencies were no longer under direct government control. This means that emergency or contingency planning has to involve, in appropriate ways, the private sector and the wider public. This involvement covers a wide spectrum of roles, ranging from the vigilance required of members of the public in, for example, reporting suspicious objects or behaviour in public places, through the statutory responsibilities for emergency planning and preparedness required of, for example, the water industry, to encouragement to local businesses to form local business continuity or resilience fora. In part, this public–private sector inter-relationship in emergency response is reflected in the new civil contingencies legislation with its listing of Category One Responders – the public sector – and Category Two Responders – mainly those private sector bodies with critical national infrastructure responsibilities. The public–private relationship is also visible in fora such as 'London First'.

However, in terms of the domestic management of terrorism in the UK, we need to recognise that these public–private sector relationships are both complex and diverse in character. For example, the private sector has a range of particular forms of vulnerability. In the case of a commercial retail chain with a nation-wide network of branches, the loss of one branch may only be of minor consequence, whereas the loss of the central supply and logistics facilities could be catastrophic.[2] By contrast, a small or medium sized enterprise, with a very localised market, could be permanently put out of business by a major incident, as happened to about 60 per cent of businesses affected by the 1996 Provisional IRA bombing of Manchester. The points set out below by 'London Prepared' represent a standard presentation of major incident impacts upon business including that of 9/11:

1   80 per cent of businesses affected by a major incident close within 18 months.
2   90 per cent of businesses that lose data from a disaster are forced to shut within two years.
3   58 per cent of UK organisations were disrupted by September 11. One in eight was seriously affected.[3]

Particular attention has long been paid to the data loss vulnerabilities of companies (see Chapter 15 on cyber-crime and cyber-terrorism) and according to the DTI only 20 per cent of companies have an IT disaster recovery plan and only 8 per cent have ever tested their plan.[4]

Even where the public sector has a more direct relationship with private sector undertakings, this may still be through several layers of decision-making powers. For example, whilst the DfT has provided one year's funding for 16 dedicated CBRN posts in the BTP, the continuity of that funding was dependant upon the commitment of funds by the private sector rail operators.[5] In another example, related to 'soft' targets, like places of entertainment, the training and licencing of door-keepers ('bouncers') is the responsibility of the Security Industry Authority under the Private Security Industry Act 2001. However, the costs of training involved and process time delays may prove to be obstacles to comprehensive implementation of this scheme. For example, it was found that in Hampshire and the Isle of Wight in May 2004 only 14 doorkeepers out of an estimated 2,000 employed in the area were actually registered by the SIA.[6] Although the Home Secretary does hope that, eventually, the fully trained and accredited complement of security industry staff would form a major component of '… the eyes and ears of the community …'.[7]

In this chapter, a number of aspects of the topic will be covered. The role of the CTSAs will be examined; two projects, which examine counter-terrorism relationships between the public and private sectors will be discussed; and some general themes on the private sector response will be identified. However, at the outset we need to be clear about what is explicitly or implicitly required from the private sector in counter-terrorism and emergencies. Moreover, some of the relevant expectations of the private sector are already well established through health and safety and occupational health requirements, regulations on the care and handling of hazardous materials, risk assessment requirements and crime prevention measures related to the security of premises and staff. Why does the public sector seek to involve the private sector beyond the key Category 2 Responders?

1 Terrorists attack private sector locations as well as obvious 'government' or infrastructure targets, for example, the Bali nightclub.
2 Private sector staff, especially security staff and security systems (particularly CCTV), are more widely deployed than public sector police and security forces. Therefore the private sector can be seen as providing significant extensions of 'controlled space'.
3 Private sector bodies can be designated by legislation as part of the 'policing' of certain activities, for example, the widely spread requirement to report suspicious financial transactions, controls exercised by pharmacists and the strict laws governing the sale of firearms.
4 The move, in urban areas, to concentrate certain activities such as clubs and restaurants or shopping malls in particular locations means that any emergency would be better handled by preparedness by the retail operators and their staff in those areas. For example, discussions with the emergency services on evacuation routes and evacuation points and how to handle bomb alerts.

In general this wider private sector would be involved through the mechanisms of:

• Public information – for '…an informed and supportive public …'.
• Alerting information – '… aimed at specific sectors and at those who carry responsibilities for public safety …'.
• Public warnings – given when clear advice can be given so that '… the public can help put themselves out of the way of danger'.[8]

CTSAs' advice as a way of enhancing counter-terrorism and promoting business resilience and continuity

Although Sir Robert Peel laid upon the police the primary task of the prevention of crime, this task, in practice, has always tended to come second to the investigation of offences and the apprehension of offenders. Certainly in 'cop culture', being a crime-prevention officer was not seen as a career enhancing move of similar status to membership of the Flying Squad or equivalent special unit. However, well before 9/11, crime prevention had assumed a higher police task profile, with the policy goal of 'designing out crime' being placed in section 104 of the Crime and Disorder Act. This promoted a partnership requirement on local forces and local planning authorities, in respect of city centre recreational use locations and shopping precincts. Similar multi-agency partnerships have also been evident in schemes to reduce crime and promote urban regeneration on problem housing estates or high-rise blocks.

To this, pre-9/11 higher profile for crime prevention, has been added the enhanced post-9/11 requirement for the police, through NaCTSO and forces CTSAs, to reach out to a wider business and industrial environment than previously came within the responsibility of MI5's T4 department (now NSAC). Whilst all localities will have individual as well as generic counter-terrorism security needs, the volume of actual and potential demand for CTSA-type services has led to a number of overarching initiatives. These are all designed to provide simple and effective information and advice links for the private sector. Most recently launched has been the new MI5 NSAC website, which was developed with input from NaCTSO. This site complements information available from the Home Office 'terrorism' website and the Cabinet Office CCS 'UK resilience' website. The MI5 'Security Advice' website provides:

- General good practice advice on: physical security, managing staff security – the 'insider threat', protecting your information, planning for an emergency, business continuity and top 10 guidelines.
- Detailed advice on specific forms of attack. The two listed to date are: bomb protection and specific threats to information.

This website is used by CTSAs as a major open-source point of reference for the business community.

Paralleling this development, former AC David Veness, both on his own initiative and in his role as Secretary of ACPO TAM, promoted two projects to assess business counter-terrorism advice needs. These are Project 'Trinity' and Project 'Unicorn'.[9] 'Trinity', developed during 2003 by NaCTSO, was based upon two concepts:

- 'Trinity' – comprising information strategies, business continuity and protective security.

The presence of the 'Trinity' components would allow, once a business has these in place, for it to achieve:

- 'steady state' – where a business is said '… to be in the optimal state to prevent and recover from a terrorist attack – irrespective of the threat level'.

'Trinity' and 'steady state' make up NaCTSO's Commercial Sector Strategy (CCS), which is designed to provide more focused '… dense networks supporting the concept of "sharing is protecting" using open source information within neighbourhoods, business districts and business sectors'. The CCS will link the network of local CTSAs with their local business communities and local authority emergency planning officers.

The advisory information is disseminated through a briefing booklet, CD-Rom, regional workshops and local CTSA activities. The CCS will provide a means of fulfilling the police contribution to the roles and responsibilities of emergency services, as set out in the civil contingencies legislation, section 4(1) with the provision of advice on Business Continuity Information Strategies and Protective Security. A good example of the local availability of advice is provided by the example of the Thames Valley Police 'Crime Reduction' website which includes for '… the business community in the Thames Valley area …' five pages entitled 'Advice to business on chemical or biological attack' based upon inputs from the MI5.[10]

If the new MI5 website and the NaCTSO 'Trinity' approach are taken as major representatives of new public sector approaches to counter-terrorism 'help' for business in the private sector one can see, to what extent, they would meet the private sector concerns as expressed in surveys of the participants in two NaCTSO/ESRC Project Workshops run in February and April 2004. A total group of 70 attended these Workshops and they represented major areas of private sector activity: banking and financial services, transport, utilities, telecommunications, manufacturing, major branded products, major retail chains, the construction industry and consultancy services. Of the total of attendees, 20 per cent returned completed questionnaires, which provides a reasonable survey sample set of data from which the following points emerged. The two major government counter-terrorism/emergencies-related websites, 'ukresilience' and 'homeoffice.gov/terrorism' were used by 71.4 per cent of the respondents. However, 35 per cent of the survey sample still felt that more specific information was needed on the nature of the terrorist threat.

Project 'Unicorn'

Whereas 'Trinity' looked at what the public sector counter-terrorism agencies could provide, by way of help, to the general business community, 'Unicorn' looks the other way and addresses the question as to how the private sector could help the police. 'Unicorn' focused on how the commercial sector in London could help what are called the Guardian Group of (Police) Forces (GGF) in their counter-terrorism role in the Metropolitan area.[11] The Project was commissioned by AC Veness in May 2003 and was supported by eight major commercial sponsors.[12] The project's aim was to:

> Assess the options for enhancing the counter-terrorism effort of the GGF by harnessing the response and capability of the commercial sector and looking for commercial solutions, thus improving the overall co-operation between the GGF and the commercial sector in countering or responding to terrorism.

For the purposes of this section, project 'Unicorn' will be discussed mainly in terms of what GGF learnt about the commercial sector's views on counter-terrorism in the UK. Discussion will also consider 'Unicorn's' role as an example of police outreach to the commercial sector.

The 'Unicorn' Project team found that five significant themes emerged from its study and some of these themes have also been found in the course of the ESRC St Andrews/Southampton Project. These are:

1   The commercial sector felt that there was a lack of a coordinated and structured government counter-terrorism communications policy.
2   The commercial sector felt that there was an absence of an identifiable and publicised centre for counter-terrorism in London.
3   The 'Unicorn' Project felt that potential existed for the private security industry to form part of a 'wider police family' through the role of accreditation envisaged by the Police Reform Act 2002 and under the auspices of the SIA.
4   The 'Unicorn' Project found that there was a need for a better understanding of the CBRN threat.
5   The 'Unicorn' Project found, as has been the experience from workshops run by the ESRC Project with NaCTSO, that counter-terrorism needs, in corporate terms, to move up from recognition by security managers to recognition as a corporate problem at board level.

In addition, Project 'Unicorn' also found that, as of 2003, companies were experiencing variable levels of support and contact from government departments and agencies. In particular, companies complained of the absence of a publicly available government counter-terrorism strategy document. There was also corporate concern that Britain did not have a single, national, public alert/threat warning system, as exists in the USA. As a consequence, companies are producing various forms of 'in-house' alert systems, based upon a wide variety of sources, including, where available, 'vellums'.

Project 'Unicorn' reflected upon what kind of 'drivers' might help to shape a deeper partnership between the wider business community and government agencies. The first 'driver' that 'Unicorn' identified was that there could be the growth of a shared culture of ownership of 'intelligence', as much intelligence can be derived from open sources and also major companies have well developed networks and methods for gathering intelligence related to their commercial operations. This 'driver' could be linked to an expanded understanding of the CNI extending beyond the traditional clients of MI5, to other sectors such as the food industry. Second, the private sector has been brought into closer and more structured relationships with government agencies because of the increased reporting requirements and increased security conditions imposed on certain activities under recent counter-terrorism legislation. Two examples of these new requirements are those relating to the reporting of suspicious transactions and the security of laboratories. In this context, 'Unicorn' made a simple but significant observation that '... the public takes fire precautions and drills for granted; the same should be true for counter-terrorism procedures'. This point was also corroborated by discussions with the private sector at the ESRC Project/NaCTSO workshops, where security and health and safety managers felt that some aspects of counter-terrorism response required of companies could be mainstreamed into health and safety regulations by the Health and Safety Executive.

The 'Unicorn' Project noted the obvious forms of counter-terrorism help that could be provided by the commercial sector, such as communications, transport, civil engineering and construction. However, 'Unicorn', from its studies, was also able to identify two particular commercial sectors that might have special contributions to make to the counter-terrorism response. First, there is the defence industry with products relevant to tasks like surveillance and perimeter protection and, second, the emerging homeland security sector, which offers 'spin-off' products from defence applications, such as CBRN testing kits. Nevertheless, the products of the homeland security sector need to be approached with some caution, as their transferabilty from defence applications to the commercial environment may not always produce the desired results. An example reported to an expert meeting related to a new CBRN detection system deployed on commercial premises in London, which caused a considerable number of false alarms necessitating repeated attendance by blue light services.[13]

The private sector's role as a potential contributor of human resources to the counter-terrorism response

'Unicorn' particularly highlighted the potential contribution that the private sector could make to counter-terrorism response because of the large resource represented by the nearly 500,000 employees of the private security industry. This human resource was of particular interest to the GGF because the emerging regulatory regime for the private security industry should mean that its previously poor reputation would be tackled and a better trained and skilled workforce would become available. The other linked human resource was identified as the company 'security managers', who were described by 'Unicorn' as '... an influential segment of the PSI', especially as many of these managers tended to have a police, military or security service background. One possibility that 'Unicorn' floated, was the exploration of the feasibility of collaborative training between senior PSI managers and senior police service managers. At a lower level of responsibility, 'Unicorn' noted the existence of plans to licence the approximately 80,000 people employed nationwide as door supervisors ('bouncers'); 11,000 of these people work in the GGF area of London. The consideration of the counter-terrorism utility of this group has significance from the recognition of the vulnerability of 'soft' targets, as shown by the Bali night-club bombing.

For the GGF, these possible emergency personnel sources represent a much greater human resource pool than is available, in terms of their normal reserves. Currently, the GGF only has available about 900 special constables. An interesting industry initiative here is that the retail industry in London is permitting '... release from work for [SIA] training and for some activities of special constables ...'.[14] In contrast, in the area bounded by the M25, there are approximately 38,000 people employed in private sector security posts. At present, the only public sector reserve enhancement that the GGF can expect, is that by the end of 2004 some 1,450 police CSOs will be appointed under powers provided in the Police Reform Act 2002. Not withstanding the attractiveness of considering the utilisation of this large private sector human resource reserve, the 'Unicorn' Project noted that PSI employees could not, at present, also become special constables and that even the CSOs were not intended to have a counter-terrorism role.

What is very evident, from project 'Unicorn', is that three years after 9/11 there were still gaps in government counter-terrorism policy coverage, insofar as there is public knowledge of it, and that there are still gaps in the outreach to the wider private sector community. The significance of this conclusion for the police in general and the GGF in particular is reflected in the following points:

1   The public sector needs information about the forms and levels of trained support that it could call upon from the wider public, beyond the traditional voluntary services such as Red Cross, St John's and the WRVS.
2   If the commercial sector enhances its counter-terrorism awareness and its own consequent 'due diligence' response, that will greatly improve the potential levels of business continuity and resilience.
3   In particular, the PSI, broadly defined, offers a valuable human and other resource multiplier potential for incident and consequence management. This was illustrated after one of the 7 July London bombings when a Marks & Spencer's store near one of the Tube Stations allowed people with damaged clothes to just come in and select fresh clothes from the store.

Private sector response – general issues

A common feature of business surveys is that 'preparedness' to meet resilience challenges such as terrorism is a variable attribute partly dependent on business size.[15] In November 2003 NaCTSO and 'London First' surveyed 152 businesses across London which fell into the four employee-size categories of the EC's business classification survey. In this sample 40 per cent were large businesses, 22 per cent medium, 21 per cent small and 17 per cent micro. The survey found that 65 per cent had a written security policy and 59 per cent a business continuity plan but these results were '... skewed towards the large and medium sized businesses'. In general, the survey found that counter-terrorism advice was not '... effectively reaching the small business sector', a factor with some implications for the potential service disruption to local communities. It certainly is not the case that information is unavailable, it can be found online from a variety of sources ranging through the police CTSAs, MI5, government regional offices and local authority emergency planning departments.[16] However, more generally it appears that '... the majority of businesses do not perceive themselves to be a primary target for terrorist attack ... [though] ... the larger the business the more likely it is to view itself as a primary target'.[17] Additionally, businesses, especially small and medium sized enterprises, are already striving to cope with a wide range of government statutory and advisory requirements. This point was made forcibly to a police officer inquiring about control procedures in a chemical supply company. The officer was directed to look at the massive folder of control procedures that the company was obliged to comply with in respect of transactions.[18]

Marks & Spencer have posted a very useful analysis of their experience in the 1996 Manchester city centre bombing on the 'London Prepared' website and the following general issues can be drawn from this case study:[19]

*   Marks & Spencer were at their company's level 2 security status but that status, unlike level 1, did not involve the permanent manning of the CCTV systems.
*   Two pre-planned store evacuation sites were unusable, the first because it was too near the suspect vehicle, the second because it came within the police wider cordon area. Therefore personnel had to be evacuated to an unplanned point – Victoria Railway Station – not a safe location as the blast shattered the station roof injuring 240 people including 10 Marks & Spencer staff. Now Marks & Spencer have secondary evacuation points for all stores at least 600–800 metres from the store.
*   Importance of realistic emergency training exercises – Marks & Spencer commented that 'One of the most important issues we had to face was the Manchester management team had never experienced the devastation caused by the two London bombs at St Mary Axe and Bishopsgate. In consequence, they had no relative scale of experience to the damage assessment and devastation that they had witnessed to the perimeter of our store'.
*   The importance of post-incident care of staff.
*   The need to be prepared for the positive and negative aspects of media attention.

In addressing their post-incident lessons Marks & Spencer came up with their own '4Ps' strategy: 'people' issues, 'press', 'product' (maintaining corporate reputation) and 'premises' (knowing accurately the contents of premises is vital for salvage purposes). The post-incident strengths of a large business are well illustrated by the fact that Marks & Spencer could announce, four weeks after the bombing, that they would open two new sites in Manchester to re-establish their trading position.

Several points of general relevance to the private sector–public sector links in counter-terrorism arise from this case study:

1   Is it feasible for private sector alert states to reflect, in content, more closely public sector alert states? The company's CCTV could have been important in detecting a potential suicide bomber.
2   Evacuation area plans may need to have greater flexibility in location terms.
3   Private sector preparedness and resilience will need to be the subject of continual monitoring through the appropriate procedures of the relevant government departments and private sector mechanisms such as insurance requirements.

Notes

1 Lewis, Leigh (2004) Terrorism – policing the unknown', Speech to the Police Federation Annual Conference, 20 May, Bournemouth, available at www.homeoffice. gov.uk/docs3/speech_policefed.html, accessed 3 June 2004.
2 Information from ESRC/Willis Group Workshop, October 2003.
3 London Prepared, 'Business continuity advice', available at www.londonprepared. gov.uk/business/businesscont/, accessed 27 July 2004.
4 New Business, 'Make your business continuity plans now', available at www. newbusiness.co.uk/cgi-bin/showArticle.pl?id=2065, accessed 27 July 2004.
5 House of Commons Transport Committee, Twelfth Report of Session 2003–04 (2004) *British Transport Police*, HC 488, June, London: The Stationery Office, Ev.5, Q.33.
6 *Hansard*, House of Commons Debates, 16 June 2004, col. 883, 'Door Staff Registration', Mr Andrew Turner, MP (Isle of Wight), available at www.publications. parliament.uk/pa/cm200304/cmhansard/cm040616/debtext/40…, accessed 28 July 2004.
7 Oral Evidence to the Defence and Home Affairs Committees joint inquiry into 'Homeland Security', HC 417-I, 2 March 2004, Q.25.
8 Oral Evidence by Sir David Omand to the joint Home Affairs Committee and Defence Committee inquiry into 'Homeland Security' HC 417-I, 2 March 2004, Q.75.
9 Information on 'Trinity' and 'Unicorn' was kindly supplied for the use of the ESRC Project by the Head of NaCTSO. See also the paper/lecture by A.C. Veness.
10 Thames Valley Police, Crime Prevention website, www.thamesvalley.police.uk/crime-reduction/ad_bus.htm, accessed 28 July 2004.
11 The Guardian Group of Forces comprises the Metropolitan Police Service, City of London Police and those parts of the BTP and MDP stationed in London.
12 See reference to Unicorn in Veness, D. (2003) 'The fight against terrorism: achieving a new balanced normality', *RUSI Journal*, 148(4), August, p. 17.
13 DADA, Committee Meeting 2004.
14 Oral evidence by the Home Secretary to the joint Home Affairs Committee and Defence Committee inquiry into 'Homeland Security', HC 417-I, 2 March 2004, Q.25.
15 A number of 'checklists' are available to businesses, e.g. 'Guide to Business Continuity Management', PAS 56:2003, BSI & BCI, see also Stokes, M. and Platten, M. (2004) *Measuring and Rewarding Business Resilience – An Insurer's Perspective*, Zurich Management Services Ltd.
16 See, for example, from a random online search: Buckinghamshire County Council Emergency Planning Unit (2004) 'News & information update', July, available at www.buckscc.gov.uk/emergency_planning/news_information_update.htm, accessed 28 July 2004, and the Government Office for the East Midlands 'resilience' home pages at www.go-em.gov.uk/resilience/civl-contingencies.php?x=0, accessed 28 July 2004.
17 NaCTSO (2004) *NaCTSO and London First 2003 Business Survey Summary*.
18 Information from Project Chemical Terrorism Workshop, March 2004.
19 Marks & Spencer, *The Manchester Experience*, available at www.londonprepared. gov.uk/business/businesscont/, accessed 27 July 2004.

Part IV

Civil contingencies and emergency response

17 UK draft Civil Contingencies Bill 2003 and the subsequent Act

Building block for homeland security?

Frank Gregory

Introduction[1]

Unlike the USA, the UK has chosen not to have a single main response framework to post-9/11 emergencies, as represented by the US DHS. The UK government's response has three separate but related elements: civil contingencies legislation, specific anti-terrorism measures including export controls on WMD materials, and a linked civil protection capabilities enhancement programme. This chapter focuses on the first of these – the Civil Contingencies Bill 2003 (Command Paper 5843), which proceeded in Draft form to its Committee stage before a joint House of Commons and House of Lords Scrutiny Committee in Autumn 2003, and went in its final form (Bill 14, 53/3, 7 January 2004) through Parliament in November 2004.

It is important to note that this legislation represents much more than just a response to 9/11. It has its origins in an emergency planning review ordered by the Deputy Prime Minister following the fuel and flood crises of 2000. Moreover, it is also a long-overdue updating of UK legislation in this area as the previous Emergency Powers Act was passed in 1920. Although the Civil Protection in Peacetime Act 1986 (c.22), which originated in a Private Bill sponsored by the National Council for Civil Protection, did allow civil defence resources to be used for emergencies other than military attacks. However, the Act clearly does reflect the impact of 9/11 on UK contingency planning, a process described by Professor Peter Hennessy as putting the UK '... on the way to becoming a proper civil defence nation for the first time since the Second World War ...'[2] and by the government as '... reflecting the move from Cold War civil defence to modern civil protection'.[3]

Three key terms are used in the legislation and the Cabinet Office's Consultation Document:[4]

- Emergency – a situation or event that threatens human welfare, the environment, or the security of the UK (author's précis).
- Civil protection – '... concerned with events or situations that are likely to have an impact on numerous individuals and that generally require a timely and immediate response to limit the harm to the public'.

- Resilience – '… the ability – at every level – to anticipate, pre-empt and resolve challenges into healthy outcomes'.

The Act itself represents an enabling framework to address emergencies, civil protection and resilience.[5] It has no new provisions relating to the role of the military as section 2 of the Emergency Powers Act 1964 (c.38) will remain in force. This will continue to provide '… the legislative underpinning for Military Aid to Government Departments'.[6] The military's new support contribution, the CCRF, has been under development since late 2002 and CCRF units of around 500, mainly reservists, are potentially available, *subject* to the demands of other military duties, in up to 12 hours call-out time in each region.[7] Furthermore, no new duties are placed on the security and intelligence services although the Emergency Planning Society (EPS) has suggested that local authority emergency planning officers will need better access to confidential information, for example 'Vellums',[8] if they are to meet the enhanced emergency planning requirements.[9]

The Act also does *not* contain any specific budgetary or other forms of resource enhancement provision. Furthermore, it has to demonstrate adherence to good governance principles by considering the burdens and impact of legislation. However, critics of the Act have suggested that the government has perhaps underestimated these in its Regulatory Impact Assessments. So, clearly the Act does not represent a 'big problem/big bucks' type of response. The government's approach to resilience, as a key element in contingency management, has five strands and includes some financial provisions:

- improved horizon scanning activity to identify and assess potential disruptive challenges and so develop integrated responses;
- increased investment in capabilities that underpin emergency responses;
- an enhanced counter-terrorist framework including investment in operational facilities and new legislation;
- an emphasis across government on improved business continuity arrangements;
- the new civil contingencies legislation as represented by this Act.

The initial aims of the legislation were supported by 94 per cent of local authorities, on whom many new responsibilities fall under the Act, because it is felt that, building on existing local networks and, subject to adequate funding, it '… will drive up standards, … end the piecemeal approach and improve consistency across the country'.[10]

The Bill stage of legislation

The Bill was designed to deliver '… a single framework for civil protection …'[11] in the UK and was widely commented on from many quarters. For example, the Chief Executive to the Highland Council described the Bill as '… placing significant new emphases on anticipating and dealing with risk, prevention, resilience and or business continuity'.[12] Liberty (the National Council for Civil Liberties) considered that the Bill was '… the most powerful piece of peace time legislation ever proposed, in seeking to grant the Government unprecedented and draconian powers'.[13] Indeed, because of the powers in the Bill, the House of Commons Defence Select Committee felt that the government should actually say whether it would have used such powers in respect of recent emergencies, such as floods and the fuel crisis.[14]

Part 1, section 1 of the Bill covered local arrangements for civil protection and provides definitions of an emergency and threats to human welfare. In addition, it specified terrorism as defined in section 1 of the Terrorism Act 2000, as one of the threats to security referred to in the Bill. One of the criticisms of this part of the Bill was that it proposes a very wide range of possible occurrences, which could be deemed *emergencies*. Part 1, section 2 of the Bill referred to contingency planning duty, which is defined as the duty to assess, plan and advise. This duty is laid upon any person or body listed in Part 1, Schedule 1 and includes a requirement to give advice and assistance to business. Those listed are termed Category 1 responders and these include the local authorities and the emergency services. An important omission that has been commented upon, was the absence, in Part 1, of any reference to central government's national responsibilities.[15] The legislation provided for Category 1 responders to receive the cooperation of those bodies listed under Part 3 of Schedule 1 (Category 2 responders), for example, power, water or telecommunication utilities, railway operators, airport and harbour operators and the health and safety executive. This is an important provision because, reflecting the consequences of the policies of privatising nationalised industries, as Sir David Omand, the former Security and Intelligence Coordinator has noted, 'Nowadays the "critical national infrastructure"… is almost entirely in private hands …'.[16]

Part 2 of the Bill detailed the actual emergency powers that are proposed and included a new regional element in contingency management in subsection 24. This subsection allows for the appointment of an emergency coordinator for Wales and Scotland and for a regional nominated coordinator for each English and Welsh region. This innovation reflects the importance that the government attaches to the relatively new regional government tier. However, some questions have been raised about the 'value added' of the regional level in contingency management. Partly this is because the regional offices' roles are limited to planning facilitation, support and aiding linkages to central government. Additionally, there is concern that the government's regional boundaries do not always reflect actual working or even infrastructure linkages. For example, Deputy Chief Constable Alan Goldsmith of the Lincolnshire Police pointed out, in Oral Evidence to the Joint Committee on the Bill, that in the East Midlands Region there were no linkages between Lincolnshire and Northhamptonshire.[17]

Emergency powers, set out in Part 2, in response to a situation deemed by the appropriate Minister to come within the scope of this legislation could be promulgated under the Act either by a Royal Proclamation or, by an innovation of this Act, through a Declaration by a Secretary of State, if the formalities of a Royal Proclamation were difficult to observe. In either case emergency powers can only, initially, last for 30 days. The powers may not be used to require people to provide military or industrial service or to prohibit strikes. Among the powers that may be promulgated are those to requisition, destroy or confiscate property (with or without compensation), the prohibition of assemblies and the prohibition of movement or travel. The Cabinet Office argued, in the Consultation Document, that three guiding principles, the 'triple lock', are a guard against possible misuse of the powers. These are 'seriousness' to warrant emergency powers, genuine need for special legislation and application in the minimum geographical area possible.[18] However, as the House of Commons Defence Select Committee pointed out, the requirement to meet this 'triple lock' criteria was not specified in the Bill.[19]

Responses to the Bill

There were a number of trenchant comments about civil liberties and human rights. These criticisms referred to: the wide parameters of the definition of emergency, the subjective element in the determination of the need to promulgate emergency powers and the challenge to human rights protection. Liberty made the point that, in practice, the UK has only declared 12 states of emergency since 1920, the last being in 1974 and '… only ever in times of industrial unrest'.[20] Similarly, it was noted by Mr Philip Selwood, of the Ambulance Services Association, in Oral Evidence to the Joint Committee on the Bill, that '… most major emergencies, particularly in the capital, have been resolved without such legislation'.[21] The EPS and the Local Government Association (LGA) consider that more precision should be introduced in the Bill. For example, the Bill should contain a 'trigger point' for an event to be considered as a serious threat. This trigger point could be derived from the terminology used in the government's *Dealing with Disaster* document.

Given the increased responsibilities placed upon Category 1 responders, especially local authorities, a significant number of criticisms refer to the Bill containing no specific clauses on the financing of civil protection. This is seen as particularly problematic because the then very small and earmarked civil defence grant (£19 million) was being subsumed in the General Revenue Support Grant to local authorities. The government's view is that the '… current level of funding is sufficient to support the basic responsibility of local authorities that flow from the Bill.[22] Both the EPS and the LGA hotly disputed this view. Arguing that even, as now, the top tier authorities spend an additional £17 million on emergency planning and the district authorities spend an additional £4 million, the total is not even really sufficient for current needs. In fact, 90 per cent of the respondents to the draft Bill felt that the present funding allocations were insufficient. Moreover, it has been pointed out '… underfunding of a statutory obligation to plan for emergencies is likely to lead to either inadequate performance of the statutory duty or funds transferred from other services …'.[23]

In addition to these criticisms of what might be termed recurrent expenditure provision, the EPS pointed to a need for capital grants to fund infrastructure improvements to meet enhanced risks. The EPS said 'We find it surprising that the new "CBRN Guidance for Local Authorities" states that local authorities should consider having backup emergency control centres, when previous Government advice has been that there is no funding available for one such centre, let alone two'.[24] Finally, on the financial side there is concern that the government has done nothing to address, as it once indicated it would, the placing of the discretionary Bellwin Scheme for compensating local authorities on a statutory footing as a central contributions fund to cover all costs including from terrorist attacks. Terrorist attacks were not covered in the Bellwin Scheme and compensation came from special *ad hoc* provision.[25] The government did not review the Bellwin Scheme during the passage of the Bill but after the Bill became law a review by the Office of the Deputy Prime Minister concluded that the scheme remained 'fit for purpose' whilst offering some possibilities of potential routes to extra funding.[26] An outcome that is not likely to seem very positive from a local authority's perspective.

During the Oral Evidence sessions before the Joint Committee on the Bill, Mr Douglas Alexander, MP, Minister of State at the Cabinet Office, indicated that the government was quite willing to consider meeting some of the concerns, including the provision of some formal statement of central government responsibilities, in the preparation of the final version of the Bill to go before Parliament.[27] Particularly, he gave assurances that the government would look at ways of incorporating the 'trigger' definition of 'emergency' and the 'triple lock' safeguard provisions into the actual legislation. He also accepted that perhaps the range of potential categories of 'emergency' situations had been drawn too widely in the draft Bill. The urgent need to address such issues, in the final Bill, of a too all-embracing set of definitions of emergencies, the need for the 'triple lock' safeguard to be in one clause or adjacent clauses and clarification of key terms such as 'serious' was also stressed by Joint Committee on the Bill.[28]

Not surprisingly, the Minister felt that the current and projected financial allocations were adequate. However, this is certainly a challengeable assumption. First, until all enhanced contingency planning and risk assessment work required by the legislation has been carried out, and this work and the related resource provisions have been audited or otherwise subject to inspection, it will be impossible to know how requirements and resources match up. Second, the Minister referred to recent funding increases to local authorities and emergency services being of the order of 35 per cent. However, for emergency responses any increases are from a previously very low baseline. These funding concerns were strongly supported in the Report of the Joint Committee on the Bill.[29] The Joint Committee also noted the similar concerns raised by some of the utilities, for example, BT, Western Power Distribution and CE Electric UK, over the potential costs and human resource demands required by the Bill for information provision, additional training, participation in enhanced cooperation fora[30] and because the legislation set national response standards for Category 1 and 2 responders.[31]

The Minister, predictably, responded robustly to questions about whether the government should have actually provided for a UK Department of Homeland Security by re-emphasising the Home Secretary's primary responsibility for the safety and security of the population, the action-coordinating role of the Cabinet Office, CCS, and the value of relying upon the expertise of particular 'lead departments', as required by particular emergencies. However, opinion outside government is still not fully convinced about the adequacy of those arrangements. For example, the 2003 Report of the Commons Science and Technology Select Committee, whilst accepting that the UK did not need an actual Department for Homeland Security, did '… recommend the creation of a Centre for Home Defence as a Government agency …' under the Home Office.[32] This was because the Committee did not feel that the Home Office, as the 'lead' counter-terrorist department, had sufficient oversight expertise to direct efforts to counter potential CBRN terrorist threats. Whilst the Joint Committee on the Bill was unable to comment on this proposal in its Report it did put forward its own strong recommendation that a Civil Contingencies Agency should be set up, reporting to the Home Office and Parliament, to provide a source of contingency management expertise and to audit the outcomes of the contingency planning required in the Bill. Indeed, given Home Secretary John Reid's very public comments on the state of the Home Office as an effective government department one can reasonably suggest that there may have been some negative impacts on its 'lead department' counter-terrorism responsibilities

The Civil Contingencies Bill as laid before Parliament in January 2004[33]

Referring to the revised Bill, Home Office Minister Hazel Blears said of concerns about balancing emergency powers and civil liberties '… it is always difficult to get the balance absolutely right but that is what we are striving to do'.[34] Indeed, the Director of Liberty, Shami Chakrabarti, noted that the '… government has taken a step in the right direction …' although the Director still felt that the '… present proposals remain worrisome …'.[35] An important related change to the Bill came in January 2004 with the government withdrawing clause 25 which had sought to treat emergency regulations as primary legislation and was thus immune from challenge under section 3 of the Human Rights Act.[36]

In brief, the final version of the Bill did show important changes reflecting notice taken of criticisms of the draft Bill. First, there had been some reduction of the potential scope of the Bill (see Part 1(1) and (2) and Part 2(19)(1) and (19)(2)) with the removal of the vague causal factor of a threat to political, administrative or economic stability. Also education has been removed from the list of activities whose disruption could cause emergency powers to be introduced. However, these new limitations have to be set against the new Part 1(2)(4) which allows a Minister to add '– a specified event or situation or class of event or situation –'[37] as falling within the scope of Part 1(1)(a)–(c) as constituting an emergency. Thus it has been pointed out in the legislation '– the definition of emergency still contained a catch-all element'.[38] Second, and importantly, the government did place the 'triple lock' safeguards within the Bill at Part 2(21) which is linked to Part 2(20). Moreover, parliamentary scrutiny and oversight powers have been increased by Part 2(27). The Responders Schedules have been made more comprehensive by the inclusion of the Chief Constable of the PSNI and local Health Boards in the list of Category 1 responders and by adding road transport routes to Category 2 responders by virtue of listing 'The Secretary of State, in so far as his functions relate to matters for which he is responsible by virtue of section 1 of the Highways Act 1980 (c.66) (highway authorities)'.

The Civil Contingencies Act 2004 (c.36) received its Royal Assent in November 2004 and came into force in April 2005. The Act plus accompanying non-statutory measures is expected, according to the Cabinet Office to '… deliver a single framework for civil protection in the UK'.[39] Civil liberties groups remained concerned about the potential scope of the Act. Statewatch called the Act 'Britain's Patriot Act'[40] and was particularly concerned that, unlike the Emergency Planning Act 1920, the requirement for the, publicly, very high profile requirement for a State of Emergency to be declared by a Royal Proclamation was replaced by the lower visibility means of either the Sovereign making an Order in Council for emergency regulations (Part 2, 20(1)) or a senior Minister promulgating emergency regulations (Part 2, 20(2)).

In their commentaries on the Act local authorities have laid stress on what they term the '… two key new concepts …' arising out of the Act. First, there is the introduction of the statutory process of the Local Resilience Forum (LRF), chaired by the local Chief Constable, to provide the 'principal forum for multi-agency cooperation under the Act'. Second, the Act requires systematic risk assessment, risk and information provision which must be carried out by the LRF and for which duties the LRF must produce a Community Risk Register.[41] Additionally for local authorities, from May 2006 the duty under the Act (Part 1, 4(1)) for local authorities to give business continuity advice came into force. However, police forces draw a distinction in practice between the published risk assessments which will only cover non-malicious events, that is, hazards and risk assessments relating to threats such as terrorism. Threat-based risk assessments will, of course, be carried out but for obvious reasons their contents will not be published. Although the police forces do identify 'typical threat scenarios that are being considered …' and give the examples of conventional attacks using explosives, CBRN threats and electronic attacks which might affect utilities and communications.[42] Furthermore, where public or private sector bodies might be affected by such threat assessments they can expect to receive advice either directly from the NSAC or the CTSAs within each police force.

Conclusion

The main practical relevance of the Act for the domestic management of terrorism in the UK, post-9/11, is to be found only partly by the inclusion of terrorism (defined under Part 1, 18(1) by reference to section 1 of the Terrorism Act

2000 (c.11)) as one of the three types of 'emergency' covered by the Act (Part 1, 1(c)). For the domestic management of terrorism in the UK, it is argued that the significance of the Act lies, first, in the necessity for both Category 1 and 2 responders to factor in terrorism as part of their emergency risk assessment and risk management duties, as required under the Act (Part 1, 2(a)–(h)). Second, in respect of the response to terrorism the Act is significant, *if* the government's powers to monitor and enforce, if necessary, responders' duties (Parts 1, 9, 10 and 11) are rigorously and regularly used with respect to both the public and private sectors.[43] There are two examples of comprehensive national monitoring exercises. First, the Regional Capability Mapping Exercise which was led by the Department for Communities and Local Government in 2003–4. Second, there is the more comprehensive National Capabilities Survey, launched in February 2006. It is stated that 'The survey will play a key role in assessing the UK's readiness to respond to a range of disruptive challenges, be they terrorist attacks or natural hazards such as flooding. The results of the survey will help to improve our understanding of national preparedness and inform priorities for future investment, exercises and policy development.'[44]

The Act thus offers a reasonable framework for addressing contingency planning and response, in respect of terrorism, based upon more comprehensive assessments. The Act has also been backed up by the issuing of two guidance documents by the Cabinet Office CCS: *Emergency Preparedness* and *Emergency Response and Recovery*. However, for the Act to be a true 'building block' for homeland security or civil protection, there still remains the key assumption that appropriate financial and other resources will be available. Also, the important elements of the nature of central government oversight, the capability of 'lead departments' and the regional level contribution may need further consideration.

(An earlier version of this chapter was published in (2004) *Jane's Intelligence Review* 10(1), January, pp. 18–21.)

Notes

1 For convenience, unless otherwise indicated in the text, all references to the legislation are taken from the final version of the Bill as passed in 2004.

2 Hennessy, Professor P. (2003) 'The secret state revisited: part I', *RUSI Journal*, 148(4), August, p. 19.

3 Cabinet Office (2003) *Draft Civil Contingencies Bill*, Consultation Document, June, p. 9.

4 Ibid., pp. 12–15. Details from the draft Bill are taken from (2003) *The Draft Civil Contingencies Bill*, Cm. 5843, Cabinet Office, June.

5 For a comprehensive assessment see Walker, C. and Broderick, J. (2006) *The Civil Contingencies Act 2004: Risk, Resilience and the Law in the United Kingdom*, Oxford: Oxford University Press.

6 Cm. 5843, op. cit., p. 29.

7 Seventh Report of the Commons Defence Select Committee (2003) *Draft Civil Contingencies Bill*, HC 557, Session 2002–2003, London: The Stationery Office, July, Minutes of Evidence, 26 March 2003, paras. 208–21.

8 'Vellums' are low-security classified briefing papers.

9 Cunningham, P., Chair, Local Authorities Professional Issues Group, Emergency Planning Society (2003) *Response of the Emergency Planning Society to the Draft Civil Contingencies Bill*, Emergency Planning Society, 1 September.

10 Councillor P. Chalke, CBE, Deputy Chairman of the Local Government Association, Oral Evidence to the Joint Committee on the Draft Civil Contingencies Bill, 9 September 2003, 2002–03, HC 1074, HL 184.

11 Cabinet Office, op. cit., p. 5.

12 The Highland Council (2003) *Civil Contingencies Bill*, Report by the Chief Executive, 11 September, submitted as a response to the Draft Bill.

13 Liberty (2003) *Response to the Draft Civil Contingencies Bill*, London: Liberty (National Council for Civil Liberties), August.

14 HC 557, op. cit., para. 61.

15 Ibid., para. 24.

16 Omand, Sir David, Security and Intelligence Coordinator and Permanent Secretary, Cabinet Office (2003) 'The secret state revisited: part II', *RUSI Journal*, 148(4), August, p. 26.

17 Deputy Chief Constable Alan Goldsmith, Lincolnshire Police, Chair of the ACPO Emergency Planning Committee, Oral Evidence to the Joint Committee on the Bill, 9 September 2003.

18 Cabinet Office, op. cit., p. 28.

19 HC 557, op. cit., p. 30.

20 Liberty, op. cit.

21 Mr P. Selwood, Chair of the Ambulance Services Association Civil Emergencies Committee, Oral Evidence to the Joint Committee on the Bill, 9 September 2003.

22 Cabinet Office, op. cit., p. 20.

23 Barclay, C. (2004) *The Civil Contingencies Bill, Bill 14 of 2003–2004*, House of Commons Library Research Paper 04/07, 15 January, p. 26.

24 Cunningham, Emergency Planning Society, 1 September 2003, op. cit.

25 Ibid.

26 Walker and Broderick, op. cit., pp. 278–9.

27 Mr Douglas Alexander, MP, Minister of State at the Cabinet Office, Oral Evidence to the Joint Committee on the Bill, 16 October 2003.

28 Report of the Joint Committee of the Lords and Commons on the Draft Civil Contingencies Bill (2003) *The Draft Civil Contingencies Bill*, HL 184/HC 1074, Session 2002–2003, November, online version, <parliament.uk>), Summary of Recommendations.

29 Ibid.

30 Ibid., paras 115–18.

31 Ibid.

32 Eighth Report of the Commons Science and Technology Select Committee (2003) *The Scientific Response to Terrorism*, HC 415-I, Session 2002–2003, London: The Stationery Office, November, p. 77, and see also HL 184/HC 1074, op. cit., para. 256.

33 See further the (2004) *Civil Contingencies Bill [Bill 14] Explanatory Notes (Bill-14 – EN)*, January, London: The Stationery Office.

34 As cited in (2004) *The Times*, 7 January.

35 Barclay, op. cit., p. 44.

36 Walker and Broderick, op. cit., p. 218.

37 Civil Contingencies Bill (Bill 14).

38 Barclay, op. cit., p. 17.

39 Cabinet Office (2004) *Civil Contingencies Bill gets Royal Assent*, 18 November, available at www.cabinet office.gov.uk/newsroom/news_releases/2004/041118_ccbill.asp, accessed 27 June 2006.

40 Statewatch (2004) *UK Civil Contingencies Bill: Britain's Patriot Act – Revised and Just as Dangerous as Before*, available at http://statewatch.org/news/2004/jan/12uk-civil-contingencies-bill-revised.htm, accessed 27 June 2006.

41 See particularly *Civil Contingencies Act 2004*, available at www.devon.gov.uk/index/democracycommunities/publicsafety/emergencies/em…, and similarly www.eastsussex.gov.uk/community/emergencyplanningandcommunitysafety/e, accessed 28 June 2006.

42 *Civil Contingencies Act 2004*, available at www.dyfed.powys.police.uk/Civil-Contingency-Act.sht, accessed 28 June 2006.

43 See further comments on the issues of auditing and embedding resilience in Walker and Broderick, op. cit., pp. 27–9 and p. 296.

44 *National Resilience Survey, 2006*, available at www.ukresilience.info/preparedness/ukgovernment/survey.shtm, accessed 28 June 2006.

18 The emergency response

Progress and problems

Anthony Richards

Introduction

The emergency response to a major terrorist incident falls under the purview of the fourth 'P' of the government's counter-terrorism strategy – 'preparing' for the consequences.[1] In the course of our research to assess the preparedness of our emergency services and other emergency responders for a major terrorist attack in the UK a number of personnel from the fire and rescue service, the ambulance service, the police, and local authorities were consulted. The general impression is that while London has made significant progress in its emergency preparedness this has not necessarily been replicated outside the capital.[2] Indeed, while the London Resilience Forum is seen as a role model for other regions in the country, the regional tier advocated in the Civil Contingencies Bill is as yet underdeveloped outside London. It is natural enough to prioritise our capital city when enhancing our emergency response (and this was clearly demonstrated by the 7 July 2005 attacks and attempted attacks two weeks later) but the nature of the threat (including simultaneous bomb attacks and a willingness to hit 'soft' targets if other targets are 'hardened') informs us that any major cities in the UK could be earmarked for attack.

This is not to say that London's preparedness could not be improved. Our research has identified the urgent need for the emergency services, and particularly the fire and rescue service, to be able to detect and identify biological and chemical agents at the scene of an incident. This in turn will enable the emergency responders to use the appropriate Personal Protection Equipment (PPE), rather than having to fall back on the all hazards gas suits, and will therefore allow maximum mobility and operational duration. It will also allow the ambulance service to administer the right antidotes more quickly. In addition, our research has discovered the need to review decontamination procedures with a view to moving towards what former Assistant Commissioner of the Metropolitan Police, David Veness, has termed 'post-bucket' decontamination.[3] The issue of emergency service communications also needs considerable attention, especially after the failings highlighted by the London Assembly report into the 7 July 2005 attacks.

The Civil Contingencies Act, the Capabilities Programme and Dealing with Disasters

In July 2001 the government established the Civil Contingencies Secretariat (CCS) in order to review emergency planning arrangements in England and Wales. While it was initially set up in response to the fuel protests, the foot and mouth disease outbreak, and flooding in 2000, it was given a whole new impetus after the terrorist attacks on New York on 11 September 2001. In June 2003 the Cabinet Office launched the draft Civil Contingencies Bill which aimed 'to set our clear expectations and responsibilities – from front line responders through the regions and to central government departments' and to 'deliver robust performance management of civil protection activity at all levels to ensure operational effectiveness and financial efficiency'.[4] The Civil Contingencies Act, when it was approved by Parliament in 2004, was the first wholesale revision of UK emergency legislation since the 1920s.

Emergency planning is a devolved responsibility in Scotland but the Scottish Executive agreed that 'the civil protection provisions in [the] Civil Contingencies Bill being introduced in Westminster should extend to Scotland'[5] through the Civil Contingencies Resilience Unit in the Justice Department. In Northern Ireland civil protection is the responsibility of the Central Emergency Planning Unit (CEPU) in the Office of the First and Deputy First Minister. Although the province is considering the implications of the Civil Contingencies Bill as a whole it also has its own 'Northern Ireland Standards in Civil Protection'.

Coordinated through the CCS has been the new Capabilities Programme which 'is the core framework through which the Government is seeking to build resilience across all parts of the United Kingdom'.[6] The programme consists of 17 workstreams, each of which is the responsibility of a designated lead department,[7] and covers all parts of the UK.

On the same day as the Civil Contingencies Bill was produced the revised third edition of *Dealing with Disasters* was published which 'collates the principles of co-operation which guide the multi-agency response to, and management and resolution of, a major incident'[8] and which 'provides the Government's core guidance to emergency planners and local responders'.[9] This latest edition, however, was described by the Cabinet Office as an interim revision and that 'a more substantial revision leading to a fourth edition will be undertaken to take account of changes which arise following the introduction of new civil contingencies legislation' and this would pay more attention to 'the response to CBRN incidents, mass evacuation, decontamination, widespread emergencies, public information and so on'.[10] In Scotland *Dealing With Disasters Together* was published in April 2003 while *A Guide To Emergency Planning Arrangements in Northern Ireland*, which draws from 'and closely follows' *Dealing With Disaster*, was published in July 2004.

There has been much discussion and debate over the new civil contingencies legislation. One issue that led to an amendment of the Civil Contingencies Bill revolved around the matter of human rights. Concerns were raised that the Bill as it stood could have undermined human rights, largely because the definition of an emergency was seen as too broad and so could have led to unnecessary denial of freedoms. In the draft bill an emergency was defined as 'an event which presents a serious threat to human welfare, the environment, political, administrative, or economic stability, and the security of the UK or part of it' but, under pressure from human rights organisations and other groups, the government amended this definition to an event which 'threatens serious damage to human welfare, the environment or the security of the UK or part of it' hence excluding threats to 'political, administrative, or economic stability' as justification for enacting emergency powers.

In the numerous responses to the draft Civil Contingencies Bill from, for example, local authorities, the emergency services and the Emergency Planning Society (EPS), a number of other issues have been raised. There has, for instance, been much debate over the definition of an emergency, and as to who should be Category 1 and Category 2 responders, and there has been criticism over the underdevelopment of, and confusion over, the function of the regional tier,[11] as well as reservations over the lack of central coordination through the nomination of different lead government departments for different types of emergency.[12] One of the most common criticisms of the Bill, however, is that while it outlines extra responsibilities for the emergency services and local authorities it reveals very little on how these duties will be resourced.

London's emergency response

London Emergency Services Liaison Panel, the London Regional Resilience Forum and the London Resilience Team

As noted above, our research leads us to the conclusion that emergency preparedness outside the capital is not as advanced as it is in London, to some degree because the 'regionalisation' (envisaged in the civil contingencies legislation) of our response has yet to develop and also because equipment takes longer to 'roll out' on a nationwide basis (such as that under the Fire Service's New Dimensions project). As the London Regional Resilience Forum (LRRF) is seen as the role model for other regional resilience teams it would seem logical to assess London's emergency preparedness first in order to identify areas for improvement that may then be of use to other regions as they develop their own responses.

The problem of Irish terrorism over a period of 30 years has meant that the emergency services in London have acquired extensive experience in responding to terrorist related emergencies. In the early years of the 'Troubles' the different services were not that well coordinated – for example, the police would be interested in gathering evidence, ambulance service personnel would walk over it and the fire service would be dousing it.[13] Greater coordination was initially achieved through the London Emergency Services Liaison Panel (LESLP) which was established in 1973 and which 'tied things together'. Through the LESLP the emergency services have acquired a greater understanding of:

1   dealing with large numbers of casualties;
2   dealing with a fairly large area of devastation;
3   working carefully together.[14]

The LRRF and London Resilience Team (LRT) were formed in the aftermath of 11 September 2001. The Forum 'oversees the work of London Resilience, … [and] is composed of senior officials representing the main emergency organisations'.[15]

It appears that the LRT has worked well, providing a coordinated response from the emergency services and other agencies. In fact, one senior London Ambulance Service source remarked how this compared favourably with his experience of the US emergency services in Washington. Recounting his visits there following 11 September 2001, he stated that there were some examples of good practice but very little liaison and that as a result there is duplication of the police and fire department roles in New York. His impression of the US response was 'that there is lots of kit, greater urgency but not so much coordination' whereas:

> in London there is a fantastic level of coordination – we know it's going to work. On a 9/11 scale I don't think anyone can say that we're totally prepared for that. But we are now thinking the unthinkable. We are confident of dealing with any incident in London.[16]

Problems of response

We have, however, identified a number of problems that require attention, and some of these relate to coordination. It has already been noted elsewhere that the nature of the terrorist threat that we face, which includes the aim of causing mass casualties amongst civilian populations, means that there is a possibility that terrorists will try to use unconventional materials in their attacks, perhaps through the detonation of a 'dirty bomb' with the subsequent dispersal of a chemical or biological agent. Knowledge of the ideological orientation of terrorists and the fact that today's Al-Qaeda or Global Salafi Jihad terrorists aim to bring about mass casualties should inform and underpin our emergency preparedness.

The 'hot zone'

The fire and rescue service currently takes responsibility for safety within the 'hot zone' cordon, making sure that people have the right Personal Protection Equipment (PPE). With the possibility that CBRN materials may now be involved, however, a senior London Fire Service source has expressed his increasing uneasiness about this safety role – 'Who are the fire service to say that the ambulance service or the police haven't got a sufficient level of PPE?'. For example, if there is a CBRN incident in the London Underground how do they know that the police and ambulance service have the right PPE equipment and the right level of training for a particular environment? So it has been suggested that each of the emergency services should begin to think about being responsible for their own safety in these zones, albeit that the fire service would provide overall coordination.[17]

Chemical and biological detection/identification equipment

Our research has found that the *main issue of concern* for the emergency services in London, however, has been the lack of adequate chemical and biological detection/identification equipment. Part of the reason for this is that much research in this area has traditionally focused on detection/identification in a military environment. The knock-on effect of inadequate detection/identification capability is that where it is perceived that there has been a release of an agent, the fire service has to default to its highest level of protective equipment (all-hazards gas suits) which then restricts the mobility and operational duration of a fireperson. The ability to detect *what* chemical or biological agent is present also facilitates further objectives, such as the aim of establishing the extent of the area that has been contaminated, and also the ability to monitor dispersal. From a medical point of view it would enable speedier treatment for victims in the 'hot zone' using the right medical intervention (that is, using the right antidotes), and ensuring that the right level of protection can be used. Indeed, it could also allow for the possibility that the hot zone itself could be reduced by the fire service. While it is acknowledged that a great deal of research has been carried out in this area the impression is that effective detection/identification equipment is taking too long to deliver to our emergency services.

Decontamination

Although it is again acknowledged that there has been ongoing research into decontamination requirements it appears that there has been little tangible evidence of progress that would take us beyond 'bucket' decontamination procedures. The Royal Society stated in April 2004 that 'human surface decontamination is still rudimentary: clothes are bagged and plenty of soap and water applied. More research is needed to determine the best technologies for generic cleansing of skin'.[18] The House of Commons Science and Technology Committee also advocated the commissioning of new research into decontamination processes and procedures to enhance this aspect of the response.[19]

Communications

In May 2002 the Chairman of the Defence Select Committee stated in relation to communications that 'the argument of different emergency services operating different systems is so bizarre that I hope something seriously will emerge'.[20] There is, however, judging from our research, clearly a long way to go before interoperable communications between the emergency services can be achieved (maybe a decade at least). It is currently no more than an aspiration, partly because there does not appear to be any central direction or control over the issue. As there are three emergency services that are separately controlled by three different ministries there is uncertainty as to where the lead is going to come from. Further obstacles include the different cultures, operational requirements and lexicons of the three services.

Interoperability would enable the ambulance service to offer advice to the other emergency services on medical issues for workers and victims, and on safety and entry for ambulance staff.[21] It could also provide worker to worker communications in the hot zone (if and when, for example, ambulance service personnel are able to enter it). Nigel Jones, from the Information Operations Capability Team of QinetiQ, noted that we need interoperable communications to improve situational awareness, to support decision-making, to facilitate the provision of direction and coordination of actions and to receive feedback 'and by so doing, help mitigate the adverse consequences of a crisis'.[22]

The issue of communications and its failings came to the fore in the London Assembly report into the 7 July 2005 bombings, which stated that 'communications within and between the emergency services did not stand up on 7 July'. In relation to underground communication it noted that it was 'unacceptable that the emergency services, with the exception of the BTP, are still not able to communicate by radio when they are underground, 18 years after the official inquiry into the King's Cross fire recommended action to address this problem'.[23] As a result emergency service personnel could not communicate effectively, 'in some cases with each other and in other cases with their control rooms'.[24]

Survivors

The London Assembly report into 7/7 found that 'the most striking failing in the response to the 7 July attacks was the lack of planning to care for people who survived and were traumatised by the attacks'. It stated that 'procedures tend to focus too much on incidents, rather than on individuals, and on processes rather than people'.[25] As valuable as emergency response exercises are, this is perhaps one lesson that only becomes obviously apparent during a real major emergency. The report noted the lack of survivor reception areas despite the estimated 3,000 people who are said to have suffered from post-traumatic stress, along with a further 3,000 who were directly affected.[26]

There is a view that the long-term medical recovery from disasters or major emergencies has not been given enough attention. Dr Ann Eyre, founder and convener of the disasters study group within the British Sociological Association, stated that 'many of the bereaved and survivors from … disasters [that is, Zeebrugge, Bradford, King's Cross, Lockerbie, Piper Alpha, Hillsborough, Clapham, Marchioness] felt their loss was compounded by the lack of understanding and effective support by those in authority … As many emergency planners will tell you, public understanding and interest still focuses primarily on the impact and immediate aftermath of disasters'.[27]

She has argued that:

Resourcing is insufficient for mitigative and planning initiatives, or for longer term recovery, despite government bleatings about being prepared for the next event and doing all they can to help the victims. This contrasts starkly with arrangements in societies like the United States where a system of federal emergency management provides national funding and support for longer term recovery activities. Many emergency management professionals are now calling for such a system to be established here.[28]

These concerns have been amplified by Rosie Murray, chair of the UK EPS's human aspects group, who also notes that there 'is ample evidence that immediate and appropriate emotional "first aid" can also reduce the long-term need for clinical psychological treatment'.[29] As there is no statutory responsibility for the social services to respond to 'human needs' after a disaster (who, in any case, are 'not a counselling agency') it is not clear as to where the responsibility should lie – the social services, the police family liaison officers (FLO)[30] or the Primary Care Trusts? The group has made the following recommendations:

- A national system for collecting and disseminating good practice in the humanitarian sphere after disasters;
- One agency clearly designated to take the lead in a multi-agency response to the human needs of individuals affected by a major incident, whether that agency turns out to be social services or some other group;
- Creation of a register of any private-sector human resources that may be used during a disaster. There should be an agreed protocol for recruitment, training, and accountability;
- Better integration of the police family liaison officers' role with the roles of local authority services during a major incident;
- A study of the potential for mutual aid agreements between local authorities to handle the human aspects of disaster response, and consideration of setting up regional disaster committees (as blue-light services have);
- An in-depth study of how existing and proposed laws affect our planning of present and future systems of human response in disasters – the Human Rights Act for instance, the Data Protection Act, or the so-called Corporate Manslaughter Bill that seeks to make company managers share responsibility if a culture of company safely [sic] is lacking and a disaster results.[31]

Perhaps Murray puts it best when she states that 'there is a desperate need at this time for someone to act as a buffer between those who are suffering and the machinery of disaster response'.[32]

The national perspective

As London's response, through the LRRF and LRT, is seen as the model or pilot for other regions in the UK one can reasonably assume that the problems of response noted above for the capital city apply, or will apply, to the rest of the UK. Over and above these areas for improvement, other regions have further inadequacies that relate to them not enjoying the high level of prioritisation accorded to London – for example, less effective coordination, and delays and time lags in equipment delivery and training on a national scale.

Resources

In the uncorrected transcript of oral evidence taken on 2 March 2004 before the Defence and Home Affairs Committees on Homeland Security,[33] Home Secretary David Blunkett stated that there had been an 'overall increase of £330 million' allocated towards countering the terrorist threat. It is assumed that this figure covers both counter-terrorism and the emergency response to terrorism and this was indeed confirmed by Cabinet Office Minister Douglas Alexander who was quoted as saying that 'we have seen, even in the last budget, an additional £330m committed to our counter-terrorism and resilience work'.[34]

In its 2004 Spending Review the government announced that:

> this Spending Review provides about £450 million of extra resources in 2006–07 and about £560 million in 2007–08. In total, spending on counter-terrorism and resilience across departments will be over £2 billion by 2007–08, compared to £1.5 billion in 2004–05, and less than £1 billion a year before 11th September 2001.[35]

The Review breakdown of the anticipated additional expenditure is shown in Table 18.1.

The additional spending on emergency planning will double that currently received by local authorities from the Civil Defence Grant (see 'Local authorities' below), while included in the £310 million and £350 million (amongst other capabilities[36]) is 'the Fire Service's New Dimension project' and 'their Firelink project, which will deliver an improved and interoperable radio communications system',[37] along with an 'enhanced capability for the police to deal with chemical, biological, radiological and nuclear incidents including Personal Protective

Table 18.1 2004 spending review: anticipated additional expenditure

	£ million	
	2006–7	*2007–8*
Intelligence	122	192
Emergency planning	20	20
Counter-terrorism	310	350[38]

Equipment'.[39] In addition, the Spending Review announced the creation of a 'Counter-Terrorism Pool' for 2005–6 for which 'resources will be set aside within the Departmental Expenditure Limit (DEL) Reserve which will be match funded from within departments' budgets to create a pool of up to £100 million pounds'.[40] In his pre-budget speech of December 2004 the Chancellor Gordon Brown announced that he was releasing a further £105 million 'for necessary security measures to counter terrorism, enhance surveillance at ports and improve civil resilience'.[41]

The police

The police role at the scene of a terrorist incident, as outlined in *Dealing With Disasters*, is 'to coordinate all the activities of those responding', take measures to protect the scene, take initial responsibility for safety management, and to collect evidence.[42] The Home Office has provided funding for the provision of PPE to all officers trained in CBRN procedures which takes place at the Police Training Centre (established October 2001) at Winterbourne Gunner.[43] In its outline of the UK's counter-terrorist strategy in July 2006 the government stated that over 7,000 police officers have been CBRN trained.[44] In addition, the police have developed national standards of operation and of procurement of CBRN equipment that would facilitate the early consideration of mutual aid.[45]

In relation to PPE, one senior police source noted the potential problem of laying out substantial resources for such equipment that may be out of date within a year. He also brought to our attention a further potential difficulty relating to public order – if you have a policy of containing people within an area until further evidence is needed as to what agent, if any, might have been used there may be a problem of large numbers of people who might want to leave immediately for fear that they may become contaminated or further affected. There is a question here as to what restraining powers the police would have in such circumstances.[46] Indeed, ACPO, in its response to the Joint Committee on the Draft Civil Contingencies Bill, was concerned that the emergency powers did not appear to meet operational requirements. While it was pleased that police would be permitted to contain people within a cordon if it was suspected that they had been contaminated 'there is no specific power of arrest and no specific authority to use force when dealing with offences proposed at clause 21(3) [relating to the prohibition of the movement of persons]'.[47] It is therefore possible that there may be serious difficulties for the police when trying to contain people within a cordon after a possible CBRN incident, including shortages of manpower to protect the integrity of the cordon and potentially public order issues in relation to people who might believe that the police would be preventing them from escaping further contamination.

The fire and rescue service

A news release on 12 March 2004 from the Office of the Deputy Prime Minister stated that:

£56 million has been invested on phase 1 of the New Dimension project providing mass decontamination equipment. A further £132 million will be spent on phase 2, which will provide urban search and rescue equipment, high volume water pumping and water safety equipment.

There has been a 28 per cent increase in core expenditure provision for fire and rescue services since 1997, from £1,237m to £1,583m in 2003 a year-on-year increase of over 4 per cent – a real increase in provision. In 2004/05, authorities will receive an average increase of 4.2 per cent and no authority will get less than a 3.5 per cent increase.

In 2004/05 Government will also distribute £60 million in capital expenditure and £100 million will be available to fire and rescue authorities under the local Private Finance Initiative.[48]

In July 2006 the government announced that '80 new Fire and Rescue Service Incident Response Units are now operationally available each containing equipment capable of decontaminating up to 400 people an hour'.[49]

In Scotland £5 million of extra funding was allocated to the Scottish Fire Service in early 2002 in the wake of the 9/11 terrorist attacks to go towards:

- three purpose built vehicles with specialist search and rescue equipment for collapsed structures;
- mass decontamination facilities;
- heat-seeking cameras for pumping appliances;
- command support facilities to improve mobilisation of fire crews and equipment in remote areas;
- heavy lifting and support equipment;
- additional protection and safety equipment for firefighters.[50]

The Civil Contingencies Bill has raised some resource implications for the Fire Service because there are potentially a number of additional duties. CACFOA (Chief and Assistant Chief Fire Officer's Association), now CFOA, in its response to the draft bill, stated that:

The level of funding for the Fire & Rescue Service is insufficient to meet the civil contingency planning and response requirements set out in the Draft Bill. The current threats to the security of the UK and the economic, environment and social sustainability of our communities require a degree of risk management significantly beyond that currently undertaken by most organisations at local, regional and national levels. From a Fire & Rescue Service perspective, additional funds will be necessary to complete intensive risk assessment in extended areas to secure the appropriate risk control and mitigation measures necessary to bolster existing resilience. Inevitably this will have a 'knock-on' effect as regards the scale of response in terms of new or upgraded plant and machinery which, in turn, demand greater levels of training to ensure competence.[51]

While the full resource implications of the civil contingencies legislation have yet to become apparent it is envisaged that there will need to be a serious commitment to providing additional funding if our emergency response aspirations are to be realised *on a national scale* as envisaged in the Civil Contingencies Bill.

The ambulance service

The government stated in 2003 that 'under a £5 million programme, the Department of Health has provided 360 mobile decontamination units and 7,250 national specification Personal Protection Equipment (PPE) suits around the country, which will enable the Ambulance Service and A&E Departments to treat people contaminated with CBRN material'.[52] This was a one-off capital injection for England.[53] Our research has discovered that in addition there was an allocation over a period of three years (£5 million for year 1, £2.5 million for year 2, £2.5 million for year 3 (ending March 2006)) from the government for Ambulance Trusts to replace equipment that is used in training, to train for CBRN awareness and to set up specialist teams.

In its response to a House of Commons Science and Technology Committee report[54] the government stated that:

> Work has started on a second-generation suit and the option of using common equipment with the Police and Fire Services is also being explored. To improve bank stock and supplies held by hospitals, 2,500 additional suits have been supplied and a stockpile established. A Memorandum of Understanding between the Department of Health and the Office of the Deputy Prime Minister ensures Fire Service support in the event of a need for mass decontamination.[55]

Indeed, it was the cooperative arrangements between the Ambulance and Fire and Rescue Services that was credited with achieving the faster than anticipated decontamination of casualties in the Operation Magpie exercise on 28 April 2004.[56] Mutual aid arrangements now also exist between the NHS ambulance services. In addition, funding has been made available for ambulance personnel to receive CBRN training at Winterbourne Gunner[57] and work is also continuing as to 'how medical aid can be extended into the warm zone in a CBRN type incident'.[58]

The Scottish Ambulance Service secured money from the Scottish Executive Health Department for a 'fairly substantial training package'. Our research has shown that 81 additional staff have been deployed in Special Operations Response Teams. The Special Operations Units include decontamination equipment, block oxygen equipment and inflatable shelters. Some equipment was funded by central government as part of the UK stockpile while the Scottish executive has also provided resources.

But, as far as England is concerned, in the longer term Ambulance Service funding will come solely from the allocation that is given to the Primary Care

Trusts.[59] Beyond 2006 there will be no further central funding. There are concerns that this may not give emergency planning the prominence it deserves, especially as the ambulance service is going to be a Category 1 responder. We need to bear in mind that Primary Care Trusts will face conflicting pressures from patients waiting for appointments, for example, and on the other hand statutory responsibilities for meeting emergency planning requirements.

The health response

The role of the NHS is not, of course, restricted to the Ambulance Service at a time of emergency. In 2002 the NHS was reorganised with the creation of 302 Primary Care Trusts which have taken control of local health care along with 28 new strategic health authorities. It is these PCTs that now have the responsibility for local health emergency planning while the 'new Strategic Health Authorities have responsibility for co-ordination of response to widespread incidents'.[60] In addition, given that very different types of major emergency could occur, whether it be the foot and mouth disease outbreak, attacks similar to those on 11 September 2001 or the deliberate release of biological or chemical agents, the Department of Health saw the clear need for an 'integrated health protection infrastructure'.[61] The result of this was the creation of the Health Protection Agency[62] which brought together the following organisations:

1   The Public Health Laboratory Service, including the Communicable Disease Surveillance Centre and Central Public Health Laboratory.
2   The Centre for Applied Microbiology and Research.
3   The National Focus for Chemical Incidents.
4   The Regional Service Provider Units that support the management of chemical incidents.
5   The National Poisons Information Service.
6   NHS public health staff responsible for infectious disease control, emergency planning, and other protection support.[63]

The HPA's roles include:

1   Advising government on public health protection policies and programmes.
2   Delivering services and supporting the NHS and other agencies to protect people from infectious diseases, poisons, chemical and radiological hazards.
3   Providing an impartial and authoritative source of information and advice to professionals and the public.
4   Responding to new threats to public health.
5   Providing a rapid response to health protection emergencies, including the deliberate release of biological, chemical, poison or radioactive substances.
6   Improving knowledge of health protection, through research, development, and education and training.[64]

Within the HPA is the Emergency Response Division, which is responsible for running exercises to test the response to major emergency situations (see the section below on 'Exercises', pp. 358ff), including those where chemical and biological agents may have been deliberately released or where a radioactive 'dirty bomb' has exploded.

At the time of a major emergency a Joint Health Advisory Cell (JHAC) will be established to provide strategic direction to the response and will consist of a number of different representatives.[65] It is the Ambulance Service and the hospital trusts, however, that provide the main frontline operational response to a major emergency.

In summary, the threats of disease or a deliberate release of an agent 'needs an unbroken and secure link from early recognition of illness, through rapid laboratory confirmation of infection, to the clinical and public health response to treat patients and prevent the infection's spread'.[66] This requires a professional response from a number of NHS bodies – whether it be the HPA,[67] the strategic health authorities, the JHAC, the Primary Care Trusts, the acute trusts, the Ambulance Service, hospital Accident and Emergency departments and so on.[68] It also means that regular exercises are needed to enhance our preparedness in the event of a real major emergency and this is a key function of the HPA's Emergency Response Division (see 'Exercises' below).

The National Audit Office Report

While the restructuring of the NHS was taking place, the National Audit Office was writing a report (published November 2002) on the state of preparedness of the NHS if a major emergency was to take place. It found that, although there had been improvements since the attacks in New York, there were deficiencies in NHS emergency planning arrangements and it stressed the need to continue testing major incident plans. The report also found that while the:

> coverage of chemical, biological and radioactive incidents was mixed, some plans were still out of date and there was scope to improve arrangements for working with other emergency organisations, such as the police and fire services ... one third of health authorities considered post September 11 that they did not test their plans frequently enough and nearly a fifth considered that testing was not effective.[69]

In relation to acute and ambulance trusts 'a third of acute and ambulance trusts reported that they had not tested their major incident plans frequently enough, and a quarter of acute trusts considered their testing was not very effective'.[70] Clearly, exercises are crucial to enhancing the quality of our preparedness and since the National Audit Office report was published the HPA has conducted a number of them (see 'Exercises' below). The National Audit Office also stated that there were 'geographical variations in the adequacy of planning arrangements'[71] and this very much echoes what our own research has shown. A survey of hospital doctors in July 2005 (reported in the *Emergency Medicine* journal) also indicated that the NHS was ill-prepared for a terrorist emergency, with a lack of preparedness for a major incident and unfamiliarity with their hospitals' major incident plans.[72]

It is not just the large number of casualties transported to hospitals after a major incident that hospitals might have to contend with. There may also be those who present themselves to Accident and Emergency departments. As noted above there is potentially a serious problem with trying to keep large numbers of people who may have been contaminated within a confined area, not least because the police may not be able to get to the scene in time but also because they may simply not have the manpower to protect the integrity of the cordon that might be needed to surround a wide area. In such circumstances it is quite conceivable that local hospital Accident and Emergency departments might be inundated with large numbers of people, many of whom may be contaminated. It would therefore be advisable that, in addition to seeking ways to prevent people leaving a contaminated area, the government ensures that hospitals would be able to cope with such a scenario.

Local authorities

Many of the emergency planning functions of local authorities pre-9/11 resonate with its current roles. The Home Office's 'Standards for Civil Protection in England and Wales' (1999) emphasised the value of multi-agency training and exercising[73] and in the event of an emergency the local authority generally provided a supporting role with the aim of continuing to deliver 'critical services' such as prioritising key services, developing strategies to maintain business as usual, establishing systems back-up, identifying alternative premises and developing a strategy for the recovery phase.[74] Since the attacks of 11 September 2001 more emphasis has been placed on exercising and emergency preparedness in general. The role of local authorities, though, is still a supporting one – for example, accommodation it owns can be made available and it can facilitate transport. *Dealing With Disasters* states that:

> Temporary mortuary provision should be an inter-agency activity with the local authority taking the lead … the identification of suitable buildings, together with arranging the necessary logistical and administrative infrastructure, should form part of the preplanning process. The plan should include storage and examination areas. It should identify separate areas for staff and the bereaved and cover access needs, ideally with separated approaches and facilities for the different groups.[75]

In the Home Office's updated (May 2004) Strategic National Guidance on *The Decontamination of People Exposed To Chemical, Biological, Radiological or Nuclear (CBRN) Substances Or Material*[76] the role of the local authority at a CBRN incident is to:

1	Organise, staff and provide logistical support at survivor reception centres; to accommodate people who have been decontaminated at the scene and who, while not requiring acute hospital treatment, need short-term shelter, first aid, interview and documentation.
2	Organise, staff and provide logistical support at rest centres for the temporary accommodation of evacuees, with overnight facilities where appropriate and invoking mutual aid arrangements with neighbouring authorities if necessary.
3	In consultation with the police establish and staff friends and relatives reception centres.
4	Lead the work of voluntary agencies in response to the incident.
5	Lead the recovery phase.[77, 78]

As the last point suggests, the local authority comes more to the fore in the recovery phase of an emergency as the emergency service involvement recedes and as it strives to get society 'back to normal'.[79] Its role includes 'the immediate and ongoing safety of the area, disposal of contaminated waste, environmental monitoring, support for business recovery, provision of information and advice and the restoration of public confidence'.[80]

Our research has shown that one of the areas that has been most wanting as far as resources are concerned has been the inadequate provision for local authorities to carry out their emergency planning responsibilities. Between 2002 and 2005 the Local Authority civil defence grant was set at £19 million a year and from 2005 will not be ring-fenced when the government transfers the grant into the mainstream Revenue Support Grant, meaning that it could be siphoned off to other priorities that may be deemed more pressing and relevant.[81] There have therefore been calls for greater transparency to illustrate that the money allocated is clearly spent on civil contingencies.[82] LGA surveys[83] in 2003 found that local authorities were spending just over £32 million in England and Wales with total expenditure (including district council expenditure) amounting to £36 million – £17 million more than the then civil defence grant. Scottish local authorities also made it clear that they did not have sufficient funding for carrying out emergency planning duties.[84]

The doubling of the resources for emergency planning that the local authorities are to receive (announced in the government's 2004 Spending Review) is therefore to be welcomed,[85] and is more in line with the government's stated position that local authorities:

> have an important role in emergency planning and dealing with the consequences of all emergencies, including those arising from terrorist attack … The ability of local authorities to respond to a major crisis has always been a key component in the resilience work of the UK as a whole[86]

It should be noted, however, that the LGA surveys above were based on *existing* responsibilities and did not take into account those additional duties outlined in the Civil Contingencies Bill. Moreover, the danger still exists that this money will be channelled into other priorities. The new responsibilities, as outlined by the Emergency Planning Society (EPS), include:

1   promoting business continuity management;
2   greater emphasis on risk assessment work;
3   preventing emergencies from occurring;
4   warning and informing the public;
5   participation in initiatives arising from the new regional tier of resilience.[87]

The Joint Committee's response to the draft Civil Contingencies Bill noted that:

Durham County Council reflected the views of many when they told us that there were completely new activities required by the Bill, including warning the public; promoting business continuity management in the community; taking action to prevent emergencies from occurring; participation in the new local resilience forums; participation in the initiatives arising from the new resilience forums; undertaking activities as directed by central government; and providing ongoing information to the public. Devon County Council, in their written response to Question 8 of the Consultation Document, pointed out that the new definition of an emergency will include, for the first time, the need to plan, and respond to, threats to the environment.[88]

In its response to the draft Civil Contingencies Bill the LGA stated that 'it is clear that the scale of the new duties under this draft Bill, especially when extended to Shire District Councils for the first time, will require a wholesale review of the funding provision'.[89] Although the additional resources allocated to local authorities are to be welcomed it will be interesting to see how these will match up to the new responsibilities outlined in the Bill. With the regional tier of response as yet underdeveloped nationally there is also some confusion as to what it would entail.[90] During the course of our research we were finding that some local responders 'knew nothing' about the regional tier let alone the resource implications of the initiatives arising from it.

Exercises

The publicity surrounding relatively recent exercises (such as the Bank Exercise, Exercise Magpie and Exercise Horizon) has perhaps left an impression that the undertaking of emergency response exercises is a recent activity and one that has only happened since September 2001. In June 2000, however, Operation Trump Card 'was [at the time] probably Britain's largest multi-site exercise, which was geared towards what could be a chem-bio threat to multi-sites in London which was very significantly supported by a range of agencies'.[91] According to a former Assistant Police Commissioner of the Metropolitan Police 'we are vigorous exercisers' and it 'is one area where probably Britain can hold its head at least highest in respect of the investment that we make in contingency planning leading to exercising'.[92]

Many of those interviewed argued that there needs to be a greater understanding of what exercises are designed to achieve before criticising them. Exercises may take place to test equipment, to test procedures or to test response times without necessarily testing all three. If, for example, procedures alone are to be tested then it may be unfair to comment on the response time. The view has been expressed to us that the holistic type of exercise which involves going through the entire procedure is too cumbersome and is not the most effective method of learning.

It therefore seems advisable to adopt a strategic approach that tests each component of our response separately and more efficiently before more holistic 'beginning to end' exercises are undertaken. While, in today's threat environment, the sense of urgency in getting our emergency response right should certainly not dissipate, it would be prudent to iron out any problems at this 'micro' stage before putting all the components together in one multi-functional test exercise that may then throw up further problems and obstacles that might, for example, be related to wider coordination issues. It is perhaps advisable for research to be carried out into how one can establish an exercise regime in which all components of a response can be tested separately and how and when they can ultimately be brought together into single holistic and integrated exercises.

On 7 September 2003 an emergency exercise took place in response to a staged chemical attack at the Bank Underground station. It was designed to 'test protocols for collaboration between the emergency services in the use of detection and identification equipment to maintain safe cordons'.[93] The following were also tested:

1   capability to perform search and rescue using appropriate PPE of casualties from a stationary train in a tunnel;
2   police testing use of their PPE;
3   ambulance testing their PPE while conducting triage and the use of appropriate antidotes;
4   testing of clinical and mass decontamination.[94]

Criticisms of the Bank exercise included:

1   it took three hours before the final 'casualty' was brought to the surface;
2   one of the decontamination units was leaking.

The exercise was, however, as far as we have been made aware, designed to test procedures and not the response time – indeed a 'staged' exercise of this type entails slowing everything down. The leak from the decontamination unit did not apparently affect its operational effectiveness. While Transport Minister Alistair Darling stated that 'some of the conclusions [of the exercise] need to remain confidential for reasons of security' the lessons learned were summarised as follows:

1   a great deal of work has already been done by government, emergency services and the Mayor of London to improve London's capability to respond to emergencies through improved equipment and planning;
2   there needs to be contingency planning, preparation and funding for responding to large scale emergencies and that this work continues to be given high priority;
3   work needs to continue to look at and prepare for alternative rescue plans for difficult environments like the London Underground;
4   work needs to continue to improve the ability of those wearing protective suits to be able to communicate under difficult conditions;
5   ambulance crews need to be able to provide earlier assessment, care and delivery of specific antidotes to contaminated casualties; and,
6   we must not underestimate the number of people and specialist equipment required to respond to such emergencies.[95]

As noted above, the HPA (Emergency Response Division) is responsible for running a series of exercises 'to test emergency preparedness in the health service community'.[96] Its website states that 'these exercises are successful in testing and improving the current emergency health plans already in place, helping to ensure that the health services can respond in a rapid and co-ordinated way to any deliberate release of chemical, biological or nuclear weapons'.[97] Exercise East Wind, for example, highlighted the potential problem of large numbers of people self-referring to hospital Accident and Emergency departments in the event of a dirty radiological bomb exploding, while Exercise Green Goblin (table top) highlighted the need for formal JHAC training.[98]

On 28 April 2004 Exercise Magpie was staged by the HPA in Newcastle to test the NHS's response to 'the deliberate release of a chemical or biological substance'.[99] Its report on the exercise stated that, in particular, the following were tested:

1   an acute hospital trust and its accident and emergency teams in the activation of major incident plans in the context of a chemical or biological attack, including the setting up of an NHS decontamination unit;
2   the command, control and communications procedures in place for the exchange of information during a CBRN incident;
3   the effectiveness of the emergency services' deployment of decontamination equipment.

The report stated that it took one hour less than anticipated to decontaminate volunteer casualties 'due to co-operative arrangements between the ambulance and fire and rescue services'.[100] There were, however, important lessons:

1   the value of multi-agency exercises;
2   health staff cannot work in the hot zone – speedier access to the hot zone is required;
3   PPE needs to be further developed (as the Department of Health is apparently doing);
4   the lack of stability of ambulance decontamination units in windy conditions;
5   disrobing contaminated clothing needs to take place more quickly;
6   there were 'difficulties for casualties trying to reclaim essential items, such as house keys, after decontamination';
7   casualties going through the ambulance decontamination units 'became extremely cold because there was no space to dress inside the units';
8   're-robe packs for casualties, which contained insulated clothing, contained inadequate footwear';
9   'casualties wanted more information and more reassurance while waiting to be decontaminated'.[101]

There were also lessons for the local NHS services and for the desktop exercise where the role of the JHAC needed to be clarified. The report also found that 'key health messages for the public need to be released to the media within the first hour of an incident'.[102]

Various recommendations were made in the report as to how these lessons could be addressed and how our response could be enhanced. The key lesson, as the report outlined, is the value of carrying out regular exercises – many, if not all, of these lessons would not have been picked up without the operation in Newcastle. Indeed, what both the Bank and Newcastle exercises have shown is that regular exercising is an indispensable part of enhancing our emergency preparedness. This was further shown by Exercise Horizon in Birmingham in July 2004 which simulated a chemical attack. The purpose of the exercise was 'to see how quickly we can get our officers together, how quickly they can get their equipment on and how quickly the equipment can be deployed',[103] but it took nearly three hours for volunteer victims to be decontaminated.[104]

In summary, the exercises that have been carried out by the HPA, the LRRF and others are to be welcomed and these should continue. It is also advisable, however, that research be carried out into how a more strategic approach can be adopted so that, rather than risk losing learning objectives in 'beginning to end' exercises, one can establish an exercise regime in which different components of a response can be tested separately before considering how and when they can ultimately be brought together into single holistic and integrated exercises. One should also be mindful of the fact that, as valuable as exercises are, they may not be able to provide some of the lessons that real major incidents do, such as some of those noted by the London Assembly report into the 7 July 2005 attacks.

Conclusion

In conclusion, there has been some significant progress in enhancing our emergency preparedness but there is still a tremendous amount of work to be done. Coordination between the different agencies in London through the LRT appears to be working well but the level of coordination in other regions is variable leading to 'varying levels of preparedness'.[105] This is related to the fact that the regional tier envisaged in the Civil Contingencies Bill has yet to develop fully outside London. We await with interest as to how this tier and the regional resilience teams will develop and to what extent they will enhance joint coordination and our level of emergency preparedness, especially when they have not had the benefit of LESLP[106] and its experience of 30 years of Irish terrorism.

This is not to suggest that London's emergency preparedness could not be improved. Our research has shown that an urgent priority is to continue to develop research into ways of improving the emergency services' ability to detect and identify chemical and biological agents. This will enable the right PPE to be used, increase opportunities for reducing the hot zone, and allow the ambulance service and medical staff to administer the right treatment and antidotes more quickly. Research is also needed to improve decontamination procedures and PPE to enable emergency responders to work more effectively and for longer periods of time. Progress also needs to be made in the whole area of communications – not just in terms of achieving interoperable communications between our emergency services but also in surmounting the difficulties of communicating in and from underground locations, as noted by the London Assembly report into the response to the 7 July 2005 attacks. The latter report also noted the failure to deal adequately with the survivors at the scenes.

Despite these emergency response issues that London needs to address it appears that other regions are not as prepared as our capital city is for a major incident. As noted above, part of the reason for this relative lack of preparedness is the underdevelopment of the regional tier of our response. Another reason is that it takes longer for equipment and training to reach other parts of the country. While it is natural that our capital city should be given top priority, it is important to remember that the threat of simultaneous attacks and a willingness to aim for 'soft' targets once others have been 'hardened' means that we must be prepared for attacks on a nationwide basis.

Notes

1 The other three being 'prevention', 'pursuing' terrorists, and 'protecting' the public.
2 Patrick Cunningham, chairman of the Emergency Planning Society's local authorities issues group, observed in February 2003 that 'the London resilience programme may have completed its work, with ministerial support, but it [resilience] appears to have stopped at the M25', in Cunningham, P. (2003) 'I call it my insomnia list', available at http://society.guardian.co.uk/publicvoices/emergencyplanning/.
3 Cited in House of Commons Science and Technology Committee (2003) *The Scientific Response to Terrorism*, 6 November, p. 53, available at www.publications.

parliament.uk/pa/cm200203/cmselect/cmsctech/415/415.pdf, from Veness, D. (2003) 'Anticipating an enduring threat', *FST Journal*, 17(10), July, pp. 5–6.

4 Cabinet Office News Release (2003) *Minister for Cabinet Office Launches Draft Civil Contingencies Bill for Consultation*, CAB 036/03, 19 June, available at www. homeoffice.gov.uk/docs2/pressnote.pdf.

5 Scottish Executive (2004) *Civil Contingencies Bill, Scottish Consultation Report*, 7 January, available at www.scotland.gov.uk/Resource/Doc/1096/0000925.pdf.

6 UK Resilience, www.ukresilience.info/contingencies/capabilities.htm.

7 The UK Resilience website (ibid.) states that the 17 workstreams fall into three categories:

– three workstreams which are essentially structural, dealing respectively with the central (national), regional and local response capabilities;
– five which are concerned with the maintenance of essential services (food, water, fuel, transport, health, financial services, etc.);
– nine functional workstreams, dealing respectively with the assessment of risks and consequences; CBRN resilience; infectious diseases – human; infectious diseases – animal and plant; mass casualties; mass fatalities; mass evacuation; site clearance; and warning and informing the public.

8 Cabinet Office News Release (n. 4).

9 Susan Scholefield, Head of the CCS, letter, 19 June 2003, available at www. ukresilience.info/contingencies/dwd/scholefield.pdf.

10 *Introductory Note, Dealing with Disasters* (revised 3rd edn), available at www. ukresilience.info/contingencies/dwd/index.htm.

11 See, for example, Memorandum from the Local Government Association (to the Joint Committee on Draft Civil Contingencies Bill), 1 September 2003, available at www. parliament.the-stationery-office.co.uk/pa/jt200203/jtselect/jtdcc/184/30909a02.htm.

12 The Chairman of Surrey's Emergency Services Major Incident Committee, Denis O'Connor, for example, in his memorandum to the Joint Committee on the Draft Civil Contingencies Bill, argued that 'recent experience during the fuel crisis and the outbreak of foot and mouth disease has shown that it [the lead department principle] does not work', Memorandum from Surrey Police, 28 November 2003, available at www.parliament.the-stationery-office.co.uk/pa/jt200203/jtselect/jtdcc/184/ 184we36.htm.

Also in evidence to the Defence Select Committee one contributor noted (of the government's response to the fuel crisis) that 'We were getting different communications, often inconsistent communications, from different departments, sometimes at the same time, and we knew more about what other departments were doing than some of the departments communicating with us', Qs 620–39, available at www.publications.parliament.uk/pa/cm200102/cmselect/cmdfence/518/2041007. htm. See also Cunningham, 'I call it my insomnia list' (n. 2).

13 As stated by a senior London Ambulance Service source.

14 Senior London Ambulance source. The panel's members include the following representatives: the Metropolitan Police Service, the London Fire Brigade, the City of London police, the BTP, the London Ambulance Service and the local authorities. The LESLP website states that: 'The group meets once every three months under the chair of the Metropolitan Police. Its purpose is to ensure a partnership approach between all the relevant agencies in the planning for, and the response to, a major incident of whatever kind. This could be anything from a terrorist attack to a natural disaster such as a severe flood, which may occur within the Greater London area', www.leslp.gov.uk/.

15 London Resilience, www.londonprepared.gov.uk/resilienceteam/. The LRT consists of experts in emergency preparedness and has members from: the Metropolitan

Police Service, the BTP, the City of London Police, the London Fire Brigade, the London Ambulance Service, the NHS, the Greater London Authority, Corporation of the City of London, Emergency Planning Department, Transport for London, London Underground, British Telecom, London Fire Emergency Planning Authority (LFEPA), the Government Information and Communications Service, the Salvation Army.

16　Senior London Ambulance source.

17　Senior Fire and Rescue Service source.

18　Royal Society report (2004) *Making the UK Safer: Detecting and Decontaminating Chemical and Biological Agents*, April, p. 41, available at www.royalsoc.ac.uk/ displaypagedoc.asp?id=9461.

19　House of Commons Science and Technology Committee report (2003) *The Scientific Response to Terrorism*, 6 November, available at www.publications.parliament.uk/pa/ cm200203/cmselect/cmsctech/415/415.pdf. For current methods of decontamination, such as the 'rinse-wipe-rinse' method which requires water, a bucket, liquid soap and a sponge or soft brush, see (2004) *Strategic National Guidance – The Decontamination of People Exposed To Chemical, Biological, Radiological or Nuclear (CBRN) Substances Or Material*, May, available at www.ukresilience.info/cbrn/peoplecbrn.pdf.

20　Bruce George, Chairman of the House of Commons Defence Committee, Minutes of Evidence, 7 May 2002, available at www.publications.parliament.uk/pa/cm200102/ cmselect/cmdfence/518/2050707.htm.

21　Richard Diment, Chief Executive, Ambulance Service Association, 'Communications Interoperability in a Crisis', Royal United Services Institute conference, 21 September 2004.

22　Nigel Jones, Information Operations, QinetiQ, 'Communications Interoperability in a Crisis', Royal United Services Institute conference, 21 September 2004.

23　London Assembly (2006) *Report of the 7 July Review Committee*, June, available at www.london.gov.uk/assembly/reports/7july/report.pdf.

24　Ibid.

25　Ibid.

26　Ibid.

27　Eyre, Dr A. (2003) 'Disaster survivors and bereaved are being listened to better', 7 March, available at http://society.guardian.co.uk/publicvoices/ emergencyplanning/.

28　Ibid.

29　Murray, R. (2003) 'We need a register of people who can help support the bereaved', 2 March, available at http://society.guardian.co.uk/publicvoices/emergencyplanning/.

30　Murray acknowledges that the FLOs have been a success but it is 'often unclear exactly where the family liaison officer is meant to refer them for ongoing support or counselling' (i.e. social services, voluntary organisations, local authority? Ibid.).

31　Ibid. Murray, R. (2003) 'We need a register of people who can help support the bereaved', 2 March, available at http://society.guardian.co.uk/publicvoices/ emergencyplanning/. See also Emergency Planning Society Human Aspects Group (HAG)　www.emergplansoc.org.uk/index.php?tab=groups&area=11&group=73, particularly *Consultation Questions Draft CCB* and *Best Practice Document* papers.

32　Murray, Rosie (2003) 'We need a register of people who can help support the bereaved', 2 March, available at http://society.guardian.co.uk/publicvoices/ emergencyplanning/.

33　See　www.parliament.the-stationery-office.co.uk/pa/cm200304/cmselect/cmhaff/ uc417-i/uc41702.htm. It should be noted that the document states that 'Any public use of, or reference to, the contents should make clear that neither witnesses nor Members have had the opportunity to correct the record. The transcript is not yet an approved formal record of these proceedings'.

34 Ensom, J. (undated) *UK Government Denies Ineffective Emergency Plans*, available at www.globalcontinuity.com/article/articleview/10235/1/30.

35 2004 Spending Review, Chapter 6: Global Security and Prosperity, available at www.hm-treasury.gov.uk/media//5EADA/sr2004_ch6.pdf.

36 Also included is 'HM Revenue and Customs work on improving security at ports; Foreign and Commonwealth Office security enhancements at UK embassies overseas; and Home Office work on enhanced border controls (ibid.)'.

37 That is interoperable within the fire service.

38 Ibid.

39 2004 Spending Review, Chapter 6: Global Security and Prosperity (n. 35).

40 Ibid.

41 Gordon Brown, pre-budget statement, 2 December 2004, available at www.hm-treasury.gov.uk/pre_budget_report/prebud_pbr04/prebud_pbr04_index.cfm.

42 *Dealing With Disasters*, ibid. (n. 10).

43 House of Commons Science and Technology Select Committee Report (n. 19).

44 HM Government (2006) *Countering International Terrorism: The United Kingdom's Strategy*, July, p. 26, available at www.ukresilience.info/publications/countering.pdf#search=%22Countering%20International%20Terrorism%20%22.

45 Senior police source, 10 March 2004.

46 Ibid.

47 See memorandum from the Association of Chief Police Officers (to the Joint Committee on Draft Civil Contingencies Bill), 28 November 2003, available at www.parliament.the-stationery-office.co.uk/pa/jt200203/jtselect/jtdcc/184/30909a06.htm.

48 Office of the Deputy Prime Minister, *Government presses ahead with the modernisation of the Fire and Rescue Service*, available at www.odpm.gov.uk/pns/DisplayPN.cgi?pn_id=2004_0057.

49 HM Government (2006) *Countering International Terrorism: The United Kingdom's Strategy*, July, p. 26 (n. 44).

50 See Scottish Executive News (2002) *Review of Fire Service emergency capability*, 22 February, available at www.scotland.gov.uk/News/Releases/2002/02/1136.

51 See www.parliament.the-stationery-office.co.uk/pa/jt200203/jtselect/jtdcc/184/30909a08.htm.

52 See www.parliament.the-stationery-office.co.uk/pa/cm200203/cmhansrd/vo030303/wmstext/30303m01.htm.

53 Wales and Scotland NHS have invested in similar equipment.

54 House of Commons Science and Technology Committee (2003) *The Scientific Response to Terrorism*, 6 November, p. 15, available at www.publications.parliament.uk/pa/cm200203/cmselect/cmsctech/415/415.pdf.

55 Government Response to House of Commons Science and Technology Committee (2004) *The Scientific Response to Terrorism*, 22 January, available at www.homeoffice.gov.uk/docs2/stc_report_reply.pdf.

56 See, for example (2004) *Health Protection Agency Publishes Lessons Learned From Exercise Magpie*, 15 June, available at www.hpa.org.uk/hpa/news/articles/press_releases/2004/040615_exer_magpie.htm.

57 The Home Secretary stated in February 2004 that senior ambulance staff in all ambulance services in the UK will have received Joint Emergency Service CBRN Incident Commander Courses. Written Ministerial Statements, Home Office, 25 February 2004, available at www.publications.parliament.uk/pa/cm200304/cmhansrd/vo040225/wmstext/40225m01.htm.

58 Memorandum submitted by the Ambulance Service Association (to the Defence Select Committee), 1 May 2003, available at www.publications.parliament.uk/pa/cm200203/cmselect/cmdfence/557/3040209.htm.

59 Unlike England, Wales, Scotland and Northern Ireland do not have Primary Care Trusts.

60 National Audit Office (2002) *Facing the Challenge: NHS Emergency Planning in England*, 15 November, available at www.dh.gov.uk/assetRoot/04/05/56/99/04055699.pdf.

61 Dr Pat Troop, Evidence to the Defence Select Committee, Q.1030, 24 April 2002, available at www.publications.parliament.uk/pa/cm200102/cmselect/cmdfence/518/2042403.htm.

62 The creation of the HPA was the main recommendation of Chief Medical Officer (2002) *Getting Ahead of the Curve*, January, available at www.publications.doh.gov.uk/cmo/idstrategy/idstrategy2002.pdf.

63 See www.hpa.org.uk/hpa/foi/foi_pub_scheme.htm.

64 HPA website, www.hpa.org.uk/hpa/about_us/about.htm.

65 This could typically include an HPA microbiologist, an HPA epidemiologist, an HPA toxicologist, an HPA expert in communicable disease control, a press officer, an environmental health officer, an HPA radiation adviser, a water company representative and so on depending on the nature of the emergency. See (2002) *Deliberate Release of Biological and Chemical Agents – Guidance to help plan the health service response*, August, available at www.dh.gov.uk/assetRoot/04/07/17/86/04071786.pdf.

66 Professor Brian Duerden, director of the former Public Health Laboratory Service, London, *Combating infection needs an unbroken chain from diagnosis onwards*, available at http://society.guardian.co.uk/publicvoices/emergencyplanning/0,12872,893559,00.html.

67 As noted above, incorporated in the HPA is the former Public Health Laboratory Service and the Communicable Disease Centre. They provide surveillance and investigation of diseases and have links with communicable disease control consultants in primary care trusts (see Professor Brian Duerden, ibid).

68 For an outline of the roles and responsibilities of the different NHS bodies see Department of Health, *Handling Major Incidents: An Operational Guideline*, available at www.dh.gov.uk/PolicyAndGuidance/fs/en.

69 National Audit Office (2002) *Facing the Challenge: NHS Emergency Planning in England*, 15 November, available at www.dh.gov.uk/assetRoot/04/05/56/99/04055699.pdf.

70 Ibid.

71 Ibid.

72 (2006) *NHS 'is Ill-prepared for Attacks'*, 17 August, available at http://news.bbc.co.uk/1/hi/health/4795651.stm.

73 Home Office (1999) *Standards for Civil Protection in England and Wales*, available at www.ukresilience.info/contingencies/pubs/sfcpew.pdf.

74 Ibid.

75 *Dealing With Disasters* (n. 10).

76 The first edition was published in February 2003.

77 (2004) *Strategic National Guidance – The Decontamination of People Exposed to Chemical, Biological, Radiological or Nuclear (CBRN) Substances or Material*, May, available at www.ukresilience.info/cbrn/cbrn_guidance.htm.

78 For a fuller outline of the role of local authorities see Home Office (2003) *The Release of Chemical, Biological, Radiological or Nuclear (CBRN) Substances or Material, Guidance for Local Authorities*, August, available at www.ukresilience.info/cbrn/cbrn_guidance.pdf.

79 Ibid. and Home Office (2000) *Recovery: An Emergency Management Guide*, available at www.ukresilience.info/contingencies/business/recovery.pdf.

80 Home Office (2003) *The Release of Chemical, Biological, Radiological or Nuclear (CBRN) Substances or Material, Guidance for Local Authorities*, ibid.

81 See, for example, the view of Patrick Cunningham, chief emergency planning officer for County Durham, Joint Committee on Draft Civil Contingencies Bill Minutes of

Evidence, Qs 80–99, 9 September 2003, available at www.parliament.the-stationery-office.co.uk/pa/jt200203/jtselect/jtdcc/184/30909p05.htm.

82 See, for example, Richard Davies, principal emergency planning officer for Leeds City Council, Joint Committee on Draft Civil Contingencies Bill, Minutes of Evidence, Qs 80–99 (n. 116), Report and Evidence, available at www.parliament. the-stationery-office.co.uk/pa/jt200203/jtselect/jtdcc/184/184.pdf.

83 Local Government Association (2003) *Emergency Planning for Districts: A Survey of District Local Authorities*, October, and (2003) *Emergency Planning: A Survey of Top Tier Local Authorities*, July, available at www.lga.gov.uk/.

84 See Scottish Executive, Civil Contingencies Bill, Scottish Consultation Report (n. 5).

85 It should be noted that this additional resourcing does not apply to Scotland because, upon the request of the Convention of Scottish Local Authorities (COSLA), the payment of the specific Civil Defence Grant stopped north of the border from April 2001. It still receives the grant through the Grant Aided Expenditure process but it is up to local authorities as to where funding priorities lie (see 'Memorandum on Emergency Planning in Scotland from the Scottish Executive', Appendix to Select Committee on Defence, March 2002, available at www.publications.parliament.uk/ pa/cm200102/cmselect/cmdfence/518/518ap06.htm).

86 See www.homeoffice.gov.uk/terrorism/govprotect/depts/index.html.

87 Memorandum from the Emergency Planning Society to the Joint Committee on the Draft Civil Contingencies Bill, 28 November 2003, available at www.parliament.the-stationery-office.co.uk/pa/jt200203/jtselect/jtdcc/184/30909a03.htm.

88 Joint Committee on the Draft Civil Contingencies Bill, Report and Evidence, available at www.parliament.the-stationery-office.co.uk/pa/jt200203/jtselect/jtdcc/184/184.pdf.

89 Memorandum from the Local Government Association to the Joint Committee on the Draft Civil Contingencies Bill, available at www.parliament.the-stationery-office. co.uk/pa/jt200203/jtselect/jtdcc/184/30909a02.htm.

90 See n. 11.

91 David Veness, Evidence to the Defence Select Committee, Q.1224, 7 May 2002, available at www.parliament.the-stationery-office.co.uk/pa/cm200102/cmselect/ cmdfence/518/2050701.htm.

92 Ibid.

93 London Prepared available at www.londonprepared.gov.uk/antiterrorism/exercise. htm.

94 Ibid.

95 Ibid .

96 HPA, Emergency Response Division, www.hpa.org.uk/hpa/erd/erd_exercises.htm.

97 Ibid.

98 Ibid.

99 Exercise Magpie, Executive Summary, Emergency Response Division, www.hpa. org.uk/hpa/erd/pdf/magpie.pdf.

100 Ibid.

101 Ibid.

102 Ibid.

103 Chief Inspector Surjeet Manku of West Midlands Police, quoted in *Britain Conducts Largest Terror Exercise*, Officer.com, available at www.officer.com/article/article. jsp?id=15057&sectionId=8.

104 (2004) *Probe after mock chemical attack*, 18 July, available at http://news.bbc. co.uk/1/hi/england/west_midlands/3903405.stm.

105 Senior Ambulance Service Source.

106 This is not to overlook the fact that Strategic Emergency Planning Groups have existed right across England and Wales (for example, the Merseyside Emergency Services joint planning group).

Part V

International dimensions and main conclusions of authors

19 International dimensions of homeland security

Paul Wilkinson

It would be absurd to pretend that the UK's homeland security can somehow be hermetically sealed from threats and problems arising from the international political strategic environment. We tend to see the problem of IRA terrorism in the last quarter of the twentieth century as a purely domestic or internal challenge, but this overlooks the fact that the IRA is constantly engaged in cross-border attacks and smuggling to raise funds for terrorism, and that it has always had parts of its support organisation, political front (Sinn Fein), and some of its key godfathers, living in the Republic. It also neglects the important role of the Irish–American sympathisers and supporters as a source of funds for the IRA, in helping to obtain weapon supplies from the USA, the key role of Libyans as a source of IRA weapons, the series of IRA attacks against British targets located in continental Europe, and the valuable support given to the Peace Process by successive US governments, and by Senator George Mitchell.[1] Above all it overlooks the huge pressure from the US on the IRA to abandon terrorism after 9/11.

The consolidation of the Northern Ireland peace process is undoubtedly one of the major achievements of the Labour government. However, it should be remembered that John Major, the former Conservative Prime Minister and his Secretary of State for Northern Ireland, Patrick Mayhew, now Lord Mayhew, deserve credit for preparing the way for the peace process with the Downing Street Declaration and the eventual achievement of a cease fire from the IRA. This gave Prime Minister Tony Blair and his new Labour government the opportunity to push ahead with a peace process which ultimately led to the Good Friday Agreement, the decommissioning of the IRA weapons and the October 2006 announcement by the Northern Ireland Independent Monitoring Commission that the IRA had dismantled its terrorism structures. The late Mo Mowlam, the former Northern Ireland Secretary for State, David Trimble (the pragmatic former leader of the Ulster Unionist Party), as well as Prime Minister Tony Blair, showed admirable determination and patience in working towards the goal of lasting peace in Northern Ireland.

The international character of the threat posed by the Al-Qaeda network has been stressed in Chapter 1. It should be obvious that success in preventing and combating Al-Qaeda can only be achieved by effective coordination of homeland security measures with a well-crafted foreign policy and *maximum* international intelligence and security cooperation with our friends and allies, within and beyond the North Atlantic alliance.

As emphasised in my chapter assessing the Al-Qaeda threat,[2] it is the most lethal and destructive non-state terrorist network we have seen in the history of international terrorism. It has global reach with a presence in at least 60 countries and, unlike the IRA and more traditional separatist groups, it does not have limited political aims and a desire to find a political pathway out of terrorism. Al-Qaeda falls into a category of what I have termed 'incorrigible' groups; Al-Qaeda's core leadership appears totally committed to its strategy of mass terror through mass killing with the avowed aim of a revolutionary change in international politics leading to the establishment of a pan-Islamist caliphate run by Al-Qaeda. This leaves the civilised world no real alternative to the policy of combining together to suppress this dangerous movement, or network of networks, which has become a major threat to human life not only in the 'front-line' states (that is, Afghanistan, Pakistan, Iraq, Saudi Arabia) but also in the homelands of Western countries and elsewhere.

The immediate response of Prime Minister Tony Blair to the unprecedented atrocities committed by Al-Qaeda terrorists on 9/11 was to express total solidarity with the USA and to pledge to stand 'shoulder to shoulder' with President George W. Bush in the 'War on Terrorism' which the President had declared in the aftermath of 9/11. The British government gave total support to the USA in its brief but very effective campaign to topple the Taliban regime in Afghanistan which had given safe haven to bin Laden and his Al-Qaeda training camps. Britain supports the government of President Karzai who came into office with the full endorsement of the UN Security Council and the establishment of the Coalition Against Terrorism which was to become the largest alliance in history. So far, so good.

At the end of 2001 there was widespread international support for the USA, although there were growing concerns that the US government was increasingly unilateralist in its decision making about the response to the Al-Qaeda threat, and that the increasingly belligerent tone of the US President's 'War on Terrorism' rhetoric was leading to a dangerous over-emphasis on seeking military solutions to the terrorist campaign waged by Al-Qaeda.

In 2002 the small but highly influential group of neoconservatives in key positions in the Pentagon won the support of President Bush for the plan for a US invasion of Iraq. This was sold to the US public as a key part of the 'War on Terrorism'. In reality, there is no evidence that Saddam Hussein was in any way complicit in the planning of the 9/11 attacks, although many US citizens may still be under the illusion that this was the case. The real motivation of the neoconservatives was to bring regime change in Iraq and to establish a democracy there which, so they believed, would help to inspire the wider democratisation of the Middle East.

Another motive was a fear (unfounded as it turned out) that Saddam had WMD which could endanger US security. (I recall attending a strategic studies conference in America in the fall of 2002 and listened, dumbfounded to an address by Paul Wolfowitz, one of the key architects of the plan to invade Iraq, while he told an audience of generals and academics that the threat posed to America by Saddam was greater than the threat from the Cuban missile crisis of 1962.)

It has also been argued that the desire to control Iraq's oil was another motive for US invasion. My personal view from the inception of the Iraq invasion plan was that it was a huge strategic mistake. Saddam was a brutal tyrant responsible for countless violations of human rights against his own people. However, unlike Al-Qaeda, he did not present a serious threat to the security of the USA or Europe. His regime was the most 'contained' state in the Middle East. It was subject to UN sanctions, was constantly over flown by US and British aircraft imposing a 'no fly zone' regime, with US military and naval forces close at hand in case he stepped out of line. The UN Security Council refused to provide a specific mandate to legitimate a military invasion of Iraq, and the US would not allow time for Dr Hans Blix, the outstanding leader of the UN weapons inspection team in Iraq, to finish his work. (If they had allowed him to complete his mission the USA would have found that Saddam had no WMD.)

Britain's Prime Minister decided to join with the USA in the invasion and the UK has had a large force of UK troops deployed in the occupation of Iraq ever since. In view of the huge number of Iraqi civilians who have died as a result of the invasion and as a result of insurgency, sectarian civil war and terrorism under the occupation, it is tragic irony that far from assisting in the 'War on Terrorism' the invasion and occupation of Iraq has been exploited to the full by Al-Qaeda which professes that it is the defender of the Muslim world, and which has used the conflict to boost its propaganda, recruitment and fundraising, and to excite even greater enmity between the USA and the Islamic world. One has only to look at the way in which images of the conflict in Iraq are used in Al-Qaeda-linked websites and videotapes to see how important the Iraq situation is as a factor in the recruitment and motivation of young Muslims in the UK and around the world.[3]

The intelligence agencies on both sides of the Atlantic concur with this analysis. No one is suggesting that the Iraq conflict is the *sole* cause of Al-Qaeda terrorism, but it has undoubtedly *exacerbated* it.

A key problem with regard to UK counter-terrorism policy, particularly with regard to the 'prevention' and 'pursuit' elements of that policy, is that the UK government has been conducting counter-terrorism 'shoulder to shoulder' with the USA, not in the sense of being an equal decision-maker, but rather as a pillion passenger compelled to leave the steering to the ally in the driving seat. The Iraq conflict has also provided an ideal targeting and training area for Al-Qaeda-linked terrorists, and deflected resources and assistance that could have been deployed to assist the Karzai government and to bring bin Laden to justice. Riding pillion with a powerful ally has proved costly in terms of British and US military lives, military expenditure and the damage caused to the counter-terrorism campaign.[4] In the early autumn of 2006 the UK was trying to help to suppress insurgencies both in Afghanistan and Southern Iraq, but with insufficient troops and inadequate equipment as a result of severe overstretch.

It is clearly a fundamental error to replace the scourge of terrorism by the even greater evil of major wars in which hundreds of thousands can be killed.[5] The military perform invaluable counter-terrorism tasks such as defending borders with major firepower, rescuing hostages and dealing with improvised explosives. But you cannot defeat a global terrorist network hidden in dozens of cities, on a battlefield. What is needed is much more sophisticated multi-pronged strategy using high-quality intelligence, police work and international cooperation to get such good information on the intentions and plans of the terrorist group that you can intervene before they carry out their attacks. This alternative strategy would also require much greater emphasis on the battle of ideas, not just by enlisting the support of the media and the public but also demonstrating *by our actions* that we uphold the values of the rule of law and the protection of human rights which we claim to believe in.

Unless this is clearly demonstrated in our foreign and security policies as well as our rhetoric we will lose this key element of the struggle against Al-Qaeda both internationally and within our own borders. Upholding human rights is not an optional extra; it is a *crucial* element in the democratic response to terrorism.[6]

Another key lesson that can be drawn from the experience of the UK's participation in the US-led 'War on Terrorism' is the importance of retaining sovereignty over our own foreign policy. Being a good friend and ally does not mean doing everything your more powerful ally wants you to do: indeed, a good ally, like a candid friend, should be prepared to warn when it believes a particular policy planned by its ally would be dangerous to the national security interest and highly counter-productive. At very least, if the UK government believes its national interests will not be served by a particular proposed policy it should politely but firmly refuse to participate, just as Harold Wilson refused to deploy British troops to join the USA in the Vietnam War.

Such differences in the past have not destroyed the UK's friendly relations with the USA. The UK owes it to its citizens to be more democratically accountable in its conduct of foreign policy and to ensure that we retain maximum independent sovereign control and freedom of manoeuvre. This is of cardinal importance when decisions on going to war are concerned: we should take care of our valuable armed forces by ensuring that they are not deployed in 'missions impossible' with too few troops and inadequate equipment and weaponry. General Sir Richard Dannatt was surely right to warn in October 2006 of the grave consequences of extreme overstretch for the future of the British Army. Sir Richard was performing his duty as an honest soldier in highlighting the vital need for realism in the conduct of British policy in an increasingly turbulent world.[7]

The consequences of military overstretch for UK homeland security

It is sometimes overlooked that the UK's armed forces play a key role in our homeland security. Although the Home Office is the lead department in tackling terrorism, and the Security Service and the Police have prime roles in protecting against terrorism within UK territory, the armed forces, with their unique capabilities to prevent, deter, coerce and disrupt, are an indispensable part of our multi-pronged counter-terrorist efforts.

The military contribution comes under the framework of Military Aid to the Civil Power or Military Aid to the Civil Authorities (MACA). In the event of a major terrorist emergency, units of armed forces can be called upon by COBR to carry out specific tasks. Specific military resources of direct value for such purposes are the SAS, SBS, NBC Regiment, II EOD Regiment, and the scientific experts at Porton Down and other MoD establishments. In addition, we should bear in mind that the MoD has responsibility for protecting 160 key sites.

The UK's response to terrorist attack on the homeland would obviously be multi-agency, but there is no doubt that if available – I repeat, if available – regular units and well trained reservist units could make a huge contribution in terms of community support, crisis management, rescue, consequence management, disaster recovery and restoration of normality.

In *theory* there should be a CCRF of 70,000 available, but in reality this is no more than an idea on paper. Local emergency planners needing military assistance would have to hope that regular units with their special skills and equipment could be spared. Herein lies a key problem: our armed forces are suffering from an unprecedented degree of overstretch. The MoD is struggling to meet all the commitments HM Government has taken on overseas.

In view of the key role of our armed forces in the War on Terrorism it is inexplicable to me that the government is reducing the Army's strength from 108,000 to 102,000; that the RAF is to be cut by 7,500 personnel and the Royal Navy by 1,500. It seems *incredible* that the Army is to lose four infantry battalions when they are in such heavy demand in so many missions. As for enhancing our rapid deployment capability, the MoD has reduced our helicopter strength and the number of air-portable light armoured vehicles. A key factor that defence planners need to take into account is that there are no easy exits from terror wars. Even Mr Donald Rumsfeld, one of the architects of the invasion of Iraq, has admitted in a secret Pentagon memo leaked to the press:

> Today, we lack the metrics to know if we are winning or losing the global 'War on Terror'. Are we capturing, killing or deterring or dissuading more terrorists every day than the Madrassas and the radical clerics are recruiting, training and deploying against us?

Mr Rumsfeld's question is as pertinent today as it was when he posed it.

The major point I have been making is that there is a worrying mismatch between our armed forces' current responsibilities and likely future tasks and the numbers of 'boots on the ground' and other defence assets to carry them out. But terrorism for non-state actors is only *one* of the many security challenges facing the UK. The IAEA states that up to 40 countries are capable of manufacturing nuclear weapons. We live in a volatile and unpredictable strategic climate in which threats to peace and security can emerge very rapidly. This is not the time to reduce the strength and versatility of our armed forces.

It would be disastrous if the UK and other democracies followed a policy of appeasing Al-Qaeda and its affiliates. But, in our conduct of foreign policy future UK governments would be wise to ensure: (1) that key decisions, especially those concerning military intervention overseas, are made with full awareness of the likely consequences in terms of a potential increase in vulnerability to international terrorist attacks against the UK homeland; (2) that the UK government has independent sovereign control over the decision to commit or withdraw our armed forces; (3) that the military intervention should be seen to be proportionate and legitimate in the context of the UN Charter and international law; (4) that the intervention should not be counterproductive in strategic terms, for example, by causing the deaths of far more civilians than were killed by the terrorism at home; and (5) that when UK troops are deployed on an overseas mission they are deployed in sufficient numbers and with adequate appropriate equipment to do the job. In this author's view, *none* of these conditions was met in the case of the UK's role in the invasion and occupation of Iraq.

There is no doubt in the mind of this author and the British military commanders he has spoken with, that the British Army is suffering from acute overstretch. Roughly a fifth of our troops are committed to overseas operations including 7,200 in Iraq, 5,600 in Afghanistan and 8,500 in Northern Ireland. Troops are suffering from a shortage of appropriate equipment (for example, lack of helicopters in Afghanistan), lack of military hospitals, and inadequate overall troop numbers to wage two major insurgencies in Iraq and Afghanistan simultaneously. General Sir Richard Dannatt's remarkable interview, published by the *Daily Mail* on 13 October 2006, spoke volumes about the effect of this overstretch on the future of the British Army. In an interview with the BBC he warned that the British Army was in danger of being 'broken' if something was not done to address this problem as a matter of urgency.

International efforts to combat Al-Qaeda terrorism

In spite of the setbacks in the struggle against Al-Qaeda described above there have been some very positive developments in the international response, in all of which the UK is playing a major part and which need to be taken into account if we are to get a more balanced assessment:

- In spite of deep divisions among members of the Coalition Against Terrorism over the invasion of Iraq, international intelligence cooperation in counter-terrorism especially at the bilateral level, has continued to improve. For example, the UK, Spain, France and Germany have continued to cooperate closely with the USA in sharing intelligence on the Al-Qaeda network despite their opposition to Washington's policy in Iraq.
- EU member states (especially Spain, Germany, France and the UK) have shown considerable success in using their criminal justice systems to try

persons suspected of involvement in Al-Qaeda-linked terrorism. The US government's apparent determination to circumvent their own highly respected Federal Criminal Court system and to resort to detention without trial for terrorist suspects is baffling and deeply damaging to America's reputation as a champion of democracy and the rule of law.

- One of the most encouraging developments in international response has been the un-dramatic but vital work of capacity building in the developing countries, for example the assistance programme of the Foreign and Commonwealth Office in disseminating expertise in anti-terrorism law, policing and intelligence work and the work of the international agencies such as the International Civil Aviation Organization, the International Air Transport Association and the Airports Council International in enhancing aviation security and of IMO in maritime security.

- The valuable progress in counter-terrorism made by the EU following the Madrid and London bombings, for example, through the European Arrest Warrant mechanism, and the enhanced intelligence sharing and judicial cooperation procedures through EUROPOL, SITCEN, and EUROJUST. This cooperation provides a useful model for other regional intergovernmental organisations and it is particularly encouraging that the UK took a very useful role during the British Presidency, following the 7 July London bombings, to further enhance the EU cooperation in this key field.

Major weaknesses in the international response to terrorism

If asked to pinpoint major weaknesses in the international response to terrorism I would stress four massive problems:

- In view of Al-Qaeda's serious efforts to acquire CBRN weapons, much more intensive efforts are required to tighten and police the international arms control and counter-proliferation regimes to enable them to encompass prevention of proliferation to non-state groups. Far more than changes in national legislation and policy pronouncements are required. We urgently need powerful international agencies to police such regimes. The IAEA is an encouraging, though far from perfect model. We need to build similar mechanisms to deal with chemical and biological weapons.

- Many governments still show a lack of political will and courage to take an unambiguous stand against terrorism whoever the perpetrators and whatever their self-professed cause. There are no good terrorists. Terrorism is a brutal attack on the most basic human right of all, the right to life. It should be outlawed and suppressed wherever it occurs. Until this happens we will continue to see more atrocities like the 9/11 attacks, the Beslan school massacre, the Bali bombings, the Madrid and London bombings and hundreds of other acts of mass murder.

- There has been a tragic failure to wage the battle of ideas against the extremists who preach hatred and incite people to commit terrorism. All democratic governments, including our own, have a special responsibility to actively promote democratic values, the role of law and human rights. Moreover, this cannot simply be accomplished by radio and TV programmes and political speeches. Action counts far more than words in the difficult world of upholding democratic values and human rights. If the behaviour of democratic states flatly contradicts our stated values we lose our credibility in the battle of ideas worldwide.

- Closely interwoven with the battle of ideas against the promoters and preachers of terrorism is the struggle to uphold basic human rights. While it is true that some extreme human rights campaigners elevate human rights into a totally impractical and irresponsible rejection of all collective moral and political obligations that make the enjoyment of human rights possible, most citizens of democracies and many who are working to democratise their countries would be shocked if we were told that some of our most cherished civil liberties (for example, habeas corpus, the right to a fair trial, freedom of speech, freedom of religion, freedom of movement, freedom of assembly, freedom of expression) were to be suspended in the name of state security. If we throw away our basic liberties in the name of dealing with the terrorism threat we will have done the terrorists' work for them.

As Joseph S. Nye, Yukio Satoh and I recommended in our Trilateral Commission report Addressing the New International Terrorism (May 2003):

> Dialogues about the protection of civil liberties in the face of security threats should be a regular feature of the meetings of the home security officials and should be reinforced by meetings of judicial officials and parliamentarians. Assistance programmes must include attention of human rights issues. Not only are such values central to the definition of the civilisation that we seek to protect, but overreactions to insecurity that infringe civil liberties undercut the sort of attractive power that is essential to maintain the support of moderate opinion and to deprive terrorists from recruiting new converts.

Notes

1 See, Mitchell, G. (2000) *Making Peace*, Berkeley, CA: University of California Press.
2 See Chapter 2 of this book.
3 For Al-Qaeda's use of the internet and videotapes in its propaganda see Peter Taylor's excellent series of programmes on 'The new Al-Qaeda' made for the BBC's *Panorama* programme.
4 See Gregory, F. and Wilkinson, P. (2005) 'Riding pillion is a high risk policy in tackling terrorism', *Chatham House Briefing Paper*, London: RIIA and ESCR.
5 See (2003) 'His answer to terrorism lies not in war', *Christian Science Monitor*, March, 6, available at www.csmonitor.com2003/0306/pl17s01-wogi.html.
6 For a fuller explanation of this thesis, see Wilkinson, P. (2006) *Terrorism Versus Democracy: The Liberal State Response* (2nd edn), London: Routledge.
7 See, interview with General Sir Richard Dannatt (2006) *Daily Mail*, 13 October.

20 Main conclusions of the authors

Project team

Assessing the threat

It would be patently absurd to attempt to assess the UK's preparedness for future terrorist attack without first trying to judge the nature and severity of the terrorist threats to the UK. These efforts to analyse the main threats are contained in Part II of this book. The editor opens with an assessment of the threat posed by the Al-Qaeda network. Taking into account Al-Qaeda's stated aims, ideology, track record and modus operandi, he concludes that although it is by no means the worst threat to human security it is without doubt the most lethal and dangerous terrorist movement to have emerged in the history of modern non-state terrorism. This is because it is explicitly committed to mass killing, has global reach, has an absolutist ideology and has typically used coordinated no-warning suicide attacks which are extremely difficult to prevent. Moreover, although the Al-Qaeda network has suffered many severe blows during the 'War on Terrorism' it has shown that it can adapt and become stronger by exploiting changes in the strategic environment.

For example, it has been able to take full advantage of the invasion, occupation and conflict in Iraq in order to intensify its propaganda war, recruitment, and fund-raising. The editor concurs with the assessment given by the UK's intelligence chiefs in October 2006 which warned that the UK is a number one target for Al-Qaeda, and that the UK's vulnerability to further attack was increased because of the large number of UK Muslims travelling to Pakistan, where many extremists and militants and supporters of Al-Qaeda are based, and the large number of Pakistanis entering the UK, and making return trips to Pakistan.

Dr Tamara Makarenko surveys a wider range of extremist international groups in Chapter 3. She shows how a number of these groups 'have used the UK as a base from which logistical operations have been organised in support of acts of terrorism conducted in other countries' (p. 37). However, she concludes, although 'the greatest threat posed by foreign-based terrorist groups for much of the past decade has been indirect (that is, contributing to criminality and community tensions) via the support structures they have established' (p. 37), 9/11 changed all this and the British government increasingly recognised that the UK had now become 'a vulnerable and likely target for international terrorist groups' (p. 37).

Dr Makarenko observes that 'it is essential that the motivations, capabilities and support structures of foreign-based terrorist groups are monitored closely and continuously ...' (p. 38).

The assessment of the CBRN Threat by Dr Jez Littlewood and Professor John Simpson (Chapter 4) opens with a candid admission that 'Providing an accurate, timely and verifiable assessment of the threat posed by ... CBRN weapons is an impossible task. It would require not only access to information held by the intelligence and counter-terrorism communities, but also detailed knowledge of the capabilities, intentions and motivations of a wide variety of terrorist groups' (p. 57).

However, in the light of their cautious and thorough examination of the evidence available to them Littlewood and Simpson conclude: '... it is both dangerous and foolish to discount entirely the threat posed by the terrorist use of CBRN weapons. There is certainly a sufficient amount of information to warrant serious concern about terrorist interest and desire to use such weapons, even if some of this may have been a self-generated threat. Those seeking to guard against the use of CBRN must not fall into apathy about its actual threat simply because little has occurred since 11 September 2001. However, responding to the threat must not be driven by hyperbole or worst case scenarios. The response requires a broad, measured, and clear-headed approach to manage the threat, and any use, of such weapons. Any CBRN response must be part of an overall threat assessment and be managed as part of an all-disasters plan' (p. 75).

In Chapter 5, Dr Anthony Richards provides an assessment of the domestic threat from terrorist activity relating to the Northern Ireland conflict and from animal rights extremism. In summing up and updating his findings on the IRA, Dr Richards quotes the finding of the IMC in its Tenth report that 'there has now been a substantial erosion in PIRA's capacity to return to a military campaign without a significant period of build-up', and that senior IRA figures have tried to stop members engaging in criminal activity, although 'there are indications that some members, including some senior ones, (as distinct from the organisation itself) are still involved in crime, including offences such as fuel laundering, money laundering, extortion, tax evasion and smuggling' (p. 86). Nevertheless, Dr Richards observes, the IMC's findings on the IRA are 'very encouraging'.

In assessing the threat from the Real IRA, Dr Richards concludes that it continues to pose a threat and he notes: 'Existing in the form of two factions (between whom there is a 'good deal of infighting') it has also continued to train and recruit' (p. 90). Moreover, 'While they continue with attacks on security personnel in Northern Ireland they both also 'recognise the propaganda value of a successful attack on the UK mainland' (p. 92).

No assessment of the terrorist threat in Northern Ireland would be complete if it excluded the loyalist terror groups. In summing up his conclusions on the UDA, Dr Richards concludes that it remains a threat to the rule of law in Northern Ireland, 'despite the apparent efforts of some affiliated to the group to steer the organisation away from violence and organised crime' (p. 96). The LVF also 'remains a threat for as long as it maintains the capacity to use violence to protect its hugely profitable criminal exploits' (p. 97). The LVF has been engaged in a feud with the UVF and the IMC has reported that the UVF has been responsible for a number of murders in relation to the feud. The IMC stated in its April 2006 Report, that the UVF still remained 'active, violent and ruthless' despite reports in February 2006 that it was about to disband.

In his assessment of the threat from militant animal rights extremists, Dr Richards shows that there is evidence that a combination of police and legislative action has helped to quell the intimidation that surrounded the HLS episode. However, he warns: '... animal rights extremism is still a serious issue to be dealt with, especially as the core of activists are very determined, very surveillance and security aware, and legally well briefed.[1] Also of concern was the establishment of a three-day animal rights extremist "training camp" in September 2004 (widely reported in the British media), which apparently "offered workshops on strategy and tactics".[2] The government, under pressure from drugs manufacturers and the pharmaceutical industry, appears to be taking a firmer line against animal rights extremists by attempting to curtail their ability to intimidate. Given that at least some of the hardcore activists that have been behind the more violent protests are the same people that have been at the heart of animal rights extremism in the last few decades (when bombs were planted and letter bombs were despatched), and if the government proves to be successful in preventing extremists from intimidating those that they target, the danger is that more extreme tactics will be adopted' (p. 108).

Enhancing the UK's preparedness

Frank Gregory's chapters on the lead department system, intelligence and police services and the Civil Contingencies Act 2004, all deal with key issues in the domestic management of terrorism in the UK. His analyses are also set within the context both of the relevant parts of the government's 'Contest' counter-terrorism strategy and the wider, but related, general issues of the long over-due modernisation of the UK's civil contingencies response system.

He notes, with regard to the Civil Contingencies Act, that its relevance to counter-terrorism lies in the requirement for both Category 1 and Category 2 responders to factor in terrorism as part of their risk assessment and risk management duties. However, he draws attention to the fact that the Act's significance, in the counter-terrorism field, depends crucially upon the capability of particular 'lead departments', notably the Home Office, and upon rigorous compliance monitoring and the provision of adequate resource levels through such mechanisms as the National Capabilities Survey. In another chapter he reflects upon the variable characteristics of the contribution that can be made by the private sector in areas such as preparedness and capability enhancement.

A particular theme in the public discussions of the UK's response to 9/11 has been the question of whether the UK should follow the US example and create a single but multi-functional, Department of Homeland Security. In Chapter 6, Gregory concludes that the performance-related evidence on the US DHS, to date, does not suggest that to be a suitable model to emulate. He further notes that the system in other EU states is generally similar to that in the UK. However, he does suggest that, perhaps, the attempts by both Canada and The Netherlands to introduce clearer and more empowered counter-terrorism contingencies management systems merit further reflection. This is particularly relevant as, first, although the Home Office 'leads' on counter-terrorism, it does not actually control the delivery of much of the response and, second, the 2006 *Capability Review of the Home Office* by the Prime Minister's Delivery Unit found not only a range of poor performance indicators but, as well, that of the seven Home Office Public Service Agreement targets *not one* mentioned terrorism. Gregory concludes that there is a need for the government to reflect upon a more effective top-level counter-terrorism management system with greater transparency and accountability. Such a system would need to be capable of overseeing an implementation focused annual audit of counter-terrorism activities, enforcing the implementation of agreed targets where necessary and have the resources for lateral thinking as well as current task management.

Professor John Simpson and Dr Jez Littlewood examine the efforts to reduce the threat of CBRN terrorism in Chapter 7. They argue that 'Arms control, disarmament, non-proliferation and counter-proliferation all have some role to play in countering the threat from CBRN. Such agreements play a normative role and a legal role' (p. 142). They recommend 'utilising many of the mechanisms that already exist for addressing clandestine trading and/or state-to-state trading in materials, equipment and technology …' (p. 152), and that a successful strategy against terrorism at the national level rests with an effective governance system that cuts across all agencies of the federal government, state, local and private sector.

Simpson and Littlewood stress the importance of the intelligence in UK anti-terrorism and anti-proliferation policies. Intelligence has thus become central to both UK anti-terrorism and anti-proliferation policies. Intelligence sharing and cooperation has been a core element of UK counter-proliferation policy, as well as an important element in its international capabilities.[3] Pakistan's role as both a nuclear proliferator and as a base for anti-Al-Qaeda operations was public knowledge, but the activities of A.Q. Khan remained hidden until Libya decided to disarm. Pursuing a multilayered UK strategy of multilateral, bilateral and unilateral indirect and direct action when confronted by the new proliferation threats was a natural continuation of existing policies for officials: by contrast, those outside government had tended to focus on the more visible and accessible WMD Treaty regimes. This gap closed as more information emerged about clandestine proliferators and international terrorists networks, though the UK government 'remained deeply uneasy … with the aggressive and unilateral approach taken by the Bush administration'.[4]

After 9/11 the terrorist proliferation threat became a central driver of global WMD counter-proliferation policies. Concerns about global terrorist networks increased when information emerged from Afghanistan that some elements of Al-Qaeda had been planning to use WMD for terrorist purposes. Whether the network was attempting to acquire WMD precursors and technology through clandestine A.Q. Khan-type procurement channels remained unclear. This led to increased emphasis on countering threats at source via interventionist counter-proliferation policies and export controls.[5]

However, Simpson and Littlewood do not under-estimate the problems involved in countering CBRN threats to the UK. They stress that: 'The nature of possible CBRN terrorist threats to the UK involves a much wider and more complex set of activities than those of terrorism using conventional explosives or car and lorry bombs or pre-9/11 airline hijacking' (p. 152).

They remind the reader of the numerous international counter-proliferation, arms control and disarmament initiatives and mechanisms that already exist, and in which the UK is playing a leading part. These include: United Nations activity through UNSCOM, UNMOVIC, the strengthening of IAEA, the three treaty-based regimes (the BWC, the CWG and NPT), the PSI, the NSG and the Australia Group.

Simpson and Littlewood remind us that the UK has played an active role in these international efforts. They emphasise that, in their view: 'it is erroneous to suggest that a completely new set of policies needs to be devised and implemented to manage this threat. While it is certainly true that terrorist interest in CBRN weapons raises new and different challenges to state-led proliferation of WMD, the policy responses developed ... to prevent the proliferation of nuclear, chemical and biological weapons are, in many cases, valid in addressing newer threats' (p. 152).

They return to this theme in their general conclusions. In an encouragingly positive conclusion they observe while by no means complete, 'Efforts since 9/11 across a range of areas – proliferation, finance, state-support, etc. – do appear to have reduced the terrorist CBRN threat' (p. 158). Simpson and Littlewood summarise their overall conclusions on reducing the CBRN terrorism threat as follows: 'In simple terms ... the management of the problem posed by terrorism at all levels with a set of policies that includes arms control and counter-proliferation, but which in fact go much further and are outside the ... Home Office. Prevention includes upholding the moral, normative, and legal prohibitions related to WMD such as the 1925 Geneva Protocol, the NPT, BWC, CWC and other Treaties. Terrorists must not only be prevented from acquiring the materials to develop a weapon from the UK, but from abroad also, underlining the necessity of export controls and enforcement of non-proliferation obligations and activities such as the PSI. The security and safety of laboratories and scientists abroad has to be supported where controls are sub-standard, as in the CTR activities under the G8 Global Partnership' (p. 154).

'Hence, in the domestic management of terrorist attacks, the role of the Foreign and Commonwealth Office is important. When enforcement of international norms or treaties becomes necessary, the MoD and the armed forces play a clear role. In controlling the export of substances and materials, the DTI has the lead. Intelligence and law enforcement agencies have a role in all such aspects as well' (p. 155).

'Clearly this is not a single policy or strategy which is wholly integrated or linear in its creation. It has grown organically, and has been pieced together in recognition of the problem. Despite the shock of 9/11, wise heads realised there was no need to reinvent the wheel to counter CBRN threats: what was required was holistic thinking and joined up government' (p. 155).

In Chapter 8, 'The UK and the threat of nuclear terrorism: A case study of organisational responses', John Simpson once again reaches very positive conclusions: 'Four years after 9/11, it is clear that a major effort has been made both to strengthen the security surrounding the civil nuclear industry and to ensure that these improvements are sustained, despite significant structural changes in that industry in the meantime. The main instrument for this has been new security methodology and regulations based on several differing pieces of legislation. The process now in place starts with assessment of design-based threats to plants and transport operations, infused with intelligence information on actual threats, and the subsequent development of SSPs or Transport Security Plans. Initial responsibility is then placed on the plant operators and their security organisations to implement these plans, backed up by OCNS inspections and the legislative authority to prosecute those in non-compliance. Yet there has been a certain amount of serendipity about these developments. Many were already in train for very different reasons prior to 2001, although 9 /11 gave them more momentum and financial and legislative priority than would probably otherwise have been the case' (p. 177).

However, Simpson also stresses the constraints and limitations of the overall planning: 'The evidence in the public domain suggests that the overall planning of a regulatory-based security system for UK nuclear sites has been both comprehensive and incisive. At the same time, it has been constrained by existing bureaucratic limitations and the process has evolved in an uneven manner. Legislation, and its implementation through regulations, has occurred in a somewhat piecemeal manner, suggesting it has encountered problems over prioritisation. This is illustrated by the lateness of the decision to legislate on making unauthorised entry into a civil nuclear site a criminal offence. There have also been limitations on resources arising in part from the contradictions inherent in the independent funding of OCNS's regulatory role and the central management and regulation of the human resources to fulfil it by the DTI' (p. 178).

A common theme in Gregory's analyses of both the intelligence services and police response to 9/11 (Chapters 9 and 10) is the problem of the continually rising demand, as noted again by the Director-General of MI5 in November 2006, for counter-terrorism surveillance resources and the impact of that demand on the performance of non-terrorism related tasks. He notes the positive benefits, in terms of public service and accountability of MI5's more visible presence in the domestic management of counter-terrorism through its website and the work of the NSAC. He also draws attention to the establishment of JTAC as an example of good practice in inter-agency intelligence sharing and analytical work. On the police response, Gregory comments upon the continuing tensions between a decentralised police system and the acceptability of any proposals for reform, in the counter-terrorism field, that carry with them elements of a centralised policing system. He also notes that the very proper emphasis on public safety in 'Contest' means that the intelligence services and police will move towards pre-emptive responses even if this means losing some evidence-gathering opportunities. This can generate a problem in terms of a more convictions/clear-up focused performance indicator approach with regard to policing. It can only be hoped that the ACPO TAM Chair, ACSO Andy Hayman will achieve his stated objective by the end of 2006 of getting the police service's gearing right between investigations, intelligence gathering and protective security.

Dr Tamara Makarenko in Chapter 11 assesses security issues surrounding immigration and asylum. Her main conclusions are that counter-terrorism responsibilities cannot be limited to the traditional security structures of a nation, such as intelligence, law enforcement and defence. Other government departments have inherent strengths that can be harnessed and ultimately contribute to the success of a national counter-terrorism strategy such as the Home Office's Immigration and Nationality Directorate.

When observing immigration and asylum issues in particular, Dr Makarenko highlights that although there are indications that certain individuals have manipulated immigration laws to secure residence in the UK, there is no available evidence indicating that terrorists favour any specific form of entry onto British territory (p. 248).

Although terrorists and criminals have manipulated the immigration system in the past, it is not the only avenue through which illicit actors can enter Britain. In fact, another worrying trend is the apparently growing number of British-born youths 'going through an identity crisis' that 'extremists are quick to exploit' (p. 249).

'Based on the link between Algerian terrorism and Al-Qaeda, and evidence that many Algerian asylum seekers are unaccounted for, the dangers of an asylum-terrorism link – even if limited – warrant consideration' (p. 249).

'Sporadic examples of the asylum–terrorism relationship in the UK, although not necessarily reflective of a wider trend, are reflective of the ways in which terrorists can manipulate an immigration policy that is ill-defined, or well-defined but not functional because of insufficient manpower and resources' (p. 249).

'Exacerbating the potential problems of this situation is the fact that the numbers of illegal immigrants are largely unknown' (p. 250). It is therefore recommended that a better grasp of this issue is ascertained, especially as it may relate to terrorism and/or serious and organised crime.

'British efforts to secure its territorial integrity have been undermined from within – through reputational damage caused by immigration scandals, however primarily as a result of limited resourcing and manpower. Even if additional resources and manpower can be attained, a successful policy and subsequent enforcement will be determined by the ability of the Immigration and Nationality Directorate to maximise their current operational efficiency. This will be influenced significantly by political priorities, and dictated by the institutional need of 'meeting targets' (p. 250).

The UK government faces numerous challenges 'in evolving an effective and efficient nationality, immigration and asylum policy that balances the benefits of immigration with any potential tensions.

A key factor in developing an effective immigration and asylum policy that circumvents political sensitivities is to ensure that future processes incorporate the advice and guidance of all relevant communities. Dedicated public education, combined with community consultation, will ensure that asylum and immigration debates do not inadvertently feed into the creation of fear or the misperception that asylum and immigration are key causes of an internal terrorist threat.

In addition to promoting inter-communal dialogue to dispel common myths of asylum, immigration and insecurity there are obvious benefits in continuing the consultation process regarding the utility of identity cards and biometrics. It is integral within a democracy to ensure that human rights of all citizens are safeguarded; however, it is also the responsibility of government to initiate schemes that would significantly contribute to the security of its citizens. A key dynamic therefore is the need to gauge individual human rights against the rights of a nation.

Paul Wilkinson assesses the effectiveness of the measures to enhance the protection of the UK civil aviation in the wake of 9/11 in Chapter 12. His main conclusions are: 'Pre-9/11 the UK had already developed one of the most effective and comprehensive civil aviation security systems in the world. The trigger for the major improvements made from the late 1980s to the mid-1990s was the Pan Am flight 103 bombing over Lockerbie in December 1988, the largest act of mass murder within the UK's jurisdiction in modern history, causing 259 fatalities of passengers and crew and 11 deaths on the ground. In the wake of Lockerbie the government made a thorough review of existing security and initiated the following reforms: enhanced access control, staff search, 100 per cent checked baggage screening, a new methodology of screening, 100 per cent staff screening, staff pre-employment background checks, training for security staff and the introduction of the Maritime and Aviation Security Act to help establish a legal framework of legal obligations for the aviation industry and a system of inspection to ensure full implementation and the power to suspend companies found to be in breach of the regulations' (p. 263).

'Problems and weaknesses, for example, failures to carry out effective employment background checks for airport and airline ground staff have been identified, and no vigilant aviation security expert from TRANSEC would ever claim that the UK has eliminated all the loopholes and weaknesses in the system UK-wide. *Nevertheless*, by comparison with the USA and our EU neighbours, the UK's airport security prior to 9/11 was widely regarded as one of the best among the first world countries.'

'9/11, however, and the continuing Al-Qaeda threat of suicide hijackings, suicide sabotage bombings, and MANPAD attacks, raise new and much more severe challenges. Recent intelligence derived from terrorist plans captured from a terrorist suspect's computer in Pakistan has confirmed that Al-Qaeda has plans to attack Heathrow. The threat is real and very severe' concludes Wilkinson.

The seriousness of the Al-Qaeda threat against civil aviation appears to have been confirmed in the Summer of 2006 by the large number of arrests in the UK and Pakistan in connection with an alleged plot to blow up nine or 10 airliners leaving Heathrow on transatlantic routes, using IEDs made of liquid explosives and assembled by the terrorists on board the aircraft. The authorities became convinced by the intelligence that they were receiving that the plot was about to be carried out and made a large number of arrests because they believed this was vital to thwart an attack. However, they could not be sure that they had identified all the alleged participants in the conspiracy and therefore decided to introduce emergency airport security measures aimed at preventing passengers from taking liquids on board aircraft (with the exception of liquids purchased at duty-free shops once the passenger/s have passed through security for departures). The potential threat from liquid explosives has been well known to sophisticated terrorist groups and aviation security experts for many years. Action is now needed to ensure that aviation security staff, procedures and screening systems are updated to counter the threat from a whole range of liquid agents and non-nitrogenous explosives. Some airline chiefs complain about extra security measures, but all the evidence from passenger opinion surveys shows airline passengers would prefer to be safe than sorry.

The major means of prevention of attacks on UK aviation targets is our counter-terrorism intelligence secured with the cooperation of the Security Service, MI6, GCHQ, Special Branch, the MPSB and the military, all of which share intelligence with their counterparts overseas. However, because both proactive intelligence efforts and airport boarding-gate security may fail to pre-empt an Al-Qaeda-style attack, we need to consider fresh ways of enhancing in-flight security, including new technologies of remote control, and we need to win over the aviation professions, especially the airline pilots, to acceptance of some radical innovations to strengthen our defences against these new and emerging threats.

'Lastly, but most urgent of all, the study concludes that the UK authorities need to improve radically their strategic planning and crisis management capabilities to face the challenge of having to deal with a situation in which terrorist suicide hijackers have seized control of one or more airliners and are heading for their targets'. The chaos caused at Heathrow when new security measures were imposed in August 2006 underlined the urgent need for greatly improved crisis management capabilities.

Dr Peter Lehr in Chapter 13 examines the measures taken since 9/11 to enhance maritime security in the UK. He concludes that much is being done to bring UK shipping and ports up to the IMO's security standards. However, he also finds there is much work still to be done and highlights some of the problems involved.

In Chapter 14, Anthony Richards deals with enhancing public information on terrorism. His main conclusions are: 'The challenge for the government is to get the balance right. Creating a culture of excessive anxiety may lead to mass panic if and when incidents do occur and this could lead to far greater numbers of casualties than the incidents themselves cause. On the other hand, the government must provide adequate information on the nature of the threat and what the British public can do to not only counter the threat but also to help themselves and others in the event of a major emergency. The government has to some extent done this. The key challenge, however, is to tackle the apathy of the vast majority of people without raising the anxiety of the minority that do actually take notice of the advice issued by government' (p. 293). He therefore recommends the following: that government place more emphasis on a national education programme to enhance the public's knowledge of the types of threat that we face. He believes that the public can be better prepared psychologically for a major terrorist attack without causing panic. Also, that government endeavours to centralise the source and provision of information to limit the confusion that might arise from information being disseminated from multiple sources (that is, Home Office, MI5, HPA, and so on). And that government assesses the impact of public information at the time of an incident on: public order, the transport network and the emergency response.

Darryl Howlett (Chapter 15) assess the UK's cyber-security policy and apparatus as follows: 'For those with cyber security responsibilities, the task of matching the source or sources of threat with a particular attack or set of attacks, given the range possible is a complex one.[6] This is because electronic attack could originate from a range of sources including: terrorist; state sponsored; organised crime; activist; hackers/crackers; and individuals or groups who develop malicious software such as viruses, known as malware, or conduct malicious computer operations in order to gain unauthorised access to specific sites.[7] Similarly, because there are several potential types of attack much effort is often required to match the attack with a particular source or sources (as it could originate from multiple sites).[8]

'Developing appropriate responses to these situations is thus an activity where both traditional and innovative thinking has been required.[9] Where this has been particularly relevant is in relation to the potential for cyber disruption or attack on the CNI.[10] Attention has subsequently focused on establishing the nature and interdependencies inherent in this infrastructure. As outlined in 2004 by Sir David Omand, the person then responsible for overseeing policy in this area, at the heart of the "UK government's counter-terrorism strategy is the 'protection' of the public and the UK's CNI"'[11] (p. 305).

'Official pronouncements indicate that the CNI has been redefined over the last few years.[12] Originally the CNI comprised six sectors, later the CNI was expanded to eight and then to 10 (communications, emergency services, energy, finance, food, government and public service, health, public safety, transport and water).[13] These 10 CNI sectors have subsequently been divided into 39 sub-sectors'[14] (p. 305).

'Identifying the linkages between the CNI and any vulnerabilities, particularly the potential for acute failure that may cause disruption in a relatively short period of time, is helpful to those who have to devise appropriate policy responses.[15] The UK has consequently been on a learning curve in respect of the CNI in the context of the new security environment.[16] Concomitantly, an outreach programme has been devised to assist in this process: "a dialogue is now underway with the industry or sector bodies, companies or trade associations to discuss vulnerabilities, resilience, and protective security issues. And security in this context means physical, personnel and information security"'[17] (p. 305).

'A key question in the outreach programme has been determining what constitutes "national criticality"?[18] Two methods are used for making this judgement: "in consultation with the organisation NISCC determines that it operates a nationally critical service that is supported by an information system; or, the organisation has an information system that is a key dependency of a nationally critical service operated by another organisation"'[19] (p. 305).

'There are also varying degrees of criticality between the 10 CNI sectors and their constituent 39 sub-sectors.[20] In this context, NISCC makes a distinction between two kinds of information dependency. One kind is "inter-sector", which is considered "easier to identify" due to the inherent nature of the dependencies.

'As an example, the emergency communications used by the emergency services are nationally critical because if they are not in operation, lives could be lost as a result of crime, fire or medical emergencies that are not responded to quickly enough. These emergency communications systems depend on electricity to operate, which in turn depends on fossil fuels to power the back-up generators. In short, the emergency services sector has key inter-sector dependencies on the electricity, gas and oil industries'[21] (p. 306).

'The second kind of information dependency identified by NISCC is "intra-sector". This is considered more complex due to the variation between the sectors involved.

'As an example, a finance sector payments system may depend on a closed financial network infrastructure, a key intra-sector dependency of the UK CNI. As a contrasting example, telecommunications providers will route traffic across each other's networks depending on cost, thus making it difficult to separate out telecommunications providers in terms of criticality'[22] (p. 306).

'The broad outline of the UK's policy for CNI protection was announced on 25 January 1999. This policy was devised to provide strategic direction for the public and private sectors. In the public sector the objective has been to enhance protection by improving IT security and developing advice and response tools; in the private sector the task has been to improve coordination between this sector and government'[23] (p. 306).

As Darryl Howlett explains, this is still the essence of the UK's policy for CNI protection. The NISSC and CSIA were established to minimise the risks to the CNI from electronic attack and to provide overall strategic guidance and to promote partnerships between the public and private sectors.

In Chapter 16 Gregory reflects upon the variable characteristics of the contribution that can be made by the private sector in areas such as preparedness and capability enhancement.

Frank Gregory concludes that there has been considerable progress in enhancing counter-terrorism and promoting business resilience and continuity through improvements in police–private sector cooperation: 'to the pre-9/11 higher profile for crime prevention, has been added the enhanced post-9/11 requirement for the police, through NaCTSO and forces CTSAs, to reach out to a wider business and industrial environment than previously came within the responsibility of MI5's T4 department (now re-numbered T1). Whilst all localities will have individual as well as generic counter-terrorism security needs, the volume of actual and potential demand for CTSA-type services has led to a number of overarching initiatives. These are all designed to provide simple and effective information and advice links for the private sector. Most recently launched has been the new MI5 NSAC website, which was developed with input from NaCTSO. This site complements information available from the Home Office "terrorism"website and the Cabinet Office CCS "UK resilience" website. The MI5 "Security Advice" website provides:

- General good practice advice on: physical security, managing staff security – the 'insider threat', protecting your information, planning for an emergency, business continuity and top 10 guidelines.
- Detailed advice on specific forms of attack. The two listed to date are: bomb protection and specific threats to information.

'This website is used by CTSAs as a major open-source point of reference for the business community.'

'Former AC David Veness, both on his own initiative and in his role as Secretary of ACPO TAM, promoted two projects to assess business counter-terrorism advice needs. These are Project "Trinity" and Project "Unicorn".[24] "Trinity", developed during 2003 by NaCTSO, is based upon two concepts:

- "Trinity" – comprising information strategies, business continuity and protective security.

The presence of the "Trinity" components would allow, once a business has these in place, for it to achieve:

- "steady state" – where a business is said "… to be in the optimal state to prevent and recover from a terrorist attack – irrespective of the threat level".

'"Trinity" and "steady state" make up NaCTSO's Commercial Sector Strategy, which is designed to provide more focused "… dense networks supporting the concept of 'sharing is protecting' using open source information within neighbourhoods, business districts and business sectors". The CCS will link the network of local CCTAs with their local business communities and local authority emergency planning officers' (p. 324).

'The advisory information is disseminated through a briefing booklet, CD-ROM, regional workshops and local CTA activities. The CCS will provide a means of fulfilling the police contribution to the roles and responsibilities of emergency services, as set out in the civil contingencies legislation, section 4(1) with the provision of advice on Business Continuity Information Strategies and Protective Security. A good example of the local availability of advice is provided by the example of the Thames Valley Police "Crime Reduction" website which includes for "… the business community in the Thames Valley area …" five pages entitled "Advice to business on chemical or biological attack" based upon inputs from the MI5'[25] (p. 325).

'If the new MI5 website and the NaCTSO "Trinity" approach are taken as major representatives of new public sector approaches to counter-terrorism "help" for business in the private sector one can see, to what extent, they would meet the private sector concerns as expressed in surveys of the participants in two NaCTSO/ESRC Project BC Workshops run in February and April 2004. A total group of 70 attended these Workshops and they represented major areas of private sector activity: banking and financial services, transport, utilities, telecommunications, manufacturing, major branded products, major retail chains, the construction industry and consultancy services. Of the total of attendees, 20 per cent returned completed questionnaires, which provides a reasonable survey sample set of data from which the following points emerged. The two major government counter-terrorism/emergencies-related websites, "ukresilience" and "homeoffice.gov/terrorism" were used by 71.4 per cent of the respondents. However, 35 per cent of the survey sample still felt that more specific information was needed on the nature of the terrorist threat' (p. 325).

Frank Gregory notes, with regard to the Civil Contingencies Act (Chapter 17), that its relevance to counter-terrorism lies in the requirement for both Category 1 and Category 2 responders to factor in terrorism as part of their risk assessment and risk management duties. However, he draws attention to the fact that the Act's significance, in the counter-terrorism field, depends crucially upon the capability of particular 'lead departments', notably the Home Office, and upon rigorous compliance monitoring and the provision of adequate resource levels through such mechanisms as the National Capabilities Survey.

He gives a cautious welcome to the Civil Contingencies Act for providing a badly needed up-to-date legislative basis for emergency planning, but he voices concerns about whether the appropriate financial resources will be available, and problems of coordination, especially at the regional level. The Act will provide a reasonable framework for addressing contingency planning and response based upon more comprehensive assessments.[26] The Act comes into force in two parts. Part 2, relating to emergency powers came into effect in December 2004 but Part 1 relating to local arrangements for civil protection will be implemented gradually as the supporting regulations and guidance are developed.[27] For example, police forces, through their Counter-Terrorism Security Advisers have established an annual review process for vulnerable locations under a 'traffic lights' categorisation which reflects the evolution of contingency management at all such locations within a force area.[28] In some cases contingency planning must reflect specific additional regulatory considerations. For example, TRANSEC, in regulating industry compliance in respect of shipping and ports activities has to ensure that requirements laid down in the ISPS Code, EU Regulation Enhancing Ship and Port Facility Security and the UK's Aviation and Maritime Security Act 1990 are met by the relevant Responders under the Civil Contingencies Act.[29]

'However, for the Act to be a true "building block", for homeland security or civil protection, there remains the key assumption that appropriate financial resources will be available. Also, the important elements of the nature of central government oversight, the capability of "lead departments" and the regional level contribution need further consideration'.

Dr Anthony Richards provides an analysis of the progress and problems in the UK's emergency response planning and capabilities in Chapter 18. He provides a brief historical background on the emergence of the Civil Contingencies Act 2004, the Capabilities Programme and the *Dealing With Disasters* publication providing guidelines for emergency planners. He then looks in more detail at London's Emergency Response and the work of the LESLP, established in 1973, and the LRRF and LRT set up in the aftermath of 9/11. The LRF's task is to oversee the work of London Resilience.

Dr Richards provides a case-study of London's emergency response from which he is able to draw some key lessons on the problems of response which have wider relevance to the planning of emergency response to terrorist attack in the UK generally: 'Our research has shown that an urgent priority is to continue to develop research into ways of improving the emergency services' ability to detect and identify chemical and biological agents. This will enable the right PPE to be used, increase opportunities for reducing the hot zone, and allow the ambulance service and medical staff to administer the right treatment and antidotes more quickly. Research is also needed to improve decontamination procedures and PPE to enable emergency responders to work more effectively and for longer periods of time. Progress also needs to be made in the whole area of communications – not just in terms of achieving interoperable communications between our emergency services but also in surmounting the difficulties of communicating in and from underground locations'.

'The issue of communications and its failings came to the fore in the London Assembly's report into the 7 July 2005 bombings, which stated that "communications within and between the emergency services did not stand up on 7 July". In relation to underground communication it noted that it was "unacceptable that the emergency services, with the exception of the BTP, are still not able to communicate by radio when they are underground, 18 years after the official inquiry into the King's Cross fire recommended action to address this problem".[30] As a result emergency service personnel could not communicate effectively, "in some cases with each other and in other cases with their control rooms".'[31]

'The London Assembly report into 7/7 found that "the most striking failing in the response to the 7 July attacks was the lack of planning to care for people who survived and were traumatised by the attacks". It stated that "procedures tend to focus too much on incidents, rather than on individuals, and on processes rather than people".[32] As valuable as emergency response exercises are, this is perhaps one lesson that only becomes obviously apparent during a real major emergency. The report noted the lack of survivor reception areas despite the estimated 3,000 people who are said to have suffered from post-traumatic stress along with a further 3,000 who were directly affected'[33] (p. 348).

'Despite these emergency response issues that London needs to address it appears that other regions are not as prepared as our capital city is for a major incident. Part of the reason for this relative lack of preparedness is the underdevelopment of the regional tier of our response. Another reason is that it takes longer for equipment and training to reach other parts of the country. While it is natural that our capital city should be given top priority, it is important to remember that the threat of simultaneous attacks and a willingness to aim for "soft" targets once others have been "hardened" means that we must be prepared for attacks on a nationwide basis.'

In Chapter 19, Paul Wilkinson contributes a brief analysis of the international dimensions of UK Homeland Security. He reminds readers that the UK has faced very different threats in the forms of Northern Ireland-related terrorism and the international terrorism of the Al-Qaeda network and its affiliated groups and cells. The UK government has applied very different policies in response to these two major types of threat. In the case of Northern Ireland the government, in cooperation with the government of the Republic of Ireland, and with valuable encouragement and support from the US government and the EU, has patiently pursued a political pathway out of the violence. By October 2006 it looked as though this policy has been successful. However, in dealing with the Al-Qaeda threat the UK had adopted a mixture of the 'war model' and the 'criminal justice model', because there was no political pathway available to end the violence.

However, the 'War on Terrorism' policy adopted by President George W. Bush's administration was adopted by Prime Minister Tony Blair, despite very considerable opposition in the Labour Party and in the country as a whole. Wilkinson has consistently argued that this was a fundamental strategic mistake. There is no evidence that Saddam was involved in plotting the 9/11 attacks, and following the invasion of March 2003, British troops, like their US colleagues have been locked into a struggle against Iraqi insurgents and terrorists which, by October 2006 looked unwinable. There were too few troops deployed to obtain basic stability. In fact, all the evidence points to a descent into a full-scale sectarian civil war.

Sadly, one of the consequences of this conflict has been to provide a big boost to Al-Qaeda, providing it with a gratuitous propaganda lift, more recruits, greater financial support from sympathisers and an abundance of civilian and military targets in Iraq. Another consequence has been that President Karzai's government in Afghanistan, who now desperately needs more troops to help him deal with a revived Taliban insurgency, cannot obtain any more military aid from the UK because our armed forces are hopelessly overstretched.

Among the dangerous consequences of 'riding pillion' to President George W. Bush's policy in Iraq are: it has robbed the UK of flexibility in foreign policy in the Middle East – it has exacerbated the overstretch of the British Army (as strongly argued by General Sir Richard Dannatt), and it has contributed to the sense of grievance against UK foreign policy among young Muslims who are targeted for recruitment by Al-Qaeda-linked organisations.

As argued elsewhere (Wilkinson and Gregory, 2005), 'riding pillion' to the foreign policy of a more powerful ally is a high-risk policy. Being a good ally does not necessarily entail falling in with every request made by the more powerful partner. On the contrary, it could be argued that in circumstances where you have a sound basis for believing that your stronger ally is in danger of embarking on a policy that involves dangers that they have underestimated or failed to foresee, it is one's duty to refrain from 'riding pillion' and to warn them of the possible risks. Harold Wilson sensibly declined the US request to join it in the Vietnam War. The USA refused to back the UK and France over the Suez venture in 1956. In neither case did this destroy our close alliance.

Last but not least, in relation to the problems of emergency response to mass-casualty terrorist attack in the event of prevention and deterrence failing, the USA has rightly undertaken a wide range of measures to strengthen its homeland security following the 9/11 attacks. The UK is not so far advanced but the police and emergency services have been planning, training and exercising in preparation for a major terrorist emergency. The response of the Metropolitan Police and the London emergency services to the bomb attacks on 7 July, despite some serious weaknesses convincingly demonstrated the benefits of intensive emergency planning and preparation. Other countries and major cities will have observed the value of these contingency preparations, and one hopes they too will swiftly develop improved emergency response capabilities. They could save hundreds of lives.

Notes

1 Police source.
2 (2004) 'Animal rights activists hit training camp to sharpen up battle plans', *Guardian Unlimited*, available at www.guardian.co.uk/animalrights/story/0,11917,1297859,00. html . See also Nugent, H. (2001) 'Animal fanatics give lessons in death', *The Times*, 6 September.
3 The Foreign and Commonwealth Office emphasised the importance of international cooperation and intelligence sharing in a December 2003 document outlining its international priorities. International terrorism and the proliferation of WMD were stated as having 'emerged as potentially the most catastrophic dangers to our (UK's) national security in the early twenty-first century'. (2003) *UK International Priorities – A Strategy for the FCO*, Cm. 6052, 9 December, p. 1.
4 Op. cit., p. 17.
5 The Foreign and Commonwealth Office clearly states that as 'there is no panacea' or 'one-size-fits-all' policy to counter WMD threats, 'the Government uses the tools that it judges will be most effective in each case'. See, *Counter-Proliferation Strategy, Terrorism & Security, UK Priorities*, available at www.fco.gov.uk/servlet/Front?page name=OpenMarket/Xcelerate/ShowPage&c=Page&cid=1065432164878.
6 Presentation at Workshop, November 2003.
7 Presentation at Workshop, November 2003.
8 Presentation at Workshop, November 2003.
9 Presentation at Workshop, November 2003.
10 Lukasik *et al.*, op.cit.
11 Sir David Omand, Keynote speech, 1 July 2004, at launch of RUSI Homeland Resilience Programme, 8 July 2004, available at www.ukresilience.info/contingencies/rusi.htm.

12 Omand, ibid., p. 6.
13 'What is the Critical National Infrastructure?', op. cit., pp. 1–2.
14 (2005) 'What is national criticality?', *NISCC Quarterly*, 04/05, p. 2, available at www.uniras.gov.uk/niscc/docs/re-20051230-01143.pdf?lang=en.
15 Lukasik *et al.*, op. cit.
16 Omand, op. cit, p. 6.
17 Ibid., pp. 6–7.
18 'What is national criticality?', op. cit., p. 2.
19 Ibid.
20 Ibid.
21 Ibid., p. 3.
22 Ibid.
23 Presentation at Workshop, November 2003, D. Howlett.
24 Information on 'Trinity' and 'Unicorn' was kindly supplied for the use of the ESRC Project by the Head of NaCTSO. See also the paper/lecture by A.C. Veness.
25 Thames Valley Police, Crime Prevention website, www.thamesvalley.police.uk/crime-reduction/ad_bus.htm, accessed 28 July 2004.
26 For general information see Cabinet Office, CCS (2004) *Civil Contingencies Act 2004: a short guide*, Cabinet Office.
27 The Civil Contingencies Act 2004 (Contingency Planning) Regulations 2005, SI 2005, No. 2042, July 2005.
28 Information from Project Workshops and discussions with CTSAs.
29 Compliance Regime for Ports and Shipping, www.dft.gov.uk/stellent/groups/dft_transsec/documents/page/dft_transsec_0304…, accessed 5 September 2005.
30 London Assembly (2006) *Report of the 7 July Review Committee*, June, available at http://www.london.gov.uk/assembly/reports/7july/report.pdf.
31 Ibid.
32 Ibid.
33 Ibid.

Appendix 1

Select addresses of UK internet sources on terrorism

CSTPV, University of St Andrews
www.st-andrews.ac.uk/intrel/research/cstpv

Foreign and Commonwealth Office
www.fco.gov.uk

Home Office
www.homeoffice.gov.uk/

MI5 Security Service
www.mi5.gov.uk/

Ministry of Defence
www.mod.uk/defenceinternet/home

Mountbatten Centre, Southampton University
www.mcis.soton.ac.uk/index.php

Select addresses on international internet sources

Canada's Counter Terrorism Program
www.csis-scrs.gc.ca/en/newsroom/backgrounders/backgrounder08.asp

Centre for Democracy and Terrorism
www.cdt.org/policy/terrorism.

Commentary published by the Canadian Security Intelligence Service
www.csis-scrs.gc.ca/en/publications/commentary.asp

Counter-terrorism bills and proposals
www.epic.org/privacy/terrorism

Counter-Terrorism Home Page
www.counterterrorism.com

Electronic Frontier Foundation
www.eff.org

Emergency Response Guide to Terrorism
www.emergency.com

EUROPA
http://europa.eu.int

Federal Emergency Management Agency
www.fema.gov

Institute for Counter Terrorism Studies
www.potomacinstitute.org/academiccen/icts/icts.htm

International Association of Counterterrorism and Security Professional
www.iacsp.com

International Policy Institute for Counter-Terrorism
www.ict.org.il

MIPT (Oklahoma City National Memorial Institute for the Prevention of
Terrorism)
www.mipt.org

Office of the Coordinator for Counterterrorism, US State Department
www.state.gov/s/ct

Patterns of Global Terrorism
www.state.gov/s/ct/rls/pgtrpt

Terrorism Group Profiles
http://library.nps.navy.mil/home/tgp/tgpndx.htm

The Terrorism Research Centre
www.terrorism.com

Terrorist and Insurgent Organisations
www.au.af.mil/au/aul/bibs/tergps/tg98tc.htm

US Department of Defense
www.defenselink.mil

US Department of Homeland Security
www.dhs.gov/dhspublic/index.jsp

William R. Nelson Institute of Public Affairs
www.jmu.edu/orgs/wrni

Appendix 2

List of proscribed terrorist groups

These terrorist organisations are currently proscribed under UK legislation, and therefore outlawed in the UK.

- Forty-four international terrorist organisations are proscribed under the Terrorism Act 2000 (www.homeoffice.gov.uk/security/terrorism-and-the-law/terrorism-act/).
- Of these, two organisations are proscribed under powers introduced in the Terrorism Act 2006 (www.homeoffice.gov.uk/security/terrorism-and-the-law/terrorism-act-2006/), as glorifying terrorism.
- Fourteen organisations in Northern Ireland are proscribed under previous legislation.

The information about the groups' aims was given to parliament when they were proscribed.

17 November Revolutionary Organisation (N17)

Aims to highlight and protest at what it deems to be imperialist and corrupt actions, using violence. Formed in 1974 to oppose the Greek military Junta, its stance was initially anti-Junta and anti-US, which it blamed for supporting the Junta.

Abu Nidal Organisation (ANO)

ANO's principal aim is the destruction of the state of Israel. It is also hostile to 'reactionary' Arab regimes and states supporting Israel.

Abu Sayyaf Group (ASG)

The precise aims of the ASG are unclear, but its objectives appear to include the establishment of an autonomous Islamic state in the Southern Philippine island of Mindanao.

Al-Gama'at al-Islamiya (GI)

The main aim of GI is through all means, including the use of violence, to overthrow the Egyptian government and replace it with an Islamic state. Some members also want the removal of Western influence from the Arab world.

Al Gurabaa

Al Gurabaa is a splinter group of Al-Muajiroon and diseminates materials that glorify acts of terrorism.

Al Ittihad Al Islamia (AIAI)

The main aims of AIAI are to establish a radical Sunni Islamic state in Somalia, and to regain the Ogaden region of Ethiopia as Somali territory via an insurgent campaign. Militant elements within AIAI are suspected of having aligned themselves with the 'global jihad' ideology of Al-Qaeda, and to have operated in support of Al-Qaeda in the East Africa region.

Al-Qaeda

Inspired and led by Osama Bin Laden, its aims are the expulsion of Western forces from Saudi Arabia, the destruction of Israel and the end of Western influence in the Muslim world.

Ansar Al Islam (AI)

AI is a radical Sunni Salafi group from northeast Iraq around Halabja. The group is anti-Western, and opposes the influence of the USA in Iraqi Kurdistan and the relationship of the KDP and PUK to Washington. AI has been involved in operations against Multi-National Forces-Itaq (MNF-I).

Ansar Al Sunna (AS)

AS is a fundamentalist Sunni Islamist extremist group based in Central Iraq and what was the Kurdish Autonomous Zone (KAZ) of Northern Iraq. The group aims to expel all foreign influences from Iraq and create a fundamentalist Islamic state.

Armed Islamic Group (Groupe Islamique Armée) (GIA)

The aim of the GIA is to create an Islamic state in Algeria using all necessary means, including violence.

Asbat Al-Ansar ('League of Parisans' or 'Band of Helpers')

Sometimes going by the aliases of 'The Abu Muhjin' group/faction or the 'Jama'at Nour', this group aims to enforce its extremist interpretation of Islamic law within Lebanon, and increasingly further afield.

Babbar Khalsa (BK)

BK is a Sikh movement that aims to establish an independent Khalistan within the Punjab region of India.

Baluchistan Liberation Army (BLA)

BLA are comprised of tribal groups based in the Baluchistan area of Eastern Pakistan, which aims to establish an independant nation encompassing the Baluch dominated areas of Pakistan, Afghanistan and Iran.

Basque Homeland and Liberty (Euskadi ta Askatasuna) (ETA)

ETA seeks the creation of an independent state comprising the Basque regions of both Spain and France.

Egyptian Islamic Jihad (EIJ)

The main aim of the EIJ is to overthrow the Egyptian government and replace it with an Islamic state. However, since September 1998, the leadership of the group has also allied itself to the 'global Jihad' ideology expounded by Osama Bin Laden and has threatened Western interests.

Groupe Islamique Combattant Marocain (GICM)

The traditional primary objective of the GICM has been the installation of a governing system of the caliphate to replace the governing Moroccan monarchy. The group also has an Al-Qaeda-inspired global extremist agenda.

Hamas Izz al-Din al-Qassem Brigades

Hamas aims to end Israeli occupation in Palestine and establish an Islamic state.

Harakat Mujahideen (HM)

HM, previously known as Harakat Ul Ansar (HuA), seeks independence for Indian-administered Kashmir. The HM leadership was also a signatory to Osama Bin Laden's 1998 fatwa, which called for worldwide attacks against US and Western interests.

Harakat-Ul-Jihad-Ul-Islami (HUJI)

The aim of HUJI is to achieve through violent means accession of Kashmir to Pakistan, and to spread terror throughout India. HUJI has targeted Indian security positions in Kashmir and conducted operations in India proper.

Harakat-Ul-Jihad-Ul-Islami (Bangladesh) (Huji-B)

The main aim of HUJI-B is the creation of an Islamic regime in Bangladesh modelled on the former Taleban regime in Afghanistan.

Harakat-Ul-Mujahideen/Alami (HuM/A) and Jundallah

The aim of both HuM/A and Jundallah is the rejection of democracy of even the most Islamic-oriented style, and to establish a caliphate based on Sharia law, in addition to achieving accession of all Kashmir to Pakistan. HuM/A has a broad anti-Western and anti-President Musharraf agenda.

Hezb-E Islami Gulbuddin (HIG)

Led by Gulbuddin Hekmatyar who is in particular very anti-American, HIG desires the creation of a fundamentalist Islamic State in Afghanistan and is anti-Western.

Hizballah External Security Organisation

Hizballah is committed to armed resistance to the state of Israel itself and aims to liberate all Palestinian territories and Jerusalem from Israeli occupation. It maintains a terrorist wing, the External Security Organisation (ESO), to help it achieve this.

International Sikh Youth Federation (ISYF)
ISYF is an organisation committed to the creation of an independent state of Khalistan for Sikhs within India.

Islamic Army of Aden (IAA)
The IAA's aims are the overthrow of the current Yemeni government and the establishment of an Islamic State following Sharia Law.

Islamic Jihad Union (IJU)
The primary strategic goal of the IJU is the elimination of the current Uzbek regime. The IJU would expect that following the removal of President Karimov, elections would occur in which Islamic-democratic political candidates would pursue goals shared by the IJU leadership.

Islamic Movement of Uzbekistan (IMU)
The primary aim of IMU is to establish an Islamic state in the model of the Taleban in Uzbekistan. However, the IMU is reported to also seek to establish a broader state over the entire Turkestan area.

Jaish e Mohammed (JeM)
JeM seeks the 'liberation' of Kashmir from Indian control as well as the 'destruction' of America and India. JeM has a stated objective of unifying the various Kashmiri militant groups.

Jeemah Islamiyah (JI)
JI's aim is the creation of a unified Islamic state in Singapore, Malaysia, Indonesia and the Southern Philippines.

Khuddam Ul-Islam (Kul) and splinter group Jamaat Ul-Furquan (JuF)
The aim of both KUI and JuF are to unite Indian administered Kashmir with Pakistan; to establish a radical Islamist state in Pakistan; the 'destruction' of India and the USA; to recruit new jihadis; and the release of imprisoned Kashmiri militants.

Kongra Gele Kurdistan (PKK)
PKK/KADEK/KG is primarily a separatist movement that seeks an independent Kurdish state in southeast Turkey. The PKK changed its name to KADEK and then to Kongra Gele Kurdistan, although the PKK acronym is still used by parts of the movement.

Lashkar e Tayyaba (LT)
LT seeks independence for Kashmir and the creation of an Islamic state using violent means.

Liberation Tigers of Tamil Eelam (LTTE)
The LTTE is a terrorist group fighting for a separate Tamil state in the North and East of Sri Lanka.

Mujaheddin e Khalq (MeK)
The MeK is an Iranian dissident organisation based in Iraq. It claims to be seeking the establishment of a democratic, socialist, Islamic republic in Iran.

Palestinian Islamic Jihad – Shaqaqi (PIJ)
PIJ is a Shi'a group which aims to end the Israeli occupation of Palestine and create an Islamic state similar to that in Iran. It opposes the existence of the state of Israel, the Middle East peace process and the Palestinian Authority.

Revolutionary Peoples' Liberation Party – Front (Devrimci Halk Kurtulus Partisi – Cephesi) (DHKP-C)
DHKP-C aims to establish a Marxist–Leninist regime in Turkey by means of armed revolutionary struggle.

Teyre Azadiye Kurdistan (TAK)
TAK Kurdish terrorist group currently operating in Turkey.

Salafist Group for Call and Combat (Groupe Salafiste pour la Predication et le Combat) (GSPC)
Its aim is to create an Islamic state in Algeria using all necessary means, including violence.

Saved Sect or Saviour Sect
The Saved Sect is a splinter group of Al-Muajiroon and disseminates materials that glorify acts of terrorism.

Sipah-E Sahaba Pakistan (SSP) (Aka Millat-E Islami Pakistan (MIP) – SSP was renamed MIP in April 2003 but is still referred to as SSP) and splinter group Lashkar-E Jhangvi (LeJ)
The aim of both SSP and LeJ is to transform Pakistan by violent means into a Sunni state under the total control of Sharia law. Another objective is to have all Shia declared Kafirs and to participate in the destruction of other religions, notably Judasim, Christianity and Hinduism.

Note: Kafirs means non-believers: literally, one who refused to see the truth. LeJ does not consider members of the Shia sect to be Muslim, hence they can be considered a 'legitimate' target.

Libyan Islamic Fighting Group (LIFG)
The LIFG seeks to replace the current Libyan regime with a hard-line Islamic state. The group is also part of the wider global Islamist extremist movement, as inspired by Al-Qaeda. The group has mounted several operations inside Libya, including a 1996 attempt to assassinate Mu'ammar Qadhafi.

Proscribed Irish groups

- Continuity Army Council
- Cumann na mBan
- Fianna na hEireann
- Irish National Liberation Army (INLA)
- Irish People's Liberation Organisation
- Irish Republican Army (IRA)
- Loyalist Volunteer Force (LVF)
- Orange Volunteers
- Red Hand Commandos
- Red Hand Defenders
- Saor Eire
- Ulster Defence Association (UDA)
- Ulster Freedom Fighters (UFF)
- Ulster Volunteer Force (UVF)

Index